The Fast Carriers

The Forging of an Air Navy

by Clark G. Reynolds

Naval Institute Press
Annapolis, Maryland

Originally published in 1968 by McGraw-Hill Book Company.
Reprinted with minor changes by the Naval Institute Press, 1992.

Library of Congress Cataloging-in-Publication Data

Reynolds, Clark G.
The fast carriers : the forging of an air navy / by Clark G. Reynolds.
p. cm.
Originally published: 1st ed. New York : McGraw-Hill, 1968. With minor changes.
Includes bibliographical references and index.
ISBN 1-55750-701-5 (acid-free paper)
1. Aircraft carriers—United States—History. 2. United States. Navy. Fast Carrier Task Force. 3. World War, 1939–1945—Naval operations, American. 4. World War, 1939–1945—Aerial operations, American. I. Title.
V874.3.R4 1992
359.3′255′0973—dc20 91-39437
CIP

Printed in the United States of America on acid-free paper ♾

9 8 7 6 5

Unless otherwise credited, all photos are official U.S. Navy

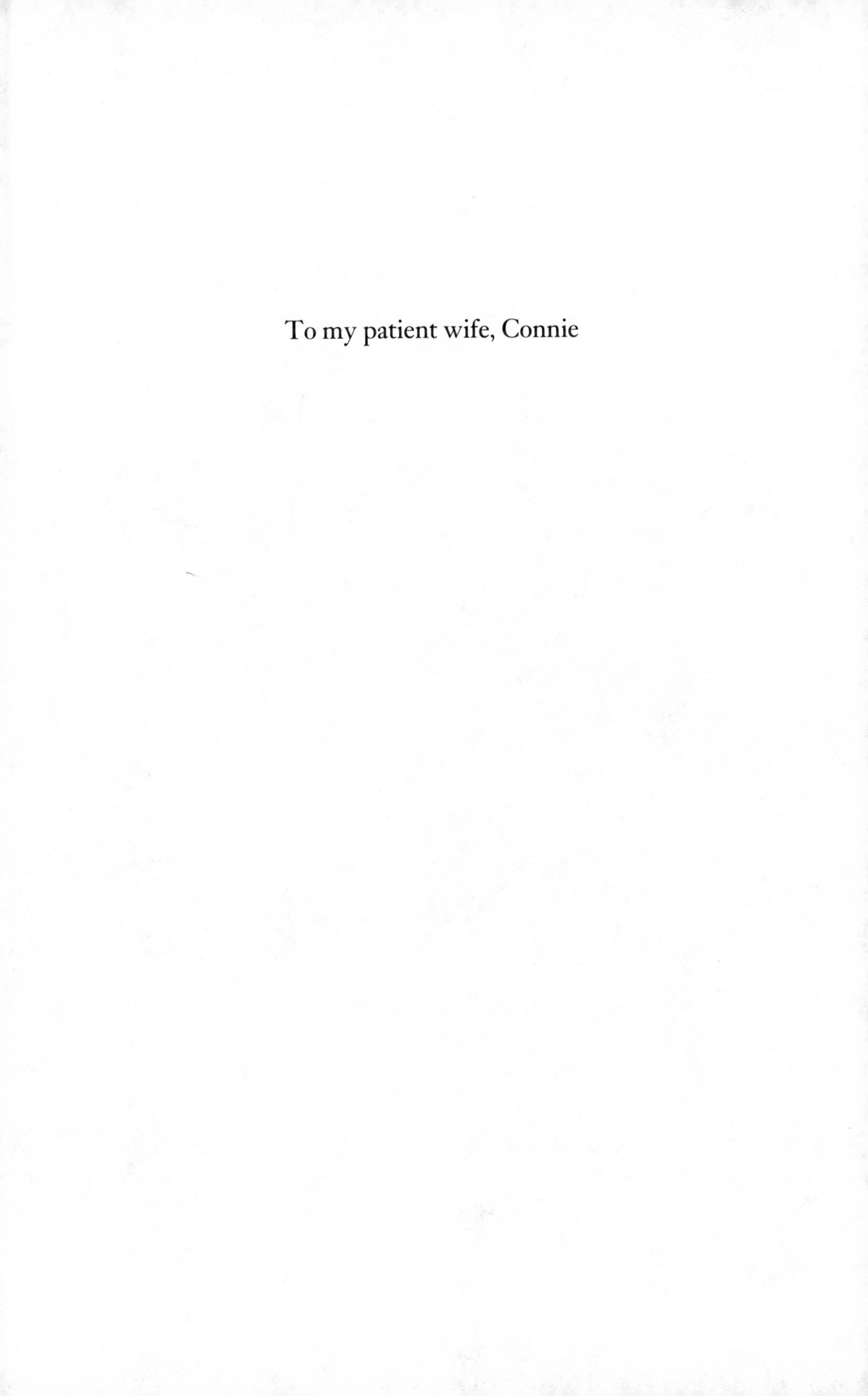

To my patient wife, Connie

Contents

Maps

Preface to Reprint

In the 100th anniversary issue of the *U.S. Naval Institute Proceedings* (October 1973), Associate Editor Robert A. Lambert selected *The Fast Carriers* as one of the ten best English-language naval books of the years 1873–1973. The book, he wrote, "is naval history in a classic mold combining scholarship and documentation with the author's willingness to pass critical judgment on personalities and events, along with ability to handle bureaucratic squabbles and the fight against the foreign enemy."

This assessment followed the *Proceedings'* selection of *The Fast Carriers* as the most notable naval book of the year 1969 (December 1969 issue) and the same journal's four-page review (August 1969 issue) by Vice Admiral David C. Richardson, a wartime Navy pilot and then Commander Sixth Fleet, who concluded that "this is a book to be studied, not one to be read in a casual manner for amusement. It is not a book of sea stories. The documents cited are documents of quality; the individual viewpoints presented are those of people who were in key positions. By employing these elements carefully and thoughtfully, the author has provided an intensely interesting book for all of those involved and especially for those who make the Navy a profession."

This generous acceptance by the Navy profession of a work critical of certain Navy personnel came as a pleasant surprise to the writer, who had expected a response similar to that of the late military historian Louis Morton, whose acid reviews had laid low many an author. Disturbed that this writer had, for example, dared to question the judgments of the eminent semi-official Navy historian of World War II, Samuel Eliot Morison, official Army historian Morton told the popular reading audience in *The New York Times Book Review* (12 January 1969) that the judgments of Reynolds in the book are "often harsh and sweeping, reflecting, one suspects, the views of the aviators rather than the reasoned conclusions of the historian." Rarely does a reviewer enjoy double jeopardy, but happily in this case Morton did, for nearly two years later he did a *volte-face* by informing the history profession in the *American Historical Review* (December 1970) that "Reynolds' volume has real value as a definitive account. . . ."

Other reviews fell in between Morton's extremes. Gerald E. Wheeler also had two chances, calling the book "excellent" in *The Journal of American History* (September 1969), which was a condensed version of his review in the *Naval War College Review* (June 1969). The *Marine Corps Gazette* (August 1969) called it "priority reading," while *Military Affairs* (February 1970) suggested that the book's frankness was "a refreshing and probably healthy change from the usual watered-down approach." The *Houston Post* (9 February 1969) topped the reactions of the popular press by heralding the book as "a standard reference on the subject," with the writing "direct, clear, and concise." And Allan R. Millett in the *Maryland Historical Review* (Winter 1969) used the words "an important book," "substantial contribution," "iconoclastic," "sound and stimulating," and "an entertaining, well-written, broadly researched, and intelligently conceived book."

Of course, many judgments and stylistic details in the book received adverse comment as well, some deserved, but the writer is gratified to observe that in the two dozen years since the book first appeared no historian has challenged the facts, thesis, or particular major interpretations (save for the usual supporters of Spruance at the Philippine Sea). Indeed, certain authors have merely tended to rely heavily on the scholarship in this work, notably Russell Weigley in *The American Way of War* and the Belotes in *Titans of the Seas*, the latter (p. x) regarding *The Fast Carriers* as "unique" and " 'must' reading for any serious student of naval warfare." The biographers have had a mixed response, Potter writing on Nimitz and Merrill and Frank on Halsey making full use; the latter in his *Halsey* (p. 122) called this volume "the definitive study regarding carrier operations in the Pacific." And naval officers Buell and Dyer writing on Spruance and Turner respectively not surprisingly chose to ignore the challenges made about their subjects in *The Fast Carriers*. The book also received honorable mention from Theodore Ropp (who in fact supervised the original dissertation) in the 40th anniversary issue of the journal *Military Affairs* (April 1977).

Inasmuch as *The Fast Carriers* has, thus far at least, stood the test of time and historiographical evaluation, there is no reason for the original text to be altered in any significant way. The writer is therefore pleased to introduce to a new generation of readers a revised edition that is different only in corrected minor errors, an updated bibliography, and the inclusion of some previously unavailable but important documentary materials.

Finally, the writer is pleased to direct the reader to what may be regarded as a companion volume to *The Fast Carriers—Admiral John H. Towers: The Struggle for Naval Air Supremacy,* which treats the evolution of fast carrier aviation from its origins to the early Cold War years through the man who was most instrumental in it over the preceding three decades. *Towers* adds new details to the wartime history of the fast carriers as well.

Clark G. Reynolds
Charleston, South Carolina
August, 1991

Preface

American naval history, particularly that of the Navy's air arm, has too often been told in superficial terms. The reason is twofold. First, the normal conservatism of the silent service discourages frank, critical, or controversial history; the United States Navy prefers to shelter its revered heroes from the illuminating probes of the historian. Second, as a result of the above, a *genre* of military pop literature has emerged, propounding a message no deeper than, "Look, mom, I'm flying!" The latter type of book includes picture histories, blood-and-guts battle tales, and some of the multivolume military history series or anthologies rapidly produced by amateurs, journalists, or irresponsible publishing houses.

The latter problem is serious, because it affects American attitudes and understanding—or lack of it—not only toward military history but toward military affairs and warfare in general. If the lay reader sought information on the aircraft carriers, for instance, he might consult a pop tome by Roger Caras under a series editorship of Martin Caidin, *Wings of Gold: The Story of United States Naval Aviation* (New York, 1965). So historically incomplete is that book, however, that not once is the Fast Carrier Task Force of World War II even mentioned—the very subject that fills the entire present work. Such bad histories can best be eliminated by sound scholarship, responsible publishers, and a more sophisticated reading audience.

The cautiousness of the military establishment toward critical histories will probably never change, although solid scholarship may convince its spokesmen that frank history is at least preferable to mythology, ignorance, or misunderstanding by the public. To borrow some words from one of the U.S. Navy's most honored yet controversial figures, Admiral Halsey: "It is the duty of historians and students to seek to know how combat commanders think and reason. After weighing all factors carefully, they must reach their own conclusions." (From the preface to Frederick C. Sherman's *Combat Command*, p. 8.) In this spirit, the present volume was undertaken.

Writing the complete analytical history of the Fast Carrier Task Force, including its contribution to the transformation of the U.S. Navy from a battleship-oriented to an air-centered navy, has been only slightly hindered by the reservations of a few participants. Most officers and families of the United States and British navies approached by the writer were most helpful and cooperative. To these people the writer is deeply indebted and hopes they will not mind being listed in the bibliography instead of in the preface. Special thanks, however, are due Mrs. John H. Towers and Mrs. Frederick C. Sherman, who generously allowed the writer to use their late husbands' private papers, also to Major Charles M. Cooke, Jr., USAF, for the use of his father's papers. Commander John H. Arbick, RCN (Ret.), was especially helpful in sending his own papers for perusal.

The writer has enjoyed untiring assistance from several mentors, archivists, historians, and colleagues throughout his research. Theodore Ropp of Duke University was instrumental in shaping the course of this project during the writer's graduate education; good suggestions were also made by Harold T. Parker, Irving B. Holley, and Robert H. Connery of that institution. Frank Robert Reynolds, the writer's uncle, and A. Russell Buchanan of the University of California at Santa Barbara provided early impetus, while archivist Mrs. Mildred D. Mayeux greatly facilitated research at the Navy's Operational Archives. Captain Stephen W. Roskill, RN (Ret.), kindly read and criticized the sections of the book dealing with the Royal Navy, and Lieutenant Commander P. K. Kemp, RN (Ret.), was very generous in providing much information from Admiralty records. Equally helpful were U.S. Navy historians Adrian O. Van Wyen, Aviation History Unit, and Lee M. Pearson, Naval Air Systems Command, also Susumu Nishiura, Chief of the War History Office of Japan. The keen, inquiring mind of William H. Russell of the United States Naval Academy opened new horizons in the realm of naval philosophy.

The final draft was written during the summer of 1967 with the assistance of a United States Naval Academy Research Grant.

To all the above persons and institutions the writer extends his sincerest thanks. He only hopes the final product measures up to some of their expectations.

Clark G. Reynolds
Orono, Maine
August 1968

Abbreviations

AAF	United States Army Air Forces
B.P.F.	British Pacific Fleet
BuAer	Bureau of Aeronautics
CASU	Carrier Aircraft Service Unit
Cincpac	Commander-in-Chief, Pacific Fleet
Cincpoa	Commander-in-Chief, Pacific Ocean Areas
CNO	Chief of Naval Operations
ComCarDiv	Commander Carrier Division
Cominch	Commander-in-Chief, United States Fleet
ComAirPac	Commander Air Force Pacific Fleet
ComBatPac	Commander Battleships Pacific Fleet
CV	Heavy (or medium) aircraft carrier
CVB	Battle (or large) aircraft carrier
CVL	Light aircraft carrier
DCNO(Air)	Deputy Chief of Naval Operations for Air
IJN	Imperial Japanese Navy
JCS	Joint Chiefs of Staff
RCN	Royal Canadian Navy
RN	Royal Navy
Servron	Service squadron
TF	Task Force
TG	Task Group
USNA	United States Naval Academy
VB	Carrier bombing squadron (or single plane)
VBF	Carrier fighter-bomber squadron (or plane)
VF	Carrier fighting squadron (or plane)
VT	Carrier torpedo squadron (or plane)

Dramatis Personae

THE FOUNDING FATHERS

WILLIAM A. MOFFETT

Director of Naval Aviation *1921*

Chief, Bureau of Aeronautics *1921–1933*

"Billy" U.S. Naval Academy 1890 (31st in a class of 34); Naval Observer 1922 (age 52). Tough, resolute, but a soft-spoken Southern gentleman. "Father of Naval Aviation."

JOSEPH MASON REEVES

Commander Aircraft Squadrons, Battle Fleet *1925–1931*

Commander-in-Chief, United States Fleet *1934–1936*

"Bull" or "Billy Goat" USNA 1894 (38/47); Naval Observer 1925 (age 52). Inspiring, outspoken, forceful speaker; willing to experiment. Laid early tactical foundations for the fast carrier task force.

ADMINISTRATIVE REFORMERS

JOHN H. TOWERS

Commander Air Force Pacific Fleet *1942–Feb 1944*

Deputy Commander-in-Chief, Pacific Fleet *Feb 1944–Jul 1945*

Commander Second Fast Carrier Force, Pacific *Sept 1945*

"Jack" USNA 1906 (31/116); Naval Aviator No. 3 1911 (age 26). Serious, courteous, quiet-mannered, receptive to ideas of others; outspoken advocate of naval aviation, leadership of which was inherited from Moffett, but, in his own words, "a flier who always kept one foot wet"; excellent administrator.

JAMES V. FORRESTAL

Under Secretary of the Navy *1940–Apr 1944*
Secretary of the Navy *Apr 1944–end of war*

Naval Aviator No. 154 (World War I; age 26). An intensely dedicated administrator, completely absorbed in his work; dynamic civilian leader of the Navy open to fresh ideas.

HIGH COMMAND

ERNEST J. KING

Commander-in-Chief, United States Fleet and
Chief of Naval Operations *1942–end of war*

"Ernie" or "Dolly" USNA 1901 (4/67); Wings 1927 (age 48). Hard as nails, profane, uncompromising; as dominating leader of the wartime Navy impatient with crusading younger aviators. "Temper?" said his Naval Academy yearbook, "Don't fool with nitroglycerine!"

CHESTER W. NIMITZ

Commander-in-Chief, Pacific Fleet and
Commander-in-Chief, Pacific Ocean Areas *1941–end of war*

USNA 1905 (7/114). No aviation experience, in fact nervous when riding in airplanes. Intelligent, thorough administrator; stern, patient, tactful, firm leader, endowed with hard common sense; excellent judge of men and questions of strategy; sensitive to criticism but could admit mistakes; enjoyed storytelling, taking long walks, and playing tennis.

RAYMOND A. SPRUANCE

Commander Central Pacific Force and
Commander Fifth Fleet *May 1943–end of war*

USNA 1907 (25/209). Little experience or interest in aviation; tactically oriented to battleships. Brilliant strategist and coordinator of complicated naval operations; quiet, pleasant, precise, calculating; a thinker, relaxed to good music; aloof, publicity-shy, also lazy and heavily dependent upon key advisers.

FAST CARRIER COMMANDERS

MARC A. MITSCHER

Commander Carrier Division Three *Jan–Mar 1944*
Commander Fast Carrier Force, Pacific Fleet *Jan–Aug 1944*
Commander First Fast Carrier Force, Pacific *Aug 1944–Jul 1945*

Deputy Chief of Naval Operations (Air) *Aug 1945–end of war*

"Pete" USNA 1910 (108/131); Naval Aviator No. 33 1916 (age 29). So quiet and soft-spoken to be barely audible; slight, bald, but tough and wiry; a leader's leader, commanding the respect of all aviators; said Ernie Pyle after meeting him, "From now on, Mitscher is one of my gods."

WILLIAM F. HALSEY, JR.

Commander South Pacific Area and Force *1942–Jun 1944*

Commander Third Fleet *1943–end of war*

"Bull" to the press. USNA 1904 (43/62); Wings 1934 (age 52). Gruff, exuberant, aggressive; all fighter, consequently not meticulous in planning; conscious of public morale and his own public image; a very late comer to aviation.

JOHN S. MCCAIN

Chief, Bureau of Aeronautics *1942–Aug 1943*

Deputy Chief of Naval Operations (Air) *Aug 1943–Jul 1944*

Commander Second Fast Carrier Force, Pacific *Jul 1944–Aug 1945*

"Slew" or "Jock" USNA 1906 (80/116); Wings 1936 (age 52). Fearless, aggressive, showy, personally pleasant, but also profane, nervous, occasionally hotheaded and often sloppy in appearance (spilling tobacco while rolling own cigarettes) and in operations.

FREDERICK C. SHERMAN

Commander Carrier Division Two *1942–Jul 1943*

Commander Carrier Division One *Jul 1943–Apr 1944; Aug 1944–Jul 1945*

Commander First Fast Carrier Force, Pacific *Jul 1945–end of war*

"Ted" or "Fightin' Freddie" USNA 1910 (24/131); Wings 1936 (age 47). Explosive, zealous, demanding, showy, irritable due to own ego and bad teeth problems; an intelligent, superb tactician, loving a good fight; though normally quiet and calm in battle, took risks and preferred independent command; outspoken for naval aviation.

THE THINKERS

DEWITT C. RAMSEY

Commander Carrier Division One *1942–Jul 1943*

Chief, Bureau of Aeronautics *Aug 1943–Jun 1945*

Chief of Staff, Com Fifth Fleet *Jul 1945–end of war*

"Duke" USNA 1912 (125/156); Naval Aviator No. 45 1917 (age 28). A pioneer aviator with keen administrative abilities; well-liked by contemporaries.

Arthur W. Radford

Commander Carrier Division Eleven *Jul–Dec 1943*
Chief of Staff, ComAirPac *Dec 1943–Feb 1944*
Assistant Deputy CNO (Air) *Mar–Oct 1944*
Commander Carrier Division Six *Oct 1944–end of war*

"Raddy" USNA 1916 (59/177); Wings 1920 (age 24). Administrator *par excellence;* a tough-minded leader under stress; quiet, calm, decisive, serious, having a slow, deep manner of speech; respected.

Forrest P. Sherman

Chief of Staff, ComAirPac *1942–Nov 1943*
Deputy Chief of Staff (Plans), Cincpac *Nov 1943–end of war*

"Fuzz" USNA 1918 (2/199); Wings 1922 (age 26). Brilliant, quiet, well-read, a near-genius; highly respected by all for his mind, but also feared for his ruthless ambition.

Donald B. Duncan

Commanding Officer, USS *Essex* (CV-9) *1942–Nov 1943*
Assistant Chief of Staff (Plans), Cominch *May1944–Jul 1945*
Commander Carrier Division Four *reporting Aug 1945*

"Wu" USNA 1917 (24/182); Wings 1921 (age 24). Keen administrative sense; superb shiphandler; much-sought-after for his mind.

THE FIGHTERS

Alfred E. Montgomery

Commander Carrier Division Twelve *Jul 1943–Mar 1944*
Commander Carrier Division Three *Mar 1944–Jan 1945*
Commander Air Force Pacific Fleet *Jul 1945–end of war*

"Monty" USNA 1912 (29/156); Wings 1922 (age 30). Impatient, sarcastic, irascible, except in battle, then calm and thoughtful; exploded violently at times, suffering from migraine headaches; difficult to please; not popular but highly respected.

J. J. Clark

Commanding Officer, USS *Yorktown* (CV-10) *Apr 1943–Feb 1944*
Commander Carrier Division Thirteen *Feb–Jun 1944*
Commander Carrier Division Five *Jul 1944–Jun 1945*

"Jock" or "Jocko" USNA 1918 (47/199); Wings 1925 (age 31). Hardhitting taskmaster, inspiring confidence up and down; Cherokee Indian heritage contributed to fighting spirit; tough, unrelenting advocate of do-it-yourself; old leg injury caused limp; prewar ulcers kept diet to milk and light foods; loud, boisterous voice.

JOHN W. REEVES, JR.
Commander Carrier Division Four *Oct 1943–July 1944*

"Black Jack" USNA 1911 (74/193); Wings 1936 (age 47). Tough, fiery, impatient for battle.

GERALD F. BOGAN
Commander Carrier Division Four *Jul 1944–end of war*

"Jerry" USNA 1916 (26/177); Wings 1925 (age 30). Pugnosed, outspoken, smart, tenacious combat leader, loving a scrap; a thorough teacher in the ways of carrier combat.

RALPH E. DAVISON
Commander Carrier Division Two *Jul 1944–May 1945*

"Dave" USNA 1916 (3/177); Wings 1920 (age 24). Highly intelligent, articulate, well-read; always quiet, friendly manner; fun-loving.

SIR PHILIP L. VIAN, RN
Admiral Commanding, First Aircraft Carrier Squadron *Nov 1944–end of war*

Royal Naval College 1911. Nonaviator, but excellent ship and force handler. Seemingly natural instinct for fighting at sea; calm and cold personally; occasionally impatient, also outbursts of foul language; difficult to please; immaculate, formal dresser always.

THOMAS L. SPRAGUE
Commanding Officer, USS *Intrepid* (CV-11) *Aug 1943–Mar 1944*
Commander Carrier Division Three *Feb 1945–end of war*

"Tommy" USNA 1918 (19/199); Wings 1921 (age 26). An aviator's aviator, excellent tactician, bold, always seeking perfection; friendly; calm in battle; much respected.

SHORT-TERMERS

CHARLES A. POWNALL
Commander Carrier Division Three and
Commander Fast Carrier Forces, Pacific Fleet *Aug 1943–Jan 1944*
Commander Air Force Pacific Fleet *Feb–Aug 1944*

"Baldy" USNA 1910 (81/131); Wings 1927 (age 39). Pleasant, affable, too polite to wield authority ashore or afloat; apparent distaste for combat, perhaps due to Quaker origins.

Samuel P. Ginder

Commanding Officer, USS *Enterprise* (CV-6) *April–Oct 1943*
Commander Carrier Division Eleven *Dec 1943–Apr 1944*

"Sam" or "Cy" USNA 1916 (99/177); Wings 1921 (age 26). A good administrator and planner, but used somewhat silly procedures afloat; a worrier.

William K. Harrill

Commander Carrier Division One *Apr–Jul 1944*

"Keen" USNA 1914 (37/154); Wings 1921 (age 29). A polished gentleman; indecisive, a worrier, unsuited for combat command.

The Fast Carriers

An aircraft carrier is a noble thing. It lacks almost everything that seems to denote nobility, yet deep nobility is there. A carrier has no poise. It has no grace. It is top-heavy and lop-sided. It has the lines of a cow. It doesn't cut through the water like a cruiser, knifing romantically along. . . . It just plows. . . . Yet a carrier is a ferocious thing, and out of its heritage of action has grown its nobility. I believe that every Navy in the world has as its No. 1 priority the destruction of enemy carriers. That's a precarious honor, but it's a proud one.

Ernie Pyle, 1945

One:
Fast Carriers, 1922–1942

"A small, high-speed carrier alone can destroy or disable a battleship alone, . . . a fleet whose carriers give it command of the air over the enemy fleet can defeat the latter," Admiral William S. Sims told Congressional inquisitors, concluding that therefore "the fast carrier is the capital ship of the future."[1] The year was 1925. Sims, the outspoken former wartime American naval commander in Europe, defined the fast carrier as "an airplane carrier of thirty-five knots and carrying one hundred planes," a weapon which was "in reality a capital ship of much greater offensive power than any battleship."[2]

Like many nineteenth-century-educated military and naval officers, Sims had been a skeptic in the earliest period of aviation. The dreadnought was undisputed champion of the seas in those happy, deceivingly carefree days following the turn of the century. Every nation which could afford these magnificent battleships built or bought them and put them on display. The people of the United States, beguiled by their own big-navy philosopher-historian, Alfred Thayer Mahan, were no exception; they eagerly participated in the Age of the Battleship.

One day during the autumn of 1909, American fleet units rested at anchor in the Hudson River off New York City for one of their festive public appearances. Diplomats and admirals were present to observe an unusual demonstration: the flight of an airplane over the fleet. Wilbur Wright, one of the two brothers who had first flown a piston-driven aircraft only six years before at Kitty Hawk, piloted the plane in a highly successful flight that impressed the audience. Among the observers were then Commander Sims, future Navy Assistant Secretary Franklin D. Roosevelt, and Lieutenant Ernest J. King.[3] Little did they realize the consequences of what they had seen or how it would one day affect the lives of the latter two.

Three years later, during the fall of 1912, a similar demonstration impressed the Japanese Emperor and other high dignitaries at the grand naval review off Yokohama. First Lieutenant Yozo Kaneko, IJN, landed a seaplane near the imperial flagship and took off from the water, while a second floatplane and a nonrigid airship flew over the Japanese fleet.[4] Like the Americans, the Japanese were to develop naval air techniques for a quarter of a century before the two navies were pitted against each other in a great air-sea war.

1. Great Britain

The British, rather than the Americans or Japanese, were the first to assign aircraft to ships on a regular basis; they also invented the aircraft carrier. After the failure of the heavy-gunned, lightly armored battle cruiser to fulfill its reconnaissance and attack roles at the battle of Jutland in 1916, the Royal Navy turned to the carrier for the solution. Two crude carriers were completed by the end of World War I, though neither saw action, followed by three others over the ensuing decade. In April 1918, however, all British military and naval aviation was unified in the Royal Air Force, and fleet air was reduced after the war to a pitiable condition in deference to the land-based strategic bomber forces. Throughout the 1920s it was represented at the Admiralty only by a lowly captain in charge of a small Naval Air Section.[1]

Despite its five experimental carriers, Britain took little interest in naval aviation until the rise of Nazi Germany in the mid-1930s. In 1937, the Navy finally succeeded in having the Fleet Air Arm transferred back from the RAF to the Navy, but the changeover took two time-consuming years to complete. Administratively, a rear admiral was appointed to sit on the Board of Admiralty as Assistant Chief of Naval Staff (Air), upgraded the following year, 1938, to be Fifth Sea Lord and Chief of Naval Air Services with the rank of vice admiral.[2] In ships, Britain completed its first modern fast, 30-knot, 60-plane carrier in 1938, the 22,000-ton *Ark Royal.* Keels were also laid for four 31-knot, 72-plane, 23,000-ton carriers of the *Illustrious* class. These, plus two modified versions begun later, comprised Britain's wartime fast carrier fleet. In naval aircraft, the Fleet Air Arm entered World War II sadly deficient, as a result of two decades of virtual neglect. Only antiquated biplanes, inferior monoplanes, and modified land planes were available until American Lend-Lease aircraft arrived.

Carrier operations in the Anglo-German war were dictated by geography more than any other single factor. Assigned the role of protecting sea lanes between bases in the British Isles and Gibraltar, Malta, Alexandria, and Singapore, the new carriers were equipped with armored flight decks to withstand heavy bombing attacks from land-based enemy planes. In addition, each eventually mounted 16 4.5-inch dual-purpose guns and numerous 40mm and 20mm antiaircraft batteries, plus whatever defense the carrier's fighters could provide. Though the ships were well-protected, the bulky armor took up space from the fuel tanks and aircraft storage areas, thus cutting down cruising radius and carrier squadron sizes.[3]

As long as Britain maintained her bases in the Atlantic and Mediterranean, the carriers were seldom faced with excessively long voyages and could often count on friendly land-based air. After two older carriers were sunk very early in the war, a German U-boat torpedoed *Ark Royal*, which foundered while in tow late in 1941, but *Illustrious* and her sister ships fared better. At Gibraltar the Royal Navy based Force H—a task force consisting of one fast carrier, one battleship or battle cruiser, several cruisers and destroyers; centrally located, this force could operate at a moment's notice in Atlantic or Mediterranean. In November 1940 old Swordfish torpedo bombers from *Illustrious* caught all six of Italy's battleships at Taranto and torpedoed three of them. The three were put out of action (one for good), and the Italian fleet abandoned Taranto. The following March aircraft from carrier *Formidable* drove off an Italian force at the battle of Cape Matapan, and in May 1941 *Ark Royal* played an important role in the sinking of the German battleship *Bismarck*, this time in the Atlantic.

Since Britain's primary mission through mid-1944 was keeping open her sea lanes, her fast carriers normally operated singly with escorts in fulfilling that mission. Since many carriers were needed to combat the U-boat, however, the Royal Navy relied upon the small, slow, but economically and rapidly produced escort carriers to carry the burden. Large numbers of these craft would not be available until the industry of allied America could turn them out, starting in 1943. Until then, Britain paid for the mistakes of the interwar period and very nearly lost the Battle of the Atlantic. Thus preoccupied, she suffered devastating losses in the Far East against Japan when that country went to war, forcing Britain to withdraw her fleet from Ceylon early in 1942.

Great Britain fought on doggedly against her continental adversaries Germany and Italy, using most of her resources and fleet. Her fast carriers helped hold the line, but they could never operate continuously in a concentrated multicarrier force until operations shifted from the defensive to the offensive. By that time, the main fighting front would shift to the plain of western Europe, and Britain's fast carriers could be released to return to the Far East.

2. *Japan*

Great Britain played a major role in the growth of Japanese carrier aviation. In addition to sending many advisers to train the Japanese in carrier operations, Britain suggested to Japan and the United States at the Washington Conference of 1921–1922 that each country convert two of its uncompleted battle cruisers into fast carriers.[1] Both countries endorsed the idea, and the United States converted two of the *Lexington* class into 33,000-ton, 33-knot, 75-plane carriers. Likewise, Japan in 1927 produced the 26,900-ton, 32.5-knot, 60-plane *Akagi*, followed in 1930 by the 29,600-ton, 28.3-knot, 72-plane ex-battleship *Kaga*. Until these two ships appeared, the tiny, 7470-ton, slow, 25-knot *Hosho*, commissioned in 1922, acted as an experimental vessel for Japan.[2]

Unlike Britain, Japan never unified its air forces, hence the Naval Air Service matured rapidly and successfully. In 1927 the Navy created two key administrative posts, Combined Naval Air Command at Imperial General Headquarters and a Bureau of Aeronautics whose chief held the rank of vice admiral.[3] In July of that year each junior officer in the Navy was required "to undergo a short course of instruction in aviation," [4] and if he expected to achieve flag rank he eventually had to qualify as an aviator or hold command of an aircraft carrier or seaplane tender.[5] Pilot training was highly selective, with about only 100 new aviators chosen every year. After up to eight years of vigorous training, only the best pilots were rotated to carrier duty, hence the carriers maintained a very skilled elite of flyers.[6]

Though reinforced in 1933 by the small, 10,600-ton *Ryujo*, the Japanese Combined Fleet relied generally upon *Akagi* and *Kaga* for aerial reconnaissance, patrol, and horizontal and torpedo bombing.[7] By the mid-1930s Japan had initiated her policy of expansion in the Far East and therefore embraced the carrier as an integral part of her military defenses. Ever since the end of World War I the Japanese had regarded as a potential threat only one nation, the United States, which was also developing aircraft carriers for operations in the vast Pacific. Alarmed, Japan began open competition against America in building carriers.

The advances of the U.S. Navy in carrier aviation led the Japanese to conclude—correctly—that in war the odds would weigh "heavily in favor of an attack force" of enemy carriers approaching Japan.[8] Japan therefore hoped to eliminate the enemy carriers, by force if not by diplomacy. British naval analyst Hector C. Bywater observed in 1934 that Japan wanted "the total abolition of aircraft carriers on the ground of their essentially aggressive character." Casting a keen glance into the future, he declared that Japan feared carriers "more than any other naval craft. She dreads the possibility of large enemy carriers steaming across the Pacific to send off swarms of bombing planes against Tokyo and other populous centers" constructed of light, inflammable materials.[9] But Japan failed to eliminate carriers through diplomacy, and late that year she abrogated her treaty commitments, effective the last day of 1936.

The best defense against American carrier attacks was Japan's own carrier force, reasoned Rear Admiral Isoroku Yamamoto, in 1933 Commander Carrier Division One and two years later Chief of the Bureau of Aeronautics. Yamamoto pressed for appropriations for more carriers and initiated the design and construction in Japan of modern naval aircraft. He succeeded in both endeavors, as new planes—especially the superb Zero fighter—and carriers joined the fleet toward the end of the decade, while the older carriers were completely modernized. When Yamamoto became Vice Minister of the Navy late in 1936, Vice Admiral Koshiro Oikawa, another former ComCarDiv 1, succeeded to the post of Chief of the Bureau of Aeronautics. Within three years Yamamoto became Commander-in-Chief Combined Fleet and Oikawa Navy Minister in the Tojo cabinet, giving naval aviation representation in the highest operational and political echelons.[10]

But not all naval officers shared the enthusiasm of Yamamoto and the aviators. Admiral Zengo Yoshida, Fleet commander in 1938, refused even to ride in an airplane.[11] The airmen, whose carriers were integrated into the First (battleships) and Second (cruisers) fleets, wanted a separate fleet for the carriers. Carrier planes dramatically supported the Army in China in 1937, and two years later Navy planes successfully bombed a mockup of the American carrier *Saratoga* at the Kashima Bombing Range. When the controversy broke into the open, the older, conservative admirals held firm to their traditional faith in the battleship as capital ship of the fleet by supporting the construction of the giant 75,000-ton *Yamato*-class superbattleships.[12]

Japan's admirals planned to fit their fast carriers into traditional strategic plans for defending the homeland. Japanese naval philosophy was basically defensive: to intercept and repel any invading force in local waters. This objective appeared in the ships, constructed like Britain's to operate with short cruising radii, within range of bases near Japan or occupied Asia. Consequently fleet maneuvers in the 1930s were held near Japan against a theoretical attack by an American fleet. When the enemy fleet approached the battleships of the Combined Fleet, Japanese leaders would send a "flying squadron" of cruisers around the flank and rear of the enemy, thereby defeating and repulsing the invader. Such tactics had been displayed by Japan in her wars against China in 1894–1895 and Russia in 1904–1905.

The fast carriers would scout for the battleships, then join the cruisers (Second Fleet) as part of the modern flying squadron to entrap and defeat the enemy navy. The carriers were to disperse and attack the enemy from different directions, especially at night using aerial torpedoes. Another key element of this strategy was Japan's system of "unsinkable carriers"—the many islands of the Central Pacific mandated to Japan after World War I: the Marianas, Carolines, and Marshalls. In 1934 Japan began constructing airfields on these islands in order to complete an interlocking defensive air network. An invading enemy fleet would therefore run the additional risk of severe bombing by land-based planes.[13]

The aviators resented this secondary role, especially after their leading carrier tactician saw a newsreel late in 1940 showing four American carriers operating together. Commander Minoru Genda suddenly realized that four or more fast carriers operating in one concentrated tactical formation could mutually defend each other against air attack with a greater volume of antiaircraft fire and fewer defensive fighter aircraft. As air operations officer to ComCarDiv 1, Rear Admiral Jisaburo Ozawa, Genda was in a position to influence policy. He therefore passed his idea up the chain of command, thus initiating the action that would create the first fast carrier task force of World War II.[14]

Genda's appeal for a four-carrier task force was most opportune. CarDiv 1, the modernized *Akagi* and *Kaga,* had been reinforced in 1939 by CarDiv 2, the new 16,000-ton, 34-knot, 55-plane carriers *Soryu* and *Hiryu.* Furthermore, by October 1941, a new carrier division would be formed from the brand-new 25,675-ton, 34.2-knot, 72-plane carriers *Shokaku* and *Zuikaku.* A separate fleet of four to six fast carriers would be most effective, or so the brilliant Genda informed Fleet commander Yamamoto. Yamamoto listened intently, and with good reason; in January 1941 he began—ever so secretly—to plan for an attack on the United States Fleet base at Pearl Harbor, Hawaii, in the event his government decided on war.[15] Such an attack could only be accomplished by a swift, powerful force of aircraft carriers.

The aviators won their case. On 10 April 1941 the Navy General Staff created the First Air Fleet, Vice Admiral Chuichi Nagumo. Nagumo, a specialist in torpedoes, had had vast experience in all ship types except carriers; equally unfortunate, his qualities of leadership had begun to wane by this point in his career.[16] Nevertheless, he also became ComCarDiv 1 and inherited Commander Genda as his air operations officer. CarDivs 1 and 2 became heavy carrier task groups, while CarDiv 3 and a new CarDiv 4 became light carrier groups. Along with the First Air Fleet, the Navy established the Eleventh Air Fleet, comprising major land-based attack air forces, under Vice Admiral Nishizo Tsukahara.

Soon Admiral Nagumo accepted Genda's concept and initiated fleet maneuvers to test it. Two cruising formations were thereupon developed during 1941. One followed the Japanese naval tradition of dispersing ships to trap an enemy fleet. The two large carrier divisions would launch planes from different areas, the planes converging simultaneously over the target, a tactic that had been accepted in principle since 1936. The second formation was also traditionally Japanese in purpose but new tactically. The purpose was to support the Army ashore. The tactic was concentration; the two divisions of two large carriers each would operate in a box formation 7000 meters from one another for tight, efficient launching procedures and especially for better mutual antiaircraft defense.[17] In neither case would any ship type larger than destroyer be used as escort in the carrier formations. Battleships and cruisers continued to operate independently. And destroyers, maximum sixteen to a carrier formation, provided too few antiaircraft barrels to defend the carriers adequately. The main shield therefore remained the defensive fighter patrols.

As Japan's political leaders deliberated war, the strategic planners discussed the means. The Army wanted to push into Southeast Asia and the Dutch East Indies, supported by the Combined Fleet, including Nagumo's four carriers and Tsukahara's land-based air. Admiral Yamamoto agreed in principle, except that he feared the United States Battle Fleet at Pearl Harbor would cross the Pacific and fall upon his left flank, relieving the Philippines and interrupting the Army's lines of communications to the south. Yamamoto therefore conceived the carrier air attack against Pearl Harbor to sink those battleships. Before proposing the plan to the Navy General Staff, he sought the advice of an experienced naval aviator—Rear Admiral Takijiro Onishi, Tsukahara's chief of staff and one of the highest-ranking, most respected, and yet most controversial pilots in the Navy. Onishi liked Yamamoto's plan but told the fleet commander that he would need all of his four large carriers to hit Pearl. Since the attack would involve carriers and not the planes of Tsukahara's command, Onishi referred the plan to Commander Genda of Nagumo's staff.[18]

Genda labored over Yamamoto's scheme for the attack on Pearl Harbor and concluded it was feasible. But, insisted the calculating aviator, complete secrecy was essential and the carrier striking force should include six heavy carriers. The two new ones would be *Shokaku* and *Zuikaku*, completed in August and September 1941 respectively. Genda's conclusion convinced Yamamoto his plan would work, and in July—when Japan decided for war—Yamamoto initiated mock air attacks on Hawaiian-type topography at Kagoshima Bay.[19] By 1 October the First Air Fleet—Japan's fast carrier task force—included Nagumo's CarDiv 1, *Akagi* and *Kaga;* Rear Admiral Tamon Yamaguchi's CarDiv 2, *Hiryu* and *Soryu;* and Rear Admiral Chuichi Hara's CarDiv 5, *Shokaku* and *Zuikaku.*

Yamamoto's plan, a bold one, met with considerable opposition—from the Army, whose leaders felt Tsukahara's land-based air was insufficient to cover the southward invasions; from the Navy General Staff, whose conservative battleship admirals found the plan too risky; and even from Vice Admiral Nagumo, who had become cautious in his later years. But Yamamoto insisted, and was supported by the resourceful Yamaguchi of CarDiv 2. There were other obstacles. No Japanese carrier had ever refueled from a tanker at sea, since the big battle had always been planned for the western Pacific near Japanese bases. Therefore *Kaga* refueled while underway in September to prove it could be done. Commander Genda recommended that only Japan's best naval pilots be used, and so Yamamoto upset all personnel patterns in the Naval Air Service by assigning the best 400 naval aviators to the First Air Fleet. Finally, so enamored had Japan's carriermen become with attack that they had turned over most reconnaissance and search functions to land-based patrol planes; on the Pearl Harbor strike the carriers would have to do their own searching. It was a risk, but Yamamoto was a gambler.[20]

Time threatened Japan. For various political and military reasons she had to attack American forces at Hawaii by mid-December 1941, and so on 3 November the Navy General Staff finally agreed to Yamamoto's plan to attack Pearl Harbor. Without a moment to lose, Yamamoto assembled the two new *Shokakus* with the four other heavy carriers for a final rehearsal—the first and only time the six fast carriers engaged in a full drill together as one task force.[21] Late in November Nagumo's carriers sailed eastward, while the invasion forces escorted by the light carriers approached the South China Sea. The Pearl Harbor Attack Force refueled en route, then on 7 December launched its devastating attack on the American Battle Fleet, disabling or sinking most of the battleships. The Japanese planes did not locate the American carriers, but Admiral Nagumo did not linger to look for them. His mission accomplished, the battleships neutralized, Nagumo broke off the attack and headed for the fueling rendezvous and home.[22]

Immediately after the attack, the six-carrier force broke up, never to reassemble in that strength. Fulfilling the traditional Navy function of supporting the Army, the fast carriers supported landing forces at Wake and Rabaul in the Pacific and at key points in the Dutch East Indies. Nagumo took most of his carriers to the latter area, where their planes sank the British carrier *Hermes* and bombed Darwin, Australia, and Trincomalee, Ceylon. But the major effort was supporting the Army, leading Nagumo to keep his carriers concentrated in Genda's tight box formation. Thus Japan's fast carrier force from December 1941 through April 1942 did not deploy for a fleet action—neither by dispersing to converge on an enemy force, by sending off torpedo bombers in night air strikes, nor by maneuvering to receive a major enemy air attack.[23]

In short, Japan's fast carrier task force—First Air Fleet—had been little more than a "flying squadron" to support Army operations, directly with close support and indirectly by long-range air raids on the Allied naval bases at Pearl Harbor, Darwin, and Trincomalee. The battleship remained the backbone of the Japanese fleet, though the carrier had assumed an enhanced position in the Navy. The carrier did not replace the battleship, nor was it integrated with the battleship into a common tactical formation. The fast carriers of Japan had not been tested in a naval battle.

Japan's strategy, as always in Japanese history, remained defensive. Once the U.S. Fleet was eliminated and the East Indies conquered, plans called for the establishment of a defensive perimeter from Wake through the Marshalls and Gilberts to New Guinea and the Solomons. The fleet, with the interior position, could operate from Singapore in Malaya, Rabaul in the Bismarck archipelago, or Truk in the eastern Carolines to meet a threat at any point in the perimeter. Meanwhile, Japan's ally, Hitler's Germany, guaranteed the defeat of Russia and Britain, with the result that the United States would sue for peace.[24] Strategically, observed one contemporary critic, "A defensive navy is nothing more than a strip of floating Maginot Line that can be propelled to points where an enemy intends to land."[25] Realizing this weakness, Admiral Yamamoto wished to insure the destruction of the American base at Pearl Harbor and to sink the carriers that had been absent on 7 December 1941.

First, however, the Army desired air cover for its operation to seize Port Moresby, New Guinea, and the southern Solomons. The Navy obliged by providing Rear Admiral Hara's CarDiv 5, *Shokaku* and *Zuikaku,* and one light carrier. This time, however, two American carriers were waiting, and early in May 1942 the two small carrier forces clashed in the first carrier battle in history, the battle of the Coral Sea. U.S. planes sank the light carrier and severely damaged *Shokaku,* while the Japanese lost 70 planes. Japan's bombers damaged both American carriers, one of which had to be abandoned and sunk. Japan also captured the southern Solomons, but its forces turned back from Port Morseby as a result of the carrier battle. The worst result for Japan was the heavy damage to *Shokaku* and plane losses to *Zuikaku*'s air group; both carriers were thus placed out of action for many weeks.

Ignoring the temporary loss of CarDiv 5, Admiral Yamamoto

determined to complete the neutralization of Pearl Harbor. His weapon again would be the airplane, but his objective was twofold. The entire Combined Fleet would accompany an invasion force to Midway Island in the western Hawaiian group. Presumably the Americans would commit their remaining two or three carriers to defend Midway. Nagumo's four carriers or Yamamoto's battleships, far superior to the enemy, would destroy the unescorted U.S. carriers. The Japanese Army would then land on Midway, capture it, and convert the airfield into a base for Vice Admiral Tsukahara's 11th Air Fleet, which would then begin the systematic bombing of Hawaii. With the carriers sunk and Pearl Harbor under constant air attack, the United States might then realize the fruitlessness of trying to fight in the Pacific.

The details of Yamamoto's Midway operation were unbelievably complicated, which Yamamoto enjoyed and which was typically Japanese. Landing forces would attack Midway and the Aleutian Islands to the north. The U.S. carriers, rushing north to relieve the Aleutians, would be engaged by Nagumo's carriers or by Yamamoto's battleships, which were still operating separately. Ignoring the obvious lesson of Pearl, the Japanese continued to regard the battle line as the main attack force. The carriers might still be overwhelmingly powerful, but Yamamoto refused to concentrate all his available carriers under Nagumo, and rightly so, since both landing forces needed air cover. As a result, Nagumo's CarDiv 1 of *Akagi* and *Kaga* and Yamaguchi's CarDiv 2 of *Hiryu* and *Soryu* formed the First Carrier Striking Force; Rear Admiral Kakuji Kakuta's CarDiv 4 of the new 24,140-ton *Junyo* and the old light *Ryujo* formed the Second Carrier Striking Force in the Aleutians; Captain Sueo Obayashi's 11,262-ton light carrier *Zuiho* covered the Midway landing force; and Yamamoto kept tiny *Hosho* with the battleships.

The aviators did not like the plan. It violated the principle of concentration as envisioned by Genda, which was indispensable for the defense of the carriers. Admiral Yamaguchi therefore recommended that the entire fleet be reorganized into three task fleets with three or four carriers in the centers screened by battleships, cruisers, and destroyers. Yamamoto refused. The carrier command was weakened by the fact that Commander Genda, charged with planning the details of the operation, received from nonaviator Nagumo none of the expert criticism he was used to getting from

Onishi and Yamaguchi. Commander Mitsuo Fuchida, *Akagi's* air group commander, later lamented the necessity of the fast carriers' covering the Midway landing, which required "a fixed schedule" and deprived the fast carriers of "the flexibility of movement that was imperative for a successful fleet engagement." Furthermore, Yamamoto in battleship *Yamato* would be too far from the carriers should his air-oriented leadership be required at a critical moment.[26] Finally, had Yamamoto waited two months he would have had three more large carriers, *Shokaku*, *Zuikaku*, and possibly *Hiyo*, sister ship of *Junyo* commissioned in July—a possible total of eleven carriers.

But Yamamoto was a gambler and the Navy General Staff was flushed with a victory drunkenness that not even the rebuff at Coral Sea had affected. One thing the Japanese fleet commander feared —and rightly so—was the speed with which industrially powerful America would recover from the initial shock and damage wrought by Japan's offensive. Thus, early in June the many-pronged Japanese attack was launched, with catastrophic results. While the Aleutians proved an easy target, the American three-carrier force was elusive. Until the latter could be pinpointed and a fleet engagement brought on, Nagumo assumed the box formation for attacking Midway's defenses and had his torpedo bombers armed with bombs. When his scout planes finally sighted an American carrier, Nagumo did not attack because too few fighters were available to escort his bombers. He stuck to his decision over the proddings of Yamaguchi and in the absence of Yamamoto, and even in the face of repeated but unsuccessful land-based bombing and carrier-based torpedo attacks on his own ships.[27]

Nagumo's orthodoxy cost him his entire force. Still in the concentrated box, four carriers defended only by two battleships, three cruisers, and eleven destroyers, Nagumo belatedly shifted to preparations for fleet engagement. Without dispersing his two carrier divisions according to Genda's original doctrine, Nagumo ordered his planes—just back from bombing Midway—regassed and rearmed with torpedoes for attacking enemy ships. At this vulnerable moment the American dive bombers caught Nagumo's low-flying defensive fighters completely by surprise, diving straight down to score several direct hits on the Japanese carriers. Initial bomb hits ignited the aviation gas and ammunition on the decks, starting uncontrollable fires on the carriers, which began to maneuver apart aimlessly. One by one Nagumo's carriers sank, *Soryu*, *Kaga*, *Akagi*, and finally *Hiryu*. Japan's fast carrier force had lived a short and exciting life—fourteen months from inception to destruction.

At Midway, Japan learned the most important lesson about fast carrier operations—the hard way. The carrier, the new backbone of any large fleet, required maximum antiaircraft (and antisubmarine) protection with all available battleships, cruisers, and destroyers. Four carriers were sufficient to defeat the two, three, or even four carriers the Americans might have had at Midway *provided* the rest of the Combined Fleet had been used to protect Nagumo's flattops. The three smaller carriers covering land forces were needed to lend air support during the landings, except that the landing in the Aleutians was unnecessary and the one at Midway was not attempted because of Nagumo's defeat. Seven or eight carriers concentrated under Yamamoto's command could have defeated the American navy and *then* supported the landing at Midway. Command of the air and sea should precede any landing.

On 14 July 1942 the Navy finally reorganized the Combined Fleet around the carriers and land-based air forces. The main fighting fleet was designated Third Fleet, under Vice Admiral Nagumo, based at Truk—two carrier divisions of three carriers each surrounded by defensive circles of battleships, cruisers, and destroyers. Nagumo retained direct command of CarDiv 1, now consisting of *Shokaku*, *Zuikaku*, and *Zuiho*. The superb Yamaguchi had gone down with *Hiryu* at Midway, so command of CarDiv 2 went to Rear Admiral Kakuta, who had successfully covered the Aleutian landings; the carriers were *Junyo*, *Hiyo*, and *Ryujo*. CarDivs 3, 4, and 5 no longer existed.[28] Fortunately for Japan, while she had lost more than 250 planes with the sinking carriers at Midway, most of the highly trained pilots (average 700 hours training in the air prior to assignment in the fleet) had merely jumped overboard and been rescued by destroyers.[29] So Japan still had a six-carrier force, but only the two *Shokakus* carried as many as 75 planes each.

The sting had been taken out of Japan's offensive, and new targets became those within range of Admiral Tsukahara's 11th Air Fleet, which moved from the Marianas to Rabaul. In construction, the emphasis changed overnight from battleships to carriers, including many conversions and much new construction. Working at full capacity, however, Japanese industry would be unable to float another carrier armada of many heavy carriers until late 1944. This race of industry therefore became a major battleground.

3. United States

The American experience with carrier aviation compared in many ways with the early British administrative difficulties and the Japanese tactical problems. The differences were that, unlike Britain's, the Navy's air force succeeded in remaining in the Navy, and, unlike Japan's, the United States Navy was faced with having to cross the broad Pacific in wartime and therefore to develop an offensive fast carrier doctrine as soon as ships became available.

United States naval aviation emerged from World War I enjoying considerable freedom in its relations with the bureaus of the Navy Department. Most of its pilots had been processed through a flexible Naval Reserve Flying Corps, aptly administered by Lieutenant John H. Towers. With the war over, however, naval aviation lost its privileges and faced criticism from two major sources. The Chief of Naval Operations (CNO), Admiral William S. Benson, felt naval air should be administered at a very low level, while General Billy Mitchell of the Army Air Service argued that naval and Army air should be combined into an independent air force.[1] Mitchell's philosophy, like that of Douhet in Italy and Trenchard in Britain, was to destroy enemy nations solely with land-based strategic bombers. Mitchell complicated matters by criticizing Admiral Benson for the CNO's poor treatment of the Navy's air.

Voices of protest immediately arose from air-minded admirals. The General Board, which advised the Secretary of the Navy on naval matters, issued a statement in June 1919: "A naval air service must be established, capable of accompanying and operating with the fleet in all waters of the globe." [2] Admiral Sims, President of the Naval War College, initiated aviation studies at that advanced school for future admirals [3] and informed his friends in Congress that a superior fleet of aircraft carriers would "sweep the enemy fleet clean of its airplanes, and proceed to bomb the battleships, and torpedo them with torpedo planes. It is all a question of whether the airplane carrier, equipped with 80 planes, is not the capital ship of the future." [4] Finally, Admiral Benson, fed up with General Mitchell's criticisms, in February 1920 agreed to give naval aviation bureau status, hoping to silence his critics.[5] Mitchell must also be given credit for showing the vulnerability of battleships to air attack, and thereby contributing to the growth of naval aviation, when his land-based bombers sank several old target battleships in 1921, especially the ex-German *Ostfriesland* in July.[6]

On 10 August 1921 the Bureau of Aeronautics, the Navy's first new bureau in sixty years, was established under Rear Admiral William A. Moffett as Chief. With bureau status, the naval airmen had no fears of an unfriendly CNO, as the bureaus were responsible only to the Secretary of the Navy in the interest of maintaining strong civilian control. The Bureau of Aeronautics (BuAer) was unique in that it represented an aspect of fleet operations that required the direct attention of all the other bureaus—construction, personnel, supplies, engineering, medicine, and ordnance—which made it something of a superbureau. But it remained small and tightly administered under Moffett, to whom the CNO and other bureau chiefs would turn for advice on air matters. So well did Moffett perform his duties in building up all aspects of naval aviation that he was reappointed three more times as Chief of BuAer. In 1933 a fatal airship accident put an end to his twelve years in office.

Moffett's major headache during the 1920s was Billy Mitchell's almost hysterical crusade to unify Army and Navy air into one service. Matters came to a head in September 1925 when, following the crash of a Navy dirigible, Mitchell publicly accused the leaders of both services of virtual murder and treason for operating with a weak air policy that allowed such catastrophies. Again Mitchell's outspokenness aided naval air, though he was court-martialed for his indiscreet remarks. The President immediately appointed an air policy board under Dwight Morrow which studied all aspects of military and commercial aviation during the fall of 1925 and listened to proponents and experts of all its facets.

Congressional legislation resulted from the Morrow Report in 1926 and set the course for naval and particularly carrier air for the next fifteen years. Along with calling for more naval aircraft, this legislation accomplished two major reforms. First, it established the office of Assistant Secretary of the Navy (Aeronautics), giving naval aviation representation at the top civilian level. This office fell vacant in 1932 as a Depression economy measure, but not before it had helped reinforce the position of Navy air. Second, the legislation ruled that all commanding officers of aircraft carriers, seaplane tenders, and naval air stations be qualified aviators.[7] As a temporary measure, interested senior officers were to be given a short course in aviation training to qualify them as "naval observers" and thus for air commands.

A few senior captains took the naval observer's course, among them Joseph Mason Reeves, Harry E. Yarnell, and Frederick J. Horne, leading the carriers in their early maneuvers. Two groups arose among the qualified aviators. One was comprised of those officers who had been pioneers, flying Navy planes since pre-World War I days. Their leader became Captain John H. Towers (Naval Aviator No. 3), and the group included such commanders and lieutenant commanders as P. N. L. Bellinger (No. 8), George D. Murray (No. 22), Marc A. Mitscher (No. 33), and DeWitt C. Ramsey (No. 45). These men were very junior in 1927 when the first fleet carriers came out. The other group, the "latecomers" to aviation, were senior commanders and captains who had spent most of their careers in battleships or other non-air duties and who jumped on the air bandwagon in their forties. Their qualification as pilots was important as it gave naval air much-needed rank in the higher Navy echelons. One typical member of this group was Commander Frederick C. Sherman, who had commanded a submarine division and two destroyer divisions; he had been gunnery officer on a battleship and executive officer on a cruiser before entering flight training; he earned his wings in 1936 at age forty-seven. Other such notables were Captains Ernest J. King (1927; age forty-eight) and William F. Halsey, Jr. (1934; age fifty-two).

Another problem involving command relationships was the clash between the new aviators and the older non-air battleship admirals and captains. The latter naturally did not subscribe to any new weapon that threatened to destroy the battleship. Furthermore, they found greasy airplanes a nuisance on their quarterdecks and tended to regard the pilots as aviators first and naval officers second, which was not generally true. Since gunnery was their main punch, the battleship sailors identified themselves with the Bureau of Ordnance, known throughout the Navy as the Gun Club.

Fortunately, these old conservatives were soon overruled by progressive air-minded colleagues who learned to appreciate the advantages of fleet aviation. Three such men were Admirals William V. Pratt, Montgomery M. Taylor, and Frank M. Schofield. As the two 33,000-ton *Lexington*-class converted carriers, authorized at the Washington Conference, neared completion these men joined the aviators in voicing the need for a carrier policy in the fleet. In April 1927 a board under Admiral Taylor met to consider the problem and recommended that carriers defend the Battle Fleet as well as engage in "scouting and offensive operations at a distance from the battle line." [8] The Taylor Board included Admirals Moffett and Schofield, Captains Reeves and Yarnell, and Lieutenant Commander Mitscher.

This general acceptance of naval aviation in the top echelons of the Navy even before the first fast carrier was commissioned was also the result of general strategic requirements. Immediately after World War I the naval building race developed that resulted in the Washington Disarmament Conference, but American strategists continued to regard Japan as the next potential enemy. Consequently, American naval strength shifted from the Atlantic to the Pacific late in 1922. In Fleet Problem I, held in the Pacific the next year, two battleships acted as simulated carriers and demonstrated the great need for carriers in that ocean. Two years after that, in Fleet Problem V, tiny *Langley* launched ten aircraft in a small but significant demonstration of carrier air power.[9] To enhance carrier striking power, Captain Joseph Mason Reeves began to formulate air tactics at San Diego that same year of 1925, and in 1926 Lieutenant Frank D. Wagner led his fighter squadron in the first demonstration of dive bombing in the Navy.[10]

Fleet Problem VII, held in the Caribbean in 1927, again including *Langley*, showed the need for carrier mobility in the face of changing weather and enemy fleet movements. This led to the recommendation that Commander Aircraft Squadrons—the carrier admiral—be given "complete freedom of action in employing carrier aircraft. . . ." [11] Thus, before the U.S. Navy had even employed fast carriers it had learned a basic lesson for successful fast carrier operations: mobility and freedom of movement from the battle line.

The appearance of fast carriers *Lexington* (CV-2) and *Saratoga* (CV-3)[12] in late 1927 and their subsequent operations bore out these lessons. In the much-publicized Fleet Problem IX in 1929 Vice Admiral Pratt allowed Rear Admiral Reeves to take *Saratoga* in a high-speed run and surprise air attack on the Panama Canal, which was defended by an opposing fleet and carriers. *Saratoga* achieved devastating success. The only trouble was that when the carriers got within range of the enemy's big guns the battleships promptly sank them. The conservative battleship admirals seized on this vulnerability; Admiral Henry V. Wiley, Commander-in-Chief of the Fleet, remarked that there was "no analysis of Fleet Problem IX fairly made which fails to point to the battleship as the final arbiter of Naval destiny." [13]

As far as most non-air admirals were concerned, the carrier was the "eyes of the fleet"—primarily for reconnaissance, the logical substitute for the battle cruiser—but evidence mounted in favor of its attack role. Admiral Pratt became CNO in 1930 and stressed that carriers be placed on the offensive in the war games, a recommendation echoed by commanding admirals in every fleet exercise thereafter.[14] One of the most telling exhibitions was Rear Admiral Yarnell's sneak air attack on Pearl Harbor with *Lexington* and *Saratoga* at dawn on Sunday morning, the seventh of February 1932—anticipating the Japanese feat of ten years later.[15] Yarnell thereupon recommended six to eight carriers be used to confront Japan in the Pacific.[16]

The problem of independent carrier operations beyond the main fleet was complicated by the fact that all of America's battleships —pre-1922 vintage—could make only 21 knots and therefore could not keep up with the 25- to 33-knot fast carriers. To let the carriers operate beyond the main battle line would seriously weaken carriers and battle line alike if enemy aircraft were threatening. A detached fast carrier force would be particularly risky in an amphibious operation, which demanded command of the sea and air, hence the presence of heavy fleet units. In May 1937 this question arose with Fleet Problem XVIII.

The carrier commander noted, "Once an enemy carrier is within striking distance of our fleet no security remains until it, its squadrons, or both, are destroyed." Admitting that leaving the main force was a gamble, he said the fleet would be "playing for high stakes" and that the greater gamble was waiting to receive the enemy's air attack. The fleet commander disagreed and tied the carriers down to flying patrols over the battleships and to supporting the landing forces. Thus restricted, *Langley* was sunk by air attack, *Saratoga* and *Lexington* were heavily bombed, while the latter also received serious damage from a lurking enemy submarine. The landing was successful, but the fleet had lost its air. To the airmen in this war game, the mistake was in restricting the mobility of the carriers. This very situation would plague wartime commanders in the Pacific during 1943–1944, especially during the Saipan landings in June 1944.[17]

With these rapid changes in carrier doctrine, a syllabus of fighting instructions for the fleet was most difficult to compose. Nevertheless, a *War Instructions* was issued in 1934; about carriers this document could say only that they were "simply mobile airplane bases and their use depends upon the employment of their aircraft" [18]—a general statement indeed!

Meanwhile, personnel changes were taking place. In 1934 Admiral Joseph Mason Reeves—a naval observer—became Commander-in-Chief of the U.S. Fleet, a boost for air. The big change, however, came the year before with the tragic death of Admiral Moffett. He had picked as his successor Captain Jack Towers, the most senior early-day naval aviator but almost too junior a captain to achieve flag rank as Bureau chief.[19] Instead, Rear Admiral Ernest J. King, a latecomer but highly qualified for the job, was appointed Chief of BuAer. The pioneer airmen and their younger colleagues in the Towers group greatly resented the selection of a latecomer over their acknowledged leader. King made an excellent Chief of Bureau, but he had not gotten along well with Moffett or with Moffett's pet officers, Towers included. King refused to accept the supremacy of the Towers-Moffett group of younger aviators, who felt, said King, "that if one were to fly one had to be born with wings."[20] From 1933 forward, no love was lost between Ernie King and Jack Towers.

Slow naval rearmament began during the mid-1930s under the aegis of President Franklin D. Roosevelt, a very naval-minded Chief Executive. First the Vinson-Trammell Act of 1934 included appropriations for two new carriers and many naval aircraft. That year the first American carrier built as such from the keel up, *Ranger* (CV-4), was commissioned. Other carriers to follow were *Yorktown* (CV-5) in 1937, *Enterprise* (CV-6) in 1938, *Wasp* (CV-7) in 1940, and *Hornet* (CV-8) in 1941. With the ships and planes arose the need for pilots, and a series of Congressional bills was passed in 1935 and after, calling for 6000 Naval Reserve pilots.[21] In contrast to the long-term selective process of the regular Japanese Naval Air Service, these pilots were given 12 to 15 months of preflight and flight training, after which they were commissioned and ordered to active duty. The so-called naval aviation cadets complemented the regular Navy career pilots and formed a solid nucleus for an enlarged wartime naval air force.[22]

With the expansion in the fleet, changes occurred in the high command of the carriers. Rear Admiral King stepped down as Chief of BuAer in 1936 and was succeeded by Rear Admiral A. B. Cook, another latecomer to air. Three years later, Rear Admiral Towers took over the post, the first pioneer aviator to hold it. In the Pacific, the billet of Commander Aircraft Battle Force came to be known as the "Carrier Command." Vice Admiral King held it in 1938, and in 1940 it went to Vice Admiral William F. Halsey,

Jr., a salty leader who came to aviation after a long career in destroyers. The Navy entered the war using the tactical doctrine for carriers established by Halsey in March 1941.[23]

Until mid-1940 the carriers participated in battle-line maneuvers, including landing operations, independent tactics, and one new vital function: at-sea refueling. In June 1939 *Saratoga* refueled from a fleet tanker off California, initiating the logistical procedures necessary to support the fast carriers in the open Pacific against Japan.[24] After the last fleet problem, XXI, in 1940, the airmen stated a belief that was to continue throughout the war: that only naval aviators could understand the intricacies of carrier operations and that therefore only they were qualified to dictate the movements of a carrier fleet.[25] At that time, 1940, all the aviators wanted was freedom from the battle line, but during the war this would mean control over the entire fleet.

As war approached, American naval aviation was still oriented around the small administrative organization of BuAer. The Bureau was woefully unprepared for the demands of large-scale procurement and training, but at least Towers was Chief and he had had the experience of mobilizing planes and pilots before World War I. In addition, to assist naval air preparations at the top levels, the office of Assistant Secretary of the Navy (Air) was reestablished in September 1941.[26] Unhappily, naval planes were so inferior to what the Japanese had that the Navy got top priority over the Army in new aircraft-production contracts. But time was running out; some of the new planes would not be ready by the scheduled date, which happened to be about the time the fighting started.[27]

By the fall of 1941 the Navy had six fast heavy carriers (excluding the smaller *Ranger*) plus two new fast battleships which could accompany them if necessary. Carrier doctrine was flexible but still subordinated to and part of the battle line. The six carriers, like Japan's, probably could have operated in one single tactical formation, but they were split up between the Atlantic and Pacific as the Germans and Japanese threatened to bring America into the war. The Navy could only wait for more ships and better planes—and hope for more time.

Many people within and outside the Navy on the eve of American entry into the fighting doubted that the fast carrier would revolutionize naval warfare. One such person was naval analyst Bernard Brodie, who wrote in 1941:

> The carrier . . . is not likely to replace the battleship. . . . The carrier can strike over a vast range and at the most swiftly moving targets, but she cannot strike with the accuracy and forcefulness that is characteristic of the large naval gun within the limits of its range.[28]

Pearl Harbor sank this theory—five battleships put out of action by attacking planes from six fast carriers.

Two:
Weapon of Expediency, 1942–1943

The Japanese attack on Pearl Harbor began World War II in the Pacific as a fast carrier war. If the British carrier attack at Taranto had failed to convince American naval leaders of the revolutionary nature of naval operations in the new war, the 400-plane attack at Pearl erased all doubt. Furthermore, the Japanese sank five battleships (two of which were never refloated), thus eliminating most of the battle line. The few remaining old battlewagons retreated to California while the carriers and submarines held the line in the Pacific. The mission of the American carrier from 7 December 1941 to the spring of 1943 was singular: to defend Allied bases and lines of communication and to escort convoys to forward bases.

1. On the Defensive

All operations during this period were conducted on an emergency basis. Strategy and forces committed were determined by what was expedient to avert defeat. At first, *Ranger* and *Wasp* remained in the Atlantic, with all other carriers soon based at Hawaii: *Lexington, Saratoga, Yorktown, Enterprise*, and *Hornet*. These few capital ships—which the carriers had indeed become—operated separately in single task formations. This expedient was necessary because (1) many separate missions had to be carried out simultaneously, (2) the fear of having "too many eggs in one basket" pervaded the high command, and (3) early losses quickly reduced the number of available carriers. *Saratoga* left the war zone after being torpedoed by a submarine in January 1942, *Lexington* sank after receiving much battle damage at the battle of the Coral Sea in May, and *Yorktown* went down as a result of similar circumstances and untested damage control at Midway in June.

Because the carriers could only be as successful as the men who commanded them, personnel assignment remained a problem throughout the war. There could be no latitude for error, and peacetime officers who failed to measure up to the demands of wartime would be quickly replaced. Important command assignments in aviation were made more or less by agreement between the Chief of BuAer, Rear Admiral Towers, and his counterpart in personnel, Rear Admiral Chester Nimitz. Pearl Harbor raised the question of which men should command the theaters to which fast carriers were assigned, the fleets in which they operated, and the task forces they comprised. Obviously, admirals who understood naval aviation and fast carrier operations were needed, preferably qualified aviators. But in 1941 very few such "carrier admirals" existed, while all but two (Towers and Bellinger) of the pilot flag officers were "latecomers" to air. The most important commanders therefore would be those on top, the men who would assign the admirals to command theaters, fleets, and carrier task forces.

The initial choices by President Roosevelt, Chief of Naval Operations Admiral Harold Stark, Secretary of the Navy Frank Knox, and Rear Admiral Nimitz were singularly fortunate. First, Admiral Ernie King, commanding the Atlantic Fleet, was made Commander-in-Chief United States Fleet (Cominch). Second, Nimitz himself was promoted to full admiral and made Commander-in-Chief Pacific Fleet (Cincpac) and Pacific Ocean Areas (Cincpoa). Both men remained at these posts for the duration, while in March 1942 King assumed the additional job of Chief of Naval Operations (CNO).

Ernest J. King (United States Naval Academy, Class of 1901) had a reputation as a taskmaster in both administration and operations. He demanded the best from every subordinate, punishing those who failed him and rewarding those who turned in good scores. His temper was quick, his manner cold. He was at ease fighting the military chiefs of Great Britain as well as his counterparts on the Joint Chiefs of Staff (JCS), General George C. Marshall of the Army and General H. H. "Hap" Arnold of the Army Air Forces. King's ability to coordinate the many fronts, ships, and men as well as help hammer out Allied grand strategy suited him admirably for the dual billet of Cominch-CNO. And King was equal to the task. He was an experienced leader not only in air but also in battleships, destroyers, submarines, and staff. To the carriermen he was a pilot but also a latecomer. His relationship with Jack Towers remained formal.[1]

Chester W. Nimitz (USNA '05) equaled King in brains and surpassed him in his ability to get along amicably with his people. A stickler for detail and form, Nimitz delegated authority and interfered with his subordinates only in serious emergencies or when he lacked adequate information. For these attributes he commanded a tremendous loyal following throughout the war. His career had been in submarines and surface ships but never in air. His broad experience in handling personnel, however, suited him well for commanding the Pacific war, where air would be only one problem of many. Along with carriermen, Nimitz would have to deal with people in submarines, auxiliaries, battleships, amphibious operations, logistics, the Marine Corps, and the Army—which included his cantankerous peer, General Douglas MacArthur.

The first use of carriers in the Pacific created an early headache for Nimitz—the conflict between the battleship admirals and the carrier admirals. Every morning Nimitz held a conference of his top commanders at Cincpac headquarters, Pearl Harbor. Since the battleships had been put out of action, all surface operations involved the air admirals and captains. The surface non-air admirals began to feel as if they had been thrust into a secondary position, and at least two of them, Pye and Theobald, became quite violent in their protests at these meetings. Nimitz used his excellent tact to calm them by telling stories.[2] But the fact remained that the battleship group had little to say in the area of carrier operations.

The leader of the carriermen in the Pacific was the Commander Aircraft Battle Force, Vice Admiral William F. Halsey, Jr. Halsey (USNA '04), who had held this job for several months, had been slated for relief when the war started,[3] but Halsey had a reputation as a slugger and inspiring leader, which makes the difference in wartime. His suggested relief, Rear Admiral A. B. Cook, did not enjoy such a reputation. Cook (USNA '05), formerly Chief of BuAer, was fiery, disagreeable, and too often inconsistent. So Halsey kept his job for many more months and Cook remained on the beach throughout the war.

With Halsey at Pearl Harbor were two other prominent air admirals, Rear Admiral Pat Bellinger (USNA '07), who commanded the land-based and amphibian patrol planes, and Rear Admiral Aubrey W. "Jake" Fitch (USNA '06), local carrier division commander. Especially important at this early stage of the carrier war were the individual carrier captains who would have to advise non-air task force admirals and who were next in line for flag rank themselves. Among these were Captains Frederick C. "Ted" Sherman of *Lexington* and George D. Murray of *Enterprise.* These two men represented exact opposites in carrier leaders. Murray (USNA '11), an early pioneer flyer, had a superb sense of administration, the charming personality of a true gentleman, and a near-spotless career in carriers, his one mistake having occurred in November 1941 when he swung *Enterprise* in front of an advancing battleship, causing a minor collision. Sherman (USNA '10), a latecomer to air, was headstrong, outspoken, and a taskmaster; he was also a fearless, extremely skilled shiphandler and tactician.

When *Hornet* arrived in the Pacific, fresh from commissioning, she brought as captain the tiny figure of a man who had been more closely identified with the top echelons of naval aviation since the early days than perhaps any other officer save Towers and Bellinger: Captain Marc A. "Pete" Mitscher (USNA '10), a very soft-spoken, intelligent, and effective leader who knew people, equipment, and the enemy. Mitscher was simple and direct, even stubborn, but most important he was a born leader.

The key non-air operational commanders early in 1942 were Vice Admiral Wilson Brown and Rear Admirals Frank Jack Fletcher, Raymond A. Spruance, and Thomas C. Kinkaid. Of note here is Fletcher (USNA '06), an extremely able officer who had had absolutely no experience with carriers. When the shooting started, the outgoing Cincpac, Admiral Husband E. Kimmel, had had to choose between Fletcher and aviator Fitch as senior flag officer. Nonaviator Kimmel selected Fletcher, which had unfortunate results in the first combat operations as Fletcher did not know how to use his carrier air effectively.[4] It was the first of several incidents that greatly irritated carrier commanders seeing their ships misused.

Besides the limited number of carriers and the uncertain command arrangement there was the problem of aircraft: sad testimony to American unpreparedness for war against Japan. The basic fighter was the Grumman F4F Wildcat, good but not good enough against the Japanese Zero. The dive bomber was the Douglas SBD Dauntless, rugged, effective, dependable, and versatile enough to triple as fighter, scout, and bombing plane. The torpedo plane was the Douglas TBD Devastator, the only "torpecker" in the fleet, old, slow, unmaneuverable, and generally antiquated; the Navy had already contracted for its replacement. For each carrier, the air group included 72 planes: 18 fighters (VF), 36 scout-dive bombers (VSB), and 18 torpedo planes (VT), with the emphasis on planes that could "see" for the fleet as well as attack.

For the first four months of 1942 Vice Admiral Halsey commanded the carriers in air raids on Japanese positions in the Gilberts and Marshalls, at Wake and Marcus islands, and then led the supreme raid of them all—delivering Jimmy Doolittle's Army bombers from the decks of *Hornet* for a strike on Tokyo in April. During this period each of the carriers formed a separate task force with its own screen of cruisers and destroyers. In multicarrier operations such task forces steamed together but separated before the attack, the planes rendezvousing near the target, a procedure much like the Japanese concept of dispersion.

A note on semantics is important here: these operations were conducted by task forces of *single* fast carriers; these units were not *multi*carrier task forces of several carriers operating within one defensive screen of escort vessels.

The exception to the above rule during 1942 was the strike on Lae and Salamaua, New Guinea, by *Lexington* and *Yorktown* under Wilson Brown. Knowing nothing of carrier operations, Admiral Brown appointed Captain Sherman of *Lexington* as his "air commander." Sherman had great faith in multicarrier operations and kept the two fast carriers tactically concentrated throughout the long-range flight of the planes. No enemy planes attacked this makeshift fast carrier task force, but Sherman was satisfied "that two or more carriers could work together in combat as a team."[5]

In April 1942, with the carriers assuming such an important role, Admiral Nimitz reorganized his command, attempting to replace the old prewar Battle Force system with a workable wartime Pacific Fleet. The air units were now divided up into patrol wings (which had been Scouting Force), utility wings, and carriers. Vice Admiral Halsey remained as Commander Carriers Pacific Fleet.[6] Three separate aviation commands soon proved unworkable, but another reorganization could not take place again until the big pending battles were fought.

By the time Doolittle bombed Tokyo, the Japanese had conquered all of Southeast Asia, the Dutch East Indies, the Philippines, and the Central Pacific islands. Even as *Enterprise* and *Hornet* were returning to Hawaii from the Tokyo operation, the Japanese moved toward the last Allied stronghold in New Guinea, Port Moresby. However, the United States Navy had broken the Japanese code, enabling Admiral Nimitz to know Japanese intentions. He immediately dispatched Fletcher with Fitch's *Yorktown* and *Lexington* task force and Kinkaid's cruisers to the Coral Sea, where Fletcher coordinated air operations rather sluggishly.[7] But with Fitch as his air commander, Fletcher could boast the sinking of a Japanese light carrier on 7 May. The next day *Shokaku* and *Zuikaku* slugged it out with *Lexington* and *Yorktown* in the final phase of the battle of the Coral Sea. Admiral Fitch, with Ted Sherman in *Lexington,* used Sherman's tactic of keeping the two carriers together in the same destroyer screen. This might have worked well, but the two ships maneuvered apart while under Japanese air attack and thus weakened their defenses. Both American carriers therefore sustained damage, while *Lexington* suffered internal explosions and had to be scuttled. Her loss put Ted Sherman out of a job.

In these early air battles Japan's aerial elite flew against the best the U.S. Navy could offer. Training and equipment gave the Japanese an edge. At this time the average Japanese carrier pilot—including even the senior instructors—had logged 700 hours of flight time during training; his American counterpart had only 305 hours before assignment to a squadron.[8] Also, the Japanese flew the light, swift Zero, better in practically every respect than the F4F Wildcat. American aerial tactics and pilot skill kept fighter losses down, but more fighters were essential to escort bombing planes as well as to cover the fleet. As a result, following the Coral Sea action several more fighters were added to each carrier air group. This improved the carrier's chances for survival. Another American practice proved indispensable—the rotation of pilots from combat to training duties where they could pass on their knowledge to new trainees. The Japanese maintained their carrier pilot elite, which made their losses very difficult to replace.

Admiral Halsey had missed the battle of the Coral Sea because of the lengthy Tokyo mission, and a bad skin rash took him out of all operations for the next few months. He was especially chagrined because naval intelligence reported the Japanese fleet was headed toward Midway. Halsey therefore selected as his replacement his cruiser commander, Rear Admiral Ray Spruance. Though not an aviator, Spruance (USNA '07) had served for several months with Halsey's carriers and now Spruance inherited Halsey's carrier-oriented staff. His chief of staff became Captain Miles Browning, an explosive individual professionally and socially but unquestionably an expert in carrier operations. Quiet, meticulous, thorough, and downright brilliant, Spruance had had several tours at the Naval War College and enjoyed a reputation as a highly qualified strategist.

When Halsey turned over the carriers to Spruance, the senior fleet commander became Fletcher. Fitch in the meantime had gone to San Diego to pick up *Saratoga*, returning to the war zone after repairs from torpedo damage. But "*Sara*" would arrive too late for the battle of Midway, leaving three nonaviators to command the carriers—Nimitz, Fletcher, and Spruance, with Rear Admiral Kinkaid leading the cruisers.

The key to victory at Midway was Spruance's handling of his orders and his staff. Admiral Nimitz ordered Fletcher and Spruance to govern their attacks on the enemy fleet "by the principle of calculated risk." Though Fletcher had tactical command, Spruance ended up operating practically independently. With Browning advising him and George Murray running his flagship *Enterprise*, Spruance split up his two-carrier force into two parts prior to the battle, allowing Mitscher in *Hornet* to operate independently. These two groups closed with the Japanese fleet, with Fletcher in *Yorktown* coming up just as the battle on 4 June began. As the two fleets closed, Captain Browning made one of the shrewdest calculations in naval history. He figured that if Spruance launched his bombers two hours ahead of schedule, they would catch the Japanese carrier planes refueling on deck, making those ships vulnerable to fires. This was indeed calculated risk, but Spruance took it. Following Browning's advice he launched his attack planes. The antiquated TBD torpedo planes were practically annihilated and the SBD dive bombers could not find the Japanese fleet. The strike leader began looking around, however, and by great good luck sighted Admiral Nagumo's four carriers. Attacking, his planes sank them all—*Hiryu, Soryu, Kaga, Akagi.*[9]

Fletcher had less good fortune, although *Yorktown*'s planes had been in on the kill, and had in fact located the target independently. The last Japanese air attack succeeded in damaging *Yorktown*, which was prematurely abandoned and then sunk by a submarine. Two days after the battle, Fitch arrived with *Saratoga* and, being senior to Spruance, took over command of the carriers.

Credit for the momentous victory must be shared by many, especially the valiant Devastator pilots who perished and the determined Dauntless pilots who pressed home their killing attacks. At the high command levels, Admiral Nimitz wisely gave his task force commanders freedom of movement, while Spruance relied on the expert advice of Halsey's air staff. Final credit for the well-timed attack on the Japanese carriers went to the aviator Miles Browning, who was rewarded with the Distinguished Service Medal: "By his judicious planning and brilliant execution, [he] was largely responsible for the rout of the enemy Japanese fleet in the Battle of Midway." [10]

Midway ended the main Japanese offensive, and both sides withdrew to repair their losses. Neither Japan nor the United States would seek battle as openly as before, since neither navy could afford more losses. Admiral Nimitz recalled Spruance from sea duty to be Deputy Cincpac and chief of staff, while Fletcher remained at sea. Nimitz and Spruance combined the best of two excellent minds, but, significantly, neither was an aviator. The highest-ranking airman on the Cincpac staff was, in fact, a captain, in early 1942 Captain Arthur C. Davis.

Nimitz, however, had his "type" commanders, those admirals who had administrative control, logistically and sometimes operationally, over each ship or plane type: the patrol wings, carriers, battleships, cruisers, destroyers, and submarines of the Pacific Fleet. Vice Admiral Halsey, still bedridden, was relieved as Commander Carriers in July 1942, and shortly thereafter the unmanageable division of air units into the three types of patrol, carrier, and utility was eliminated. On 1 September 1942 all three were merged into one air type commander, to be known as Commander U.S. Naval Air Forces Pacific Fleet, shortened in October to Commander Air Force Pacific Fleet. ComAirPac, initially Rear Admiral Fitch, became the controlling aviator in the Pacific, administering aviation personnel, equipment, and ships; as a type command it "received planes from the Bureau of Aeronautics and men from the aviation-training commands and assigned them to squadrons, provided for squadron training and the shakedown of ships, and saw that all units were maintained in a state of combat readiness." [11] But ComAirPac did not occupy a policy-making position on Cincpac staff. No aviator did.

Admiral King laid down a new law regarding carrier doctrine immediately after the battle of Midway. The loss of *Lexington* in the Coral Sea and the four Japanese carriers at Midway while operating in multicarrier formations convinced King that this tactic was unsafe, at least with the existing dearth of escort vessels. He therefore expressly forbade any two carriers operating together in the same screen and tactically concentrated formation.[12] Each carrier would wear the flag of an admiral and would have its own escorting screen of cruisers and destroyers. This policy is especially interesting since the Japanese reacted to Midway in exactly opposite fashion by forming multicarrier task groups of three carriers each.

The early battles of 1942 had provided valuable experience for the carriermen, and all fast carrier captains were promoted to rear admiral. This meant that the carrier task forces would be commanded increasingly by experienced pilots who had handled carriers in battle. By August 1942 Nimitz's available carrier task force commanders included Vice Admirals Fletcher (non-air) and Halsey, and Rear Admirals Mitscher, Murray, Sherman, Leigh Noyes, and Kinkaid (non-air).

With the promotions to admiral, an entire new set of carrier captains appeared, all of them early-day pilots who had spent their entire careers in aviation and who had established good records as administrators and leaders. Captain DeWitt C. "Duke" Ramsey (USNA '12) had *Saratoga;* his ability had been a major factor in gearing BuAer for war and he was highly respected by Ernie King. Captain Charles P. Mason (USNA '12) took over *Hornet;* he was Naval Aviator No. 52 and had recently been laboring to open up new training facilities for wartime pilots. Captain Arthur C. Davis (USNA '15) commanded *Enterprise* after two years as aviation officer to Cincpac; among his accomplishments was playing a major role in the development of the famous Norden bombsight. Captain Forrest P. Sherman (USNA '18) had *Wasp* and was recognized as one of the most intelligent officers in the Navy; he brought his ship to the Pacific after it had delivered planes to beleaguered Malta in the Mediterranean.[13]

The only other major change was in equipment. The TBD Devastator, utterly useless in fast carrier battles, was discarded in favor of the new Grumman TBF Avenger, a rugged torpedo bomber that had been overdue in joining the fleet.

Now that the carriers had successfully held the defensive, the course of the war shifted and Allied planners began to consider a limited offensive. On 2 July 1942 the Joint Chiefs of Staff decided that the first major objective to be captured in the Pacific would be Rabaul, the big new Japanese base on the island of New Britain in the Bismarck archipelago. General Douglas MacArthur, Allied commander in the Southwest Pacific, wanted to advance in a series of swift operations up the Solomon Islands and New Guinea to take Rabaul. Since his land-based Army Air Force bombers could not reach that far without building airfields, MacArthur wanted Nimitz's carriers to cover his flanks.[14]

Admirals King and Nimitz were aghast. Having lost two carriers because of inferior quality and quantity of planes along with inadequate antiaircraft protection, they were not about to expose these same ships to the confined waters of the Solomon Sea where carriers would be sitting ducks for Japanese land-based air and submarines. MacArthur apparently regarded the carriers as an expendable auxiliary to his thrust on Rabaul and thence back to the Philippines, where American resistance had ceased in April. MacArthur preferred to use his own land-based air force under Major General George C. Kenney as his main air arm, while the carriers could assist and also neutralize Japanese airfields and fleet units in the Central Pacific.[15]

MacArthur's proposal forced the Navy to reflect upon its strategy. One thing was certain; the fast carriers needed operating room and could not be dangerously exposed to land-based air attack. Another matter to be considered was the placing of the few remaining carriers at the disposal of someone who did not appreciate their uses as mobile, long-range strategic capital ships. Regarding strategy, the Navy agreed to a compromise. The Solomons–New Guinea area was divided into two parts, (1) the South Pacific Force, a subarea under Nimitz's over-all command and Vice Admiral R. L. Ghormley's direct command, and (2) the Southwest Pacific Area, under MacArthur. Both would cooperate in a limited offensive toward Rabaul. Immediately, the Navy would use its carriers to cover Marine Corps landings at Tulagi and Guadalcanal in the southern Solomons in August 1942. MacArthur would use Army, Allied air forces, and his own small Seventh Fleet to work up the Papuan peninsula of New Guinea. As for MacArthur's attitude toward carriers, the Navy thereafter refused to place fast carriers under his direct tactical command.[16]

To support operations in the Navy's South Pacific campaign, a new command was established, Commander Air Force South Pacific, composed of land-based patrol planes, seaplanes, bombers, and fighters. The first commander was Rear Admiral John S. McCain, a rugged sailor and latecomer to aviation. Carriers in this area remained administratively under ComAirPac Fitch at Pearl Harbor, but operated tactically under the South Pacific commander, Ghormley.

The Guadalcanal operation was one heartbreak after another for the carriers. For the initial landing on 7 August 1942 Vice Admiral Fletcher had three carriers. He flew his flag in *Saratoga;* nonaviator Kinkaid was in *Enterprise;* and Noyes, a newcomer to the Pacific, operated in *Wasp.* Fletcher did a terrible job. Once the Marines were ashore he informed the assault commander, Rear Admiral Richmond Kelly Turner, that he was pulling out a day early. To the chagrin of his own airmen he feared the possibility of *Shokaku* and *Zuikaku* and the three light carriers at Rabaul threatening his force. So indeed he did withdraw, only to allow Japanese surface units to sink several American cruisers off Savo Island the next night. His admirals did little to change his mind; Noyes would not even forward Forrest Sherman's recommendation to pursue the withdrawing Japanese ships.[17]

The first six weeks after Savo were as rugged for the carriers as for the troops on Guadalcanal sweating out the first island jungle campaign. Admiral Fletcher continued with his lack of aggressiveness, while he and his uncertain admirals were flown from carrier to carrier for repeated conferences. Japan's Admiral Nagumo brought about the battle of the Eastern Solomons on 24 August, using *Shokaku*, *Zuikaku*, and *Ryujo;* and Fletcher did some poor guessing. *Enterprise* was hit, but Captain Art Davis brought her out, while the American planes sank light carrier *Ryujo.* Then, seven days later, an enemy submarine torpedoed *Saratoga* for the second time during the war, taking her out of action for three months. Fletcher was reportedly wounded by the blast, thus terminating his service in carriers, which was perhaps fortunate. He spent the last two years of the war isolated in the remote North Pacific. On the other hand, Captain Duke Ramsey of *Saratoga* was promoted to rear admiral and ordered to remain in the Pacific.

Matters worsened. The aviators complained of having to operate in confined waters, while advocates of the multicarrier task force deplored the separation of the carriers as an air defense measure.[18] On 15 September *Wasp* was torpedoed while escorting a convoy to Guadalcanal, and Captain Forrest Sherman, unable to save her, ordered his ship scuttled. Her admiral, Leigh Noyes, who had been burned during the action, was criticized for crossing the same track twelve times in three days, thus giving the submarine a chance to pin him down.[19] Noyes was immediately ordered to Pearl Harbor for temporary duty as ComAirPac. This released Jake Fitch, who was transferred to the South Pacific as land-based-air commander. The incumbent there, Rear Admiral McCain, received orders to go to Washington to be Chief of BuAer. These changes were in effect by mid-October.

Rear Admiral George Murray and Captain Charlie Mason with *Hornet* managed to rough-up Japanese planes and shipping on 16 October in the South Pacific, clear evidence that carriermen in command of carriers could achieve an aggressive attitude. Unfortunately, though, with only *Hornet* and *Enterprise* remaining, there were more admirals than carriers. Standing by to take over carrier task forces were Vice Admiral Halsey, now recovered from his illness, and Rear Admirals Duke Ramsey and Ted Sherman. At last, however, Admirals King and Nimitz appreciated the price of indecision and on 18 October 1942 they ordered Halsey to relieve Ghormley in command of the entire Solomons operation.

The instant old "Bull" (as the press called him) took over, morale skyrocketed in the South Pacific. In addition, two new fast battleships arrived under Rear Admiral W. A. "Ching" Lee (USNA '08), a highly respected ordnance expert who had never operated battleships with carriers in combat—but then nobody had. Added to these were nine cruisers, 24 destroyers, George Murray with *Hornet*, and Tom Kinkaid with the repaired *Enterprise*, now commanded by Captain Osborne B. Hardison. Halsey needed all this, for eight days after he assumed command Admiral Yamamoto committed practically all of Nagumo's carrier strength in another attempt to drive the Americans from Guadalcanal—*Shokaku*, *Zuikaku*, *Junyo*, and *Zuiho*.

The battle of the Santa Cruz Islands lasted two days. *Hornet*-based SBDs pounded *Shokaku* for her second beating in six months. But Admiral Kinkaid fumbled in committing his carriers to battle, the Japanese got the jump on him, and their bombers hit *Hornet*, engulfing her in flames until she sank. *Enterprise* was also bombed, but the real hero of the battle was new fast battleship *South Dakota*, whose many antiaircraft guns claimed dozens of attacking planes. The battle convinced Halsey of the folly of operating carriers in these confined waters, so he withdrew the last survivor, *Enterprise*, to the south. Ted Sherman and others were also convinced that operating carriers in separate task forces was folly, but this became a moot point with only one carrier left until *Saratoga* returned.[20]

Halsey had one more major task before him—to turn back a

final Japanese effort to retake Guadalcanal. The result was the Naval Battle of Guadalcanal, 13–15 November 1942. It was not a fast carrier action, although *Enterprise* planes shuttling out of the airfield at Guadalcanal helped sink an enemy battleship and seven transports. Also, CarDiv 2 carriers *Junyo* and *Hiyo* were part of the Japanese force. Rear Admiral Kinkaid handled *Enterprise*'s and Fitch the land-based air. Real honors went to Admiral Lee, whose two battleships fought a very successful night engagement with a Japanese force. This three-day battle, which won Halsey his fourth star, ended Japan's attempt to retake Guadalcanal and led to both navies' withdrawing their carriers and battleships from major operations for a full year.

The Guadalcanal campaign disappointed most naval air commanders because the carriers had been denied their mobility, because carrier task forces had again been commanded by less-skilled non-airmen, notably Fletcher and Kinkaid, and because King's order of one carrier per task force frustrated many. As for mobility, Halsey now withdrew his two carriers from the range of land-based enemy planes. In the problem of command, all task forces built around carriers were to be commanded by aviators henceforth; Kinkaid, ordered to the North Pacific, was the last non-airman to fly his flag from a fast carrier.[21] Vice Admiral Jack Towers, relieved by McCain as Chief of BuAer, assumed the post of ComAirPac in October 1942, thus lending his expertise to solving carrier problems in the Pacific. Duke Ramsey hoisted his flag in *Saratoga*, Ted Sherman in *Enterprise*.

The remaining problem at the outset of 1943 was the single-carrier versus multicarrier task force. Ironically, the two points of view were represented by the two task force commanders, Ramsey and Sherman. Halsey remained a somewhat disinterested party, since his concern was consolidating the Allied position at Guadalcanal, and Fitch's land-based air was more important to him than the two carriers, now confined to escorting convoys beyond the range of Japanese planes. Halsey did, however, continue King's order early in January 1943 for carriers to operate separately. Admiral Sherman, finding this "contrary to my doctrine," discussed the order with Halsey on the twentieth and found that "we agree perfectly." But Halsey listened to both sides, then reversed his opinion in March, leading Sherman to conclude that "Ramsey has been doing some dirty work at the cross-roads." [22]

Halsey was willing to leave the debate up to the carrier admirals, since he had become a theater commander. He had not participated in a carrier battle at all, leading only air raids early in 1942, and for all his wonderful attributes as a combat leader it is doubtful that he ever really became interested in doctrinal theory. He was more the fighter than the thinker, and this particular issue was hardly relevant to the Solomons campaign early in 1943.

But Sherman and Ramsey, deeply concerned with the future of fast carrier operations in the Pacific, recommended to Halsey that they be allowed to experiment with *Saratoga* and *Enterprise* in double-carrier task formations. Halsey agreed, and alternately Sherman and Ramsey traded off commanding both carriers. Sherman, concerned with maximum antiaircraft defense, concluded the multicarrier force was proved feasible by these trials. Ramsey, interested in efficient flight and cruising patterns, concluded the opposite.[23] Halsey sided with Ramsey, who was following Ernie King's original dictum, and the matter rested for the moment.

The carrier situation remained critical. *Enterprise* needed an overhaul, yet big old "*Sara*" could not be counted on to stand alone in the South Pacific and dodge torpedoes successfully should she be attacked again. Admiral King therefore called upon the British for help. The Admiralty was somewhat reluctant to dispatch a carrier from the Atlantic–Mediterranean, as the fighting still raged in North Africa, where the Allies had landed in November 1942. But the Pacific situation being critical, fast carrier *Victorious* was dispatched to Pearl Harbor, where she arrived on 4 March 1943 to begin familiarization training with Pacific Fleet units. On 28 April *Enterprise* started for home and an overhaul, while Admiral Sherman reported to Fitch for temporary duty. Ramsey and *Saratoga* held on alone until *Victorious* arrived in the South Pacific on 17 May. The two Allied fast carriers then operated together for the next two months.[24]

The spring of 1943, though quiet in the Solomons, was otherwise a busy one for the Allies in the Pacific. The Japanese had captured two Aleutian islands, Attu and Kiska, during the Midway campaign. Vice Admiral Kinkaid, using forces which included land-based air under Rear Admiral J. W. Reeves, Jr., executed the recapture of these islands. The minor cruiser-destroyer battle of the Komandorski Islands in March ended in a draw, but the Aleutians were regained by late summer. In New Guinea, General Kenney's Army medium bombers waged a fierce battle with enemy planes and transports, sinking several of the latter in the battle of the Bismarck Sea in March. Admiral Yamamoto then sent his carrier pilots from *Zuikaku*, *Junyo*, *Hiyo*, and *Zuiho* to land bases to operate against MacArthur's forces in eastern New Guinea. Kenney's flyers gave these planes such rough treatment that Yamamoto had to recall the remnants on 16 April. Two days later American planes ambushed Yamamoto's plane and shot it down, robbing Japan of its greatest naval leader.[25]

For a brief moment, in May 1943, there was a relative lull in the Pacific war. When it passed, Halsey would begin moving north up the Solomons toward Rabaul and new fast carriers would begin arriving at Pearl Harbor to open a second Pacific "front." But if the carriers were to be used effectively in either area—South or Central Pacific—much remained to be done in doctrine. As Ted Sherman noted angrily in his diary in April, ". . . the Navy high command in my opinion shows . . . no proper conception of handling carriers. We have yet to have a permanent two or more carrier task force trained to operate together. . . ." This problem, Ernie King permitting, would have to be resolved in the Pacific. Nor, noted Sherman, "has naval aviation a proper voice in developing the higher strategy and policy of the war." [26] This problem concerned many airmen who were actively fighting for such a voice. Their battlefield was Washington, D.C.

2. *Battle of Washington*

United States naval aviation entered World War II as unprepared administratively as it had been 25 years before when America had entered World War I. This time it had bureau status, but even this was inadequate. For in 1941 naval aviation, symbolized by its carriers, "reached into every part of the naval establishment from one of the coordinate bureaus," and, with its rapidly growing size, was "bursting the bounds of a single bureau." [1] From Pearl Harbor until the summer of 1943, while battles raged against Japan in the far Pacific, the aviators at the Department of the Navy in Washington waged a growing battle to gain an appropriate high position in the policy-making and administrative hierarchy of the Navy.

The first problem was simply BuAer's meeting the demands of the fleet by procuring better and enough airplanes and then distributing them where they were most urgently needed. Simultaneously, it had to produce enough pilots to fly these planes. Constructing new carriers was also important, but the responsibility of studying this problem rested in large measure with the General Board and the Bureau of Ships.

When the war broke out, BuAer enjoyed no system of planning, either for the number of planes needed or for their distribution throughout the fleet. In July 1940 Congress had authorized the procurement of 15,000 Navy aircraft, and BuAer had responded by constructing naval air training centers during 1940–1941 for exactly this number of naval aviators to be under instruction at capacity. The major bases were at Chicago and Jacksonville, though many cadets went to Alameda, Norfolk, Pensacola, San Diego, and Seattle.[2] By Pearl Harbor only 5000 planes had been produced, and the original figure of 15,000 suddenly appeared minuscule next to the actual need. Consequently on 16 January 1942 Congress raised the authorization to 27,500 aircraft. Training centers and airfields sprang up all over the country, coordinated generally through the efforts of a very skillful director of training, Captain Arthur W. Radford. But these were emergency measures, devoid of systematic planning.[3]

Fortunately, Rear Admiral Towers, Chief of BuAer, had been instrumental in shaping naval air policy in 1917 and could anticipate some of the pitfalls. Equally important was his head of the Program and Allocations Section, Lieutenant Commander George W. Anderson, Jr. Anderson (USNA '27), already known for his talents as a pilot and administrator, was in charge of programs and policy planning, including the procurement and assignment of aircraft. Towers and Anderson collaborated closely in the early days of the war to get BuAer's policy planning on a wartime footing. In such an important post, Lieutenant Commander Anderson required knowledge of the larger picture of the war effort. Towers therefore made Anderson his unofficial assistant and took him to all important meetings, "which normally would have been closed to all except top policy-making officials. . . ." These meetings gained for Anderson "an insight into war plans and operating strategy which undoubtedly influenced many of the decisions made by this section."[4]

Towers and Anderson laid the foundations for the inauguration of planning systems that were undertaken during the summer of 1942. Later a director of the Aviator Planning Section was appointed, Captain Harold B. Sallada. Still, difficulties were tremendous, as BuAer had to coordinate not only aircraft procurement and pilot training but also spare parts, shore air bases, and the new carriers as they came out. Requirements continued to rise, as for example on 15 June 1943 when BuAer's authorized inventory was raised from 27,500 airplanes to 31,000. Planning improved, but much of it remained on a makeshft basis throughout the battles of the Atlantic against the U-boat and of the Pacific against the Japanese navy in 1942. As new carriers began massing for the 1943 offensive in the Pacific, coordinated aircraft procurement and assignment were far from perfect.[5]

In carriers, the Bureau looked forward to the new 27,100-ton fast fleet carrier *Essex* (CV-9), authorized in 1938 and laid down in April 1941. In June and July 1940, along with the 15,000 naval planes, Congress authorized the construction of ten more carriers of this class. Two weeks after Pearl Harbor, two more *Essex*es were called for. These ships took time to build, especially as changes had to be made from lessons learned in battle. To augment these fast ships the Navy in January 1942 decided to undertake "a desperate experiment," the conversion of the light cruiser *Amsterdam* of the *Cleveland* class into an 11,000-ton light carrier, renamed *Independence* (CVL-22). Two more conversions were authorized in February, three in March. These ships would carry only half the planes of an *Essex*-class heavy carrier, but would make over 31 knots and could therefore supplement the *Essex*es.[6]

The General Board, although comprised almost entirely of retired nonaviator admirals, had laid much of the groundwork for the designs of *Essex* and *Independence*. After *Saratoga* was removed from the fighting shortly after Pearl Harbor by one torpedo hit, the Board studied the vulnerability of America's carriers and concluded that the Navy needed "some tougher carriers . . . which can engage in offensive operations without being easily placed out of action by a few light bombs, one or two torpedoes or medium sized projectiles." On 14 March 1942 the Board recommended the design of a 45,000-ton armored-deck carrier capable of making 33 knots and carrying six squadrons of planes (36 VF, 48 VB, 36 VT). Admirals King and Towers, in "complete agreement," endorsed the proposal immediately.[7]

The battle of Midway provided additional stimulus to the carrier construction program. In July 1942 Congress authorized funds for fourteen more carriers. One was canceled six months later, but keels were eventually laid for ten more *Essex* class heavy or "medium" carriers (CV) and three for what came to be known as the *Midway* class battle or large carrier (CVB) of 45,000 tons. In addition, three more converted *Independence*-class light carriers (CVL) were called for, making a total of nine carriers of this class. BuAer then had its authorized wartime carrier strength before the start of the Guadalcanal campaign, although the keels for three more *Essex*es and two light carriers of a new class were laid down before the end of the war.

BuAer in mid-1942 could therefore expect to have no less than 35 to 40 fast attack carriers in commission or building before final victory. In addition, to meet the demands of antisubmarine warfare in the Atlantic, the Navy had by this time planned on at least 32 of the tiny, slow escort carriers (CVE), plus many more being built for the Royal Navy. Also, BuAer had planned to procure 27,500 aircraft by June 1945. That great had been the impact of carrier aviation on modern naval warfare.

By way of contrast, the traditional battleship played a very minor part in the Navy's construction plans. In mid-August 1942 the "Gun Club" could boast only six new battleships in commission since early 1941, and these were the first since 1923; two *North Carolina*-class (35,000 tons, nine 16-inch guns) and four *South Dakota*-class (35,000 tons, nine 16-inch guns). But these could make only 27 knots and therefore could not always keep up with the 33-knot carriers in high-speed operations. The battleship admirals, however, had somewhat impressive plans: six battlewagons of the *Iowa* class (45,000 tons; nine 16-inch guns; 33 knots) and five superbattleships of the *Montana* class (60,500 tons; twelve 16-inch guns). But Pearl Harbor, coupled with the sinking of the British *Repulse* and *Prince of Wales* out of Hong Kong by Japanese air several days later, had sealed the future of the battleship. By mid-1943, as the new carriers began arriving in the Pacific, only two of the *Iowa*s had been commissioned, and on 21 July 1943 authorized construction of the five *Montana*s—none of which had been started—was canceled.[8] Eventually, only four of the six *Iowas* were completed.

Yet on 7 December 1941—despite the sinking of the old battleships—the administrative structure of the Navy Department was built upon the battleship as capital ship of the fleet. Any reorientation to air or to anything else would upset a system of command and promotion that had been gradually molded since the days of Mahan fifty years before. Conservative forces within the Navy would resist such a change, despite the exigencies of war. The aviators disagreed, and throughout 1942 and 1943—anticipating the eventual carrier-led offensive in the Pacific—the airmen sought to strengthen their position in Washington.

Important for the reorientation of naval administration to the realities of modern naval warfare was a broad-minded civilian leadership. President Franklin Roosevelt watched the Pacific war with deep interest that perhaps stemmed from his first encounter with airplanes over ships in 1909. His Secretary of the Navy, Frank Knox, was not a particularly outstanding Department head, but he had a first-rate Under Secretary, James V. Forrestal, to whom he gave a free hand. Forrestal, who had earned his wings in the World War I reserves as Naval Aviator No. 154, was a superb administrator and friend to new ideas such as the aviators presented. Forrestal's only problem was Admiral Ernie King, but Knox acted as "a sort of emotional buffer" between Forrestal and King until "a kind of frosty mutual respect" grew up.[9] The other key civilian was the airmen's own Secretary, Artemus L. Gates, Assistant Secretary of the Navy (Air). Gates, like Forrestal, had qualified to fly during the first war as Naval Aviator No. 65; his administrative background was broad and his political contacts important.[10]

Under the direct authority of the Secretary of the Navy were the bureaus, which meant that a bureau chief such as Rear Admiral Towers could legally bypass the CNO on BuAer matters. BuAer, being concerned with material and procurement, worked through the management end of the Secretary's office. In addition, BuAer maintained considerable control over its own personnel assignments, much to the displeasure to the Chief of Personnel, Rear Admiral Randall Jacobs. Jack Towers gladly accepted this freedom from his old antagonist, King, and from Jacobs, who was reputed to be King's "man."[11] King, however, wanted to centralize all procurement, especially air's, under CNO, and in May 1942 he ordered the reorganization of the Navy Department. On 15 May Towers received orders appointing him Assistant CNO (Air) directly under King, while Jacobs simultaneously welcomed control over "all personnel functions now performed by other bureaus and offices." King, however, had failed to consult President Roosevelt and Secretary Knox on the changes. When FDR found out he became enraged and personally ordered King to rescind the order.[12] So the Chief of BuAer continued to work under Knox through Gates. And Towers was rescued from King.

Just as important for the growing influence of the aviators as a friendly civilian regime was a friendly military regime, namely Admiral King. King, wearing the two hats of CNO and Cominch, maintained two separate offices. Since the office of CNO handled logistics and fleet readiness, the aviators had no real concern over its control. In fact, King turned over the functions of CNO to his Vice CNO, Vice Admiral Frederick J. Horne, who worked closely with Assistant Secretary (Air) Gates, who in turn dealt with BuAer. Horne (USNA '99), last of the active naval air observers, had commanded *Saratoga* in 1930 and the Aircraft Battle Force in 1936–1937, but was conservative enough to oppose any reorientation of the Navy high command to air.

Admiral King as Cominch was of greater concern to the aviators since this office controlled fleet command, administration, policy, and strategy. Chief of Staff to Cominch at the beginning of 1943 was Vice Admiral Richard S. Edwards, whose fine mind made him King's closest adviser throughout the war. The two key divisions under Cominch were plans and operations, each of which included one aviator captain to advise the assistant chiefs of staff heading these divisions. In early 1943 King's planning officer was Rear Admiral Charles M. "Savvy" Cooke, a nonaviator as brilliant as his nickname implies. Cooke's aviator planning officer was Captain Matthias B. Gardner. The airmen made their first inroads to the top command echelon in March 1943 when Rear Admiral Art Davis, who had brought the damaged *Enterprise* out of the Solomons, became King's operations officer. Davis' assistant for air, and therefore King's air officer, was Captain Thomas P. Jeter. These were the key staff officers who helped King plan the Pacific offensive during 1943.[13]

During late 1942 and early 1943 King began to feel pressure from the aviators in both offices, CNO and Cominch. His attempt to reorganize the Navy Department and thus control BuAer did not set well with Towers, who had objected strongly. King, though defeated by President Roosevelt, decided to transfer the troublemakers out of Washington, and as soon as the ComAirPac job opened up King sent Towers to take it over. Towers got promoted to vice admiral, but he was apparently withheld from going to sea by King's order. Rear Admiral John S. McCain replaced him as Chief of BuAer in October 1942. McCain, being a latecomer to aviation, could not fill Towers' shoes as the leader of the aviators in Washington, which King knew very well. Coarse and outspoken in two languages—"English and profane" [14]—McCain was no more popular with the dignified non-airmen of Washington than with the Towers men. But he suited Ernie King's needs, and King respected him as a leader.

Problems of BuAer mounted, however, requiring King to look again toward reorganization. One difficulty surrounded the fate of naval aircraft after they had been procured by BuAer and sent to the fleet. In 1941 and 1942 BuAer sent planes wherever they were most urgently needed. In the spring of 1943, however, shortages began to disappear, and no policy existed for replacing or repairing old or damaged planes. Also, pilots were suffering from fatigue after extended operations. BuAer handled personnel in training, but rotating air groups in the forward areas was a fleet matter. And as more planes and more men headed west to the Pacific, aviation logistics became a problem that could affect the entire conduct of the war. King reasoned, rightly, that this matter belonged under his authority as Cominch.[15]

Simultaneously with this need, the aviators' protests mounted over their lack of representation at the higher command levels. Although King was a latecomer aviator, Horne an observer, and Rear Admiral Art Davis in the operations post, the airmen wanted an official command and policy billet with three-star rank, held by one of their own number. As some of these men envisioned such a change, it would give naval aviation virtual autonomy from the rest of the Navy, much like that of the Army Air Forces with respect to the Army. A "Chief of Naval Air" was not exactly contemplated—though some aviators wanted this—but rather a senior aviator who would be responsible only to Cominch-CNO. And they were supported in the spring of 1943 by none other than Secretary Knox, who pointed out to President Roosevelt that no airmen then on duty were handling operational policy at the office of the CNO.[16]

In May 1943 Ernie King made his move to solve the logistical-operational problems facing BuAer in order to pacify the aviators and to achieve his long-awaited reorganization of the Department under his authority. He recommended to Roosevelt and Knox the establishment of four Deputy CNO's—in Operations, Material, Personnel, and Aviation, each to be "supervisory and technical in character." Such a change would downgrade the bureaus to "executive technical agencies." [17]

King failed to convince the President, the civilian Navy heads, or the bureau chiefs that such a sweeping change was advisable in wartime, but the arguments for a Deputy for Air did achieve results. The President approved this one aspect of the proposal, and in July King announced his plan to elevate one naval aviator to the rank of vice admiral to be his deputy on all matters concerning aviation, "to correlate and coordinate all military aspects including policy, plans, and logistics of naval aviation. . . ." [18] From BuAer the divisions of Planning, Personnel, Training, Flight, and Marine Corps air were to be transferred to the new office, which would also recommend to the Bureau of Personnel duty assignments for aviators.[19]

The title of the office and its first occupant were important. King called it Deputy CNO (Air), which brought it into a nebulous relationship with the Vice CNO, Vice Admiral Horne. Furthermore, as part of the CNO organization it would be a "nuts-and-bolts" type of billet, concerned with fleet readiness and logistics only. It would have little to do with policy and fleet operations, which is exactly what happened. The DCNO (Air) in 1943–1945 relied on his own "spy" in the Cominch office for information regarding policy matters. This individual was King's air officer, Captain Wallace M. Beakley, who relieved Captain Jeter in December 1943.[20] Had King wanted this billet to share in policy and planning, he would have titled it Deputy Cominch (Air) or Deputy Cominch–DCNO (Air). As for the first aviator for the job, King had only two available vice admirals, Towers and Fitch. He had no desire to recall Towers to Washington, and Fitch was doing good work in the vital South Pacific. The best solution was to "fleet up" McCain from BuAer, promoting him to vice admiral. He was an aviator, had the experience and knew the problems of BuAer, and was loyal to King.

On 18 August 1943 the post of DCNO (Air) was established under Vice Admiral McCain. The position was not quite what the aviators wanted, but it was an important step in the right direction. DCNO (Air) now established aeronautical logistical policies above the bureau level, while BuAer became a technical agency to carry out DCNO (Air)'s programs. The new Chief of the downgraded BuAer was Rear Admiral Duke Ramsey, a veteran of BuAer activities.

King's efforts at centralization—overcentralization, said many—were not only opposed; they were resented by civilian and naval leaders, including many aviators. One reaction was the suggestion that King's responsibilities of Cominch–CNO be divided as they had been at the outbreak of war. At the conference of Allied leaders at Quebec in August, Secretary Knox, most likely at Under Secretary Forrestal's instigation, suggested to King that he take personal command in the Pacific as Cominch and lead the new offensive; Horne could remain in Washington as CNO. King replied that Nimitz was doing a fine job there and that he, King, would prefer to direct the Navy's many-fronted war from Washington.[21] This is not to say that King did not want to go to sea. He probably would have loved it. Witness the feelings of Admiral Harry Yarnell, former Asiatic Fleet commander, who wrote to King in October 1943, "You should get away from Washington with its politics, petty squabbles, speech writing, and all the distractions that take time and energy, all of which should be concentrated on how we can lick the Jap. That is the one big job for the Navy." Yarnell suggested that King hoist his flag on a warship and lead the fleet back across the Pacific.[22] Many in the Department wished he would do just that; the idea gained support throughout the fall of 1943.

Admiral Yarnell reappeared at the Navy Department during the summer of 1943, four years following his retirement, stirred up several hornet's nests in about three months, and then passed into obscurity. These "nests" were no less than (1) a poll to sound out naval aviators' feelings about their role in the prosecution of the war, (2) the initiation of postwar studies for the size of the peacetime Navy, and (3) the reopening of the debate over unification of the armed forces. Harry E. Yarnell (USNA '97) had been in naval aviation longer than Admiral King; he had commanded an air station and Atlantic Fleet air squadrons and had attended the Naval War College before earning his naval air observer's wings in 1927. Yarnell had brought *Saratoga* into commission and had served as Commander Aircraft Battle Force, 1931–1933. He had commanded the Asiatic Fleet during Japanese expansion in the Far East (1936–1939) before retiring. He was recalled to active duty in 1943; by whom is something of a mystery, since he undertook the airmen poll with only the "approval" of Vice Admiral Horne, King having apparently no part in its initiation.[23] In any case, Yarnell's three problems were timely and germane; they became the major areas of conflict during the battle of Washington until after the end of the war.

The question of who would command the Navy and its carriers in the "aero-amphibious" phase of the Pacific war then about to begin was first asked openly by Captain Logan C. Ramsey in the *United States Naval Institute Proceedings* for May 1943. Ramsey, a naval aviator, suggested that such operations be commanded by a naval officer, "preferably one who has had considerable contact with, or experience in, aerial operations." [24] Yarnell took up this question, put it into a form letter, and early in August 1943 sent it to several score of top fleet commanders and naval aviators from vice admiral to senior lieutenant, "in order to get the best thought possible on this problem." [25] He also asked for the airmen's feelings regarding wartime unification of the armed services. On the major question, Yarnell received a spirited response: the aviators were of one mind about their subordinated position in the naval hierarchy.

The airmen developed two themes. First, aircraft carriers were being used on the defensive, which was improper. Second, all major command staffs needed an aviator. As for defensive use, said Captain Harold Sallada of the CNO's office, "Unless a change is made the ever-increasing potentialities of Naval Aviation may continue to be restricted by fleet plans—the mobility of Naval Aviation will be wasted." [26] Commander J. S. "Jimmy" Thach, a veteran fighter pilot and aerial tactician, noted that the "handwriting on the wall" showed "that Naval aviation is not an auxiliary or arm of the Navy but is the PRIMARY WEAPON—both offensively and defensively—with other branches as arms of the Navy." [27] Rear Admiral Calvin T. Durgin, commanding fleet air at Quonset Point, R.I., summarized the airmen's explanation for mishandled carriers, namely "that our aircraft carrier Task Forces, despite their victories, have been handled with [a] lack of full aggressive affectiveness, when commanded by non-aviator OTC's [officers in tactical command] who lack experience in and knowledge of the air groups." [28] Captain C. R. "Cat" Brown of the Joint War Plans Committee recommended therefore "that either the commander or chief of staff in all echelons should be a naval aviator." [29] Captain Matt Gardner from the office of the CNO pointed out that at that time (August 1943) Nimitz's Cincpac staff had one naval aviator (Captain Ralph A. Ofstie), Atlantic Fleet had one, a commander, Halsey in the South Pacific had only a lieutenant commander aviator, while the new Central Pacific Force staff had but one aviator with the rank of commander.[30]

The general tone of the aviators was anger, for at last they could blow off steam. What particularly irked them was the "damned aviator" attitude demonstrated by many non-air officers. Here was the opportunity to bypass conservative non-air seniors who would not otherwise put up with such rebellious talk. As far as the men at home were concerned—Sallada, Thach, Durgin among them—their words went to Admiral Yarnell alone and caused no one embarrassment. But when Yarnell's form letter reached Pearl Harbor, it hit like a bombshell.

Admiral Nimitz, a nonaviator with only one airman on his Cincpac staff, took a dim view of Yarnell's survey. He immediately disqualified himself from commenting on aviation matters, as "my background lacks intimate association with Air over any extended period. I therefore feel that my personal contribution will be limited to comment on papers being forwarded to you, and viewed largely from the broader aspects of the case." Nimitz then challenged Yarnell for bypassing the chain of command by initiating "the direct interchange of views on this subject between yourself and officers in the Fleet." He questioned Yarnell's authority to conduct this survey and concluded, "I can more intelligently handle future related correspondence if you will inform me on this point."[31] In an effort to reestablish the chain of command, Nimitz had in the meantime sent a form letter of his own to all flag officers commanding air units under his command, asking for their comments on the Yarnell letter and urging frankness and full expression of views.[32]

This move exposed the key non-air fleet commander to the airmen's feelings, and one of the first broadsides Nimitz received was from "Fightin' Freddie" Sherman, who had been smoldering in the South Pacific ever since the battle of the Coral Sea. Sherman declared that present organization and methods for sea war were "antiquated." Because of the revolutionary change in applying the bomb, torpedo, and gun in warfare, "surface ships must be integrated and coordinated with naval air forces, rather than the reverse. The best personnel to do this are naval aviators." Then, practically slapping Nimitz in the face, Sherman opened fire: "Naval aviators, as officers trained and experienced in naval aviation, should have the dominant voice in determining all naval policy and not just naval aviation policy. . . . I recommend . . . [that an order be issued, proclaiming] that it is the Navy Department's policy for the Navy to become a Flying Navy and that hereafter the following positions will be filled only by active naval aviators as part of the aeronautical organization of the Navy"—Cominch (King was not an "active" aviator), CNO, Chief of Personnel, half of the

General Board, "Commanders-in-Chief of all major fleets," obviously including the Pacific, and commanders of all mixed forces which included air.[33] Period. End of statement.

Nimitz, normally calm and collected, reacted rather violently to this and the other letters received on the subject.[34] The object of his anger became his air type commander, the leader of the airmen, Vice Admiral Jack Towers, since Ted Sherman had returned to the South Pacific. Fortunately, Towers' chief of staff was Captain Forrest P. Sherman (no relation to Ted), a very persuasive individual who had won Nimitz's respect and admiration. This Sherman wrote to Admiral Yarnell via Nimitz echoing what other airmen were saying, but much toned down and stressing integration of air and non-air rather than the extreme view of total takeover by the aviators. Sherman pointed out that his views on the matter had not changed in his 22 years in naval aviation,[35] and he recommended "that aviation units are operated either by competent commanders of extended aviation experience or by commanders whose staffs include sufficient competent senior officers with extensive aviation experience. . . ." [36] Nimitz approved Sherman's letter, sending it on to Yarnell. Meanwhile Yarnell answered Nimitz's letter that he was acting on Vice Admiral Horne's authority, which apparently satisfied Nimitz, who wrote no more on the matter.[37]

Admiral Towers waited until everyone else had had his say, then on 4 October 1943 he wrote a long memorandum to Nimitz, ranging over the whole field of naval aviation. Criticizing the new office of DCNO (Air) as "unsound, probably is illegal, and is confusing and overlapping," Towers recommended that Cominch be abolished and replaced by a Chief of Naval Staff, including "one Deputy Chief, with the rank of Admiral . . . [and] that either Chief or Deputy Chief must be a naval aviator." Aviation in the Pacific Fleet Towers regarded as "sound," but he made one important recommendation that no doubt interested Nimitz, as events were to prove. "Establish in each major Fleet command organization," wrote Towers, "the position of Deputy Commander in Chief, with rank next below that of Commander in Chief, and establish the policy that either the Commander in Chief or the Deputy in each case be a naval aviator."

Drawing upon his 32 years experience as a pilot, Towers contradicted those in the Navy who were denying that a "damned aviator" attitude existed: "I contend that the Navy as a whole has not been progressive in its attitude toward application of aviation to naval warfare." He underscored the historical problems of naval aviation: "It was pushed onto the Navy by aviators and a very limited number of senior far-seeing officers [which would have to include King and Yarnell]. Unfortunately, resentment was aroused, and continues. This is not conducive to good team work." Towers then turned to a defense of aviators as good line officers and ship commanders, a crusade which he had waged for years. He spoke on behalf of "outstanding naval officers in aviation . . . who would have been outstanding regardless of specialty." Thus, said ComAirPac, "The naval and national interests better would be served if the best ones were given positions in which their views perforce would be translated into policies and actions." [38]

Admiral Yarnell collected his data, 127 replies out of 300-plus form letters sent out, wrote his Report on Naval Aviation, and submitted it to Secretary Knox and Vice Admiral Horne on 6 November 1943. Concluding that "we are not using Naval air power in the war as fully as might be done," Yarnell listed a very one-sided set of recommendations. Most drastic was that the DCNO (Air) be given the rank of full admiral, a seat on the Joint Chiefs of Staff comparable to that held by the Chief of the Army Air Forces, and authority to direct naval air forces rather than simply advise the CNO. Furthermore, "it is highly desirable that the Commander in Chief in the Pacific be an aviator," which would have meant relieving Nimitz; or barring that, Cincpac should have "an operations officer for Air, with the rank of Rear Admiral." [39]

The aviators had thus made their bid for power—in the Navy Department and in the Pacific where the new fast carriers would soon lead the offensive. In Washington, Ernie King would not be budged. But in the Pacific, two reasonable suggestions had been made: the appointment of two key staff officers to Nimitz, one a Deputy Cincpac to advise on air matters and the other an operations officer for air. This need would become more pronounced during the first campaign involving fast carriers.

The two other issues raised by Yarnell complemented the campaign of the air admirals. One was the question of unified over-all command in one Department of War to improve coordinated planning in the top wartime echelons. Yarnell published an article on the subject in the August 1943 *Naval Institute Proceedings*, while his form letter to the aviators had asked their views. The replies varied widely, the consensus being to keep naval aviation in the Navy no matter what else happened in the unification movement.

A major dispute was brewing, however, over the general uses of air power; the Army Air Forces argued for strategic bombers, while the Navy aviators replied for fleet-supporting aircraft. Captain Cat Brown summarized the problem in his letter to Yarnell on 9 August 1943:

> . . . the quarrel is between the proponents of "support aviation" and those who would like to see the airplane used as a separate weapon such as . . . for strategic bombing. Mixed into this, of course, are all the narrow fixations and elements of personal ambition which human frailty is heir to.
>
> But the honest proponents of each school of thought have much on which to base their contentions. Those who would like to see the airplane used as an effective weapon in support of ground and surface forces say that they have no quarrel with strategic bombing but point out the incontrovertable fact that, when organized in a separate air force, aviators are prone to give lip service to support aviation and the war effort suffers thereby.
>
> Those who favor a separate air force claim, with much justification, that the ground forces and the Navy are not really interested in strategic bombing. . . .[40]

This cogent analysis pertained not only to air power discussions in 1943 but those that had racked the military in 1925 and those that would again undermine unity during the postwar period. For the Navy's part, aircraft and the fast carrier were to support the offensive against Japan, strategically by sinking the Japanese fleet and destroying the Japanese air force and tactically by supporting Marine and Army ground forces at the beachheads. Strategic bombing of Japanese industry by heavy bombers lay in the distant future.

Yarnell's *Proceedings* piece reopened the eyes of the Army airmen who had been relatively silent on the matter of a separate air force since the Billy Mitchell court-martial and the Morrow Report of 1925. Unifying the armed services with a separate Army, Navy, and Air Force appealed to Army planners, but following President Roosevelt's stand on reorganizing the Navy, they realized that no general reorganization around unification could be attempted during wartime. The postwar period was better suited to an administrative battle, but thus had begun Army Air's rejuvenated interest in autonomy in a unified defense structure.[41]

What interested the naval aviators in 1943 about the postwar period was not defense reorganization but the size and composition of the postwar Navy. Admiral C. C. Bloch of the General Board first considered a postwar Navy in a memorandum to Vice Admiral Horne on 10 June 1943. He suggested a balance of 12 battleships and 12 large carriers, but also 20 smaller carriers and 5000 aircraft.[42] Horne, realizing the importance of thinking about demobilization and the postwar Navy, on 26 August appointed Admiral Yarnell as Head of the Special Planning Section to consider the problem. Working practically alone, although in the midst of his Report on Naval Aviation, Yarnell threw himself into the task and presented Horne with a final draft proposal on 22 September. He called for three "fully manned Task Forces," each consisting of three carriers, two battleships, six cruisers, and 18 destroyers. The airmen would predominate.[43]

By the time the first major operation in the Central Pacific involving fast carriers got underway in November 1943, the naval airmen were improving their position substantially within the Navy. Whether they succeeded—at the Cominch–CNO level, at Cincpac headquarters, or in the postwar Navy and defense establishment—would depend entirely on the performance of the new fast carriers in the war against Japan.

Three:
Mobilizing the Carrier Offensive

The pending arrival of many new carriers in the Pacific had a profound effect on shaping Allied strategy during the summer of 1943. The war had bogged down in the Southwest Pacific area, specifically in New Guinea, where General MacArthur's forces were battling the Japanese. In the South Pacific area—the Solomon Islands—Admiral Halsey was making ready to drive north from Guadalcanal toward the key Japanese base at Rabaul. In the Central Pacific Admiral Nimitz remained relatively idle, waiting for the new warships to arrive. Fast carriers could do little in the confined waters around New Guinea and the Solomons, and Navy planners would take no chances in repeating the losses suffered during the air aspects of the Guadalcanal campaign. Therefore land-based air fought in South Pacific skies, while the new carriers went to Hawaii.

The Central Pacific was the logical choice for the offensive; in this region prewar naval strategists had fought their mock battles, and in this region Japanese island airfields and the still-formidable Japanese fleet commanded all approaches. Here a reconstructed United States Pacific Fleet could draw its opponent into battle and thus pave the way for a swift offensive against the Empire, Japan's home islands. For this reason in June 1943 the high-level Joint Strategic Survey Committee recommended that Allied strategy in the Pacific be reoriented from MacArthur's Southwest area to Nimitz's Central.[1] Many Army officers, especially MacArthur, protested strongly for the obvious reason that the Southwest Pacific and the Army would be subordinated to Nimitz and the Navy. But General George Marshall, Army Chief of Staff, had to agree that the tremendous new carrier armada could not be allowed to stagnate, and on 15 June the Joint Chiefs of Staff informed MacArthur that

Central Pacific forces would attack the Marshall Islands, and possibly the Gilberts, beginning mid-November 1943. The operation would be Navy, oriented around two new experimental weapon concepts, the fast carrier task force and the Navy–Marine Corps amphibious assault team.[2]

Much of the Army's opposition, shared by the semi-independent Army Air Forces, was based on the vulnerability of carriers to Japanese land-based air attacks. Allied leaders meeting at Casablanca in May 1943 had decided that a Central Pacific offensive should go forward, but MacArthur and his supporters wanted Nimitz's carriers only to guard the flank of MacArthur's drive up the New Guinea coast. The carriers, in the Army's thinking, could engage in hit-and-run raids while General Kenney's land-based Air Force handled the main supporting role. This assumption that the vulnerable carriers would be inadequately defended stemmed from earlier experience in the war and from the old AAF cliché that land-based air power had made navies obsolete. The forceful Admiral King dispelled these fears for the Joint Chiefs, but the first major offensive action would have to provide the evidence that the fast carriers could hit and stay.

Strategic discussions during the summer resulted in a Joint Chiefs directive on 6 August 1943 calling for a dual advance across the Pacific. Nimitz, to obtain advanced bases for attacking the Marshalls, would seize the Gilbert Islands beginning 15 November 1943, followed up by landings in the Marshalls on New Year's Day 1944. Halsey, working through the central and northern Solomons, would neutralize or capture Rabaul by 1 February 1944. The Central Pacific forces would then aim toward mighty Truk, fortress and fleet anchorage of the Combined Fleet in the eastern Carolines; neighboring Ponape would be taken on 1 June 1944. Simultaneously, MacArthur would cross northern New Guinea to assault Hollandia from the sea on 1 August 1944. Nimitz would land at Truk one month later and continue on to the Palau Islands in the western Carolines on the last day of 1944.[3]

The ultimate goal of these two drives was the Luzon "bottleneck," that strait of water between the China mainland from Hong Kong to Amoy, the island of Formosa, and the northern tip of Luzon in the Philippines. By landing on the Chinese coast, on Formosa, or on Luzon in 1945 Allied forces would cut the flow of Japanese ships carrying vital raw materials such as oil and rubber from the East Indies to the Empire. After the bottleneck had been "corked" Allied forces could seize Malaya to the west and the Ryukyu Islands in the north in 1945–1946. Final operations against the four home islands of Japan, including blockade and possibly invasion, could be carried out in 1947–1948. All these long-range plans assumed victory in Europe in 1944, which led Admiral Savvy Cooke of Cominch staff to point out that the American people might well tire of the prospect of another four years of war after the defeat of Germany. He recommended both enemies be defeated in 1946, and this view eventually was accepted. Such were the first concrete plans for the counteroffensive against Japan that would be spearheaded by the new fast carriers.[4]

1. New Weapons

The American fast carrier of 1943 was one product of a community of industry, science, and technology the like of which the world had never before seen. Applying its best minds to a vast reservoir of raw materials and skilled technicians, the United States molded a modern war machine with unprecedented speed and unforeseen results. The fast aircraft carrier for the Pacific war, only one fragment of this techno-industrial complex, was one of the most important products of America's warmaking capability that burst upon the fighting fronts of the world after the spring of 1943.

The *Essex*-class carrier surpassed every other "flattop" that had preceded it. *Saratoga* was bigger but less maneuverable and could carry fewer planes. *Enterprise* compared in many respects but was older and required modernization, which she got during the summer of 1943. The 45,000-ton *Midway*-class "battle" carrier was still on the drawing boards. *Essex* displaced 27,100 tons and was manned by 150 officers and 2550 men, along with 175 officers and 130 enlisted of an air group and, if an admiral was aboard, 35 officers and 65 enlisted in "flag country." Possible total: 3105 persons.[1] The *Independence*-class light carrier, displacing 11,000 tons, carried a crew and air group of 159 officers and 1410 enlisted personnel.

Along with the flight deck, the major activity on the carrier centered around several important command and communications centers. The captain's bridge, located forward on the "island" superstructure, was the command post of the ship. One level below was the signal and flag bridge, from which the air officer directed flight operations and the admiral directed the task force. Adjacent to the signal bridge were gunnery control, radio air plot, and the photographic laboratory, all equipped with the latest communications equipment. The hub of aviation activity was air plot, which monitored all pertinent data to pilots and aircrewmen in their ready rooms or to their planes while they were airborne. Flag plot, also located off the signal bridge, housed the radar equipment which recorded ship dispositions and the location of all aircraft in the vicinity. The captain, flag plot, and air plot got their information from the Combat Information Center (CIC), a usually chaotic communications room suspended below the flight deck on the gallery deck.

Advanced communications equipment held the key to successful fast carrier task force operations in the Pacific. The debate over single- versus multicarrier task force operations was resolved to a large extent by developments in radar. This British invention (*ra*dio *d*etection *a*nd *r*anging) served two purposes—tracking ships and tracking airplanes. Ship tracking, performed by the Position Plan Indicator (PPI), enabled a multicarrier force to maintain a high-speed formation at night or in foul weather. All supporting vessels could then provide continuous mutual antiaircraft protection. Every new carrier and screening vessel had a PPI; the older ships were getting them. In addition, the new ships (and older ones, when modernized) carried the Dead Reckoning Tracer (DRT) for purposes of general navigation and the tracking of surface ships.[2]

Aircraft detection was essential for the fighter director in air plot to direct his combat air patrols and for the gunnery officer to direct his antiaircraft batteries. Each *Essex*-class carrier was equipped with air search radars to determine the composition and vertical formation of incoming flights. The only problem with the Mark 4 radar in 1943 was that its horizontal sweep could not detect low-flying planes between the horizon and 10 degrees above it. A new Mark 12 radar was due when the new carriers went into combat, thus filling the one gap in the radar's performance, but production delays kept it out of the fleet until the first half of 1944.[3]

What radar could not tell was the identity of incoming planes, and again the Navy adopted a British device, the IFF (Identification, Friend-or-Foe). With the IFF turned on inside a friendly airplane, ships had no worry. If a plane did not respond to an IFF signal, the ship assumed him to be hostile; woe unto the Yank who forgot to flip on his IFF, and there were many. This gadget was installed on all American warships and planes during the second half of 1943.

Radio, which had begun to transform naval warfare thirty years before, was vital to the prosecution of carrier warfare. Until mid-1943 the ship could talk to its pilots at long range, but very often the enemy would listen in. In addition, single channels restricted the volume of radio traffic. For the new fast carriers, American science developed a four-channel very-high-frequency (VHF) radio that permitted four separate conversations from one ship, all short-ranged so the enemy could not listen in. Simultaneously, combat intelligence officers could communicate over one channel to their counterparts in another ship, the fighter director officer could direct his pilots from air plot on another channel, the ship could maintain contact with its defensive combat air patrol and antisubmarine planes over the force, and the fourth channel could be used for training purposes at sea. Effective use of the new radio equipment, such as proper assignment of channels to avoid overcrowding, could only be learned in battle.[4]

Radar and radio were essential to coordinated antiaircraft fire, which was the carrier's sole defense without its planes. By the summer of 1943 the standard antiaircraft weapons were the 5-inch/38-caliber dual-purpose gun, Swedish 40mm Bofors cannon, Swiss 20mm Oerlikon cannon, and the VT or proximity-fuzed shell. Though radar never actually did control antiaircraft fire during the war, the combination of all these weapons fired visually was devastating. So effective a defense did the 40mm provide that official historians have claimed that it "contributed as much as any other weapon to saving the warship from the oblivion which was so freely predicted for it by air power experts during the early part of the war." Yet in mid-1943 *Essex*'s 17 quad 40mms (68 barrels) were surpassed in importance by the 65 or so single-mount 20mm guns used for very close-in defense against attacking planes. The light carriers mounted only two 40mm quads and nine twin 20mms.[5]

The major defensive firepower of the fast carrier was provided, however, by the 5-inch/38 gun armed with the proximity-fuzed shell. This weapon, double-mounted in six turrets flanking the island of *Essex*, had a long-distance range of 10 miles, ceiling of 6 miles, and could fire 12 to 15 rounds per minute. The proximity (or VT, "variable time") fuze had been added at the beginning of the year. Until 1943 all American antiaircraft shells had detonated on impact, a highly unreliable defense against the swift, small airplane. American scientists labored for two and a half years to produce the proximity fuze, a radio transmitter and receiver built into the head of the shell that would gauge its own distance from the target before detonating. When the shell was 70 feet from an enemy plane, a strong ripple pattern of radio waves set off a chain reaction of triggers, culminating in detonation; a near-miss usually finished an airplane. The effectiveness of the 5-inch gun was therefore increased three or four times. A few VT-fuzed shells had been used at the end of the Guadalcanal campaign, but the new device would be first put to the test on a large scale aboard the fast carriers.[6]

The so-called "Sunday punch"—the main offensive battery—of the fast carriers was its air group. American industry met the timetable of new aircraft for the new carriers. New fighters, new scout/dive bombers, and new torpedo bombers were either in commission or undergoing trials by the summer of 1943. Each *Essex*-class ship would have three squadrons—36 fighters, 36 scout/dive bombers, and 18 torpedo planes. The light carriers had about one-third this strength, 24 fighters and nine torpeckers.

The new carriers could not take the war to Japan without a fighter plane to match the celebrated Zero. The F4F Wildcat had held its own against the Zero, but it was inadequate to maintain command of the air. Following the battle of Midway three of the Navy's leading fighter pilots, Lieutenants Butch O'Hare, Jimmy Thach, and Jimmy Flatley, had told President Roosevelt that the Navy needed "something that will go upstairs faster," something "with climb and speed." [7] Two superb fighters followed. One, the Chance-Vought F4U Corsair, had first been conceived before the war, but design changes quickly brought it into the Navy inventory. The Corsair entered combat as a land-based Marine Corps fighter in February 1943 and soon earned the reputation among the Japanese as the Whistling Death. But the long cowling, low cockpit, and weak undercarriage made the Corsair undesirable for carrier operations.

Grumman Aircraft Engineering Corporation came up with the solution, its own new fighter. During the Midway campaign, a Zero from *Ryujo*, one of the two Japanese light carriers attacking the Aleutians, had crash-landed on an isolated island in that chain.

The wreckage had been recovered by American forces and shipped to the United States for tests. BuAer flyers and engineers were amazed to find the Zero's superior performance was achieved with a mere 1000-horsepower engine but at the sacrifice of armor protection and high-altitude capabilities.[8] Plunging into a round-the-clock effort to produce a fighter to defeat this Zero, Grumman's engineers constructed a new experimental airplane in less than three months, the XF6F Hellcat. A new high-altitude 2000-horsepower Pratt and Whitney engine gave the Hellcat an extra 30 miles per hour over the Zero and almost 2000 feet higher ceiling (up to 22,800 feet).[9] The new plane could outdive and outclimb the Zero, while its heavier engine allowed for heavier guns, armor to protect the pilot and fuel tanks, and self-sealing gas tanks of rubber encased in a canvas hammock to nullify the effect of bullet punctures.[10] The first production F6F appeared in November 1942, while the first squadrons arrived in Hawaii with the new carriers. They were untried in combat.

The Hellcat's armament was six .50-caliber machine guns, three fixed on each wing, a heavier firepower than the Zero's two 20mm and two 7.7mm guns. The .50, which fired more than 1000 rounds per minute, had become most popular of the Navy's machine guns by 1943 because it could pierce armor and because new suspended containers carried more ammunition for it than previously. Always looking for better and more destructive weapons, however, the Navy had begun experimenting with the 20mm cannon, and in June 1943 the Bureaus of Ordnance and Aeronautics were ordered to start top-priority development of a forward-firing 3.5-inch rocket for fighters.[11]

The hero of the battle of Midway, the rugged Douglas SBD Dauntless scout/dive bomber, did not have the range or speed of the new fighter, nor could it carry the bombload now required by the carriers. The Navy had therefore contracted the Curtiss Wright Company to build a new dive bomber, the SB2C Helldiver. The new plane suffered along with the new factory which produced it. Difficulties with both slowed production, but during the spring of 1943 the first Helldivers joined the new carriers for trials. The results were disastrous; wingfold and arresting gear malfunctioned, fuselage and wing skin wrinkled, tailwheels collapsed, and the hydraulic system leaked. Frustrated carrier skippers returned the SB2Cs to the factory for further work.[12] Meanwhile the fast carriers had to depend on the old Dauntless for dive bombing. The first corrected Helldivers did not reach the Pacific until the early fall of 1943, and then only in limited numbers. In armament, the SBD-5 carried two .50-caliber fixed and two .30-caliber flexible machine guns and up to 2250 pounds of bombs. The SB2C-1 had four fixed .50-caliber and two .30 flexible machine guns; it could carry 2650 pounds of bombs or one torpedo. [13]

Grumman Aircraft also accounted for the Navy's first-line torpedo bomber, the TBF-1 Avenger, the *only* torpedo plane after the battle of Midway. Rugged and versatile, the "turkey" could drop a torpedo or 1600 pounds of bombs, while thought was being given to arming it with rocket launchers. It could defend itself with two .50-caliber fixed machine guns, one .50-caliber in a rotating dorsal turret, and one flexible .30-caliber "stinger" gun, the latter located aft of the bomb bay.[14] Not content with this already-aging plane, the Navy soon contracted for a slightly improved version, the TBM-3 built by General Motors. BuAer also placed high hopes in a brand-new torpedo bomber, Chance Vought's TBU, which incorporated "everything we have learned about planes of this type," according to Rear Admiral Ralph Davison, Assistant Chief of BuAer, in September 1943. "The last word" in torpedo bombers, said Davison, "there is no other torpedo plane in the world to match it." [15] Initially unsuccessful, development was taken over by Consolidated Aircraft, which relabeled the plane the TBY-2 Seawolf.

The roles of the bombers were ill-defined by 1943. Originally (during the 1920s) designed as scout planes to give the fleet "eyes," the VS scout type had been adapted to dive bombing as the VSB after 1927. With the advent of extensive bulky radio gear and airborne radar in 1942–1943, the small VSB could not fully perform both its bombing and scouting missions. Its range was extended with the use of droppable fuel tanks, but technology soon eliminated the VSB as a scout. After November 1943 it became a full-time dive bomber, VB. The bulky torpedo plane could accommodate much communication equipment, and late in 1943 it took over many of the scouting functions. Also, early in 1944, the fighter plane could be equipped with a lightweight airborne radar set for reconnaissance purposes. Still, the torpedo plane was rated as a VT or even a VTB, the fighter as a VF or later VBF, both planes doubling as bombers but usually not as scout planes. The U.S. Navy did not have a suitable long-range scout plane for the fast carriers. It had, like the Japanese Navy, sacrificed its traditional information-getting ability in the interest of the attack mission.

A new enemy threat to pending carrier operations was Japanese night air operations. Rear Admiral McCain, while commanding naval air in the Solomons in 1942, had been dismayed by the single Japanese "washing-machine Charlie" that flew over Guadalcanal and dropped a few 100-pound bombs just to keep the troops awake. Having no night fighters, American forces had had to sit there and sweat out these nuisance raids.[16] McCain recommended that something be done, and when in October 1942 he became Chief of BuAer he instituted studies to deal with Japanese night-flying aircraft. Captain Arthur W. Radford, in charge of naval air training, alerted his flight instructors to the new menace. A team of Marine Corps aviators returned from England in June 1943 with the information that the British "have found out very definitely that [the] twin-engine night fighter is a necessity."[17] BuAer thereupon turned to Grumman again, as that company had been developing a heavily armed radar-equipped twin-engine night fighter, the XF7F Tigercat. The first production model of this airplane flew in December 1943.[18]

In the meantime the Navy needed a night fighter and adopted the land-based F4U Corsair as a makeshift solution. Commander W. J. "Gus" Widhelm trained a detachment of five radar-equipped Navy night Corsairs during the summer and then took it to the Solomons for combat testing. If proved successful, the night Corsairs might conceivably be placed aboard the fast carriers, as Japanese night air attacks were increasing in the Solomons, an indication of what might appear in the Central Pacific. Admiral Nimitz therefore suggested to Vice Admiral Towers that four-plane night-fighter detachments be placed aboard each new carrier, but Towers preferred to await the results of Widhelm's experiment.[19] So the new fast carriers went to war without a night defensive capability.

The fast carrier task force, then, would be initiating several new pieces of equipment in battle: the *Essex*-class heavy carrier, the *Independence*-class light carrier, the F6F Hellcat fighter, multichannel VHF radios, and the PPI and DRT radars. Supporting these ships would be the proximity-fuzed 5-inch/38 shell, an arsenal of 40mm and 20mm antiaircraft guns, and a host of new and modernized older battleships, cruisers, and destroyers.

2. *The Japanese*

The Japanese decision after the Naval Battle of Guadalcanal in November 1942 to abandon that island marked a turning point in Japan's hopes to win the war. Unable to afford the losses in fighting for Guadalcanal, Admiral Yamamoto had to give up his attempt to engage and destroy the remnants of the American fleet. He could only wait until that fleet was reinforced by American industry, and then victory would be impossible. The hope of Axis victory in Europe was also dashed, after the Allied invasion of North Africa that same month and the surrender of the German army before Stalingrad two months later. Then in May 1943 the German army in North Africa surrendered. Guadalcanal was evacuated in February, the Japanese garrison at Attu in the Aleutians was annihilated in May. Yamamoto made one final attempt to reverse Japanese fortunes in April by sending the planes from four of his carriers to battle American air forces in the Solomons and New Guinea. Badly battered, these squadrons had to be recalled by Yamamoto, who was himself ambushed in the air and killed days later.

These setbacks led the Japanese Emperor to deem it "essential to end the war without a moment's delay," and in April 1943 peace moves were begun within Japanese political circles.[1] The change in Japan's strategy from offensive to defensive was not lost on Japan's enemy; Admiral Towers announced to his aviators in April that "the enemy has definitely gone on the strategic defensive and . . . his limited air strength is being conserved for employment against worthwhile shipping targets." [2] In late June Halsey's forces jumped off from Guadalcanal by attacking New Georgia Island in the central Solomons; it fell within two weeks. As other islands fell to the South Pacific drive, cruiser-destroyer battles ensued, sometimes joined by land-based air. Then on 8 September Italy surrendered, freeing some British vessels in the Mediterranean for service in the Indian Ocean against Japan.

Though the more realistic leaders of Japan sought to make peace, in mid-1943 the militant faction led by Prime Minister Hideki Tojo still prevailed. In September Japanese strategists held an Imperial Conference to decide general policy for prosecuting the remainder of the war. Although every effort was to be made in countering American and British advances in the following year, Japan would "rapidly build up the decisive battle strength, especially air power, and prosecute the war . . . on our own initiative . . . at the latest by around the middle of 1944. . . ." [3] Japan was therefore losing the battle of industry. Whereas new American ships and planes became available in mid-1943, Japan's would not be ready for another year.

In August 1943 the Third Fleet Striking Force—Japan's fast carrier task force—consisted of six carriers, all but two of which were conversions. CarDiv 1 included the veteran *Zuikaku* and *Shokaku*, plus light carrier *Zuiho*. CarDiv 2 was comprised of the two sister conversions, 24,140-ton *Hiyo* and *Junyo*, which each carried 54 planes. In addition, this division included the new 13,360-ton light carrier *Ryuho*, conversion completed in November 1942. The only other carrier then available was the old *Hosho*, antiquated and inactive. Supporting the carriers was a formidable battle force of the two *Yamato*-class superbattleships, five modernized older battleships, and ten heavy cruisers.

Emergency conversions were going forward to reinforce the fleet by mid-1944. Two 11,190-ton sister converted light carriers, *Chitose* and *Chiyoda*, were due in the fall. Two older battleships, *Ise* and *Hyuga*, were having their after turrets removed in favor of short flight decks. But carriers new from the keel were to comprise Japan's new fleet. The 29,300-ton 75-plane fast carrier *Taiho* was to be the first and most advanced of the new ships, with an armored flight deck. After the battle of Midway, the Modified Fleet Replenishment Program of 1942 planned for 15 modified *Hiryu*-class carriers and 5 improved *Taiho*s, a program comparable to America's with the *Essex*es. Building all these new vessels on Japan's weakening industrial base soon proved unrealistic, but several of the new *Hiryus* were laid down. Finally, Japan had its own "battle" carrier of the *Midway* variety, the mammoth 64,800-ton *Shinano*, converted from a *Yamato* battleship hull to be a ferry and supply ship for other carriers; she was due in the spring of 1945.[4]

In aircraft and pilots the Japanese had decidedly declined from their earlier superiority. The Zero fighter had been modified but it still suffered from lack of armor. American .50-caliber slugs hitting most Japanese planes could knock off wings or expose the fuel tanks to .50-caliber incendiaries, making the planes highly inflammable. Japan employed a large variety of bombers, especially land-based. When the American offensive began these planes could operate between islands—the "unsinkable carriers"—to trap enemy ships, theoretically. The fatal weakness was in pilots. Japan's insistence on a trained elite, plus the lack of rotating veterans to training duties, had begun the attrition of the Japanese navy's best aviators (the army pilots remained in China). By mid-1943 the average Japanese pilot had trained 500 hours in the air, contrasted to 700 hours at the time of Pearl Harbor. By comparison, United States naval aviators had improved from 305 to 500 hours of flying training in that year and a half.[5]

In doctrine, the Japanese had applied the lessons of Midway, although American naval leaders had no way of knowing this. The Japanese penchant, and Yamamoto's, for dividing up the fleet during major operations had been quickly scrapped in favor of tactical concentration. The carrier had been made the nucleus of the Combined Fleet, with battleships and lesser vessels providing antiaircraft protection. Experience in multicarrier operations enabled the Japanese to continue the practice, using three carriers per task group. This formation was used throughout the Guadalcanal battles in late 1942.

Admiral Nagumo's defeat at Midway and failure to turn the tide at Guadalcanal led to his replacement as Commander-in-Chief Third Fleet by Vice Admiral Jisaburo Ozawa. Ozawa (JNA '09), though not an aviator, had commanded a cruiser, then a battleship, and had been chief of staff Combined Fleet before becoming ComCarDiv 1, 1939–1940. After leading a battleship division he had commanded part of the forces, including one carrier, in the conquest of the East Indies in 1942. Unexposed to the Midway disaster, Ozawa took over Third Fleet in November 1942 and began refreshing his keen mind to the intricacies of carrier warfare. He did not have the services of Commander Genda, who after serving two months on Vice Admiral Tsukahara's staff returned to Tokyo with that officer at the end of 1942. Tsukahara became Chief of BuAer; Genda joined Imperial Headquarters.

Ozawa, also relieving Nagumo as ComCarDiv 1, was assisted by the new ComCarDiv 2, Rear Admiral Takaji Joshima, appointed in August 1943. Joshima was not an aviator either, but his seaplane carriers had been major participants in the Guadalcanal and Solomons campaigns. Both Ozawa and Joshima flew their flags ashore at Rabaul, along with Vice Admiral Jinichi Kusaka, Tsukahara's relief as Commander 11th Air Fleet. The carrier planes were used to attack American forces in the Solomons, while the carriers remained at Truk. Also based at Rabaul was the Commander-in-Chief Combined Fleet, until April 1943 Admiral Yamamoto and after his death Admiral Mineichi Koga, a nonaviator but very aggressive officer.

The United States Pacific Fleet therefore faced a somewhat formidable adversary in the summer of 1943. Based at Truk, the Japanese Third Fleet of six carriers and assorted supporting vessels could seriously challenge any American advance. Additional air strength was available from Japan's "unsinkable carriers," the interlocking system of island airfields. The longer Japan harbored this strength, the stronger its fleet and naval air force would become. Two more carriers were expected by the end of 1943, perhaps three more by the following summer. Pilot training was also essential to the success of this fleet, and again time was the vital factor. But trained pilots, land- and carrier-based, were being squandered in the defense of Rabaul and the Solomons; by the end of 1943 Japan had lost more than 7000 aircraft and an equal number of pilots and aircrewmen, a staggering figure.[6]

By the autumn of 1943 the Japanese fleet was not ready to fight a major battle.

3. *Command and Doctrine*

Two general concepts of warfare dominated American military thinking during World War II. One was based on continental warfare: large armies marching across great land masses, supported by land-based strategic and tactical air forces. Practiced by the United States Army and its own subservice, the Army Air Forces, this school of strategy had led to the successful landings in North Africa in November 1942, Sicily in July 1943, and Salerno, Italy, in September 1943. The other concept was victory through sea power, advocated by the United States Navy and its subservice, the Marine Corps. This school of thought envisioned great naval battles, amphibious assaults on enemy outposts, and naval blockade. The American effort to gain command of the sea had led to the battles of Midway and Guadalcanal and those in the Solomons.

Not coincidentally, the Army had gained predominance over the conduct of the war against continental Germany and the Navy over that against island-nation Japan. The Army, though depending on the Navy to provide and protect its logistics on the high seas, planned to invade northern Europe and conquer

Germany by land. Its air force would assist by bombing Axis industry. The Navy planned to regain key islands in the Central and South Pacific as a prelude to air and sea blockade of the Japanese homeland. Its Marines would assault these islands while the fleet eliminated Japanese air and naval interference. The Army in the Southwest Pacific under General MacArthur complemented this strategy by pushing across New Guinea.

In theory, the separation of authority between the Army in Europe and the Navy in the Pacific was logical. But the Navy's strategy for the counteroffensive against Japan was based only on theory. Success depended on two untried concepts, the amphibious doctrine of the Fleet Marine Force and the new fast carrier task force. Until February 1943, when the Marines took it over, amphibious training and operations had been divided between the Army and Marines, with the only Marine experience the unopposed landing at Guadalcanal in August 1942. As for the carriers, discussed above, they had not operated effectively in support of landings at all, much less in multicarrier formations.

For these reasons, many Army and Army Air Force generals opposed Navy control of the Central Pacific offensive; the new amphibious and carrier forces were too new and untried to form the basis of the new campaign. General MacArthur was the most vocal of the Navy's opponents. He wanted his Southwest Pacific theater to remain primary, with an Army-type advance to the Philippines and possibly to China supported by General Kenney's Army air. The Navy, in MacArthur's view, should cover his northern or right flank. When the Joint Chiefs decreed in favor of the Navy-centered Central Pacific offensive, Army leaders tried to restrict Admiral Nimitz by making him primarily Commander-in-Chief Pacific Ocean Areas (Cincpoa), the coordinator of ship movements, rather than accepting him as Commander-in-Chief Pacific Fleet (Cincpac), in which capacity he would command the offensive forces. Also, as Cincpoa, Nimitz would be under tighter control of the Joint Chiefs, and the Army commander at Pearl Harbor would have greater authority in the Central Pacific. But the Navy resisted, and Nimitz remained in control as commander of the Pacific Fleet and Central Pacific theater, far removed from the Joint Chiefs.[1]

The Army was understandably concerned about the disposition of its forces in the new theater. In August 1943 it replaced its old prewar defensive-oriented Hawaiian Department with the

Headquarters, U.S. Army Forces, Central Pacific Area, geared to the new offensive. The commander was Lieutenant General Robert C. Richardson, Jr. On 6 August the Army and Navy commanders at Hawaii were directed to begin preparing for amphibious operations against the Gilbert Islands, which brought the problem of command to a head.[2] Since Nimitz and the Navy prevailed, the Army suggested that a joint Army-Navy planning staff be appointed under Nimitz. On 6 September Nimitz agreed to this, but to insure his absolute command, he separated the Joint Planning Staff from the main Cincpac administrative office, a practice that was soon to prove impractical.[3] On 24 August the Fifth Amphibious Force was established at Pearl Harbor under the command of Rear Admiral Richmond Kelly Turner, who had commanded amphibious forces in the South Pacific under Admiral Halsey. To the Army's and particularly to General Richardson's disappointment, the Navy and Marines assumed and maintained control of amphibious operations in the Central Pacific.

By March 1943 the Navy had assumed full responsibility for all amphibious operations, the chief agency being the Marine Corps. The Army, in conjunction with the British, would continue preparations for landing on the continent of Europe, such landings (Salerno, Anzio, Normandy, and Marseilles) to be merely preludes to larger land campaigns to follow. But the Marine Corps would develop the amphibious doctrine that was to characterize the many landings in the Central Pacific, landings that were to be total campaigns in themselves. To update its *Landing Operations Doctrine* for the new offensive, the Corps in August added 50 new pages, the last major revision of this manual during the war.[4]

Another manifestation of the Army's preoccupation with continental objectives was its use of tactical air forces. The amphibious landings in the Central Pacific would require close air support of a sort foreign to the Army Air Forces, which had been developed on the glamour of air-to-air combat in the Eddie Rickenbacker tradition of World War I and on the strategic-bombing crusade of the Billy Mitchell school. Tactical Army air used in support of ground forces had changed after World War I to "attack in depth"—interdiction bombing of rear troop and supply concentrations and lines of communication such as railroads and bridges so common in the European theater.[5] The Marine Corps air arm, on the other hand, had developed close support to within 200 yards of friendly front lines, a practice which the Army Air field manual of

July 1943 regarded as "difficult to control, expensive, ineffective and dangerous to our own troops." [6] To the Army flyers the Central Pacific would turn out to be "a monotonous sort of war . . . involving relatively little combat with enemy planes . . . [which] rarely permitted the successful application of tactics taught in the AAF schools." [7]

Since the major effort of Army tactical air would be in Europe, the AAF could not be expected to alter its training doctrines to conform to conditions in a secondary theater. But to the Navy the Pacific was the primary theater of operations, where close air support had to be learned and perfected. Marine Corps aviators had begun to work on this doctrine during maneuvers in 1935, but the real advances in technique were being made in mid-1943 by land-based Marine and Navy pilots in the central Solomons and by Army pilots in New Guinea. For the Central Pacific offensive, these techniques would have to be transferred to the fast carriers and their air groups. Only the Navy was in any position to do this, even though, ironically, the first close air support coordinator in the Central Pacific turned out to be an Army Air Force colonel.

The Navy, then, assumed control over the Central Pacific offensive, which would consequently result in a contest between the United States Pacific Fleet and the Imperial Japanese Navy for command of the sea. To achieve this end, the United States Navy and Allied naval units had three major objectives: to sink or immobilize the Japanese fleet, to neutralize or capture and develop enemy air and naval bases in the Central Pacific, and to seal off the Japanese home islands with an air-sea blockade. If and when full-scale invasions were made against such large land masses as China, the Philippines, or Japan itself the Army would have a legitimate claim for sharing in the over-all command of the Central Pacific theater.

One of the principal Army objections to a Navy-centered offensive was, again, the fleet's supposed vulnerability to Japanese land-based air attack. The Pacific Fleet, built around its new fast carriers, did face tremendous problems, which at least one perceptive naval writer fully appreciated in the spring of 1943. Franklin G. Percival, writing in the May *Naval Institute Proceedings*,[8] pointed out that indeed the key problem of a fleet of a dozen carriers and a dozen battleships with supporting craft was sufficient antiaircraft and antisubmarine protection to give it "untrammeled movement." "The outstanding unsolved problem is the defense of aircraft carriers . . . the Achilles' heel of our present system of waging offensive war." Percival had part of the answer, the battleship: "a well-designed battleship will add more to the anti-aircraft strength of the fleet than any single vessel of any other type." To this he should have added the increasing numbers of antiaircraft batteries on the carriers themselves as well as on the escorting cruisers and destroyers. Also, the defensive fighter-plane cover would be essential. The real difficulty—which Percival did not see—was developing an adequate multicarrier task formation that would give the carriers maximum protection.

Such a fleet of fast carriers and battleships with "overwhelming superiority in striking and resisting power which is necessary to annihilate the opposing fleet," Percival pointed out, would need sufficient ammunition plus a well-protected floating drydock for repairing ships. What Percival was hinting at was mobile logistics that could enable the new fleet to maintain its general mobility. "The potentialities of such a fleet," he said, "would open a new chapter in the history of naval warfare."

In the campaigns against Japanese-held islands, Percival continued, "such a fleet can cover a landing with a greater volume of supporting gunfire, and then afford an invaluable sustained support afterward." For the assaults, Percival again lauded the battleship: "It can still deliver a more devastating bombardment of any shore position within range of its guns." Equally important, the mobile fast carriers "would eliminate the necessity for an island-by-island advance. The strategic short cuts made possible by such freedom of movement will bear some thought." In other words, Percival had seen what strategists in the Pacific were soon to discover, that a mobile fast carrier force could neutralize and thereby allow the amphibious forces to bypass certain well-defended enemy islands. And such a powerful fleet, said this writer, would not have to hit and run; it could hit and stay.

Percival, like the naval aviators, had foreseen the effectiveness a well-managed fast carrier–fast battleship fleet would have in defeating Japan. Like them, he had no doubts about which ship type would form the nucleus of this fleet when battle was joined. "The outcome of the engagement," Percival echoed the aviators, "will, of course, be decided largely by superiority in the air. . . ."

The key to an effective fleet strategy, then, lay in the development of a sound new fast carrier doctrine and the appointment of qualified admirals to formulate this doctrine and then put it into practice. And since men precede ideas and doctrine, success in the first fleet operations of the new offensive would depend on the men who commanded the first fast carrier task forces. The naval aviators in Washington had begun to press their point that only airmen should be appointed to this task, and they had made an important administrative gain in the creation of the office of DCNO (Air). But it was in the Pacific, at Pearl Harbor, that the issue had to be resolved. There the aviators had begun to give Admiral Nimitz no peace in pressing their case.

Over-all credit for the victory at the carrier battle of Midway in June 1942 had gone to Admiral Nimitz and Rear Admiral Spruance. Neither was an aviator, and Nimitz did not even like to ride in airplanes. The senior naval aviators at Midway had been Spruance's temporary chief of staff, Captain Miles Browning, and the captains of the three carriers, Murray, Mitscher, and Buckmaster. Following the battle, Nimitz appointed Spruance, reputed to have one of the finest strategic minds in the Navy, to be his chief of staff at Cincpac headquarters. When the fighting shifted to the South Pacific in August 1942, the carriers and aviators went there. But Nimitz and Spruance remained at Pearl Harbor, considering their strategy and plotting the future course of the war in the Pacific. Without a senior air admiral on the staff to handle aviation requirements, they established the office of ComAirPac on 1 September 1942.

The obvious choice for ComAirPac was Jack Towers, elevated to the rank of vice admiral. Ernie King wanted him out of Washington, but probably not in an operational capacity where Towers could distinguish himself. As matters stood, Towers was senior to Spruance by one year and now another star. Operationally, Towers rated command of a fleet in October 1942, when he reported in the Pacific. Nimitz, who had been Towers' peer as a bureau chief on the eve of the Pearl Harbor attack, did not welcome this crusader for air with any enthusiasm, particularly in light of Admiral King's coolness toward the man. So Towers arrived in Hawaii with the support of almost no top commander, a situation he had experienced throughout his career as he had battled to gain acceptance of naval aviation throughout the fleet.

What King's actual instructions were to Nimitz regarding Towers will probably never be known, but from the nature of ComAirPac's specified duties, it was obvious that Towers was to be kept out of operations. Though ComAirPac was to advise Cincpac on all aviation matters, his major work was to prepare tactical instructions and doctrine for naval aviation in the Pacific, to prepare and maintain operational air units and carriers prior to their combat service, to analyze the strategic situation in regard to the needs and capabilities of naval aviation, and to establish "policies regarding organization, maintenance, and employment of [Pacific] Fleet aviation." [9] In short, Towers was to build and maintain a carrier air force but not command it. ComAirPac was to be a "nuts-and-bolts" type of job, the very same fate that befell the post of DCNO (Air) when it was created the following summer.

Whereas Towers enjoyed little popularity among the high command at Pearl Harbor, he remained the acknowledged leader of all pilots who had been flying in the Navy since they were junior lieutenants. He therefore had his pick of aviators, and as more carriers were put out of action during the fall of 1942 more top airmen became available. In particular, Towers saved the brilliant Forrest Sherman, captain of the sunken *Wasp*, from utter rejection for losing a ship, by appointing him to be chief of staff; Towers also took on *Wasp*'s former air group commander, the able Wallace M. Beakley, as his assistant operations officer for carriers.

Ignoring the cool attitude of the Cincpac staff, Towers and his own ComAirPac staff set about systematizing the integration of naval air material into Pacific Fleet strategy and operations. Gradually Nimitz came to accept and to admire the work of the ComAirPac staff. One of the reasons was Nimitz's great respect for Forrest Sherman, who was as persuasive as he was intelligent and served more than once as intermediary between the disagreeing Nimitz and Towers. Until the summer of 1943 the problem of ComAirPac becoming operational as a "field" commander did not arise, since Nimitz had only two carriers most of the time and these were under Halsey in the South Pacific. But the carrier admirals looked to the day when they could run the carrier war themselves; the vocal Ted Sherman wrote to Halsey on 28 March 1943 "recommending a Comdr. Carriers Pacific with [the] rank of V. Adm. and that I be it." [10] Had such a post been created then, either Towers or Ted Sherman would have qualified for it, but such a supreme carrier commander did not suit Admiral Nimitz's needs at that time.

During the spring of 1943, officially 15 March, in anticipation of the new ships and planes soon to arrive in the Pacific, Pacific Fleet forces were reorganized into three separate fleets, the Third, Fifth, and Seventh. The Seventh, commanded successively by Vice Admirals A. S. Carpender and Tom Kinkaid, comprised the naval forces operating under MacArthur in the Southwest Pacific; Nimitz provided the ships, MacArthur maintained operational command. The Third Fleet, Admiral Halsey, was actually a theater command, the South Pacific, with the same command arrangement between Nimitz and MacArthur. The Fifth Fleet comprised those ships of the Central Pacific whenever they began arriving; they would be under the direct operational control of Admiral Nimitz. Not until 1944 was this fleet referred to by number; it was commonly known in 1943 as Central Pacific Force.

In forming a command staff for the new campaign in the Central Pacific Nimitz did not alter the position of aviators under his authority. Cincpac staff still had one aviation officer, Captain Ralph Ofstie, though another, Captain Cato D. Glover, reported to the Joint Planning Staff later that summer. Cincpac's Plans Officer, so important in helping to shape Pacific strategy, was a battleship-oriented officer, Captain James M. Steele. Rear Admiral Ray Spruance, chief of staff, reputed to think and act just like Nimitz, was selected to command the new Central Pacific Force or Fifth Fleet with the rank of vice admiral. So the aviators did not have one of their own number to lead the new carrier-centered fleet. And Spruance did not appoint airmen to his key staff posts. His chief of staff, Captain C. J. "Carl" Moore, was best known as a strategic planner, particularly in the Navy's War Plans Division at the beginning of the war. Uninterested in assigning the other members of the staff, Spruance left this up to Moore, who selected Captain Emmet P. Forrestel to be operations officer.[11] "Savvy" Forrestel, an excellent officer, was experienced in battleships and not at all in aviation. And, since Spruance often left decision-making to his key advisers, Moore and Forrestel would be instrumental in running the Central Pacific campaign. Were Spruance to fight another Midway in late-1943, however, he would not have a Miles Browning to advise him. He had but one aviator on his staff for nuts-and-bolts chores, Commander Robert W. Morse, who was very junior to the rest of the staff.

The new fleet was officially established on 5 August 1943 as Central Pacific Force under Vice Admiral Spruance. A vacancy for chief of staff to Nimitz had thus opened up, but Cincpac did not fill it with an aviator. Instead he appointed Rear Admiral Charles H. "Soc" (for one as intelligent as Socrates) McMorris, distinguished cruiser commander at Guadalcanal and in the Aleutians. McMorris' attributes as a planner were that he could cut through mountains of data to perceive a problem correctly and that he had a clear memory to use this information.[12] But he too had had no experience with air. Jack Towers remained as ComAirPac.

Significantly, most of the combat carrier admirals were in the South Pacific fighting the Japanese as Nimitz began shaping the new Central Pacific Force during the spring. Halsey was South Pacific and Third Fleet commander, with Captain Browning still his chief of staff. Vice Admiral Jake Fitch commanded all South Pacific air, Rear Admiral Pete Mitscher the land-based portion in the Solomons, and Rear Admiral Duke Ramsey the carriers *Saratoga* and *Victorious*. Ted Sherman, for lack of ships, had no command, but was standing by there, as he was a close favorite of Halsey. Along with Towers these five air admirals were perhaps the most highly qualified to command any new fast carrier force. And several of them expected to.

Admiral Halsey, building up for his central Solomons campaign in June, had been waiting patiently for some of the new carriers to bolster his thin surface forces. While the carriers would not operate in confined waters, they could give Halsey's flanks more protection as the South Pacific forces neared their objective, the big enemy base of Rabaul. Then Halsey discovered that the first of the new fast carriers, *Essex*, was going to Pearl Harbor and not the South Pacific, which meant that his theater was not to get priority in ships. Furthermore, without *Essex*, Ted Sherman would be left, as he put it, "holding the bag without a task force." Halsey protested to Nimitz, leading to some difference of opinion between the two men during May 1943.[13]

Meanwhile, the new carriers had begun to leave the United States. After initial shakedown cruises in the Caribbean area, each carrier was inspected and released by Commander Air Force Atlantic Fleet, Vice Admiral Pat Bellinger. Passing through the Panama Canal, jurisdiction of each ship passed to ComAirPac, Vice Admiral Towers. Air groups for each carrier were provided at one of several places along this route, final assignment being made by Commander Fleet Air West Coast, Rear Admiral Charles A. "Baldy" Pownall. They were then sent west to Hawaii. The first was *Essex* (CV-9), Captain Donald B. Duncan. "Wu" Duncan, one of Ernie King's favorite planning officers, had brought out the first escort carrier, *Long Island* (CVE-1), and had now molded the first new fast carrier into combat readiness after many modifications to the original design. *Essex* entered Pearl Harbor on 30 May. The next carrier was the new *Yorktown* (CV-10), Captain J. J. "Jocko" Clark, a part-Cherokee Indian who was known as a hard-driving fighter. Clark had rushed his first ship, an escort carrier, to completion in record time and then had participated in the North African landings. *Yorktown* arrived in Hawaii on 24 July. Several new light carriers of the *Independence* class also reported during the summer.

Admiral Halsey, observing these developments from afar, apparently convinced Nimitz that Ted Sherman deserved a carrier command, for early in June Sherman was ordered to Pearl Harbor to hoist his flag aboard *Essex* as ComCarDiv 2. Reporting 7 June, Sherman initiated training operations with *Essex* and *Enterprise* until the latter vessel departed for the States and overhaul on 14 July. Towers observed these very successful maneuvers, which were due not only to Sherman's ability but to several able subordinates, among them Captains Duncan and H. S. Duckworth, Sherman's chief of staff, and Commander Truman J. Hedding, exec of *Essex*. Sherman was pleased to participate in preparing for the new offensive, but he found actual planning for carrier operations nebulous and slow.[14]

One of the reasons for doctrinal uncertainty was that everyone was waiting for the new fleet doctrine, known as PAC 10. Throughout the spring a group of planning officers headed by Admiral Spruance and including representatives from ComAirPac had been laboring to prepare a new syllabus of tactical fighting instructions for the Pacific Fleet. On 10 June 1943 PAC 10 was issued to the Fleet. In carrier operations it emphasized flexibility and demanded only one thing, concentration of carriers and supporting screens when under enemy air attack. It cited the success of the British carriers when concentrated in the Mediterranean and criticized the single-carrier formations of American carriers during the battles of 1942. Multicarrier task forces, for which Ted Sherman had argued so forcibly, had finally been accepted, a necessity which "increases in importance as the number of carriers increases and as their speed decreases [because of these greater numbers]. . . . In large [fleet] dispositions [concentration] becomes mandatory."[15]

In offensive fast carrier operations, PAC 10 was less specific, stating that "doctrine and tactical orders for offensive air action by carrier air groups is contained in Air Type publications." This meant that Admiral Towers and ComAirPac staff had the responsibility of developing offensive doctrine. Noted PAC 10, "No special plans are provided herein, since such actions usually develop suddenly from reports of air search, and the Officer in Tactical Command is limited by time and conditions to ordering the attack and specifying the objective."[16] In short, Spruance's planners would leave air doctrine up to the experts, Towers and company. But application of the doctrine in battle was still a sticky proposition, since the Central Pacific commander, Spruance, was not an aviator and had no aviation advisers. Apparently Towers was not to go to sea by Ernie King's order, which left Ted Sherman, who was eminently qualified to command the carriers at sea and therefore to become Spruance's air commander.

Towers, an early-day pilot, and Ted Sherman, a latecomer to air, had never served together, and the suave Towers disliked Sherman's bombastic manner, with the result that Towers did not include Sherman as one of his own close followers. Nevertheless, both men understood the problems of the fast carriers, and they spent much time discussing these problems in Hawaii. Towers told Sherman the latter could be carrier commander for the Central Pacific except that two men senior to Sherman (USNA '10) had already been ordered to Pearl Harbor, Rear Admirals Baldy Pownall (USNA '10) as ComCarDiv 3 and John H. Hoover (USNA '07) as ComCarDiv 4. Sherman would therefore not be senior carrier admiral. Towers offered to recommend that *Essex* be sent to the South Pacific, to which Sherman replied that he wanted both available carriers, *Essex* and *Saratoga*, "together in either place," Hawaii or the South Pacific.[17] Sherman obviously wanted his multicarrier formation.

Then, suddenly, on the night of 16 July Admiral Sherman received orders to relieve Duke Ramsey as ComCarDiv 1 aboard *Saratoga* in the South Pacific. Ramsey had been selected to become Chief of BuAer, and Halsey no doubt wanted his number-one carrier commander returned. But Sherman was ordered to leave his flagship, *Essex*, within 24 hours, leading him to regard his transfer as a demotion and suggesting that he was not wanted at Pearl Harbor by ComAirPac, which may have been the case.[18] Sherman departed the Central Pacific, leaving the post of senior carrier admiral to Hoover or Pownall. Hoover soon assumed control of all land-based air, including that of the AAF, in the Central Pacific, leaving Pownall to head up the carriers. Unfamiliar with the merits of the various air admirals, with whom he had never served, Admiral Spruance "had no preference for that assignment," [19] and so on 6 August 1943 Admiral Nimitz appointed Pownall carrier commander. Pownall simultaneously handed over command of West Coast fleet air to Rear Admiral Pete Mitscher.

Though Halsey had lost his bid to have more carriers in the South Pacific, his land-based air proved sufficient. By the time Sherman relieved Ramsey as ComCarDiv 1 at Noumea on 26 July, battles were raging on land, in the air, and in the waters around New Georgia Island. Hoisting his flag aboard *Saratoga*, Sherman enjoyed a multicarrier force for only a few days; HMS *Victorious* departed on 31 July to return to the British fleet. Sherman saw no action, as Halsey still preferred not to commit his one carrier to any unnecessary risk. Complained Sherman of Halsey's attitude, "He is keeping [his carriers] at sea . . . [and] will not use them under present conditions in a raid or operation where they might get hit by shore-based air. He considers them his main reliance against attack by [the] Jap Fleet." [20] With *Victorious* gone and no immediate help to be expected from Pearl Harbor, Halsey could hardly be blamed for his reluctance to expose his last flattop to unnecessary risk.

Sherman had discovered one of Halsey's few cautions, the great respect the old fighter had for land-based planes against surface ships. The sad experiences of heavy Japanese air attacks on his naval forces off Guadalcanal had convinced Halsey of the effectiveness of such planes. At that moment, August 1943, his pilots were still battling good enemy flyers based at Rabaul, though Allied superiority was growing. Aside from the Doolittle raid against Tokyo in April 1942, Halsey had never experienced fast carrier mobility on the high seas. He did not therefore have the same faith in multicarrier operations as did his experienced juniors, Jack Towers and Ted Sherman. And old "*Sara*" was sluggish and understrength compared to the new *Essex*-class ships.

Although Halsey was an aviator and Sherman his favorite, the new ships which arrived in the South Pacific were not carriers but battleships, cruisers, and destroyers. On 30 July Halsey ordered Sherman to initiate maneuvers "in coordination of surface types in fleet dispositions," but with only one carrier along with four battleships, seven light cruisers, and fifteen destroyers Sherman could hardly operate as a carrier task force. And though *Saratoga*'s captain, John H. Cassady, and Air Group 12 performed magnificently during the maneuvers on 3–4 August Sherman could not help but lament, "Feel that I am kind of out of the picture down here with one old C.V." Such maneuvers continued during the late summer and early fall, but without carriers Sherman regarded them as "antiquated, being designed from a surface ship [as opposed to carrier] standpoint. Too little training as one fleet." [21]

The ship situation at Pearl Harbor was quite the reverse. During early summer several new heavy carriers arrived, *Essex, Yorktown,* and the new *Lexington* (CV-16), with light carriers *Independence* (CVL-22), *Princeton* (CVL-23), and *Belleau Wood* (CVL-24). In addition there were new support ships—two cruisers, two battleships, and twenty destroyers. With the many carriers arrived several new carrier admirals. Rear Admiral Alfred E. Montgomery (USNA '12) hoisted his flag in *Essex* as ComCarDiv 12. Rear Admiral Arthur W. Radford (USNA '16), ComCarDiv 11, served as carrier training officer especially with the light carriers. Finally, Rear Admiral Pownall arrived and hoisted his flag aboard *Yorktown.*

This rapid increase in carriers and air flag officers brought the issue of fleet doctrine to a head. Towers and his ComAirPac planners, using PAC 10 as a basis, had their own very definite ideas of how the new Central Pacific Force should be organized and commanded, and Admiral Nimitz had no choice but to consult them once he had established the new fleet and been ordered to attack and capture the Gilbert and Marshall islands. On 11 August 1943 Cincpac addressed a memorandum to Towers asking for a definite policy statement on carrier employment. Nimitz noted that the enemy was on the defensive, that American naval strength was increasing, and that it was therefore time to establish "a new concept in planning and development." [22]

At last the aviators had been called upon to give their expert advice on the use of the new fast carriers in the Central Pacific offensive. Drawing upon all the available minds then at Pearl Harbor, Towers called a meeting on 16 August to discuss a new carrier policy. Present were four ComAirPac staff officers, four carrier division commanders, and seven carrier captains. Ranging over the broad spectrum of carrier operations, these men settled upon the composition and size of carrier air groups and carrier divisions, the former 36 VF, 36 VB, and 18 VT, the latter one heavy and one light carrier eventually to be increased to two or three heavies and perhaps two lights according to their availability. Thus the multicarrier doctrine was put into practice.[23]

The full impact of the aviators' deliberations reached Admiral Nimitz with Towers' formal statement on fast carrier policy, dated 21 August 1943. The fast carriers, declared Towers, were (1) to attack the enemy on land and sea, the carriers being the principal offensive element of the fleet, (2) to provide direct air support for amphibious operations, and (3) to provide air support to task forces in which carriers were not the principal element. Carrier planes would gain command of the air and destroy the enemy air force, conduct air searches, provide fighter cover in landings, and maintain combat air patrols over the fleet. Their effectiveness depended upon tactical concentration; splitting up the carriers would dissipate their strength.

Then Towers pressed his case for command of the new ships. "On the degree of skill and imagination with which this powerful force is employed," he wrote, "may depend the difference between a reasonably expeditious victory in the Pacific and a long drawn out and exhaustive [*sic;* exhausting] war." Towers observed, "Carrier air operations are highly specialized and should be conducted by officers thoroughly trained therein. To be 'air-minded' is no substitute for long aviation experience." He declared that senior commanding officers of large naval forces should either be aviators or have senior staff officers who were aviators, pointing out that "operations and logistics cannot be divorced." [24]

Towers was making clear the obvious, that ComAirPac could not possibly handle logistics and maintenance without having some authority over air operations. Either Towers himself or another senior aviator such as Fitch should command the Central Pacific Force, or, barring that, Spruance's chief of staff should be an aviator. The force of Towers' letter on carrier doctrine was heightened when, simultaneously, Admiral Harry Yarnell's form letter on naval aviation arrived from Washington. It fell like a well-timed bomb.

Upset that Yarnell had brought the matter into the open just as the Central Pacific command was being established, Nimitz on 19 August issued his own letter to each of the aviator flag officers suggesting they reply to Yarnell's letter through the chain of command. Towers told Nimitz that these individuals were too busy planning operations to spare the time to formulate an answer to

Nimitz's letter. Pushed too hard by Towers, Nimitz exploded angrily and informed ComAirPac in no uncertain terms that he would nevertheless await the formal replies of the newly arrived air admirals.[25] Towers' formal paper of 21 August on carrier policy further aggravated Nimitz, who openly disagreed two days later with several of ComAirPac's statements about naval air.[26] Nimitz, defending his selection of non-airman Spruance to command the fleet, repudiated Towers' entire line of reasoning. "To put it bluntly," said Towers in a letter to Admiral Yarnell, "his reaction was to the effect that I did not know what I was talking about." Bitterly reflecting upon the many months of frustration at Pearl Harbor, Towers concluded, "Based on my experience out here, I am inclined to believe that the official Fleet recommendation [on carrier doctrine] will be to hold fast to the status quo!" [27]

Nevertheless, the bargaining position of the aviators was solid, for more carriers were arriving and being absorbed into the plans for forthcoming operations. In addition, large numbers of aircraft accompanied them to the Pacific, creating an inventory not theretofore enjoyed in the war against Japan. ComAirPac needed a more systematic logistical policy for integrating new planes into the fleet as well as some replacement policy. Admiral Nimitz held a three-hour conference on over-all logistics for the fleet on 26 August, at which Towers pronounced the great necessity "of carrying forward logistics connected with aviation to a speed far greater than is normally accepted for logistic support as a whole." Rear Admiral Kelly Turner, Nimitz's amphibious commander and himself a latecomer aviator, strongly supported Towers.[28] Two days after this meeting Nimitz raised the question of carrier admirals with Spruance and Towers in a closed meeting of the three men, thereby increasing ComAirPac's role in over-all planning.[29] Despite the friction, which was old hat to crusader Towers, his position within the Pacific command structure was rapidly being strengthened.

The case of the airmen could be proven indisputably by deeds, and during August the planners at Pearl Harbor decided that several of the new ships should be put to the test in battle. First, Admiral Pownall was to prepare for a hit-and-run strike against the Japanese outpost at Marcus Island in the north-central Pacific. He would have two heavy carriers, one light carrier, one fast battleship, several cruisers and destroyers. If this operation proved successful, as the airmen anticipated, more of a similar type would follow.

Throughout the summer, as the admirals argued, ComAirPac's staff officers had been formulating an improved cruising formation based on increased antiaircraft protection. Rear Admiral Montgomery had inherited Ted Sherman's chief of staff, Captain H. S. Duckworth, when Sherman returned to the South Pacific.[30] Contributing the expertise of Sherman's ideas to new multicarrier formations, Duckworth worked closely with Admirals Montgomery and Radford as the carriers trained. When Pownall arrived and received his orders to attack Marcus Island, he had no staff and immediately appealed for volunteers. Montgomery loaned him Duckworth as chief of staff, while Towers gave him Captain Wallace Beakley from his own staff to be air operations officer. Other junior officers from ComAirPac staff also joined Pownall for the operation. Between them, Duckworth and Beakley contrived the air and ship operations plan, which Pownall enthusiastically accepted.[31] ComAirPac was going to demonstrate the skills of his new carriers with his own people.

Although there was no break in the preparations for the Gilberts–Marshalls operations and no easing of the tension between Nimitz and Towers, Baldy Pownall was assembling the first American fast carrier task force for combat.[32] The public received its first hint of events at Pearl Harbor when Vice Admiral McCain, the new DCNO (Air), issued a statement to the press on 30 August 1943, the thirtieth official anniversary of American naval aviation. On this date in 1913, when naval air had consisted of nine qualified pilots including Lieutenant Jack Towers, the General Board had recommended to the Secretary of the Navy that "the organization of an efficient naval air service should be immediately taken in hand and pushed to fulfillment." [33] Now McCain told the people that twelve carriers had been built since the attack on Pearl Harbor and that "huge task forces, spearheaded by carrier-based aircraft, are poising for new pile-driver blows against the enemy." [34]

The feeling at Pacific command headquarters in August 1943 was one of extreme relief and awe at the daily growing armada. Twenty months before, the Pacific Fleet had been resting on the bottom of Pearl Harbor. Now there were ships and more ships. And as the new *Yorktown* steamed out of the Harbor on 22 August en route to attack Marcus, the tower on Ford Island blinked out a final, appropriate message: "You look good out there, honey." [35]

Four:
Fast Carrier Task Force on Trial

The landings in the Gilbert Islands, projected for mid-November 1943, were to involve more than the baptism under fire of the new fast carrier forces and new Marine Corps amphibious forces. They would possibly result in the first fleet engagement in one year, the first with large numbers of carriers since Midway, and the first during the war with many battleships. The Japanese, as Admiral Nimitz probably realized, in September had begun to anticipate an attack somewhere in the Central Pacific.[1] The Japanese Third Fleet, including the three carriers of CarDiv 1 and many battleships based at Truk in the eastern Carolines, was being prepared to resist such an enemy offensive (CarDiv 2, as a result of aviation fuel shortages caused by submarine sinkings of tankers, had gone to Singapore to train pilots).

But of even greater concern to Japan than the Gilberts or Marshalls was Rabaul on the island of New Britain in the South Pacific. Halsey's forces penetrated the Central Solomons during the summer and began to establish airfields within easy striking range of Rabaul. To augment his land-based air Halsey still had old *Saratoga* and its escorts, on 4 August designated Task Force 38. In October American surface forces advanced on Bougainville in the northern Solomons, placing Rabaul in peril as Bougainville was within fighter range of the great base. If Japan could reinforce and hold Rabaul, American naval forces massing in the Central Pacific might be diverted to the Solomons. This diversion of strength would give the Japanese Navy and shipbuilding industry more time to strengthen the defenses of the Empire.

Admiral Nimitz hoped the Japanese would commit their fleet in the defense of the Gilberts. His "private ambition" was to sink the carriers *Shokaku* and *Zuikaku*, sole survivors of the Pearl Harbor attack force. He told General Holland Smith of the Marines that the happiest day of his life would be "when I reach my office to find a message on my desk reporting that we have sunk these two carriers."[2] By November the Pacific Fleet would outnumber the Japanese in carriers, eleven to six. Vice Admiral Spruance, who would command the Central Pacific Force during the Gilberts landing, did not relish the prospect of a naval battle. Rather, he wanted to launch a swift, overwhelming assault, using his carriers to complement the bombardment, and *then* perhaps to think about a surface battle.[3]

In late August, however, the question of optimum use of fast carriers—as a long-range mobile striking force or as amphibious support ships—seemed in the distant future. The new ships and planes had engaged only in training exercises; the new Hellcat fighters had yet to face an enemy fighter in battle; and the green crews and pilots had never been under fire. For this reason Admiral Nimitz released several of his new carriers for hit-and-run raids against enemy outposts. In addition, the fast carriers would soon be called upon to beef up Halsey's South Pacific campaign.

1. Battle Training and Doctrine

Marcus Island, in 1943 equipped with an airfield and weather station, lies 2700 miles from Pearl Harbor but only a thousand miles from Japan. Task Force 15 formed on 23 August 1943 north of Hawaii for the purpose of attacking Marcus, destroying its planes and installations, and then withdrawing quickly. Rear Admiral Baldy Pownall, task force commander, flew his flag aboard *Yorktown,* while Rear Admiral Monty Montgomery rode in *Essex* in "make-you-learn" status. Actually, neither man had any experience operating in battle with the new carriers but Montgomery was junior and assumed the role of observer. In addition, the force included light carrier *Independence,* Captain George R. Fairlamb, fast battleship *Indiana,* Captain William M. Fechteler, two light cruisers, and ten destroyers.

Task Force 15 was supported by a small logistic unit and a lifeguard submarine. The former, one fleet oiler escorted by one destroyer, fueled the big ships en route to the target and again on the retirement. The carriers and battleships refueled the tiny destroyers every third or fourth day. The submarine, on station near the target throughout the attack to retrieve downed aviators, was the idea of

Admiral Pownall. Pownall, interested in his pilots' morale as much as their lives, had gone directly to Vice Admiral Charles A. Lockwood, Commander Submarines Pacific, before the operation and asked for a sub. Lockwood admitted such duty would not be "all beer and skittles" for his submariners but agreed with Pownall's motives and assigned *Snook* to cover Marcus. Admiral Nimitz endorsed the scheme, which evolved into the Lifeguard League, a standard practice during every subsequent fast carrier operation.[1]

On *Yorktown* Pownall and his staff labored over the plan of attack. Captains Duckworth and Beakley, handling ship dispositions and ship-air coordination, kept the three carriers at the center of a circular formation of destroyers, with the battleship and cruisers forming an inner circle. Theoretically, the vulnerable carriers thereby enjoyed maximum antiaircraft protection. This cruising disposition was the result of ComAirPac studies, including the ideas of Admiral Ted Sherman; the Marcus operation was the test, although air attack on the force was not anticipated. Captain Jocko Clark of the flagship and his air group commander, Jimmy Flatley, drew up the plan of the air strikes on the target itself.[2] Intelligence on Marcus was skimpy, based entirely on data obtained by Admiral Halsey during his raid on Marcus in early 1942, a year and a half before. Beakley, using the flight patterns of Marcus-based patrol planes of 1942 and guessing the Japanese had characteristically not deviated from these patterns, plotted the task force's approach. Almost everyone else on the staff doubted his reasoning, but Beakley stuck to it.[3]

On 27 August, after going far to the north, the ships began two days of refueling from the tanker, then picked up a weather front and followed it all the way to the launching area. Before dawn on the morning of the attack, 31 August, force radars registered an enemy patrol plane returning to Marcus, just as Beakley had calculated. The Japanese had not changed their flight pattern since the beginning of the war, and Task Force 15 followed the "snooper" back toward his base.[4] The sea was dead calm, but the sky was clear with the planet Mars glowing in the direction of the target—an omen of the day's work. The carriers maneuvered to give their planes suitable air speed by churning up to 30 knots and heading for any breeze. Destroyers swung in front to mark a launching horizon with their lights, and the big-gun ships gave the carriers sea room. At 4:22 A.M. the first Hellcat rolled down *Yorktown's* deck and into the sky.

The American carrier planes caught the enemy on Marcus "with their pants down in the cold grey dawn," according to Admiral Pownall.[5] Strafing fighters on the first sweep destroyed seven parked Japanese "Betty" torpedo bombers, while the attack planes hit the airstrip and buildings. The TBFs carried single 2000-pound "blockbusters", the heaviest bombs carried by them to that time; the SBDs dropped 1000-pound fragmentation "daisy cutters." Five deckload strikes were flown against Marcus, two each from *Essex* and *Yorktown* and one from *Independence*. Enemy antiaircraft was initially heavy and claimed three planes; unfortunately, submarine *Snook* could not locate the survivors, who were eventually captured.[6] No enemy planes interfered, since the closest Japanese air base to Marcus was at Iwo Jima, 700 miles away.

Throughout the morning the three-carrier task force operated successfully, rearming and refueling planes, closing the distance to Marcus to 110 miles, then turning around. No enemy planes or submarines threatened the force, making the operation relatively unexciting. Nevertheless Admiral Pownall was upset. En route to the target he had admonished Captain Clark for some close-quarters shiphandling of *Yorktown*; and now, during the strikes, he appeared on the captain's bridge moaning to Clark and navigator George Anderson, "Why did I ever come to carriers?"[7] This startling remark brought silence from his listeners. Pownall then began to make decisions that indicated he feared risking his ships to sinking. He refused an all-out effort to rescue some airmen, rejected several suggestions to bombard Marcus, and then ordered his ships to get out of enemy waters as fast as possible.[8]

Despite Pownall's apparent timidity the Marcus strike was an unqualified success; it established the prototype of the fast carrier task forces to follow. The multicarrier formation, with its heavily concentrated antiaircraft barrels, required fewer fighters to fly defensive combat air patrol.[9] The smooth execution of the new cruising formation brought Admiral Pownall's praise to those primarily responsible, Captains Duckworth and Beakley; "too much economy in talent on these staffs is dangerous for an extensive and exacting operation." Planes had also performed well, but the admiral thought the bulky TBF torpedo bomber a nuisance for light carriers and recommended the *Independence*-class ships carry only fighters, a full squadron of 36 F6F Hellcats.[10] Of Pownall's remarks, only this latter recommendation was not accepted by higher echelons.

While Marcus had become a live target for the new carriers and was of little value to the Japanese, other islands fitted into the overall scheme of the Central Pacific offensive. One of these was Baker, a strategically located islet due east of the Gilberts. With airfields on Baker, on the recently occupied Phoenix Islands southeast of it, and on the Ellice Islands to the southwest, the United States would have a triangle of air bases for land-based strikes against the Gilberts. The occupation of Baker completed the triangle.

As the ranking aviator afloat, Pownall had commanded the Marcus operation, so the ranking battleship admiral conducted the occupation of Baker. Rear Admiral Willis A. "Ching" Lee, Commander Battleships Pacific, ironically led a force without battleships—Task Force 11—for the mission on 1 September 1943. Rear Admiral Arthur W. Radford, ComCarDiv 11, provided air cover with planes from light carriers *Princeton* and *Belleau Wood.* The occupation took place without a flaw. A destroyer provided fighter-director services, and several days later these directors used their radar to vector Radford's Hellcats in shooting down three enemy flying boats.[11]

The Marcus and Baker affairs, minuscule against the great operations before and after, accentuated the problem of command for the new offensive. Continuing the airmen's line, Admiral Pownall recommended to Nimitz that "a naval aviator of sufficient rank with the necessary carrier experience under war time conditions" command the new carrier forces.[12] What Pownall did not discuss was the quality of leadership needed. Pownall himself had displayed a lack of aggressiveness which could prove dangerous in a more demanding operation. In his own force, one high-ranking officer had already cracked under the strain of command responsibility in combat; Captain Fairlamb of *Independence* had lost his breakfast and apparently his composure on the bridge and was relieved as soon as the ships returned to Hawaii.[13] So the carriers needed not only an aggressive, knowledgeable fleet commander, but officers of the same character in the lower echelons.

Admiral Nimitz realized the need for administering his dual responsibility as Fleet and Pacific Ocean Areas commander, but he was not prepared to relinquish his tight authority over the fleet—to the Joint Staff, the Army, or his own insistent advisers. He therefore requested, on 27 August, that an officer with the rank of vice admiral be assigned as Deputy Cincpoa to administer ship movements throughout all areas of the Pacific, leaving Nimitz to concentrate on commanding the Pacific Fleet in the new offensive. The officer assigned by Ernie King was Vice Admiral John H. Newton, an able administrator with wartime experience in cruisers. The arrival of Newton on 19 October was accompanied by another change. Rear Admiral Soc McMorris was upgraded from chief of staff to be Deputy Cincpac, a fancier title conferred, significantly, on another nonaviator.[14]

Meanwhile Nimitz decided to establish the post of Commander Carriers Pacific and to confer it upon the senior carrier division commander, Rear Admiral Pownall, thus giving the airmen some administrative recognition of their new importance. No doubt Nimitz's thinking in this action was nebulous. He could not (and perhaps would not) appoint Towers, who was a vice admiral senior to Spruance, the Central Pacific Force commander; the new ComCarsPac like ComBatPac would go to sea. He therefore informed Spruance that his choice was the next in line, Pownall. Spruance informed Pownall upon the latter's return from Marcus on 8 September, and Pownall informed Towers. When the latter two men discussed the new post, they could not decide what Pownall's duties would be, administrative and shore-based or operational and afloat. Spruance wanted Pownall to have a large staff, while Towers, already administrative-logistical head of the new carriers in the Pacific, regarded the post as unnecessary.[15]

As soon as Pownall's Task Force 15 and Radford's carriers from Task Force 11 returned to Pearl Harbor, another battle-training mission was planned. Rear Admiral Montgomery meanwhile took *Essex* and *Yorktown* to San Francisco on a "logistical mission" to bring back men and vehicles.[16] Pownall then hoisted his flag aboard *Lexington* (CV-16), Captain Felix B. Stump, for an air raid against Tarawa atoll, principal island target for the Gilberts operation. Radford joined him with *Princeton*, Captain George R. Henderson, and *Belleau Wood*, Captain A. M. Pride. Again designated Task Force 15, this collection of ships would test the advantages of the multicarrier task force when comprised mainly of light carriers. Escorting were three light cruisers and ten destroyers.

The Tarawa strike followed the pattern of Marcus, with the important exception that photographs were to be taken of the landing beaches for the November assault. One oiler refueled the force, and Captain Beakley again correctly based his intelligence of the enemy on year-and-a-half-old data. This time 25 Seventh Air Force bombers preceded the Navy attack with a bombing strike on the night of 17–18 September, while submarine *Steelhead* arrived on station to provide rescue services. Again, unhappily, Rear Admiral Pownall displayed signs of nervousness and irrationality. On the final run-in on the eighteenth he stayed up all night preparing a memorandum on what should be done in case he was a casualty, something which doctrine had long ago firmly established. Furthermore, he countermanded the plan of his operations officers to make a key navigational turn before dawn. As a result the lead destroyers at first light could see breakers hitting the reef, Air Force bombers over Tarawa, and Japanese planes taking off. The course change was then ordered with only moments to spare before the task force would be upon the target.

Expecting Japanese interference from the big air base at Kwajalein in the Marshalls, the fighter directors on *Lexington* prepared for their first of many intercepts. Only three enemy planes appeared, however, and these were easily "splashed" by defensive Hellcats. The attacking fighters and bombers destroyed several enemy planes and small boats at Tarawa, then turned to hit neighboring Makin and Apamama. Antiaircraft fire claimed two carrier planes, while careful enemy camouflage spoiled the effectiveness of the bombers. Good oblique photographs were taken of the landing beaches but they did not show the reefs clearly. Worse, the plane taking the vertical pictures was one of the two shot down. So important were these for planning the Tarawa landing in November that Pownall's staff recommended sending another plane to complete the task. But Pownall refused, again nervous over risking his ships. He was justified in his expectation of enemy interference; that it did not come Admiral Towers attributed to "a definite element of luck." Nevertheless, the verticals were still missing.[17]

In fact, the air raid on Tarawa alerted the Japanese to a possible invasion of the Gilbert Islands, and as the attack was under way on 18 September the Mobile Fleet—three carriers, two battleships, and ten cruisers, plus destroyers—sortied from Truk. The fleet anchored at Eniwetok in the northern Marshalls on the twentieth, found no American fleet threatening, and returned to Truk.[18] The Japanese, unknown to Admirals Nimitz and Spruance, were going to commit their fleet to the defense of the Gilberts and Marshalls. Spruance would get his sea battle after all.

The Japanese had to weigh the relative importance of Rabaul against that of the Gilberts–Marshalls carefully. The immediate real threat was against the former, particularly as Halsey moved into the northern Solomons. Therefore on 30 September Imperial Headquarters designated Rabaul "the ultimate point of resistance." [19] And since the best means of air defense of Rabaul was to use the airfields there, the Japanese decided to commit the air groups of CarDiv 1, *Shokaku, Zuikaku,* and *Zuiho,* to the defense of Rabaul. These pilots, the last of the elite that had survived Midway and subsequent air battles, were to leave their carriers at Truk and fly to Rabaul. The fleet would thus be stripped of its planes if the Americans moved into the Central Pacific. As these planes were about to make the transit, reports of a move toward the Marshalls caused the flight to be postponed.

When Task Force 15 returned to Hawaii Admiral Pownall recommended that a standardized Pacific Fleet fighter direction doctrine be adopted to make procedures for intercepting enemy planes more comprehensible. Feeling exposed in moonlight, he wanted four night fighters placed on board each carrier, thus supporting Admiral Nimitz's earlier suggestion to Towers. And again he urged the light carriers trade in their torpedo planes to create a light carrier air group of all fighters.[20] The Fighter Director School at Pearl Harbor was already attempting to develop a standard doctrine, but the real lessons would come from battle. Admiral Towers rejected night carrier aircraft since no specially equipped night fighters were yet available.[21] And no less a person than Ernie King ordered the CVLs to maintain an air group of 24 F6F fighters and nine TBF torpedo bombers.[22]

The day after Task Force 15 struck Tarawa, 19 September, Admiral Nimitz held a special conference following the regular morning Cincpac meeting to discuss prospective operations. Among those attending were Spruance, Towers, McMorris, and Captain Forrest Sherman. Towers called for another carrier strike before Operation GALVANIC—the Gilberts landings. Because the anticipated battleships for GALVANIC would not yet be available for another battle-training mission, ComAirPac urged "as large a carrier force as possible" to provide maximum protection.[23] Admiral Spruance agreed, and Towers appointed Rear Admiral Montgomery to do the planning, a sound choice enhanced by the fact that Montgomery had reclaimed Captain Duckworth as his chief of staff and principal planning officer.[24] Now Montgomery appointed Duckworth to draw up the plans for the new operation—a two-day strike on Wake Island in the Central Pacific.[25]

During the planning of the Wake operation Admiral King arrived at Pearl Harbor to discuss with Nimitz the forthcoming carrier and amphibious operations and to inspect submarine facilities.[26] On 25 September Montgomery, with Towers, Radford, Sherman, and Duckworth in attendance, briefed Cominch on the plans for prospective operations.[27] Montgomery, who would command the carriers at Wake, planned to operate six carriers, the largest concentration of carriers in a single formation since the Japanese had done it in the attack on Pearl Harbor. As an experiment Montgomery would vary his cruising dispositions between a single task group of six carriers, two groups of three carriers each, and three groups of two carriers each.[28] Experience gained in this operation would be invaluable for GALVANIC.

As part of the experiment, Task Force 14 was divided into two "cruising groups" of unequal size. The First Cruising Group, under Montgomery, included *Essex* and *Yorktown* and a bombardment unit of four light cruisers. Supporting these cruisers were *Independence* and *Belleau Wood* under Rear Admiral Van Hubert Ragsdale, who was scheduled to command an escort carrier group in GALVANIC. The Second Cruising Group, under Radford, included *Lexington* and light carrier *Cowpens* (CVL-25) and a bombardment unit of three heavy cruisers. Task Force 14 featured an escort of 24 destroyers, a logistic support unit of two oilers, and lifeguard submarine *Skate*.[29]

Task Force 14 launched its first strikes in a very dark predawn of 5 October, and for the first time the carrier planes met Japanese fighters over the target. Thirty Zeros gave battle to a force many times their number with the obvious result: most were shot down. This swift action drew first blood for the F6F Hellcat, proving its superiority over the Zero. In addition, three times as many bombs were dropped on Wake as at either Marcus or Tarawa. The Japanese retaliated by sending two flights of six fighters and six bombers each from the Marshalls. Ragsdale's combat air patrol intercepted and drove away these interlopers, which landed on Wake, then escaped back to their base that night.[30] The few enemy planes encountered, plus antiaircraft fire, on the fifth and sixth claimed 12 American planes. These losses were heaviest of the three raids, though rescue sub *Skate* retrieved six airmen from the drink.[31] The cruisers also pounded Wake on both days.

Wake, last of the practice runs, was an unqualified success in terms of fast carrier task force doctrine. Captain Duckworth, who had planned the operation, after the war judged that "virtually all the techniques of ship handling for a multi-carrier force which were later used successfully had their origins in this operation." [32] The circular formation had been proved feasible with six-, two-, or three-carrier task groups, and the latter was adopted for GALVANIC. The effective use of radar in directing defensive fighters was only a matter of time and practice. And carriers, commanded by aviation flag officers, operated efficiently and effectively.

The Japanese response to the attack on Wake went beyond the 24 planes staged in from the Marshalls. Fearing the United States was beginning the Central Pacific offensive, the Mobile Fleet sortied in mid-October from Truk to Eniwetok and north toward Wake. Finding no sign of enemy activity, the ships returned to Truk on the twenty-sixth. Obviously Wake had been a mere diversion, which left the Japanese to concentrate on the defense of Rabaul. At the end of the month the planes from *Shokaku*, *Zuikaku*, and *Zuiho* left their carriers for Rabaul.[33] Stripped of these planes, not only the Fleet but also the Gilberts and Marshalls were deprived of their main air defense. Should the American Pacific Fleet move before these planes returned from Rabaul, the outer defense line would be lost.

Admiral Towers concluded that Japanese air defenses were weak, but he had no idea how weak. Remembering heavy Japanese air losses in New Guinea and the Solomons and now assessing the weak resistance at Tarawa and Wake, Towers concluded that "in future carrier operations in the Central Pacific, enemy air opposition might be little more effective than it has been to date," even if concentrated more heavily.[34] Less optimistic admirals such as Spruance and Turner did not share this view, but their big gun and amphibious forces had not yet experienced such overwhelming success as enjoyed by the fast carriers.

2. *Debate over Doctrine*

As the assault date for the Gilberts approached, Admiral Nimitz realized he had to resolve the confusion of command and employment of the fleet. Not only were the aviators insisting on command of the fleet, they were now openly conflicting with the battleship and amphibious admirals over the optimum use of the fast carriers in GALVANIC. Nimitz and his staff, all non-airmen, Spruance and his staff, all non-airmen, and Rear Admiral Kelly Turner, the amphibious commander, wanted the flattops tied down to the beaches as offshore artillery. The aviators wanted mobility to use their offensive power, an idea expressed as long before as Fleet Problem VII in 1927, when the recommendation had been made that the local carrier commander have "complete freedom of action in employing carrier aircraft in order to obtain their efficient use." [1] In 1943 the carrier commander had no such freedom.

In October the issue came to a head. On the fourth Admiral Towers composed his long letter to Nimitz, the last shot in the stir over the Yarnell inquiry, in which he pointed out the continuing resentment of many non-airmen toward aviators and in which he recommended either Cincpac or Deputy Cincpac be an aviator.[2] The next morning Nimitz held a special conference to discuss Operation GALVANIC, and Towers complained of too much caution in the planning. Spruance worried about Japanese air attacks, especially at night, fears shared by Admiral Pownall.[3] Towers had to leave that afternoon for a logistics conference at San Diego with Rear Admiral Mitscher,[4] but Captain Forrest Sherman, his chief of staff, took up the fight.

Sherman tangled with no less a person than "Terrible" Turner over the employment of the fast carriers at the Gilberts. In Spruance's office Turner declared bluntly that he wanted the carriers used defensively for close air support alone; Sherman countered by saying the carriers should have mobility. They could then not only provide support for the assaulting infantry, but they could destroy enemy air power at its source—airfields in the Marshalls. Simultaneously Vice Admiral Jake Fitch arrived from the South Pacific and conveyed his irritation at the "poor treatment being given aviators," first to Nimitz, then in a meeting with Spruance, Forrest Sherman, and Captain Ralph Ofstie, the one aviation officer on Nimitz's staff. Fitch "stressed the necessity for increasing morale by better promotion, a more liberal policy for awards, less of the 'damned aviator' complex by other officers, better publicity, etc." [5]

These events began to have an impact on Admiral Nimitz. Most convincing perhaps was the evidence of the Wake strike, captured on color movie film by wing-gun cameras on *Yorktown* fighters; Forrest Sherman dramatically showed their films during one debate over the effectiveness of carrier air.[6] The battleship orientation of the South Pacific forces under Admiral Ching Lee was unrealistic, the airmen felt,[7] while Nimitz's own planning officer, a battleship man, had shown a failure to grasp the full implications of offensive carriers. Spruance tended to think along battleship lines, and although he sent his aviation officer, Captain R. W. Morse, on the Tarawa strike, he never involved Morse in planning.[8] Nimitz had begun to see the merit in the airmen's arguments, and in doing so he initiated hurried changes.

On 12 October, just after Towers returned from California, Nimitz summoned him and asked which aviator Towers would recommend to be the new Cincpac planning officer. Towers listed the three most intelligent and experienced carriermen in the Pacific Fleet: Rear Admiral Arthur Radford, ComCarDiv 11; Captain Forrest Sherman, Towers' own chief of staff; and Captain Donald B. Duncan, commanding officer of *Essex.* Nimitz felt Duncan needed more sea experience, so he passed him over. Ironically, Ernie King grabbed up Duncan to be Cominch planning officer with the rank of rear admiral, so Duncan did not stay at sea anyway. Of the other two men Nimitz asked Towers which, if he were Cincpac, he would choose. Towers favored Sherman, with whom he had worked the closest, but said he wanted either Duncan or Radford to replace Sherman on the ComAirPac staff. Nimitz agreed, and on the twentieth Sherman was ordered to be Cincpac plans officer and Radford to be chief of staff to Towers, effective immediately following the Gilberts landings.[9] Sherman would relieve Captain James M. Steele, who then assumed command of battleship *Indiana.*

Though this personnel change marked a major victory for Jack Towers, he had an equally pressing concern over finding experienced and suitably senior air admirals to command the fast carriers in GALVANIC, and this question of seniority aroused feeling among some of the battleship admirals. Vice Admiral Spruance decided to place the battleships in carrier task groups where they could lend their many antiaircraft batteries to defending the carriers, which could in turn provide air cover for the battleships. If the enemy fleet approached, the battleships could pull out of the carrier formations to form the Battle Line. But as long as the battleships were in the carrier groups, the local carrier division commander would have tactical command, despite the possible seniority of the local battleship division commander. For the Gilberts, however, Towers had senior-enough experienced air admirals available —Pownall (USNA '10), Ted Sherman ('10), and Montgomery ('12). Radford ('16), brilliant and expert, was the exception. Except for the latter case the battleship and cruiser admirals were equal or junior in rank to the carrier task group commanders.

Other junior air admirals Towers assigned to the escort carriers, Rear Admirals Van H. Ragsdale ('16) and Henry Mullinix ('16).

Experience and seniority were two of three prerequisites for carrier command; the other was the unrelenting determination of a fighting leader. And many peacetime officers, aviators included, simply could not meet this third requirement for combat command. For example, in October Ernie King sent out to the Pacific one of his favorite airmen, Rear Admiral Alva D. Bernhard, who was senior to all the task group commanders ('09) but who was wanted by no one at Pearl Harbor. Bernhard had an excellent peacetime record, but he enjoyed no reputation as a leader and spent the Gilberts operation in the ignominious position of "aviation adviser" to Admiral Spruance. Rear Admiral George Murray ('11), though a veteran of the early Pacific battles, did not qualify as an aggressive leader and remained Stateside in a training command. Other, more junior aviators with good peacetime records whom Towers did not want in the war zone were Rear Admirals Osborne B. Hardison ('16) and Andrew C. McFall ('16). The once-aggressive Charlie Mason had fallen ill and never fully recovered the ability to command at sea.

About his existing commanders Admiral Towers had some misgivings. Pownall, he knew from his loaned-out staff officers, had behaved erratically in both the Marcus and Tarawa strikes. Nevertheless, Nimitz appointed Pownall Commander Fast Carrier Forces Pacific Fleet, so Towers had no choice but to wait and see. Ted Sherman Towers regarded as an unknown quantity. Though Sherman boasted a long and fine combat record, it was somewhat mortgaged by an offensive, outspoken personality. Towers had never served with Sherman, who had been a latecomer to air, and even felt that the latter was using aviation to advance his own career. Montgomery and Radford, both early-day pilots, Towers knew and trusted. The other fast carrier division commander, John H. Hoover, assumed command of all land-based air in the Central Pacific, so Towers sent for Rear Admiral J. W. Reeves, Jr., from the Aleutians. "Black Jack" Reeves ('11), another latecomer to aviation, would be available for the Marshalls operation. The fast carriers lost the services of Captain Duckworth, who had been at sea almost continuously since 1941. He was sent home to become chief of staff to Admiral McFall in a training command. The new fast carrier chief of staff was Captain Truman J. Hedding.

The many air admirals were accompanied to the Pacific by new fast carriers, air groups, and escort carriers. *Bunker Hill* (CV-17), Captain J. J. Ballentine, and *Monterey* (CVL-26), Captain L. T. Hundt, arrived at Pearl Harbor during the fall and were joined by the modernized and refurbished *Enterprise* (CV-6), Captain Matt Gardner.[10] *Bunker Hill* brought with her the many-times modified Curtiss SB2C-1 Helldiver dive bomber. But Bombing 17 was the only squadron with the new plane. The new fighters and torpedo planes assigned for scouting had been equipped with special new airborne radar, though techniques had to be perfected. So, during GALVANIC—for the last time—the old SBD Dauntless would be used for protective scouting as well as dive bombing.[11]

As the size of the carrier forces grew, so did the office of ComAirPac, in its continued role of materiel and now also in operations. In the former, Captain Fred W. Pennoyer, Jr., labored to distribute the tremendous flow of new planes and spare parts from the United States. In operations, Captain Beakley transferred to Washington as Ernie King's air officer, but Towers brought in his old BuAer planner, Commander George Anderson, then navigator of *Yorktown.* The fact that Towers had finally convinced Nimitz that ComAirPac should participate in operational as well as logistic planning became clear when, on 29 November, a Plans Division was established on the staff.[12] Towers appointed as head of Plans Commander Frank W. Wead. "Spig" Wead (USNA '16), an early-day aviator who had been crippled in an accident and forced to retire in 1927, had achieved fame as a film writer and was recalled to active duty at the outbreak of war. He lent his keen knowledge of naval aviation to ComAirPac during this period of expansion until relieved of all active duty in July 1944.

But as Towers shaped his fast carrier forces for GALVANIC, and generally with Admiral Nimitz's cooperation, he could not dissuade the non-air commanders from tying down the carriers off the beaches. Admirals Ragsdale and Mullinix would employ planes from the tiny escort carriers to bomb Japanese defenses, supplemented by planes from Pownall's fast carriers. Cautious Spruance and Terrible Turner wanted it this way, since the landing forces needed maximum support and naval air close support was still an uncertain experiment.

The Pacific Fleet had no close air support doctrine when Captain Harold B. Sallada organized the Pacific Fleet Amphibious Forces Support Aircraft unit in November. Admiral Turner felt close support should be put on a permanent basis, though few at Pearl Harbor agreed with him and no naval officer had the experience. Certainly Sallada was not ready to contribute any systematic air support to GALVANIC, but he did report aboard battleship *Pennsylvania* to direct air support at Makin. The only experienced Central Pacific air support director was an Army Air Forces officer, Colonel William O. Eareckson, who had handled the few air strikes during the landings at Attu in the Aleutians the previous May.[13] Eareckson was therefore appointed over-all Acting Support Air Commander at Tarawa. Unfortunately, battleships were ill-equipped in communications gear to handle radio traffic between air support directors and the Air Support Control Units and Air Liaison Parties on the beach. To add to the difficulties, though some carrier squadrons rehearsed with amphibious forces at Hawaii in October,[14] too few pilots understood amphibious procedures adequately, an ignorance reflected by the men who briefed them on targets.[15]

Admiral Spruance's great concern for maximum air support at the beaches was complicated by his fear of a Japanese fleet sortie from Truk to intercept the landing. Spruance wanted his amphibious forces secured on the beach before he fought any fleet engagement. He therefore concluded that prelanding shore bombardment and bombing would not begin until the actual morning of the assault. Earlier commitment of these ships and planes would alert Admiral Koga, Japanese Fleet commander, who might then attempt to prevent the landing. Any possible devastation of the objective by a prolonged bombardment of several days was therefore sacrificed in the interest of achieving surprise.[16] This reasoning followed Allied practices at Sicily the preceding July and at Salerno in September, both of which, however, had had very dubious results.

Should a surface battle develop, it would be fought along traditional Jutland-type lines with obvious variations due to the new element of air. Unlike his situation at Midway, Spruance now had a formidable battle line of five new fast battleships under Rear Admiral Ching Lee, Commander Battleships Pacific, aboard *Washington*. However, cruiser and destroyer shortages required Spruance to use these battleships with their many antiaircraft batteries as part of the circular formations of the two fast carrier task groups stationed off Makin, nearest Truk and the Marshalls, Pownall's and Radford's. Fleet tacticians did not yet regard battleships as essential to the antiaircraft protection of the fast carriers, as seen by Montgomery's and Sherman's carrier task groups, escorted by only cruisers and destroyers, when repelling Rabaul-based Japanese air attacks in November.

Spruance solved the absence of a formed permanent battle line with an ingenious compromise. Should the Japanese fleet approach, Lee would withdraw the battleships from the carrier task groups, form his battle line, and assume tactical command for battle *à la* Jutland. The carriers remained protected, which satisfied the air admirals, but did Spruance really envision a naval battle without carriers?

Incredibly, as if all the experience since 7 December 1941 had been erased, the battleship admirals were to resume tactical control over the fleet for a gunnery duel along World War I lines. It appeared to many frustrated battleship men that the formalist battle tactics evolved over the centuries since the days of Rooke and Byng and destroyed by the airplane had now returned. But such a paradox could never exist in reality, because the airplane would never allow it. Unfortunately, however, Spruance followed the traditional approach to battle, and the possibility of a battleship engagement near Makin added weight to his reasons to keep the carriers, which required battleship escort, "in as close tactical supporting distance of the Northern [Makin] Attack Force as the nature of their air operations and their fuel situation permits." [17]

The overriding importance of a fleet engagement was not lost to Spruance. Should the Japanese fleet sortie for battle, Spruance told his commanders, its defeat "would at once become paramount" since the consequences of destroying a major part of Japan's fleet "would go far toward winning the war. . . ." [18] Once the enemy fleet was eliminated, all subsequent landings would go forward unopposed by surface forces. This realization of Spruance's is important in understanding his philosophy of battle. As long as he could form his battle line, Spruance was confident of victory. Secondarily, carriers could provide air cover and support the landings and possibly engage the enemy's carriers. This was the Spruance of 1938–1940 when he had commanded battleship *Mississippi.* This was not the Spruance of Midway, operating under the necessity for calculated risk while on the strategic defensive with a weapon of expediency and a borrowed staff of strangers. Spruance, now on the strategic offensive, faced the possibility of a surface battle with certainty. He knew what battleships could do and he knew their commanders, with whom he had served over three decades. And to advise him was his erudite chief of staff, old friend, and colleague Captain Carl Moore, only four years removed as operations officer to Commander Battle Force, the prewar battle line. To these men the battlewagon remained capital ship of the U.S. Navy.

Spruance's willingness to remain on the tactical defensive during the landings while relying on his superior battleships to protect his other forces may have been sound judgment in the days before the airplane, but success in the new war—or so the aviators maintained—was based on the swift striking power of the fast carrier. Battleships could wait for the enemy fleet to sortie, but the carriers could not, for they were particularly vulnerable to air and submarine attack. A surer means of protecting landing and support forces alike was to send the carriers north to attack enemy airfields and sub bases—and surface units if they appeared.

Instead, Spruance, whose experience and thinking differed from that of the airmen, assigned each of the four fast carrier task groups to a defensive sector. Pownall's TG 50.1 formed a "Carrier Interceptor Group" between the Gilberts and Marshalls. As well as intercepting Japanese air attacks from the north, this group was permitted to attack the airfields at Mili and Jaluit in the southern Marshalls. Radford's TG 50.2 formed the "Northern Carrier Group" to cover and support the Northern Attack Force at Makin Island. Montgomery's TG 50.3, the "Southern Carrier Group," would cover and support the Southern Attack Force at Tarawa atoll. Ted Sherman's TG 50.4, *Saratoga* plus light carrier *Princeton* (which joined in October), would hasten north from the Solomons to form a "Relief Carrier Group" and neutralize the airfield at Nauru, west of the Gilberts, as well as stand by for any emergency.[19]

Defensive sectors, the aviators knew very well, would attract Japanese land-based planes by the score, something any South Pacific veteran would never have allowed. Certainly Halsey would not have, after his troubles holding onto Guadalcanal the year before. Mobility was the only defense when carriers lay within range of enemy air bases and long-range bombers. In heavy ships the carrier force would be formidable for repelling air attacks—five battleships, three heavy cruisers, and three antiaircraft light cruisers. But only 21 destroyers could be assigned to the 11 carriers, hardly enough at fewer than two "tin cans" per flattop.

Admiral Pownall preferred to agree with Spruance in most matters—the two men were very congenial, perhaps too much so for combat planning—but even Pownall could see his carriers would be dangerously exposed, particulary if the Japanese instituted the night air attacks as they had over Guadalcanal. And the carriers, which could put up a heavy fighter patrol during the day to help remedy the shortage of destroyers, had no night fighters.

Pownall studied the operation carefully with Admiral Radford, then on 14 October both men approached Towers to complain that the planned use of the fast carriers was "dangerous." Towers sympathized and told them to go see Spruance. They did, repeated their fears, and asked Spruance to release the carriers from their defensive sectors. Spruance refused, pointing out that such changes would be too sweeping and that he simply feared the consequences of separating the carriers from the other support groups.[20] At the Cincpac morning conference of 17 October Spruance admitted that placing them on the defensive constituted "an improper use of carriers." Towers agreed and emphasized the need for striking the main Japanese air bases in the northern Marshalls, particularly Kwajalein.[21] But Spruance, precise and careful in his planning, decided to adhere to his established operation plan. Those Jap carriers at Truk bothered him, but even when all three task group commanders at Pearl, Pownall, Radford, and Montgomery, went in a body and protested to Spruance he still would not budge.[22] Nimitz, who had had enough troubles with the aviators, did not interfere; it was Spruance's show, and Nimitz trusted him implicitly. The operation plan stood, and the airmen went into battle apprehensive.

3. *Battle*

While the Central Pacific admirals debated and prepared for GALVANIC, Admiral Halsey in the South Pacific sent his Task Force 38, *Saratoga* and *Princeton*, into battle on 1 November 1943, the first time fast carriers had seen action in that theater since Guadalcanal days late in 1942. That day Ted Sherman's two carriers supported Halsey's landings at Bougainville. Operating well to the west in open waters, they launched two strikes against the Buka–Bonis airfields at the northern end of the island. Another strike on the second eliminated the 20 or so planes that could have interefered with the landing. Task Force 38 then withdrew to the south of Guadalcanal to refuel.[1]

Halsey's bold landing triggered an immediate Japanese response. Satisfied that the huge carrier strike on Wake had only been a raid and that the threat to Rabaul took temporary precedence over the defense of the Gilberts, Admiral Koga released the carrier planes of CarDiv 1 to transfer from Truk to Rabaul. On the first these 173 aircraft from *Zuikaku*, *Shokaku*, and *Zuiho* landed at Rabaul, bringing its air strength to about 375 planes.[2] In addition, Koga dispatched Vice Admiral Takeo Kurita with seven heavy cruisers, one light cruiser, and four destroyers to Rabaul on the first; these would run south to destroy Halsey's shipping, which was protected only by light cruisers and destroyers.

Halsey did not have the news of these movements when Sherman's two carriers withdrew to the south on 2 November. His greater concern that day was his own covering force, which included four light cruisers, engaging a Japanese force of two heavy and two light cruisers in the sea battle of Empress Augusta Bay, site of the landings at Bougainville. No sooner had this enemy surface force been repulsed and turned back toward Rabaul than, on the fourth, search planes reported Kurita's heavy cruisers anchored at Rabaul.

His toehold on Bougainville now seriously threatened, Halsey had no choice but to commit his tiny carrier force. The best chance of success was to attack the cruisers by surprise while they were anchored at Rabaul, but the risk would be terrific. Offensively, if he sent all the planes from *Saratoga* and *Princeton*, about 100, they would be hopelessly outnumbered by whatever the Japanese had, not to mention antiaircraft fire. Defensively, the stripped carriers would have to be covered by land-based fighters from southern Solomon airfields. This unorthodox plan would also place the two flattops, old, slow-turning "*Sara*" and the small, vulnerable *Princeton*, within range of land-based air, a situation into which Halsey hated to place any ship. The Admiral "sincerely expected both air groups to be cut to pieces and both carriers stricken, if not lost. . . ."[3]

Other factors worked in Halsey's favor, however. Air Group 12, Commander Howard H. Caldwell, had been in the Pacific for exactly one year without seeing action, but during this time it had trained to precision as a team. It had become a cracker-jack outfit, due in large measure to the fighter-escort tactics evolved by Fighting 12's dynamic skipper, Commander J. C. Clifton. "Jumpin' Joe" Clifton had trained his Hellcat pilots to fly on top of the dive bombers and torpedo planes to cover them from diving Zero interceptors. Now Jumpin' Joe told his pilots, "It is our job to escort the bomber and torpedo planes and to get them in there, get them out and get them home; no dogfighting. It's our problem to escort."[4] Clifton also had the services of Hank Miller's *Princeton* group, veterans of the Tarawa strike. To cover the carriers during the strike Halsey had land-based planes fly out from Solomon Island fields. Finally, Fightin' Freddie Sherman, if anyone, could make the plan work.

Since Miles Browning had been replaced as chief of staff by nonaviator Rear Admiral R. B. "Mick" Carney in July, Halsey relied mainly on his air operations officer, Commander H. Douglas Moulton, for air planning. Moulton and other staff members prepared the plan and the dispatch to Admiral Sherman. Halsey studied the message, and fearing the worst but having no choice, handed it to Carney, saying simply, "Let 'er go!"[5]

Task Force 38 sped north at 27 knots to commence launching planes at 9 A.M., 5 November. Howard Caldwell led the flight in his TBF Avenger, one of 23 from both carriers. Twenty-two trusty old SBD Dauntless dive bombers joined him. Jumpin' Joe Clifton led all the Hellcats, totaling 52. Halsey could expect at least 150 planes at Rabaul, despite repeated Army Air Force bombings during previous weeks. He could not know that the remainder of Japan's carrier elite had swelled Rabaul's air defenses to more than twice that number.

As the 97 American planes approached the target, the enemy prepared a reception. Above a curtain of heavy flak circled 70 Zero fighters, ready for their dogfights with the new Hellcat. But the frantic maneuvers of the many ships in Simpson Harbor revealed the attack had been something of a surprise. The next surprise followed quickly. Waiting patiently for Clifton's fighters to leave the bombers when the latter began to dive, the enemy interceptors refrained from attacking the flight. When the dive bombers nosed down into their 75-degree dives,[6] the torpeckers dropping to the deck for masthead drops, Clifton's Hellcats stayed locked onto the bombers. Fighters dived through the flak, tightly maintaining formation with the bombers, an extremely difficult tactic for a fighter type to execute. The Japanese Zeros could not lure the fighters away for an air battle and would not give chase through their own antiaircraft fire. Below, ships twisted and scurried about, but the bombers pressed on, abandoned by their escorts only moments before they released their bombs and torpedoes. Then explosions and plumes of smoke erupted in Simpson Harbor, and the bombing planes pulled out to rendezvous with the fighters for the flight home.[7]

Antiaircraft fire peppered the formation but with limited effectiveness. Two hundred bullet holes in the *Princeton* Hellcat flying wing on Commander Caldwell's Avenger failed to bring the F6F down. And on the return flight Clifton's fighters maintained their tight cover. Of the 97 planes in the strike, relatively few failed to return: five Hellcats, two Avengers, and one Dauntless. The rest flew back to the carriers, where a friendly combat air patrol greeted them. Joe Clifton landed aboard *Saratoga* and rushed up to the flag bridge to tell Freddie Sherman the good news. Then Task Force 38 high-tailed it away to the south.

Left behind at Rabaul were four heavily damaged heavy cruisers and two wounded light cruisers, leaving the Japanese surface fleet temporarily crippled. Ted Sherman, as jubilant as Halsey and every Allied leader up the chain of command, hailed the accomplishment as "a glorious victory, a second Pearl Harbor in reverse."[8] Sherman was not far wrong, for now Japan's battleships had lost their valuable cruiser protection. Along with other air and Solomons surface actions, Japan's cruiser force of eleven in September had dropped to four after this attack.[9] The damaged cruisers limped back to Truk, to the planeless carriers and the unprotected battlewagons. Bougainville was safe for Halsey's advance; heavy ships would never again come to Rabaul.

The fifth of November heralded the arrival of three more carriers in the South Pacific. Admiral Nimitz, finally yielding to Halsey's appeals for more carrier support, had dispatched Alfred Montgomery with Task Group 50.3 to reinforce the South Pacific Force prior to GALVANIC. The new group brought battle-seasoned *Essex*, now under Captain Ralph Ofstie, the new *Bunker Hill* with the untried SB2C Helldiver bombers, and *Independence*, now commanded by Captain Rudy Johnson. These ships remained at Espiritu Santo for three days while the admirals desperately sought more destroyers to beef up their screen. Ted Sherman, who had never seen the likes of five carriers in one pack, appealed to Halsey for all five to be combined in one task force for another strike against Rabaul, again from the south.[10]

Halsey had the same idea, but opposed the single task force. Wanting to knock out Rabaul air for good he ordered Sherman's two air groups to hit the big base from the north, Montgomery's three from the south. Halsey set the attack day for the eleventh and pointed out "Five air groups . . . ought to change the name of Rabaul to Rubble." [11] On this occasion Montgomery's carriers would send a full strike to Rabaul, and their combat air patrol would be assumed by two land-based Navy F4U Corsair squadrons. One of these was Fighting 17, the famous "Skull and Crossbones" squadron led by Tommy Blackburn, which had first trained on *Bunker Hill* before winning plaudits in the Solomons. Now Blackburn would use the tail hooks on his F4Us to land and refuel on *Bunker Hill*.[12] If Task Group 50.3 was attacked, the Japanese would have a fight on their hands against the much-feared "Whistling Death" Corsair.

The 11 November strikes on Rabaul confirmed the striking power and mobility of the new fast carrier task forces. *Saratoga* and *Princeton* planes bucked heavy weather to get in close with a few hits, but *Bunker Hill*, *Essex*, and *Independence* fared better later in the day. They torpedoed one light cruiser and destroyer, the latter sinking, and sank another destroyer with bombs. The 90 or so fighters tangled with a few of the 68 Zeros over Rabaul and shot down six. When the planes headed home, however, the Japanese launched retaliatory strikes.

The moment of truth for the multicarrier task group was at hand. A heavy land-based air attack of 120 planes descended upon a force of three carriers defended by only the antiaircraft guns of its carriers and destroyers, the cruisers having been detached to support Halsey's beachhead, plus fighters from five squadrons. Montgomery's combat air patrol intercepted the first enemy bombers 40 miles from the force and went to work. More planes came on, pressing the attack when they sighted the three carriers. Montgomery bellowed over the loudspeaker on *Bunker Hill*, "Man your guns and shoot those bastards out of the sky!"[13] Instantaneously, 5-inch, 40mm, and 20mm bursts filled the sky, along with Zeros and Hellcats, while Captains Ballentine, Ofstie, and Johnson adroitly swung their ships to avoid falling bombs and torpedoes. The early-afternoon action lasted 46 minutes, but the carriers held their own, driving off the attackers and sending over two dozen enemy planes into the sea. American losses amounted to 11 aviators. This aerial victory, plus many battles by land-based planes over Rabaul, resulted in a severe blow to Japanese naval aviation.

The two overwhelming victories of the fast carriers at Rabaul proved many things that originally were supposed to have been first tested at the Gilberts. Most important, Halsey's landing force at Bougainville had been rendered secure by carriers operating offensively against a major Japanese fleet and air base. Furthermore, without battleships or even cruisers, the multicarrier formation had survived a heavy air attack by destroying and repulsing land-based enemy planes. Halsey had taken a risk which had succeeded, then he had used his reinforced carrier task forces to reduce his objective. In addition, the American Navy pilot had again proved himself superior to the Jap, with much credit going to the superior Hellcat and Corsair. Also, the new SB2C Helldiver won the praise of earlier doubters; even the skipper of Bombing 9 on *Essex*, which still flew the SBD, remarked that 90 per cent of the bomber pilots were now "all for them."[14] The TBF Avenger took honors in torpedoing enemy cruisers, but the aerial torpedoes left much to be desired due to malfunctions.

These lessons Vice Admiral Spruance and his GALVANIC commanders had no time to appreciate, absorb, or even consider. It was certainly too late to change the operations plan, though Spruance probably did not want to do so anyway, for the other three fast carrier task groups had sortied from Pearl Harbor the day before the second Rabaul strike, 10 November. But jubilation pervaded Cincpac and ComAirPac headquarters, and on the thirteenth Admiral Nimitz proclaimed defiantly, "Henceforth, we propose to give the Jap no rest."[15]

And the Jap would have no rest. His losses at Rabaul upset any possibility of successfully defending the Gilberts, or the Marshalls for that matter. The carrier strikes, plus repeated attacks by General Kenney's Army planes, had convinced Japan that Rabaul was unsafe for shipping, though Japan's admirals were not yet willing to give it up as an airdrome. But with Bougainville in American hands, Rabaul would soon be within range of Halsey's land-based fighters. On 13 November Admiral Koga recalled the survivors of his carrier planes that had gone to Rabaul two weeks before. Of the 173 planes sent from CarDiv 1, Koga had lost half his fighters and practically all of his attack planes in various air actions around Rabaul. His carriers became little more than hulks until fresh pilots could be trained, a process that took a minimum of six months. With seven cruisers out of action, his battleships stood naked against enemy ships. The Japanese fleet at Truk was helpless, while effective air defenses for the Gilberts and Marshalls no longer existed.

The United States Pacific Fleet appeared quite the opposite, brimming with power and full of fight. Late on the eleventh Ted Sherman's Task Force 38 received its new designation, Task Group 50.4, and along with Montgomery's TG 50.3 headed north to join the Central Pacific Force. Simultaneously, Pownall's TG 50.1 and Radford's TG 50.2 rendezvoused with their battleships and oilers north of the Phoenix Islands and separated in the final approach to the target. Eleven American fast carriers descended upon the Gilbert Islands, now undefended by surface or air forces. Only weakened land-based air and submarine forces in the Marshall Islands offered any hope for Japan.

Task Force 50 formed the first actual Fast Carrier Task Force,[16] but its very newness and the Rabaul emergency handicapped it in addition to its already unattractive defensive role. The early division of the carriers because of Rabaul meant that Sherman and Montgomery did not participate in last-minute rehearsals, and neither received a briefing on plans for the Tarawa assault, both necessary for a well-timed landing. Also, no preparations had been made for countering Japanese night air attacks, except the personal initiative of Rear Admiral Radford. His flagship, *Enterprise*, had arrived in Hawaii with a new air group deficient in night training. So Matt Gardner, the skipper, had asked Jack Towers to give him a veteran air group for GALVANIC while the other worked up in Hawaii. Air Group 6 had been provided, commanded by Medal of Honor winner Butch O'Hare. When Radford hoisted his flag on the "Big E" he immediately formed a three-plane night fighter team led by O'Hare.[17] The other carriers had no such night defense.

Softening up the target beaches, Makin and Tarawa, had begun several days before the Central Pacific Force arrived by Rear Admiral Hoover's long-range land-based air from the South Pacific. Montgomery's task group struck first, bombing Tarawa on 18 November, two months to the day after the previous fast carrier visit. The next day the other groups joined in. Pownall's planes struck airfields at Mili and Jaluit in the southern Marshalls, Radford's bombed Makin, and Sherman's successfully eliminated Japanese air strength at Nauru. The first three task groups maintained their stations in accordance with the defensive sectors assigned in the operations plan, while Sherman turned east to escort garrison convoys toward the objective.

The planned battleship-cruiser-destroyer bombardment of Tarawa, the most heavily defended of the two main targets, began less than three hours before the assault, augmented by planes from the escort and fast carriers. But close air support proved very poor and inefficient from the start. Montgomery's absence from the final prelanding briefing led to his planes' tardiness by one-half hour, leading to a lull in battleship fire as the ships waited for the planes. When the planes did strafe and bomb the beach, the pilots did not concentrate on specific targets but switched around, thereby destroying only few targets. Colonel Eareckson, trying to coordinate the planes from a battleship, suffered a communications breakdown resulting from the concussions of the ship's salvos. So coordination suffered, along with effectiveness because of the general ignorance among the carrier pilots of close support procedures. *Essex* pilots were naïve enough to believe they had completed their mission by destroying Tarawa's defenses. The truth struck everyone as soon as the Marines hit the beach and casualty figures began to mount.[18]

The other definite weakness involved protection of the carriers in their defensive sectors. To get the jump on Japanese air strikes each task group sent ahead 30,000 yards one special radar picket destroyer to direct fighters against incoming planes.[19] But even this was not enough, for on the evening of 20 November long-range Betty torpedo bombers from Kwajalein and Maloelap—airfields Pownall had not been allowed to strike—attacked Montgomery's task group off Tarawa. Airborne combat air patrol and antiaircraft fire from *Essex*, *Bunker Hill*, and *Independence* brought down nine of them, but one succeeded in torpedoing the latter ship. Several men died on *Independence*, which had to retire from the war zone for repairs that took the ship out of the war for six months.

This loss of *Independence* to a dusk torpedo air attack gave Admiral Towers, observing from Pearl Harbor, sufficient evidence to demand that Spruance's defensive carrier sectors be abandoned. The next morning, 21 November, Towers asked Admiral Nimitz to call an immediate special conference, which Nimitz did following the regular morning meeting. Towers, supported by Soc McMorris, Nimitz's deputy, asked Cincpac to modify the operations order that had restricted the carriers' mobility. He reminded Nimitz that he, Towers, had opposed the plan and pointed out that Pownall, Radford, and Montgomery had protested in a body to Spruance, who had overridden their objections. When Nimitz asked why Spruance had taken this attitude, Towers and McMorris blamed it on Spruance's fear that the Japanese carriers would come out of Truk to threaten the landings. With the torpedoing of *Independence* fresh in everyone's minds, Towers argued that, because more dusk air and possibly submarine attacks would continue, the fast carriers should be sent north to attack enemy bases in the Marshalls.[20]

Towers spoke with more authority than merely as the airmen's leader demanding recognition. He had the evidence of Rabaul to support his arguments, and now that his and other air admirals' arguments had been ignored a valuable warship was out of action for many months. Furthermore, Forrest Sherman, a rear admiral since the tenth and now in his last three days as chief of staff to Towers, had won Nimitz's confidence and was now supporting Towers fully. So did Soc McMorris, Cincpac's non-air deputy. Spruance, notwithstanding the presence of air "adviser" Bernhard, had no such advice from his staff. Nimitz listened to the various expressions, then accepted Towers' argument and on the spot instructed McMorris and Sherman to draft a "despatch of instructions" to Spruance to send the fast carriers north to strike the Marshalls as soon as the opportunity arose.[21]

Spruance did not immediately change his plans. The troops needed close air support at Makin and Tarawa, and it had begun to improve as the troops pressed forward. Support therefore continued until the twenty-third, when resistance ended on Betio, the major atoll at Tarawa. Simultaneously, Makin and Apemama fell to the invaders. But the Japanese air attacks continued, two small flights from the Marshalls being destroyed by planes of TG 50.1 on the twenty-third and twenty-fourth. Then the submarines struck. In the predawn darkness of the twenty-fourth escort carrier *Liscome Bay* took a torpedo that sent her down quickly; losses were 644, including Rear Admiral Mullinix. Naval air thus lost a promising officer who would have probably soon acceded to a fast carrier division command. The loss of another carrier under-

Founding Fathers aboard USS *Langley*, September 1926. LEFT: Joseph Mason Reeves RIGHT: William A. Moffett

Fast Carrier Commander aboard USS *Lexington,* August 1944 Marc A. Mitscher

Above left: Administrative Reformers at Pearl Harbor, March 1945 LEFT: James V. Forrestal RIGHT: John H. Towers

Below left: High Command aboard USS *Indianapolis,* July 1944. LEFT TO RIGHT: Chester W. Nimitz, Ernest J. King, Raymond A. Spruance.

FAST CARRIER COMMANDERS

William F. Halsey, Jr.

John S. McCain

Frederick C. "Ted" Sherman

THE THINKERS

DeWitt C. Ramsey

Arthur W. Radford

Forrest P. Sherman

Donald B. Duncan

THE FIGHTERS

Alfred E. Montgomery

J. J. "Jocko" Clark

Gerald F. Bogan

John W. Reeves, Jr.

Ralph E. Davison

Sir Philip L. Vian, RN (*Courtesy Imperial War Museum)*

Thomas L. Sprague

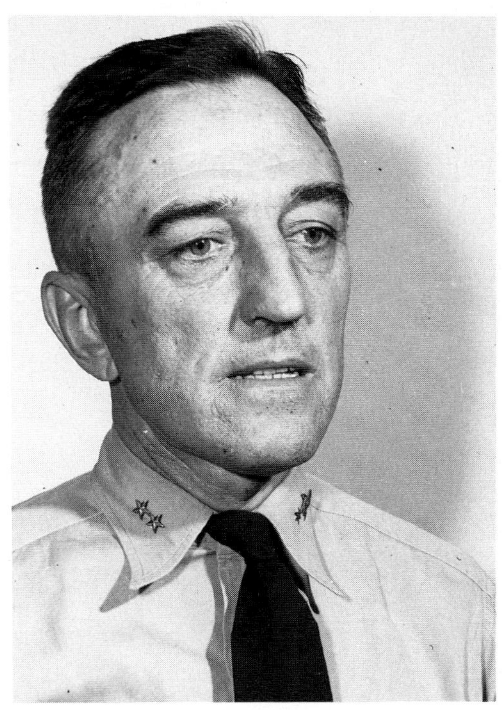

SHORT-TERMER

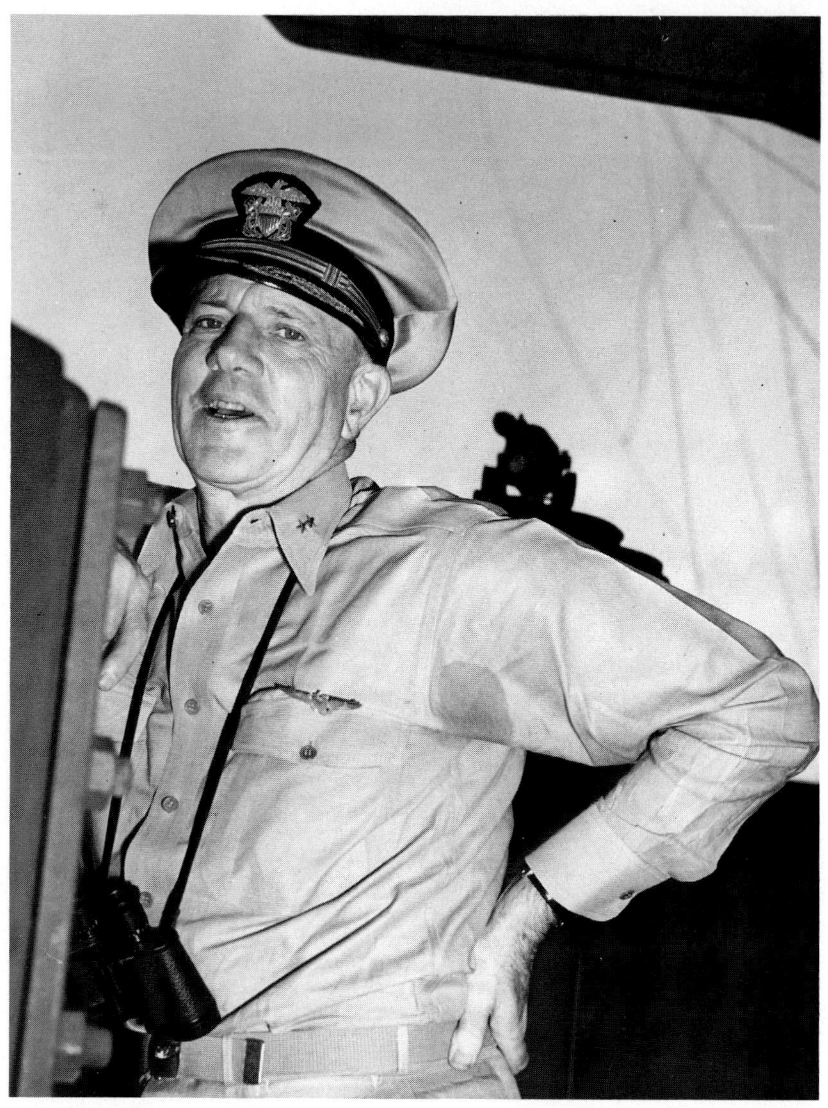

Charles A. Pownall

scored the vulnerability of carriers in restricted waters, though of course the escort carriers had no choice but to remain off the beaches—restricted by their slow speed and single mission of support.[22]

Japan's major retaliatory tactic, as the carrier admirals had feared, revealed itself in night torpedo attacks. A single Japanese plane, dubbed "Tojo the Lamplighter" by the American crews, appeared several evenings to drop flares over Radford's carriers off Makin. On the night of 26 November about 30 such planes, torpedo bombers, flew in from the Marshalls to hit Radford. But Radford, unlike his colleagues, was ready with O'Hare's night team. *Enterprise* launched two Hellcats, including O'Hare's, and one radar-equipped Avenger, flown by Lieutenant Commander John L. Phillips, skipper of Torpedo 6. Before they could rendezvous, Phillips jumped two Bettys by surprise and shot them down. Then, as the two fighters jockeyed into position on each side of the TBF, more shooting developed. O'Hare's plane went into the sea, probably brought down by .50-caliber fire from the TBF's turret. The Japanese planes, thrown into confusion by all this unexpected activity, maneuvered and fired wildly, then returned to base. O'Hare was never found—a tragic loss to the fast carriers —but he had proved night interception was feasible.[23]

A few more aerial actions occurred during GALVANIC, but by the end of organized resistance on the target islands on 28 November Japanese air attacks had also ceased. Seventy-one Marshalls-based planes had been shot down during the month, along with several more staged in from Truk. The last 32 Japanese carrier fighters had been sent to the Marshalls, where most were shot down.[24] But more enemy aircraft remained north of the Gilberts, and if American shipping and garrison forces in the Gilberts were to remain unmolested these planes would have to be eliminated. In contrast to Japanese losses American carrier losses for all of November—including Rabaul—was 47 planes. And submarine *Plunger* picked up several pilots at the Gilberts.

At last Admiral Spruance could act on the instruction dispatch sent by McMorris and Sherman. He sent *Saratoga* and *Princeton* back to Pearl with Arthur Radford, who as Towers' new chief of staff could continue experimenting with night carrier defenses. He ordered Pownall to leave two carriers under Ted Sherman, *Bunker Hill* and *Monterey*, north of the Gilberts for insurance and take the rest around the Marshalls for a large-scale attack on Kwajalein.

All planning had to be done hastily on board ship, a procedure foreign to the methodical and precise Spruance. But seizing the tactical initiative and maintaining operational flexibility had proven decisive with the fast carriers at Rabaul and before that at the Coral Sea and Midway. Unfortunately, it would not during the strike on Kwajalein. Initiative in the midst of combat requires aggressive leadership, an attribute which Rear Admiral Baldy Pownall lacked.

The six-carrier striking force rendezvoused far to the east of the Marshalls on 1 December. Pownall's TG 50.1 included the same ships as before, *Yorktown*, *Lexington*, and *Cowpens*, while Montgomery's TG 50.3 had been reshuffled, *Essex*, *Enterprise*, and *Belleau Wood*. Air groups had also been altered on the *Essex*-class ships to give them more fighters, 38, and fewer dive bombers, 28.[25] There were no night fighters, however. With O'Hare dead, John Phillips assumed command of Air Group 6 and with Radford gone made no attempt to continue night flying. The force would have to await specially equipped planes and properly trained pilots to engage in this very complex business; otherwise they would continue to shoot each other down. Pownall's mission was to neutralize enemy air at Kwajalein and to obtain photographs of the atoll for the landings there scheduled for January 1944.

The fast carriers in the Kwajalein strike enjoyed their first real flexibility since the beginning of the Gilberts operation. Pownall brought his two task groups to the launching area from the northeast on 4 December, surprising the Japanese, who were accustomed to his strikes from the south. But here the tremendous possibilities of the raid ended, and a succession of errors began. Intelligence concerning the target was lacking and target coordination faulty. Commander Charlie Crommelin, the normal target coordinator from *Yorktown*, had been wounded over Mili earlier and replaced by E. E. Stebbins, an SBD pilot unfamiliar with the F6F to which he had been assigned to fly. When the planes roared in over Kwajalein, their bombs, torpedoes, and strafing missed the mark so badly that few installations and ships suffered damage. In a 45-minute attack Pownall's planes destroyed four Japanese merchant vessels and 55 aircraft, 28 of which had been airborne. As the planes withdrew a few pilots noticed many Bettys parked unscathed on the airfield at Roi atoll. The land-based multiengine Betty (Allied code name for the Mitsubishi Zero-1 torpedo bomber) had an extraordinary range of 3000 miles, twice that of any American carrier plane, and was capable of carrying radar, self-sealing tanks, and a 5- to 7-man crew.[26] These planes would have to be destroyed in the second strike, lest they launch night torpedo attacks against Task Force 50 as it retired from the area.

But Pownall had no desire to remain in Marshalls waters long enough for a second strike, though he did send a few planes to attack Wotje Island. Captain Jocko Clark of *Yorktown*, the force flagship, and the squadron commanders of Air Group 5 pleaded with Admiral Pownall to launch a second strike, but he would not be persuaded. Then, about noon, two flights each of four Kate torpedo planes attacked the carriers and were all shot down. As one pressed its attack against the flagship, *Yorktown*'s antiaircraft gunners kept lowering their fire until they were shooting into one of their own heavy cruisers. At this point Pownall yelled up to Captain Clark, "Cease fire! Cease fire! You are firing at that cruiser!" Clark ignored the order, and his gunners brought down the attacker. Recovering the Wotje strike, Task Force 50 headed for friendly waters, but heavy seas slowed down the destroyers and thus all ships. Everyone knew what would come at dark, and several times that afternoon Jocko Clark pounded *Yorktown*'s chart desk with his fist, exclaiming, "Goddammit, you can't run away from airplanes with ships!" [27]

Cruising at 18 knots, Task Force 50 prepared for a night attack. Shortly after 8 P.M. it came. Guided by snoopers that had shadowed the ships during the afternoon and aided by a brilliant gibbous moon, 30 to 50 Japanese Bettys began several hours of aerial torpedo attacks. Without night fighters Pownall relied on individual ships' maneuvers and antiaircraft fire. Captain Felix Stump of *Lexington* later paid tribute to Pownall, who "without doubt . . . saved us from a coordinated attack by changing course all the time." [28] The two task groups separated to ward off the attackers by independent evasive movements. The attack was erratic, sometimes heavy, and at other times only threatening. It reached its most difficult moment one-half hour before midnight when a torpedo struck the stern of *Lexington*. She lost steerage, but superb efforts by steering engine room operators soon regained it, and the last attack was beaten off by ships' fire and the fact that the moon set at 1:30 A.M. on the fifth.[29]

Pownall had completed only part of his mission by destroying some enemy planes and ships and by obtaining photographs of Kwajalein. He had seriously jeopardized his carriers by placing them on the defensive to land-based enemy air attack at night in Japanese waters. The fact that the task force escaped intact was the result of his own maneuvering skill and that of his ship captains, the superb gunnery of the antiaircraft crews, and great good luck. He had failed to neutralize all Japanese air in the Marshalls, which intelligence soon reported to have withdrawn to Nauru. Admiral Spruance ordered Pownall and Montgomery to return to Pearl and detached a strong surface force to Nauru to bombard the airfield there. Odd that battleships should be used to attack an airfield, but nevertheless Ching Lee and five battlewagons carried out the mission on 8 December. Needless to say, they were covered by Ted Sherman with *Bunker Hill* and *Monterey*. They destroyed the few planes that had remained at Nauru and then continued on to the South Pacific. Not surprisingly airman Sherman, who admired Lee as a commander, lamented that a carrier-battleship force should be led by a nonaviator.[30]

Ironically, while the Central Pacific air admirals who could have used more combat experience returned to Hawaii, the most experienced of them returned to action in the South Pacific. Ted Sherman reported back to Halsey, who wanted him, on 12 December 1943 as Commander Task Group 37.2 with *Bunker Hill* and *Monterey*. While the Central Pacific Force was idle,[31] Halsey began to encircle Rabaul by capturing islands and establishing airfields to the east and north. On Christmas Day Sherman's two carriers struck Kavieng, New Ireland, north of Rabaul, then eluded night torpedo air attacks by rapid maneuvering and by laying down a smoke screen. The same ships hit Kavieng again on New Year's Day and 4 January 1944. Several Japanese planes were shot down, while Sherman's forces suffered light damage.[32] The raids proved disappointing, as targets were few, but they at least contributed to the over-all pressure on Rabaul.

The Gilberts campaign ended when Task Force 50 returned to Pearl Harbor early in December 1943. Mistakes had been made with the new fast carriers and the new amphibious forces, but many of these mistakes had been foreseen by the aviators. Others had not been anticipated. Said one Marine Corps historian, "There had to be a Tarawa . . . the inevitable point at which untried doctrine was at length tried in the crucible of battle." [33] In spite of these mistakes, the success at Rabaul and the fumbling over Tarawa and Kwajalein vindicated everything the air admirals had been claiming. The fast carrier task force emerged from GALVANIC triumphant.

4. Battle of Washington

"Every possible encouragement must be given to the development of a full-grown [strategic, land-based] air force rather than an apron-string force tied down to slow and vulnerable aircraft carriers," declared one suddenly unconvincing writer in the *U.S. Naval Institute Proceedings* for December 1943. "In the face of such world air power the aircraft carrier must wither and die. The great expense necessary to provide a floating base for so small a number of planes should not be tolerated much longer." [1]

The "great expense" had been justified in the first step of the Central Pacific offensive, leading the Navy—including its conservative elements—to accept naval aviation and the fast carrier as the dominant element of the Pacific war. Already, three more fast carriers of the *Essex* class had been commissioned: *Intrepid* (CV-11), the new *Hornet* (CV-12), and the new *Wasp* (CV-18). Another, *Franklin* (CV-13), had been launched. During 1943 construction had continued so that by mid-1944 the Navy expected another two to be ready for combat. By the end of the new year, yet another four would be added. And the keels of more—many more—had been laid and more would be laid down during 1944. Perhaps most impressive was the laying of the keels of two "battle carriers" of the class to be known as *Midway* late in 1943.

The Navy had also begun to think seriously of its postwar organization, the groundwork for which had been laid by Admiral Harry Yarnell. Vice Admiral Horne, the Vice CNO and last of the naval air observers, took over postwar planning from Yarnell in the fall of 1943 and issued his first tentative demobilization and postwar plan on 17 November. In it he gave naval aviation the "dominant" position with 42 per cent of the postwar budget, 27 fast carriers as opposed to 13 battleships, and a greater percentage of aviation officers than ever before. After he had studied his estimates and had received comments from interested officers, he had second thoughts about such a large budget for naval air. But when Horne touched upon the subject of limiting the number of carriers to be kept in commission after the war, Vice Admiral McCain, DCNO (Air), countered with the recommendation on 2

December that none of the Navy's flattops at war's end be decommissioned, giving the Navy *40* carriers "less battle losses." [2]

The airmen thus joined battle with the conservatives within the Navy Department. It would also soon be joined with the advocates of a separate Air Force who would underplay the role of naval aviation. In the Pacific, the battle was already being fought and won. The next time the fast carriers went into battle they would enjoy new importance in the Pacific Fleet under a new, dynamic leader—Mitscher—and with a new designation—Task Force 58.

FLEET ORGANIZATION

MARCUS TASK ORGANIZATION
31 August 1943

Task Force 15

CTF 15—Rear Admiral C. A. Pownall (ComCarDiv 3)
Chief of Staff—Captain H. S. Duckworth
Yorktown—Captain J. J. Clark; Air Group 5
Essex—Captain D. B. Duncan; Air Group 9
Independence—Captain G. R. Fairlamb, Jr.; Air Group 22

BAKER TASK ORGANIZATION
1 September 1943

Task Force 11

CTF 11—Rear Admiral W. A. Lee (ComBatPac)*
CTU 11.2.1—Rear Admiral A. W. Radford (ComCarDiv 11)
Princeton—Captain G. R. Henderson; Air Group 23
Belleau Wood—Captain A. M. Pride; Air Group 24

TARAWA RAID TASK ORGANIZATION
18 September 1943

Task Force 15

CTF 15—Rear Admiral C. A. Pownall (ComCarDiv 3)
Chief of Staff—Captain H. S. Duckworth
Lexington—Captain F. B. Stump; Air Group 16
Princeton—Captain G. R. Henderson; Air Group 23
Belleau Wood—Captain A. M. Pride; Air Group 24

WAKE TASK ORGANIZATION
5–6 October 1943

Task Force 14

CTF 14—Rear Admiral A. E. Montgomery (ComCarDiv 12)
Chief of Staff—Captain H. S. Duckworth
CTG 14.12—Rear Adm. Montgomery
Yorktown—Captain J. J. Clark; Air Group 5
Essex—Captain D. B. Duncan; Air Group 9
CTU 14.5.3—Rear Admiral V. H. Ragsdale (ComCarDiv 22)
Independence—Captain R. L. Johnson; Air Group 22
Belleau Wood—Captain A. M. Pride; Air Group 24
CTG 14.13—Rear Admiral A. W. Radford (ComCarDiv 11)
Lexington—Captain F. B. Stump; Air Group 16
Cowpens—Captain R. P. McConnell; Air Group 25

RABAUL TASK ORGANIZATIONS
1–11 November 1943

South Pacific Force—Admiral W. F. Halsey, Jr.
Chief of Staff—Rear Admiral R. B. Carney*
CTF 38—Rear Admiral F. C. Sherman (ComCarDiv 1)
Saratoga—Captain J. H. Cassady; Air Group 12
Princeton—Captain G. R. Henderson; Air Group 23
CTG 50.3—Rear Admiral A. E. Montgomery (ComCarDiv 12)
Essex—Captain R. A. Ofstie; Air Group 9
Bunker Hill—Captain J. J. Ballentine; Air Group 17
Independence—Captain R. L. Johnson; Air Group 22

GILBERTS TASK ORGANIZATION
15–26 November 1943

Central Pacific Force—Vice Admiral R. A. Spruance*
Chief of Staff—Captain C. J. Moore*
CTF 50—Rear Admiral C. A. Pownall (ComCarDiv 3)
Chief of Staff—Captain T. J. Hedding
CTG 50.1—Rear Adm. Pownall
Yorktown—Captain J. J. Clark; Air Group 5
Lexington—Captain F. B. Stump; Air Group 16
Cowpens—Captain R. P. McConnell; Air Group 25
CTG 50.2—Rear Admiral A. W. Radford (ComCarDiv 11)
Enterprise—Captain M. B. Gardner; Air Group 6
Belleau Wood—Captain A. M. Pride; Air Group 24
Monterey—Captain L. T. Hundt; Air Group 30

CTG 50.3—Rear Admiral A. E. Montgomery (ComCarDiv 12)
Essex—Captain R. A. Ofstie; Air Group 9
Bunker Hill—Captain J. J. Ballentine; Air Group 17
Independence—Captain R. L. Johnson; Air Group 22
CTG 50.4—Rear Admiral F. C. Sherman (ComCarDiv 1)
Saratoga—Captain J. H. Cassady; Air Group 12
Princeton—Captain G. R. Henderson; Air Group 23
Commander Support Aircraft—Colonel W. O. Eareckson, USAAF

27 November–5 December 1943

Task Force 50

CTF 50—Rear Adm. Pownall
CTG 50.1—Rear Adm. Pownall
Yorktown, Lexington, Cowpens
CTG 50.3—Rear Adm. Montgomery
Enterprise, Essex, Belleau Wood
CTG 50.4—Rear Adm. Sherman
Bunker Hill, Monterey

6–11 December 1943

Task Group 50.8

CTG 50.8—Rear Admiral W. A. Lee (ComBatPac)*
CTU 50.8.5—Rear Admiral F. C. Sherman (ComCarDiv 1)
(After 12 December 1943 Task Group 37.4)
Bunker Hill, Monterey

---

*Nonaviator

Five:
Task Force 58

The combined Allied planners concluded on 2 December 1943 that an air and sea blockade of Japan be the ultimate objective of all operations in the Pacific.[1] Both MacArthur's Southwest and Nimitz's Central Pacific forces would continue separately toward a common objective: the area of Formosa–Luzon–China, where "a major assault" would take place during the spring of 1945. The Japanese fleet must be destroyed "at an early date" but flexibility would be the keynote of Allied strategy. The planners emphasized "the importance of the provision of aircraft carriers of all sorts for our future operations against Japan." They also stressed that "preparations are made to take all manner of short cuts made possible by developments in the situation," an idea made the more feasible by the mobility and striking power of the fast carriers.

The target, Formosa–Luzon–China, once reached, would enable the indirect blockade of Japan to commence, for Japan's raw materials passed by sea from the East Indies to Japan through this so-called Luzon bottleneck. The exact landing place, be it northern Luzon, the island of Formosa, or the coast of China, would be determined later. The blockade was to include mining, air and submarine attacks on Japanese shipping and harbors, "and intensive air bombardment from progressively advanced bases." The latter provision referred to the new very-long-range B-29 strategic bomber, which could be based in China or in the Marianas Islands. If invasion of Japan proper became necessary, the Allied military must be prepared to execute it.

But in late 1943 the questions of Formosa versus Luzon versus China and blockade versus invasion lay in the seemingly distant future. So flexible was strategy at this time that the top strategists and planners could not decide on the precise targets to capture on the road to the Luzon bottleneck and Japan. Rabaul was being encircled by Halsey's South Pacific forces, even though Japan continued to bolster Rabaul's defenses. Late in January 1944 Rear Admiral Takaji Joshima and the planes of CarDiv 2 arrived at Rabaul from their training at Singapore. With the decimation of CarDiv 1 aircraft in the defense of Rabaul and the Gilberts in November, these pilots represented the last carrier pilots with training sufficient to challenge Allied command of the air in the Solomons. But they too quickly fell victim to the Solomons "meat grinder"—Halsey's land-based air.[2] Satisfied that Halsey had sealed the fate of Rabaul, the Pacific planners focused on Truk—mighty Truk, "Gibraltar of the Pacific"—which one day soon would have to be captured. From this great Japanese fleet anchorage in the eastern Carolines Admiral Nimitz desired to fly his own flag. But before Truk could be approached, American forces first had to invade and occupy the Marshall Islands.

On 3 December 1943 a new Pacific timetable called for the seizure of the Marshalls during January 1944,[3] followed by Ponape Island near Truk on 1 May 1944; from Ponape land-based planes could begin to soften up Truk. One month later Nimitz would assist MacArthur in taking Hollandia on the northern coast of New Guinea. Then, on 20 July, the Central Pacific Force would attack Truk. On 1 October 1944 they would land at Guam and other Marianas islands, enabling B-29 strikes to commence from these islands by the last day of the year.[4]

Even the question of which of the Marshall islands to assault plagued the strategists. Before GALVANIC the plan for Operation FLINTLOCK had called for the Central Pacific Force to capture the three Marshall islands closest to Pearl Harbor—Kwajalein, Wotje, and Maloelap. The two other key islands, Mili and Jaluit in the south, could be neutralized by air strikes. General Holland Smith, feeling that three islands being assaulted simultaneously would constitute too great a task, recommended Wotje and Maloelap be taken first, then Kwajalein. After the heavy losses at Tarawa, Smith and Admiral Kelly Turner agreed that the assault of three such islands simultaneously would be impossible. Furthermore, the capture and development of Tarawa and Makin as forward air and supply bases meant FLINTLOCK, once launched from Hawaii, would be supported from the Gilberts. If the three or any one of the initial three target islands were taken, American lines of communication would be in constant peril from Japanese airfields on Mili and Jaluit. These southern islands could of course be neutralized by land-based air from the northern Marshalls, meaning complete bomber strips had to be captured. In turn this required the taking of Wotje and Maloelap, as Kwajalein apparently had no large bomber field.

Then, Pownall's carriers returned from the Kwajalein raid in early December 1943 with fresh photographs of the atoll showing a nearly completed new bomber strip. Rear Admiral Forrest Sherman, in his new role as Cincpac planning officer, immediately suggested a direct assault on Kwajalein, bypassing Wotje and Maloelap; "we can let them wither on the vine," he said. Nimitz and Soc McMorris bought the idea, but the amphibious commanders, led by Spruance, objected. Kwajalein, encircled by airfields at Wotje and Maloelap to the east and at Mili and Jaluit to the south, would further be open to air attacks staged in from Japan through Eniwetok to the west. The amphibious commanders could not forget the horrors of Marshall-based night air attacks off the Gilberts, and these had come from only one direction. An occupied Kwajalein would be virtually surrounded.

Nimitz did not waste time. Calling together his top commanders two weeks before Christmas, he opened the floor for discussion. Spruance argued "as strongly as I could" for landings at Wotje and Maloelap, thus keeping Hawaii at his back and insuring secure lines of communication. Admiral Turner and General Smith emphatically agreed. When each man had finished, Nimitz announced, "Well, gentlemen, we are going to Kwajalein."[5] The Joint Chiefs of Staff quickly approved Nimitz's decision, and on 14 December FLINTLOCK was changed to the capture of Kwajalein only. Twelve days later Admiral Spruance asked and obtained permission to include the seizure of Majuro atoll with its fine anchorage between Maloelap and Mili.[6]

The fact that Nimitz decided against the advice of Spruance and Turner, his most trusted commanders, suggests the impact of the aviators' reasoning on Cincpac. Before GALVANIC the caution of Spruance and Turner had governed Nimitz's approval of their plan to restrict the fast carriers on the defensive. The persuasive Forrest Sherman now had Nimitz's ear, and Nimitz listened to the keen intellect of this young aviator with much respect. Air power would neutralize all the islands around Kwajalein; Admiral Hoover's planes from the Gilberts and later from Kwajalein itself could bomb them regularly, while the ever-growing fast carrier

Japan from the South Pacific

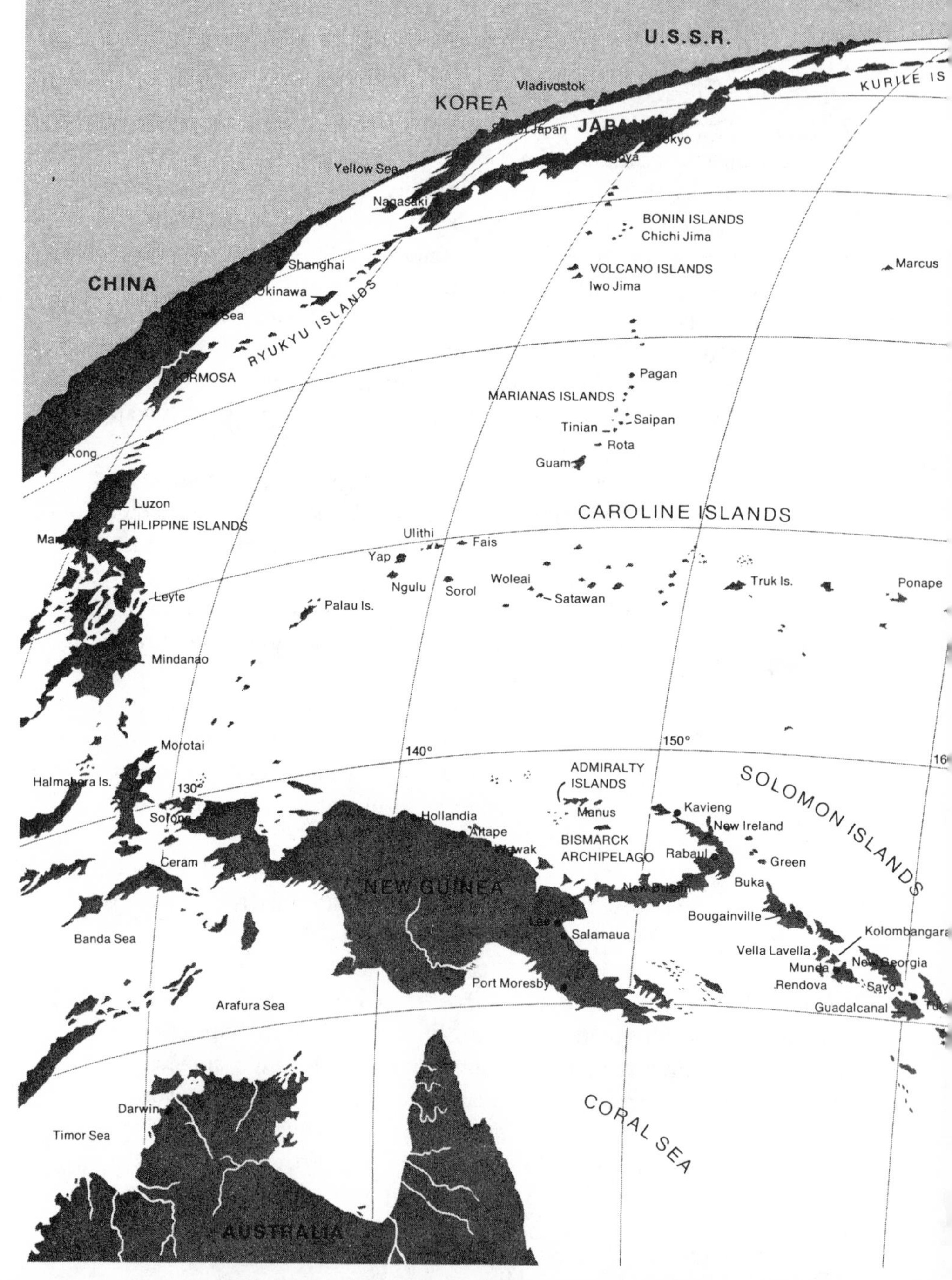

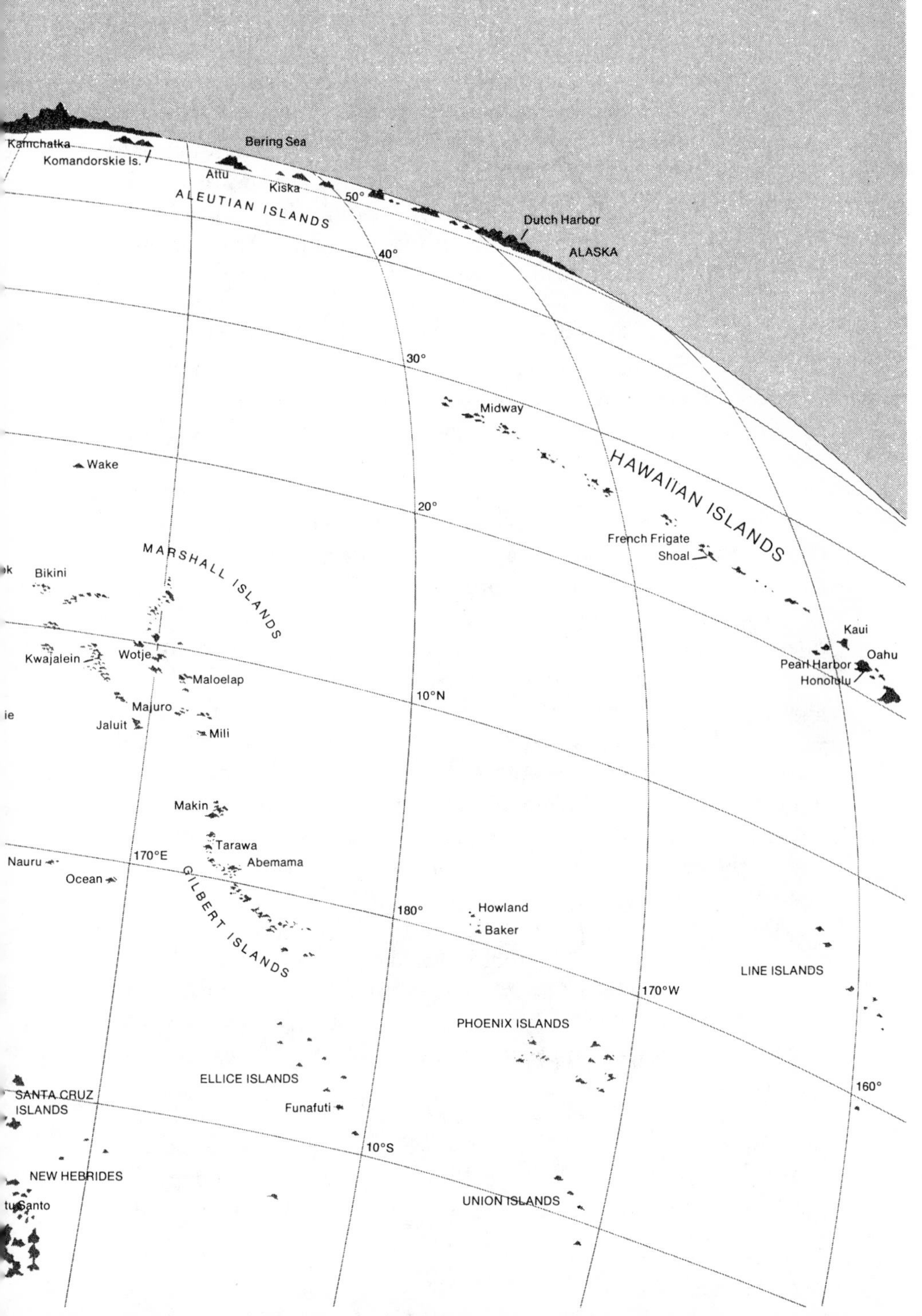
Kamchatka
Komandorskie Is.
Bering Sea
Attu
Kiska
ALEUTIAN ISLANDS
50°
Dutch Harbor
ALASKA
40°
30°
Midway
Wake
HAWAIIAN ISLANDS
20°
French Frigate
Shoal
MARSHALL ISLANDS
Bikini
Kaui
Oahu
Pearl Harbor
Honolulu
Kwajalein
Wotje
Maloelap
10°N
Majuro
Jaluit
Mili
Makin
Tarawa
Abemama
170°E
Nauru
Ocean
GILBERT ISLANDS
180°
Howland
Baker
LINE ISLANDS
170°W
PHOENIX ISLANDS
ELLICE ISLANDS
SANTA CRUZ
ISLANDS
Funafuti
160°
10°S
NEW HEBRIDES
Santo
UNION ISLANDS

task force would eliminate fresh threats from Truk, the Marianas, or Japan. The November strikes against Rabaul and the undisputed command of the air during GALVANIC gave Nimitz all the confidence he needed to bypass all the Marshall Islands but Kwajalein.

This idea of bypassing lesser islands to get the larger ones—"leapfrogging"—was not new in the Pacific. It had been suggested by military strategists and planners as early as 1940 and revived by Franklin Percival in the May 1943 *Proceedings*. It had been practiced in the North, South, and Southwest Pacific theaters in mid-1943: Admiral Kinkaid had leaped Kiska to take Attu in the Aleutians in May; Admiral Halsey had bypassed Kolombangara to seize Vella Lavella in the Solomons in July; and General MacArthur had hopped Salamaua to get at Lae, New Guinea, in September. Admiral Towers had been convinced of the feasibility of island-hopping in January 1943 by Major General Charles F. B. Price, Marine Corps commander at Samoa. Towers had developed the idea with Forrest Sherman, then his chief of staff. With all this evidence for leapfrogging, Nimitz had decided to bypass certain Gilbert islands for Tarawa and Makin and now to do the same thing in the Marshalls in favor of Kwajalein.[7]

But leapfrogging on a grand scale had not been seriously considered. General MacArthur of course favored bypassing the entire Central Pacific, but once the forces of that theater had commenced their offensive the capture of certain key targets was assumed: Rabaul, Truk, Guam, and Formosa. Yet several people were beginning to have second thoughts about one or more of these targets. When Admiral King met with Admirals Nimitz and Halsey at San Francisco on 3–4 January 1944 he stressed to them that the key to the entire Pacific was the Marianas. Forrest Sherman suggested that reaching the Marianas might be facilitated by bypassing Truk altogether, thus planting the idea of hopping a major objective.[8] Going on to Washington, a few days later Halsey informed King he saw "no need to storm Rabaul or the secondary base Kavieng." Halsey felt he impressed King with his reasoning.[9] All at once, the idea of bypassing both Rabaul and Truk received serious attention.

Simultaneously, Jack Towers presented an even more bizarre plan: bypass Truk and the Marianas, keeping them neutralized with land-based air. Rabaul and the Bismarck archipelago along with the Marshall Islands would have to be captured for their bomber fields, hence these could not be leapfrogged. Also useful for airfields and a good fleet anchorage were the Admiralty Islands, 600 miles south of Truk and just north of New Guinea. Towers believed Truk would be too expensive to assault, although as early as April 1943 he had recommended its capture.[10] Since then, however, the defending garrison had doubled to about 9000 troops and dug into a mutually defensible interlocking complex of six islands and 11 lesser islets.

Two Marine divisions would be necessary for the assault, supported by 17 battleships, 15 escort carriers, 24 cruisers, 187 destroyers and destroyer-escorts, and 17 fast carriers divided into five task groups—most of the Pacific Fleet's surface strength. The effort would be gigantic and losses high. Towers rejected the capture of the Marianas Islands on the grounds that if occupied they would be an exposed salient pointing toward Japan. He further reasoned that these islands were unsuitable for B-29 bases and were too far from Japan to provide the B-29s with fighter escort.[11]

On 5 January 1944 Towers submitted a memorandum to the Cincpac staff incorporating these ideas and recommending that Truk and the Marianas be bypassed. He pointed out the objective of the Luzon bottleneck would be reached more quickly if the Central Pacific Force went by way of the Bismarcks, Admiralties, Palaus, and Philippines, which should be reoccupied. Agreeing entirely with MacArthur, Towers insisted that "*only*" from the Philippines could air and submarine bases be established to intercept Japanese shipping, and only from the Philippines could an invasion of the Chinese mainland be mounted. Towers offered a new timetable: bombard Truk with a diversionary raid on 1 June 1944, capture Palau on 1 July, begin air attacks on the Philippines on 1 August, and invade the southern Philippines two months later.[12]

Forrest Sherman first read the recommendation and praised his former boss for showing "careful thought." Sherman agreed that the capture of the Philippines was necessary and that Truk could be neutralized by air attack. He pointed out that the Marianas was only the last objective for 1944 and not the ultimate objective. Sherman then passed on the memo to Soc McMorris, recommending it be shown to Nimitz. McMorris, equally impressed by Towers' ideas, endorsed them, "This *is* a good paper. The idea of bypassing Truk is sound, if feasible, but it will surely have to be neutralized if by passed and we will require a fleet base [obviously Palau] short of the Philippines." McMorris gave the paper to Nimitz, who studied it, then wrote "Concur" next to McMorris' notes, and forwarded the paper with comments to Admiral King.[13]

The economy of one main drive along the north coast of New Guinea by both Central and Southwest Pacific forces appealed to many high commanders and gained momentum at Pearl Harbor throughout January. On the thirteenth Nimitz restated his recommendation for the occupation of Kwajalein in the Marshalls, the Carolines (Truk included), the Marianas and Philippines, but he suggested Palau might be substituted for Truk. He then called a conference of top Pacific command representatives to meet at Pearl Harbor on 27–28 January to discuss strategy.[14]

From the Southwest Pacific came Lieutenant General Richard K. Sutherland, MacArthur's chief of staff, and Major General George C. Kenney, theater air commander. From the South Pacific, now becoming a backwater of the war, came Rear Admiral Mick Carney, chief of staff to Halsey, who had been detained in the United States. And Nimitz had all his Central Pacific planners there, Lieutenant General Richardson of the Army, Towers, Calhoun (logistics commander), McMorris, and Sherman. In premeeting discussions Generals Richardson and Kenney considered pooling all forces for the one advance along the New Guinea coast to the Philippines. They were pleasantly surprised to find their views in accord with those of Towers, Sherman, and Carney, while Calhoun added that such a route would be better logistically. In the formal conference everyone agreed that the Philippines had to be retaken, while all but Admiral McMorris supported a general advance along the New Guinea–Palau route. Capture of the Marianas was not considered essential, and the leapfrogging of Truk seemed highly advantageous.[15]

"The meeting finished with everyone feeling good and ready to work together and get the war over," recalled General Kenney later, and at the luncheon following the conference Admiral Nimitz "spoke about now seeing an end to the war," which looked clearer "to everyone there." [16] No decisions were reached, as such matters of high strategy could be decided only by the Joint Chiefs of Staff. But Sutherland and Sherman were dispatched to Washington to present the ideas of the meeting to the JCS. Formidable barriers would confront them. First of all, a possible offensive via New Guinea led General MacArthur to insist on over-all command and that Halsey be his fleet commander.[17] Such a flouting of Admirals Nimitz and Spruance would be unacceptable. Furthermore, General Hap Arnold, Army Air Forces chief, wanted the Marianas for the B-29s.

The final decision of whether to bypass Truk and/or the Marianas would rest on the outcome of the Marshalls operation. If the Japanese resisted strongly and jeopardized the beachhead, the New Guinea advance might be preferable. If the fast carriers performed as unevenly as they had in the Gilberts they might be best subordinated in a southern advance. But if the Central Pacific Force triumphed, leapfrogging could be adopted in addition to a two-pronged offensive toward the Luzon bottleneck. FLINTLOCK held the key.

1. Command Shakeup

The perfect balance for fleet commander in the Pacific would have been a high-ranking admiral who had had extensive experience in both carrier operations and in non-air activities. The one individual who met these requirements was the Commander-in-Chief of the United States Fleet himself, Admiral Ernest J. King, as both Secretary Knox and Admiral Yarnell had both suggested late in 1943. Now, in January 1944, Under Secretary Forrestal proposed that the Office of CNO be abolished, that Vice Admiral Horne, the Vice CNO, remain in Washington as Chief of Logistics and Material, and that Admiral King go to the Pacific as "Admiral of the Navy and Commander, United States Fleet." President Roosevelt and Secretary Knox supported Forrestal's recommendation.[1]

King immediately understood Forrestal's intentions: to get King out of Washington and allow Forrestal, the strong man behind Knox, to strengthen civilian control over the wartime Navy. The rank of "Admiral of the Navy" anticipated the five-star rank then being considered for the highest officers in the Navy (and Army); historically, it was a plum enjoyed only by one other individual, Admiral George Dewey. Forrestal's thinly disguised maneuver might have had some administrative merit, but it ignored several operational realities. First, the Navy needed its top admiral on the JCS. Second, the United States Fleet included ten numbered fleets across the world, not just in the Pacific. One of these, the Tenth, antisubmarine forces in the Atlantic, King personally supervised. Third, King fought almost alone with other Allied strategists for greater emphasis being given to the Pacific theater.

Ernie King's presence was felt in the Pacific despite his physical absence, for he exerted great influence on Admiral Nimitz and Pacific strategy. King's participation was deliberate; after inadequate reports of the amphibious phases of GALVANIC reached him, King sent a stinging note to Nimitz demanding greater details on all amphibious operations.[2] Also Cominch, though not sympathetic to Admiral Towers' needs, did weigh the importance of having aviators in key positions in the Pacific. King advised Secretary Knox on 29 January that air representation in key posts had been poor, "because of the scarcity of seasoned officers qualified in aviation." King, supported by Horne, did not think Cincpac need necessarily be an aviator, but he did agree with Admirals Yarnell, Towers, and others that "there should be aviators of adequate rank on the staffs of all fleet and force commanders."[3] Meanwhile, the aviators themselves continued their chest-beating for the public; on 23 January, at the launching of the new fast carrier *Hancock*, Rear Admiral Duke Ramsey, Chief of BuAer, declared that the carrier had replaced the battleship as the backbone of the fleet.[4]

King, ignoring the claims of the aviators, allowed Admiral Nimitz to use aviators however he wished on the Cincpac staff, but Nimitz had already realized the inadequacy of his administrative organization. Before GALVANIC Nimitz as Cincpac–Cincpoa had had two deputies, Vice Admiral Newton as Deputy Cincpoa and Rear Admiral McMorris as Deputy Cincpac. This arrangement did not spell out duties sufficiently, and in December Nimitz reorganized his offices again. He made Newton Deputy Cincpac–Cincpoa, in charge of all logistics and administration, particularly in the Pacific Ocean Areas (including the North, South, and Southwest Pacific). Nimitz named McMorris Chief of Joint Staff, in charge of Fleet plans, operations, staff coordination, preparation and supervision of strategic and operational planning.[5]

This change had far-reaching importance for the air admirals and the carrier war. With Newton handling logistics and McMorris operations, on 11 December 1943 Rear Admiral Forrest Sherman became Assistant Chief of Staff for Plans. For the first time Cincpac's planning officer became an aviator, and the post was also elevated to the number-two staff officer to Cincpac with the rank of rear admiral.

From December 1943 until the end of the war this staff arrangement continued. McMorris (USNA '12), active and tenacious, remained senior adviser on fleet matters, but it was the young aviator Sherman (USNA '18) who balanced McMorris' strong views and put all staff ideas into carefully detailed papers.[6] Sherman's excellent performance in these first weeks on Nimitz's staff led to the upgrading of his post to Deputy Chief of Staff on 23 March 1944, which placed Sherman in the realm of plans and operations though he continued to concentrate on planning.

Sherman's proximity to Cincpac still did not give aviators what they wanted, an aviator as either number-one or number-two man in the Pacific. This difficulty, however, was soon resolved. When Nimitz and Sherman flew to San Francisco to meet with Ernie King in January 1944, along with strategic matters they discussed possible command changes in the Pacific. One decision marked a major victory for the airmen: Vice Admiral Towers would become Deputy Cincpac–Cincpoa at the conclusion of FLINTLOCK. In addition, the post would be upgraded from pure logistics and administration to include all matters of aviation. Vice Admiral Newton would go to Admiral Halsey as deputy commander in the South Pacific. Between Jack Towers and Forrest Sherman, Admiral Nimitz would have the best aviation advisers in the Navy.

These administrative changes advanced the cause of the aviators—the proper employment of carriers—considerably, but such employment still depended on the operational commanders, and the staff of Commander Central Pacific Force had no aviator. Captain Bobby Morse played as small a role in staff operational planning as did his counterparts from the Army and Marine Corps. Most decisions were influenced by Carl Moore and Savvy Forrestel, both intelligent, dedicated men, completely loyal to Spruance and, like him, inexperienced in air operations. The three men functioned smoothly together, and Spruance saw no need to upset his staff organization by replacing one of these men with an aviator. Besides, Spruance would rarely take tactical command of the fast carriers, so he did not need and therefore had no Miles Browning. He could depend upon his fast carrier commander.

Unfortunately, Rear Admiral Baldy Pownall did not display the aggressiveness Towers and the other air admirals felt his job warranted. After suspicious behavior on the Marcus and Tarawa raids during the fall, Pownall had seriously jeopardized his carriers by unaggressive use of them during the Kwajalein strike of 4 December. When that task force returned to Pearl Harbor, Captain Jock Clark of *Yorktown* went directly to Cincpac headquarters with his aerial photographs of the enemy ships and planes left behind at

Kwajalein. When Clark showed these pictures to Forrest Sherman, Sherman gasped and called to Soc McMorris in the next room, "You want to see the fish that got away?"[7] Clark and several *Yorktown* officers then prepared an unsigned "White Paper" setting forth what had happened during the recent operations and calling for more aggressive leadership of the fast carriers. Clark showed the paper to Towers and Radford, who were duly impressed.[8]

On 23 December 1943 Admiral Nimitz convened a special conference at his headquarters, including only himself, Towers, McMorris, and Sherman. The topic was command of the fast carriers. Towers "strongly recommended changes to bring about more aggressive use of carrier forces" and specifically asked that Pownall be relieved as senior carrier division commander by Rear Admiral Marc A. Mitscher, then Commander Fleet Air West Coast. Sherman seconded Towers' choice, because of Mitscher's availability as well as his intimate association with carrier operations from *Langley* days to the battles of the Solomons, where Mitscher had commanded land-based air. After discussing this proposal, Nimitz and McMorris agreed to bring in Mitscher for the next operation after FLINTLOCK. That very day they sent word to Mitscher that he would report soon as ComCarDiv 3. Two days later the same four officers discussed the matter, with Sherman recommending that Mitscher be brought in immediately for the Marshalls. Nimitz was favorable but he asked McMorris to sound out Spruance first.[9]

Spruance, inexperienced in the niceties of carrier command, had seen no fault in Pownall's actions during the Gilberts campaign and could not understand why Pownall was being considered for relief. Spruance's attitude, however, did not influence Nimitz's decision, for Nimitz ordered Pownall's relief without even informing Spruance.[10]

Pownall received notice of his relief following the regular Cincpac morning meeting on 27 December. Along with Towers, McMorris, and Sherman, Nimitz asked Newton, Spruance, and Pownall to remain. Then Nimitz informed Pownall that he was being criticized "on the grounds of being too cautious in his operations" and cited Jocko Clark's report without mentioning Clark by name. Nimitz remarked that he was disappointed at the lack of carrier effectiveness in the Kwajalein raid, pointing out that the carriers should be employed to do their utmost, despite the risk involved. Pownall appeared surprised and hurt over this criticism and defended his hasty departures from Marcus and Kwajalein, but he did not convince his listeners.[11] By this time Admiral Halsey, en route to Washington, was at Pearl Harbor and he too concurred with the appointment of Mitscher. Nothing could be decided, however, until the Pacific commanders consulted with Ernie King in San Francisco.

Meanwhile, other changes were taking place in regard to the fast carriers. Rear Admiral Arthur Radford had reported as chief of staff to ComAirPac, thus leaving a vacancy in task group command. Ted Sherman still had CarDiv 1 and Monty Montgomery CarDiv 12, while CarDivs 4 and 11 were vacant. To fill the former Towers called on Rear Admiral J. W. Reeves, Jr. "Black Jack" Reeves (USNA '11), though a latecomer to air, enjoyed a reputation as rugged, outspoken and combat-seasoned first wartime skipper of *Wasp* and then Navy air commander during the Aleutians campaign. Into the ComCarDiv 11 post arrived Rear Admiral Samuel P. Ginder (USNA '16), a young career aviator whose wartime experience had been limited to shore billets and skipper of *Enterprise* prior to and during her overhaul period. He was unproved in combat.

During December 1943 the planning for FLINTLOCK proceeded, but before long the old argument over employment of the fast carriers arose. It could not have come at a better time for the aviators and at a worse time for Spruance, since the issue of Pacific commanders was soon to be discussed at San Francisco. Again, Spruance feared the loss of or damage to his carriers if they were committed too early in the operation. He and Pownall planned to begin the air bombardment of the Marshalls two days prior to the landing, which was scheduled for 31 January 1944. This marked a major improvement over the single-morning shelling at Tarawa. But Pownall, supported by Spruance, insisted that the escorting fast battleships, now a standard component of the fast carrier task group, not join in the bombardment until the day before the landings, fearful that they would be needed to defend the carriers against enemy air or surface-ship attacks.[12]

As 1943—the remarkable year that had begun with only two prewar carriers on hand—drew to a close, Towers and Pownall argued daily over the employment of the great carrier armada in the invasion of the Marshall Islands. Pownall's pending relief did not foster cooperation between Pownall and Towers, who was obviously "pulling the strings" on air matters in the Pacific. In addition, Spruance supported the softspoken Pownall, whom he liked very much. Then, on the first day of the new year, Admirals Nimitz and Forrest Sherman departed for San Francisco, leaving McMorris as acting Cincpac.

On 3 January 1944 Towers ordered Pownall to assemble his flag officers and their chiefs of staff at the ComAirPac office. After Pownall, Reeves, Montgomery, and Ginder arrived, Towers called for a poll on the matter of a prenoon bombardment by the fast battleships on 29 January, the same day the carriers would hit the target. Everyone voted for it, and Pownall had to agree. But the next day, the fourth, Pownall called his own meeting and invited Spruance. This time Spruance reiterated his fears of the Truk-based Japanese fleet attacking his exposed carriers. Towers and his chief of staff Radford had more confidence in their carriers and insisted on maximum carrier and battleship bombardment of the objective, as the amphibious commanders wanted. Spruance and Pownall opposed this view, calling for carrier strikes on the twenty-ninth and joined by fast battleship shelling on the thirtieth. Finally, McMorris as acting Cincpac threw his weight behind Towers, settling the matter, though Spruance eventually got his way.[13]

The picture changed completely on 5 January with the arrival of Pete Mitscher, who immediately—that morning—relieved Pownall as ComCarDiv 3. The next day the fast carriers were designated Task Force 58 and Mitscher took command. Also on the sixth, Nimitz and Sherman returned from San Francisco with news of the command shakeup. Towers would become Deputy Cincpac–Cincpoa while Pownall was placed "in temporary status to relieve Towers" as ComAirPac. But now aviation policy would be transferred with Towers to his new post; ComAirPac would become only a "nuts-and-bolts" logistical office. Nimitz wanted Pownall to be available to Mitscher during planning, an empty concession, but Spruance agreed to take Pownall aboard his flagship on the Marshalls operation "as an adviser on aviation matters." Pownall rode as an observer, the same fate assigned Alva Bernhard at the Gilberts. The permanent changes would not become effective until the Marshalls were secured, sometime in February.[14]

Though Mitscher was the most available air admiral to command Task Force 58, at least three others wanted it—Towers, McCain, and Ted Sherman. Slightly senior for task force command especially under Spruance (USNA '07), Towers ('06) had the experience that eminently qualified him for the post. Both Forrest Sherman and Matt Gardner, skipper of *Enterprise*, tried to talk him out of the new Deputy Cincpac job in favor of the carrier command.[15] Towers, however, was duty-bound to accept the new post he had battled for; Cincpac's deputy should be an aviator. Also, the carrier command was still a two-star billet, which would have meant a demotion for Towers. Finally, Ernie King may have kept him from sea command. No doubt King wanted Vice Admiral Slew McCain (USNA '06) to remain in Washington until the new DCNO (Air) office was working efficiently, which kept sea-dog McCain tied to his desk several months longer. Ted Sherman, classmate of both Pownall and Mitscher ('10), suffered from a sharp personality that hampered his chances. When he learned of the Towers–Pownall–Mitscher shift he concluded, correctly, "I apparently am left out on a limb as usual." [16]

January 1944 was a busy month at Pearl Harbor, as high brass looked in on preparations for FLINTLOCK. Naval air representatives called on Towers: Assistant Secretary (Air) Di Gates and Rear Admirals Duke Ramsey and George Murray. Most important, however, was the arrival of Under Secretary Forrestal on the twenty-first to witness the Kwajalein landings. Forrestal's admiration for the young, vigorous aviators he had first met in Washington made his appearance most opportune.[17] Further, he and Towers shared a common bond: the intense dislike of Ernie King. Though he stopped only briefly at Pearl Harbor, Forrestal had chosen an operation which would demonstrate the carriers at their finest. The Under Secretary was a valuable ally.

Probably no naval aviator was dissatisfied with the selection of Pete Mitscher as fast carrier commander. Neither brilliant nor outspoken, Mitscher understood the three factors that would shape his new command: warfare, people, and aviation. Quiet enough to be barely heard, Mitscher could be understood often by his stern, severe expressions. His vast experience in naval air since pre-World War I days combined with his skillful qualities of leadership inspired a devotion and personal following among junior officers unequaled by any other naval aviator. And the fast carrier commander knew how to fight. He had launched Doolittle's bombers from *Hornet* to bomb Tokyo and had sent the heroic Torpedo 8 on its tragic but important mission against the superior Japanese fleet at Midway. Mitscher's admirals and pilots knew he knew how to fight, and they followed him. It took a man of such stature and forcefulness to handle the likes of Ted Sherman, Monty Montgomery, and Black Jack Reeves. But he would never interfere with their work, unless absolutely necessary: "I tell them *what* I want done. Not *how!*" [18]

Mitscher enjoyed absolute command of Task Force 58 in the event of a carrier battle, but if a surface engagement threatened he yielded to the fast battleship commander, Rear Admiral W. A. Lee. Ching Lee (USNA '08), a highly respected, brilliant, and aggressive tactical leader, was in an anomalous position. As "type" commander for battleships in the Pacific (as Towers was for air), Lee rode aboard a battleship in Mitscher's screen virtually as an observer. If a surface action ensued, he assumed command of Task Force 54, the fast battleships forming into the Battle Line. But in such a battle, Spruance might assume tactical command. Lee could never maneuver with his own battle forces and never had the opportunity even to assemble all his ship commanders.

Lee took the subordination of the battleship to the carrier with good grace, but many of the lesser battleship people haughtily continued to reject the supremacy of the flattop. Nevertheless three of the four battleship admirals in the carrier task groups for FLINTLOCK were senior to the air admirals in command. When the new fast battleships *Iowa* and *New Jersey* reported to Ted Sherman in the South Pacific in January, their captains and admiral strutted into the preoperation conference resplendent in new gray uniforms and boasting a "we're-here-to-win-the-war" attitude. Sherman, clothed in the crumbled khakis typical of all South Pacific veterans, snorted, "I don't care whether or not you can shoot your 16-inch guns, but you'd better know how to use your antiaircraft batteries!" [19]

Central Pacific Force command was not well balanced at the outset of the Marshalls operation. Spruance the nonaviator still maintained his surface-oriented staff and his faith in Ching Lee. But to Spruance's lasting credit he realized from the GALVANIC experience that battleships were ideal as antiaircraft weapons as well as capital ships, and he now permanently assigned them to the carrier task groups. Spruance's uncertainty about his carrier commanders, however, only heightened as a result of the sweeping changes made without his even being consulted.[20] Aviators Towers and Forrest Sherman had gained the ear of Nimitz by assuming the very positions closest to Cincpac that only Spruance and McMorris had heretofore enjoyed. Their first change had been to replace the agreeable Pownall with the unknown quantity of Mitscher without even consulting Spruance, who did in fact object. Regarding Mitscher on a trial basis for FLINTLOCK, Spruance assigned Pownall to his own personal staff as aviation adviser. But Spruance's fears of Mitscher were only out of ignorance, for as Admiral Halsey later observed, "Putting Ching Lee and Pete Mitscher together was the smartest thing the Navy ever did. You had the best surface tactics and the best air tactics the world has ever known." [21]

By the same token Mitscher immediately became involved in the dispute over length of bombardment and employment of the carriers in the Marshalls. Listening with misgivings to Spruance's arguments for a two-day prelanding bombardment and continued close support during and after the assault, Mitscher voiced his first disagreement with the fleet commander. He worried that Spruance might restrict the carriers to offshore artillery chores at the Marshalls, and Spruance did not change his plan. Only when the operation got under way would Spruance and Mitscher agree on the employment of the fast carriers.

The only other major command problem involved the amphibious forces. Rear Admiral Kelly Turner continued in command of the assault phase, while Major General Holland Smith commanded the landing forces once ashore. After the Gilberts operation General Richardson, Central Pacific Army commander, resented the Marines having this authority and recommended to Admiral Nimitz that the Army replace the Marines as the major landing force in the Central Pacific. The evidence of heavy Marine losses at Tarawa was plain, but Nimitz demurred and Ernie King killed the recommendation.[22]

When Admiral Mitscher hoisted his flag aboard Jocko Clark's *Yorktown* on 13 January 1944, the commanders for FLINTLOCK were firm:

FLEET ORGANIZATION

Cincpac-Cincpoa—Admiral C. W. Nimitz*
- Deputy Cincpac-Cincpoa—Vice Admiral J. H. Newton*
  - Chief of Joint Staff—Rear Admiral C. H. McMorris*
  - Assistant Chief of Joint Staff—Rear Admiral F. P. Sherman
- ComAirPac—Vice Admiral J. H. Towers
  - Chief of Staff—Rear Admiral A. W. Radford
- Commander Central Pacific Force—Vice Admiral R. A. Spruance*
  - Chief of Staff—Captain C. J. Moore*

CTF 51 (V Phib Force)—Rear Admiral R. K. Turner
CTF 54 (ComBatPac)—Rear Admiral W. A. Lee*

Task Force 58

CTF 58—Rear Admiral M. A. Mitscher (ComCarDiv 3)
Chief of Staff—Captain T. J. Hedding
CTG 58.1—Rear Admiral J. W. Reeves, Jr. (ComCarDiv 4)
Enterprise—Captain M. B. Gardner; Air Group 10
Yorktown—Captain J. J. Clark; Air Group 5
Belleau Wood—Captain A. M. Pride; Air Group 24
CTG 58.2—Rear Admiral A. E. Montgomery (ComCarDiv 12)
Essex—Captain R. A. Ofstie; Air Group 9
Intrepid—Captain T. L. Sprague; Air Group 6
Cabot—Captain M. F. Schoeffel; Air Group 31
CTG 58.3—Rear Admiral F. C. Sherman (ComCarDiv 1)
Bunker Hill—Captain J. J. Ballentine; Air Group 17
Monterey—Captain L. T. Hundt; Air Group 30
Cowpens—Captain R. P. McConnell; Air Group 25
CTG 58.4—Rear Admiral S. P. Ginder (ComCarDiv 11)
Saratoga—Captain J. H. Cassady; Air Group 12
Princeton—Captain G. R. Henderson; Air Group 23
Langley—Captain W. M. Dillon; Air Group 32
Commander Support Aircraft—Captain H. B. Sallada

*Nonaviator

2. *Open Secret Weapon*

The invasions of the Gilbert and Marshall islands were launched from Hawaii, while a few ships were staged out of Funafuti in the South Pacific. Logistically, fleet tankers had supplied oil and aviation gas at the half-way point to and after the air strikes, but the rest of the supplies had to be loaded at Pearl Harbor or Funafuti. For operations beyond Kwajalein, advance bases and great numbers of tankers would be needed. Anticipating this requirement, in October 1943 Admiral Nimitz had ordered Vice Admiral William L. Calhoun, Commander Service Force Pacific Fleet, to form two mobile service squadrons for the Central Pacific offensive. These at-sea logistical forces would become a secret weapon enabling the fast carriers to remain at sea for extended periods; they were "the logistical counterpart to the airplane carrier." [1]

Service Squadron 4 had fueled the fast carriers for GALVANIC under the control of Rear Admiral Hoover, but the major unit was to be Servron 10, forming at Pearl Harbor for FLINTLOCK. Based at Majuro as soon as that important atoll-lagoon was taken, this squadron—to service the fast carrier forces exclusively—would be comprised of provisions stores ships, barracks ships, oil tankers, hospital ships, destroyer tenders, net cargo ships, net tenders, repair ships, submarine chasers, picket boats, rearming boats, buoy boats, harbor tugs, salvage tugs, self-propelled lighters, ammunition barges, salvage barges, repair barges, floating drydocks, floating cranes, "and other types considered necessary" to serve any part of the carrier force, including its escorts.[2]

Based at Majuro and other advanced bases as the American Navy moved westward, Servron 10 would repair and service vessels at the anchorage and send out fleet oilers to replenish the carrier forces at sea. During GALVANIC 13 oilers had provided the entire Central Pacific Force with its fuel; each oiler carried 80,000 barrels of fuel oil, 18,000 barrels of aviation gasoline, and 6800 barrels of diesel oil.[3] This number of oilers would grow steadily as the war shifted westward. Fortunately Admiral Spruance had an expert logistical officer, Captain Burton B. Biggs, to keep the fleet replenished efficiently.

In general, this form of the mobile service squadrons continued throughout the rest of the war. Early in 1944 escort carriers were added to the servron for antiaircraft and antisubmarine protection, also to ferry replacement aircraft to the fast carriers. But the principle of the floating logistical base did not change, and as the fighting pressed toward Japan the carrier and service forces became even more interdependent, giving the U.S. Navy an unprecedented operating range.

Administratively separate from Calhoun's Service Force was ComAirPac's aviation logistics, the facilities for providing, servicing, and repairing Navy planes in the combat area. Until the buildup of the summer of 1943 these logistics had been part of the general supply establishment under Calhoun. Then, on 26 August, Admiral Towers had asked for an accelerated aviation logistics program to accommodate the many planes arriving in the Pacific for shore bases and for carriers. Admiral Nimitz had responded by placing all shore-based Carrier Aircraft Service Units (CASU) under ComAirPac's jurisdiction on 17 September.[4] This transfer was realistic, as the carrier-based counterpart of the CASU, the Carrier Aircraft Service Division (CASDIV), could be interchanged with the CASU. When the 96-plane *Essex*-class carrier air groups began arriving in the Pacific Towers enlarged the small CASU/CASDIV organization to 17 officers and 516 enlisted personnel per unit.[5]

Aviation logistics did not work effectively as planes continued to flow into the Pacific simply because there were so many of them and no policy existed regarding their deployment. Neither did policy cover when and if planes should be retired, repaired, or simply withdrawn from combat, nor the method by which spare parts should be distributed to the CASUs. The problem had been voiced throughout the Pacific by the end of 1943; Admiral Yarnell had considered it important enough to bring to the attention of the Secretary of the Navy in his survey of naval aviation.[6] Since ComAirPac assumed responsibility for this difficulty, the DCNO (Air), Vice Admiral McCain, wanted an aviator to tackle it. He picked Arthur Radford, much to the chagrin of both Towers and Radford, as Towers wanted Radford to remain in the Pacific. Nevertheless Radford received orders to return to Washington following FLINTLOCK to find a solution for aviation supply and maintenance problems in the Pacific.[7]

Despite this problem Central Pacific logistics had reached its final form by the time of the Marshalls invasion. Never glamorous and usually involved in back-breaking work, the logistical support units of the fast carrier forces became an open secret weapon that enabled the fast carriers to baffle and frustrate the enemy by their mobility. Without such floating logistics the fast carriers could never have developed into the fighting force that would carry the war to the home islands of Japan.

3. *Kwajalein to Truk*

PAC 10, the fleet tactical doctrine adopted in June 1943, remained in effect, although a few revisions led to a new official statement of doctrine, USF 10A, issued on 1 February 1944. The carriers were to remain "tactically concentrated" in multicarrier formations as before, with extreme latitude being left with the officer in tactical command.[1]

One major improvisation for the fast carriers to arise out of GALVANIC was night fighters. Immediately after Admiral Radford had returned from the Gilberts in December 1943 to take up his duties as chief of staff to ComAirPac, he had begun to formulate a night fighter policy. His own experience in carrier training and with O'Hare on *Enterprise* made him well suited for the task. On 16 December he issued an emergency night fighter training syllabus to each fast carrier captain. Each large carrier would form and train at least two night fighter teams of one TBF torpedo plane and two F6F fighters, or two TBFs, or two F6Fs. Every air group was to experiment with various combinations until a suitable doctrine evolved. Using ships' fighter directors and radars, the planes would maintain visual contact to avoid shooting each other down. Commander Phillips of Torpedo 6 was made officer-in-charge of night training, soon to be joined by Commander W. J. "Gus" Widhelm of Night Fighting 75 from the Solomons.[2]

Phillips' radar-equipped Avengers and escorting Hellcats achieved early success, thanks to a new shipboard radar on *Enterprise,* and on 8 January 1944 each large carrier was assigned a "Bat" team of one Avenger and two Hellcats.[3] These teams were makeshift, strengthened soon by the arrival of several specially equipped and trained F4U Corsairs and pilots.[4] Another major factor in improved night air operations was the return of Air Group 10 to *Enterprise;* its torpedo skipper, Lieutenant Commander William I. Martin, specialized in night torpedo plane attacks using the ASB radar. Air Group 6 transferred to the new *Essex*-class carrier *Intrepid* (CV-11), Captain Thomas L. Sprague. Both *Enterprise* and *Intrepid* received four-plane night Corsair teams, while *Yorktown* and *Bunker Hill* got less-trained but still effective teams of four night Hellcats each.[5]

Defense of the carriers also involved questions of the day fighters and bombers. Spruance, concerned for his carriers' safety, wanted more fighters committed to combat air patrol, a measure Towers strongly opposed because it would weaken strike groups over the target.[6] One beauty of the multicarrier formation was its compactness, requiring fewer defensive fighters, and as enemy air attacks had thus far been small the problem did not become acute in the Marshalls or Carolines. In attack planes *Bunker Hill* remained the only fast carrier with SB2C Helldivers. The plane, though plagued by constant modifications—900 by February 1944 [7]—and though aerodynamically vicious enough to earn the nickname "The Beast," had proved its effectiveness, especially in carrying the 2000-pound blockbuster, which its predecessor, the Dauntless, could not do. More "2Cs" would arrive in the Pacific with the new air groups.

The main changes resulting from the lessons learned at Tarawa and Makin involved the quantity of support for the assault forces.

It had been inadequate, and Admiral Turner recommended preliminary land-based air attacks on the target area for weeks in advance of the landing. Also, "the assault should be preceded by several days (not hours) by deliberate [ship] bombardment and day and night air attacks. Defenders should be given no rest day or night for at least a week prior to the landing. . . . Prior to the landing the selected beaches should be subjected to a devastating bombing and bombardment. . . ." [8] Admiral Hoover's land-based planes did begin to hit the Marshalls early in January, but their targets were primarily airfields, not defenses, neither of which they destroyed. Admiral Spruance's reluctance to commit his fast battleships more than two days early further frustrated Turner's wishes. Much would therefore depend upon the fast carriers.

Admiral Turner had been pleased with close air support techniques in GALVANIC and recommended similar techniques "be generally adopted as standard." He especially praised the planes of the fast and escort carriers at the Gilberts for "continually strafing enemy positions with great accuracy, coming down to within 30 or 40 feet of the ground and firing as little as ten feet ahead of the Marines." [9] The Army Air Forces had a different view. When effective heavy bombardment preceded the landings at Cape Gloucester, a key position opposite Rabaul on New Britain, late in December 1943, the AAF concluded that "pre-assault bombardment seems to have had more significance than the close support of ground soldiers after they had contacted the enemy; perhaps the most important job of the air forces during the actual invasion was to protect the amphibious forces from enemy air attacks." [10] This apology for ineffective close support doctrine illustrates how foreign were conditions in the Southwest Pacific theater to those in the Central Pacific. The carriers of the latter had both to command the air over the beach and to clear a path for the foot soldier.

The confused control of air support at the Gilberts passed with the appearance in the Pacific of new specialized amphibious command ships (AGC). Proved at the landings in the Mediterranean, the AGC centralized all amphibious command and control, from ship-to-shore movement to bombardment. Commander Support Aircraft occupied three compartments for his enlarged staff of 12 officers and 38 enlisted men in each AGC.[11] Two major islands would be assaulted in the Kwajalein atoll, Roi-Namur and Kwajalein Island. Each assault would have its own AGC and support aircraft commander. Captain Sallada (USNA '17) remained with Admiral Turner for Kwajalein, while Captain Richard F. Whitehead joined the Roi-Namur command ship. Whitehead (Massachusetts Naval Militia '16), a longtime naval aviator who had been completely sold on the need for effective close air support, had gone ashore at Tarawa as an observer and was scheduled to relieve Captain Sallada, soon to be promoted rear admiral.

Several innovations had been adopted by the air support experts. To enhance strafing, one squadron of TBF Avengers was armed with rockets, which were far more devastating than .50-caliber machine-gun fire. Also, the Support Air Control Unit ashore was strengthened, in the event ship-to-air communications failed (as at Tarawa) and to act as liaison with landing force commanders ashore. Commander Support Aircraft relieved the carriers of their control over Target Combat Air Patrol and assumed responsibility over local air target selection using these standby planes.[12] Perhaps the one great weakness of Navy close air support doctrine was the failure of pilots to heed the signals of friendly troops, with the result that the latter had been strafed at Tarawa.[13] Improved proficiency was the obvious solution to this problem.

Task Force 58 sortied from Pearl Harbor late in January 1944, the last sortie of the fast carriers from Hawaii. After the Marshalls campaign Hawaii would be left far in the rear as the Central Pacific Force surged westward. Admiral Mitscher commanded a striking force of 12 fast carriers, including two new light carriers, *Langley* (CVL-27) and *Cabot* (CVL-28), 650 airplanes, eight fast battleships, plus cruisers and many destroyers. Unknown to American naval intelligence, the last of Japan's best veteran Navy pilots had been spent at Rabaul and over the Gilberts. No carrier pilots remained, so when word of the American fleet sortie reached Truk Admiral Koga ordered the evacuation of most of his major units to Palau. Remaining behind to defend the Marshalls were 150 planes, many of them the Bettys that had attacked Pownall's carriers in these same waters on 4 December 1943. En route to the target Mitscher's planes engaged in practice exercises, while extensive preattack briefings led to the assignment of specific targets for each pilot.

The prelanding bombing and bombardment followed Admiral Spruance's original plan, thus overruling the objections of the air and amphibious commanders to a prolonged shelling. The carriers attacked the Marshall Islands on 29 January, and the battleships remained in the screen. The latter then closed on the beaches to begin shelling on the thirtieth, being relieved the next day by the regular invasion bombardment vessels. Along with Task Force 58 Admiral Turner softened up the beaches with seven old, World War I-vintage battleships, many cruisers and destroyers, and planes from eight escort carriers under Rear Admirals Ralph Davison and Van Ragsdale. Several lesser islets of the atoll fell on the thirty-first, as did the great Majuro atoll and lagoon. The Army and Marines assaulted Kwajalein and Roi-Namur islands on 1 February.

Whatever fears Admiral Spruance may have entertained about the Japanese airfields surrounding Kwajalein atoll were allayed when Task Force 58 struck on the twenty-ninth. Reeves' planes struck Maloelap while Ginder's bombed Wotje. Montgomery's air groups attacked the airdrome on Roi; Sherman's hit Kwajalein Island. The few Japanese planes over Roi became early victims of *Essex, Intrepid,* and *Cabot* Hellcats, which then strafed the many parked planes on the airstrips. By midmorning Mitscher's airplanes commanded the skies over the target areas, a supremacy that remained unchallenged. To insure that the Japanese did not stage in planes through Eniwetok Sherman shifted to that island the next three days, while Ginder moved to Maloelap for two days after which his group joined Sherman off Eniwetok. Montgomery spent the next five days pounding Roi-Namur in close support. Reeves used the same period to strike Kwajalein Island. Hoover's land-based air worked over Mili and Jaluit. The fast carriers lost 17 fighters and five torpedo planes to enemy action and 27 other planes operationally.[14]

From 31 January to 3 February the planes took directions from air support commanders in striking enemy defensive positions. With the heavy bombardment these strikes—more than 4500 flown—so dazed the Japanese defenders that resistance was much weaker than in the Gilberts.[15] The new AGCs worked wonderfully and contributed to the successful operation. On 4 February Kwajalein atoll fell. That day three of the fast carrier task groups headed for the new anchorage at Majuro, leaving Ginder's TG 58.4 to continue pounding Eniwetok. The operation had been near-perfect.

The new base at Majuro, 2000 miles west of Pearl Harbor, was the real plum of the Marshalls campaign, although the Kwajalein bomber field was no small prize. Service Squadron 10 arrived at Majuro, where Servron 4 was merged into it. Commercial tankers could now bypass Hawaii and be directly routed to Majuro. For the carriers ComAirPac established a carrier-aircraft replacement pool at Majuro for 150 to 300 planes which could be ferried to distant-operating Task Force 58 by escort carriers now being especially assigned to Servron 10.[16]

The overwhelming victory at Kwajalein had been easy compared to the uncertainty throughout the Gilberts operation, but this success could not have been possible without the GALVANIC experience. Kwajalein had fallen with such ease that the Pacific timetable needed hasty revision. The Japanese had revealed glaring weakness in the vicinity of the Gilberts and Marshalls despite the proximity of mighty Truk, meaning that a follow-up landing might be launched immediately. The original timetable called for the capture of Kavieng in the South Pacific campaign to encircle Rabaul. Spruance preferred to move against Eniwetok, however, as it was closer to Kwajalein and had a good airfield. Admiral Nimitz adopted this reasoning as soon as Kwajalein fell; he radioed Spruance suggesting Eniwetok be taken with the fresh reserve troops still afloat. Nimitz also contemplated a carrier strike on Truk in the hope of bringing on a fleet engagement.[17]

The original date for capturing Eniwetok atoll had been 1 May 1944, with Truk not to be hit by an air raid before late March 1944.[18] But Kwajalein had changed all that, so Spruance took Nimitz's proposal to his amphibious commanders, Turner and Holland Smith. Turner, in perfect sympathy, endorsed the plan, whereupon Howlin' Mad Smith immediately produced an operation plan he had already drawn up for such an exigency.[19] As for Truk, Mitscher had no doubt that his planes could give it a shellacking, though losses might be heavy. So Spruance replied to Nimitz in the affirmative, and on 10 February he got the go-ahead for Eniwetok–Truk.[20]

The brief lull at Majuro enabled Admiral Mitscher to make a few changes in personnel. For the first time since the new carriers had arrived in the Pacific, some of their skippers were being promoted to flag rank. And, instead of being returned to the United States for breaking-in as rear admirals, as was the standard practice, they were kept in the Pacific. Jocko Clark, fighting skipper of Mitscher's flagship *Yorktown*, was appointed Commander Carrier Division 13, a new billet; his relief was Captain Ralph Jennings. J. J. Ballentine, bright, intelligent captain of *Bunker Hill*, became chief of staff to ComAirPac; his relief was Captain Tom Jeter. And

"Slats" Sallada, Commander Support Aircraft, took over an escort carrier division; his relief was Captain Dick Whitehead. All three men were detached at Majuro.

For task group commanders, Mitscher had only a few difficulties. Montgomery, though quiet, was every bit as obnoxious as Black Jack Reeves and Fighting Freddie Sherman, and petty jealousies arose among them. Sam Ginder, junior to Montgomery by four years, to Reeves by five, and to Sherman by six, had performed less satisfactorily than the others, Mitscher felt. Ginder flew his flag aboard old, less maneuverable *Saratoga*, and Mitscher left his task group to cover Eniwetok when the other three groups went to Truk. Of the four carrier task group admirals, probably Sherman was the most frustrated. Senior to and more combat-experienced than Mitscher, he felt he rated more influence in the over-all planning. Admitting his own oversensitivity, Sherman thought to himself in his diary, "I am tired of playing second fiddle to these boys." [21]

On 11 February Admiral Spruance assembled his commanders aboard his flagship, battleship *New Jersey*, for what Ted Sherman called "a rather meaningless talk." The Truk strike, said Spruance, would be commanded by himself in his flag battleship, although air operations would be under Mitscher in *Yorktown*. If the Japanese fleet offered battle, as usual Spruance would assume command, using Ching Lee's Battle Line of six fast battlewagons (the two others remained with Ginder). Sherman for one found the operation too battleship-oriented, for again Spruance seemed to disregard the impact of the carriers upon any possible surface engagement. However, after Spruance had finished talking, Baldy Pownall, still acting as air adviser to Spruance, briefed the carrier admirals.[22]

Three task groups comprised the Truk attack force: Reeves' TG 58.1 with Matt Gardner's *Enterprise*, Ralph Jennings' *Yorktown*, and Mel Pride's *Belleau Wood;* Montgomery's TG 58.2 with Ralph Ofstie's *Essex*, Tommy Sprague's *Intrepid*, and Malcolm Schoeffel's *Cabot;* and Sherman's TG 58.3 with Tom Jeter's *Bunker Hill*, Bob McConnell's *Cowpens*, and Lester Hundt's *Monterey*. Ginder's TG 58.4 covered the Eniwetok landings with John Cassady's *Saratoga*, George Henderson's *Princeton*, and Gatch Dillon's *Langley*.

When Task Force 58 sortied from Majuro on 12–13 February, it comprised the first independent carrier strike of that size in the war—nine fast carriers—more powerful than the six-carrier Japanese force that had bombed Pearl Harbor. And Truk was every bit as important to the Japanese Fleet as was Pearl to the United States Fleet. Of Truk naval intelligence knew little. The Japanese had hidden and fortified it as their main Central Pacific fleet anchorage, earning it the sobriquet "Gibraltar of the Pacific." Mitscher could only say, "All I knew about Truk was what I'd read in the *National Geographic*, and the writer had been mistaken about some things." [23] His pilots had definite feelings concerning Truk. For instance, Commander Phil Torrey, skipper of Air Group 9 on *Essex*, said, "They didn't tell us where we were going until we were well on the way. They announced our destination over the loudspeaker. It was Truk. My first instinct was to jump overboard." [24]

No sooner had the carriers cleared Majuro than Ted Sherman began using his old independent techniques, specifically no signals, leaving the escorts to form on the flag carrier during flight operations. He had enjoyed independent carrier force command since late-Guadalcanal days, even at Rabaul and the Gilberts. Now, for the first time, he was subject to a tight, three-task-group cruising formation, the tightest to that time. Admiral Spruance immediately criticized him and ordered him to conform to PAC 10, which he begrudgingly did, noting that it was "a funny command status" that enabled a non-airman to issue carrier cruising orders to an aviator admiral.[25] Servron 10 oilers rendezvoused with the force 640 miles northeast of Truk on the fourteenth and fueled the big ships. These oilers then returned to Kwajalein to take on oil from commercial tankers in preparation for the post-strike refueling, a procedure that now became standard.[26]

A predawn-launched, 72-plane fighter sweep on 17 February opened the air attack against "impregnable" Truk; launching point was 90 miles to the northeast. The idea of an all-fighter sweep belonged to Mitscher, to clear the air of Japanese fighters and give the bombers a clear approach to the target.[27] It certainly beat Joe Clifton's technique of having the fighters hug the bombers all the way in. Clifton, incidentally, missed the Truk strike as his *Saratoga* planes were working over Eniwetok.

Lieutenant Commander Herb Houck's Fighting 9 from *Essex* later recorded some impressions regarding their arrival over Truk. Lieutenant John Sullivan: "Our first sight of Truk was a black curtain of AA. They held it until we got over the target but they weren't too sharp. We surprised them. Their ships were at anchor, dead in the water, and that made them duck soup. It was wonderful! We never had such a setup before." Lieutenant (jg) Marvin Franger: "Right over the center of Truk all hell broke loose. God damn! That was the worst scared I ever was. . . ." Lieutenant (jg) William Arthur: "I watched flak following just behind another plane in a sort of impersonal fascination. It wasn't till later that it occurred to me the same thing was following me." Then the Hellcats tangled with the Zeros. Herb Houck: "It was our superior pilots and superior tactics [that] gave us victory over the Japs. Sometimes they just kept coming at us and they must know they will be knocked down." Lieutenant (jg) Eugene A. Valencia, who shot down three enemy planes: "These Grummans [Hellcats] are beautiful planes. If they could cook, I'd marry one." [28]

About 80 Japanese planes and heavy, inaccurate flak challenged Mitscher's sweep, but only half the Zeros sought to engage. For most of the morning the air battle raged, resulting in the loss of 50 Zeros and four Hellcats. By noon, the U.S. Navy controlled the air over Truk. The carrier planes then strafed the parked aircraft on three strips and destroyed or damaged about 150 in all, leaving another 100 undamaged. Eighteen incendiary-laden Avengers augmented the strafing. In shipping, the attackers were disappointed to find only two light cruisers and two destroyers, along with some 50 auxiliaries and transports. The bombers went directly to work and had a field day. Before Task Force 58 left Truk, about 140,000 tons of enemy shipping lay sunken or piled up on the beach.

During the air attack Admiral Spruance formed a small battle line of two fast battleships, two heavy cruisers, and four destroyers to engage the few Japanese warships attempting to escape from Truk lagoon. The battleships' scout planes did the reconnaissance work, while Commander "Brute" Dale of *Bunker Hill* spotted ships' fire against the Japanese light cruiser and two destroyers that gave battle. *Cowpens* Hellcats covered the surface force, alerting the big ships to avoid threatening torpedo wakes emanating from the enemy "tin cans." One SBD was splashed by friendly fire, but the cruiser and one can were sunk, while the other destroyer got away, this action being fought shortly after noon on the seventeenth. One aviator who observed this handiwork pointed out, "This is how we can win battles in the future. Teamwork is the answer. We find them and slow them down. The battlewagons close in and pretty soon there aren't any more 'possibles' and 'probables.' They're all 'definitely sunk'!" [29]

That night the excitement continued. A six-plane strike of Kate torpedo bombers succeeded when one of the planes eluded a *Yorktown* night fighter to plant a "fish" into the side of *Intrepid.* Night fighter direction had failed in its first employment.[30] Tommy Sprague, after assessing damage to his ship, had to retire to Pearl for many months of repairs to *Intrepid; Cabot* and several cruisers and destroyers escorted the stricken ship. Then the night specialists of Torpedo 10 on *Enterprise* carried out a very successful radar night attack with twelve TBM Avengers armed with 500-pound bombs. Another 60,000 tons of shipping left the Japanese registry as the torpeckers scored many direct hits. For the first time in U.S. naval history, the fleet had exercised an all-weather air capability in combat.

The next day the carrier planes struck again, but opposition amounted to only light antiaircraft fire. The planes bombed installations on the main islands but encountered no Japanese aircraft. Spruance's battle force rejoined the carrier screens after having circled Truk, and during the afternoon Task Force 58 retired from the area, leaving behind only the lifeguard submarines engaged in their marvelous rescues of downed aviators. The fast carrier force had destroyed more than 250 Japanese planes and about 200,000 tons of enemy shipping, along with inflicting extensive damage to the base and airfields. The Japanese shot down 17 American planes, of which 26 crewmen were lost, and they put carrier *Intrepid* out of action for several months.

With Truk under attack on 17 February, the assault on Eniwetok took place without fear of interference. Sam Ginder's task group worked over the Eniwetok islets on the eleventh and thirteenth, wrecking most of the atoll's defenses. On the seventeenth Ginder returned with Van Ragsdale's three escort carriers for more bombing. Rear Admiral Harry Hill commanded the expeditionary force, assisted on the command ship by the new Commander Support Aircraft, Captain Dick Whitehead. Close air support was minor, however, since the Army commanders did not fully appreciate it, but the carriers launched several strikes and many combat air patrols over the force.[31] The Marines and Army assaulted the first atoll at Eniwetok on the seventeenth and pushed across the rest of the islets until Japanese resistance ceased on the twenty-second. The carriers stood by until 28 February.

Meanwhile Task Force 58 did not return to Kwajalein or Majuro but remained deep inside Japanese waters. Servron 10 oilers refueled the force on the nineteenth, then returned to Majuro. Admiral Spruance, who also returned to the new advanced base, released Admiral Mitscher to head even farther west for air strikes against the Marianas, a bold objective indeed! *Intrepid* and *Cabot* had already left, and *Enterprise* departed as well, bombing bypassed Jaluit on the twenty-first. Mitscher now had two balanced task groups of three flattops each: Montgomery's 58.2, *Essex, Yorktown*, and *Belleau Wood*, and Sherman's 58.3, *Bunker Hill, Monterey*, and *Cowpens*.

For the first time Mitscher had independent command over his ships, with the result that he soon faced his first major decision. As the force made its final run-in toward the launching point on the night of 21–22 February an enemy Betty sighted it and escaped to report Mitscher's presence. But Mitscher wasted no time in deciding what to do; the overwhelming success at Truk underscored his confidence. "We have been sighted by the enemy," he informed his crews; "we will fight our way in." [32]

Fight they did. Beginning at 10 P.M. enemy torpedo bombers launched repeated attacks. Although Mitscher had night fighters available, the faulty night-fighter direction that had led to *Intrepid's* torpedoing kept the planes on board.[33] The events of this night compared with the action of 4–5 December 1943 off Kwajalein (from which *Lexington* was still in the yards recovering) except that Mitscher was running in instead of away. Most of the enemy attack fell upon Montgomery's group, where Mitscher was riding, but skillful maneuvering kept the ships undamaged. Mitscher radioed over to Ted Sherman, "But where the hell were you?" Fighting Freddie replied, "Japs like your company better than mine." [34] Antiaircraft guns splashed about ten enemy planes, the rest breaking off before dawn.

Mitscher launched his predawn strikes against Saipan and Tinian from a position 100 miles west of the targets in order to face into the wind for launch and recovery. Many of the 74 planes that rose to intercept Mitscher's Hellcat sweep were shot down; several dozen others on Saipan and Tinian were strafed and bombed. An F6F which strayed away located a new airfield and more planes at Guam, which was then attacked. Several enemy transports were sunk by the bombers, while others fled into the open sea where five of Admiral Lockwood's submarines awaited them. The submarines scored many hits on succeeding days, bringing the total enemy tonnage lost as a result of the strike to 45,000 tons. Japanese planes destroyed in the Marianas came to 168, American planes six. Also, Mitscher's planes took many photographs of the beaches at Saipan, where the landings would take place. Task Force 58 retired for Majuro during the afternoon.[35]

As the ships headed for "the barn"—home—the normally inarticulate Mitscher hailed his intrepid sailors; "After the Nips' loss of face at Truk, we expected a fight, we had a fight, we won a fight. I am proud to state that I firmly believe that this force can knock hell out of the Japs anywhere, anytime. Your standard is high. I can only congratulate all hands on an outstanding performance and give you a stupendous 'well done.' "[36]

The Truk–Marianas raids by Task Force 58 revolutionized naval air warfare. By giving the fast carriers "extreme mobility," as Jack Towers and his air admirals had insisted, they could destroy the enemy's air power and discourage his fleet from interfering at an amphibious operation. Thus, Towers now concluded, the mission of the fast carriers was strategic, not merely tactical, guarding the beaches. Task Force 58 succeeded because of surprise, intelligent selection of targets, superior ordnance, good timing, "and the qualitative and quantitative superiority of our planes and pilots."[37] When Secretary Knox said Navy pilots were scoring 13:1 victories over the Japanese in aerial combat, *Yorktown*'s crack Air Group 5 countered with the claim that its odds were 95:1, a fair indication of the muscle in Task Force 58.[38]

February 1944 had changed the complexion of the war in the Central Pacific. The Marshalls had been cracked and Truk battered, leaving the Marianas wide open to attack and invasion. Doubt and uncertainty were erased by Task Force 58's proven superiority over anything the Japanese could send up in the Pacific. Truk's reputed strength had been a myth, Allied strategists now realized. Changes would have to be made in Central Pacific strategy.

4. *Striking Westward*

The impunity with which Task Force 58 had attacked Truk and the Marianas demonstrated the basic flaw in Japan's chain of "unsinkable carriers": they could not move. Once neutralized by mobile carrier air, these islands could be bypassed and then kept neutralized by Admiral Hoover's land-based air forces. The night after Spruance left Truk, 19 February, Captain Carl Moore, his chief of staff, recommended to his commander that such a strategy be used on Truk. Baldy Pownall, still riding aboard, was impressed with Moore's memorandum and forwarded a copy to Nimitz.[1] This source added strength to the growing feeling that Truk should be bypassed.

In any case, the rapid clearing of Kwajalein and Eniwetok for airfields, the neutralization of Mili, Jaluit, Maloelap, Wotje, and Truk, and the development of Majuro as a fleet anchorage enabled Nimitz to accelerate the Pacific timetable. On 1 March he informed Admiral King that a major amphibious assault could be made in June, either on Truk or the Marianas, depending on the analysis of photographs taken by carrier planes of both places. This new recommendation would move up the target date from 20 July if it was Truk, from 1 October if it was the Marianas.[2]

Meanwhile, in late February and early March 1944, General MacArthur's forces attacked the Admiralty Islands north of New Guinea, resulting in another strategic controversy. The Admiralties include the great anchorage of Seeadler Harbor and surrounding Manus Island, which would become—like Majuro—another major fleet base for the advance westward. Manus lay on MacArthur's Southwest Pacific right flank and on Nimitz's Central Pacific left flank, and both men claimed they would develop the base for their own use. But MacArthur wanted it only for his Seventh Fleet (Vice Admiral Kinkaid), while Nimitz intended that Manus be administered by his Third Fleet commander, Admiral Halsey. The issue was critical, as any future strategy involved Manus. Nimitz would base the fast carriers there for his proposed eventual invasion of Formosa, bypassing the Philippines; MacArthur would base his fleet there for his proposed liberation of the Philippines, which he had sworn to do. These differences reverberated all the way up to the JCS, where they became "the most controversial single problem" during March 1944.[3]

All these strategic issues were resolved when Admirals Nimitz and Forrest Sherman journeyed to Washington for discussions on Pacific strategy with the President and the JCS on 11 and 12 March. Ernie King relied on Sherman to review the issues, although the Manus controversy became somewhat tense when MacArthur's representatives held forth. Nevertheless, the two days of talks led to decisions which "greatly clarified the situation."[4] Good aerial photographs had demonstrated the feasibility of landing in the Marianas, while Task Force 58 had made the assault on Truk unnecessary. The JCS therefore ordered Nimitz to continue the neutralization of Truk and to land at Saipan on 15 June; he was to plan for an assault on Formosa in February 1945. MacArthur, on the other hand, would go ahead and secure New Guinea but cancel the Kavieng operation, then assault the southern Philippines, notably Mindanao, late in 1944; he was to plan for landings on Luzon in February 1945.[5]

The JCS directive compromised the situation. Both Southwest Pacific and Central Pacific forces would direct offensives toward the Luzon bottleneck. Both would use the base at Manus, both would be mutually supporting. Although some problems were merely postponed, and although some Pacific commanders registered surprise at the JCS ignoring the recommendation for one big offensive from the southwest,[6] the new plan was realistic. The Japanese, trying to meet the Allied counteroffensive into the western Pacific, would not be able to stop two drives simultaneously. Also, though the Marianas were a salient exposed to air attack from Japan (Towers' criticism against taking them), the Fast Carrier Task Force could win command of the Philippine Sea to the west, thus insuring the safety of occupying forces and B-29s based in the Marianas.

These decisions eliminated the importance of Rabaul, now left behind by the deep penetrations of Task Force 58 into Japanese waters and by MacArthur's occupation of the Admiralites. The invasion of Rabaul was never again discussed, and with Truk effectively neutralized the Japanese withdrew the last surviving planes of CarDiv 2 from Rabaul on 20 February 1944. The seizure of Manus, Green, and Emirau islands in February and March—west, north, and east of Rabaul respectively—completed the encirclement of that great Japanese base. Routine "milk-run" bombings of Rabaul by land-based planes began early in March. Later that month the fighting on Bougainville in the Solomons ceased, bringing a close to the South Pacific campaign. Admiral Halsey was now out of a job as Commander South Pacific, but as Commander Third Fleet he reported in May to Admiral Nimitz for further assignment.

Another officer due for a change was Vice Admiral John H. Towers. With the completion of the Marshalls operation he could be elevated to be Nimitz's deputy, in which capacity he would have "great operational and planning responsibility and would be in a position to influence strategy and tactics as well as techniques and administration." Rear Admiral Pownall would then return to Pearl Harbor as ComAirPac, "a position which is primarily concerned with administration and maintenance."[7] But Pownall did not want to return to Hawaii. He preferred to remain at sea on Admiral Spruance's staff and had Spruance recommend that Captains Fred Pennoyer and Raöul Waller, ComAirPac maintenance and personnel officers, be sent to the fleet at Majuro where Pownall could assume his duties as ComAirPac.[8]

Towers went directly to Admiral Nimitz after the morning Cincpac conference on 22 February and showed Nimitz a copy of Spruance's despatch. Towers pointed out that the continued presence of Pownall on Spruance's staff would lead to confusion, not so much because of the administrative and logistical nature of ComAirPac but simply because of continued differences of opinion of "a broad operational nature" between Spruance–Pownall on the one hand and Nimitz–Towers on the other. Towers was referring to Spruance's conservative use of carriers during amphibious operations and to Pownall's tendency always to support Spruance. By eliminating Pownall from the fleet, Spruance could deal with only one aviator, Rear Admiral Mitscher, his carrier commander. Pownall at Pearl Harbor would be occupied with logistics, operational air matters there being left to Towers. Nimitz accepted Towers' reasoning, rejected Spruance's proposal, and ordered Pownall to return to Pearl. On the 28th Pownall relieved Towers as ComAirPac, whereupon Towers fleeted up to Deputy Cincpac–Cincpoa, replacing Vice Admiral Newton.[9]

Other changes were made in the Pacific air command. Ted Sherman, at sea since early 1943, went home on leave early in March, still disgruntled that he had not been given a higher post.[10] He reported to San Diego for temporary duty as Commander Fleet Air West Coast, relieving Rear Admiral William Keen Harrill. Harrill (USNA '14), a longtime aviator, had been shore-based most of the war but now took over Sherman's old post as ComCarDiv 1. Another new carrier admiral was Rear Admiral Frank D. Wagner, ComCarDiv 5, who had been relieved as Assistant DCNO (Air) by Rear Admiral Radford. Radford's relief as chief of staff to ComAirPac was Rear Admiral John J. Ballentine. Two other prominent air officers at Pearl Harbor were Captain Cato D. Glover, Jr., Assistant War Plans Officer to Cincpac, and Commander George Anderson, whom Towers managed to have shifted over to his staff as "special assistant."

The major change involved Pete Mitscher. He had so conclusively proven his mettle to King, Nimitz, and Spruance as fast carrier leader during February that on 16 March he was upgraded from senior carrier division commander to be Commander Fast Carrier Forces Pacific Fleet, and five days later was promoted to the rank of vice admiral. Simultaneously, Spruance was elevated to full admiral, and John Hoover and Ching Lee became vice admirals. Rear Admiral Montgomery relieved Mitscher as ComCarDiv 3.

Another major innovation was the assignment of a nonaviator to be Mitscher's chief of staff. This was a consequence of airman Towers' appointment to be Deputy to non-airman Nimitz, just as airman Halsey's chief of staff, Mick Carney, was non-air. Ernie King now felt air and surface should be completely integrated at the top commands as qualified officers became available. Significantly, no top aviator was yet assigned to Admiral Spruance's staff or to Vice Admiral Lee's battleship staff. Spruance and Lee had only junior aviation advisers who enjoyed no influence on operations.

The new surface officer assigned as TF 58 chief of staff was Captain Arleigh A. "31-Knot" Burke, a distinguished destroyerman from the Solomons. Initially, because of their different backgrounds, Mitscher and Burke did not get along. Mitscher tried to make a figurehead of Burke by going directly to Captain Hedding, his aviator deputy chief of staff. Burke, every bit as individual as Mitscher, would not cooperate, so the men locked horns. But soon a frosty mutual respect grew up, and as spring gave way to summer the frost melted. Mitscher and Burke soon became an inseparable team.[11]

To the career naval aviator, Task Force 58 represented the first team, the major leagues, so that vice admirals to ensign pilots sought duty with the fast carriers. The DCNO (Air), Vice Admiral Slew McCain, even flew out from Washington to Majuro to try to persuade Mitscher to relinquish his command and go home for a rest. Mitscher was still tired from his early campaigns, but giving up his command was out of the question. Frank Wagner had managed to get Radford recalled to Washington so he could get out to the Pacific—to Radford's undying resentment. And when Radford reported to Washington he elicited a promise from McCain that he would be returned to the Pacific as soon as he completed his work—a promise McCain did not honor. Once with the fast carriers, however, each officer had to meet Mitscher's requirements, including the staff of 140 officers and men. For the staff Mitscher began to pick his own people, most prominently his new operations officer, Commander Gus Widhelm, whom he had not seen since the battle of Midway.[12]

The next scheduled operation, Hollandia, brought together Central and Southwest Pacific forces briefly, a phenomenon not to be repeated until both reached the Luzon bottleneck separately. Nimitz was to use Task Force 58 to neutralize Japanese air forces in the Palau Islands and then employ it for close air support during the Hollandia landings. The Hollandia affair had been planned for several weeks by the combined staffs of Nimitz, MacArthur, and Halsey, during which time they had clashed over the Manus question. The climax to the planning came on 25 March 1944 when Nimitz and Forrest Sherman, fresh from the discussions in Washington, arrived at Brisbane, Australia, to coordinate the use of the fast carriers during the landings.

Nimitz expressed great fear that his fast carriers would be brought within range of the 200 or 300 Japanese planes based at Hollandia and neighboring New Guinea airfields. Then there were the planes in the Palaus that could strike from the north, but Nimitz told MacArthur of the planned strikes there in a few days. On the matter of the Hollandia planes, Nimitz made General Kenney promise to knock out most of them by 5 April. The landing would take place on the fifteenth. In addition, Nimitz had dispatched *Saratoga* to the Indian Ocean to join the British in tying down Japanese planes in the East Indies. This last joint meeting, despite General MacArthur's "moments of forensic oratory" (noted Forrest Sherman), "established a background for better cooperation in the future" between the two theater commanders and staffs.[13]

Several fast carrier operations preceded the Hollandia landings. Carrier *Lexington*, fresh from West Coast repairs to her rudder damaged in the December Kwajalein strike, launched battle-practice air strikes against bypassed Mili on 18 March, though the two-battleship, one-carrier force was under battleship command, Ching Lee's. Admiral Mitscher then hoisted his flag in *Lexington*. On the twentieth Emirau was occupied under cover of carrier-based air from *Enterprise* and *Belleau Wood* under Black Jack Reeves and two escort carriers under Ralph Davison. At the same time another new *Essex*-class carrier reported to Majuro, the new *Hornet* (CV-

12), Captain Miles R. Browning, the flagship of Rear Admiral Jocko Clark, ComCarDiv 13. No available command was open for Clark, but Mitscher would have one for him soon, so Clark joined Task Force 58 in "makee-learn" status.

Worth particular notice was the return of Miles Browning, tactical hero of Midway, to the Pacific after an absence of almost one year. Browning still typified the irascible combat commander and learned veteran carrierman so sorely needed in the Pacific. Indeed, during his two years on Admiral Halsey's staff, Halsey had several times recommended him for flag rank. But Browning's wild streak continued to interfere with both his personal and professional lives, so that he angered many of his peers in the Pacific Fleet, not the least of whom was Mitscher.[14] Downright ineptness as captain of the new *Hornet* led to his eventual dismissal from command on 29 May 1944, and he was exiled to an Army post on the plains of Kansas for the duration of the war and his career.

Admiral Mitscher readied Task Force 58 for strikes against the Palau Islands, a distant target that would subject his carriers to more day and night air attacks. Night air operations annoyed Mitscher—who, although he now had ample night fighter teams, did not care to keep his air departments awake at night. This being the case he did not encourage night air training, causing his night pilots to lose their keen proficiency. Deck crashes resulted, leading to greater reluctance on the part of the task force commander to employ night interceptors. Nevertheless, since the Japanese had already proved their effectiveness in night attacks, a solution had to be found. One idea put forth was a special night carrier, but neither ComAirPac nor Mitscher took action on the proposal at this time.[15]

For the Palau strike, Admiral Spruance assumed over-all command in heavy cruiser *Indianapolis*, but as usual left tactical command of the carriers to Mitscher, and since the operation was one big carrier raid Mitscher maintained command throughout. Lee would assume tactical command should the Japanese elect to give battle with their battleships. For the first time, two of the task groups contained four carriers, Montgomery's and Ginder's, though Jocko Clark was riding with Montgomery's group and Mitscher with Ginder. Reeves had three carriers.

Task Force 58 sortied from Espiritu Santo on 23 March, swinging south to avoid Truk-based search planes. However, the latter sighted the carriers on the twenty-fifth and alerted the Japanese Fleet, which then fled Palau for points west. Admiral Koga took an airplane that never reached its destination, probably because of weather; Koga was lost, after Yamamoto the second Japanese Nimitz to die. Japanese torpedo planes made their usual nocturnal visit to Mitscher's advancing ships on the night of 29 March, but the Force's antiaircraft fire drove them off.

PALAU STRIKES
March–April 1944

Commander Central Pacific Force—Admiral R. A. Spruance*
Chief of Staff—Captain C. J. Moore*
CTF 58—Vice Admiral M. A. Mitscher (ComFastCarForPac)
Chief of Staff—Captain A. A. Burke*

CTG 58.1—Rear Admiral J. W. Reeves, Jr. (ComCarDiv 4)
Enterprise—Captain M. B. Gardner; Air Group 10
Belleau Wood—Captain A. M. Pride; Air Group 24
Cowpens—Captain R. P. McConnell; Air Group 25
CTG 58.2—Rear Admiral A. E. Montgomery (ComCarDiv 3)
Bunker Hill—Captain T. P. Jeter; Air Group 8
Hornet—Captain M. R. Browning; Air Group 2
Cabot—Captain M. F. Schoeffel; Air Group 31
Monterey—Captain S. H. Ingersoll; Air Group 30
CTG 58.3—Rear Admiral S. P. Ginder (ComCarDiv 11)
Yorktown—Captain R. E. Jennings; Air Group 5
Lexington—Captain F. B. Stump; Air Group 16
Princeton—Captain W. H. Buraker; Air Group 23
Langley—Captain W. M. Dillon; Air Group 32

*Nonaviator.

At dawn on the thirtieth Mitscher launched his fighter sweep of F6F Hellcats from 90 miles south of the target. These planes easily eliminated the 30 airborne Zeros, then joined the bombers in concentrating on the large volume of merchant shipping at Palau. Many new bombing techniques were used. Two squadrons of SB2C Helldivers carried more bombs in conventional dives to score more hits proportionately than the SBDs. Steep-diving Hellcats dropped light bombs at low altitudes with limited success, but their strafing had a devastating effect. The TBF Avengers excelled in both masthead bombing and torpedo attacks; eight "turkeys" ganged up on a lone Japanese destroyer by attacking from eight surrounding positions—the "can" could not escape and was blown to bits.

The all-purpose Avengers also engaged in aerial mining of Palau waters, the first and only time this was done by fast carrier planes during the war. The new squadrons on *Bunker Hill* and *Hornet* and the veteran unit on *Lexington* performed the work against intense antiaircraft fire. They laid down their mines, many of which had been delay-fuzed, successfully, with the result that undamaged shipping at Palau was trapped there for another six weeks—until the mines were swept. However, the task of aerial mine-sowing had been dangerous for slow, exposed Avengers. The job was thereafter passed to land-based long-range bombers. During the night, 60 Japanese planes flew into Palau from distant bases, affording Mitscher's boys more targets the next day.

On the thirty-first Montgomery's and Ginder's groups returned to bomb Palau, while Reeves' struck Yap Island to the northeast. All three groups attacked Woleai on 1 April. A few planes also visited Ulithi, but Palau afforded the only profitable targets during this raid. Along with several dozen Japanese planes destroyed in the air and on the ground, Mitscher's air groups and the delay-armed mines claimed about 130,000 tons of Japanese shipping at the Palaus. They missed the Japanese fleet, which had fled to Singapore, Borneo, and the homeland, but the raid had indirectly cost Admiral Koga his life. Of 44 airmen who ditched at sea, lifeguard submarines, destroyers, and seaplanes retrieved 26—an unprecedented record though still not good enough for Mitscher. Task Force 58 had neutralized Palau, thus relieving Nimitz and MacArthur of anxieties about their northern flank during the Hollandia operation.[16]

Smooth though the Palau raid appeared, it involved the first major crisis over task group command. During the operation Rear Admiral Sam Ginder had worried himself to the point of becoming totally ineffective as task group commander. Fortunately, Captain Truman Hedding of Mitscher's staff had been assigned temporarily to Ginder's staff, and he immediately had taken charge. When Task Force 58 returned to Majuro Mitscher went to see Admiral Nimitz, who had arrived there accompanied by Forrest Sherman, Pownall, and others of the Cincpac staff for a visit. Mitscher "expressed dissatisfaction with the way Ginder had handled his task group," whereupon Nimitz gave Mitscher the authority to relieve Ginder. Mitscher did so immediately and lost no time in appointing the well-known fighter Jocko Clark to the post. The same thing had happened to Captain George Fairlamb of *Independence* at Marcus, and he too had been relieved without hesitation.[17]

Ginder had not been a coward, nor had he done anything deliberately wrong. In fact, he had had an excellent record both in peacetime and during the war, until he achieved carrier division command. Then, apparently, he began to worry about the heavy responsibilities he had to shoulder, which had undermined his emotional composure and eventually his physical alertness. Ginder had issued a newspaper called *Tallyho Ack-Ack* that was read over his ships' loudspeakers daily, much to the embarrassment of readers and the consternation of listeners. Mitscher had left Ginder behind during the Truk raid, then assigned Hedding to help him during Palau. But Ginder's worries mounted and his confidence weakened until he had become visibly nervous and unsure of himself during the last operation. He was thus unsuited to command in combat, but he was still valuable in administration, so Nimitz placed him in charge of the aircraft replacement escort carriers for the duration.

Mitscher wanted admirals who would not only fight but would also seek out the enemy and look for a fight. Jocko Clark perhaps fitted this requirement more than any other of Mitscher's admirals; coincidentally, he was the first carrier admiral Mitscher appointed after taking command. Though very junior, Clark (USNA '18) had an eagerness for battle that impressed Mitscher. The latter had hoisted his flag aboard Clark's *Yorktown*, had retained him for task group command, and—beginning at Hollandia—throughout the rest of the war Mitscher always kept Clark's task group closest to the enemy—in the van going in and in the rear coming out. Montgomery, Reeves, and Ted Sherman were equally eager fighters, especially Sherman, who went so far as to defy Mitscher on occasion. But the boss wanted such cantankerous individuals, knowing if they fought among each other and with him they would also fight the enemy. To such combat leaders Mitscher knew he could delegate authority and know the job would be done. Sometimes these men got into each other's way, in which case Mitscher's excellent qualities as a strong coordinator came into play.

At first, Mitscher's decision to replace Ginder with Clark created a stir at Pearl Harbor. Again, the mild-mannered Spruance and Pownall teamed up to keep Ginder at least in fast carrier planning, so again Jack Towers requested a special conference to discuss Ginder's case and to support Mitscher's decision. On 19 April Nimitz, Towers, McMorris, and Forrest Sherman discussed the matter, first in the presence of Pownall and Ballentine, then without them. In the last situation, Sherman stated bluntly that Mitscher did not want Ginder with the fast carriers and that Mitscher blamed Pownall for stalling Ginder's detachment. Cincpac respected Mitscher's perogatives as the tactical commander, so Commander Task Force 58 never again had such a personnel change challenged.

Another change involved designations. After the end of the fighting in the South Pacific theater in March, there was no reason for Nimitz to split his operations into South and Central Pacific. All were now in the Central, so on 14 April 1944 he abolished the title Central Pacific Force in favor of Fifth Fleet, the title by which the Force had been known administratively (hence Task Force 58). Simultaneously, all forces under Admiral Halsey became known as Third Fleet. Both fleets continued under Cincpac's authority. The same day Admiral Spruance shifted his flag to Pearl Harbor to begin planning the Marianas campaign, leaving Mitscher on his own until June.

Fifth Fleet participation in the Hollandia operation was unnecessary and therefore anticlimactic to all the coordinated planning and the Palau strikes. Hollandia, New Guinea, contrasted to Eniwetok, the last coral atoll to be assaulted in the Pacific, in that several large airfields served this huge island. But General Kenney's bombers smashed all New Guinea air early in April, while Task Force 58 had ruined Palau as a staging base for the Japanese.

The fast carriers sortied from Majuro on 13 April under Mitscher's direct command—three task groups of four carriers each under Clark, Montgomery, and Reeves. They feinted toward Palau again, then commenced air attacks along the New Guinea coast on the twenty-first. Only snoopers from the west harassed Clark's ships. The next day the troops landed under a perfected close air support system whereby Commander Support Aircraft controlled both target selection and air defense of the entire Seventh Fleet amphibious force. A force fighter director performed this function as a regular staff member. Since Hollandia was a Seventh Fleet operation under MacArthur's Southwest Pacific command, air support was commanded by Air Force Colonel Eareckson in a destroyer. But he had little to do; the Japanese offered only token resistance, and soon air controllers took over ashore.[18] Mitscher launched his long-unused night fighters to watch for enemy night torpedo-plane attacks and to make noise over the jungle where Japanese might be trying to sleep.[19] On the twenty-fourth the Task Force withdrew to the new anchorage at Manus, where its oilers were waiting.

HOLLANDIA–TRUK OPERATIONS
April–May 1944

Commander Task Force 58—Vice Admiral M. A. Mitscher
  Chief of Staff—Captain A. A. Burke*

CTG 58.1—Rear Admiral J. J. Clark (ComCarDiv 13)
  Hornet—Captain M. R. Browning; Air Group 2
  Belleau Wood—Captain John Perry; Air Group 24
  Cowpens—Captain R. P. McConnell; Air Group 25
  Bataan—Captain V. H. Schaeffer; Air Group 50
CTG 58.2—Rear Admiral A. E. Montgomery (ComCarDiv 3)
  Bunker Hill—Captain T. P. Jeter; Air Group 8
  Yorktown—Captain R. E. Jennings; Air Group 5
  Monterey—Captain S. H. Ingersoll; Air Group 30
  Cabot—Captain M. F. Schoeffel; Air Group 31
CTG 58.3—Rear Admiral J. W. Reeves, Jr. (ComCarDiv 4)
  Enterprise—Captain M. B. Gardner; Air Group 10
  Lexington—Captain E. W. Litch; Air Group 16
  Princeton—Captain W. H. Buraker; Air Group 23
  Langley—Captain W. M. Dillon; Air Group 32
Commander Support Aircraft—Colonel W. O. Eareckson, USAAF

* Nonaviator.

Along with the neutralization of Palau, the integrity of the Hollandia landing forces had to be preserved by the continued neutralization of Truk. Therefore South Pacific-based B-24 Liberator bombers had executed the first land-based daylight raid on Truk on 29 March and were surprised by 90 Japanese fighters who gave battle. The bombers shot down 31 planes and shot up more on the ground, losing two of their own number.[20] Truk had obviously been restored as an operative airdrome and would have to be attacked in force again. Nimitz passed the word to Mitscher at Manus, and Task Force 58 immediately sortied, twelve carriers strong, to finish off Truk. As *Yorktown*'s Plan of the Day informed that ship's crew, "Today we start a two-day return engagement at that popular theater which was so receptive on our last visit.

This time we intend our performance to knock them completely off their feet." [21]

A predawn fighter sweep on 29 April began the second carrier air battle over Truk, followed immediately by a Japanese torpedo-plane attack on Task Force 58. Patrolling Hellcats and ships' antiaircraft fire drove off the attackers, while Japanese ack-ack over Truk was equally intense. Also, 60 Zeros challenged the F6Fs, but the Japanese pilot showed less ability in each successive encounter, and Mitscher's flyers won control of the air over Truk by midmorning. The next day the bombers destroyed more planes on the ground, bringing the total to 90 destroyed. Twenty-six carrier planes with 46 men went into the drink, but over half were picked up, 22 by lifeguard submarine *Tang* alone. This operation finished Japanese designs to utilize Truk as a major airfield, though the big complex still bristled with antiaircraft guns and a few airplanes.

The work of the carriers completed, Mitscher detached his heavy surface ships to get in a few licks. The cruisers bombarded Satawan Island on 30 April, while Vice Admiral Lee formed the Battle Line to shell Ponape on 1 May. Mitscher set his course for Majuro with Task Groups 58.2 and 58.3 and assigned Clark's 58.1 to give the battleships air cover. For one hour on the afternoon of the first the big ships shelled Ponape and drew no reaction. The Japanese sought out the carriers, especially at low altitude where the old Mark 4 radar could not detect their planes. But Jocko Clark was one up. He had instituted visual fighter directors on the carriers who spotted an incoming flight of four planes at low level and directed their destruction by patrolling F6Fs.[22] Lee and Clark then headed for Eniwetok, now an auxiliary anchorage relieving the load on Majuro.

A one-month breather followed the Hollandia–Truk foray, giving Mitscher the opportunity to make final preparations for the Marianas operation. In particular, he needed to replace some of his veteran air groups with new units; Air Group 5 on *Yorktown* had been in every battle since the Marcus strike in August 1943. In January 1944 the ComAirPac staff had established a rotation schedule for air groups on a basis of six to nine months of combat operations. In April the intensive pace of the Central Pacific offensive caused this tour to be shortened definitely to six months.[23] Under this program, six air groups were rotated home in May for regrouping, reequipping, and reassignment. In addition, more carriers reported for duty. *Essex*, fresh from overhaul, returned, and the new *Wasp* (CV-18), Captain C. A. F. Sprague, arrived. So did the last of the new *Independence*-class light carriers, *San Jacinto* (CVL-30), Captain Harold M. Martin.

Now that so many carriers were available, 15 with three others under repair or overhaul, another task group command billet opened up. Already Mitscher had four carriers per group, with no intention to increase the size. So a new group of three flattops was formed. Two men were immediately available to command it, Rear Admirals Keen Harrill (ComCarDiv 1) and Frank Wagner (ComCarDiv 5). Wagner did not, however, measure up to Admiral Mitscher's formula for leadership; boastful and irritating, he lasted only a short time before transfer to the Southwest Pacific in June for the duration. Harrill was equally untried but seemed to hold promise, so Mitscher assigned him to "makee-learn" status.

With two new carriers, three new air groups, and one new admiral, Mitscher decided on a battle practice operation against Marcus and Wake. He formed Task Group 58.6 under Rear Admiral Montgomery, including *Essex*, *Wasp*, and *San Jacinto*. The strike also involved several experiments along with the training. Specialists in target selection had joined the ComAirPac staff; they intended that each pilot be prebriefed on his assigned target before takeoff in order that bombs not be wasted on insignificant targets. The Marcus–Wake raids would prove or disprove the value of this technique.

Montgomery's force departed Majuro on 14 May 1944, then divided as it approached Marcus. *San Jacinto* steamed to the north and west searching for enemy picket boats, while *Essex* and *Wasp* attacked the island on the twentieth. Heavy antiaircraft fire made bombing accuracy extremely difficult and negated the use of rockets, where a long glide was needed. The next day weather interfered, and Montgomery broke off the attack. *San Jacinto* rejoined, then on the twenty-fourth all three carrier air groups attacked the installations on Wake. Damage to both islands was sufficient to isolate them from the Marianas operation, but prebriefed target selection had failed. Admiral Pownall as ComAirPac concluded that each island target was unique, and selection would have to be left to tactical air commanders who could correlate their attack potential with certain primary targets.[24]

As May 1944 ended, the greatest battle of the Pacific war since

Midway was about to begin. With overwhelming numbers of ships, planes, and pilots, Task Force 58 was capable of covering the landing at Saipan Island as well as fighting the Japanese carrier-battleship fleet. Seven months of overwhelming aerial victories had molded it into this excellent condition. The Marianas campaign would prove to be the final test for the Fast Carrier Task Force.

Six:
Battle of the Fast Carriers

Saipan Island was Japan's command post for defense of the western Pacific. Along with neighboring Tinian, Guam, Rota, and Pagan, it forms the main islands of the Marianas group, in 1944 situated in the very center of Japan's network of "unsinkable carriers." With the many airfields in the Marianas, Japan staged through planes from Japan and the Bonin-Volcanos in the north to all points east and south—Wake, Truk, New Guinea, and the Palaus. Fleet units could anchor there, but facilities were limited. In American hands, the situation in the Marianas would be reversed; very-long-range B-29 Superfortresses could bomb Japan, while air and supply units could be staged west toward new targets.

Defensively, the Japanese occupied the interior position, meaning they could shift their forces conveniently to any threatened point in the Pacific. And with Admiral Nimitz holding the Marshalls and General MacArthur the northeast coast of New Guinea, they did not know where the next blow would fall, the Marianas or Palau-western New Guinea. Had American and Japanese military, naval, and air forces been evenly matched the Japanese could have stopped an attack at either of these points. This was in fact their strategy during the spring of 1944. Unfortunately for Japan, the United States was so greatly superior militarily that it could continue its two-pronged advance in the Central and Southwest Pacific with almost equal strength. When such a superior force operates from the exterior position, the interior position loses its otherwise inherent advantages.

1. The Japanese Fleet

By 1941 or even 1942 standards, the Japanese Mobile or Third Fleet was practically brand-new. At the top it had lost two supreme commanders, Yamamoto and Koga, in air mishaps. The new Commander-in-Chief Combined Fleet, Admiral Soemu Toyoda, assumed command in May 1944 aboard a light cruiser permanently based in Tokyo Bay. In addition to his physical separation from the fleet, Toyoda had had no experience in aviation, which made him doubly hampered to direct an air-centered defense of the western Pacific. But his chief of staff, Vice Admiral Kusaka, had had wide experience in naval aviation as a prewar carrier admiral and then as land-based air commander in the defense of Rabaul. Furthermore, Admiral Toyoda's new air operations officer was Captain Mitsuo Fuchida, whose 3000 hours of flying time had included the attack he had led at Pearl Harbor. Also stationed at Imperial Headquarters was the brilliant Commander Minoru Genda.[1]

Air defense of the western Pacific would be the responsibility of First Air Fleet, under the direct command of Naval General Headquarters. In February 1944, with the aerial evacuation of Rabaul, all land-based planes had been withdrawn to western bases, the four big ones in the Marianas (Guam, Tinian, Saipan, and Rota), two in the western Carolines (Babelthuap in the Palaus and Yap), and one in the Volcanos (Iwo Jima). Air Fleet headquarters was at Tinian under Vice Admiral Kakuji Kakuta, the veteran air commander whose carriers had covered the Aleutian landings in 1942. Theoretically, Kakuta would have over 1600 airplanes on the seven islands to concentrate at any threatened point.[2] Also, it should be noted in passing that headquartered at Saipan was the "commander in chief of the fleets of the central Pacific region and commander in chief of the 14th Aerial Fleet," Vice Admiral Chuichi Nagumo, victor of Pearl Harbor and goat of Midway whose new post meant nothing.

If the land-based air forces failed to repel the invaders, the carriers would have to do the job. In March 1944 the First Task Fleet had been established from the Third Fleet, both under Vice Admiral Jisaburo Ozawa. Ozawa had been Third Fleet commander since late 1942 but had fought no sea battles since that time. As Third Fleet commander he paralleled Spruance, as First Task Fleet commander he paralleled Mitscher, an administrative organization that had serious limitations. In addition, he assumed the post of ComCarDiv 1. As a fleet command he and his staff were eminently suited, but they could not qualify—by American standards—for either carrier post. Neither Ozawa nor "his entire senior, operations, and air staffs" had any experience in fighting enemy carriers.[3]

The other three carrier flag officers suffered from equal inexperience. Rear Admiral Takaji Joshima had been ComCarDiv 2 since August 1943; before that he had commanded the carrier *Shokaku* during the Pearl Harbor attack and had served under Kusaka at Rabaul. But he and all but one of his staff lacked experience in carrier battles. That one was his air staff officer, Lieutenant Commander Masatake Okumiya, who had served on Kakuda's staff during the Aleutians campaign. Only Rear Admiral Sueo Obayashi, ComCarDiv 3, had commanded at the battle of Midway, but his ship was light carrier *Zuiho* attached to the assault force and therefore out of the main battle. Rear Admiral Chiaki Matsuda became ComCarDiv 4 upon its re-establishment in May 1944 (it had been abolished after Midway); his experience was entirely in ordnance, culminating in the 1942–1943 command of superbattleship *Yamato*.

In carrier production the Japanese still trailed the United States by one year, and had only one new fleet carrier ready for combat, 29,300-ton *Taiho* (75 planes). A magnificent ship with armored flight deck and many antiaircraft guns, *Taiho* became Ozawa's flagship. The other carriers of CarDiv 1 were Coral Sea veterans *Shokaku* and *Zuikaku* (75 planes each). The rest of the Japanese fast carriers were conversions. The 1942 former merchant ships *Junyo* and *Hiyo* (54 planes each) teamed with 13,360-ton converted submarine tender *Ryuho* (36 planes) to form CarDiv 2. The ships of CarDiv 3 were small flattops of the CVL variety, former sub tender *Zuiho* (30 planes) and new 11,190-ton converted seaplane tenders *Chitose* and *Chiyoda* (30 planes each). CarDiv 4 included the most unusual warships in the world, *Ise* and *Hyuga*, battleships whose after main batteries had been replaced by a short flight deck. These hermaphrodite carriers could launch planes which would have to land ashore. The Japanese decided not to commit this division yet, so it never figured in the Marianas campaign. All of Japan's carriers had radar, but Admiral Ozawa doubted whether the operators had mastered its use.[4]

In aircraft, the Japanese Navy was inferior qualitatively and quantitatively. A new version of the Zero was coming out, but it took second place to the Grumman Hellcat in capability. A new bomber also appeared, but instead of going to the more experienced bomber pilots of CarDiv 2 it went to the green aviators of CarDiv 1, the fault of poor administration.[5] Ozawa's large carriers of CarDiv 1 carried 79 fighters, 70 dive bombers, 51 attack (including torpedo) planes, and seven reconnaissance aircraft.[6] The converted carriers of Joshima's CarDiv 2 had a smaller strike force of 81 Zero fighters, 27 dive bombers, 18 attack and nine scout planes. Obayashi's CarDiv 3 of only 90 planes was to provide bombing services only, but because of the short flight decks of these converted CVLs bombers could not gain sufficient momentum for launch. Therefore, at the last minute, the bombers were removed in favor of 63 lighter-armed Zero fighter-bombers.[7] In addition, CarDiv 3 carried 12 torpedo and six attack planes.

Airplane performance in the last analysis depends on the men who fly them, and here the Japanese Navy suffered what would prove to be its fatal weakness. The land-based naval aviators were all post-Truk trainees, raw and still new to the cockpit; Vice Admiral Kakuta expended many of them by shifting them repeatedly to various threatened points in the Pacific, a practice that cost him dearly in operational crashes.[8] The carriers faired similarly. Their senior air group commanders had dropped ten years in age since 1942. CarDiv 1 had lost its veteran pilots at Rabaul and in the Marshalls, so that by May 1944 its pilots had less than five months of training. Some veterans of CarDiv 2, trained at Singapore during the fall of 1943, had escaped from Rabaul in February to give Ozawa *some* experience in his air groups, but ideally their skill could be sharpened only by many more months of practice. CarDiv 3, organized after the first Truk affair, boasted pilots of less than three months in the cockpit. Cumulatively, the average Japanese Navy pilot had trained 275 hours in the air, or almost half that of his predecessor one year before. His American counterpart had at least 525 hours flying time before assignment to a carrier.[9]

After fleeing Palau and the approach of Task Force 58 in late March, Third Fleet reassembled at Tawi Tawi, a secluded anchorage between Mindanao and Borneo in the Celebes Sea. There the pilots were to resume training, but green pilots could not be allowed to jeopardize the carriers so their drills were held ashore. Unfortunately, the airstrip at Tawi Tawi had not been completed, and flight training was suspended throughout May.[10] The carrier air groups therefore lacked coordination and unity, combat experience, night qualification, and general familiarization with fast carrier operations.[11] They were not ready for battle and would not be for many months by their own standards.

Tactically, the Japanese had long since abandoned their separated fleet units and since July 1942 had adopted the carrier task group comprised of three carriers escorted by battleships, cruisers, and destroyers. In June 1944 Admiral Ozawa concentrated his battle line of four battleships under Vice Admiral Takeo Kurita, Commander-in-Chief Second Fleet, with the light carriers in CarDiv 3, while a fifth battlewagon accompanied CarDiv 2. Interspersed thoughout the three task groups were seven cruisers and 28 destroyers. These ships, with the nine carriers and 450 aircraft, formed the largest Japanese fighting force during the war, but also the most undertrained and inexperienced.

United States naval intelligence correctly estimated the strength of this "new Japanese First Striking Fleet." It carried planes, so Admirals Spruance and Mitscher were informed, "equivalent in number to those carried by 4 *Essex* (CV) and 3 *Independence* (CVL) class carriers." Furthermore, by the end of May 1944, American intelligence surmised that the Japanese had concentrated over 400 land-based planes in the Marianas and Palaus with which to repel the American fleet.[12]

The only question facing the enemy of Japan was if and how the Japanese would commit their fleet to defend the Marianas. The

MARIANAS CAMPAIGN

Commander-in-Chief Combined Fleet—Admiral Soemu Toyoda
    Chief of Staff—Vice Admiral Jinichi Kusaka
  Chief, Bureau of Aeronautics—Vice Admiral Nishizu Tsukahara
  Commander-in-Chief First Air Fleet—Vice Admiral Kakuji Kakuda
  Commander-in-Chief Third Fleet—Vice Admiral Jisaburo Ozawa

    ComCarDiv 1—Vice Admiral Ozawa
      Taiho, Shokaku, Zuikaku
    ComCarDiv 2—Rear Admiral Takaji Joshima
      Junyo, Hiyo, Ryuho
    ComCarDiv 3—Rear Admiral Sueo Obayashi
      Chitose, Chiyoda, Zuiho

Japanese high command, however, had no doubts. Saipan was too valuable; it *had* to be defended at all costs.

2. *American Battle Tactics*

The United States Fifth Fleet in June 1944 comprised the most powerful battle fleet the world had ever known. For a carrier action, Task Force 58 included fifteen fast carriers. For a surface engagement, the Battle Line could form with no less than seven new fast battleships. The Pacific Fleet command for the mammoth Marianas operation and possible naval battle included practically all veterans of carrier operations and amphibious attacks.

The expectation of a major naval battle during the assault on Saipan provided the major difference between this operation and the Gilbert and Marshall campaigns, at which Admirals Nimitz and Spruance had considered but not really anticipated the appearance of the Japanese surface fleet. This opportunity every American naval officer in the Pacific had awaited eagerly, and few doubted the outcome of such a battle. Admiral Nimitz believed that the Japanese would use "every bit of strength" they could muster to defend the Marianas, but the Fifth Fleet had "plenty of muscle" to meet such a challenge, enough in fact "to make a decisive engagement favorable to us." When reporters informed Cincpac that a Japanese radio broadcast had suggested a naval battle was pending, Nimitz declared, "I hope they stick to that idea. I don't know anything more we can do to provoke these people into a fleet action." [1]

Nimitz clearly demonstrated confidence in his commanders' ability to win such a major battle, but in doing so he took too much for granted. The United States Navy had never in its 150-year history fought what could be termed a major fleet action involving great numbers of ships on the scale of Trafalgar (1805), Tsushima (1905), or Jutland (1916). The shock of Pearl Harbor and the extraordinary good luck of American forces at Midway had made all previous wars and surface engagements seem suddenly irrelevant. The airplane had seen to that, as was further demonstrated by the smashing blows at Rabaul and Truk. But historical forces, antedating World War II by many generations of admirals, so influenced American fleet battle tactics in 1944 that Nimitz would not achieve the crushing naval victory he so confidently expected during the Marianas campaign.

FLEET ORGANIZATION

Commander-in-Chief United States Fleet—CNO—Admiral E. J. King

Commander-in-Chief Pacific Fleet—Cincpoa—Admiral C. W. Nimitz*

Deputy Cincpac-Cincpoa—Vice Admiral J. H. Towers
Chief of Joint Staff—Rear Admiral C. H. McMorris*
Deputy Chief of Staff—Rear Admiral F. P. Sherman
ComAirPac—Rear Admiral C. A. Pownall
Chief of Staff—Rear Admiral J. J. Ballentine

Commander Fifth Fleet—Admiral R. A. Spruance*
Chief of Staff—Captain C. J. Moore*
CTF 51 (Amphibious Force)—Vice Admiral R. K. Turner
CTF 58—Vice Admiral M. A. Mitscher
Chief of Staff—Captain A. A. Burke*

CTG 58.1—Rear Admiral J. J. Clark (ComCarDiv 13)
Hornet—Captain W. D. Sample; Air Group 2
Yorktown—Captain R. E. Jennings; Air Group 1
Belleau Wood—Captain J. Perry; Air Group 24
Bataan—Captain V. H. Schaeffer; Air Group 50

CTG 58.2—Rear Admiral A. E. Montgomery (ComCarDiv 3)
Bunker Hill—Captain T. P. Jeter; Air Group 8
Wasp—Captain C. A. F. Sprague; Air Group 14
Monterey—Captain S. H. Ingersoll; Air Group 28
Cabot—Captain S. J. Michael; Air Group 31

CTG 58.3—Rear Admiral J. W. Reeves, Jr. (ComCarDiv 4)
Enterprise—Captain M. B. Gardner; Air Group 10
Lexington—Captain E. W. Litch; Air Group 16
San Jacinto—Captain H. M. Martin; Air Group 51
Princeton—Captain W. H. Buraker; Air Group 27

CTG 58.4—Rear Admiral W. K. Harrill (ComCarDiv 1)
Essex—Captain R. A. Ofstie; Air Group 15
Langley—Captain W. M. Dillon; Air Group 32
Cowpens—Captain H. W. Taylor; Air Group 25

CTG 58.7 (Battle Line)—Vice Admiral W. A. Lee (ComBatPac)*

Commander Support Aircraft—Captain R. W. Whitehead

* Nonaviator.

The origins of fleet tactics lie in the Age of Sail, from the first English broadside fired in action against the French fleet off Shoreham in 1545.[2] Slowly, over a period of two entire centuries, British tactics developed into a rigid pattern, codified in the Permanent Fighting Instructions, violation of which at one time meant death.[3] These so-called "formalist" tactics demanded strict line of battle, tight control by the commanding admiral, and therefore the possibility of withdrawal from an unfavorable situation. Risk, personal initiative by subordinates, division of forces, or any other deviation was intolerable. The British navy fought many battles using formalist tactics, but few resulted in a clear decision. The obvious weaknesses in this concept, like equally rigid tactics in land warfare, led to its modification during the worldwide war of the American Revolution, 1777–1783.

The new school of "meleeist" tacticians advocated exploitation of the initiative to achieve concentrated firepower against one part of the enemy battle line, then overpowering it piecemeal. Certain risks were involved, but the rewards of a complete victory were generally greater. The chief proponent of the melee concept was Admiral Viscount Horatio Nelson, final conqueror of the French fleet during the Anglo-French wars of 1793–1815. So devastating were Nelson's victories and so thorough his tactics at Cape St. Vincent, the Nile, and Trafalgar campaign and battle that they immediately became legendary and brought to an exciting climax the age of sailing-ship battles.[4]

Ironically, Nelson's lessons disappeared immediately after the wars ended, leading to a revival in the British Navy of the conservative formalist doctrine throughout the transition of naval technology from wood and sail to steam and steel. The appearance of the armored battleship around 1890 along with the big-battleship navies stressed by Captain Alfred Thayer Mahan led to the ultimate in battle fleets, the British Grand Fleet, after 1906 centered around its new, powerful dreadnoughts. The architect of this navy, Admiral Sir John Fisher, was so engrossed in his material accomplishments (the dreadnought and the battle cruiser) that he gave little attention to tactics and ended up endorsing rigid formalism. So did his wartime Grand Fleet commanders, Admirals Sir John Jellicoe and David Beatty.

The great battle fleet action off Jutland in the North Sea in May 1916 was not won decisively because of this uncritical adherence to mid-eighteenth-century tactical doctrine. Vice Admiral Beatty began the action by driving south with his battle cruisers in an attempt to cut off the approaching German battle cruisers from their base in Germany; then Jellicoe would appear with the battleships and seal the trap. Beatty made one major error and almost committed another. Formalism required complete information be passed on to the Fleet commander so he could form his line; scouting was one function of the battle cruisers. As Beatty pressed south, the main German battleship force suddenly appeared, and Beatty turned about but not without losing some ships to enemy fire. His mistake was his failure then to keep Jellicoe informed of German strength and movements. His near-mistake was in almost getting trapped himself between the German battle cruisers and battleships.

As Beatty rejoined Jellicoe, with the entire German High Seas Fleet close behind, Jellicoe deployed his battle line in the classic maneuver to "cap the enemy T." He succeeded, as the point of the advancing German column met the concentrated salvos of the British battle line. Heavily damaged by this deadly fire, the German ships, many badly damaged, turned away. Here Nelsonian melee tactics had called for "general chase" to break up the retreating foe and to exploit his confusion by concentrating on key portions of the enemy fleet. But the Fisher–Jellicoe formalism allowed no such thing, and Jellicoe maintained his line. The German fleet pressed forward again, again to have its "T" capped, and again turned away. Jellicoe maintained his line, neither offering pursuit nor allowing individual action by subordinate commanders. By this point, darkness had covered the North Sea with the two fleets running on parallel courses south, Jellicoe keeping the Grand Fleet between the German ships and their home base. Night action being foreign to British doctrine, he planned to reopen the battle at dawn.

Again, lack of information hampered Jellicoe's plans. Admiralty intelligence in London had information that the German fleet would attempt to break through the rear of Jellicoe's column. This information was not passed on, and before Jellicoe could learn that his rear was engaged the German battleships had passed through his formation en route to their base. Lacking information and a night doctrine, Jellicoe did nothing. The battle was over. Technical shortcomings and fear of torpedoes had added to Jellicoe's woes in the battle, but his failure to achieve an overwhelming victory may be attributed mostly to poor tactics.

Had the German fleet been destroyed, the Grand Fleet would have been released from continuing its watch over German warship movements, and in fact another battle almost ensued ten weeks later. Furthermore, the inland waters of the Baltic remained in German control due to the fighting potential of the High Seas Fleet. Neither Jellicoe nor his successor Beatty even attempted to modify the formalist orientation of fleet tactics following Jutland. In December 1917 the Grand Fleet was reinforced by the Sixth Battle Squadron, five dreadnoughts of the United States Navy, which had finally come of age. This navy immediately adopted British principles and tactics.

During the twenty years after World War I, neither British nor American tacticians found reason to change the tactics of Jutland. In another war, they reasoned, another Jutland would be fought, the only difference being the substitution of the aircraft carrier for the battle cruiser. Also, more emphasis was given to night tactics, especially by the Japanese navy. At the United States Naval War College during the 1920s and 1930s junior officers studied and restudied the battle of Jutland along formalist lines. While the carriermen were evolving their own radical battle theories in the fleet, the battleship experts—"Gun Club"—were preparing tactics for a super-Jutland at the Naval War College.

One of the foremost tactical theorists at the College was Raymond A. Spruance, who spent no less than three tours of duty there in the period 1926 to 1938. In his last tour, 1935–1938, Captain Spruance was student, then head of the Tactics Section, and finally head of the overall Department of Operations. During these years, two key men closely associated with Spruance were none other than Commander C. J. Moore in the Senior Tactics class and Captain Richmond Kelly Turner in tactics, strategy, and operations classes as student then instructor.[5] Leaving the Naval War College as leading experts in battleship tactics, Spruance assumed command of the battleship *Mississippi,* Moore became operations officer to Commander Battle Force, and Turner took command of heavy cruiser *Astoria.* When Admiral Spruance became Commander Central Pacific Force in 1943 he specifically requested that his old friends and colleagues Moore and Turner be assigned as his chief of staff and amphibious commander—and they were. Spruance, Moore, and Turner had determined the tactics of tying down the carriers at the Gilberts, and the same three men drew up the operations plan for the Marianas. And for the actual legwork of decision-making in the Central Pacific, Spruance depended heavily upon Moore and Savvy Forrestel, operations officer and longtime ordnance expert.

Spruance therefore was battleship-trained in the formalist tradition. He could delegate command, but his operations plans were always precise and thorough, which was essential to the success of his many complex campaigns, especially those involving amphibious forces. His one great battle experience at Midway had been a fluke. He was thrown into an emergency situation with a strange staff and new tools of warfare, plus melee-type orders calling for operations governed by "calculated risk." Spruance had simply allowed that staff and those weapons to execute these orders and to win the battle for him. Then, just as quickly, he had left the carriers for staff duty. His next command assignment came a year later, the Gilberts operation. There, with the keen advice of Moore and Turner, he had eagerly planned for battle using his Battle Line of new fast battleships. But the Japanese had chosen not to commit their surface fleet at the Gilberts.

Spruance was a formalist in the tradition of Fisher and Jellicoe. He preferred to leave nothing to chance, to plan for every possibility. An amphibious operation required such precision. But he had confidence in his amphibious commander, Turner, and he knew his amphibious support commanders, all frustrated battleship officers relegated to leading old battleships in laying down monotonous barrages. He had great respect for Vice Admiral Ching Lee, his fast battleship commander, who had led battleships night and day at Guadalcanal; with seven battlewagons Lee could fight the surface battle long awaited by the prewar, Jutland-oriented naval tacticians. Of his aviators and carriers Spruance knew less, the result of his own ignorance, inexperience with them, and the lack of a senior air officer on his staff. And knowing less, he could not meticulously plan for the role of the carriers in his campaigns. PAC 10 had decreed that decisions regarding carriers be left up to the local commander—Mitscher—as new situations arose. And this stipulation meant uncertainty, initiative by subordinates breaking the plan of battle, hence risk or, historically speaking, the use of melee tactics.

The big naval battle Spruance wanted, and by tying down the carriers at the Gilberts he relied on his battleships to engage the enemy battle line. Since then, however, he had lost this prerogative. To be sure, the Battle Line could be formed, but the fast carriers were now to provide the main punch of the fleet, operating offensively, away from his main amphibious forces. This destroyed the neat package of the formalist philosophy. The fast carriers were still tactically alien to him, and he necessarily regarded their use with caution. The conditions for another Jutland might have existed in November 1943, but by June 1944 and the imminence of the big battle these conditions seemed to be fading.

The fast carriers embodied the meleeist doctrine. Mobile and long-ranged in their capability to give battle, they had to remain flexible. Personal initiative was assumed; each pilot had to use his own judgment, as did carrier captains and admirals, to maneuver away from enemy attacks. Great risk was therefore involved in any carrier battle, for a carrier was not merely less effective tied to a formalist doctrine, it was downright vulnerable—to ships' fire, bombing planes, and submarines. It *had* to keep moving, and the battleships—with their protective antiaircraft batteries—had to move with the carriers. But Towers, Mitscher, and the other carriermen had no doubt that their carriers would carry the day. They knew their weapons as Spruance knew his battleships, and they had unbounded faith in them. Of this assurance regarding carriers Spruance could not boast.

None of this discussion is intended to imply that Spruance did not still want to destroy the Japanese Mobile fleet. Going into the Marianas operation he told General Holland Smith that he hoped to inflict enough damage to the Japanese fleet to take it out of the war. Having done this, Spruance reasoned, he would dispose not only of the threat to the American forces in the Marianas "but would facilitate subsequent operations by removing the menace of the Japanese Navy, always a potential danger to the amphibious operations we were undertaking at increasing distances from our bases." [6]

So Spruance had the long-range view in mind. But how was he going to achieve it—by the formalist tactic of tying down all carriers and battleships to the beach for a certain if less spectacular or thorough victory, or by the meleeist tactic of releasing Task Force 58 to seek out and destroy the Japanese surface fleet once and for all by accepting certain variables and risks? If Spruance's record was any indication, he would obviously do the former. But new forces were at work—the fast carriers, which required a revision of his traditional thinking. This view was projected by none other than Spruance's over-all boss, the Commander-in-Chief

United States Fleet, Admiral Ernie King, in March 1944. King's statement, in his annual report to the Secretary of the Navy, is such a thorough affirmation of the melee school that it deserves quotation in full:

> One of the mental processes that has become almost a daily responsibility for all those in command is that of calculating the risks involved in a given course of action. . . . Calculating risks . . . is not reducible to a formula. It is the analysis of all factors which collectively indicate whether or not the consequences to ourselves will be more than compensated for by the damage to the enemy or interference with his plans. Correct calculation of risks, by orderly reasoning, is the responsibility of every naval officer who participates in combat. . . .

King added that the calculation of risks in combat had been "properly discharged" thus far.[7]

If Spruance did not know how the Japanese would challenge his forces, Vice Admiral Jack Towers did. On 13 June 1944, two days after Task Force 58 had begun pounding the Marianas, Towers suggested to Forrest Sherman that the "Japs might well proceed within 600 miles of [the] Marianas and from that point launch their aircraft with the intention of landing in the Marianas after an attack on our forces, thus keeping their ships out of range of our carrier aircraft."[8] Unhappily, the ambitious Sherman had begun to move away from his old boss to devote full attention to his new and higher-ranking one, Nimitz. The old working relationship was beginning to deteriorate, and now Sherman did nothing about Towers' very sound idea. So the next day before the regular morning meeting Towers went directly to Nimitz with his concept of the Japanese plan and suggested that Spruance "be advised of this possibility." Towers' reasoning impressed Nimitz enough to call a special meeting on 15 June to discuss it. Towers recommended ordering Spruance to send Task Force 58 west to seek out the Japanese fleet should it be committed, but again Sherman demurred. However, Nimitz ordered Admiral McMorris to draw up a dispatch for Spruance relating the discussion at the meeting.[9]

Armed with this expert opinion from an aviator, Spruance awaited reports of Japanese fleet movements. Unfortunately, he suffered the same fate as Jellicoe at Jutland in not receiving such information as completely as he should have. As we shall see, airborne and submarine radio and radar were sadly deficient in supplying the fleet commander with quick, accurate information. And complete information regarding enemy movements was absolutely essential for any formalist commander before he would dare commit (or risk) his forces in offensive action.

Raymond Spruance was the logical choice to command the American fleet in the Marianas campaign and the anticipated battle. As a strategist he had few peers, and as a tactician he had the necessary credentials. But technology had antiquated many of the tactics he had earlier learned and helped to formulate. As over-all operational commander, he could have remedied this weakness in either of two ways. First, he could have added a senior aviator (rear admiral) to his staff to give him the expertise that Miles Browning had provided at Midway. Or he could have given his carrier commander complete tactical freedom to fight the fleet battle. But events were moving so swiftly that Spruance could see no need to take either action. As a formalist, he relied upon his fellow formalist tacticians, vintage 1937, and maintained rigid control over his fleet in battle.

Though Spruance enjoyed relative freedom to conduct this campaign, Admirals King and Nimitz could have influenced Spruance's personnel and tactics. King had months before assigned nonaviators to be chiefs of staff to air admirals Halsey and Mitscher, but he had not yet assigned aviators to head the staffs of battleship-oriented Spruance and Lee. But he *had*, as noted above, made known his views on the need for calculated risk, the very orders Nimitz had issued to Spruance at Midway. The unqualified successes of Spruance and the fast carriers since November 1943 had led both King and Nimitz to trust Spruance's tactics implicitly and to assume he would use the strategic mobility of the carriers at the Marianas as well as he had at Truk. Or they uncritically took for granted Spruance the formalist would use melee tactics. In this groundless assumption they were sadly mistaken.

3. *Attack on the Marianas*

Along with the fast carrier admirals, Mitscher, Reeves, Montgomery, Harrill, and Clark, several other air flag officers joined the Fifth Fleet for the great battle. Vice Admiral Slew McCain, the DCNO (Air), came all the way from Washington to ride as an observer with Spruance in flagship *Indianapolis*, which he boarded 26 May. Because McCain was scheduled to relieve Mitscher several months later, he brought with him his future operations officer,

Commander J. S. "Jimmy" Thach. Rear Admiral Ralph Davison, the first of many junior escort carrier admirals to fleet up to fast carrier command, went aboard *Yorktown* in "makee-learn" status. In addition, Admiral Turner's bombardment force included eight escort carriers under Rear Admirals Slats Sallada, Felix Stump, and Gerald F. Bogan. Again, Captain Dick Whitehead was Commander Support Aircraft. Mitscher's chief of staff was still nonaviator Captain Arleigh Burke, but Mitscher also retained pilot Captain Truman Hedding as deputy chief of staff. There is no reason, beyond his passion for a small staff, that Admiral Spruance could not have worked out a similar arrangement on his own staff.

Participating vessels in the Marianas operation numbered more than 600. Task Force 58 included seven heavy and eight light fast carriers, seven fast battleships, three heavy and seven light cruisers, and an unprecedented total of 60 destroyers. The bombardment force, along with the eight escort carriers, was comprised of seven prewar "old" battleships, six heavy and five light cruisers, and many destroyers. Two escort carriers attached to the service squadrons provided replacement aircraft. To all this, Admiral Nimitz provided the services of over two dozen submarines; the ensuing operation and naval battle would become "the high points of the war" for submarines operating in support of the fleet.[1]

A major concern of Admiral Spruance was the protection of support ships and landing craft from enemy air, surface, and submarine attack day or night—for he still had vivid memories of the relatively slight but successful Japanese counterattacks in the Gilberts. His best antiaircraft defense was the combat air patrol fighters of the fast and escort carriers, in addition to the many 5-inch/38 cal., 40mm, and 20mm ack-ack guns.

Defensive fighters could be most effectively employed by sophisticated fighter direction, insured by the recent installation of the new Mark 12 and Mark 22 shipborne radars which scanned the vertical plane to detect all incoming flights of enemy planes up to 150 miles away. Hasty packaging of these sets for immediate deployment had resulted in some flaws, but the ships also maintained visual scanning to assist fighter directors.[2] Lieutenant Joseph R. Eggert on *Lexington* coordinated fighter direction for Task Force 58, assisted by a fighter director officer on each of the four fast carrier task group flagships. The amphibious command ships also carried fighter directors to protect the transports and landing craft.

But these had yet to be used against enemy planes; the carriers had done all fighter direction at the Gilberts and Marshalls.[3]

Defense against submarines and surface ships also depended largely on the antisubmarine and search patrols of carrier aircraft. The dependable destroyers carried the latest sonar submarine-detection gear, but occasional doubts over the nature of a contact could always be eliminated by visual aerial verification. Enemy surface ships were not supposed to elude patrolling planes, but if they did shipboard search radars could scan as far as their antennae could "see" to the horizon. In the old battleships of the amphibious force this distance was never more than 30 miles, or just outside the range of large-caliber enemy naval guns. This fact more than any other required Admiral Spruance to have absolutely correct information regarding enemy fleet movements. Not inconceivably an enemy battleship might suddenly appear on the horizon and begin shelling the offshore shipping—a highly unlikely but nevertheless real possibility.

Long-range detection of enemy fleet movements would best insure the security of the Saipan landing forces, and for this Spruance relied upon Vice Admiral Lockwood's far-ranging subs, shore-installed high-frequency radio direction finders (HF/DF), long-range patrol bombers and seaplanes, and radar-equipped carrier search planes. All these information-gathering tools had peculiar shortcomings which compromised Spruance's ability to rely upon them. The submarines patrolled Ozawa's own back yard, but they could see an enemy fleet only from the water level of the periscope and could not ascertain the size and composition of an enemy naval force. Furthermore, some radio transmissions were not always clear and took precious time to be verified at submarine headquarters in Hawaii, then forwarded to the Fleet. HF/DF could pinpoint an enemy radio transmission but also told nothing of size and composition. Navy patrol planes suffered from serious radio transmission difficulties. Army bombers were poor for patrol because of the inexperience and reluctance of their pilots in locating and accurately reporting enemy naval units over open water.

Even without these tools, the fast carriers still bore the burden of gathering their own information, and in this respect they were badly deficient. Overemphasis on attack functions had led to the degeneration of the scouting function of the ship type known only a few years before as the "eyes of the fleet." The S for scout in

SBD and SB2C meant little. The SBD had flown its last scout mission off the Gilberts, while the new SB2C had been adopted more for its bigger bombload than for any reconnaissance value. The first Helldivers to get airborne radar were those of Bombing 7 in the new carrier *Hancock*, then undergoing shakedown in the Caribbean. By the end of 1944 all SB2Cs were to carry search radars as standard equipment, but this was of little consolation to Admiral Spruance in June. As a makeshift substitute, 37 TBF/TBM Avengers provided the Fifth Fleet with airborne radar that could "see" enemy ships up to 32 miles ahead of the plane.[4] Unfortunately these "turkeys" were very slow in flight, but they did incorporate three pairs of eyes (though the radioman had a poor view) rather than the two crewmen of the dive bomber or the single pilot of the fighter.

Without an adequate scout-bomber, the ComAirPac organization thus turned to the single-seat fighter. The F6F Hellcat, with a theoretical one-way range of over 500 miles, was equipped for search. In June 1944 only the night F6F-3N Hellcats and night F4U-2 Corsairs carried airborne radars, and Mitscher had available 24 of the former and three of the latter. Along with performing general night work these planes could search for enemy ships or aircraft 65 miles, 25 miles, five miles, or one mile ahead of the plane using a rotating beam of radio waves searching a conical area of 120-degrees dead ahead. But these radars were not always dependable. All airborne radar could detect aircraft ahead, but generally this was restricted to five miles in sighting a single plane. Besides, shipboard radar did all the fleet's aircraft detection in mid-1944.[5] Airborne early-warning radar lay in the future.

In intelligence, then, Admiral Spruance was seriously hampered by inadequate tools and a generally lackadaisical attitude on the part of the Bureau of Aeronautics toward providing him with adequate scout planes. The major reason for this, understandably, was the sacrifice of certain activities in order to prove the new strategic attack mission of the fast carriers to opponents within and outside the Navy. In any case, a formalist naval tactician was likely to use extreme caution when deprived of complete information; witness Jellicoe at Jutland. To act on inadequate intelligence was to invite extreme risk, reasoned the formalist, and Spruance had a landing force as well as a battle fleet to protect.

Of the two major weapons for pounding Saipan and engaging the Japanese fleet, the carrier and the battleship, the carrier offered the most versatility and firepower in new as well as tried techniques. The F6F-3 Hellcat fighter could carry light bombs, while the TBF-1C Avenger torpedo bomber was equipped with launcher posts for the new power-packed 3.5-inch forward-firing wing rockets. The major doubt existed over the new SB2C-1C Curtiss Helldiver, now replacing the SBD-5 Dauntless, which was making its last appearance with the carriers during this operation. Most of the air groups seemed to find the new dive bomber acceptable, but Jocko Clark regarded it so much a "beast" (the nickname given it by pilots who found it a difficult airplane) that he wanted to trade in most of his 2Cs for Avengers.[6] But the SB2C-1C version carried hard-hitting 20mm wing cannon, replacing the .50-caliber machine guns, and the SB2C-3 version had such an improved hydraulic system that Captain Ralph Ofstie of *Essex* lauded the Helldiver after the May attack on Marcus. Captain Ernie Litch of *Lexington* even suggested replacing some Avengers with SB2Cs.[7]

For the Marianas operation, Task Force 58 carried 448 Hellcat day fighters, 27 Hellcat and Corsair night fighters, 174 Helldiver bombers, 59 Dauntless bombers, and 193 Avenger torpedo bombers. In addition, the escort carriers provided about 80 TBM Avengers and 110 FM fighters, improved versions of the F4F Wildcat.

The pilots held the key to the success of these planes. Each naval aviator had had 300 hours of flying time before going to carriers and two years of over-all training before seeing combat. By June 1944 the average American naval pilot had flown 525 hours during training, compared to the 275 hours of his Japanese adversary. In fact, so thorough had the Bureau of Aeronautics been in providing pilots to the fleet that it had accumulated a huge backlog of pilots in training by 1944, and in March and again in June instituted cutbacks in pilot training. The overwhelming superiority of these aviators was difficult for even some of the admirals to accept. An overemphasis on defensive fighter tactics led a returning Air Group 5 pilot to declare that "fighter pilots could and should be inculcated with the certain knowledge that they have the best planes, that they are flying and fighting with adequate numbers of the best pilots, backed up by the greatest fighting fleet in the history of the world." [8] Better than anyone, naval aviators knew how good they were.

Task Force 58 demonstrated its overwhelming strength with the attack on the Marianas. Departing Majuro on 6 June 1944 and refueling from Servron 10 oilers two days later, it enjoyed good weather in approaching the target for the scheduled predawn strike on 12 June. Admiral Mitscher felt he could get in an afternoon fighter sweep one day early, thus avoiding a certain "all-out attack during the night" by Japanese land-based air and also breaking the pattern of always launching strikes before dawn.[9] Admiral Spruance accepted Mitscher's reasoning, and Mitscher hastily adjusted his plans. Under Plan Gus, named for operations officer Commander Gus Widhelm, he detached radar, fighter-direction, and rescue destroyers 20 miles ahead of Jocko Clark's van group. Under Plan Johnny, for Widhelm's assistant Lieutenant Commander John Myers, the fighters were readied for an afternoon strike on Saipan, Tinian, and Guam. Plan Jeepers, named for a well-worn expression of gunnery officer Lieutenant Commander Burris D. Wood, rescheduled regular bombing strikes for the next morning.

At 1 P.M., 11 June, 192 miles east of Guam, each fast carrier began launching fighters to the number of 211, while ten attack planes joined in, carrying spare life rafts. Jocko Clark's planes strafed Guam and Rota before encountering about 30 Japanese fighters, which they easily shot down. Antiaircraft fire, however, was very thick. Over Tinian, Hellcats from *Monterey*'s Fighting 28 in Montgomery's task group entered a landing circle of Betty bombers, which they quickly shot up. Reeves' and Harrill's planes faced clouds of smoke from pots the Japanese had lit to obscure Saipan, but two Avengers and four Hellcats swooped down to 500 feet to obtain good photographs of enemy installations. The bomb-laden Hellcats cratered and strafed airfields, claiming a total of about 150 enemy planes for the day, most of them parked. Eleven Hellcats were shot down and three pilots rescued. The score seemed disappointingly low, but within those few hours the fast carriers had swept the Marianas of Japanese planes.[10]

On the succeeding three days prior to the 15 June assault, fast carrier bombers and fighters worked over the Marianas. Antiaircraft fire was severe, "the heaviest . . . encountered by this squadron [*Belleau Wood*'s Fighting 24] in its nine months of combat experience . . . ," but, noted the skipper of Bombing 14 on *Wasp*, the veteran pilots "have overcome most of their earlier nervousness in attacking defended targets and are able to press their attacks with increased accuracy."[11] Nervousness continued to plague the rocket-carrying Avenger pilots, who were dangerously exposed to ground fire during their low, slow approach to launch rockets. Mitscher wanted to conserve his bombs for the possible naval battle, so the TBFs used the rockets against land targets. On the thirteenth Torpedo 16 from *Lexington* lost its popular skipper, Lieutenant Commander Robert H. Isely, during such an attack; this led to pilot objections to the rockets, which were subsequently shifted to fighters.[12] The same day Lieutenant Commander William I. Martin of *Enterprise*'s Torpedo 10 also took a hit while dropping bombs, but he jumped in time for his parachute to open just feet above the water. Making valuable observations of the landing beaches, he then swam out to sea and was rescued.

The prelanding neutralization strikes also yielded some shipping targets. Harrill's planes, while strafing tiny Pagan Island to the north, attacked a convoy on 12 and 13 June, sinking ten transports and four small escort vessels. A *Yorktown* bomber located another convoy far to the east of Guam on the twelfth, so the next day Jocko Clark dispatched 20 bomb-laden Hellcats guided by two radar-equipped night fighters to attack it at long range. The radar succeeded in locating the ships, but the fighter pilots had so little experience in bombing ships that they managed to damage only one vessel. *Hornet* planes also dropped warning leaflets to the Chamorro natives on Guam. On the night of the fifteenth Montgomery's and Reeves' ships beat off a small Yap-based torpedo plane attack by skillful maneuvering, night fighters, and ack-ack.

The other capital ship of Task Force 58, the fast battlewagon, proved almost useless in the prelanding softening-up of Saipan. Its gunners had been trained to fight ships and airplanes, but knew nothing of target selection and firing techniques against the beach. Lee's battleships displayed this ineptitude throughout 13 June; they might just as well have remained with the fast carriers.[13] But no matter. The experts under Kelly Turner would arrive the next day to join the carrier planes in hitting the defenses on the island. The big babies had to be saved to show their stuff in the fleet engagement everyone anticipated.[14]

Carrier and battleship fire teamed up best in the escort carriers and old battleships of the landing support force. Rear Admiral Jesse B. Oldendorf controlled seven battleships, six heavy cruisers, five light cruisers, and over two dozen destroyers for the pinpoint fire that commenced on the morning of 14 June and continued throughout the landing on the fifteenth. It fell with devastating accuracy, as a result of the gunners' training at the shore bombardment range in Hawaii under the tutelage of Marine Corps shore fire control experts. In fact, the rehearsals for the Saipan assault held in Hawaii during May had actually included one day of ship and air cover.[15] The planes in that rehearsal, of course, had been land-based at Hawaii, replaced in the real event by the escort carrier squadrons directed by Captain Dick Whitehead from amphibious command ship *Rocky Mount.*

Close air support came of age in the Marianas, but not entirely to the satisfaction of the Marines. Commander Support Aircraft, using a team of 15 officers and 46 men afloat and a smaller air support unit ashore after 15 June, coordinated requests for support missions from the 41 air liaison parties (each having one officer and five men) with each battalion and regiment. Certain target priorities were established, which meant time lost in executing many requests from advancing troops. Also only one radio circuit, "the support air request net," was available for all these transmissions to *Rocky Mount.* Liaison and control sometimes became unwieldy, especially with the additional coordination of ship and artillery fire. The Marines wanted decentralized control of air support as well as their own pilots especially trained for this kind of work, recommendations that duly went forward. In any case, close air support was effective as it had never been before and, combined with the gunnery of the old battleships, laid down an excellent barrage.[16]

For the Marines, the three and one-half days of prelanding shelling beginning with the fighter sweep of 11 June was an unprecedented amount of heavy support, though they could always use more. Of that first sweep Japanese Sergeant Tokuzo Matsuya noted in his diary: "For about two hours, the enemy planes ran amuck and finally left leisurely amid the unparalleledly inaccurate antiaircraft fire [a view not shared by the pilots]. All we could do was watch helplessly." And when the fast battleships moved in on the thirteenth Sergeant Matsuya lamented: "The enemy holds us in utter contempt." [17] The fast carriers broke off supporting the beachhead on 17 June, leaving the escort carriers alone to assist the Marines from the air on their drive across the island.

Despite the air and heavy gun support, Japanese resistance at Saipan was typically tenacious, forcing General Holland Smith on the fifteenth to commit his floating reserve, one Army division, in support of the two assaulting Marine divisions. This reserve had been scheduled to assault Guam on the eighteenth, an operation Admiral Nimitz now postponed. Three full divisions were thus put ashore and had to be supported by gunfire, aircraft, and logistical forces from the sea. Japanese fleet, air, and troop reinforcements had to be kept from reaching Saipan at all costs.

The very presence of the Fifth Fleet off the Marianas kept enemy troop convoys from arriving after the landings on 15 June, and until the Japanese fleet started to move the major threat was air attack from the north. (As we shall see, a distinct threat from the south had already been eliminated at its source). Admiral Spruance, using intercepted radio intelligence decoded from an aviation code book captured during the Hollandia operation, knew the Japanese were staging aircraft from the homeland into the Bonin and Volcano islands to the north, principally Iwo Jima and Chichi Jima. These planes were to be sent south to attack American forces engaged in the landing. Spruance therefore directed Admiral Mitscher to dispatch two fast carrier task groups north to eliminate that menace.

Dividing one's fleet before or during a naval engagement violated a concept adhered to in the U.S. Navy since Alfred Thayer Mahan had warned against the practice fifty years before. But Spruance was taking no risk, since he directed the strikes to take place on 16–17 June, after which these detached ships would rejoin Task Force 58 before any battle could take place. Should the Japanese fleet sortie from Tawi Tawi before the Jima strikes could be completed, Spruance would be able to recall these two groups in time to meet the enemy navy in full force—which is actually what happened. But concentration of forces for battle was an inviolate formalist dictum, and neither Spruance nor other tacticians at that time were expected to deviate from it.

Mitscher selected Admirals Harrill and Clark to go north, though neither wanted to. Jocko Clark, the fighter, complained that he did not want to miss the big battle with the Japanese fleet. To which Captain Burke cleverly replied that Mitscher's staff agreed with Clark, that, in fact, it was a very dangerous and difficult mission. Part-Cherokee Indian Clark swallowed the bait without hesitation and said that he was rarin' to go north to knock out Japanese air in that neighborhood.[18] Keen Harrill, on the other hand, complained that his task group was too low on fuel to make the trip, despite the expert advice of his staff to the contrary. Mitscher therefore ordered Harrill to go north.[19] In doing so, however, he established a unique command arrangement. Distrusting the reluctant Harrill and placing great confidence in his fighting bull Clark, who was four years junior to Harrill, Mitscher gave neither man tactical command. Rather, he told them to cooperate as independent commanders but to remain "tactically concentrated."

Harrill continued to resist going north, informing Clark of the fact when the two task groups rendezvoused north of the Marianas on 14 June. In disbelief, Clark flew over from *Hornet* to *Essex* to sound out Harrill. Sure enough, Harrill did not want to go, giving many reasons: low fuel, missing the battle, heavy weather over the Jimas, etc. So Clark and Captain H. E. "Blackie" Regan, Harrill's chief of staff, spent several hours trying to talk Harrill into obeying his orders. Finally Clark declared, "If you do not join me in this job I will do it myself!" [20] Having independent command, he could, so Harrill finally consented to go. Harrill's indecisiveness, however, revealed that he was unequal to the demands of responsible command in combat and was falling into the category of Baldy Pownall and Sam Ginder.

That night, 14 June, Admiral Spruance received information that the Japanese fleet had sortied from its anchorage, and he ordered Clark and Harrill to cut short their strikes to one day, 16 June, then rendezvous on the morning of the eighteenth off the Marianas for the battle. Characteristically, Clark charged north at full speed to get in an attack on the fifteenth and thus have the two days he felt he needed. When he was 135 miles from Iwo Jima on the afternoon of the fifteenth, Clark launched his planes, which swept the skies over Iwo of two dozen Zeros and then bombed shipping and installations at Iwo, Chichi, and Haha Jima with much success. Harrill dragged his feet coming up, preferring not to launch planes in the very heavy weather, but managed to get off his combat air patrol. Then, at day's end, Harrill informed Clark he was going to terminate the operation after this one day and rejoin Mitscher. Angrily, Clark roared over the voice radio that despite what Harrill did *he* was staying to finish the job. A tense moment of silence followed on the *Essex* flag bridge, after which Harrill let out an agonized wail, clutching his hands to his temples and bemoaning Clark's severe indictment. But he stayed with Clark the next day.[21]

Clark put two night fighters over Chichi Jima during the night to keep Japanese night planes from taking off and grounded at dawn, thus eliminating the necessity of a predawn fighter sweep. This ruse succeeded, but the steadily worsening weather had already caused a deck crash and fire on *Belleau Wood*, and by the morning of the sixteenth no planes could be launched from any of the badly pitching carrier decks. During the afternoon the skies cleared somewhat, enabling Clark to put three more strikes into the air against Iwo. Harrill launched no planes. That night the seven carriers turned south to rejoin Mitscher. Spruance's northern flank was secure for the time being.

4. Spruance's Decision

Correctly assessing the original strategic intentions of American commanders in the Pacific, the Japanese had planned for the main attack to come somewhere near the western Carolines or Palau. They therefore distributed their 500 available land-based Navy planes between the Marianas and New Guinea with a view toward concentrating these planes with the Mobile Fleet for a crushing victory against the United States Pacific Fleet. When General MacArthur's forces leapfrogged up the New Guinea coast from Hollandia to Wakde and Biak in May 1944, the Japanese therefore dispatched planes and ships to strengthen their western New Guinea defenses. These reinforcements were beaten off by MacArthur's land-based air and light surface forces, so early in June Admiral Toyoda sent superbattleships *Yamato* and *Musashi* to the Molucca Islands for an attack against MacArthur's shipping at Biak.

Japanese expectations and Pacific strategic preferences had, however, been reversed by the American Joint Chiefs of Staff in March 1944 by the decision to seize the Marianas. When Mitscher's fighter sweep struck these islands on 11 June Admiral Toyoda realized his error and ordered his forces to concentrate for the defense of Saipan, Tinian, and Guam. Unfortunately Admiral Kakuta's land-based air had suffered so heavily during the Biak attacks that very few planes could rally to the defense of the Marianas after the almost 200 planes were destroyed on the eleventh. In the north, as we have seen, air reinforcements from Japan were grounded or destroyed in the Jimas by heavy weather and Jocko Clark's carrier strikes. This placed the onus of repelling the Americans on Vice Admiral Ozawa and the Mobile Fleet. On the morning of 13 June this force departed Tawi Tawi for passage through the Philippine Islands and San Bernardino Strait into the Philippine Sea. About 300 miles east of the Philippines these ships would rendezvous with the *Yamato* force coming up from the south and proceed together to attack the American fleet.

Admiral Spruance received his first intelligence that the Japanese fleet had begun to move within hours after its departure from Tawi Tawi on 13 June. Quick calculation told him that battle could not possibly be joined before the seventeenth, but he cut short the Clark-Harrill foray north to the sixteenth to be sure his carriers were concentrated in time for battle. Susequent intelligence enabled him to revise his estimate for battle at no earlier than the morning of the eighteenth, at which time Clark (TG 58.1) and Harrill (TG 58.4) were to rendezvous with Montgomery (TG 58.2) and Reeves (TG 58.3).[1]

Relying exclusively on American submarines for his intelligence, Spruance learned the most influential piece of news—as events were to prove—on the evening of the fifteenth. Submarine *Flying Fish* reported the main Japanese fleet clearing San Bernardino Strait, and *Seahorse* reported the *Yamato* battleships several hundred miles south of that position, moving northward. True to their naval tradition, then, from Tsushima in 1905 to Midway in 1942, the Japanese appeared to Spruance to be laying a trap by dividing their fleet.[2] Little did Spruance know that in fact the Japanese forces were converging on a common point for a concentrated movement against him. In any event, the battle anticipated by all was imminent.

On 16 June Spruance made preliminary decisions. That morning he boarded *Rocky Mount* to discuss matters with his trusted amphibious commander, Kelly Turner. To shield the beachhead most effectively from enemy fleet interference, these men and their advisers—including the third member of the prewar Naval War College triumvirate Carl Moore—decided on three changes. First, Task Force 58 would be reinforced by five heavy cruisers, three light cruisers, and 21 destroyers from Turner's fire support force. Thus strengthened, the fast carrier force on the morning of 18 June would steam westward in search of the enemy fleet. Second, to guard against a possible flank attack by the reported southern force of Japanese ships, the seven fire-support old battleships and three cruisers would form their own battle line 25 miles west of Saipan. Third, at nightfall on the seventeenth, all transports would retire 200 miles to the east of Saipan well beyond the danger of air or surface attacks, and would remain there until after the battle. Only the eight escort carriers and a handful of landing craft and destroyers would remain to support the forces ashore.

Spruance concluded correctly from available intelligence that a carrier-vs.-carrier battle of the Midway variety was in the making, and he therefore made the enemy carriers the primary target for his own carrier bombers when the battle opened.[3] If Spruance did not at once appreciate Ozawa's possible air tactics he soon received a sound piece of friendly advice when the Towers–McMorris message arrived on the sixteenth (fifteenth Hawaii time). To repeat, Towers suggested that the Japanese carriers might remain 600 miles out, and shuttle planes into Guam, thus remaining beyond the range of Mitscher's planes; Ozawa's planes could attack Task Force 58 both coming and going.[4] Admiral Mitscher needed no prompting from Towers to guess Japanese motives, and on the night of 16–17 June he ordered Clark and Harrill to steam and search to the southwest following their operations against the Jimas. If they failed to locate the Japanese fleet, they were to meet their schedule by arriving at the rendezvous on the eighteenth.[5]

As for the fast battleships, Spruance made a very wise decision. When the carriers rendezvoused, Admiral Lee would form his Battle Line fifteen miles ahead of the carrier task groups. Lee's orders were to "destroy enemy fleet either by fleet action if the enemy elects to fight or by sinking slowed or crippled ships if enemy retreats." By this early maneuvering into battle formation, Spruance eliminated the time lost and confusion that would ensue if Lee tried to draw out his battleships when the battle was joined. And when the fight did begin Lee would have tactical command of his own movements just as Mitscher would of his; said Spruance: "I shall issue general directives [only] when necessary. . . ."[6]

On the morning of 17 June, as Montgomery's and Reeves' carrier task groups turned over all air support at Saipan to the "jeep" carriers, Clark's and Harrill's launched search planes to the extreme range of 350 miles to seek out Ozawa's ships. When these planes returned empty-handed, the plan called for return to Saipan waters. Jocko Clark had other ideas. Recalling Admiral Beatty's near-successful attempt to cut off the German battle cruisers in the 1916 battle of Jutland, Clark reasoned that he and Harrill could do the same: continue southwestward, swing in behind the advancing Japanese fleet, and cut off its retreat. Caught in the vise of strong carrier forces, the Japanese fleet could be annihilated; Clark, Harrill, and Mitscher would do what Beatty and Jellicoe had failed to do 28 years before.[7]

Tactically, Clark's bold plan reeked of meleeist aggressiveness. It consequently involved a certain amount of risk, since such a division of forces—anathema to historian Mahan as well as to the formalists, and wonderful to Lord Nelson and his "band of brother" lieutenants—would cut Mitscher's force to eight carriers and seven battleships, and the Clark–Harrill force to seven carriers and no battleships. The latter, according to intelligence, did not face the threat of another enemy fleet coming out from the Philippines, unlike the surprised Beatty at Jutland. But enemy land-based air in the Philippines and Ryukyus comprised a possible threat, plus the fact that Ozawa could throw his entire force against Clark and Harrill—and destroy them. This possibility led one of Clark's pilots to remark: "What I want to know is, who's trapping whom?" [8] It was bold but not unprecedented. In the meleeist tradition, once the enemy has committed himself—as Ozawa had—victory could best be assured by bold and intelligent initiative. Hard-hitting Jocko Clark was such a leader, but there was a serious problem with regard to Harrill.[9]

Clark needed permission to execute his plan, but he could not get it. He could not radio his ideas to Mitscher because Japanese radio direction finders might pinpoint the transmission, thus giving away the scheme, luring enemy subs to the carriers, and telling Admiral Ozawa that the American fleet was at least temporarily split. Clark did talk over the voice radio to Rear Admiral Ralph Davison, riding as an observer in *Yorktown*, and Davison endorsed the plan. But Harrill flatly refused. Twice defied by Clark, Harrill said he had had his fill of independent operations and was going to make the rendezvous on schedule. He thereupon changed course and left. Clark, reduced to four carriers, had no choice but to return with Harrill, a decided disappointment.[10] Mitscher later told Clark that he had been correct, but Admiral Spruance would surely have vetoed such a proposal.[11]

Given available intelligence on 16 June, Admiral Mitscher expected the Japanese fleet to approach from the southwest along the line of Davao–Palau–Yap. "However," he told Admirals Reeves and Montgomery, "they may come from the west." [12] During the night of 17–18 June, however, submarine *Cavalla* reported a large enemy force coming from the west, so that at daybreak of the eighteenth Spruance informed Mitscher and Lee: "In my opinion the main attack will come from the west but might be diverted to come from the southwest." [13] He did not worry much about the northern flank now, well covered by Clark and so far quiet as an active enemy operating area.[14] By midday of 17 June, when Spruance issued his battle plan, everyone was anxious to begin the battle. And Spruance left no doubt as to his intentions: "Actions against the enemy must be pushed vigorously by all hands to ensure complete destruction of his fleet."

On the morning of the eighteenth Admiral Mitscher welcomed the return of his two meandering task groups and made calculations for battle. By pressing westward during the day—Lee's battleships in front covered by Harrill, followed by (north to south) Clark, Reeves, and Montgomery in line abreast 12 miles between them—Task Force 58 could launch search planes to pinpoint Ozawa's carriers before sunset. Then, during the night, Ching Lee—past master of night battleship fighting off Guadalcanal—could close in for the gunnery duel. Mitscher therefore asked Lee during the morning, "Do you desire night engagement? . . . Otherwise we should retire to the eastward tonight." Lee replied immediately, "Do not, repeat not, believe we should seek night engagement." This answer surprised Mitscher and his staff, who were "most disappointed,"[15] as were "most people" at Admiral Nimitz's headquarters in Hawaii.[16]

Lee's reasons for refusing a night surface battle could have been uttered by Admiral Jellicoe when he was pacing the German fleet during the night at Jutland. Lee told Mitscher: "Possible advantages of radar [which, of course, Jellicoe had not had] more than offset by difficulties of communications and lack of training in fleet tactics at night." He added, however, that he "would press pursuit of damaged or fleeing enemy . . . at any time."[17] In other words, two decades of studying Jutland plus wide experience in combating Japanese night tactics had not improved American capabilities for a night action one bit, nor had Lee's healthy respect for Japanese night torpedo attacks by air or destroyers changed. Part of this negligence can be attributed to the swift pace of operations that had disallowed fleet battle practice at night, but also to Admiral Spruance's naïve assumptions at the Gilberts, at Truk, and now before the Marianas that a surface engagement was even possible in broad daylight in the presence of many hundreds of airplanes. Being a formalist like Lee, leaving nothing to chance, Spruance then quickly supported Lee's decision and agreed to the alternative, a night retirement toward Saipan.[18] Little did these battleship-weaned tacticians realize that *only at night* could a pure surface action take place in the presence of fast carrier forces.

When Spruance elected to return to cover Saipan closely on the night of 18–19 June, Admiral Mitscher, Commander Widhelm, and nonaviator Captain Burke—now well versed in the fine points of carrier operations—were mystified. They "could not understand why the Commander Fifth Fleet would throw away the tremendous advantages of surprise and initiative and aggressiveness." These assets would surely be lost if Task Force 58 had to steam eastward. In the first place, the fast carriers would be tied to the beaches again, just as at the Gilberts. They would have to remain defensive and receive the attack of 400 or 500 carrier- and possibly also land-based planes on 19 June. Secondly, unless they headed west at night on 18–19 June, they would continue to operate near Saipan on the nineteenth because they had to steam into the wind, eastward, to launch and recover aircraft. Conversely, the Japanese fleet was approaching into the wind, giving the enemy the advantage in speed of launch. Task Force 58, as long as it cruised to the east, could not close toward the enemy, westward, unless it had recovered all planes—an impossibility if under enemy air attack. "This fact," remarked destroyerman Burke at the end of the war, "was general knowledge and is an elementary consideration in carrier warfare. It is a consideration, however, that nonaviators are apt to overlook unless they had a great deal of experience in carrier warfare." [19] Spruance and his staff had had very little.

Mitscher's aviators, from rear admirals to ensigns, were similarly anxious to go west. The senior task group commander, Black Jack Reeves, was angry over the delay, and fired a curt message to his boss that he intended Spruance to see. He wanted to stop wasting time and get under way. Mitscher, used to such reverberations from his restless subordinates, played along by answering that Reeves' suggestions were "good but irritating" and that those "higher up . . . certainly know the situation better than we do." [20] Doubtless Mitscher wondered whether Spruance had all the information. Down in the ready room of Bombing 14 on carrier *Wasp*, Lieutenant Joseph E. Kane wrote in his diary of the anticipated dawn strike against the Japanese fleet on the nineteenth:

> Word is that we're going out after the Jap fleet. Might intercept them tomorrow. . . . If we do catch them, I'm supposed to be on the first strike with Art and Al. Sure is going to be rough—no matter how you look at it. Gives you plenty to think about, particularly about getting to the states—not [by] Christmas—but getting back period.[21]

Lee's decision not to fight his battleships at night changed Spruance's attitude and therefore the entire plan of battle. As long as he had assumed his Battle Line could pave the way, Spruance had spoken confidently of destroying the enemy fleet. Now, on the eighteenth, without the possibility of a gunnery duel, Spruance became less sure of how best to employ his carriers. He often repeated his desire to let the carriers get in the first blow, but they could not do this at night; only radar-aided big guns could do so. To increase the range between Task Force 58 and Saipan during the night worried him, for he received no new intelligence on the enemy fleet all day 18 June. Spruance could only conclude, therefore, that the Japanese were coming in the two last-reported groups, from the west and the southwest. Task Force 58 maintained its southwesterly course throughout the afternoon of the eighteenth, while Spruance worried.

By now Mitscher had concluded that Spruance would maintain tactical command throughout the battle, despite its obvious nature as a potential carrier duel.[22] He was understandably unhappy about it, for he had not yet been so restricted by Admiral Spruance. Now Lee's reluctance had fouled a beautiful plan. Captain Burke came up with one last possibility to get Lee into a fight. He recommended Lee's battleships cruise 25 miles ahead of the carriers for a surface battle at dawn of the nineteenth. Mitscher the pilot doubted the wisdom of this, since an air attack would hit them at dawn, in which case he wanted the battleships in the rear protected by his planes. Doubting also whether Spruance would accept it, Mitscher did not forward the recommendation.[23]

On the morning of the eighteenth, when Spruance had supported Lee's decision to avoid a night action, he had also introduced an old idea from GALVANIC that increasingly dominated his thinking as the hours wore on and the tension mounted. At that time he had informed Mitscher and Lee: "Task Force 58 must cover Saipan and our forces engaged in that operation." The reported Japanese southern force, now ascertained to be a lesser force if it did exist, bothered Spruance. Japanese precedence pointed clearly to the two-pronged attack, as did a recently captured Japanese tactical manual and propaganda broadcasts predicting it.[24] Small wonder Spruance feared the divided approach by the enemy.

Commander Fifth Fleet was correct, lacking reliable information to the contrary, in assuming the Japanese would hit him from two directions. But if the main attack came from the west, as intelligence indicated would happen, what could he expect from the southwestward quarter? Any Japanese strike there would have to be diversionary, therefore comparably small and possibly expendable. It would probably be comprised therefore of battleships, older ones at that, a cruiser or two, and destroyers. The evidence of Midway suggested air cover would have to be provided in the form of one or maybe two light carriers. Its mission would be a shock action—upsetting American defensive plans by shooting up the shipping and beachhead, then running. Admiral Mitscher and his carrier staff, studying this possibility, concluded that such a southern force could inflict heavy damage only with "an inordinate amount of luck," and therefore Mitscher could not believe the Japanese would take such a risk.[25]

Furthermore, should such a secondary force evade air and radar searches to achieve a surprise at Saipan, would not the Japanese be the more surprised? All shipping had retired to safety 200 miles to the east, while the beachhead had been secured and the troops were pushing inland by the eighteenth. The only targets, then, would have been a formidable battle line of seven old battleships (two with 16-inch guns, the others 14-inch), three cruisers, and five destroyers, covered by eight escort carriers armed with about 75 bomb-laden Avengers and 120 Wildcat fighters. Even had the Japanese been foolish enough to waste their two 18.1-inch-gunned super *Yamatos* in such a diversion, Admiral Oldendorf's seven battlewagons were more than a match. Even more surprising to the Japanese, had they identified the ships in this line, would have been the discovery that four of them had been victims of the Pearl Harbor attack. Admiral Mitscher's staff believed that a secondary Japanese surface force attack on this fire support line "would have resulted in the annihilation of such a small force."[26]

Still another element could defend Saipan if Task Force 58 headed west, and this was Task Force 58 itself. What Admiral Spruance did not seem to understand about carriers was that enemy ships could not run around a fast carrier task force. Had a southern surface force with good luck evaded air searches by the newly arrived seaplanes off Saipan, those scouts from the carriers, and patrol bombers from New Guinea, it could not last long after making its presence known at Saipan. The reason is that Task Force 58 could steam over 200 miles to the west and still be within range of the beaches. If a diversionary battleship force survived the mauling given it by Oldendorf's guns, then its cripples and luckier survivors would face carrier strikes from the west—in their rear. The Fifth Fleet remained tactically concentrated within the range of its aircraft, or a circle with a diameter of at least 400 miles. Or so reasoned the aviators, of whom Spruance was not one.[27]

The idea of dividing Task Force 58 by leaving, say, a four-carrier task group near Saipan and taking the other 11 fast carriers west to deal with Ozawa was never considered. Spruance required overwhelming force to deal with the Japanese fleet, and no formalist tactician violated the "no-division-of-force" rule of his training. But, under the circumstances as they were or as they might have been, such a division was not actually necessary, not when his operating radius was over 200 miles.

The surest means of a victory, however, was to head west for a carrier strike against the main body of the Japanese fleet. The big carriers, backbone of any future operations, would be in that force, and they must be eliminated. Between noon and 8:30 P.M., however, no new intelligence reached Spruance, and the carriers, by constant course changes to operate search planes, covered only 115 miles to the westward. At the latter moment night had arrived, and Spruance turned Task Force 58 eastward, retiring back toward Saipan. Then, about 10 P.M., he received a radio direction report pinpointing a Japanese radio transmission more than 300 miles to the west, his only piece of intelligence received all day 18 June. It substantiated the fact that part of the Japanese fleet was approaching from the west.

Admiral Mitscher greeted the radio direction report with enthusiasm. The main enemy force lay 355 miles to the west-southwest. If Task Force 58 reversed course again to the westward at 1:30 A.M., 19 June, it would come within 200 miles of the Japanese fleet at five o'clock—the optimum distance for a carrier strike. After making these calculations, Mitscher turned to Arleigh Burke and in words worthy of his predecessor Nelson said, "It might be a hell of a battle for a while, but I think we can win it." [28] He ordered Burke to request permission from Spruance to implement his plan. At 11:25 P.M. Captain Burke called flagship *Indianapolis* by voice radio: "Propose coming to course 270° at 0130 in order to commence treatment [of the enemy] at 0500. Advise." [29]

Spruance, tense from the lack of definite intelligence and tired from continuous combat operations for more than a week, now had to face the problem directly. There were two ways to defeat the enemy, who was theoretically advancing in two prongs. According to the formalist tradition, Task Force 58 could fall back on Saipan to form a veritable battle line of defensive aircraft. These could concentrate on incoming enemy planes and ships just as a battleship line could cap an enemy *T*. But, if the enemy carriers stayed out of range, they might escape to fight again. In such a battle, Spruance would repel the enemy attack and thereby win the battle, but he would not destroy the Japanese fleet. To the meleeist's way of thinking, Task Force 58 could let any flanking force try its luck. Such a divided enemy fleet would mean the main force was weakened. If Mitscher threw all his force against only part, even the main part of this fleet, he would probably destroy its main ships and planes, thus achieving tactical concentration. The enemy fleet would never fight again, even should the smaller flanking force survive its diversionary mission.

That Spruance had already made his decision when Burke called over is suggested by his subsequent actions to obtain more tangible support for his tactics. At 11:46 P.M. he was handed an intercepted message—not yet intended for his eyes—from Admiral Lockwood to submarine *Stingray* asking for amplification of a radio message that had apparently been "jammed" by the Japanese. Spruance immediately assumed that *Stingray*, 175 miles east-southeast of the radio direction contact, had located a Japanese southern force and was having difficulty transmitting the news. He furthermore concluded that the earlier radio bearing on the western Japanese force must be indefinite, located somewhere in a 100-mile area, originator unknown (possibly a decoy), size of force unknown.[30] For reasons all his own, he placed more faith in a garbled radio message than in a definite fix. (The transmission, incidentally, was merely a routine operational damage report.)

Spruance discussed the situation with Captain Moore and other members of his staff in the flag mess, looking over a large chart of the Philippine Sea. Then he wrote out a reply to Mitscher's request, remarking to his staff that he did not trust the radio bearings received and that he feared an end run around the Saipan shipping by a secondary enemy force. He then asked if anyone had any questions, but none of his staff did—not even Captain Bobby Morse, his aviation officer, since he had just come off the flag watch at midnight and knew none of the pertinent facts.[31]

At 12:38 A.M., 19 June, Spruance replied to Mitscher:

> Change proposed in your . . . message does not appear advisable. Believe indication given by *Stingray* more accurate than that contained in [Cincpac radio bearing]. If that is so, continuation

> as at present seems preferable. End run by other fast ones [carriers, battleships?] remains a possibility and must not be overlooked.[32]

Mitscher and the TF 58 staff were stunned. On the strength of this one "indication"—now mentioned to Mitscher for the first time—Spruance retained the fast carriers on the defensive. He had not sought the advice of his air experts, neither Mitscher nor Mitscher's deputy chief of staff Captain Hedding, who had seen first hand the results of carriers on the defensive in GALVANIC, nor any other war horses such as Black Jack Reeves and Monty Montgomery. Even Arleigh Burke, as outspoken a non-airman as there was before he had joined Mitscher, later summed up the frustration of the carrier staff: "Our airmen . . . our procedures and skill and combat activity were much superior to the Japanese. . . . Therefore, the decision was not one of winning or losing the battle . . . [but of] how well we could win." The aviators in the task groups shared Mitscher's frustration; some uttered Horace Greeley's old frontier slogan, "Go West, young man, go West!" Mitscher had taken all the liberty he dared in trying to influence Spruance; said Burke: "We had done everything that we could to persuade him of what we thought was an error." [33]

For a formalist, Spruance's tactics of caution and no-risk were sound, especially when he lacked complete information. But carriers demanded melee tactics, based on mobility and initiative to get in what the aviators called their "Sunday punch." Spruance did not think thus. By midnight he was tired, which must have affected his decision to assume the most sure way out of the crisis. And as the night wore on he received more vague intelligence to tighten his resolve. At 1:05 A.M. Spruance learned that submarine *Finback* had seen searchlights five hours before at a point northeast of the radio-bearing report. This indicated a *third* possible enemy force, an unreasonable assumption, but it added to the conflicting intelligence and "further confirmed Commander Fifth Fleet in his decision to continue to the eastward." [34] The final irony of this hectic night was that a seaplane had picked up all 40 of Ozawa's ships on its search radar at 1:15 A.M. but awkward atmospheric conditions would not convey the transmission. Spruance got that information seven hours too late, yet had it been received immediately it still might not have influenced his decision.[35]

By dawn, Task Force 58 would be hugging the Marianas, where carrier-based Japanese planes would attack them. It was a defensive role, and no one doubted that the Japanese attack on the fleet would fail. Mitscher had his aircraft gassed and pilots readied throughout the night for the air battle and also for the chance that the Japanese fleet just might get within range. For the latter possibility the air admirals anxiously awaited the morrow.

5. Battle of the Philippine Sea

Vice Admiral Ozawa accommodated Admiral Towers' expectation by planning to launch from beyond the range of Mitscher's planes and shuttle his airplanes to Guam. He further anticipated Admiral Spruance's caution and concluded that the victor of Midway would remain within 100 miles of Saipan.[1] Overblown battle claims by Vice Admiral Kakuda led him to expect considerable assistance from a land-based air force that had been whittled down to almost nothing, but Ozawa knew the general position of Task Force 58 from good scouting reports from his longest-range planes. He therefore enjoyed an edge over Spruance in intelligence.

One contact led Rear Admiral Obayashi, ComCarDiv 3, to launch a premature strike at 4:30 P.M. on the afternoon of 18 June, but these planes were recalled by Ozawa's order. During the night Ozawa prepared to commence the big battle after sunup, and at 8:23 he radioed Admiral Kakuda to be ready to coordinate air operations. This was the transmission pinpointed by Cincpac radio direction finders. At 9 P.M. Ozawa divided his force into two parts. After some necessary maneuvering, Obayashi's three small light carriers and Vice Admiral Kurita's battle force (which had joined on the sixteenth) assumed the role of vanguard, 100 miles ahead of the large carriers under Ozawa and Joshima. At dawn, when the van would be 280 miles and the main body 400 miles from Task Force 58, Ozawa would begin launching his strikes. Should Mitscher hit him first, Kurita's antiaircraft guns and Obayashi's 60 fighters could delay the attacker and enable Ozawa to launch or recall his main fighter force.

In fairness to Admiral Spruance, it should be noted that the Japanese *did* divide their fleet, though it remained tactically concentrated, by 100 miles—a separation of ships Spruance himself never would have undertaken in battle. Had Ozawa sent Kurita and Obayashi on a successful "end run," as Spruance feared, to hit Saipan beaches, the battle off Saipan would have been constituted as follows: Japan (Kurita and Obayashi)—three CVL (60 fighter-bombers, 25 torpedo bombers), four BB (two with 18.1-inch guns, two with 14-inch guns), six CA, and nine DD; United States (Oldendorf and Sallada)—eight CVE (120 fighters, 75 torpedo bombers), seven BB (two with 16-inch guns, five with 14-inch), three CL, and five DD. This is assuming Mitscher would have gone west, taking Lee's battle line along. Since the Avengers were loaded with rockets and light bombs for close support ashore, they would probably not have been very effective against ships. The issue most likely would have been decided by the battleships —and Admiral Mitscher's bombers roaring in from the west.

Had Ozawa sent his van on the "end run" he would of course have stripped his main body of its main escort strength, leaving one battleship, three heavy and two light cruisers, and 19 destroyers to defend his six large carriers, a force weaker than the escort which had vainly supported the doomed carriers at Midway. Such a plan would therefore have been very risky, even assuming Kakuta's land-based air force had been at full strength. Had Ozawa seriously considered an end run he would have sent only a portion of the van, knowing that such an expedition would probably be a one-way affair. In fact, some admirals recommended to Admiral Toyoda in Tokyo that battleships *Fuso* and *Yamashiro* be sent from Japan on a suicide run to the beach, at least relieving pressure on the Saipan garrison, but Toyoda vetoed the idea.[2] And Ozawa had learned from the Americans to concentrate his fleet—no end run.

At 5:30 A.M. 19 June, the moment Mitscher had hoped to strike the Japanese fleet, Task Force 58 turned northeast into the wind and began launching the dawn search, antisubmarine, and combat air patrols. One fighter patrol from *Monterey* shot down a Japanese search bomber but missed another, which escaped to inform Ozawa of the latest position of Task Force 58. The sun rose at 5:45, "ceiling and visibility unlimited." At 6:19 Spruance changed course to the west-southwest toward the advancing enemy fleet and asked Mitscher to neutralize Guam and Rota if the Japanese fleet was not located that morning. Rear Admiral Montgomery protested Spruance's request by telling Mitscher that "the maximum effort of the force should be directed toward [the] enemy force at sea."[3] Mitscher compromised by sending a fighter force to Guam, thus conserving his bombs. This mission illustrates that even while cruising westward toward the enemy fleet the carriers could still cover the islands; and they could do so at distances of 200 or even 300 miles, the maximum range of their fighters. Spruance, from the McMorris–Towers dispatch of the sixteenth and the general tactical situation, knew that the Japanese planes could land and refuel at Guam. Mitscher's fighters could therefore upset the Japanese program by intercepting planes (or ships) coming from this southern flank.

At 7:20 the Hellcat patrol from *Belleau Wood* reported planes taking off from Guam and requested assistance to meet them. These Japanese planes probably included the last 19 to leave by-passed Truk, plus about 30 more that had survived the carrier attacks on Guam. Jocko Clark dispatched reinforcements, and after more land-based planes were detected coming up from the southwest a lively series of dogfights developed near Guam. Between 8 and 9 A.M. Navy Hellcats splashed 35 Japanese aircraft. At the latter hour Spruance received the delayed PBM contact of 1:15 A.M. placing the Japanese fleet 360 miles to the west, but it was too late to do anything about it. One hour later the first Japanese carrier planes registered on Task Force 58 radar screens. Also, Spruance could not yet discount the possibility of an end run.

Commencing at early twilight, Admiral Ozawa launched scout planes from the battleships and cruisers in Kurita's van, some of which were shot down by Mitscher's combat air patrol but not until they had reported Mitscher's position to their admiral. Then, about 8:30, Rear Admiral Obayashi began launching a strike of 16 fighters, 45 fighter-bombers, and eight torpedo planes from CarDiv 3 in the van. One hundred miles to the west, Ozawa's own CarDiv 1 commenced its launch at 8:56. This strike from the large carriers necessarily had more planes: 48 fighters, 53 bombers, and 27 torpeckers. At 9:10 Warrant Officer Sakio Komatsu, taking off from flagship *Taiho*, spotted a torpedo heading straight toward his ship, whereupon he immediately crash-dived into it, taking his own life but exploding the "fish." A second torpedo—both of them were fired from American submarine *Albacore*—went undetected and slammed into the starboard side of *Taiho*, causing what appeared to be only minor damage. Rear Admiral Joshima launched a small strike of 15 fighters, 25 fighter-bombers, and seven torpeckers at 10:00, and Ozawa sent off a fourth raid from the main body: 30 VF, 36 VB, 10 VBF, and six VT.[4]

At 9:50 Task Force 58 radars registered Obayashi's planes 130 miles to the west, and Lieutenant Joe Eggert's fighter directors went to work. Using the two radio channels common to all ships (many new ships had four channels), he and his four task group counterparts began a busy day of directing Hellcats to the intercept. First, Mitscher recalled his fighters from the embattled skies over Guam, which were now generally clear of enemy land-based planes. Then he ordered all 192 Avengers, 174 Helldivers, and 59 Dauntlesses in the force launched to clear the area and orbit east of Guam, leaving the flight decks free to handle fighters. Mitscher gained a precious fifteen minutes to do this when the incoming Japanese carrier planes began circling at 20,000 feet 100 miles out (and 200 miles from Guam).[5] With the bombers gone, 450 Hellcats began to operate from the carriers.

From the moment the first Hellcat pilot yelled "Tallyho!" upon sighting an adversary, the air battle developed into the worst slaughter of Japanese planes during the war in the Pacific, and led one jubilant pilot to remark, "Hell, this is like an old-time turkey shoot."[6] Hence this great air fight of 19 June 1944 has come down through history as the Marianas Turkey Shoot.

American superiority in the air came as no surprise to the veterans of Rabaul, the Gilberts, the Marshalls, and Truk, though the new post-Truk flyers marveled at the relative ease it took in splashing enemy "Zekes." For instance, Lieutenant (jg) Alex Vraciu of Fighting 16 nailed six Japs to become an ace, while another pilot flying between carriers on a ferry hop opened fire in amazement when a Zero flew right into his sights. From 10:30 A.M. until about 3 P.M. F6F Hellcats, including some night fighters, filled the sky over Task Force 58 and up to 60 miles to the westward. For the first time in the Central Pacific campaign, atmospheric conditions produced contrails which initially alarmed even some veterans into thinking the Japanese had produced a secret weapon.[7] Instead, these vapor trails gave the ships' crews a dazzling spectacle of the war's greatest air-sea battle. Each of four Japanese raids met destruction, though a few planes got though the F6Fs to drop their bombs only to be splashed by the intense antiaircraft fire. Of all the ships in Task Force 58 only battleship *South Dakota* received a direct bomb hit, though others sustained near-misses. And many bombs were required even to slow down a fast battlewagon.

As the air battle raged, the planes and ships drifted toward Guam, the Japanese trying to land, the American carriers needing the wind to operate aircraft. During the afternoon Admiral Montgomery suggested to Mitscher that the Guam airfields be cratered to make landings hazardous. Mitscher agreed and ordered the orbiting bombers to do the job, which they did well. Straggling enemy planes continued to operate near Guam during the late afternoon and on into the night, but the main Japanese carrier attack was spent by 2:30 P.M.

The Marianas Turkey Shoot ended with the Japanese suffering aircraft losses ten times greater than those of Task Force 58. Of 373 carrier and some 50 land-based planes that began the action, Japan lost over 300 in the great air battle. Mitscher lost 18 fighters and 12 bombers, but managed to rescue some of the air crews. For all Mitscher knew, however, Ozawa still had 200 planes, all nine carriers, and his battle line. Thus while victory in the air had been spectacular, it had been only a half-victory. The enemy was still at large and a formidable threat.

But Ozawa was having his troubles keeping afloat. *Taiho* had been damaged by *Albacore*'s torpedo, and other American submarines threatened. Twenty minutes after noon three torpedoes from submarine *Cavalla* ripped into mighty *Shokaku*, starting fires and causing the veteran of Pearl Harbor and the Coral Sea to fall out of formation. Then, as the last of Ozawa's major raids dissipated over Guam, two of his heavy carriers exploded and sank. Gas fumes touched off a bomb magazine in *Shokaku*, breaking up the carrier and sending her down shortly after 3 P.M. *Taiho*, her torpedo damage magnified by inefficient damage control, was torn apart by a huge explosion around 3:30, starting fires and putting the great ship in a sinking condition. Admiral Ozawa transferred his flag to a cruiser, and shortly after 5 P.M. Japan's newest carrier rolled over and sank. Twenty-two additional planes went down with *Shokaku* and *Taiho*.

Despite the PBM report of 9 A.M. giving the size and earlier position of Ozawa's force, Spruance had no definite information throughout the day. For all he knew, Ozawa had split up his fleet for the end run; in fact, Ozawa had sent his van 100 miles ahead. At 11:03 A.M. Black Jack Reeves asked Mitscher to send some of the orbiting scout bombers on a search-strike 350 miles out. Mitscher, anxious to find the location of the enemy force, replied: "Approved. Approved. Wish we could go with you."[8] But force fighter directors had jammed all available radio channels, leaving Reeves unable to contact his bombers. As the day wore on and the carriers drifted eastward conducting their continuous flight operations, the difficulty in locating the Japanese fleet increased.

At 3 P.M. Spruance returned tactical command of the carriers to Mitscher, still recovering planes and unable to move westward. Spruance had not accepted the fact that only one Japanese force existed and at 4:30 informed Mitscher: "Desire to attack enemy tomorrow if we know his position with sufficient accuracy. . . . If not, we must continue searches tomorrow to ensure adequate protection of Saipan."[9] With the entire Fifth Fleet lying 50 miles off the Marianas and Japan's carrier air might destroyed, Spruance had surely succumbed to overcautiousness. Even Nimitz tried to nudge Spruance to press westward for a decisive engagement. After the Japanese fleet replenished, wrote Cincpac, "we may have another chance at it. If they come back, I hope you will be able to bring them to action."[10] But Spruance was tired, having fought the greatest air battle of the war and contemplating its being renewed on the morrow. And without accurate information—though he knew at what positions the two carriers had been torpedoed—his doubts only continued.

By darkness, however, it was obvious to everyone that the Japanese attack was over, and Spruance notified Turner to recall his shipping to the Saipan beaches from its haven 200 miles to the east. He also allowed Mitscher to detach one task group to remain off Guam. This was an unusual, though very correct, denial of tactical concentration on the part of Spruance in the face of the enemy, but the enemy was now about 300 planes weaker. The immediate reason for splitting Task Force 58 this way was again Keen Harrill. Dragging his feet, the cautious Commander Task Group 58.4 had failed to top off his destroyers and was therefore low on fuel. He asked Mitscher if his task group could stay behind. Mitscher agreed, with obvious disgust. Jocko Clark, on the contrary, fueled his destroyers of Task Group 58.1 and told Mitscher so: "Would greatly appreciate remaining with you. We have plenty of fuel." Mitscher declared without hesitation: "You will remain with us all right until the battle is over."[11]

Task Force 58 was thus deprived of the air groups on *Essex*, *Langley*, and *Cowpens*, especially *Essex*'s "hot" Fighting 15 of Commander David McCampbell, which had turned in one of the high scores of the day. The four night fighters of *Essex* worked over Guam and

Rota during the night, shooting down three planes, and at dawn the carrier's day squadrons destroyed many more planes on the ground.

At 8 P.M. the other three task groups finally turned northwestward in pursuit of the elusive enemy fleet. Mitscher regassed his planes for a daylight attack, though many of his pilots had trouble settling down after the biggest day of their lives. There was also the additional apprehension that the Japanese would attack with their usual cunning night torpedo aircraft, but this did not occur. Mitscher had to race to try to catch Ozawa, who (unknown to Mitscher) had begun his withdrawal at 8 P.M. Ozawa originally intended to resume his attacks on the twentieth, but a tally of his losses quickly discouraged him. He did enjoy the advantage over his adversary of knowing the latter's whereabouts. For his information Mitscher had still to rely upon the long-range PBM seaplanes now operating from Saipan waters.

Some criticism has been directed at Admiral Mitscher for his failure to launch night searches from the carriers. Professor Morison attributes the failure to two factors, Mitscher's humanitarian concern for his pilots, who might get lost in the vast darkness of the Pacific night, and his general reluctance—"a sort of mental block"—to use night fighters, a nuisance to tired deck crews.[12] Certainly these explanations account for a part of the story. But many of the 27 night Hellcat and Corsair pilots had fought in the Turkey Shoot, while the bombers had orbited monotonously east of Guam for several hours; these men needed sleep if they were to attack Ozawa's fleet the next day. The night fighter pilots had been equipped and trained only for short-range intercepts of the cunning enemy torpedo bombers and not for long-range searches. Also, like Lee's battleships, they had not developed an effective doctrine for large-scale night operations and were therefore unreliable. Better to save them for defensive purposes and eliminate the loss of mileage and time that would result from turning into the wind (eastward) to launch and recover planes. The indictment of Mitscher should not be for his tactical failure to launch search planes that night, but for his earlier failure to develop an adequate day-night air search capability.[13]

At dawn the carriers launched air searches to the northwest, continuing throughout the day. One of them from *Lexington* stretched 475 miles out before coming home empty-handed. Spruance had heard nothing of the Japanese fleet since the *Cavalla* torpedoing of *Shokaku* at noon 24 hours before; he would be satisfied to find that cripple—if it was still afloat—and sink it. To this end Vice Admiral Lee's battle line formed the van in the pursuit northwestward. After noon Mitscher placed his strike groups on standby, and everyone waited eagerly for some news. When the sun crossed the meridian, length of daylight loomed increasingly large in Mitscher's plans.

At 3:40 P.M. 20 June, Lieutenant R. S. Nelson of *Enterprise*'s Torpedo 10 made contact. By 4:05 Mitscher knew that the Japanese Mobile Fleet was about 275 miles west-northwest of Task Force 58 and seemed to be taking on fuel, a highly embarrassing moment to be attacked (witness Midway). Mitscher made rapid calculations and ascertained the uncomfortable fact that an immediate strike would leave half an hour of daylight to press home an air attack, followed by a return flight and recovery at night. Such night landings had been made after the battle of Midway two years before,[14] but not immediately following an air attack, and many 1942 pilots had qualified in night landings before the war. This was not true of the day-oriented wartime-trained flyers.

If Mitscher wanted to hit the enemy fleet, this might be his last chance. It would entail a certain amount of risk to his pilots' safety, and his rebuff from Admiral Spruance the night before when he had recommended heading west made Mitscher "a little reluctant" to suggest this long-shot strike against the enemy fleet. He asked the opinion of his operations officer, Commander Gus Widhelm. Widhelm considered a moment, then replied that such a strike was possible, but added, "It's going to be tight." [15] So Mitscher, in true Nelsonian style, threw caution to the winds and informed Spruance that Task Force 58 was shooting its bolt. He would launch two deckload strikes to hit the enemy fleet. Admiral Lee's battle line could close during the night and sink straggling cripples. Spruance concurred.

Time was of the essence, and at 4:10 P.M. pilots scrambled in record time from ready rooms to planes. Eleven minutes later the carriers swung eastward into the wind. Four minutes after that flight-deck officers waved plane after plane down their decks in rapid succession. All the big carriers launched planes: *Yorktown*, *Hornet*, *Bunker Hill*, *Wasp*, *Lexington*, and that noble veteran, "The Big E." All CVLs but *Princeton*—which was to join in the second strike—launched: *Bataan*, *Belleau Wood*, *Cabot*, *Monterey*, and *San Jacinto*. Flight leader was Lieutenant Commander B. M.

"Smoke" Strean of *Yorktown*'s Fighting 1. Behind his Hellcat were 215 carrier planes: 84 F6s, 54 Turkeys (TBF-TBM), 51 Beasts (SB2C), and 26 Old Reliables (SBD) in their last carrier battle. In a record ten minutes these planes had cleared the decks to rendezvous, then headed west, climbing very slowly in order to conserve fuel. At 4:36 the carriers swung northwestward again.

Several minutes had passed when Lieutenant Commander Ralph Weymouth, skipper of *Lexington*'s Bombing 16, intercepted a corrected position report which placed the enemy fleet 60 miles farther west. This eliminated any possibility of a second strike, which Mitscher immediately canceled.[16] By quick individual calculation, each pilot discovered that the new bearing would strain his fuel supply to the limit, possibly beyond it. The idea of a night water landing was not inviting, especially when chances for rescue narrowed, and the normal intercom chatter died out as these young men kept their thoughts to themselves. But their leaders reviewed possible alternatives to this dreaded fate. Lieutenant Commander J. D. Arnold, leading *Hornet*'s Air Group 2 and one of the last group commanders to fly an Avenger instead of a fighter, "decided . . . it would be best to . . . attack, retire as far as possible before darkness set in, notify the ship . . . then have all planes in the group land in the same vicinity so that rafts could be lashed together and mutual rescues could be affected." [17]

After two hours and 300 miles of flight, at 6:40 P.M. Smoke Strean and his lead planes sighted the Japanese fleet. Six oilers and six destroyers comprised one group, which appeared to have just broken off fueling (though, in fact, no ships had yet been refueled). Off in the distance, fanned out from west to northwest, were the warships: CarDiv 3 and the battle line, CarDiv 2 ten miles to starboard, and CarDiv 1, *Zuikaku* with Ozawa now aboard, about 20 miles northeast of CarDiv 2. The sun was just touching the horizon; the sudden tropical sunset would give the attackers a maximum of 30 minutes to do their work.

Lieutenant Commander J. D. Blitch of *Wasp*'s Bombing 14 figured "that this time we would chase the Jap Fleet instead of running away from it [and I] . . . decided to knock out the fleet oilers in order to prevent a speedy retirement, which would require refueling by them." [18] With time so short, each plane attacked immediately and independently, with no coordination even attempted by squadron commanders. Lieutenant Joe Kane of Bombing 14 "was still undecided about my target. Then [I] saw one of the ships firing quite heavily—apparently at me." He dived his SB2C down, but his bomb missed in what he confessed was a poor attack.[19] Kane observed three near-misses near one oiler, part of the damage that caused two oilers to be disabled, abandoned, and scuttled.

As the other planes passed beyond the oiler group toward the warships, a large burst of flak at 24,000 feet over the Japanese fleet initiated the antiaircraft fire. Even the battlewagons and cruisers fired their main batteries as the curtain of flak formed at 10,000 feet with small calibers firing below that. Ozawa's carriers were recovering a search flight when the American planes appeared, but his flattops were able to launch about 75 planes of their remaining 100. This meager defense took its toll of 20 American planes but could not hope to repel the rest. Mitscher's boys shot down some 65 enemy aircraft, enabling the bombers to press home their attacks.

Time favored the Japanese, for if they could maneuver away from U.S. bombs for just 20 minutes darkness would engulf their fleet. This fact was painfully evident to the American pilots, many of whom experienced the additional trauma of seeing their fuel gauges drop below the half-full mark during the attack. So they attacked wildly, wasting no daylight or fuel to form up into sections or to select targets carefully. They headed toward the enemy carriers. The bombs fell, but they did not repeat the triumph of Midway. Japanese experience and the disjointed attack are part of the explanation. The major reason, however, was the armament of the torpedo bombers. Because bomb-carrying SBDs had sunk the four carriers at Midway and the torpedo-carrying Devastators had been annihilated, carrier practice had come to stress bombs. The real success at Midway, however, had been the great good luck of hitting the Japanese carriers while they were fueling planes and while the old TBDs were being shot down, diverting attention away from the dive bombers. In general, however, a well-placed torpedo lets in water much faster than a bomb hit above the water line, as Mitscher's pilots discovered in this battle. Also, the Avengers had been using bombs and rockets to hit islands since the fall of 1943 and had neglected torpedo tactics. So most Avengers now carried bombs.[20]

Carrying bombs, the Avengers caused damage but no sinkings. Torpedo 10 from *Enterprise* hit *Ryuho*, doing little damage. Dive bombers joined *Yorktown*'s Bombing 1 and *Hornet*'s Torpedo 2 in setting afire big *Zuikaku,* which was prematurely ordered abandoned until the fires were brought under control. Torpedo 28 from *Monterey,* Torpedo 31 from *Cabot,* and the new Torpedo 8 from *Bunker Hill* combined to bomb the light carrier *Chiyoda;* one bomb scored directly on the flight deck, putting the deck out of commission and starting fires. A combination of planes bombed *Junyo,* scoring several direct hits near the bridge and on the flight deck, but she survived.[21]

Honors, however, went to Torpedo 24 from *Belleau Wood,* the only squadron in the battle armed with torpedoes. Lieutenant (jg) George P. Brown led his four Avengers against *Hiyo* in CarDiv 2. Japanese gunners hit Brown's plane, forcing his gunner and radioman to bail out, but Brown kept on until the fires were extinguished by the slipstream. Whether his torpedo hit is anybody's guess, but instead of then breaking off his approach Brown "turned his plane . . . in to[ward] the carrier and . . . flew straight down the length of the ship. The surprised Japanese instinctively concentrated their fire on him, and in that moment of uncertainty" the next Avenger, flown by Lieutenant (jg) Warren R. Omark, dropped its fish—which sped "straight to the mark." [22] *Hiyo* burst into flames, and Lieutenant Brown's two crewmen watched from the water as the converted carrier sank two hours later. They were recovered the next day. Brown was less fortunate; wounded, his plane crippled, he rode it into the dark sea on the return flight.

One carrier sunk, three badly damaged, and two oilers scuttled, with 65 planes shot down—the meager score for what was to have been the greatest carrier battle of the war. But Mitscher's pilots could not continue the attack beyond 7 P.M., by which time the last rays of twilight had disappeared. The new moon on 20 June meant no moon, leaving a sky full of stars, lightning flashes, and variable degrees of overcast—useless for attacking ships and also making difficult the long flight home. Added to these problems of meteorology were the pilots' general inexperience in night operations, battle damage to planes, pilot fatigue from the long flight and hectic battle, the monotonous drone of the engines which added to the general hypnotic effect of the dark, and the knowledge that a water landing awaited those who could not reach the task force. For two hours and 250 miles, these 190 or so surviving planes and crews battled tension and exhaustion to make it back.

A few crippled planes went "into the drink" along the route because of battle damage and wounded pilots like George Brown. But mass ditchings did not occur until fuel supplies ran out within several miles of the task force. Then there were dramatic decisions made and some colorful quips exchanged. A Fighting 1 pilot announced: "Today the Navy is losing one of its best fighter pilots. I am now going in." [23] Five pilots agreed to vote on ditching together, the majority to decide it. The vote was four to one in favor, whereupon the chairman announced: "That's that! O.K. Here we go!" [24] Joe Kane of Bombing 14 was down to five gallons of gas when he headed for a light that did not turn out to be a carrier. He therefore leveled off his Helldiver at 30 feet until the engine died. Then he hit the water, scrambled out of the cockpit, inflated his raft, and helped his gunner out of the rear seat. For five hours Kane, suffering from the "dry heaves," and his crewman drifted, passed by three carriers and one cruiser before being picked up by destroyer *Bell*. Kane slept in the exec's bunk, was transferred to *Hornet* in the morning, whence back to *Wasp*.[25]

For those pilots whose fuel kept them aloft all the way back, an Air Group 16 pilot said the words for everybody: "Boy, oh boy, what a relief! We're here!" [26] The initial visual contact between ships and planes was made at 8:30, whereupon Admiral Mitscher reversed course from west to east to bring the carriers into the wind at 22 knots. The first planes entered their landing circles at 8:45, guided by the lights of the carriers.

Much legend has sprung up on the matter of the ships displaying lights, because it was a dramatic, exciting moment, and recovery was accomplished in the face of a potential submarine threat. Actually, lighted-ship was standard operating procedure for night recovery. In fact, the battle instructions for night specifically stated that if deck landing and ramp lights were not displayed pilots were to interpret this as a signal *not* to land.[27] Expecting lights, then, the returning pilots looked for them, but too often "it was a case of chasing lights that turned out to be stars." [28] Being closest to the returning planes, Admiral Clark turned on the lights of Task Group 58.1, followed almost immediately by Mitscher's order for the whole force to do the same. But Mitscher went all the way: each flagship displayed a searchlight beam, which *was* something new for wartime, while cruisers and destroyers fired starshell to illuminate the carriers. He even launched night fighters to guide in lost planes.[29]

The two-hour scramble to land began at 8:50 when a *Hornet*-based plane landed on *Lexington.* Mitscher therefore instructed the planes to land on any available carrier deck, which they did. As gas gauges neared the empty mark, "planes were stampeding in an animal panic, blind and headlong, crowding and shoving to be the first in line [to land] . . . ." Deck crashes ensued, and many planes were pushed overboard to facilitate recovery. Plane types offered some difficulty, as deck crews on *Lexington* had never handled SB2Cs, and one "airedale" on a CVL could not understand that the wings of the SBD did not fold! Planes ditched alongside, while others mistakenly attempted to land on lighted cruisers and destroyers. Many ships reported a Japanese plane trying to land, but this has yet to be substantiated. As airmen bobbed up and down in the water playing their small waterproof flashlights on the ships, destroyers weaved between the larger vessels to pick them up. Said Admiral Montgomery of the "cans," ". . . had it not been for their persistent and effective efforts, our loss of pilots would have been staggeringly large."[30]

Nerves had reached the breaking point. Commander Blitch of *Wasp*'s Bombing 14 took a shot of medicinal brandy on *Lexington*, then chewed out Admiral Mitscher for the extreme range of the flight.[31] A "Lex" bomber pilot refused the brandy offered him on *Enterprise*, saying, "I've got a bellyfull of war, and no room in it for drinks." An SBD gunner from Bombing 16 thrust his camera into a ready-room chair with the exclamation, "Take the goddam thing! I'll never use it again! I'll never fly again! *Never*!"[32]

But he and the others did fly again. The Japanese fleet was still at large, its location pinpointed by a PBM report at 1:30 A.M. 21 June. Despite fuel shortages to destroyers, Admiral Spruance wanted to press on to catch any cripples and possibly to get off an air strike at daylight. He ordered Admiral Harrill back at Guam to come forward with Task Group 58.4 and oilers and had Mitscher send out long-range searches of radar-equipped Avengers. This time Mitscher had fresh pilots to make these searches.

The stern chase was on, Task Force 58 trying to catch the Japanese Mobile Fleet before it reached the cover of land-based air from the Ryukyus or Japan. To see the carrier operations at first hand, Vice Admiral Slew McCain, who had been riding with Admiral Spruance as an observer, at 8:30 A.M. transferred by destroyer to *Lexington*, where he joined Admiral Mitscher. During the morning the searching TBFs made contact with Ozawa, but the distance was opening. A strike of bomb-laden Hellcats did not make contact, though a bombing attack by fighter pilots on ships probably would have been ineffective. At 10:50 A.M. on the twenty-first Spruance detached Lee and the Battle Line with *Bunker Hill* and *Wasp* to pursue Ozawa and locate any crippled enemy ships. Admiral Clark received *Monterey* and *Cabot* into his task organization, placing six carriers in one formation, the first time this had happened since the Wake strikes of October 1943. Air searches and Admiral Lee found nothing, so at 8:30 P.M. Task Force 58 turned around toward Saipan. Ozawa had escaped to Okinawa.

During this fruitless pursuit, search planes and destroyers combed the Philippine Sea for survivors of the dusk attack. They were rewarded by making many rescues. Mitscher's losses in aircraft had been six Hellcats, ten Helldivers (*no* Dauntlesses), and four Avengers shot down, 17 Hellcats, 35 Helldivers, and 28 Avengers ditched or pushed overboard—100 aircraft in all. Recovered near the force were 51 pilots and 50 aircrewmen; by PBMs, float planes, and destroyers during the pursuit another 36 pilots and 26 crewmen were picked up. Against these 160 men saved, 16 pilots and 33 aircrewmen were lost, plus two ships' officers and four enlisted men during the hectic recovery and deck crashes.[33]

On the twenty-third Admiral Spruance ordered most of Task Force 58 to head for home, Eniwetok, with Harrill's TG 58.4 to remain off Guam. Admiral Clark was ordered to bomb Pagan Island en route to Eniwetok. Clark did, but went out of his way northward. His Japanese-language radio listener learned that more than 100 planes had been staged into Iwo and Chichi Jima, waiting for the weather to clear before going on to attack U.S. shipping off Saipan. Clark obtained permission from Mitscher to conduct independent operations against these islands, a foray Mitscher fittingly dubbed "Operation Jocko." On 24 June Task Group 58.1 planes took off in heavy seas to strike the "Jimas." The Japanese responded with three strikes against Clark's ships, but all were intercepted by Clark's planes and repulsed. The latter two strikes actually reached the task group, but antiaircraft fire helped repel them. By 7 P.M. Clark's ships and planes had destroyed 66 Japanese planes, enough to discourage the relief of Saipan and Guam. But the Jimas were still a menace and would have to be kept neutralized.

Clark then shaped course for Eniwetok, arriving on 27 June, the last of the carrier groups to arrive. The great naval battle for the Marianas—the Battle of the Philippine Sea—was over.

Results of the two-day confrontation with the Japanese Mobile Fleet had been very impressive from the standpoint of aircraft destroyed, but discouraging on the matter of ships. In carrier planes, float planes, and land-based air the Japanese had lost about 475 planes (including most pilots and crews), plus the 66 shot down near Iwo on the twenty-fourth—a phenomenal score. In contrast, Mitscher had lost 100 planes, but only 16 pilots and 33 aircrewmen. In ships, the evidence was less conclusive. The Navy pilots could not be certain of the carriers present or sunk on 20 June, but were certain at least of *Hiyo*'s fate; possibly one or two other flattops had been sunk. This left a Japanese force of at least six and possibly seven or eight carriers, since no American had seen *Shokaku* or *Taiho* go down on the nineteenth.

True, admitted the aviators, they had won the battle. Also, they had successfully covered the beaches, so that no relief came to the Saipan garrison; organized resistance on the island ended on 9 July. But they had missed a golden opportunity to stop the Japanese fleet from ever fighting another battle. Their rejoicing was restrained.

6. *Another Jutland?*

The first official statement regarding the outcome of the Battle of the Philippine Sea hinted at the immediate disappointment over the results. Secretary of the Navy James V. Forrestal, an old aviator himself, announced within two days of the action: "Under the circumstances, our fleet did a magnificent job, but the Navy is not going to be satisfied until the Japanese fleet is wiped out." [1]

At Pearl Harbor, according to British Commander Harry Hopkins of the Cincpac staff, "Criticisms and feelings of regret were uppermost in the minds of most people." [2] Naturally Admiral Nimitz made no criticism, for Spruance was still his most trusted fleet commander. Nevertheless, Nimitz had announced before the Marianas operation his great hope of seeking out and destroying the Japanese fleet. This had been Nimitz's primary objective, though he had not stated it explicitly in Spruance's orders.[3] For the next major operation, Leyte, Nimitz would rectify this confusion by making such an order explicit. In Nimitz's

Deputy, Towers, and the airmen at Hawaii, a disappointed "I-told-you-so" attitude prevailed—the Central Pacific Force commander should have been an aviator as recommended during the squabbles of the previous fall.

In Task Force 58 disappointment was most keen. Thirty-One Knot Burke, a nonaviator who had learned his carrier tactics through continual exposure to them, wrote a scathing action report condemning Spruance for his failure to head west the night of 18–19 June. Mitscher normally signed the reports of his chief of staff without reading them, but this time Burke insisted he read it. After Mitscher had done so he commended Burke for showing it to him and pointed out that while Spruance had made a mistake, he had been under strain and influenced by the men around him and that despite this one error Spruance was still a brilliant and wonderful officer. Mitscher had Burke tone down the report, which still in its final form conveyed the bitter feeling of a job half done: "The enemy had escaped. He had been badly hurt by one aggressive carrier air strike, at the one time he was within range. His fleet was not sunk." [4]

Spruance's reasoning for not heading west that fateful night has been detailed in the preceding narrative, a view he maintained ever after. To this writer he explained: "The Japanese in their operations in the South Pacific, and later at Midway, had always operated with divided forces, from different directions. At Saipan I had no idea from what direction, or directions, they would attack. Our landings were in an early and critical stage. Our amphibious shipping to the westward [eastward?] of the beaches had to be protected from attack." [5] Said his biographer and then operations officer Savvy Forrestel: "His primary mission was to take Saipan, Tinian and Guam, and the amphibious landing on Saipan was at that time in a critical stage with troops ashore with partial supplies and a vast fleet of loaded ships in the vicinity." [6] This "vast fleet of loaded ships," however, lay 200 miles to the east at the time and was nowhere in the vicinity of Saipan.

The aviators did not quarrel with the importance of covering the Marines on Saipan. But, said Monty Montgomery, it was unfortunate "that our entire strength was deployed for this purpose and therefore not permitted an opportunity to take the offensive until too late to prevent the enemy's retirement." [7] Ted Sherman, analyzing Spruance's fear of an end run, concluded: "Spruance was still thinking in terms of a surface action. He did not grasp the tremendous power of our air weapons or their ability to strike in any direction to the limit of their fuel supply. There were no 'ends' in aerial warfare." [8] In other words, Task Force 58 could have steamed 250 miles west of Saipan and still covered it. With which Jocko Clark fully agreed, noting that the best means to protect the beachhead was to adopt an aggressive attitude toward the Japanese fleet.[9]

With much ill-feeling at Pearl Harbor, at Eniwetok–Majuro, and in the Fifth Fleet, Admiral Ernie King arrived at Saipan on 17 July and tried to pour oil on the troubled waters. His "first act on stepping ashore was to tell Spruance he had done exactly the correct thing . . . no matter what anyone else might say, especially since he had to remember that the Japanese had another fleet ready in the Inland Sea to pounce upon the many American transports . . . at Saipan." [10] Again, what transports? This was no doubt window-dressing to reassure Spruance of King's faith in him and to quiet the criticism. Otherwise, King would have to have been pulling the historian's leg: fleet intelligence in May 1944 had told nothing of another enemy fleet in the Inland Sea. It had revealed only two escort carriers and two *Ise*-class half-battleships with flight decks, which, had they sortied to reinforce Ozawa, would have taken 26 hours to get to Iwo Jima and 48 hours to reach Saipan, and through waters patrolled by American subs.[11] Spruance had never given thought to any such fleet anyway, only to the possible "end run" by part of Ozawa's nine-carrier force operating from Tawi Tawi.[12] Besides, Ernie King, the aggressive fighter, had never lost a fleet exercise and had been a pioneer in the development of offensive fast carrier tactics. His great respect for Spruance no doubt dictated his compromising attitude in this instance.

Part of the criticism involved Spruance's staff. The aviators complained that Spruance surrounded himself only with nonaviators, and that his chief of staff, Captain Carl Moore, was too junior to serve in such a capacity to a four-star admiral. Arleigh Burke went further and criticized the staff as too homogeneous in thinking and temperament.[13] These staff officers, upon whom Spruance depended heavily, never disagreed, never enjoyed the dynamic clashes that produced friction yet ideas, as on Mitscher's staff and between Mitscher and his admirals. That Ernie King accepted these arguments is borne out by the fact that upon his return to Washington in late July King relieved Carl Moore, effective 1 August

1944. Spruance's new chief of staff would be King's own operations officer, veteran aviator Rear Admiral Art Davis.[14] And forever after every non-air fleet commander would have an aviator for chief of staff.

The most important postwar interpretation of Spruance's decision was by Professor Morison, who explained Spruance's and Mitscher's divergent attitudes in terms of responsibilities. Mitscher had "an absorbing passion . . . to destroy the Japanese carriers that menaced his carriers," while Spruance "had the overall responsibility . . . to secure the Marianas . . . [and was] imbued with a strong sense of that mission . . . ." [15] I find this thesis difficult to accept, since Mitscher knew very well that Task Force 58 was in no critical danger. Its superior pilots, aircraft, and antiaircraft defenses had driven Japanese air forces from the skies for seven straight months, and it went to Saipan superior in numbers and almost certainly superior in quality. Rather, it was the Japanese carrier force that had been in critical danger. Spruance did not know his chief weapon, the fast carrier, as intimately as did Mitscher—hence his reluctance to use it aggressively in a situation that called for expertise. On the other hand, the battleship he knew better.

Morison also speculated rather wildly that a dawn strike by Mitscher's planes on the Japanese fleet on 19 June would have been less favorable than the results of the Turkey Shoot. Such an attack "would probably have sunk some of the Japanese carriers; but the Japanese planes might also have sunk some of ours." [16] This is, indeed, a very tenuous idea. First, if some (two, three?) Japanese carriers had been sunk, not many of their planes would have survived to attack Task Force 58 or the Saipan beach. Second, a full Japanese deckload strike (130 planes?) would still have been no match for the radar-directed combat air patrol Hellcats. Third, though greater losses of aircraft were expected in carrier battles, Mitscher had every reason to believe his fighters would gain supremacy of the air over Ozawa's fleet—just as they had over the Marianas in February, over Truk on two visits, and over Palau—leaving the Japanese ships at the mercy of his bombers. Crippled by Mitscher's bombs and torpedoes, these ships could have been closed and polished off by Lee's Battle Line. Finally, if Ozawa *had* split his force in two as Spruance guessed he might, a dawn strike by the full force of Mitscher's carriers followed up by

Lee's battleships could easily have annihilated the main fighting strength of the Japanese fleet—and Saipan could still have been relieved if necessary.

Professor Morison drew from the days of sail for evidence to support Spruance's decision. He selected French Admiral de Grasse's brilliant maneuver, during the battle of the Virginia Capes (September 1781), of drawing away the British fleet from the Chesapeake Bay and electing not to fight to a decision. In this manner, the sea battle was indecisive but General Washington was reinforced in front of Yorktown, and de Grasse manuvered back to support Washington and forgot ideas of a victory over the British fleet. In this manner Lord Cornwallis was compelled to surrender Yorktown and his own army, the result being the recognition of American independence by the British. The example is a good one to a point, but it fails to mention one important fact: the naval policy of France throughout the eighteenth century was *always* to eschew any major confrontation with the British Navy, even when superior, and primarily to support the army and operations ashore. De Grasse had never enjoyed a Midway, whereas Spruance had. American naval strategy called for the big battle in the British tradition as well as supporting forces ashore, the former being the gospel according to Mahan.[17]

A more proper comparison from the days of sail is the treatment of Admiral de Grasse by Admiral Sir George B. Rodney after the surrender of Yorktown. De Grasse unsuccessfully attacked the anchored smaller fleet of Admiral Sir Samuel Hood at St. Kitts in the West Indies (January 1782) before being confronted by the combined fleets of Rodney and Hood in the battle of the Saints (April 1782), also in the Indies. The conduct of Rodney and Hood provides a clue to understanding the later actions of Spruance and Mitscher, for, says Mahan, "this whole action . . . is fraught with sound military teaching." Rodney succeeded in dividing and scattering the French fleet, but he ignored the suggestions of his chief of staff, Douglas, to follow up and crush de Grasse; Admiral Hood claimed that Rodney could have taken 20 French ships, more than half the enemy fleet. Says Mahan: "Advice and criticism are easy . . . but great results cannot often be reached in war without risk and effort." Not following up the advantage "with all possible vigor," Rodney "had allowed the immediate objective to blind him to the general military objective"—destruction of the French fleet in the West Indies.[18]

Historical parallels always break down under close comparison, but in this case the general lesson is instructive. Mahan favored complete destruction of the enemy battle fleet and condemned Rodney for being satisfied with only a tactical victory. Thus with Spruance. The French fleet lived to fight again. It did not fight again, because the statesmen soon ended the war, but the surviving fleet gave France much bargaining power at the conference table. The Japanese fleet also lived to fight again, and it did.

The issue therefore comes back to formalist versus melee tactics. Like Rodney at the Saints and Jellicoe at Jutland Spruance played the cautious, calculating fleet commander. Battleship-oriented, he had assumed tactical command over a carrier action and had failed to heed the advice of the experts in prosecuting that battle. On the other hand, Spruance had been hampered by inadequate intelligence, at the same time knowing that the enemy knew his position quite well from its long-range search planes. The heavy responsibility of command and of the safety of the entire Fifth Fleet in a sustained campaign gave Spruance little time to rethink strategic missions. His one stated order from Cincpac was to seize Saipan; of that he could be certain. Decisions involving a fleet action had been properly left on an *ad hoc* basis to Commander Fifth Fleet. Thus Spruance followed his training and judgment to play it safe, but in doing so he caused an even more decisive victory to be postponed.

Mitscher and the other carrier admirals were meleeists in the Nelsonian tradition. Of Admiral Lord Nelson Captain Roskill has said that he "understood his opponent's failings sufficiently clearly to realize that hot pursuit was the most probable way of destroying the last remnants of his self-confidence, and so leading him into error." [19] The air commanders of American Fleet Problem XVIII in 1937 had embraced this philosophy for carriers: "Once an enemy carrier is within striking distance of our fleet no security remains until it—its squadrons—or both, are destroyed. . . ." Carrier operations beyond the main body of the fleet (or landing force) reduces the defense of the latter, hence the detaching of the carriers becomes a gamble, but the fleet commander "is playing for high stakes." [20] Had the Fifth Fleet embodied a meleeist rather than formalist philosophy, the actions of 19–20 June 1944 could have resulted in one of the most decisive naval battles in history.

Instead, the Battle of the Philippine Sea compares with the

battle of Jutland in 1916 in strategic consequences. At Jutland, the German ships had been badly battered when Jellicoe had crossed their *T*. At Saipan, Spruance's *T*—several hundred F6F Hellcats—destroyed Ozawa's air strike in the famous Turkey Shoot. Both battles had gone through several stages, the last being the escape of the defeated fleet at night. For two years after Jutland the British Grand Fleet had had to stand vigil over the North Sea lest the German fleet again sortie. During the summer of 1944, as Pacific planners prepared for the Philippines campaign, every move and target was selected with the menace of the Japanese fleet always in mind. So important did those six surviving carriers become to the fleet commander at Leyte Gulf that they would come very close to causing an American military calamity of the first order.

Seven:
Emergence of the Air Admirals

The summer of 1944 marked a turning point in the war not only because of the major Allied landings at Normandy, France, and in the Marianas but also in the progress and successes of naval aviation. Naval analyst Bernard Brodie, impressed by the record, could write in June that the aircraft carrier "has won for itself a place in the fleet second to none . . . [having] struck blows such as no other type of warship could deliver, and . . . is . . . the most versatile of combatant craft, both offensively and defensively." [1]

In the Pacific, the Marianas campaign demonstrated the fast carrier task force to be, in the words of ComAirPac, "a well-rounded air force, able to keep the sea for long periods until the job is done and until land-based aviation can set up bases and fully relieve the seagoing air force." [2] The defeat of the Japanese fleet and the capture of Saipan "should prove conclusively," said the ComAirPac staff, "the combat effectiveness of Navy fighter planes, pilots and tactics, and defensive abilities of Navy fighter direction, against the pick of the Japanese air force." [3]

In the Atlantic, Allied strategy had shifted from the defensive to the offensive in the year beginning June 1943. Prior to that month German U-boat wolfpacks had been devastating Allied convoys, but the change came with the formation of Tenth Fleet under the personal direction of Admiral King. Utilizing new techniques developed through "operations research" and the results of intensified industrial output, Tenth Fleet organized its counterattack against the U-boat around the new Hunter-Killer Group. Each HUK group included one escort carrier with a dozen or more Avengers and a half-dozen fighters or less, along with about half a dozen destroyers or destroyer escorts—ships and planes well-equipped with radar. Attacking U-boats offensively, each HUK group assumed the status of an independent slow carrier (top speed 18 knots) task force. Before any major landing could take place on the Continent, Allied sea lanes had to be rid of the U-boat, and by D-Day 1944 they generally were. Naval air was the major factor in winning the Battle of the Atlantic and in patrolling Allied sea lanes for the duration of the war in Europe.

In the Mediterranean, naval aviation with its techniques for supporting amphibious assaults had been conspicuous by its absence. Long-range land-based tactical air forces from North Africa had been present but largely ineffective at Sicily in July and at Salerno in September 1943; the extreme distance of their bases from Anzio helped that landing bog down after January 1944. The Pacific experience changed this inadequacy, however, and for the landings in southern France in August 1944 an Anglo-American escort carrier support force was formed. Task Force 88, Rear Admiral T. H. Troubridge RN, included nine escort carriers, two of which belonged to the American carrier division under Rear Admiral Calvin T. Durgin. For many days Hellcats, Wildcats, and Seafires bombed Nazi rolling stock and retreating army columns with much success.[4]

By the end of the summer of 1944, both the Atlantic and the Mediterranean were virtual Allied lakes, the former patrolled regularly by land- and carrier-based planes. In its final phase, the war in Europe—the Army's war—would be won on the ground and by the big bombers based in England.

The Navy's war, the Pacific war, by no means reached its final stage during the summer of 1944. Several key islands had yet to be captured in the drive westward, the Japanese surface fleet and air forces remained constant and unpredictable threats, and the road to the Luzon bottleneck was still far away. When it was reached, the liberation of the Philippines and the blockade of Japan could begin. Then there were the millions of well-trained, veteran, undefeated Japanese ground forces in China and the homeland, inviting invasion and conquest in a Pacific Normandy that still lay one or two years in the future.

For the Navy the summer of 1944 marked the last time the admirals could pause to consider their next course of action, and the last chance for major changes to be made in the fleet. When they moved again, it would be to the distant peripheral waters of Southeast Asia, against the interior bulwarks of Japan's defenses. Air, sea, and ground attacks by the Japanese would be unrelenting from the Philippines all the way to Tokyo. Therefore risks and chances had to be minimized, only trusted leaders given command responsibilities. And above all, as the aviators saw it, the fact had to be recognized once and for all that the Navy's war henceforward would be an air war. In other words, the United States Navy had to become an air navy.

1. Battle of Washington

The first six months of 1944 witnessed not only spectacular air victories in the Pacific but also equally remarkable aerial successes by the Army Air Forces over Germany. These demonstrations of air power increased the importance of aviation in both the Army and Navy. But each air force was unique. The Navy's air now determined the character of the fleet itself; the two were inseparable. The Army's air was in fact autonomous and bore little actual resemblance to the parent service. Strategic bombers and the foot soldier could survive without one another administratively and operationally. To achieve increased status, then, early in 1944 both sets of aviators began agitating, and—since defense reorganization was inconvenient during wartime—the two services focused on the postwar situation.

In the Navy, the airmen wanted control of the fleet, more aircraft carriers and pilots, and a lion's share of the postwar Navy budget. In the Army, the aviators wanted independence through unification of the Army and Navy into one Department of National Defense and the creation of an equal subservice, the Air Force.

The naval aviators enjoyed a friend in James Forrestal, who acceded to the Secretaryship of the Navy upon the death of Frank Knox in April 1944. An early naval pilot himself, Forrestal stood in direct personal and administrative defiance of Admiral King. Indeed Knox and President Roosevelt had favored dividing King's job between King as Cominch and Vice Admiral Horne as a super CNO for logistics and administration. In truth, King's work load was mounting, and the promotion of Forrestal appeared likely to reduce King's power. But Forrestal, realizing he should not jeopardize Cominch's authority during the massive operations at Normandy and Saipan, left King alone and decided during the summer of 1944 that as long as King cooperated no wartime reorganization was necessary. Forrestal therefore directed that all plans for reorganization of the Navy Department be dropped, and in November 1944 organized instead a policy group of top Navy civilians and admirals to advise the Secretary.[1]

Two other men wielded much influence on behalf of the aviators. One was Assistant Secretary for Air Artemus L. Gates, another early-day pilot who fought doggedly for aviation's place in the fleet. The other was the Deputy CNO (Air), until 1 August 1944 Vice Admiral J. S. McCain and afterward Vice Admiral Aubrey W. Fitch. Since the creation of this post one year before, the aviators had claimed that DCNO (Air) held direct authority from the CNO and therefore was equal in authority to the Vice CNO, Admiral Horne. They wanted to run all aspects of the air program from planning to procurement, and were therefore opposed by Admiral Horne and other nonpilots. Finally, Horne got King to direct that the DCNO (Air) was junior and subordinate to the Vice CNO, but this did not silence the aviators, who continued to press for their special place within the Navy's administrative hierarchy.[2]

What the aviators lacked, then, was representation at the very top levels of the flag echelon in the office of Cominch. On 1 October 1944 Admiral King streamlined his staff by creating the combined post of Deputy Cominch-CNO, which went to his chief of staff, Vice Admiral Richard S. Edwards. The new position dealt with matters of military policy, while fleet operations on the staff remained the responsibility of the chief of staff, now Vice Admiral Savvy Cooke.[3] Neither of these men had wings, and their ranking counterparts in aviation were still in the Pacific. But the next echelon of admirals in Washington included many prominent airmen: Rear Admiral Art Davis was Cominch operations officer until 1 August 1944 when he was relieved by Rear Admiral Malcolm F. Schoeffel, top man in the Naval Academy class of 1919 and recent skipper of light carrier *Cabot.* Rear Admiral Donald B. Duncan, who had brought *Essex* into commission, lent his fine abilities to Cominch as planning officer. Rear Admiral Duke Ramsey remained Chief of the Bureau of Aeronautics, and Captain Wallace Beakley was King's air officer.

These aviation zealots could not hope to revamp the Navy Department until the real powerhouses of naval air—Towers, Mitscher, the Shermans—returned from the wars. Yet, in a manner of speaking, nature was taking its course as more airmen were promoted to flag rank; the number of air admirals jumped from 34 to

54 in 1943–1944, from 20 per cent to 26 per cent of all flag officers.[4] The difference was made up in fewer "black shoes," admirals who commanded the increasingly fewer battleship divisions.

The Navy was obviously and rapidly becoming an air navy, so much so that in considering the postwar Navy Admiral Horne in May 1944 recommended to Forrestal a peacetime fleet of 21 fast attack carriers, 22 escort carriers, and only nine battleships. Horne could not accept the airmen's demands for 42 per cent of the total postwar Navy budget, including a quota of 40,000 pilots, but the trend was clear. The major stumbling block for postwar planning was the absence of any potential blue-water enemy fleet after the defeat of Japan. Even given the remote possibility of Russian and/or Chinese belligerence, these nations had no large surface fleets. Also, with the extermination of Hitlerism, no blue-water navy would be left to challenge Anglo-American naval supremacy in the Atlantic. With no "precise task" before the postwar navy as of mid-1944, the admirals looked to "a scaled down version of the wartime service."[5]

Even before the great Marianas Turkey Shoot of June 1944, the aviators had succeeded in gaining a construction program that would produce a carrier fleet of vast proportions before any postwar scaling down would take place. By 1 July 1944, the Navy had in commission ten *Essex*-class heavy carriers, plus the prewar *Saratoga* and *Enterprise*, and nine *Independence*-class light carriers. In addition, keels had been laid in 1943 for eight more *Essex*es and two *Midway*-class battle carriers; most of these vessels would presumably get into the fighting if the Pacific war lasted at least until the end of 1945, which everyone anticipated. By that time, 1 January 1946, counting from 1 January 1944 and barring sinkings, the Pacific Fleet would theoretically be able to float a huge fast carrier fleet of 20 heavy carriers, nine light carriers, and two of the big battle carriers—surely enough with which to finish the war against Japan no matter how long it lasted after 1945.

But the masterful accomplishments of the fast carriers at Rabaul, the Marshalls, and Truk enabled the aviators to get four more *Essex*-class keels laid during the first six months of 1944. By 1 July and the defeat of Japan's fleet in the Battle of the Philippine Sea by the 15 flattops of Task Force 58, naval air had won control of the skies over the Central Pacific. Surely a fleet of carriers more than twice that size would be unnecessary by 1946.

The crushing blows to the enemy fleet off Saipan in June, however, convinced Cincpac that the fast carrier program should be given top priority. Admiral Nimitz informed Admiral King that the carrier-building program should be accelerated, but when King visited Nimitz at Pearl Harbor on 14 July he expressed reluctance to give carrier construction any more emphasis.[6] King could not deny Nimitz's request, though, and immediately upon his return to Washington King agreed. To Nimitz's recommendation King replied on 31 July: "Concur in general. The carrier building program will be awarded suitable priority."[7]

Rapid completion of carriers then building was what Nimitz wanted, but the airmen and Admiral Horne also had postwar concerns. On 17 August Admiral Fitch informed Horne that the postwar navy needed three battle, 11 heavy, and 17 escort carriers.[8] But the 35 carriers in commission or building at the beginning of the summer seemed insufficient. Consequently, during the summer Navy-contracted shipbuilders laid down three more *Essex*es, another *Midway* battle carrier, and two light carriers of a new *Saipan* class. As late as January 1945 one more *Essex* was laid down. The aviators would one day have a stockpile of no less than 41 attack carriers (excluding the old *Ranger*) from which to "scale down" into a respectable postwar fleet.

One may conclude the obvious, that the admirals were cheating on their wartime budget to build ships which would never fight Japan. But they were realistic in their assumptions that public interest and hence Congressional appropriations would drop to the usual postwar lows, and the Navy would need to maintain up-to-date ships in adequate numbers during such lean years. The hearings of Senator C. A. Woodrum's Select Committee on Post-war Military Policy during the spring of 1944 already suggested the growing movement of the Army Air Forces to compete with the postwar Naval Air Force. Typical Navy silence led to the formulation of two tentative Navy demobilization plans in May and June without consultation with the other service, but in fact the entire Navy approach to its postwar requirements, beginning with the earlier Yarnell study, pointed up the general uncertainty throughout the Navy about its future.

With this lack of direction in mind, on 22 October 1944 Admiral King turned over all postwar planning to his new Deputy Cominch-CNO, Vice Admiral Edwards, and specifically to his planning officer, Rear Admiral Duncan. These two men initiated a systematic study of the Navy's postwar requirements. With the anticipated limitations on such a fleet, priorities had to be established; these priorities were fast carriers and escort carriers, then battleships. Consequently airman Duncan was a key man for the task.[9]

The threat of the AAF to the Navy lay in the postwar world, when appropriations would be thin. In the spring of 1944 the idea of unification was only vague, but practically all the Navy's key leaders opposed it. The exceptions were Secretary Knox, who died, and Admiral Yarnell, who was already retired. The others proclaimed the continued autonomy of the Navy before the Woodrum Committee hearings, with Di Gates informing that group on 15 May that "the naval air force has proven to be the most important member of the Navy team." [10] Yet two fears were beginning to worry the Navy and its airmen; first, that a separate and politically powerful U.S. Air Force would deprive the Navy's air wing of funds, and worse, that naval aviation might conceivably be placed under the over-all administration of an independent Air Force, a move that had nearly destroyed the Fleet Air Arm in Britain between the wars. These fears would mount as the end of the war approached.

The problem being a military one, on 9 May the Joint Chiefs of Staff appointed a special committee to analyze the various possibilities of postwar defense organization and to obtain opinions from all interested parties. The committee, headed by retired Admiral J. O. Richardson, included one Army major general, an AAF major general and colonel, and one naval member, the brilliant Rear Admiral Malcolm Schoeffel, King's operations officer. Significantly, as Duncan the aviator laid the groundwork for the postwar Navy, so Schoeffel the aviator represented the Navy in the unification investigation. The Richardson committee interviewed military people in Washington, Europe, the Mediterranean, the Southwest Pacific, and, in late November and early December 1944, the generals and admirals at Pearl Harbor. For months these investigators collected the best opinion in the armed services on the subject of postwar defense organization.[11]

As the war moved westward and the carriers engaged in increasingly furious air battles the closer they got to Japan, the Navy entered a new realm, public relations. The formerly "silent service" established a program to inform the public of its accomplishments and its attitudes toward the proposed unification.[12] Even as the fast carriers swept into the western Carolines in the late summer of

1944 the Navy and its airmen were opening in Washington a battle that would become full-scale in the postwar years.

Jake Fitch, for example, went on nation-wide radio on 29 August to mark the thirty-first anniversary of naval aviation and the first anniversary of the fast carrier force, initiated at Marcus Island one year before. Joined by Vice Admiral Pat Bellinger, ComAirLant, and Rear Admiral Monty Montgomery, on leave from the Pacific, Fitch told the radio audience that the carrier offensive thus far had been like "a sweet summer zephyr" compared to what was coming.[13] Rather than by the battleship admirals or Army Air generals, the brunt of this attack would be borne by the hard-pressed Japanese.

2. *Japan*

While the United States Navy talked in terms of 41 fast carriers and indulged in the luxury of postwar planning, the Imperial Japanese Navy was fighting for its life in the summer of 1944 against seemingly overwhelming odds. The loss of Saipan early in July, uncharacteristically admitted by the government to the people, shook the nation's confidence in the Navy and led immediately to the downfall of General Hideki Tojo and his military cabinet.[1] Realizing that the "loss of fleet and air forces . . . [meant] no effective defense could be mounted," [2] Japanese naval leaders concluded that defeat was inevitable, and they began to press for peace. The Emperor's Supreme Naval Adviser decided: "Hell is on us." [3] To Japan, "the loss of Saipan was the turning point in the trend of the Pacific war." [4]

Though seriously weakened by the loss of three proud ships, *Shokaku*, *Hiyo*, and the new *Taiho*, in the Battle of the Philippine Sea, the Japanese carrier fleet had one last hope for striking a major blow to the United States Pacific Fleet. In the long run Japan had lost the battle of industry, a result of shortages from submarine attacks on supply ships and of an overstrained shipbuilding industry. After Midway, the Navy had programmed for 20 fast carriers from the keel, six *Taiho*-class, eight of the 17,000-ton *Unryu*-class, and seven modified *Unryus*, but only *Taiho* and six of the *Unryus* had been actually laid down. *Taiho* had joined the fleet in time to be sunk in June, but several *Unryus* were commissioned during the summer. In addition, ships under conversion to carriers included the

64,800-ton *Shinano* and 12,500-ton light carrier *Ibuki*, both due for commissioning by early 1945 with the rest of the *Unryus*.[5]

The important question was time. Japan expected an American landing in the Philippines in November 1944. If the Americans met that timetable, as indeed they coincidentally planned to do, then Japan had four months in which to hastily train new air groups to replace those lost in the Turkey Shoot and to shake down two and possibly three new fast carriers of the *Unryu* class. On 6 August 17,150-ton *Unryu* was commissioned, followed four days later by 17,460-ton sister ship *Amagi*. Each ship carried 54 aircraft and could make up to 34 knots. Vice Admiral Ozawa immediately shifted his flag to the new *Amagi* as Commander Third Fleet and ComCarDiv 1, *Amagi*, *Unryu*, *Zuikaku*. They were joined on 15 October by 17,260-ton sister ship *Katsuragi*. CarDiv 2 was dissolved and its ships, *Junyo* and *Ryuho*, transferred to CarDiv 4, Rear Admiral Chiaki Matsuda, whose other carriers were half-battleships *Ise* and *Hyuga*. CarDiv 3 remained light carriers *Zuiho*, *Chitose*, and *Chiyoda*.

In aircraft, Zero fighters were available, and the Navy had hopes that its new 400-mph Shiden-kai fighter would soon be ready for the carriers. The actual successor to the Zero, the 390-mph Reppu fighter, lagged in development, but a prototype with an improved engine flew in October. Mass production never began for the Reppu, but the Navy would soon receive the first of 400 Shiden-kais.[6]

Theoretically, then, by mid-November 1944 Admiral Toyoda would have a fairly respectable fleet. Ozawa's fast carrier force would include five heavy carriers, four light carriers, and the two *Ise*s. The real weakness lay in untrained pilots who needed to practice in the cockpit, first ashore and then from a carrier deck. During the summer, fuel shortages caused by submarine sinkings of tankers restricted any large-scale air training operations and ship maneuvers. Even the few air operations undertaken from carrier decks in the Inland Sea of Japan resulted in deck crashes and the death of many green pilots. The Second Fleet battleships and cruisers, all having survived the Marianas campaign, had transferred to Lingga Roads near Singapore, still under the command of Vice Admiral Kurita.

In reality, the Japanese surface navy was finished, unless a miracle, very good strategy, great good luck, and general bungling on the part of the Americans combined to make the Mobile Fleet a serious opponent to the U.S. Fleet. Several thoughtful Japanese officers realized the truth, and one, Captain Eiichiro Jyo of light carrier *Chiyoda* concluded that his navy could "no longer . . . hope to sink the numerically superior enemy aircraft carriers through ordinary attack methods. . . ." He therefore recommended to Admiral Ozawa, with the full endorsement of veteran carrier commander Admiral Obayashi, "the immediate organization of special attack units to carry out crash-dive tactics" against the American fast carriers. In other words, he advocated suicide attacks.[7]

The recommendation for suicide tactics still seemed extreme to most leaders in the Japanese high command, for many good land-based pilots remained in Japan for staging south to any threatened area, along with some veteran carrier pilots. So Ozawa rejected the idea, but another high officer gave Jyo's plan serious consideration. This was aviator Vice Admiral Takajiro Onishi, then serving in the air munitions section at headquarters and earmarked to command land-based air in the Philippines in October. Onishi knew the Japanese fleet and air forces could never hope to wage a successful battle against the U.S. Navy using conventional tactics, and he began laying plans for his *kamikaze* corps of suicide planes.

Japan's enemy knew that the Imperial Navy had been badly hurt and that its planes and pilots were inferior. "This may not continue indefinitely," warned the ComAirPac staff late in July. "An improvement of Japanese aircraft even halfway to German standards would cause our carrier forces considerable difficulty." Admirals Towers and Pownall cautioned the aviators about "the potential vulnerability of aircraft carriers to effectively coordinated torpedo and bombing attacks." To exploit this weakness, they warned, the enemy would change his tactics and strategy, a thought certainly borne out by the idea for a suicide corps. The closer the fast carriers got to Japan, the more stubborn resistance would be. "Losses will be heavier. Overconfidence is not justified."[8]

3. *Innovations and Admirals*

Operations culminating in the defeat of the Japanese Mobile Fleet and capture of Saipan in early July 1944 created a minor breathing period for Admirals King and Nimitz during the Central Pacific offensive. Carrier raids and smaller landings continued throughout the summer of 1944, but without fear of enemy fleet or major air interference. This relative lull gave the high commanders the opportunity to assess their achievements, rectify mistakes, update administrative organizations and patterns, change personnel due for rotation for various reasons, and welcome new ships and weapons into the fleet.

Admiral Nimitz could count on a continuous flow of new *Essex*-class carriers for his offensive. During the summer three reported to the Pacific, *Franklin* (CV-13), *Ticonderoga* (CV-14), and *Hancock* (CV-19). New commissionings occurred at about one per month, *Bennington* (CV-20) in August, *Shangri-La* (CV-38) in September, *Randolph* (CV-15) in October, and *Bon Homme Richard* (CV-31) in November. New launchings in late 1944 were *Antietam*, *Lake Champlain*, and *Boxer*. These ships compared almost identically with the earlier *Essex*es, except for slightly longer flight decks on some of them and a small change in antiaircraft defenses. The 20mm Oerlikon had been the mainstay of carrier gun defenses, but as night operations intensified these guns gave way in prominence to more of the longer-range 40mm Bofors and 5-inch/38 with its increasingly accurate proximity-fuzed shells.[1]

The primary defense of the fast carriers remained their combat air patrol interceptors, directed to the attacker by skillful fighter director officers using radar equipment. Admiral Mitscher noted that the success of Task Force 58 in the Marianas "proved that the long and costly efforts in research, training, and the practical applications of radar have not been in vain." [2] Despite widespread transmission difficulties because of different models of radios, *Hornet*'s air officer, Commander Roy Johnson, reported coordination between fighter directors and fighters at Saipan "well-nigh perfect and interceptions . . . made like clockwork." [3] The final judge was the victim, Admiral Ozawa, who attributed U.S. carrier superiority to "the use of radar, interception of radio messages, and intercepting by radar of Japanese air attacks which [American planes] . . . can catch and eat up whenever they want to." [4] Early in the summer the Navy began to install the new Mark 22 radar, which, adapted to shipboard fire control systems, operated with the older Mark 4 and Mark 12 radars to give an even better fix on incoming bogies.[5] By the autumn each fast carrier was equipped with improved antiaircraft defenses.

With regard to new aircraft, especially fighters, the Navy was in somewhat of a quandary. The F6F-3 Hellcat, flying at speeds up to 376 miles per hour (at 17,000 feet), had defeated the Zero and every other Japanese fighter in the air, and in April 1944 production began on the F6F-5, better armored, more streamlined, and slightly faster than its predecessor.[6] With such a plane, augmented by the still land-based F4U-1 Corsair, civilian defense managers saw little need for spending large sums to produce any completely new airplanes to replace these superb fighters. For instance, in a press conference at Pearl Harbor on 18 September Di Gates remarked: "My personal feeling is that we can win the war with the kind of equipment we have. I see no reason for putting new [aircraft] types in production as long as the Corsairs and Hellcats are doing the job they are." [7] Such an attitude made aircraft development at BuAer extremely difficult. Commander Robert E. Dixon, a veteran pilot then heading the Military Requirements section of the Bureau, noted in a letter to Jimmy Flatley that "progress is upset by the semi-experts who have been with you a few days for their total war experience and come back with all the dope," namely that "what we have will win the war." Dixon stressed that "it is extremely difficult to sell new articles here unless we get some backing from you out there." [8]

Superficially, the policy of continuing to rely upon the tried veteran planes made sense, but wars are not won and technology does not advance if progress is halted. Furthermore, the Japanese might be developing new fighters to match the Hellcat and Corsair, as indeed they were: the Shiden-kai and the Reppu. There was the additional question of readying suitable aircraft for the postwar world, for the Germans and British were pioneering in jet-propelled aircraft; postwar air forces would rely upon the successors of these jets as well as new piston-driven planes. Likewise, unforeseen requirements—in the form of new airborne weapons, radar, and heavier bombloads necessary to carry the war to Japan—had begun to confront the older planes. Newly designed planes specifically suited to these needs would be more economical in the long run than the attempt to make on-the-spot modifications to existing aircraft which would compromise their existing advantages.

The major change involved fighters. In all fast carrier operations, once the fighters had gained command of the air, bombers could attack at will. Fighters carrying rockets and bombs absorbed many of the bombers' functions. And as the fleet neared Japan, shipping targets would decrease, thus lessening the need for torpedo bombing. In the spring of 1944 Admiral Nimitz, faced with long-range ordnance planning, called for 1.67 carrier air groups per fast carrier. This new requirement meant that 32 carrier air groups would be in commission by 30 June 1945 and 39 by 31 December 1945, and it also meant activating air groups six months before they would be needed in combat. Nimitz and his air planners under Towers therefore had to anticipate their needs for additional fighter planes for January 1945. In fact, they needed more fighters immediately. Admiral King accepted Nimitz's proposal and on 31 July 1944 authorized that heavy carrier air groups be changed from 18 torpedo bombers, 36 dive bombers, and 36 fighters to 18 VT, 24 VB, "with VF to capacity," or about 54.[9] Accordingly, late in August each large air group began trading in 12 SB2Cs for 12 F6Fs. All bomber pilots were checked out in fighters, and those assigned to the new Hellcats found their strange "fighter-bombers" equipped with single 500-pound general-purpose bombs. Under the prodding of Admiral Halsey all heavy carriers had their 54 fighters by November.[10]

The fighter most wanted to supplement the Hellcat was already well known as a Jap-killer, the "Whistling Death" Corsair. Originally designed before the war as a carrier plane, the "hot" F4U had been earmarked for Fighting 12 aboard *Saratoga* early in 1943. Unfortunately, pilot visibility was poor for landing, during which the plane tended to bounce. The planes were sent ashore to Navy and Marine Corps squadrons in the Solomons, where they established brilliant records. But until the carrier-landing weaknesses could be corrected, the Navy, specifically Captain Beakley of the Cominch staff, kept the Corsair off carriers. Finally, in April 1944, the Vought F4U-1 (also produced as the Goodyear FG-1 and Brewster F3A-1) qualified for carrier operations. And in October, the newer, faster (446 mph to 425) F4U-4 (and a few FG-4s) began to join Navy squadrons. Some night Corsairs had served on the fast carriers early in 1944, but these were now taken off. No more Corsairs were then assigned to the carriers, despite their qualification, simply because the F4U had become the standard Marine Corps fighter and could not be spared for carrier duty.[11]

One possible solution was to provide the Marines with a new replacement for their Corsairs, which could then be transferred to the carriers. The Bureau of Aeronautics had just the plane, the Grumman XF7F-1 Tigercat. This twin-engine, single-seat fighter and the night radar-equipped two-seat XF7F-2N were designed to operate from the new *Midway*-class battle carriers. With a speed equivalent to that of the F4U-1, this power-packed fighter carried four 20mm guns in the wings, four 50-caliber machine guns in the nose, and equipment for two 1000-pound bombs or a torpedo.[12] First flying in April 1944, the Tigercat remained a carrier plane throughout the summer. However, DCNO (Air) planners felt that if 12 Marine squadrons could be equipped with F7Fs, the Corsairs of those units could go to the fast carriers, but this not until early 1946.[13] When Assistant Secretary Gates and Admirals Ramsey and Radford presented the idea to Admiral Towers in August, Towers agreed the F7F was too large for "standard carrier use" and should be land-based. Happily, the Marines soon endorsed the F7F as "the very backbone" of future Marine aviation, especially as a night fighter.[14]

A sound solution to a difficult problem, but 1946 was too far in the future to wait for a new fighter. Besides, the F4U would complement the F6F, not replace it. The specially designed replacement would be another Grumman product for which DCNO (Air) and BuAer planners had great hopes, the XF8F-1 Bearcat. A small, speedy plane with only four 50-caliber machine guns, the first experimental model flew on 21 August 1944, having been designed and built in a record ten months.[15] This plane, and the experimental FR Fireball, Bob Dixon wrote to Jimmy Flatley, "are so much improved over what you have [in the fleet] that I feel any shortcomings they have are more than made up by their superior performance." [16] This enthusiasm led Admiral Towers to tell Gates, Ramsey, and Radford in August that if the F8Fs "turn out as well as could be expected," they could replace the F6s at least aboard the light carriers.[17] But this could not take place until the autumn of 1945.

Other less-promising though still important experimental fighters were under development in 1944 for possible use aboard carriers. Goodyear received a contract in March for 418 F2G-1 modified low-altitude, land-based Corsairs and ten F2G-2s for carriers, but this aircraft never overcame its deficiencies before the end of the war. The McDonnell Company was building the Navy's first pure jet fighter, the XFD-1 Phantom, which first flew in January 1945, but design troubles slowed progress. Higher hope was placed in the Ryan XFR-1 Fireball, a piston-turbojet with speeds equal to the F4U-1 and which first flew on 25 June 1944. But it too was so new and radical that development often lagged behind schedule.[18]

By the end of the summer of 1944, then, the Navy could expect to depend on the F6F-5 Hellcat for its main carrier fighter strength, with the F4U-1 and F4U-4 Corsairs as possible supplements whenever the Marines would part with them. One year hence, the F8F Bearcat would begin to replace the Hellcat. Also the F7F Tigercat and FR Fireball might possibly mature for carrier duty, though their employment was not likely in the near future.

All fighters, starting with the F6F-3, would be capable of service as fighter-bombers as the result of the introduction of several new weapons and bombing techniques. Techniques were the special concern of the Navy's Operations Research Group, which solved tactical problems mathematically, then trained pilots accordingly, and thereby saved many lives.[19] In weapons, fighter aircraft were going to be strengthened by four new devices, the 20mm cannon, napalm bombs, and 5-inch and 11.75-inch rockets.

The 20mm cannon, which carried much more punch than the 50-caliber machine gun, was beginning to compete with it in new planes and was especially important for fighter-bombers in the role of strafing. But existing Hellcat models in mid-1944 still continued to use the 50.

Napalm was nothing more than liquid gas in a bomb casing, which started fires when dropped. In mid-1944, this rather unpredictable method was suddenly improved by the addition of gelatine thickener to the gas, enabling the mixture to cling to a surface and burn with great intensity. Dropped in used, jettisonable fuel tanks, these fire bombs could neutralize Japanese bunkers by spreading a sheet of flame over 25,000 square feet for a full minute, then continuing to smolder for five to ten more minutes. Difficult to mix and store and somewhat inaccurate when tumbling from the plane, napalm bombs made their combat appearance in the Marianas during the summer.[20]

Rockets were the greatest innovation in the carrier's arsenal of weapons. The 5-inch shell in the aerial rocket slowed it down, thus impairing accuracy, but during the spring of 1944 production began on a bigger motor for the 5-inch rocket head, giving it even greater speed than the lighter 3.5-inch rocket. Named the HVAR (high velocity aircraft rocket) and nicknamed the "Holy Moses," this weapon went into combat in August 1944. With eight launchers mounted per fighter, each plane packed the punch of a salvo from one destroyer. So popular was the Holy Moses among pilots in Europe and the Pacific that it had to be rationed. Another rocket very dear to both Admirals King and Towers was the Tiny

Tim, 11.75 inches in diameter and ten feet long. Designed for carrier planes, the Tiny Tim was put on an emergency basis in June 1944. After being launched ineffectively from F4U Corsairs, which were not then carrier planes, the rocket was redesigned during trials to incorporate free-drop and ignition away from the plane. Once perfected, the Tiny Tim would give one plane the same effect as a 12-inch gun, a 36-plane squadron the firepower of one volley from a division of three heavy cruisers.[21]

During the summer, then, the fighters and fighter-bombers shifted from bombs to 5-inch rockets, while the dive bombers and torpedo planes reverted strictly to bombs. Against land targets, napalm, 50-caliber, and some 20mm guns were employed by the fighters.

The rather sudden demand for more fighters caused the Navy to reconsider its bombing-plane needs. In July 1944 the last SBD Dauntless left the carriers, while improved Helldiver models, SB2C-3 and later SB2C-4 planes, replaced the troublesome earlier types (which, in addition to Curtiss, had been produced by the Fairchild Company as the SBF and by Canadian Car & Foundry as the SBW). No new VSB scout bombers were programmed. In torpedo bombers, the TBF-1C Avenger was modified for higher cruising altitudes, better speed and range, and improved bomb facilities. Transferred from Grumman to the Eastern Aircraft Division of General Motors, this improved version was redesignated TBM-3. Grumman was planning to replace the Avenger with the XTB2F, like the F7F a twin-engine carrier plane. Unfortunately, progress was slow with the new plane, leading the Navy to cancel its contact in January 1945. Douglas was working on a torpedo plane, its XTB2D, which could carry 4000 pounds of bombs operating from a battle carrier; the first model flew in February 1945. The most promise shown was with Consolidated's TBY-2 Seawolf (designed by Vought as the TBU-1); the first of 1100 ordered was delivered to the Navy in November 1944. Faster than the TBM, the TBY was meant not to replace but to complement it.[22]

In sheer numbers, however, the Navy suddenly had too many bombers because of the increase in fighters. So in September Helldiver production (by Curtiss, Fairchild, and Canadian Car & Foundry) was cut back sharply from 430 to 270 planes per month. Some people wanted to replace the TBM entirely with the SB2C-4, which could launch a torpedo, though others believed the Helldiver should be junked altogether. But both planes remained with the fast carriers.[23]

When, at the end of 1943, the old scout bomber lost any pretense as a scout plane because radar was replacing visual searching and other planes carried that radar, the Navy realized it needed to develop a single plane type that could perform all types of attack functions. Such a plane should be able to dive-bomb, horizontal-bomb, drop napalm, fire rockets, launch an aerial torpedo, strafe, and even fend off enemy fighters—all this, with a powerful engine, sufficient armor and range, compactness for carrier operations, and operation by one pilot alone. Therefore, in late 1943, the old *VSB*, *VB*, and *VT* designations were dropped for new attack planes in favor of one all-purpose attack aircraft, the bomber-torpedo plane, VBT.

The Bureau of Aeronautics turned to four aircraft companies for details. Curtiss, builder of the controversial Helldiver, contracted for the XBTC on the last day of 1943. Over one year later, in March 1945, Curtiss began a second plane, the XBT2C, but neither bomber was completed in time to fight Japan and both were canceled in the early postwar period. Kaiser-Fleetwings on 31 March 1944 accepted a contract for the XBTK; a lighter plane which first flew in April 1945, it was never accepted by the Navy. Martin in January 1944 began work on the XBTM Mauler, a large, fast bomber that housed four forward-firing 20mm cannon. The first Mauler flew in August 1944, and Admiral Fitch recommended this airplane replace the Helldiver and Avenger aboard the carriers in 1946. The Mauler, which could carry over five tons of ordnance, was purchased by the Navy in January 1945. Douglas, fulfilling an August 1943 contract, dug up an old design to produce by June 1944 a makeshift VBT, the XBTD Destroyer. Only thirty Destroyers were built, but they provided the groundwork for a genuinely new and superior airplane, the XBT2D Dauntless II. On 6 July the Navy ordered 15 Dauntless IIs from Douglas. This powerful plane was designed to fly up to 344 mph with a combat radius of over 500 miles, requiring a shorter take-off from a carrier deck, and carried over a three-ton payload, including rockets, bombs, and/or torpedoes. In addition, it could mount two 20mm wing guns and APS-4 radar. Douglas and BuAer engineers labored over the prototype throughout the rest of 1944.[24]

One fleet requirement that demanded immediate attention was night capability. Like Jellicoe at Jutland, Spruance and Mitscher had been completely paralyzed by their inability to attack the Japanese fleet after night had fallen and ended the Battle of the Philippine Sea. Lack of good night-search doctrine and enough night long-range planes had further restricted Spruance's intelligence, while lack of night training for the average pilot had led to the near-disastrous night recovery and water landings of 20 June. To eliminate the possibility of the latter event's being repeated, ComAirPac henceforth required all carrier pilots to qualify in night landings before going into combat.[25] The other problems would take time to resolve, but Admiral Towers, in consultation with Soc McMorris and Forrest Sherman, on 5 July decided to designate the freshly repaired light carrier *Independence* as a night carrier and to send it into combat "as soon as possible." [26] Commander Turner F. Caldwell assembled several night fighter and torpedo plane detachments then at Pearl Harbor to form Night Air Group 41 (19 F6F-5N, eight TBM-1D), which was then assigned to *Independence*. This makeshift night unit, under Captain E. C. Ewen, sailed for Eniwetok on 17 August.

For a permanent, systematic night carrier search and attack doctrine, the air admirals wanted a night carrier task group. The main ship for this purpose was generally agreed to be *Enterprise*. Her Air Group 6 under Butch O'Hare had initiated defensive night air operations in the Gilberts. Her Torpedo 10 under Bill Martin had originated offensive night air operations at Truk. *Enterprise* night fighters had also given a "most gratifying" performance at Saipan.[27] Throughout all these campaigns, skipper of the "Big E" had been Captain Matt Gardner. As a result, *Enterprise* was earmarked for future conversion to a night carrier; Bill Martin stayed in Hawaii when his air group rotated and eventually assumed command of Night Air Group 90; and on 7 August Gardner was promoted to rear admiral and made ComCarDiv 11 to develop a night carrier group.

Admiral King envisioned a night carrier division of *Enterprise* and four escort carriers, but he was immediately dissuaded by his Pacific planners on the grounds that the latter would be too slow for fast carrier operations. He therefore agreed late in July to assign light carriers *Independence* and *Bataan* to the group along with *Enterprise*.[28] For training purposes, however, since *Enterprise* would continue as a day carrier until her current tour ended, CarDiv 11 was comprised of the old *Saratoga* and *Ranger* (CV-4), which joined the Pacific Fleet in July. The Fleet, therefore, would not have a two-night-carrier group until the end of the year. In the meantime, these two ships would qualify and train night pilots and develop night procedures and tactics off Hawaii.[29] All night aircraft were to be equipped with airborne radar. The APS-6 went into the F6F-5N, which had now completely replaced the F4U night Corsair. This set could pinpoint a carrier up to 22 miles away. The TBMs carried the ASD-1 which could see a flattop at 40 miles.[30] To implement such an effective team, night planes had to be recalled from other carriers, some equipped with the new sets, and then the pilots taught to use them. This all took time.

With these new carriers, weapons, and planes coming to the Pacific, the Navy also could boast—for the first time in the war—that it had enough planes and pilots to carry on the offensive. This being the case, pilot training was cut back on 4 June 1944. Aircraft replacement was not as simple. Admiral King in February had set the absolute ceiling on the Navy's inventory of aircraft at 38,000 planes, and he adamantly refused to allow any increase. This meant that if new planes, particularly fighters, were overproduced to meet the needs of the fleet, older planes would have to be scrapped. Such a luxury had not been anticipated, which meant that a rather sophisticated study would have to be made and a policy formulated. For this reason, Vice Admiral McCain had recalled Rear Admiral Radford from the Pacific to Washington in February.

On 12 April 1944 McCain officially appointed the "Informal Board to submit an integrated aeronautic maintenance, material and supply program," or, unofficially, the Radford Board. After three weeks Radford and his aviators formulated a policy whereby only the newest planes would be assigned to combat, and planes returning to the United States would be reconditioned and reassigned for training purposes. Radford submitted his report on 4 May and implemented his "Integrated Aeronautic Maintenance, Material and Supply Program" two days later without waiting for approval; it was that urgent. Vice Admiral Horne approved the report on 27 May, as did Secretary Forrestal on 27 June, calling it "excellent."

Still, the number of planes did not decrease, and so on 9 September Vice Admiral Fitch appointed a second Radford Board to review the program of the first board. It was found to be sound, but the second Radford report on 2 October recommended liberal junking of old planes, at home and especially in the Pacific to save transporting them back. Only enough planes should be returned to meet minimum requirements. In addition, the Radford reports made certain that adequate spare parts and mechanics who understood the new plane models would arrive in the war zone ahead of the new aircraft. Generally successful, this program seemed to be working by February 1945.[31]

The rapid pace of the war also affected the training of new carrier air groups once they arrived with their planes in the Pacific. Until the Saipan operation, each carrier had returned to Pearl Harbor to pick up its new air group and engage in a ten-day training period. In June, however, Task Force 58 abandoned its bases at Majuro and Kwajalein for new ones closer to the fighting—Eniwetok in the western Marshalls, Manus in the Admiralties, and Saipan. And even two of these bases were soon evacuated by the carriers, Manus in October and Saipan in November, in favor of Eniwetok and other anchorages closer to the enemy. Beginning in the summer, then, all new air groups trained aboard available carriers at San Diego or Hawaii, and after qualification were ferried to their ships at the advanced anchorages just prior to going into combat.[32]

The organizational structure of ComAirPac, as the above logistical and training problems illustrate, had grown considerably since the beginning of the Central Pacific offensive. The Operations and Plans divisions remained the most important units, the latter under the dynamic leadership of Commander Spig Wead, who, already crippled for many years and in failing health, stepped down in July to retire from the Navy. One key unit in Plans was the Operational Intelligence Section, headed since its inception late in 1942 by Lieutenant Commander G. Willing Pepper. Maintaining constant touch with events in the fleet, this section kept ComAirPac informed, wrote monthly analyses of aviation operations for wide distribution, and sent Commander Pepper and others aboard the carriers to observe each major operation. For the Saipan operation, this section distributed 10,000 pounds of target and intelligence material to key air units; for Leyte in October, 25,000 pounds.[33]

The summer of 1944 brought expansion. Between April and August new sections established were Air Navigation, Fleet Air Maintenance, and the Administrative Division, while in June the Gunnery and Training sections were separated. The latter development was especially important, for with the new policy of

Rear Admirals Harry E. Yarnell and goateed Joseph Mason Reeves directed the early prewar fast carrier fleet war games. Standing behind them on board flagship *Saratoga* in this 1931 photograph are Yarnell's chief of staff, Captain John H. Towers (far left), and (between the admirals) operations officer Lieutenant Commander Ralph Davison.

Sister carriers *Saratoga* (foreground) and *Lexington* lie at anchor off Diamond Head, Hawaii, early in 1931, with biplane fighters, dive bombers and torpedo planes filling their flight decks. These two "flattops," the first American "fast" (33-knot) carriers, initiated the tactical experiments that evolved into the wartime task force that spearheaded the American offensive in the Pacific war.

The Grumman F6F Hellcat, standard fighter of the Fast Carrier Task Force.

An F6F Hellcat fighter prepares to be waved off the deck of the "new" *Yorktown* (named for the "old" one sunk at Midway) during flight operations in the Chesapeake Bay, May 1943.

The Mitsubishi Zero fighter, principal Japanese interceptor throughout the Pacific war.

The Doublas SBD Dauntless scout-dive bomber, seen over the *Enterprise.*

The Grumman TBF Avenger seen launching a torpedo.

Right: The LSO—landing signal officer—of the *Yorktown,* Lieutenant (jg) Richard Tripp, gives the "cut" to a plane to land aboard.

Captain J. J. "Jocko" Clark (left) and Rear Admiral Arthur W. Radford conducting training maneuvers in Hawaiian waters from Clark's ship, the *Yorktown,* during the summer of 1943.

Plane pushers prepare to push a Hellcat aft as it is lifted from the hangar to the flight deck.

Two *Essex*-class carriers steam together, TBFs "spotted" (parked) forward with wings folded, SBDs behind, without folding wings. Radio antennas are in the "down" position.

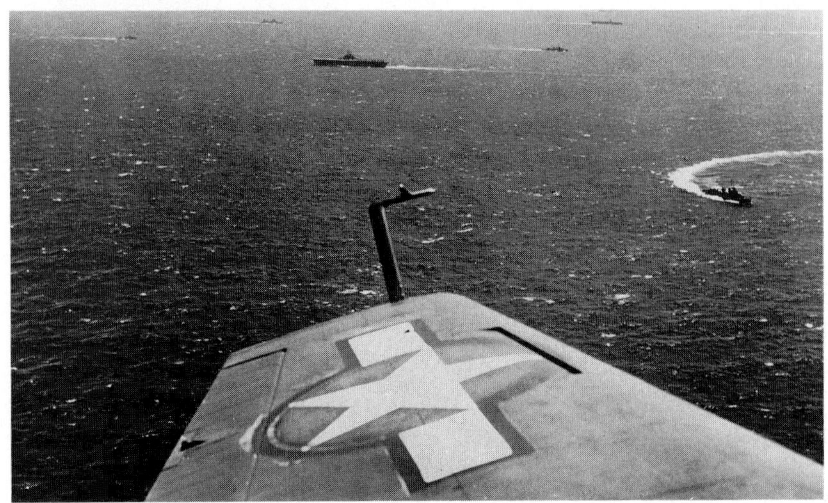

A carrier turns into the wind to launch or recover aircraft while a light carrier and escorting battleships, cruisers, and destroyers of this fast carrier task group continue on the main course.

When not in use, aircraft elevator wells were used for recreation. On the light carrier *Monterey,* blond ship's officer Ensign Gerald R. Ford tips a basketball. This photograph of the future president is courtesy of his shipmate, Robert B. Rogers.

To speed the spotting and respotting of planes on the flight decks, jeeps and tractors with two bars gradually replaced the plane pushers—as seen with this F6F on light carrier *Princeton.*

With a full deckload strike spotted aft, an *Essex*-class carrier invades the Gilbert Islands late in 1943, protected by its own 5-inch antiaircraft guns (left) and those of a battleship astern.

A TBF Avenger torpedo-bomber circles over burning Marcus Island 31 August 1943.

Commander James H. "Jimmy" Flatley, Jr., briefs his pilots of *Yorktown*'s Air Group Five in the wardroom, en route to attack Marcus Island, August 1943.

A Japanese "Emily" flying boat fills the gun camera of a Hellcat east of the Gilbert Islands during the raid on Tarawa in September 1943. The seaplane soon plummeted into the sea.

A quad 40mm antiaircraft gun frames two carriers and a fleet tanker during the autumn of 1943 while off-duty crewmen rest.

Commander J. C. "Jumpin' Joe" Clifton reports results of the raid on Rabaul to Rear Admiral "Ted" Sherman and a happy staff on the flag bridge of the *Saratoga.*

Japanese cruisers fail to escape severe damage in Simpson Harbor at Rabaul as they are pummeled by planes from the *Saratoga* and *Princeton,* 5 November 1943.

Betio Island of Tarawa atoll appears devastated following carrier strikes and shore bombardment on 20 November 1943, but inexperience in attacking fortified coral atolls led to stiff resistance by the well-dug-in Japanese, who inflicted heavy casualties.

These Avengers provide air support to the pollywog-like landing craft bringing the Army's 27th Division ashore at Makin in the Gilberts.

Admiral Pownall's planes score many hits on Japanese merchant and naval shipping in the raid on Kwajalein in the Marshall Islands, 4 December 1943.

A Japanese "Kate" torpedo plane is splashed close aboard the guns of the *Yorktown* midday of the Kwajalein raid.

Before. Carrier planes photographed lush Kwajalein Island, revealing Japanese military barracks, at the end of January 1944.

After. Kwajalein as it appeared after receiving the "Spruance Haircut" and "Mitscher Shampoo"—enabling the troops to go ashore with relative ease.

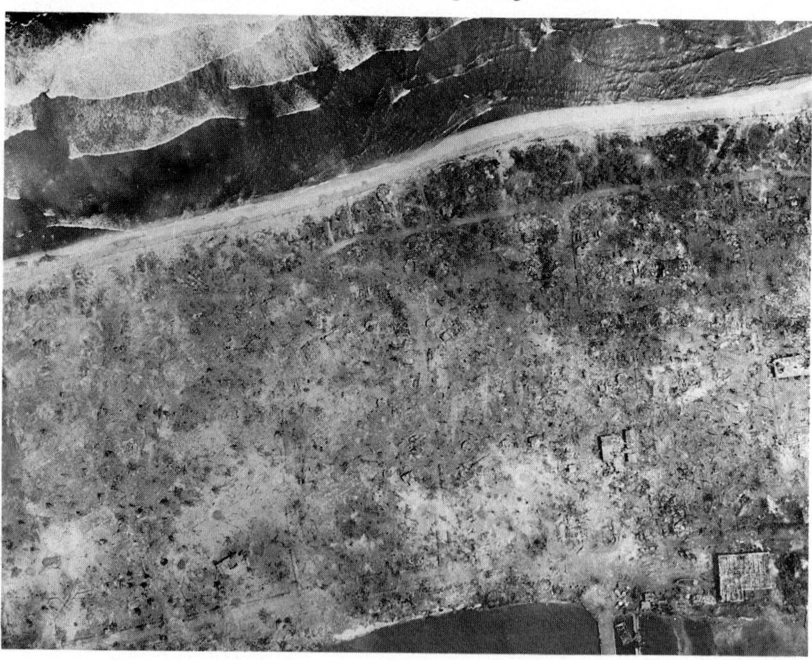

The Curtiss SB2C Helldiver dive bomber gradually replaced the SBD aboard the fast carriers during the first half of 1944.

Tons of Japanese merchant shipping at Truk lagoon are sent to the bottom by Task Force 58 planes, 16–17 February 1944.

Bombs rain down from Mitscher's planes onto the Japanese seaplane base on Dublon Island, Truk, 16 February 1944.

The *Independence*-class light carrier *Belleau Wood* repels "Betty" bombers during the Marianas raid of 22 February 1944, while the *Bunker Hill* task group can be seen throwing up flak just over the horizon beyond.

Close air support Navy-style from Admiral Ginder's task group helped Marines and Army to overrun Eniwetok during late February 1944.

A Service Squadron craft delivers bombs to a fast carrier at Majuro atoll, enabling TF 58 to remain in the forward areas without returning to Hawaii for supplies.

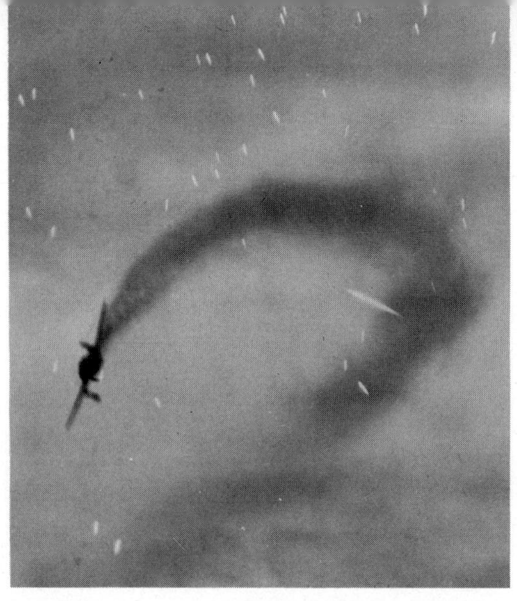

Flak from Admiral Montgomery's carriers and escort vessels brings down a "Jill" torpedo-bomber at dawn, 29 April 1944, during the run-in to Truk.

Lieutenant (jg) Hamilton McWhorter displays ten airborne kills at the end of Fighting 9's eight-month combat tour on the *Essex*—not unusual for the many battle-seasoned veterans of the fast carriers by the spring of 1944. Note VF-9's symbol of the cat on a cloud clutching a beer bottle.

Mitscher's late afternoon strike on 11 June 1944 has caught many Japanese planes on the ground at Saipan, making quick work of them.

At the height of the Marianas Turkey Shoot, 19 June 1944, Ensign Richard Meyer gives a smile to a *Yorktown* VF-1 (the "High Hat" squadron) Hellcat before sending it off, replete with belly tank.

Contrails of dogfighting carrier planes fill the sky over TF 58 during the Turkey Shoot.

Admiral Mitscher (right) directs the Turkey Shoot from the flag bridge of the new *Lexington.*

Although the Japanese fast carrier *Zuikaku* takes several hits in the Philippine Sea, she did not sink.

The Japanese Mobile Fleet twists and turns to evade the bombs of TF 58 during the Battle of the Philippine Sea, 20 June 1944.

Spruance and Mitscher discussing Guam, July 1944. BOTTOM LEFT: Lieutenant General Holland M. Smith. BOTTOM RIGHT: Vice Admiral Richmond Kelly Turner.

Above right: Carrier admirals and advisers: *Lexington,* 20 September 1944 (left to right), Vice Admiral Mitscher, Rear Admiral Carney, Commodore Burke, and Admiral Halsey.

Below right: Planes are respotted beneath the island superstructure of an *Essex*-class carrier during the raid on Formosa, 12 October 1944.

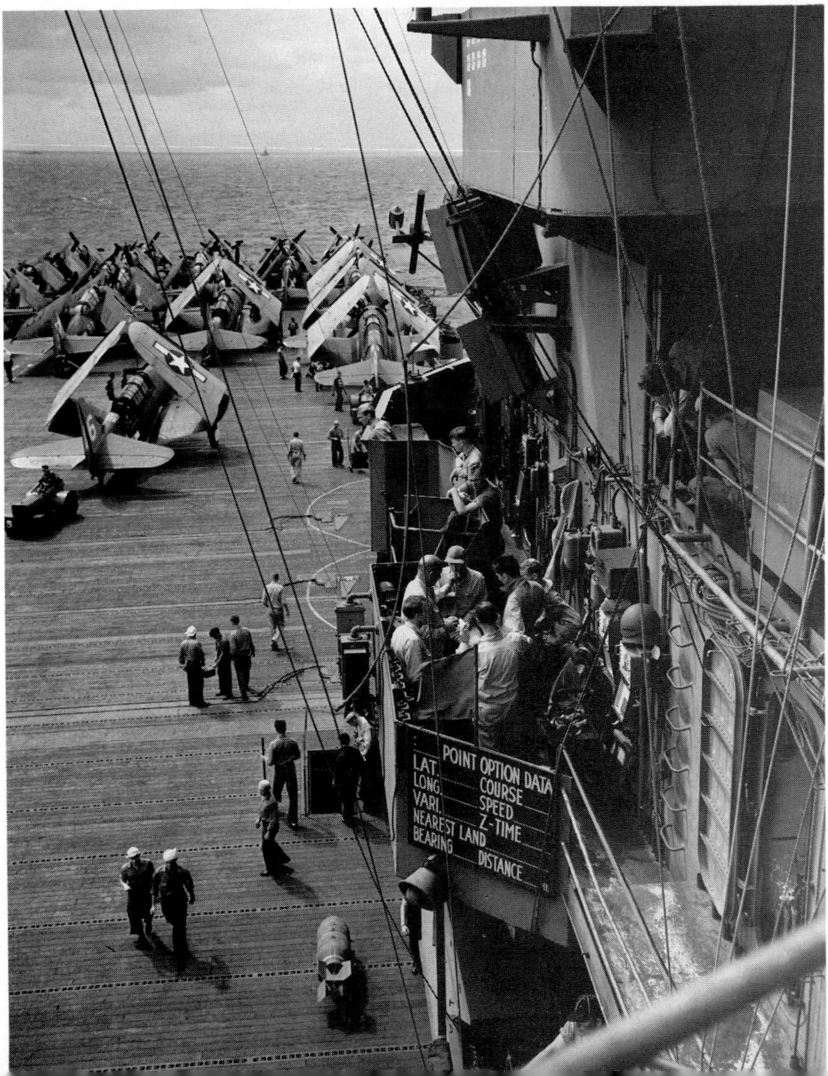

POINT OPTION DATA
LAT.
LONG.
VARI.
NEAREST LAND
BEARING
COURSE
SPEED
Z-TIME
DISTANCE

Bombs from Air Group 20 straddle a Japanese battleship in the Sibuyan Sea, 24 October 1944.

Task Group 38.2 commander Jerry Bogan (left) and operations officer Commander Robert B. Pirie (foreground) during Philippines operations.

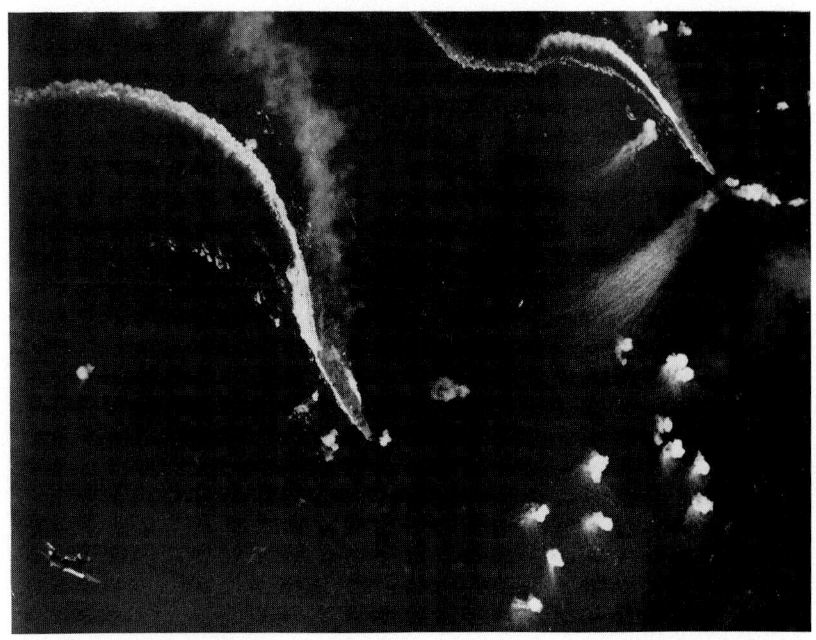

Japanese carrier *Zuikaku* (center) and a light carrier maneuver wildly to avoid bombs and torpedoes off Cape Engaño, 25 October 1944, as a Bombing 20 Helldiver from the *Enterprise* goes into its dive (lower left corner).

Vice Admiral McCain and Commander "Jimmy" Thach in flag plot of the *Hancock.*

One of two kamikaze suicide planes explodes on the hard-luck *Intrepid* 25 November 1944, killing 65 men and forcing her to return to the States for major repairs.

Rear Admiral Gardner, the new night carrier commander, visits TF 38 flagship *Hancock* in a TBM, January 1945.

Top: British Supermarine Seafire fighter (*Courtesy Imperial War Museum*)
Center: British Fairey Firefly fighter-bomber (*Courtesy Imperial War Museum*)
Bottom: British Fairey Barracuda torpedo-bomber (*Courtesy Imperial War Museum*)

Japanese oil refineries at Palembang burn under attack by British carrier planes, 24 January 1945. Note barrage balloons outlined against clouds of smoke. (*Courtesy Imperial War Museum*)

Barracudas (one being lowered) and U.S.–built Corsairs aboard the *Illustrious* after the Port Blair raid, 21 June 1944. (*Courtesy Imperial War Museum*)

Chance Vought F4U Corsair fighter-bomber.

Saratoga burning after fourth bomb hit, plus two kamikaze hits, while providing close air support at Iwo Jima, 21 February 1945. Note parked "mule" tractors in foreground.

A four-plane division of *Yorktown* Hellcats support Marines on Iwo, 21 February 1945. The assault fleet lies offshore.

Above right: Essex VF-9 pilots are briefed in their ready room before the first carrier strikes on Tokyo in February 1945.

Below right: Task Force 58 attacks anchored Japanese fleet units at Kure on the Inland Sea of Japan, 18 March 1945.

TOKYO
BOUND

Left: A kamikaze crumbles on the armored flight deck of HMS *Formidable* off Sakishima Gunto, 4 May 1945. (*Courtesy Imperial War Museum*)

Inset: A "Judy" dive bomber kamikaze just misses the *Yorktown*—against the hull of which she is outlined—off Okinawa, 29 March 1945.

Below: Yamato, the world's largest warship, rolls over and explodes after being hit by TF 58 bombs and aerial torpedoes south of Japan, 7 April 1945. A light cruiser and four of eight destroyers were also sunk.

Two tired warriers: Pete Mitscher turns over the fast carriers to Slew McCain for the last time, 27 May 1945.

HM light carrier *Glory* arriving in the Pacific for the final campaign against Japan, August 1945. (*Courtesy Imperial War Museum*)

Rear Admiral C. H. J. Harcourt, RN (left), Commander 11th Aircraft Carrier Squadron (March 1945–end of war), on the bridge of the *Indomitable* with Captain J. A. S. Eccles, RN, August 1945. (*Courtesy Imperial War Museum*)

Vice Admiral Towers (right), new TF 38 commander, and Rear Admiral Radford, veteran task group commander, on the flag bridge of the *Yorktown* at the end of the war.

Cincpac File

UNITED STATES PACIFIC FLEET
AND PACIFIC OCEAN AREAS
HEADQUARTERS OF THE COMMANDER IN CHIEF

SECRET

June 19 1944

SECRET and PERSONAL

Dear Raymond:

We are following with the closest interest your operations around the Marianas, and we share with you a feeling which I know you must have - that of frustration in our failure to bring our carrier superiority to bear on the Japanese fleet during the last few days.

We all understand, of course, that the Japanese had better information of our whereabouts through their shorebased long-range search than we had of their locations. It was exasperating to have one of the early reports of the first long-range search conducted from Saipan be delayed 8 hours in reaching you. Whether or not the situation would have been different had this delay not occurred is of course problematical.

It now appears that the Jap fleet is retiring for replenishment, and that following a short period for this purpose we may have another chance at it. If they come back, I hope you will be able to bring them into action.

The CAVALLO's report of three torpedo hits in a SHOKAKU class carrier is what I have been expecting to hear for the last two years, and I hope the report is correct. I also hope that the ship is destroyed, although her sinking simplified the problem presented the Japanese fleet, had she remained afloat in an almost salvageable condition it is possible that you would have had a chance to attack the ships attending her.

We regret the delay in starting the Guam operation, but we know we must accept the dictum of those on the spot. We hope that Guam will be less tough than Saipan.

With assurance of our keenest interest in what you are doing, and of all the support of which we are capable, and with kindest regards and best wishes.

Sincerely yours,

CWNimitz

Admiral Raymond Spruance, USN,
USS INDIANA,
Fleet Post Office, San Francisco.

Letter of 19 June 1944 from Admiral Chester W. Nimitz to Admiral Raymond Spruance.

training new carrier air groups, ComAirPac controlled *Ranger* and certain escort carriers plus an occasional fast carrier temporarily for carrier qualifications out of San Diego and Pearl Harbor. Finally, in December, the chief of staff billet was upgraded to Deputy ComAirPac.[34] ComAirPac grew with the size of the carrier and land-based naval air forces, and although Vice Admiral Towers as Deputy Cincpac controlled air policy he depended upon Rear Admirals Pownall and Ballentine, the chief of staff, for his information.

The great buildup, with the end of the Solomons and New Guinea campaigns by the summer of 1944, led to new importance for the Central Pacific forces of the Army, AAF, and Marines. The Army began to prepare its Tenth Army for major land campaigns near or in Japan in 1945, and on 21 June Lieutenant General S. B. Buckner arrived to organize that army. In July, the Army established its Central Pacific Base Command and in August U.S. Army Forces, Pacific Ocean Areas, both headquartered in Hawaii under Lieutenant General Richardson. On 1 August the new Headquarters, Army Air Forces, Pacific Ocean Areas, was activated under the command of Lieutenant General Millard F. Harmon, absorbing the administrative functions of Seventh Air Force, now reorganized into a mobile tactical air force. Also established was Headquarters, Fleet Marine Force, Pacific, under Lieutenant General Holland Smith, lifting him from the control of several Navy commanders to direct subordination to Admiral Nimitz.[35] Southwest Pacific remained independent under General MacArthur and included the Sixth Army, General Kenney's new Far Eastern Air Forces, and Vice Admiral Kinkaid's Seventh Fleet.

These massive Army, Navy, and air forces of the Central and Southwest Pacific theaters would cause certain command difficulties when they converged around the Luzon bottleneck late in 1944, as neither the Army and MacArthur nor the Navy and Nimitz would want to yield to the supreme authority of the other. However, once this great campaign got under way in September, it would have to be waged relentlessly until all major islands of the western Pacific were seized or neutralized and the merchant marine of Japan destroyed, a series of operations designed to culminate in the encirclement of Japan late in 1945 Such a sustained effort would create difficulties for the Navy in planning each successive operation. Unlike the Army, the Navy's operational planner, Commander Fifth Fleet, needed time to plan the intricacies of each major amphibious operation at Pearl Harbor, then take command of the forces involved at sea. After June 1944, however, no time could be wasted between campaigns for planning. The enemy had to be driven back without letup.

The Navy's solution was a two-platoon system of fleet commanders, whereby while one commander and staff were planning one operation at Pearl Harbor, the other commander and staff would be at sea fighting. When one operation ended, the commanders and staffs would rotate. The plan, originally conceived by Admiral Savvy Cooke late in 1943,[36] was adopted in its final form at San Francisco on 5–6 May 1944 in a meeting between Admirals King and Nimitz to which Admiral Halsey was also invited. The former two officers informed Halsey that with the end of the Solomons campaign his Third Fleet-South Pacific Area would be divided.[37] SoPac would be downgraded, while Halsey as Commander Third Fleet would rotate with Admiral Spruance in tactical command of the fleet. When Spruance had command, Nimitz's battle forces would be known as Fifth Fleet, under Halsey as Third Fleet. Task designations would be similarly altered, Task Force 58 becoming Task Force 38 and so forth. The ships would remain the same, and if the enemy became confused into thinking two separate powerful fleets were at sea—as he did initially—so much the better.

Significantly, the Third Fleet commander was an aviator, the man who had been in command of Pacific Fleet carriers at the outbreak of war and who might be expected to exercise tactical command of the fast carriers rather than depend on his carrier task force commander. That person would be, when Vice Admiral Mitscher rotated home with Admiral Spruance, Vice Admiral John Sidney McCain. Slew McCain lost no time in hastening out to the Pacific where, late in May, he had boarded Spruance's flagship to observe the Marianas operations. On 15 June, the day Spruance put his Marines and Army ashore at Saipan, Halsey handed over the South Pacific command to his Deputy, Vice Admiral Newton, and flew to Pearl Harbor, where on the seventeenth he established his headquarters. The next day he began planning post-Marianas operations.[38]

The appointment of McCain to be Mitscher's alternate caused something of a stir among the aviators, especially the early-day flyers who felt a latecomer did not deserve the top air command.

It meant that Ernie King had again bypassed Jack Towers for command at sea, this time in favor of McCain, a loyal King supporter. Furthermore, King in doing so had also rejected the man Mitscher recommended to be his own relief, Rear Admiral Frederick C. Sherman. Though a latecomer to aviation and oftentimes antagonistic to Mitscher, Ted Sherman was ready, willing, and able to assume the post; he was then taking a rest as Commander Fleet Air West Coast after almost continuous carrier duty since before hostilities. Mitscher, Sherman later recorded, "told me he had recommended me as his relief . . . [and] that high dispatches had been exchanged in which I came within an ace of relieving him instead of McCain" doing so.[39] Also, "Fightin' Freddie" was Halsey's favorite carrier admiral, but King rewarded McCain with the job after the latter had manned a desk in Washington for nearly two years.

Ernie King was beginning to take an increasingly active role in directing the fast carriers, because he could see in them the future of the Navy. His selection of McCain to rotate with Mitscher not only defied the wishes of the Pacific air admirals but created an embarrassing situation in Washington. On 24 May Secretary Forrestal announced that Vice Admiral Aubrey W. Fitch would replace McCain as DCNO(Air) on 1 August 1944. Meanwhile, with McCain's hasty departure to the Pacific, Rear Admiral Radford became acting DCNO(Air). One week later Vice Admiral Towers, representing Nimitz, arrived in Washington to discuss Pacific naval aviation matters with King as well as with Fitch, Ramsey, and Radford. McCain returned to Washington briefly in July to check out, and reneged on his promise to send Radford to sea upon the completion of Radford's aeronautics logistics study. Then, with McCain's departure, Radford found his new boss, Fitch, relying very heavily upon his advice in key decisions. But the office of DCNO(Air) was now coming under the strong influence of King, who no longer left it alone as a logistical branch under the Vice CNO (Horne). For example, King met personally with Fitch several hours each Sunday to discuss naval aviation.[40]

King also injected a major reform in the fleet which further intrenched aviation as the principal element of the U.S. Navy. He now ruled what the aviators had considered long overdue, that all nonaviator fleet and task force commanders have aviators as chiefs of staff. Furthermore, these officers—like the existing non-air chiefs of staff to air admirals—should be upgraded in rank from captain to commodore or rear admiral. Aviator Halsey already had nonaviator Rear Admiral Mick Carney, just as Mitscher had now-Commodore Arleigh Burke. The new policy led to dramatic personnel changes: nonaviator Spruance lost his trusted Captain Carl Moore for airman Rear Admiral Art Davis, Cominch operations officer; Vice Admiral Kinkaid, Seventh Fleet commander, received Commodore Valentine H. Schaeffer, of late light carrier *Bataan*'s skipper; Vice Admiral Ching Lee, Commander Battleships Pacific, was assigned Commodore Tom Jeter, recent captain of *Bunker Hill.*

This decision came as a blow to many admirals of the "Gun Club." Some of them, such as Rear Admiral Oscar Badger, downright resented aviation's takeover. Some, such as Rear Admiral Jack Shafroth, accepted aviation but criticized senior seagoing nonaviators for not taking a firmer stand against the admirals in Washington ("Just stay at your desk and never go to sea, and you will be ruler of the King's Navee"—Ernie's of course).[41] Some, like Rear Admiral Bill Fechteler, had already seen the course of events and helped write new tactical doctrine. Others, like Rear Admiral Spike Blandy, stayed in amphibious-bombardment work and away from air altogether. But most, like Rear Admiral Larry DuBose, commanding cruisers under (though five years senior to) his air task group commander (Jocko Clark), accepted in good grace the evolving nature of naval warfare and the resulting changes as they came.

By the summer of 1944 the Gun Club had lost control of the Navy, but the aviators had not quite taken over. It was only a matter of time. Until mid-1944 there had been some balance in seniority between carrier admirals and battleship-cruiser admirals in the carrier task groups. But henceforth the flood of young admirals with aviator's wings would be too great. Compared with the battleship admirals from the Naval Academy classes of 1911, 1912, and 1913 were two-star air admirals Radford, Davison, and Bogan of '16, Duncan and Sallada of '17, Forrest Sherman, Ballentine, Clark, Tommy and Ziggy Sprague of '18, and Schoeffel, Gardner, and Ofstie of '19.

The very nature of fast battleship operations broke down the Gun Club's influence at sea. With his battleships and heavy cruisers always distributed among the carrier task groups, Vice Admiral Lee was never able to maneuver his battle line or to develop doctrine, such as night gunnery; witness his decision not to engage the enemy the night of 18–19 June 1944. He could never assemble his ship captains and did not know them all personally. He and his new air chief of staff suffered a complete breakdown in communications due to a personality clash, while Lee did not like this troublesome aviator to be senior to his battleship captains. Lee never bothered to write action reports, for he never fought actions as a tactical commander. As type commander of Pacific battleships, he had no function at all, in contrast to ComAirPac, which was growing phenomenally. These factors finally led to the dissolution of the ComBatPac billet in late November, effective 15 December 1944, and the formation of two battleship squadrons.[42] The First Batron was comprised of the old battleships of the Pacific Fleet under Vice Admiral Jesse B. Oldendorf; the Second was Lee's fast battleship force. Simultaneously, of all things, new staff gunnery officers to the battleship admirals began to be aviators, obviously for assistance in antiaircraft techniques, but also a sure sign that the solidarity of the Gun Club was being completely undermined.

The summer of 1944 gave the aviators the opportunity to reassess their own top commanders, and again Ernie King played a personal role. King went to the Pacific in July to look over the situation in general, and specifically to make certain command changes. He brought with him Vice Admirals Savvy Cooke and Randall Jacobs, Chief of Personnel. On 13–14 July Cominch ranged over tactical problems with Nimitz and the aviators at Pearl Harbor, then flew out to Saipan to inspect the damage, returning to Pearl on the nineteenth. Three days later a major conference on air flag officers convened in Vice Admiral Towers' office involving King, Nimitz, Jacobs, Towers, McMorris, and Forrest Sherman.[43]

The first change came at the top, ComAirPac. Rear Admiral Charles A. Pownall, kicked upstairs in February for his lack of aggressiveness at sea, had repeatedly run into disagreements with Admiral Towers throughout the spring. Most of Pownall's recommendations were corrected or rejected by Towers, while Pownall's kind disposition led him to continue his unaggressive attitude.[44] This spirit could no longer be tolerated in the Pacific war, and King agreed that Pownall would trade jobs with Rear Admiral George D. Murray, Chief of Naval Air Training at Pensacola. When Pownall received his orders on 31 July, he protested to Admiral Nimitz that he had been "very badly treated," to which

Cincpac gave little consideration, pointing out Admiral King's statement that Pownall's appointment had only been temporary.[45] It will be recalled that George Murray had similarly failed to command the carriers successfully in the Solomons, but as an early-day pilot he was part of the Towers team and was being given another chance in the Pacific. Murray became ComAirPac on 16 August, and to the great surprise of everyone was even promoted to vice admiral in December, leading Ted Sherman to complain, "Polish up the handle of the big front door and never go to sea seems to the answer." [46]

Actually, Murray's promotion was final recognition that the ComAirPac billet had become important enough to warrant a vice admiralcy, or so decided Ernie King in September. So when in mid-December 1944 ComBatPac was abolished, ComAirPac was upgraded, with Murray becoming a vice admiral. Similarly, the ComAirPac chief of staff billet, occupied after 29 September by Captain Frederick W. McMahon, was then upgraded to Deputy ComAirPac, and McMahon was promoted to commodore.[47]

Before King's party departed for home after the morning conference on 22 July, the admirals agreed on one other major change. Rear Admiral Keen Harrill, ComCarDiv 1, had completely failed to fight aggressively at Saipan. On 29 June, while operating off Guam, Harrill was stricken with appendicitis and temporarily relieved by his cruiser commander, Rear Admiral Wilder D. Baker. Baker, who flew his flag aboard *Essex* from the twenty-ninth to 7 July, enjoyed the distinction of being the only nonaviator to command a fast carrier task group in combat during the Central Pacific offensive. Harrill went to the hospital at Pearl Harbor on 11 July, but his superiors had no plans to keep him in the Pacific. They decided to send him back to San Diego to relieve Ted Sherman as Commander Fleet Air West Coast, which was done on 1 August. Sherman returned as ComCarDiv 1.[48]

Other carrier division commanders also changed jobs. ComCarDiv 2, Rear Admiral Ralph Davison, had been riding as an observer during June and took command of Task Group 58.2 in July. ComCarDiv 3, Rear Admiral Alfred Montgomery, led TG 58.3 throughout July, then began two months of well-deserved leave in mid-August. ComCarDiv 4, Rear Admiral Gerald F. Bogan, relieved Harrill and Baker in TG 58.4 on 13 July. ComCarDiv 5, Rear Admiral Frank D. Wagner, obnoxious and unwanted, was relieved on 1 July by Rear Admiral Jocko Clark, whose old title of ComCarDiv 13 was dissolved; Clark continued to lead TG 58.1. ComCarDiv 6, a new billet, went to Rear Admiral Harold B. Sallada, who reported in makee-learn status on 11 August and served aboard several carriers until October, when he was suddenly relieved. Rear Admiral Alva Bernhard, commanding the Gilberts–Marshalls Area, became ill and went home. Meanwhile, Arthur Radford, stuck in Washington, appealed to Ernie King for reassignment to the carriers. King agreed, placed Sallada in the Gilberts–Marshalls Area, and made Radford ComCarDiv 6. The only other cardiv was Matt Gardner's night training CarDiv 11. During all these changes, Black Jack Reeves—overdue for a rest—left the fast carriers for good.

A pattern was being established for fast carrier task group command. These new division commanders, Davison, Bogan, and Sallada, transferred from the command of escort carrier divisions. These escort cardivs were, in turn, often commanded by former fast carrier captains. During the summer of 1944, such new rear admirals were Tommy Sprague from *Intrepid*, George R. Henderson from *Princeton*, Felix Stump from *Lexington*, William D. Sample from *Hornet*, Ziggy Sprague from *Wasp*, and Ralph A. Ofstie from *Essex*. Such a pipeline of promotion from ship to fast carrier task group gave the fast carriers a broad spread of experience in leadership and combat. Still, available experienced air flag officers were at a premium, and in July Ernie King told Nimitz that good air admirals and captains were so scarce that they were not to be wasted commanding atolls.[49]

On the subject of fast carrier divisions, Admiral Murray wanted to comprise each cardiv and task group of one light and two heavy carriers, maintaining that larger groups of one light and three large carriers "would be difficult and no doubt unwieldy. . . ." He was off on the wrong track, since Admiral Mitscher had decided that the four-carrier task group was of optimum size and so it would remain. But Murray did introduce a new thought. He pointed out to Admiral Nimitz that one year hence, the summer of 1945, the Pacific Fleet would have 17 heavy and nine light carriers. These could be organized into two separate fast carrier task forces of 13 carriers each. Each could operate independently and provide the fleet with more flexibility in a "one-two punch." [50] This idea, which gave the air admirals something to ponder, would erase the necessity of rotating carrier task force commanders; there would always be two available. Mitscher and McCain could command at sea simultaneously.

But that was in the future; for the present, the fleet had to accommodate the two-platoon system. Vice Admiral McCain visited several carriers and admirals the week after the Battle of the Philippine Sea and spent four days in Hawaii, till 3 July, where he conferred with his future boss, Admiral Halsey. Flying back to Washington, McCain turned over the DCNO(Air) job to Jake Fitch, then headed back to the Pacific. On 5 August 1944 the post of Commander Fast Carrier Force Pacific Fleet was replaced by two new billets, Commander First Fast Carrier Task Force Pacific (Mitscher) and Commander Second Fast Carrier Task Force Pacific (McCain).[51] However, since Mitscher had been to sea only seven months, he did not follow Spruance home but remained in command of the redesignated Task Force 38. McCain learned this, much to his chagrin, from Jack Towers the day after his arrival in Hawaii, 9 August.[52] Mitscher would remain in command for three more months, until the completion of the next major operation. Lacking any experience in fast carrier task force operations, McCain would assume command of Task Group 38.1 as a makee-learn interim assignment.

Displeased at Mitscher's refusal to go home, McCain now discovered he would have to form his own staff from scratch. Smarting because he was four years senior to Mitscher, McCain felt he ought to get part of Mitscher's staff. On 15 August McCain protested to Towers, who disagreed, saying that McCain could temporarily borrow staff officers from Jocko Clark, who would continue to ride aboard *Hornet* in TG 38.1 in an advisory capacity. Insisting someone was trying to "cut his throat," the salty, ruffled McCain left the poised, polished Towers "and dashed off to see Admiral Nimitz." Nimitz then called together Towers, McMorris, and Forrest Sherman to hear out McCain. Excited, McCain repeated his accusations, but the others merely agreed with Towers. The next day a special conference convened with the above five officers plus Admiral Halsey to discuss McCain's status. Future command arrangements were reiterated, and McCain was told he would have seniority and over-all command if Mitscher returned when McCain had the fast carriers.[53]

Generally satisfied, McCain then set about building a staff. For chief of staff, he selected the one nonaviator who had commanded Harrill's task group briefly, Wilder Baker. Along with Commander Jimmy Thach, his regular operations officer, McCain borrowed Jocko Clark's three operations experts, and later tried—unsuccessfully—to steal Clark's excellent fighter director officer. Clark's flag secretary, who compiled the best action reports in the task force, provided guidelines for McCain's staff. After two or three weeks, during which time McCain's staff depended almost entirely on its advisers, Clark's officers returned to *Hornet*.[54]

Jocko Clark did not particularly want to serve under Halsey and McCain, but he did want to serve under Mitscher again. He therefore recommended to Mitscher that as soon as McCain was broken in he, Clark, be sent home on leave, then rotated back again when Spruance and Mitscher returned. Mitscher, who considered Clark his right-hand task group commander, thought this an excellent idea and passed it on to Towers, who approved. But Forrest Sherman advised Nimitz against it, as no reliable carrier division commander would be available to relieve McCain when the latter took over Task Force 38 in November. As in so many such questions, Nimitz accepted Sherman's judgment, but Clark could go home when Monty Montgomery returned from leave to relieve McCain in command of TG 38.1. Then, suddenly, on 2 October Clark and his staff arrived by plane in Hawaii, leading Nimitz to send a reprimand to Halsey for releasing Clark without permission. Three days later Nimitz let Clark go on to California but on constant standby. On the seventh, however, Radford reported for duty, followed on the eighteenth by Montgomery. Ideally, Mitscher liked to have two carrier admirals on standby for emergencies; now he had them.[55]

Mitscher, when he returned in 1945, would have the services of three veteran admirals, Ted Sherman, Monty Montgomery, and Jocko Clark, along with Arthur Radford, who had commanded briefly in the Gilberts. He would also have available Ralph Davison and Gerry Bogan. By then, too, Matt Gardner's night task group should be ready. In the meantime, Mitscher had to finish up some loose ends in the Marianas under Spruance and then resume the drive westward, but he was awkwardly placed between Halsey, also an aviator, and McCain, who eagerly waited to relieve him.

The men and the weapons which would pit the fast carrier task forces in the final campaigns against Japan were firmly set during the summer of 1944. Sweeping changes would not be made again until Japan was literally on its knees.

4. Strategy and Carrier Sweeps

Before major strategic decisions could be made in light of the defeat of the Japanese Mobile Fleet in June 1944, Saipan had to be mopped up and the islands of Tinian and Guam to the south assaulted and captured. As in such amphibious operations, the fast carriers had two assignments, isolating the beachhead from enemy fleet and air interference and reinforcement, and providing close air support for the ground forces. Since the Japanese fleet presented no immediate threat, the carriers had only to cope with isolated though often cunning and industrious snoopers from several different distant Japanese bases. Most of the support was provided by escort carriers and land-based Seventh Air Force fighters. On the morning of 22 June, two escort carriers catapulted the first Army P-47 Thunderbolts to Aslito Field on Saipan. These planes and those of the escort carriers supported the infantry on Saipan until the island fell on 9 July.

Meanwhile Task Force 58 regrouped before going to the support of the Guam–Tinian landings in July. Three groups rested at Eniwetok, while TG 58.4 (*Essex*, *Cowpens*, and *Langley*) continued to strike Guam and Rota from 23 June through 3 July. Task group composition would change repeatedly, just as commanders, air groups, and new carriers were arriving and others rotating back to the States. Admiral Mitscher's concern was to destroy the planes and installations Jocko Clark had left behind at Iwo and Chichi Jima, so on 30 June he dispatched Clark's TG 58.1 (*Hornet*, *Yorktown*, and *Bataan*) and Davison's TG 58.2 (*Wasp*, *Franklin*, *Monterey*, and *Cabot*) to work over those islands to the north. On 3–4 July these forces attacked the "Jocko Jimas," destroying over 75 aircraft, most of them in the air, concluding with a heavy two-and-a-half-hour cruiser bombardment of Iwo.[1] So thorough was the destruction that the Japanese recalled the surviving 54 planes at Iwo and Chichi Jima to Japan.[2] Simultaneously, on the fourth planes from Black Jack Reeves' TG 58.3 (*Enterprise*, *Lexington*, *San Jacinto*, and *Princeton*) swept in on Guam in a daylight attack, followed by a night destroyer shelling. This group then retired toward Eniwetok, following TG 58.4, which had departed the day before. On 5 July Clark and Davison coming south from Iwo struck Guam and Rota, beginning the reduction of Guam's defenses in preparation for the assault.

The systematic preinvasion bombardment of Guam began on 6 July, when the task groups of Clark and Davison began rotating between Guam and Rota. For one week these forces routinely bombed their targets. By the time Task Groups 58.3 and 58.4, now under Montgomery and Bogan, joined on 13–14 July, Task Force 58 had been reorganized as a consequence of certain carriers' going home for overhaul: TG 58.1—*Hornet, Yorktown, Cabot*; TG 58.2— *Wasp, Franklin* (Air Group 13); TG 58.3—*Lexington* (Air Group 19), *Bunker Hill, San Jacinto*; TG 58.4—*Essex, Langley, Princeton.* These ships and their planes attacked targets in the Marianas for another week, joined on the eighteenth and after by the regular bombardment ships.

When the Marines and Army stormed Guam on 21 July, the island had been given the most sustained, and in Professor Morison's opinion the best, prelanding bombardment of the Pacific war.[3] During the hour preceding the landing, three of Mitscher's task groups sent full deckload strikes, 312 planes, to drop 124 tons of bombs on the assault beaches. After the landing, the fast carriers and five escort carriers continued in close support, despite protests of the troops that Commander Support Aircraft, Captain Dick Whitehead, was taking too long (up to five hours!) to answer their specific requests. Overcrowded radio networks and water-soaked radios ashore were partly to blame, though the Marines wanted tactical control over and voice contact with the Navy planes on station—a practice the Navy did not accept. Also, unfortunately, friendly troops were accidentally bombed, a constant hazard of close air support.[4]

Tinian was another story. Within range of artillery and P-47s on Saipan, this island was also pounded for many days prior to the 24 July assault. Beginning on the fifteenth the P-47s dropped napalm to ignite the undergrowth at the beaches, joined by planes from Rear Admiral Van Ragsdale's escort carriers. The fast carriers were not needed at Tinian, as planes from nearby Saipan could remain over the target for an hour and a half; Dick Whitehead could keep his headquarters ashore at Saipan; and an Air Coordinator operated over the target. Radio nets were not overcrowded, and coordination between air and artillery was very satisfactory.[5]

Organized resistance ended on Tinian on 1 August, on Guam 11 days after that, following the usual tenacious performance by American forces. The carriers had kept the Marianas generally isolated from outside enemy interference, but the Marines believed the air support techniques of the Navy and AAF on Saipan and Guam inferior to their own. The Marines preferred to have their own pilots support them, as in the Solomons, with these pilots in direct radio contact with Marine liaison parties on the battlefield. Since no airfields were available for Marine Corps fighter and dive bomber squadrons, their generals requested the assignment of four escort carriers to the Corps. The proposal took some time getting through channels, but it was finally accepted by the Navy Department on 30 December 1944. Working up their escort carrier air groups would take many more months after that, however. Until they were ready, the Marines would have to depend largely on Navy escort and fast carriers for air support.

The passing of the Marianas Islands into the hands of the United States was a major milestone in the Pacific war. Its other islands to the west and south now flanked, Japan fell back upon its inner defense line, extending along the island chains that girdle Southeast Asia, except for the Palaus, which protruded as a lone salient in the western Carolines. The harbor of Saipan served as an anchorage for the fast carriers from July to November and for the tankers of Servron 10 from August 1944 to February 1945. Guam became a Servron 10 base in September and a fast carrier anchorage in November. Even while the fighting raged on Guam Admiral Nimitz inspected it as a possible site for advanced Cincpac headquarters. But the major profit resulting from the seizure of the Marianas was realized by the AAF. Immediately after the occupation began, Navy construction battalions and Army engineers arrived to lay down huge airdromes for the new very-long-range B-29 Superfortress strategic bombers. On 24 November 1944 the first B-29 strike took off from Saipan to bomb Japan.

Before the offensive could pass from the Marianas to the Luzon bottleneck, a better fleet anchorage than Saipan or Guam was needed. In addition, Admiral Nimitz was planning the capture of Peleliu in the Palau group in September. Photographs were needed of the Palaus and several other islands as possible anchorages—Yap, Ulithi, Fais, Ngulu, and Sorol. On 22 July, then, Admiral Mitscher left Bogan's TG 58.4 to assist at Guam, and sent Clark (TG 58.1), Davison (TG 58.2), and Montgomery (TG

58.3) with their ships to do the job. The latter two groups attacked the Palaus on 25 July, while Clark's planes attacked and photographed the other atolls that day and the next three.[6]

Retiring from the western Carolines, Admirals Clark and Montgomery received orders from Mitscher to head back to the Bonin and Volcano islands to knock out a new concentration of Japanese planes and a reported Japanese light carrier. Meanwhile, Dave Davison withdrew with *Wasp*, *Yorktown*, and *Princeton*. Hastening north, Clark (with *Hornet*, *Franklin*, and *Cabot*), on his fourth visit to the Jimas since 16 June, and Montgomery (with *Bunker Hill*, *Lexington*, and *San Jacinto*) sent planes against Iwo, Chichi, and Haha Jima on 4–5 August. No light carrier presented itself as a target, but a fleeing convoy of eight freighters and three escorts did. Jocko Clark's planes sank nine of the ships, and his cruisers finished off the other two; total sunk, 20,000 tons of Japanese shipping. About two dozen grounded planes were shot up, and many installations destroyed, especially by a cruiser bombardment on the sixth.[7] Iwo Jima was open to occupation for the asking, but American strategists did not know it. Japan then began to reinforce the island until it became a virtually impregnable fortress.[8]

On 10 August, the day after Task Force 58 anchored at Eniwetok, Admiral Nimitz paid a visit and told Mitscher: "Ninety-one years ago, a Naval officer [Matthew C. Perry] opened up the ports of Japan and now another officer is doing his damndest to close them." [9] The fast carrier task force began a two-week rest period, its last before the relentless final push toward Japan. On 12 August Rear Admiral Fightin' Freddie Sherman relieved Monty Montgomery in command of TG 58.3, and on the eighteenth Vice Admiral Slew McCain replaced Jocko Clark as Commander TG 58.1. Admiral Halsey relieved Admiral Spruance on 26 August, Fifth Fleet became Third Fleet, and Task Force 58 became TF 38.

By mid-August 1944 no firm strategy had been adopted for the corking of the Luzon bottleneck and the final blockade of Japan. No major strategic decision had been forthcoming from the Joint Chiefs of Staff since 12 March 1944 when, along with the bypassing of Truk and the plans to capture Hollandia and the Marianas, the following target dates had been set forth: Palau, 15 September, for Nimitz; the southern Philippines, late in the year, for MacArthur, who pinpointed Mindanao; Nimitz to plan for Formosa and MacArthur for Luzon in February 1945.

But an inclination to bypass all of these places existed among many planners. In May at San Francisco Admiral Halsey told Nimitz he believed the Palaus and western Carolines should be leapfrogged, but Nimitz and Mick Carney disagreed.[10] Then, on 13 June, the Joint Chiefs asked Nimitz and MacArthur if they felt the Philippines and Formosa could be bypassed altogether in favor of a direct landing on Kyushu, southern Japan. Both replied in the negative; intermediate air and fleet bases were first needed in the Palaus or Morotai, then in the southern or central Philippines, before going to Luzon or Formosa to cork the bottleneck. A straight shot for Japan seemed too dangerous logistically and with regard to Japan's interior air and shipping defenses.[11]

The defeat of the Japanese fleet in the Philippine Sea and the Allied landing in France in June acted as catalysts for the resumption of strategic decision-making. The joint planners in Washington accordingly offered two general courses for the offensive against Japan. One was the quick approach; either the Bonins and Iwo to Kyushu then Honshu and Tokyo, or the northern approach through Hokkaido to Honshu. These plans, involving huge numbers of troops and ships, depended on two prerequisites: the defeat of Germany and the destruction of the Japanese surface fleet. Neither happened during the summer of 1944, with the result that these direct approaches to Japan were abandoned in favor of the alternate and longer route: the Philippines or Formosa to the Ryukyu Islands to Kyushu to Honshu.[12]

Early in July, MacArthur and Nimitz agreed that Mindanao in the southern Philippines would have to be taken after Palau, the date 15 November. But both men and their staffs entertained great respect for the Japanese air network in that area. Admiral Murray recalled later in the year, "Until September, it was not clear to us, and it was inconceivable to the enemy, that the obstacle of enemy land-based airpower . . . and backed up by the enemy carrier and surface fleet, could be overcome without prohibitive loss."[13] General Kenney on 1 July rightly criticized MacArthur for depending on the fast carriers alone to "neutralize and maintain neutralization of enemy strong points and air installations" within range of Mindanao.[14] An intermediate base was needed to provide sustained land-based air support, so MacArthur decided—with JCS approval—to assault Morotai in the Halmaheras on 15 September, the same day Nimitz's forces landed in the Palaus.

Nimitz and MacArthur agreed that the land-sea advance to Japan should be supported by land-based air all the way, which meant the capture of more intermediary bases such as Morotai. MacArthur's overriding aim was to liberate the Philippines, which he had promised the natives upon his withdrawal in 1942. The stepping stones to Manila, he said on 15 June 1944, would be Mindanao in the south on 25 October, Leyte in the central islands on 15 November, Aparri in northern Luzon 15 January 1945, Mindoro south of Luzon in February, and Lingayen Gulf north of Manila on 1 April. All of these operations, save the last, would depend entirely on land-based air. Even MacArthur's own air commander, General Kenney, criticized him for not wanting to use the fast carriers more extensively—a reversal of MacArthur's earlier hopes to depend too heavily on the carriers. Now, however, MacArthur enjoyed supporters for his revised schedule in Generals Richardson and Kenney and Admirals Halsey and Kinkaid.[15]

Admiral Nimitz, strongly backed by Admiral King, agreed to land at Leyte, where air bases could be established, but then to bypass Luzon altogether for simultaneous landings in southwest Formosa and the adjacent Chinese coast at Amoy. This would quickly plug up the "bottle" of Japanese supply lines to the East Indies and hasten the defeat of Japan. Nimitz said that Kenney's planes from Leyte and the Seventh Air Force from Palau could join the fast carriers in pounding Japanese air in the Philippines as cover for the landings. General George Marshall, Army Chief of Staff, who had profound respect for the power of the Pacific Fleet, supported Nimitz and King, as did General Hap Arnold of the AAF, since B-29s could operate from Formosa. Only Admiral William D. Leahy, wartime JCS chairman, dissented.[16]

The debate grew in intensity throughout July and August, involving all key commanders from President Roosevelt on down. On 26–28 July FDR met in Hawaii with MacArthur and Nimitz, who each calmly presented their arguments, and though MacArthur seemed to win his case, the actual decision lay with the Joint Chiefs. When Forrest Sherman presented Nimitz's case to the Joint Planning Staff (which included two naval aviators, Rear Admiral Donald Duncan and Captain P. D. Stroop) in Washington on 28 August, these zealous men—ever looking for shortcuts—asked if after Leyte the Formosa–Amoy targets might be bypassed and Kyushu invaded directly. But Sherman reiterated the need for land-based air; landings could not be made on Kyushu "without shore-based aircraft which must be counted on to support the troops continuously over a sustained period." [17]

When the Joint Chiefs convened to listen to Sherman on 1 September, he pleaded for a firm directive one way or the other so that Nimitz could initiate planning. Sherman gave 1 March 1945 as a tentative date for the Formosa–Amoy landings; by then, Germany was supposed to be defeated, prerequisite for the operation, which would use troops redeployed from Europe. But by now General Marshall had changed his mind about Formosa. Opposed to campaigns on large land masses in the Pacific, Marshall considered Luzon an easier target than Formosa and a strip of the Chinese mainland. Admiral Leahy agreed with this point of view, adding that sufficient numbers of troops for Formosa would depend on developments at Leyte—assuming Germany did not surrender by the end of 1944. Leahy therefore suggested that supplies be assembled for either the Luzon or Formosa operations, and that the Pacific planners await developments on Leyte. On 8 September, after Sherman had returned to Hawaii, the Joint Chiefs set the Leyte landings for 20 December 1944 with possible landings at Luzon or Formosa–Amoy for late February or early March 1945. Beyond Leyte, though, planning could be more precise, judging from the Japanese reaction to Halsey's carrier strikes in September.[18]

When Task Force 38 sortied from Eniwetok on 28 August with Admiral Halsey exercising tactical command, the firm dates of the Pacific timetable were: Morotai and Peleliu (Palau) 15 September, Mindanao in the southern Philippines 15 November, and Leyte in the central Philippines 20 December. Halsey's mission was twofold: to support the landings at Morotai and Peleliu, and to whittle down the 650 aircraft on 63 Japanese airfields in or near the Philippines; he had ten weeks to do it before the Mindanao operation.

For the sweep westward, Halsey and Mitscher had 16 carriers, the first time the Fast Carrier Task Force had operated at full strength since the attack on the Japanese Mobile Fleet.

For preliminaries, Davison's task group struck Iwo and Chichi Jima again from 31 August to 2 September before moving to hit Yap on the sixth, while light carrier *Monterey* raided out-of-the-way Wake on the fifth. The main event began on the sixth when the task groups of McCain, Bogan, and Ted Sherman bombed the

FLEET ORGANIZATION

Commander Third Fleet—Admiral W. F. Halsey, Jr.
Chief of Staff—Rear Admiral R. B. Carney*
CTF 38—Vice Admiral M. A. Mitscher (Com1stFastCarTaskForPac)
Chief of Staff—Commodore A. A. Burke*
CTG 38.1—Vice Admiral J. S. McCain (Com2ndFastCarTaskForPac)
Hornet—Captain A. K. Doyle; Air Group 2
Wasp—Captain O. A. Weller; Air Group 14
Belleau Wood—Captain J. Perry; Air Group 21
Cowpens—Captain H. W. Taylor; Air Group 22
Monterey—Captain S. I. Ingersoll; Air Group 28
CTG 38.2—Rear Admiral G. F. Bogan (ComCarDiv 4)
Intrepid—Captain J. F. Bolger; Air Group 18
Bunker Hill—Captain M. R. Greer; Air Group 8
Cabot—Captain S. J. Michael; Air Group 31
Independence—Captain E. C. Ewen; Night Air Group 41
CTG 38.3—Rear Admiral F. C. Sherman (ComCarDiv 1)
Essex—Captain C. W. Wieber; Air Group 15
Lexington—Captain E. W. Litch; Air Group 19
Princeton—Captain W. H. Buraker; Air Group 27
Langley—Captain W. M. Dillon; Air Group 32
CTG 38.4—Rear Admiral R. E. Davison (ComCarDiv 2)
Franklin—Captain J. M. Shoemaker; Air Group 13
Enterprise—Captain C. D. Glover, Jr.; Air Group 20
San Jacinto—Captain M. H. Kernodle; Air Group 51

* Nonaviator.

Palau Islands, continuing through the eighth. On 9 September Davison fueled his ships off Palau and then assumed a support role while the other carriers attacked airfields on Mindanao on the ninth and tenth. Easily successful, and drawing practically no enemy resistance, Halsey cut short his strikes and headed north.

Admiral Halsey was astounded by the lack of Philippine-based Japanese air strength, reaffirmed by his air strikes on the Visayas Islands of the central Philippines on 12–13 September. His planes destroyed 200 enemy aircraft, sank ships, and shot up ground targets with impunity. Then, he received a stroke of good luck in the person of one of those intrepid "boot-assed" ensigns who had been transformed into the supermen of the fast carriers—or so they believed. Ensign Thomas C. Tillar from *Hornet*'s Air Group 2 was shot down over Leyte, sheltered by natives who told him of the weak Japanese defenses there, and then was picked up by a PBY "Dumbo" seaplane. His story, passed through Jocko Clark on *Hornet*, reaffirmed Halsey's suspicions that Japan's air defenses in the Philippines were nothing but a hollow shell.[19]

No ten weeks were necessary to whittle down Jap air for Mindanao, Halsey knew immediately. In fact, with the fast carriers already in command of the air in the western Pacific, there would be no need to land on Mindanao at all. The Sixth Army could go directly to Leyte, supported by Task Force 38. At midday on 13 September Halsey boldly recommended to Admiral Nimitz just this scheme. With utmost faith in Halsey's assessment of Philippine air defenses, Nimitz and MacArthur agreed on the fourteenth and passed on Halsey's recommendation to the Allied heads of state and Combined planners then meeting at Quebec. Within 90 minutes these strategists also approved, despite the fact that the rainy season would hamper airfield construction on Leyte during November. Halsey also wanted to cancel the Morotai–Palau operations, but it was too late for that.

The new decision changed everything. Troops gathering for three various minor landings (Yap, the Talaud Islands, and Mindanao) were shifted to the Leyte operation, stepped up two whole months to 20 October. This meant other operations would also be stepped up, and with the war in Europe dragging on Nimitz would not have enough troops for his proposed Formosa–Amoy operation by February. But Ernie King held out against Luzon as the next target, complaining to General Marshall in late September that the fast carriers would be tied down for six weeks off Luzon, exposing them too long to enemy attacks. General MacArthur pointed out he would need Task Force 38 only a few days until the escort carriers and land-based air took over support chores.

The plan for the capture of Formosa and Amoy died when Admiral Nimitz turned against it. Generals Harmon and Buckner, Central Pacific AAF and Army leaders, observed that the Japanese were overrunning American Fourteenth Air Force bomber bases in China, leaving any Formosa operation without air support from that quarter. Also, troops committed to Formosa would slow down the timetable for the jump forward to Okinawa in the Ryukyus. Finally, there just were not enough troops available for such a huge operation, and there would not be for many months. Convinced, Nimitz told King of his view in a meeting at San Francisco, 29 September to 1 October 1944. Cominch still did not like the idea of tying down the carriers off Luzon, but he grudgingly agreed on Luzon.[20]

The question of subsequent targets after Luzon Admiral Nimitz answered with a new timetable he presented to King at San Francisco: Iwo Jima in the Volcanos in late January 1945 and Okinawa in the Ryukyus on 1 March. Both would be needed for air bases, Iwo for fighters to escort the B-29s as well as to provide an emergency landing airfield for crippled Superforts, Okinawa as a supply base and airfield for medium and heavy bombers. On 3 October the Joint Chiefs accepted this schedule, pinpointing the Luzon operation for about 20 December, the original Leyte date. The fast carriers would support MacArthur on Luzon, then the AAF would operate from Luzon in support of the Okinawa operation. Formosa, bypassed by these new plans, would be neutralized from the air. Lingering preferences for the eventual seizure of Formosa died in the rush of other events.[21]

Only one target was left after Leyte–Luzon–Iwo–Okinawa, Japan itself, although several admirals wanted to establish a base along the coast of China north of Formosa. *How* to defeat Japan in her home islands provided the next real debate between the Army and Navy and within the JCS. The Army favored the traditional invasion, as in Germany; the Navy—joined by the AAF—favored an air-sea blockade to starve and pound Japan into submission. For planning purposes, the JCS had ruled on 11 July 1944 that Japan be invaded, since a blockade would be too prolonged.[22] But the debate would get hotter as the war moved west and north and the fast carriers battled for supremacy of the air and sea approaches to Japan.

Unfortunately, Peleliu, the one target unnecessary to future strategy but captured nevertheless, proved to be another Tarawa in terms of American casualties. With the lessons of the Marianas to draw from, one would think Peleliu might have been a relative pushover. The air strength present appeared overwhelming. On 6–8 September the Palaus were pounded by McCain's TG 38.1, and Bogan's TG 38.2, and Sherman's TG 38.3; and before that land-based B-24s had done extensive damage. Then Davison's TG 38.4 took over the attack. Captain Dick Whitehead lent his expertise in close air support by preparing the air support plan before going home on leave and giving it to the Palau Commander Support

Aircraft, Commander O. L. Odale. On D-Day, 15 September, Odale directed the attacking planes from ten escort carriers under Rear Admirals Ofstie and Sample and Davison's TG 38.4. Davison remained on station until the eighteenth, then left air support to the escort carriers. Air support was good, often even too close, but still losses remained high.[23]

Taking their cue from American landing and bombardment habits at Guam, the Japanese had developed a new defense-in-depth. They dug into caves, advancing only between salvos and then after the troops had come ashore. The lack of opposition at the beach made the three-day battleship shelling rather worthless and minimized targets for aircraft. By the seventeenth all Marine Corps artillery was ashore, and air support was shifted to deep targets that artillery could not reach. After the fast carriers retired on the eighteenth, the air support commanders moved ashore and later the Marines flew their F4U Corsairs into the captured airfield. Using 1000-pound and napalm bombs dropped from treetop heights, these planes gave the ground forces optimum support. But air support could not decide the issue; the foot soldier had to dig out Peleliu's defenders. Most of the island was secured by 22 September, but organized resistance did not cease until 25 November. Peleliu, while hardly worth the cost, provided a warning of things to come.[24]

Much had yet to be learned about air support, but as long as Marine planes were not aboard the carriers their techniques could not be learned. Still, Navy procedures were acceptable, as the near-flawless landings at Morotai on 15 September demonstrated. McCain's TG 38.1 stood 50 miles offshore for air strikes in conjunction with six escort carriers under Rear Admirals Tommy and Ziggy Sprague. One thing Admiral Nimitz learned to appreciate about close air support was that it belonged under the administrative control of amphibious rather than air commanders, an idea Admiral Kelly Turner had finally sold to him. Therefore, on 1 October 1944 Captain Whitehead's outfit was taken from ComAirPac's administrative authority and made a part of Turner's ComPhibsPac: Air Support Control Units, Amphibious Forces, Pacific Fleet (ASCU, PhibsPac).[25] Until the Iwo operation in January, however, Whitehead and his reinforced office would not be needed; the Leyte and Luzon landings were MacArthur's affairs.

Task Force 38 completed September's activities with devastating air attacks on the Philippines: Mindanao and the Visayas on the fourteenth, Manila and the Visayas on the twenty-first, twenty-second, and twenty-fourth. Nimitz criticized Halsey for not mining Manila Bay, but Halsey refused to use mines from carrier planes because of the storage space they consumed and the vulnerability of planes dropping them. Mines were thereafter carried only by land-based bombers. There was no need to despair, however; by the end of the month Task Force 38 had destroyed no fewer than 893 Japanese planes airborne and parked, and had sunk 67 ships totaling 224,000 tons—a magnificent score.[26]

Logistically, the carriers now enjoyed several bases from which to operate in these forward areas. The major one would be Ulithi, occupied on 23 September; this great atoll and lagoon lies on the same longitudinal meridian as Tokyo, Japan. While the new anchorage was being readied by Admiral Calhoun's service forces, the fast carriers retired separately to other points. Seeadler Harbor at Manus in the Admiralties, designed as a more permanent base for both Central and Southwest Pacific forces, received McCain's TG 38.1 on 29 September. Bogan took TG 38.2 to Saipan on the twenty-eighth, while Sherman anchored TG 38.3 at Kossol Passage at the north end of the Palaus on the twenty-seventh. Davison kept TG 38.4 off the Palaus until early October, awaiting developments in the southern target islands. On 1–2 October Bogan and Sherman took their carriers into the Ulithi lagoon, which was lashed for the next three days by a violent typhoon.[27]

In October Service Squadron 10 moved its headquarters from Eniwetok to Ulithi, forty different ship types shifting their base 1400 miles across the Pacific. At Ulithi a "floating tank farm" of obsolete tankers provided a ready reserve of 400,000 barrels of fuel oil and aviation gas. In addition to Servron 10, the Pacific Fleet was served by Servron 2, which operated all repair, salvage, and hospital ships in the combat zone; Servron 8, which provided the ship pool of service vessels at Pearl Harbor; and Servron 12, building harbor facilities at Guam and Saipan.

But the fast carriers would now be obliged to range far and wide for long periods of time, and could not return even near Ulithi for fuel and replacement aircraft. To supply Task Force 38 with these requirements at sea, Fleet supply experts created the At Sea Logistics Service Group, 34 fleet oilers escorted by 11 escort carriers, 19 destroyers, and 26 destroyer escorts. Fueling at Ulithi, each replenishment group of 12 oilers would sortie for a rendezvous with the fast carriers; the "jeep carriers" would provide combat air patrols and would ferry replacement aircraft. Admiral Halsey set each fueling rendezvous at the extreme range of Japanese land-based planes, which never succeeded in disrupting any refueling operations. This Group gave the fast carrier task force its unprecedented mobility—for the next campaigns would shatter all records for endurance—and enabled American carrier planes to attack the vitals of Japan's inner defenses.[28]

By the first week in October 1944 Task Force 38 boasted excellent leaders, aircraft, ships, personnel, logistics, and a splendid record. It would need all these things for the long campaigns ahead, for another fleet battle, for many weeks in close support of ground forces, for the heaviest weather yet encountered, and for repelling the thousands of airplanes and human guided missiles Japan would hurl at the U.S. Navy. As the June ComAirPac Analysis, distributed late in July, had warned: "Losses will be heavier. Overconfidence is not justified."

Eight:
The Philippine Campaign

Once the United States was committed to the liberation of the Philippine Islands, the Leyte and Luzon operations became crucial to the survival of the Japanese Empire and war machine. Secure at Leyte, the Americans could stage aircraft, warships, and amphibious forces from west to north, to China and the East Indies, cutting Japan's vital lines of communications to her raw materials. Not only could this great supply area be "corked" at the Luzon bottleneck, but the Americans could conceivably coordinate operations with the British in India to overrun the Indies. Or they could land in China, link up with Chiang Kai-shek, and challenge Japanese superiority on the continent.

The Philippines, as in December 1941, covered Japan's eastern flank in her Southeast Asia Empire; but now, in October 1944, they were also part of the inner line of defense. They would have to be defended at all costs by the fleet based at Singapore and in Japan, by the thousands of superb ground forces in the Philippines, and by the land-based air forces staging to the threatened area from Japan, China, and other points within the defense sphere. True, hope for victory was slim, and true, the admirals and several statesmen were pressing for peace, but the great Japanese Army had yet to be tested in large-scale actions. Leyte and Luzon would provide such a test.

An American victory in the Philippines would not only free the suppressed Filipinos and shorten the war; it would guarantee Japan's defeat as a great power. The campaign would last many months and tax the patience of all combatants, especially those men of fast carrier task force who would now be tied down in the support of large-scale continental-type Army operations. But it would, therefore, prepare the carrier forces for all future operations.

The outcome of the operation has led many historians to succumb to hindsight in minimizing the potential strength of the Japanese fleet and air forces in October 1944. Realistically planning for November landings in the Philippines by the Americans, however, Admiral Toyoda could count on a carrier fleet by that time comprised of the following:

FLEET ORGANIZATION

Commander Third Fleet—Vice Admiral Jisaburo Ozawa
ComCarDiv 1—Vice Admiral Ozawa
Amagi, Unryu, Zuikaku, Katsuragi
ComCarDiv 3—Rear Admiral Sueo Obayashi
Zuiho, Chitose, Chiyoda
ComCarDiv 4—Rear Admiral Chiaki Matsuda
Ise, Hyuga (half-battleships), *Junyo, Ryuho*

As soon as those carriers damaged at the Philippine Sea battle were repaired and the new *Unryus* shaken down, Admiral Ozawa intended to take his carriers to Singapore to join up with the battleships and cruisers of Vice Admiral Takeo Kurita's Second Fleet.[1] The Mobile Fleet would then sally forth to repel the invaders. Admiral Toyoda had no choice but to commit it, for with the fleet's fuel in the East Indies and its arms in Japan, the Luzon bottleneck had to be kept open. Said Toyoda, "There would be no sense in saving the fleet at the expense of the loss of the Philippines."[2]

By November, the Japanese land-based air forces would be in better condition than if committed early. In July, the Army and Navy agreed to cooperate in the defense of the Philippines, but as in all previous battles in the Philippines Navy air would end up doing the lion's share of the work; Army pilots could not navigate over water.[3] So Navy planes would attack Task Force 38, Army planes the shipping off the beachhead. Toyoda planned to commit his land-based air first, just as he had done in the Marianas. If these planes failed to stop the landing, as in June, he would then commit his carrier air units, understrength and undertrained as they would be even in November. If both land- and carrier-based air forces did not succeed, only one course of action was left: Onishi's suicide planes. Before that last resort Toyoda would have to lose over 1000 airplanes and pilots.

But American plans would upset Toyoda's schemes. The Leyte landing was moved up to 20 October 1944, to be followed by landings of Mindoro, south of Luzon, on 5 December, and on Luzon at Lingayen Gulf of 20 December. The latter two targets are situated on the western side of the Philippines, facing the South China Sea. Once American naval forces attempted to put troops ashore in these places, their backs would be presented to air bases in China and Indochina. Operating at such great distances from their bases, the American Third and Seventh fleets would be at a distinct disadvantage geographically. This fact led most American planners to anticipate the appearance of the Japanese fleet either at Mindoro or Luzon, not at Leyte.

1. Battle for Leyte Gulf

American operations in the Philippine Islands fell within the Southwest Pacific theater under General Douglas MacArthur. Relying primarily on the land-based air forces of Lieutenant General Kenney, these forces had waged a typical Army-type land campaign across New Guinea, aided by the light surface forces of the Seventh Fleet. The commander of "MacArthur's Navy" was Vice Admiral Thomas C. Kinkaid, who as the last nonaviator to command a carrier force had lost the old *Hornet* in 1942—or he was blamed for so doing by Admiral Towers.[1]

In New Guinea, however, Kinkaid had had nothing further to do with carriers and would not have at Leyte had the original Pacific strategy been followed—that is, Mindanao captured and Kenney's planes flown from bases there to support the Leyte assault. But now all air support had to be from the sea, so Nimitz loaned eighteen escort carriers from the Central Pacific for Leyte. And when General Kenney found he knew nothing about air support procedures from ships, Nimitz furnished Captain Dick Whitehead, hurriedly recalled from his leave to be Commander Air Support Control Units at Leyte—with no cooperation from an irate Kenney.[2]

Also supporting this Southwest Pacific operation would be Task Force 38 from Nimitz's Central Pacific theater. Because Admiral William F. Halsey, Jr., assumed virtual tactical command, TF 38 was often referred to as Third Fleet, but none of the Central Pacific amphibious units took part in the Leyte operation as members of the Third Fleet. As at Saipan, the fast carriers would join

Japan's Inner Defenses

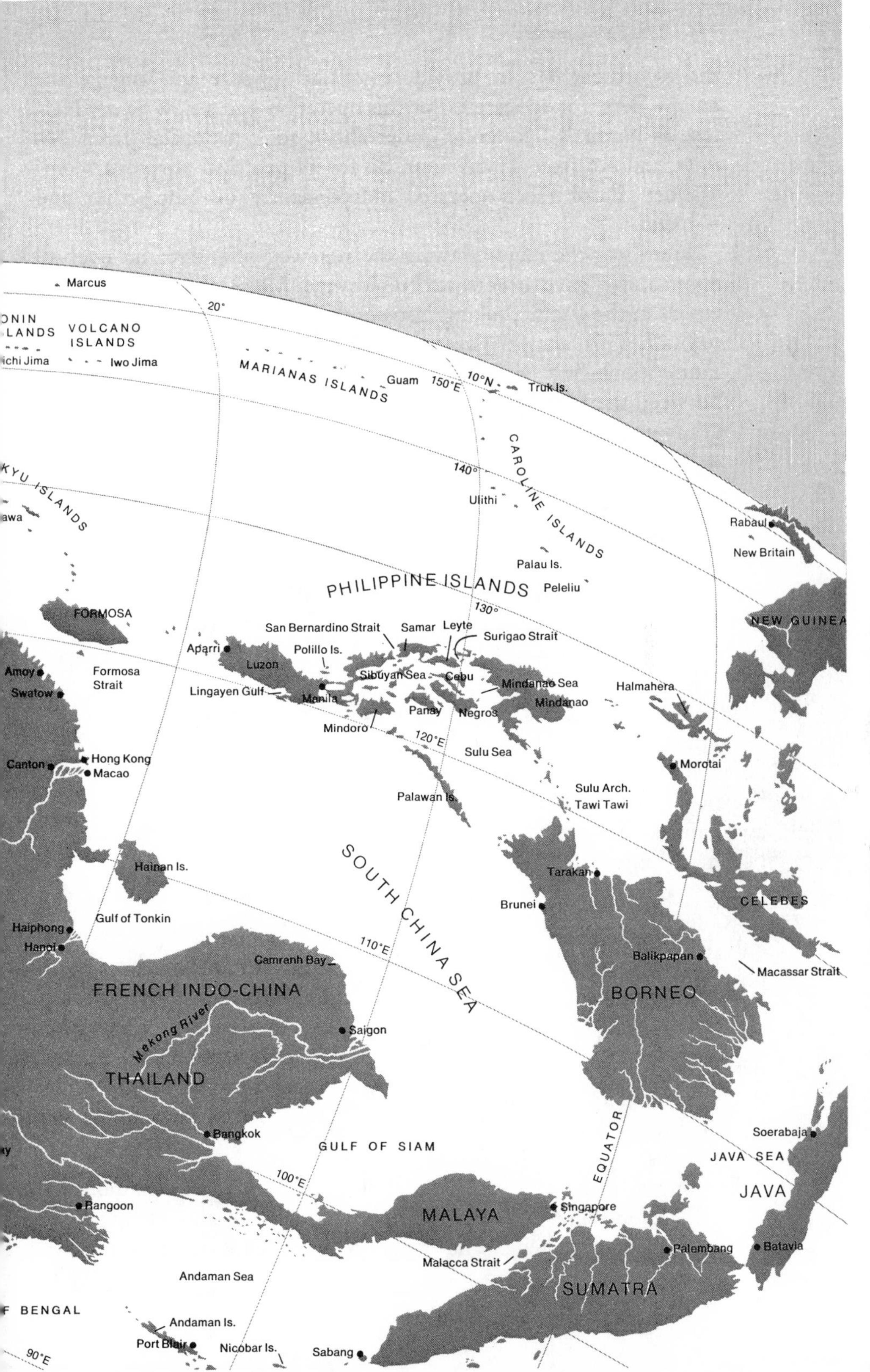
Marcus
20°
VOLCANO ISLANDS
Iwo Jima
MARIANAS ISLANDS
Guam
150°E
10°N
Truk Is.
CAROLINE ISLANDS
140°
Ulithi
Rabaul
New Britain
Palau Is.
Peleliu
PHILIPPINE ISLANDS
130°
NEW GUINEA
FORMOSA
San Bernardino Strait
Samar
Leyte
Surigao Strait
Aparri
Polillo Is.
Luzon
Sibuyan Sea
Cebu
Mindanao Sea
Halmahera
Amoy
Formosa Strait
Swatow
Lingayen Gulf
Manila
Panay
Negros
Mindanao
Mindoro
120°E
Sulu Sea
Canton
Hong Kong
Macao
Morotai
Sulu Arch.
Tawi Tawi
Palawan Is.
SOUTH CHINA SEA
Hainan Is.
Tarakan
Brunei
CELEBES
Gulf of Tonkin
Haiphong
Hanoi
110°E
Camranh Bay
Balikpapan
Macassar Strait
FRENCH INDO-CHINA
BORNEO
Mekong River
Saigon
THAILAND
EQUATOR
Bangkok
GULF OF SIAM
Soerabaja
JAVA SEA
JAVA
100°E
Rangoon
MALAYA
Singapore
Palembang
Batavia
Malacca Strait
Andaman Sea
SUMATRA
BENGAL
Andaman Is.
Port Blair
Nicobar Is.
Sabang
90°E

the escort carriers to provide close air support and engage the enemy fleet if it appeared. But this operation had a new twist; Halsey, as Nimitz's fleet commander afloat, took his orders from Nimitz, and not from MacArthur. So for all practical purposes, Commander Third Fleet operated independently of MacArthur and Kinkaid.

Here was the major flaw in the renewed offensive: no over-all commander gave orders to Nimitz and MacArthur. They were equals in the Pacific, taking instructions only from the Joint Chiefs of Staff. This being the case, Halsey had no direct, automatic communications link with MacArthur and Kinkaid. Every message between the two fleets had to be specially routed, with copies not going automatically to interested parties along any distribution list or chain of command. Such an inefficient system created communications delays, lack of information, misunderstandings, and occasional mistakes. But there could be no unity of command in the Pacific, for Nimitz would never trust MacArthur with fast carriers that might be carelessly exposed or sacrificed, and MacArthur insisted that such a large-scale operation as Leyte was strictly Army business. This system—or lack of it—invited confusion and possible disaster.

Halsey, respected by Nimitz as a fighter, was appointed to the Philippines operation to fight. Not a brilliant thinker like Spruance, he would not be hampered by the multitudinous details of another Saipan. He would be free to use the fleet, hopefully to draw out and fight the Japanese fleet, completing the task Admiral Spruance began in June. This hope Nimitz reiterated to Ernie King at San Francisco late in September.[3] And so that Halsey would not be restricted by vague orders Nimitz made explicit the orders he had only implied to Spruance in the previous operation: "In case opportunity for destruction of major portion of the enemy fleet is offered or can be created, such destruction becomes the *primary task*."[4] These were fighting orders, issued without consultation with General MacArthur and the amphibious commanders, and they gave Bull Halsey *carte blanche* to seek out and finish off the Mobile Fleet despite his other missions of search and supporting the landings.

Fighting was Halsey's job in the Third–Fifth Fleet two-platoon Central Pacific command arrangement. After the Philippines operation, throughout which he would engage only in covering operations for MacArthur, he was to yield to Spruance, who would direct the complex Iwo Jima and Okinawa landings. When these were completed, only the invasion of Japan would remain, and Halsey would certainly return to his covering role. Ernie King in the September meeting at San Francisco asked Nimitz about giving Spruance command at the Luzon beaches with Halsey to head the fast carriers for a naval engagement. This suggestion was made in the belief the enemy fleet would not come out until December and that Luzon might be Nimitz's show. King also inquired about placing Halsey directly under Spruance's command during the Iwo Jima and Okinawa operations, but Nimitz preferred to keep the existing two-platoon arrangement.[5]

When Halsey took command, he looked upon himself as the fast carrier commander, having little real use for Mitscher or McCain, the rightful carrier tactical commanders. This attitude was dangerous, for Halsey lacked the experience of Mitscher and other admirals in the fast carrier task force. Upon assuming command in late August, he hastened to visit Mitscher's flagship; "I hadn't been with the fleet for more than two years; I wanted to see what the new carriers and planes looked like." [6] Much had happened in carriers since he had delivered Doolittle's raiders to Tokyo in April 1942, and he would need the advice of experts in order to catch up on his homework.

In fact, Halsey might have profited from a "makee-learn" period for fast carrier operations along with McCain, for he was not the kind of man to depend on subordinates such as Mitscher, nor did he have a suitable staff for fast carrier task force operations. His nonaviator chief of staff, Rear Admiral Robert B. Carney, shared Halsey's fiery temperment, which was fine for cooperation but not conducive to stimulating disagreements. His operations officer, Captain Ralph E. Wilson, was also a nonaviator, while Halsey had a Marine Corps brigadier general for war plans, a carryover from his theater command. All his staff accompanied him from the South Pacific, including his flag secretary, Commander Harold E. Stassen (former governor of Minnesota) and three aviators, Commanders M. C. Cheek (intelligence), H. Douglas Moulton (air operations), and L. J. Dow (communications). Mike Cheek and Doug Moulton had left the Navy during the 1930s and only returned for the war, while they and Ham Dow had been with Halsey since 1942. His closest advisers he assembled into his "dirty trick department"—Carney, Moulton, Dow, Stassen, and Lieutenant Commander John E. Lawrence, air combat intelligence officer. Neither Halsey, any of his staff, nor McCain, had ever participated in a carrier battle or in any of the operations of Task Force 58. The experience lay with Mitscher, Burke, and the three veteran carrier task group commanders, Ted Sherman, Dave Davison, and Gerry Bogan.

Tactically, Halsey was a meleeist in the tradition of Nelson. Also, as an aviator, he would not be expected to suffer the reluctance to seek battle shown by a formalist nonaviator like Spruance. He had daring and was unafraid to take risks, but he was also sloppy in his procedures. Rather than issuing meticulous operations plans, he operated by dispatch. This being the case, he lost valuable time in sending communications—which were too often vague—and his carrier admirals never quite knew his plans. McCain was identical in his sloppiness. Both men were loved dearly by their men, but neither of them enjoyed the keen professional respect of their captains and admirals that Spruance and Mitscher did. And since the Leyte operation was complicated by the divided command situation, this old-fashioned bulldog brand of leadership was out of place.

Having missed the great carrier battles of the Coral Sea, Midway, and the Philippine Sea, Halsey intended to destroy the Japanese carriers at the first opportunity. His staff constructed a game board on the deck of *New Jersey* in "flag country" and frequently worked out possible battle situations with the Japanese fleet.[7] A major concern was the Mindoro operation, scheduled for 5 December. If the Japanese carriers did not fight for Leyte, or survived a naval battle for Leyte, they could be used most effectively to hit American shipping off Mindoro. With carriers operating in the South China Sea, Japanese planes by the hundreds could shuttle (as at Saipan) from China airfields to the flattops to Mindoro. They could trap MacArthur's amphibious forces and Task Force 38 on the west side of the Philippines and raise havoc. And if conventional bombing attacks did not work, the possibility of suicide attacks existed. Looking ahead, then, Halsey felt the carriers must be eliminated as soon as possible.[8]

When Task Force 38 rendezvoused 375 miles west of the Marianas on 7 October 1944 to begin the prelanding attacks on Japanese airfields, it represented the fast carrier task force at unprecedented strength, carrying more than 1000 aircraft:

FLEET ORGANIZATION

Commander-in-Chief Pacific Fleet—Admiral C. W. Nimitz*
Commander Third Fleet—Admiral William F. Halsey, Jr.
Chief of Staff—Rear Admiral R. B. Carney*
Commander Task Force 38—Vice Admiral M. A. Mitscher (Com1stFasCarForPac)
Chief of Staff—Commodore A. A. Burke*
CTG 38.1—Vice Admiral J. S. McCain (Com2ndFasCarForPac)
Wasp—Captain O. A. Weller; Air Group 14
Hornet—Captain A. K. Doyle; Air Group 11
Monterey—Captain S. H. Ingersoll; Air Group 28
Cowpens—Captain H. W. Taylor; Air Group 22
Hancock—Captain F. C. Dickey; Air Group 7
CTG 38.2—Rear Admiral G. F. Bogan (ComCarDiv 4)
Intrepid—Captain J. F. Bolger; Air Group 18
Bunker Hill—Captain M. R. Greer; Air Group 8
Cabot—Captain S. J. Michael; Air Group 31
Independence—Captain E. C. Ewen; Night Air Group 41
CTG 38.3—Rear Admiral F. C. Sherman (ComCarDiv 1)
Essex—Captain C. W. Wieber; Air Group 15
Lexington—Captain E. W. Litch; Air Group 19
Princeton—Captain W. H. Buraker; Air Group 27
Langley—Captain J. F. Wegforth; Air Group 44
CTG 38.4—Rear Admiral R. E. Davison (ComCarDiv 2)
Franklin—Captain J. M. Shoemaker; Air Group 13
Enterprise—Captain C. D. Glover, Jr.; Air Group 20
Belleau Wood—Captain J. Perry; Air Group 21
San Jacinto—Captain M. H. Kernodle; Air Group 51
Commander Task Force 34 (Battle Line)—Vice Admiral W. A. Lee (ComBatPac)*
Chief of Staff—Commodore T. P. Jeter
Commander Southwest Pacific Theater—General Douglas MacArthur*
Commander Seventh Fleet: Vice Admiral T. C. Kinkaid*
Chief of Staff—Commodore V. H. Schaeffer
Commander Escort Carrier Group—Rear Admiral T. L. Sprague
Commander Support Aircraft—Captain R. L. Whitehead

* Nonaviator.

Halsey's orders were first to neutralize Japanese air north of the Philippines, principally at Kyushu, Okinawa, and Formosa. These forces belonged to the Second Air Fleet under Vice Admiral

Shigeru Fukudome. Then Halsey was to shift southward to Luzon and Visayan airfields, the First Air Fleet bases under Vice Admiral Onishi. In these strikes, he naturally hoped to lure out the Japanese carrier fleet, while aboard ship scuttlebutt had it, incorrectly, that this "Hot Foot" operation would include strikes against the Chinese coast and even Tokyo.[9] Struggling against poor visibility caused by overcast, American carrier planes attacked Okinawa airfields and shipping on 10 October with great success—the closest the fast carriers had ever operated to Japan. Task Force 38 sank 19 small warships and some sampans and destroyed over 100 planes at the cost of 21 from the carriers, but most of the crews were picked up by the lifeguard submarine. On the eleventh a less-successful strike was launched against Aparri, northern Luzon. On the twelfth Halsey began four days of heavy air attacks against Formosa.

Japanese plans for a November carrier battle were wrecked. Vice Admiral Kusaka, chief of staff to Admiral Toyoda in Tokyo, on the tenth ordered Vice Admiral Fukudome to commit his land-based air to the destruction of the enemy fleet and told Vice Admiral Ozawa to transfer his 300 undertrained carrier pilots ashore. Admiral Toyoda himself flew to Formosa on the twelfth to direct the air attacks on the enemy naval air forces. That day 101 Japanese sorties and antiaircraft fire shot down 48 American carrier planes but at tremendous losses to their own planes in the air and on the ground. Overoptimistic reports by Japanese pilots led Admiral Toyoda to decide to change his air defense plans from making his stand at the Philippines to Formosa, and from the date of the landings to the present seemingly opportune moment. Late on the twelfth he ordered Rear Admirals Obayashi and Matsuda to send their carrier planes from CarDivs 3 and 4 to Formosa to join in the attack. All or nothing at Formosa.[10]

For a time, the air battle over Formosa was titanic. On the thirteenth the Japanese flew off only 32 sorties, but then launched 419 on the fourteenth and another 199 on the fifteenth. It was another Turkey Shoot. Halsey's Hellcats sent most of these green pilots into the sea, destroying even more on the ground along with some light shipping and many installations; over 500 Japanese planes failed to survive the four days at Formosa. Toyoda had sacrificed his air strength for the Philippines prematurely.

A few dauntless Japanese torpedo planes did get through, however, to hit heavy cruiser *Canberra* on the thirteenth and light cruiser *Houston* on the fourteenth and again on the sixteenth. Seriously crippled, these ships withdrew slowly toward Ulithi under tow and the escort of other cruisers, destroyers, and light carriers *Cabot* and *Cowpens*. Attempting to use these ships as bait for the Japanese fleet, Admiral Halsey managed to lure out three cruisers under Vice Admiral Kiyohide Shima from Japan. Shima soon discovered Task Force 38 was by no means defeated and sinking, and he turned around. On the seventh, search planes went after him, expecting to find a carrier and two battleships, but he got away.[11]

Formosa neutralized, Task Force 38 shifted to the Philippines to begin the isolation of the beachhead at Leyte by the twentieth, the date of the landing. On the fifteenth TG 38.4 began five days of strikes against Luzon, especially Manila, joined by TG 38.1 and TG 38.2 on the eighteenth. With the retirement of Admiral Shima's force of warships from Formosa, Admiral Halsey decided the Japanese fleet would—as suspected—wait until the Mindoro or Luzon assaults to challenge the American naval forces in the Philippines. He therefore initiated plans to rotate his hard-working carrier task groups back to Ulithi for rest and replenishment. Many of the carriers' duties could be absorbed by General Kenney's active long-range planes, now operating out of New Guinea and Morotai to hit Luzon and the East Indies.

Halsey could not know that Toyoda had used up his main air strength, including that of the carriers, in the Formosa air battle. The early American sortie and these losses now forced Admiral Ozawa to draw up an entirely new plan for the defense of the Philippines. On 17 October, confessing his inability to unite the fleet at Singapore and no longer needing the carriers for the planes they no longer had, Ozawa recommended to Toyoda that Vice Admiral Kurita's battleship-cruiser force at Singapore be placed directly under Toyoda's command at Tokyo, where the Commander-in-Chief had returned after the Formosa debacle. He recommended that his planeless carriers now be used as sacrificial bait to lure Halsey and Task Force 38 away from Leyte Gulf so that Kurita could slip in and destroy the landing force there. Said Ozawa after the war, "I expected complete destruction of my fleet, but if Kurita's mission was carried out that was all I wished."[12]

Toyoda agreed, and gave the order on the morning of 18 October. While Ozawa steamed down from Japan with his "northern force" of decoy carriers, two gun forces would penetrate the

Philippines from the west for a coordinated attack on the Leyte shipping on the morning of 25 October. Vice Admiral Kurita would pass through the central Philippines via the Sibuyan Sea and San Bernardino Strait and descend upon Leyte Gulf from the north and east of Samar Island. This "center force" included superbattleships *Yamato* and *Musashi*, two older battleships, and six heavy cruisers, plus a light cruiser and several destroyers. A second gun force of two old battleships, one heavy cruiser, and destroyers would penetrate the Sulu and Mindanao seas and Surigao Strait to strike Leyte from the south. This "southern force," commanded by Vice Admiral Shoji Nishimura, would be supported by Vice Admiral Shima and his three cruisers from Japan. In every respect, the plan was suicidal. Ozawa's carriers would be sacrificed as a lure, Nishimura's ships would face a strong battle line of old battleships at Surigao, and Kurita—if he managed to elude the fast carriers—would hardly be able to retrace his steps back to San Bernardino; Halsey's returning carriers would cut off his retreat.

So Japan had decided to give up its surface fleet in order to keep open the Philippines lifeline. In one last gigantic fleet action, the Empire of Nippon would quit its blue-water naval doctrine. In the confined waters of the continent, after this battle, land-based air and submarines would comprise the main strength of the Navy. Ozawa dissolved CarDiv 1, left the three new and untried *Unryus* at their Inland Sea anchorage, and shifted his flag from *Amagi* to old veteran *Zuikaku*. Ozawa then assumed direct command of CarDiv 3, *Zuikaku* and light carriers *Zuiho*, *Chitose*, and *Chiyoda*. These ships took on 116 planes of a possible complement of 160 on the twentieth, enough for one shuttle-strike to Luzon to make Halsey think the Northern Force was also heading for the rendezvous at Leyte. CarDiv 4, Rear Admiral Matsuda, lost any pretense as a carrier unit. *Ise* and *Hyuga* had already lost their planes to the Formosa debacle, and they were added to Ozawa's force for their 14-inch guns. The carriers of this division, *Ryuho* and *Junyo*, became aircraft ferries at the end of the month, the former going to Formosa, the latter to Borneo, then Manila.[13]

With three light cruisers and eight destroyers as escorts, Ozawa's northern decoy force of four carriers and two battleships sortied from the Inland Sea at 5 P.M. 20 October, only hours after MacArthur had stepped ashore at Leyte. At practically the same moment Admirals Kurita and Nishimura, who had left Singapore with their warships on the eighteenth, received their orders at Brunei Bay, Borneo. Both forces, the Center and Southern, sortied from Brunei for the Philippines on the twenty-second. The same day Shima's cruiser force left Japan to join Nishimura's Southern Force. By the twenty-second Vice Admiral Fukudome of Formosa's Second Air Fleet had flown in the last of about 200 available airplanes to the Philippines, and the call went out for hundreds more from China and Japan. These began arriving within days, but Vice Admiral Onishi of the Philippine's First Air Fleet had little faith in these largely untried pilots. On 19 October he activated the Kamikaze Corps of suicide planes.[14]

When the U.S. Sixth Army began its landing on Leyte Island on 20 October, it enjoyed fairly respectable air cover and support, all coordinated by Captain Dick Whitehead from Seventh Fleet amphibious headquarters ship *Wasatch*. Rear Admiral Tommy Sprague had over-all command of the 18 escort carriers which operated Hellcats, Wildcats, and Avengers. His three task units were commanded directly by himself, Rear Admiral Felix Stump, and Rear Admiral Clifton A. F. "Ziggy" Sprague. Other escort cardiv commanders present were Rear Admiral Bill Sample, Ralph Ofstie, and George Henderson, though the latter departed with two escort carriers for Morotai on the twenty-fourth. Each of these men had been captain of a fast carrier within the past year. All four fast carrier task groups patrolled, or they attacked enemy airfields, joined by Fifth Air Force bombers. From the twentieth through the twenty-third fast and escort carrier planes and the AAF met little resistance in the air and destroyed over 100 planes on the ground. The Navy planes used two captured airfields on Leyte for emergency landings.

Sixth Army moved steadily inland under this cover, hoping to gain as much ground as possible before the Japanese launched heavy counterattacks on land, sea, and in the air. Heavy rains postponed the use of the newly captured fields for AAF planes, while equipment piled up on the beach as the transports raced to unload and clear Leyte Gulf before the expected massive counterattack. Any beachhead is in danger in the early stages of a landing; especially so was that at Leyte, situated on the edge of Japan's inner defense line. This being the case, Vice Admiral Kinkaid breathed easier on the eighteenth when he learned that Shima's cruisers had fled Task Force 38 off Formosa; the absence of enemy fleet units meant that Halsey could now concentrate on guarding San Bernardino and Surigao straits, the only passages enemy fleet units could transit to get to Kinkaid's shipping.[15] Anyway, should Japanese warships appear off the beach Kinkaid had the same protection Turner had had at Saipan: Jesse Oldendorf's battle line of six old battleships (two with 16-inch guns, four with 14-inch), many escort carriers, and the fast carrier task force up to 250 miles away, the effective round-trip range of its planes.

Admiral Halsey detached McCain's TG 38.1 toward Ulithi for rest and replenishment. It was 600 miles to the east when, after daybreak on the twenty-fourth, Halsey learned that two U.S. submarines were attacking Kurita's Center Force west of the Philippines in Palawan Passage. The subs performed brilliantly, sinking two heavy cruisers and putting a third out of action, though one of the subs had to be abandoned and scuttled after the action. Halsey now knew the Mobile Fleet was going to give battle. Unfortunately, however, Halsey had waited for this definite news before stopping McCain's trip to Ulithi, and he would need TG 38.1 to bring Task Force 38 to full strength for battle. McCain had no fewer than five carriers with him, *Wasp*, *Hornet*, *Hancock*, *Monterey*, and *Cowpens*, while *Bunker Hill* had retired on the twenty-third to return to Ulithi for more fighters. The absence of these ships left Halsey with 11 fast carriers.

After carrier search planes sighted both Kurita's and Nishimura's forces shortly after 8 A.M. 24 October, Halsey went into action. He ordered his three available task groups to cover the three approaches to Leyte, Sherman's TG 38.3 (*Essex*, *Lexington*, *Princeton*, and *Langley*) off the Polillo Islands east of Luzon, Bogan's weakened TG 38.2 (*Intrepid*, *Cabot*, and the night *Independence*) off San Bernadino Strait, and Davison's TG 38.4 (*Franklin*, *Enterprise*, *San Jacinto*, and *Belleau Wood*) to the south covering Surigao Strait. Admiral Halsey also recalled McCain's TG 38.1, arranging its at-sea refueling for the next morning. By then, however, McCain might arrive too late, for he was now 600 miles east of Leyte; Halsey should have kept TG 38.1 on station until he had had definite intelligence regarding the Japanese fleet. Finally, Halsey ordered air strikes to commence, with Sherman and Davison to close on Bogan, who was nearest the line of the enemy fleet's approach.

During the morning of the twenty-fourth all three task groups were heavily engaged. To the south, Dave Davison's planes made rather ineffective attacks on the Southern Force, after which Halsey ordered this group to the assistance of Gerry Bogan, whose planes were attacking the big Center Force in the Sibuyan Sea. Meanwhile, Ted Sherman's task group came under a heavy air attack from Japanese planes operating out of Luzon. Sherman had to break off his air strikes to concentrate on defending his carriers. His Hellcats, especially those of Commander Dave McCampbell's Turkey Shoot veterans of *Essex*'s Air Group 15, shot down or turned away over 50 enemy planes. But one got through to plant a bomb on light carrier *Princeton*. The valiant ship and assisting cruisers and destroyers battled the flames, but a mighty internal explosion ripped the ship later in the day, and she had to be sunk. The Fast Carrier Task Force had lost its first carrier.

While Sherman's group continued to battle off fresh enemy air attacks, Halsey committed his full attention to the Center Force. He concluded that Kinkaid could deal with the oncoming Southern Force, which would be within range of Oldendorf's battleships around midnight, so he discontinued air strikes against that force. This decision was sound, but its execution illustrates the weaknesses of the divided Third–Seventh fleets command at Leyte. Halsey never communicated his decision to Kinkaid; the latter simply assumed he would take on the Southern Force and spent the rest of the twenty-fourth preparing for a night gunnery duel in Surigao Strait.[16]

The battle in the Sibuyan Sea lasted from 10:30 A.M. to about 2 P.M. All three task groups sent planes, which encountered almost no air opposition, this because the Japanese admirals had considered offensive air attack on Sherman's group more important than air cover for Kurita.[17] The result was the sinking of *Princeton*, but at the cost of 72,000-ton battlewagon *Musashi*. Repeatedly hit by bombs and torpedoes, this great ship fell behind in a sinking condition; she retired, and in the early evening rolled over and sank—her loss unseen but suspected by the American commanders. In addition to the loss of *Musashi* and the three cruisers to the subs, Kurita's other ships sustained damage; but he still had four battleships and six heavy cruisers plus escort ships. At 2 P.M. he turned around to the west in apparent retreat. The jubilant American aviators reported great damage to the enemy ships, leading Halsey to conclude Kurita no longer represented a serious threat. Admiral Mitscher, however, was used to exaggerated aviator reporting, and personal interviews of pilots on board flagship *Lexington* raised doubts in his mind as to the extent of the damage to the Center

Force.[18] Halsey, his flag in a battleship, had no such direct contact, and he did not choose to consult Mitscher.

Halsey did not discount the possibility of Kurita's still turning around, for at 3:12 P.M. he sent a preparatory battle plan to his task commanders covering that possibility. Four of the six battleships, two heavy and three light carriers, and 14 destroyers, he radioed, "will be formed as TF 34 under V. Adm. Lee, Commander Battle Line. TF 34 will engage decisively at long ranges." The other two fast battleships would presumably continue in support of the carriers. Quite by accident, Admiral Kinkaid intercepted this message and was gratified to know that if the Center Force turned eastward again, it too would be running into a trap like the Southern Force. The match looked even in gun ships at San Bernardino Strait: four battleships for each side, six Japanese cruisers to Lee's five, but Halsey had ten carriers to almost no Japanese planes. The flaw in all this was that Kinkaid literally believed Task Force 34 was being formed at 3:12 P.M. to guard San Bernardino Strait. Halsey then clarified his order by short-range voice radio to his subordinate commanders: "If the enemy sorties, TF 34 will be formed when directed by me." This clarification Kinkaid could not intercept.[19] He assumed the Battle Line had already been formed. But no problem. For if the Center Force did turn around, Halsey would still form Task Force 34, according to his battle plan.

With both San Bernardino and Surigao straits well covered, the question that plagued all American naval commanders was the whereabouts of Japan's carriers. Mitscher believed they were in the South China Sea, but Halsey guessed the north. Ted Sherman, "strongly suspicious of the presence of Jap carriers to the northeast," obtained permission from Mitscher to launch a search in that direction, which he did at 2:05.[20] Actually, Admiral Ozawa was doing everything he could think of to get his Northern Force detected, whereupon he could turn tail and lure the fast carriers north. He made fake radio transmissions, sent out daily air searches, and at 11:45 A.M. on the twenty-fourth launched a 76-plane strike which was obliterated by Sherman's Hellcats and antiaircraft guns about 1:30 P.M. But the Americans thought this was a land-based raid like the one that had bombed *Princeton.*

Finally, at 4:40 P.M., Sherman's searching Helldivers located the Northern Force. Only 190 miles away, Ozawa's ships were accurately reported by several search planes: one heavy and three light carriers, those two crazy flight-deck battleships, two cruisers, and destroyers. Fightin' Freddy was jubilant: "The carrier forces to the north were our meat; they were close enough so that they could not get away if we headed to the northward. . . ." Despite the loss of *Princeton*, Sherman reflected his chief's own attitude: "As the sun went down the situation was entirely to my liking and I felt we had a chance to completely wipe out a major group of the enemy fleet including the precious carriers which he [the enemy] could ill afford to lose." [21]

The same thoughts raced through Halsey's mind. Should Kurita turn eastward again toward San Bernardino, Halsey would have two forces to consider. He did not enjoy waiting on the defensive for the Japanese carriers to come south and join up with land-based air in shuttle strikes the next morning, Center Force or no Center Force. To sink carriers, one must seize the initiative, as Spruance had not done off Saipan. After dinner, Third Fleet staff "discussed at some length" the possibility of leaving Lee's battle line and one carrier group to guard San Bernardino Strait and sending the other two groups north.[22] But Halsey disagreed and decided that whatever he did, "he would keep his fleet together because the entire operation would be under potential land-based air attack." [23] He had already lost *Princeton* to Luzon-based planes, and he was determined to concentrate his forces for maximum antiaircraft protection. This was fleet doctrine stemming from Mahan and Fisher in Halsey's Academy days down to PAC 10 formulated the year before. Only the previous week, the ComAirPac Analysis for August had been distributed, warning "limited forces must concentrate in order to destroy. . . ." [24] If his forces divided, enemy land- and carrier-based air "together . . . might inflict far more damage on my half-fleets separately than they could inflict on the fleet intact." [25]

With his key advisers, Halsey considered the possibility of the Center Force turning around to the eastward again if Task Force 38 went north. Kurita's force "might plod through San Bernardino Straits and on to attack Leyte forces, à la Guadalcanal . . . and . . . might . . . inflict some damage, but its fighting power was considered too seriously impaired to win a decision."[26] The damage, exaggerated by the pilots, was emphasized by Halsey's trusted air operations officer, Commander Doug Moulton, and most of the staff accepted it. The Center Force would be capable only of a typical, indecisive hit-and-run mission as at Guadalcanal or of a last suicide effort. Halsey also believed the Center Force, if it turned around after midnight, could not enter Leyte Gulf until 11 A.M., by which time Oldendorf's battleships would have turned from obliterating the smaller Southern Force at Surigao to meet the Center Force. In that case, Task Force 38 could knock off the Northern carriers and then turn south to help corner Kurita.[27]

After listening to the views of his staff officers, who did not all support him, Halsey put his finger on the plot of the Northern Force—now 300 miles away—and declared: "We will run north at top speed and put those carriers out for keeps." [28] In doing so, said Halsey, "It preserved my fleet's integrity, it left the initiative with me, and it promised the greatest possibility of surprise." [29] At 7:50 P.M. he radioed Kinkaid at Leyte: "Central force heavily damaged according to strike reports. Am proceeding north with three groups to attack carrier forces at dawn." [30]

Sixteen minutes later, at 8:06 P.M., Halsey received the news he half-expected. An *Independence* night Hellcat had sighted the Center Force in the Sibuyan Sea, heading east at 12 knots toward San Bernardino Strait! But this turn of events did not alter Halsey's decision in the least. After passing on the contact report to Kinkaid, at 8:22 Halsey ordered Bogan's and Davison's task groups to join Sherman's off Luzon for the run north, and told McCain's to stop refueling and return for battle. Then he went to bed, having been without sleep for nearly two days. This being the case, Commander Mike Cheek, who came off his four-hour watch at midnight, decided against waking Halsey to protest the decision. In any case, Mick Carney told Cheek, the Admiral had overruled all dissension at the staff conference. Halsey was finally going to put the Japanese carriers out for keeps.

But what about Kinkaid at Leyte? After the *Independence* sighting report of the Center Force was received by Seventh Fleet at 8:24 P.M., Kinkaid heard nothing more from Halsey. Here the breakdown began in the American operation. As a result of the lack of a common chain of command, Halsey did not keep Kinkaid automatically informed of his detailed plans. And in accordance with Halsey's own habits of battle plans by dispatch—and oftentimes vague ones at that—he took no pains to outline his program for 25 October. He merely said he was proceeding north "with three groups." He made no mention of how he might handle the Center Force or of his plans for San Bernardino Strait, nor did he relay the additional *Independence* reports as they came in. He just assumed Kinkaid would fill the vacuum without adequate information.

What Admiral Halsey did not know, of course, was that Kinkaid had eavesdropped on his 3:12 P.M. vague preparatory battle plan. Kinkaid thought—as did Nimitz, reading all the dispatches at Pearl Harbor—that Task Force 34 had been formed to guard San Bernardino Strait. Four fast battleships apparently comprised the Battle Line, while the other two stayed with the carriers for the engagement with the two Northern Force half-battleships. This division of gun ships, said Kinkaid later, "was exactly correct in the circumstances." [31] But Halsey had said he was going north with three task groups, *all* his carriers until McCain returned. This meant that if Task Force 34 was guarding the Strait it had no air cover—a highly dangerous and improbable tactic so close to Luzon airfields, and one Kinkaid should therefore have questioned. He had other concerns, however, for one hour before midnight Admiral Nishimura and the Southern Force entered the western end of Surigao Strait.

By midnight, then, Kinkaid expected two night gunnery duels, Olie Oldendorf's six old battleships against Nishimura's two at Surigao Strait, Ching Lee's four fast battleships against Kurita's four at San Bernardino Strait. Both actions should occur shortly after midnight, according to the latest information.

Vice Admiral Mitscher, virtually a man without a command, was similarly confused by Halsey's vagueness. Without the precise instructions that Spruance always outlined, Mitscher only knew from an 8:29 P.M. copy of Halsey's message to Kinkaid that the carriers were going north. As for the 3:12 P.M. preparatory battle plan, Mitscher just assumed it would now go into effect and so gave appropriate orders to the two battleships that would accompany Task Force 38 north when Halsey (in battleship *New Jersey*) and TF 34 formed for line of battle off San Bernardino Strait.[32] Not until midnight, when the task groups rendezvoused off Luzon, did Mitscher learn, much to his surprise, that the Battle Line had not been formed and that Halsey and all six battleships were going north as part of the carrier screens.

Commodore Burke and Commander Jimmy Flatley, Mitscher's new operations officer, both urged Mitscher to recommend that Halsey send the battleships back to guard San Bernardino Strait. Bogan's one heavy and two light carriers (or just one, as Halsey would need the night *Independence* for the run north) could provide air support. But Mitscher, having lost tactical command weeks before and still stung by the rebuff Spruance had given his recommendation off Saipan, told Flatley: "If he wants my advice he'll ask for it." While Mitscher did not suggest the plan, Bogan almost did, but decided against it after Halsey's staff showed irritation at Bogan's urgent reporting of *Independence*'s sightings. Ching Lee, who would gladly have formed his battle line off the Strait without air cover, told Halsey the Northern Force was playing the decoy, but the Bull paid no attention. He was taking the fast carriers (TF 38) and fast battleships (TF 34) north; Kinkaid and Oldendorf could deal with Kurita and the Center Force off Leyte.[33]

Halsey's run north was more like a slow trot, for it involved night operations, which Halsey, Mitscher, and Lee did not particularly enjoy. As soon as Davison and Bogan roared up to meet Sherman at 25 knots, Task Force 38 slowed down to 16 knots at 11:30. Of all things, Halsey feared the Japanese might slip by his flank during the night—shades of the "end run"![34] At midnight Halsey turned over tactical command to Mitscher, who immediately increased speed to 20 knots; Mitscher wanted to charge north, knock off the carriers, then hurry back to attack the Center Force. Halsey ordered a 1 A.M. search from *Independence*, against Mitscher's protest that it might alert the Japanese and start them running for home. Mitscher would rather launch a well-armed search-strike than a simple search. After being launched, the search of radar-equipped Hellcats began to fly 350 miles out, but instead at 2:05 A.M. sighted Japanese ships 80 miles north of the task force. Quick calculation meant a night surface action at about 4:30 A.M.[35]

Halsey's inexperience in fast carrier operations continued to tell when, at 2:55 A.M., he ordered Ching Lee to form the battle line ten miles ahead of the carriers. Pulling six lumbering battleships out of three task formations which included carriers, eight cruisers, and 41 destroyers in the middle of the Pacific night took great skill—and much time. Mitscher did not like the idea of forming such a large battle line in this manner, and he no doubt now appreciated Admiral Spruance's foresight in forming the battle line off Saipan *before* the naval battle. Lee liked this close maneuvering at night even less than did Mitscher, and he ordered all his battleships to change to a different fixed course and slow to 15 knots, thus drawing them out of formation in a painfully slow but safe manner. Lee's chief of staff, fiery aviator Commodore Tom Jeter, protested. "Admiral, what are you trying to do? We've got to get the ships together." Said Lee impatiently: "It's too dangerous. Send the signal. All ships head this course and slow to fifteen knots." Easing out of line, battleships *Iowa*, *New Jersey*, *Massachusetts*, *South Dakota*, *Washington*, and *Alabama* then headed for the rendezvous, those on the outside having to race to join up. Then more time was lost building up speed in the center ships from 15 to the cruising speed of 20 knots.[36]

Halsey slowed down again, however, when he learned that Oldendorf was engaging Nishimura in Surigao Strait. Also, the *Independence* night fighter shadowing the northern contact lost it when the plane's radar set broke down. Just as well, for those ships 80 miles to the northeast were only the detached van of Ozawa's force, Rear Admiral Matsuda's half-battleships *Ise* and *Hyuga*, which were indeed seeking a night engagement to attract Halsey north. This group did not sight the *Independence* snoopers, but instead saw flashes of light off to the south indicating Task Force 38 was under land-based air attack. Instead these were lightning flashes from an electrical storm, but on the strength of this false report Ozawa recalled Matsuda to rendezvous with the nearly empty carriers. When 4:30 rolled around and no surface battle developed, Mitscher concluded incorrectly that his search planes had scared the Northern Force into turning around. He could only arm his bombers and wait to launch long-range search-strikes at first light.[37]

Meanwhile, down at Leyte, Kinkaid awaited the two night battles. The one in Surigao Strait began at 10:30 P.M. on the twenty-fourth with torpedo (PT) boats engaging Nishimura's ships and reached its peak at 4 A.M. on the twenty-fifth, when the surviving Japanese battleship reeled under the killing salvos of Oldendorf's battle line. Nishimura went down with his flagship, his force practically annihilated (though Shima, fearing the worst, took one look and retired safely with his cruisers from the Strait). Interested in the dawn mop-up, at 1:30 A.M. Captain Dick Whitehead recommended to Kinkaid two flights be readied aboard the escort carriers, one a fighter-torpedo strike in pursuit of cripples down Surigao Strait and the other a search to the *north* up the coast of Samar and to the northeast of Leyte. When Kinkaid asked Whitehead what he was looking for up north, the air support commander replied that he merely wanted to pick up any stray enemy ships that might slip by Lee's battle line, then assumed to be at San Bernardino. Kinkaid agreed, and at 4:30 he ordered Felix Stump to ready ten planes for the task. In addition, some PBY Catalina seaplanes were supposed to be making a night search to the north.[38]

With the Southern Force being pounded to its death by Oldendorf's covering force, Admiral Kinkaid called a staff meeting "to check for errors of commission or of omission." No one could think of anything, including his aviator chief of staff, Commodore Val Schaffer. The meeting adjourned about 4 A.M., but Kinkaid's operations officer, Captain Richard H. Cruzen, returned and said to Kinkaid: "Admiral, I can think of only one other thing. We have never directly asked Halsey if TF 34 is guarding San Bernardino." [39] Kinkaid agreed, and at 4:12 he sent a message to Halsey asking for confirmation of that fact. Halsey, surprised, received the message at 6:48, and he replied in the negative at 7:05—too late to be of any use to Kinkaid.

This almost casual negligence by Kinkaid's staff of a very crucial aspect of the operation—covering MacArthur's right flank from San Bernardino to the Gulf—suggests that Kinkaid and his advisers actually gave very little credence to the possibility of a Japanese fleet transit of San Bernardino Strait.

According to one of those almost unproveable sea stories circulated in the Navy after the war,[40] strategists at the Naval War College before and during the early part of the war had concluded the Japanese fleet would probably one day penetrate Surigao Strait, but they had disagreed over whether it would pass through San Bernardino. The chief proponent of the latter view was allegedly Captain Richard W. Bates, from mid-1941 to mid-1943 senior strategist at the College. Bates held that San Bernardino was too narrow and shallow for capital ships, so that the main battle would be at Surigao.

If this story is true, it explains the negligence and subsequent actions of the Seventh Fleet commanders at Leyte. For throughout 1942 Bates' partner in the Strategy section had been none other than Commander Dick Cruzen. At Leyte Cruzen served Kinkaid as operations officer, while Commodore Bates had joined Rear Admiral Oldendorf as chief of staff. Also, in 1941–42 Captain Oldendorf had been head of the Intelligence Department at the Naval War College and therefore knew Bates intimately.[41] Vice Admiral Kinkaid, having recently been assigned an aviator as chief of staff, leaned heavily on his black-shoe strategist Cruzen for advice. So Kinkaid with Cruzen had ignored San Bernardino until too late, while Oldendorf with Bates—after their old battleships had mauled the Southern Force—went charging down Surigao Strait after any Southern Force remnants, giving little thought to San Bernardino. By the dawn of 25 October Oldendorf's battle force was 65 miles away from the beachhead.

At daybreak of the 25th the battle for Leyte Gulf had only just begun, and information about the Japanese fleet was still vague. The Southern Force was badly beaten, but how badly Kinkaid did not yet know, so Oldendorf's battleships went in pursuit covered by well-armed fighters and torpedo planes from the escort carriers. The PBY night patrol to the north had missed seeing anything of interest, while the escort carrier search for that sector was only being launched at 6:45 A.M. Kinkaid had heard of no night surface battle fought at San Bernardino Strait and no one knew the exact location of the Center and Northern forces. Then, without any warning whatsoever, at 6:45 the Center Force was sighted visually by the escort carriers off Samar; within fifteen minutes 18.1-inch shells from *Yamato* were dropping in among the nearly helpless air support carriers. At 7:07 Kinkaid radioed in plain language to Halsey that his ships were under attack by heavy surface units of the enemy. This message, like all the others, took over an hour for transmission, reception, and delivery. Meanwhile, Mitscher had launched his searches to the north then swung them eastward, followed by deckload strikes. One hundred miles northeast of Task Force 38, Ozawa was steaming south when his radar registered Mitscher's search planes. He turned around and managed to get 40 more miles away before being sighted by Mitscher's planes at 7:10.

The attack by Task Force 38 on the Japanese Northern Force began with ten deckload strikes of Mitscher's orbiting planes, which had been waiting for the search planes to make contact. This northern phase of the battle for Leyte Gulf has had various titles, the second battle of the Philippine Sea and, for the nearest point of land on Luzon, the battle off Cape Engaño, which, in Spanish, means "mistake, deception, or lure."[42] First on the scene was Air Group 15 from *Essex*, and its skipper, Dave McCampbell, became target coordinator and directed his planes against the four carriers. Admiral Ozawa, who began launching his last 29 planes, was surprised by the intense air attack, for it was his first indication that his decoy mission had succeeded.[43]

Ozawa's ships were sitting ducks, making the whole action anticlimactic to the Battle of the Philippine Sea. Unlike the twilight melee in June, this morning attack was well executed and systematic. A heavy bombing strike sank light carrier *Chitose*, which went down at 9:37 A.M., while a torpedo struck *Zuikaku*, forcing Ozawa to transfer his flag to a cruiser. The second bombing strike set *Chiyoda* afire, eventually forcing her abandonment. Afternoon strikes led by Commanders Hugh Winters of *Lexington*'s Air Group 19 and Malcolm Wordell of *Langley*'s Air Group 44 finished two of the carriers. Pearl Harbor veteran *Zuikaku* was repeatedly bombed and torpedoed until she sank at 2:14 P.M. Light carrier *Zuiho* received a continuous pounding until she sank at 3:26 in the afternoon. Cruiser fire finished the abandoned *Chiyoda* at 4:55, against Ted Sherman's wish to take her in tow as a souvenir. Smart maneuvering, intense antiaircraft fire, and good luck saved *Ise*, *Hyuga*, and some of the destroyers from being sunk by the air strikes. These, however, were proper meat for Lee's battle line.[44]

But Halsey was not able to use his fast battleships. At 8:22 A.M. he received Kinkaid's cry for help at Leyte Gulf. Yet, quite logically, Halsey had no real fears for Kinkaid; "I figured that the eighteen little carriers [down to 16 after the departure of two for Morotai the day before] had enough planes to protect themselves until Oldendorf could bring up his heavy ships."[45] The escort carriers tried. Dick Whitehead recalled the planes chasing the Southern Force survivors, and these attacked Kurita, but the rest of Sprague's aircraft were armed for combat air patrol, antisubmarine action, and close support of infantry. Without torpedoes and heavy bombs, these fighters and TBMs could do little but make dummy runs to draw away fire from their carriers. Kinkaid turned to Whitehead (". . . I leaned heavily on his advice in combat with the enemy"),[46] who tried to reach Kenney's bombers over the Visayas for help. He could not, however, and the AAF gave no assistance in the battle.[47] Oldendorf, whose old battleships had plenty of ammunition, contrary to Kinkaid's belief, were 65 miles away in Surigao Strait and could not reach Leyte for three hours. Kinkaid, and Ziggy Sprague too, pleaded by radio with Halsey to send the fast carriers and fast battleships to save them from the pounding. Halsey had all this information by 9:30, but he could only order McCain to the rescue, and TG 38.1 was still over 300 miles from Leyte—a long flight for the planes. The carriers and battleships with Halsey needed several more hours to finish the Northern Force.

As gallant destroyers and escort carriers battled, some in vain, to save themselves, the weakness of divided command in the operation became painfully evident. Desperate, Kinkaid cried out in plain language for Lee's Task Force 34 battle line to reinforce him, but Halsey refused to turn around. At least now Kinkaid knew where Lee was, not guarding San Bernardino Strait as the preparatory battle plan of the previous afternoon had indicated. But Admirals King and Cooke in Washington and Nimitz at Pearl Harbor, also recipients of that fateful message, did not know the whereabouts of Lee. Ernie King, blue with rage, paced the floor cursing Halsey to the audience of visitor Jocko Clark.[48] Nimitz fired a coded message to Halsey, which, with the normal cryptographer's padding, said, "Turkey Trots to Water. From Cincpac. Where is, repeat, where is Task Force 34. The world wonders."[49] Kinkaid's communicators eliminated the prefixing and suffixing padding before handing their copy of the message to Kinkaid.[50] But Halsey's signalmen struck off only the first phrase, so that the latter phrase was incorporated into the meaning of the message.

"From Cincpac. Where is, rpt, where is TF 34. The world wonders," Halsey read at 10:00 A.M. Infuriated at this obvious criticism, Bull Halsey lost his temper. He grabbed his cap, threw it to the floor, and started cursing until Mick Carney calmed him down.[51] But even without the unintended suffix, Nimitz's meaning was clear; the fast battleships were not where Nimitz thought they should be. This prodding forced Halsey to take measures for the relief of Kinkaid, but not until he wasted nearly an hour thinking about it. With three Japanese carriers still afloat and the two half-battleships undamaged, at 10:55 Halsey reluctantly ordered the entire battle line south.[52] Two battleships under Rear Admiral Oscar Badger and covered by Bogan's TG 38.2 were to charge ahead at 28 knots, but not until Bogan's destroyers could be refueled.

Halsey then informed Nimitz: "Task Force 34 with me engaging carrier force. Am now proceeding with Task Group 38.2 and all fast BB to reinforce Kinkaid. . . ."[53] Characteristically, Halsey could see no reason to divide the battleships by leaving two behind to finish *Ise* and *Hyuga*; he apparently wanted overwhelming strength when Lee met Kurita. Consequently, this all-or-nothing attitude ended in nothing; the two *Ise*s escaped—and as far as Halsey was concerned, escaped to fight again. And by waiting from 8:22, when he first knew Kinkaid was in trouble, or from 9:22, when he knew Oldendorf was not available at Leyte, or from 10:00, when he received Nimitz's message, till 10:55 to go south, Halsey would also allow Kurita's four battleships to escape.

At his pace, 12 knots during refueling (1:45 to 4:12 P.M.), then 28 for Badger's two battleships and Bogan's three carriers with the other battleships to follow, no warships would reach San Bernardino Strait till 1 A.M. on the twenty-sixth or Leyte till 8 A.M. This deployment made no sense at all, for if Badger—with only two battleships and three light cruisers—and Bogan—with the night *Independence* (24 VFN, 9 VTN) and two useless day carriers—encountered Kurita's four battlewagons during the night, the result might well have been catastrophic.[54] Worse, the Japanese had become experts in night battle, most of it by visual means, while Lee's fast battleships had no experience and little opportunity to practice for it, even with radar.

But Kurita suffered from the same preoccupation as Halsey—get the carriers at the cost of all else. Around noon, after sinking only one escort carrier and damaging others, as well as finishing off two destroyers and one destroyer escort, Kurita received a false contact report on the radio that the enemy carriers were closing in from the sea. With land-based U.S. planes operating out of Leyte (though, unknown to him, only on an emergency basis), he feared being trapped in Leyte Gulf. He also believed he had been engaging—and had therefore sunk—several carriers from Task Force 38. Indeed, the stubborn American defenders sank three of his heavy cruisers. He must now head out to sea to engage the rest of the fast carriers. "The destruction of enemy aircraft carriers was a kind of obsession with me, and I fell victim to it."[55] In addition, Kurita believed the American transports had already evacuated the area of the beachhead—in this respect, he was correct, as many of them had before the battle. Finally, the Japanese commander, "under great strain and without sleep for three days and nights," made the decision at 12:30 P.M., without consulting his staff, to clear the Gulf. The action off Samar was ended. Since no American carriers appeared, and he was low on fuel, at 5:30 P.M. Kurita turned for home—via San Bernardino Strait.[56]

On a suicide mission, Kurita had failed. He worried about refueling, picking up survivors, and then enemy carriers outside the Gulf. He was supposed to engage whatever was in the Gulf, then head for the beach and any shipping he could find. This was

Japan's last naval battle; the carriers were gone, though Kurita had not received Ozawa's message announcing the decoy had worked, and the fuel for Japan's ships was going fast.

Admiral Onishi realized the stakes, and late in the morning—while Kurita was still hammering away at the Spragues—Onishi sent in the first organized flight of kamikaze suicide planes. They crashed several escort carriers, sinking one. Had Kurita pressed into the Gulf, by 2 P.M. he would have engaged Oldendorf's battle line of six battleships and the planes from McCain's five carriers roaring in from the east. Whatever Japanese ships to escape would have then faced Lee's six battleships and the other three fast carrier task groups. But Kurita did not follow the plan. In very un-Japanese fashion he decided to save what he could and headed north—much to the relief of Admiral Kinkaid and the battered, outgunned, but not outfought American sailors.

Shortly after 1 P.M., just as the Center Force retired, planes from McCain's five carriers attacked from far to the east but did little damage; destruction of the Japanese was up to Halsey racing south with Badger and Bogan. To gain information on Kurita, around 8 P.M. Halsey ordered six night Avengers launched from *Independence*. One of these reported fifteen ships at 9:45 passing along the coast of Samar into San Bernardino Strait, and the contact was maintained. On board *Independence*, Eddie Ewen and Turner Caldwell tried to convince Halsey to let them launch a night torpedo attack against the Center Force. Tired of purely routine defensive and reconnaissance work, the night carrier men wanted to show their stuff. Halsey finally agreed at 3 A.M. on the twenty-sixth, but not before a severe thunderstorm had caused the shadowing torpecker to lose his contact with Kurita. A strike of four Avengers and five Hellcats, each armed with one 500-pound bomb, was launched, but it did not relocate the Center Force.[57]

At dawn McCain and Bogan launched strikes over the Sibuyan Sea, but results were dire. Their planes managed to sink one light cruiser and damage a heavy. But Kurita soon reached Manila and safety. The complicated, confused, exhausting battle was over, and Leyte Gulf was safe for the Allies.

The United States Navy had won the battle. Losses: light carrier *Princeton*, two escort carriers, two destroyers, one destroyer escort, about 36,000 tons in all. The Imperial Japanese Navy lost the battle and 45 per cent of the ships engaged: three battleships, one heavy carrier, three light carriers, six heavy cruisers, four light cruisers, and nine destroyers, totaling 305,710 tons![58] Hampered by poor communications, lack of carrier pilots, an untrained land-based naval air force which was wiped out over Formosa, and inferior equipment, the Japanese had sacrificed their fleet in one last battle to save the Philippines and their cause. Even with the kamikaze planes, the spirit of supreme sacrifice had not been shared by Kurita. As a result, he failed in his mission and lost the battle.

2. *Critique and Consequences*

The over-all flaw in the prosecution of the Leyte operation was the lack of unity of command, a shortcoming no officer or historian has yet disputed. With Kinkaid responsible to MacArthur and with Halsey practically a free agent but taking orders from Nimitz, coordination was difficult. And radio communications being what they were—requiring at least an hour in plain language, up to five or more hours in code—effective coordination proved exceedingly difficult. Blame for the divided command, of course, might be meted out to MacArthur and Nimitz for their adamance in not yielding to the other's authority, but both had good reasons.

The question of prime responsibility for letting Kurita's Center Force penetrate San Bernardino Strait undetected and attack Kinkaid forms the real issue that will always interest historians of the battle. The criticisms have been twofold: first, Halsey bit for Ozawa's bait and was lured north, thus uncovering the Strait; second, Kinkaid failed to send air searches to the north during the night and therefore failed to guard MacArthur's right flank and rear.

Admiral Halsey began defending his actions immediately—10 P.M. the night of 25 October—by reporting to Nimitz and MacArthur that while a temporarily tight situation might exist at Leyte, "it seemed childish to me" to keep the carriers "statically" off the Strait, and so he had adopted the offensive.[1] An unusual word for describing naval operations, *childish* must have been meant in its secondary sense, denoting weakness. Despite the "atmosphere of great gloom" over the Third Fleet staff which Admiral Radford noticed after the battle,[2] Halsey held to his decision. He informed Admirals King and Nimitz officially in November of "the elimination of serious naval threat to our operations for many months, if not forever."[3] When they replied that they failed to see the basis for his conclusions, he remarked to his staff: "Let them wait and see."[4] Halsey never admitted any error in leaving the Strait open, only that he should not have run south with Lee and Bogan but rather stayed to finish Ozawa. He wrote strongly on the subject in his autobiography in 1947 and in a *U.S. Naval Institute Proceedings* article in 1952.[5] His final judgment, which others suggested to him, was: "I wish that Spruance had been with Mitscher at Leyte Gulf and I had been with Mitscher in the Battle of the Philippine Sea."[6]

Halsey's loud defense of his action did not draw any public statement from Kinkaid for ten years after the event, except for a brief speech in 1949.[7] Military writer Hanson Baldwin in 1955 wrote an essay on the battle which he submitted to Halsey and Kinkaid for comments which he then published with the essay; Kinkaid's notes were much more convincing than Halsey's but the latter's senior age may have been partly accountable. Later, Commodore Val Schaeffer, Kinkaid's chief of staff, spoke for Seventh Fleet staff when defending Kinkaid: ". . . under the circumstances existing at the time and the information which was then available to him, I fail to see where Admiral Kinkaid should have done other than what he did."[8] The Sixth Army which Kinkaid was covering concluded a Japanese victory "would have been calamitous" to its operations;[9] reported Navy Captain Ray Tarbuck of MacArthur's staff in November: "People here feel that the Third Fleet battleships [were] chasing a secondary force, leaving us at the mercy (of which there is none) of the enemy's main body."[10]

At the Cincpac level, opinion favored Kinkaid. Reported the British liaison officer to his superior: "It is considered that if the Third Fleet had remained on station, it would have been quite capable of dealing with both enemy center and northern forces. . . . It is not understood why the Seventh Fleet [Oldendorf] failed to give support to the escort carriers."[11] Captain Ralph C. Parker, head of the Analytical Section at Pearl Harbor, so strongly criticized Halsey in Cincpac's report of the battle that Admiral Nimitz had him revise and tone it down before submitting it to Cominch.[12] Vice Admiral Towers, Deputy Cincpac, put the blame on Kinkaid for the lack of air searches,[13] but Vice Admiral Murray, ComAirPac, introduced the idea that Halsey should have split his force to deal with both the Northern and Center forces. Admitting his own fault at stressing concentration in the September air operations analysis, Murray, in the October report, called for tactical flexibility: "Concentration, though usually sound, may sometimes be pursued too far, with diminishing returns. The ability to divide forces cleverly, as developed by the enemy, and to 'unconcentrate' quickly, may often be an advantage." On Cincpac's copy of this statement, someone penciled in the margin: "Gentle slap at Halsey." [14]

The feeling at Cominch headquarters was definitely critical of Halsey. After Ernie King's outburst against Halsey to Jocko Clark at the height of the battle, he told Nimitz at the end of November that Halsey was tired and ought to be given a rest. At the same time, King recommended Kinkaid be promoted to four-star admiral as soon as the new five-star rank of fleet admiral elevated Nimitz.[15] Vice Admiral Savvy Cooke, King's chief of staff, made a point of going to see Kinkaid early in 1945 to tell him he had done exactly the right thing at Leyte.[16] As with Spruance after the Philippine Sea battle, however, King saw no reason to press the issue, and when Halsey brought it up again, King said: "You don't have to tell me any more. You've got a green light on everything you did." [17] After the war, King placed equal blame on Halsey and Kinkaid, attributing Kurita's surprise off Samar "not only to Halsey's absence in the north but also to Kinkaid's failure to use his own air squadrons for search at a crucial moment." [18]

Immediately after the war, Halsey received several supporters who argued from the position that, as war correspondent Ernie Pyle put it, "every Navy in the world has as its No. 1 priority the destruction of enemy carriers." [19] The Navy Department issued a press release three weeks after hostilities ceased, saying: "In modern warfare enemy carriers are the top A-1-A priority. At whatever cost, the Jap carriers had to be hit. Admiral Halsey hit them with everything at his command." [20] Historian C. Vann Woodward, not normally a student of naval affairs but fresh from wartime intelligence duty, wrote in 1947: "It would have been a rash man indeed who would have deprecated the importance or scorned the opportunity of wiping out the enemy's carrier forces. . . . It would have seemed improbable to the point of absurdity to suggest in October 1944 that a modern naval power would stake the existence of its fleet on the gunnery of its surface ships and throw away its last carriers as an expendable diversion force." [21] And Admiral Ted Sherman pointed out in 1950 that Kinkaid should have reconnoitered north, then formed Oldendorf's battleships and Sprague's escort carriers into battle formation.[22]

Military historians did not deal too harshly with Halsey before his death in 1959. Bernard Brodie in 1947 marveled that a man who prided himself on violating the rules should act in such a conventional manner, namely, strict adherence to tactical concentration; Halsey's judgments "were not equal to his boldness, and boldness alone does not make a Nelson." [23] Samuel Eliot Morison only implied blame for Halsey in his fine 1958 volume on Leyte, but five years later—after the grand old admiral was gone—Morison echoed Brodie's criticism. He declared that Halsey's decision was a clear "mistake" and that Halsey had minimized the *Independence* midnight sightings on 24–25 October of the Center Force because "he simply did not care." Morison concluded: "Unfortunately, in his efforts to build public morale in America and Australia, Halsey . . . built up an image of himself as an exponent of Danton's . . . 'Audacity . . . always audacity' . . . [which] is the real reason for his fumble in the Battle for Leyte Gulf." [24]

Stanley L. Falk in 1966 admitted Halsey was guilty of "complete neglect" of San Bernardino Strait, and that a destroyer patrol ought to have covered it, but "Unless he could have absolute knowledge that Ozawa had no planes, his decision to go north was a proper one." Furthermore, Falk agreed with Halsey's post-battle observation that the run south with Badger and Bogan was a mistake. It let Ozawa's gun ships escape while "Kurita had the stronger force, and, had the interception succeeded, neither Badger nor Halsey, who was sailing with him, might have survived." But nearly any reasonable risk was worth the objective since defeat at Leyte would have delayed the Pacific timetable by six months.[25]

With the study of the battle by a new generation of historians which does not even remember it, much less has emotional attachments, criticism will probably be balanced between Halsey and Kinkaid. In my view, however, the burden of criticism must rest on the former.

Admiral Halsey was not a Fleet commander in the same sense as Spruance, employing amphibious forces and escort carriers as well as battle forces; he was in fact the fast carrier task force commander at Leyte, and not a very good one at that. Audacious he was by nature, prone to *ad hoc* rather than detailed planning, guilty of sloppy techniques and often vague dispatches. These traits were acceptable in the trying, doubtful days of 1942 when the simple goal was to hang on at Guadalcanal or to raid enemy island outposts. But by late 1944 the complex offensive was at its height and inefficiency was intolerable. The veterans of the Central Pacific offensive such as Mitscher, Lee, Bogan, and Sherman knew this only too well, but Halsey, too proud and too stubborn, lacked the good sense to utilize their experience. He was, indeed, a bull, attacking first and asking questions after. His experience in carriers stemmed from pre-Midway days and from the Solomons, when lack of concentrated antiaircraft strength literally meant a carrier's life. And now, in 1944, he became the first carrier admiral to lose an attack carrier (*Princeton*) since Kinkaid had lost the old *Hornet* off the Solomons two years before. So he took risks only within the inviolable 1942 rule of concentration.

Had Halsey been an efficient planner, as meticulous, experienced, and careful as, say, Mitscher, two other courses of action might have succeeded. First, as some Monday-morning quarterbacks have suggested, and as Mitscher, Lee, Bogan, and Burke had expected, Halsey could have split his forces between four battleships and three carriers to deal with Kurita and two battleships and seven carriers to handle Ozawa. This would have broken with the doctrine of concentration, in the manner of a Nelsonian meleeist, but it would have presented problems: Lee would probably have been inferior to Kurita in night gunnery, and the night *Independence* was needed in both places, to attack Kurita and to search for Ozawa. One other means of employing concentration would have required the skill of a Robert E. Lee at Chancellorsville: since the Americans were suddenly acting from the interior position tactically—defending the beachhead at Leyte—the carrier task force commander could have thrust north to hit Ozawa first, then turned south to close the door on Kurita. Such a movement would have required efficient, expert tactics and constant information on Kurita. Admiral Lee would have formed his battle line during the rendezvous (as Spruance had done at Saipan), just before midnight on the twenty-fourth, possibly making use of the first-quarter moon low in the west; then a high-speed run north for a night or dawn engagement. This maneuver would have required a constant watch over Kurita by shadowing destroyers, submarines, or aircraft—*coordinated* with Kinkaid. Halsey could then have tried his run – the so-called "Battle of Bull's Run" – south. But such tactics were simply too complex for Bull Halsey.

Vice Admiral Kinkaid had had no more experience in long-range Central Pacific amphibious operations involving large surface forces than had Halsey, except perhaps for Hollandia, which had been a pushover. His position at Leyte resembled that of Kelly Turner at Saipan—protecting amphibious forces using Oldendorf's old battleships and many more escort carriers. Turner, however, was an aviator, had helped plan for a fleet engagement since November 1943, and had kept in constant touch with Spruance as to enemy fleet movements. The divided command set-up at Leyte made coordination more difficult, but Kinkaid did have Central Pacific air support commander, Whitehead, to advise him, and Whitehead's advice to launch a search north was not executed expeditiously, something Terrible Turner never would have allowed. Something else Turner probably would not have permitted was Oldendorf's uncovering the beachhead to chase a battered Nishimura with *all* his battleships down Surigao Strait. It simply did not make good sense, as long as Kinkaid did not have good information as to the whereabouts of the rest of the enemy fleet. For this premature pursuit, Oldendorf (and his advisers) must share responsibility.

Kinkaid, then, was not careful enough in his tactics. He took Halsey too much for granted and left too much to the discretion of subordinates Oldendorf and Tommy Sprague. Such assumptions might have been allowable, again, had Kinkaid had reliable information, but from midnight to dawn of the twenty-fifth he did not know the whereabouts and movements of all three Japanese forces. Part of this responsibility was his own, part was Halsey's, and part was General Kenney's, who proved very uncooperative with his land-based Army air throughout the landing and battle.

With all these criticisms and "might-have-been-ifs," the United States Navy did win the battle, with over-all credit going to the top commanders, Halsey and Kinkaid, just as it had gone to Spruance after Saipan. Both commanders stayed on, Halsey as *de jure* fleet commander but *de facto* fast carrier commander, Kinkaid as amphibious commander for MacArthur. On the other hand, Halsey did not get promoted—as he and Congress had expected he would[26]—to the five-star rank of fleet admiral when that rank was created in December, while Kinkaid was promoted to four-star admiral the following April. One must conclude, then, that history like the Navy at the time must attribute most of the responsibility for Kurita's attack and escape to Admiral Halsey.

From the Japanese point of view, blame for defeat rested with Kurita for his failure to complete destruction of the American warships and available amphibious shipping in Leyte Gulf. For this, in December he was banished to the Japanese Naval Academy as its president, the end of his naval career. Vice Admiral Ozawa, for successfully sacrificing his carriers and luring Halsey north, became the dubious hero of the battle, and in May 1945 he relieved Admiral Toyoda as Commander-in-Chief Combined Fleet. But by then there was no fleet, and Ozawa was not even promoted to full admiral. Admiral Toyoda must be criticized for committing his planes prematurely at Formosa; 500 more Japanese aircraft thrust at Halsey during the battle might have changed its outcome considerably.

Though CarDiv 3 was sunk, Japan had one last hope of using its carrier force. She still had five carriers, all lumped into CarDiv 1 under Rear Admiral Keizo Komura: *Unryu*, *Amagi*, *Katsuragi*, *Junyo*, and light carrier *Ryuho*. But these had no planes for want of pilots, and little fuel for operations. One ship which might yet succeed, however, was *Shinano*. Her construction accelerated after the Battle of the Philippine Sea, this 68,059-ton giant was protected by 17,700 tons of armor and could carry up to 47 aircraft. Operating in the South China Sea, she might well realize Admiral Halsey's fears by shuttling planes, even kamikazes, to hit the shipping off Mindoro in December. *Shinano* was the last hope for Japan's carriers; she was launched in Tokyo Bay on 11 November 1944 and commissioned one week later.

American submarines finally drove Japan's carriers into port for good. Soon after her commissioning on 18 November, *Shinano* was loaded with 50 Oka piloted bombs (later nicknamed by U.S. sailors "baka," fool). These new kamikazes, which carried 2400 pounds of explosives in the nose, were to be dropped from the bellies of attack planes. *Shinano*'s orders were to proceed to Kure naval base, pick up an air group, and train in the Inland Sea, then to proceed with the Oka bombs for the relief of the Philippines.[27] On the twenty-ninth, however, while under way in Tokyo Bay, *Shinano* was torpedoed by American submarine *Archerfish*; poor damage control hastened her sinking later in the day. One month afterward, 19 December, carrier *Unryu*, en route with supplies through the East China Sea, was sunk by the sub *Redfish*.

One could say the Japanese surface navy was a "fleet-in-being" after the battle for Leyte Gulf, causing a potential though unlikely threat to American operations. But with the *Shinano* and *Unryu* sinkings, Japan generally kept her flattops anchored in port, along with her battleships, cruisers, and destroyers. Carrier *Junyo*, operating out of Nagasaki on 9 December, was severely damaged and put out of action by two submarines. The two half-carriers *Ise* and *Hyuga* made one of the last runs from Singapore to Japan carrying gasoline in February 1945, when they too concluded their sailing days. Oddly, carrier construction continued as late as March 1945 on 18,300-ton *Ikoma* and *Kasagi*, 17,400-ton *Aso*, and 12,500-ton converted *Ibuki*; these were 60 to 80 per cent completed when construction shifted to weapons for the defense of Japan against invasion.[28]

Development of carrier planes was equally discouraging and sealed the fate of Japan's carriers if lack of trained pilots and fuel did not. With the beginning of B-29 attacks on Japan from China in June and from the Marianas in November, fighter factories were badly damaged or completely destroyed. Construction slowed down seriously on the improved Zero ("Hamp") and the new Shiden-kai ("George"). Only eight new Reppus ("Sam") came off the production line at Nagoya before a severe earthquake combined with the B-29s to demolish the factory. In 1945, all planes and pilots were programmed for defense of the homeland, and the majority of them in a suicide capacity.[29]

On 1 March 1945 the two carrier divisions were deactivated. Rear Admirals Matsuda, ComCarDiv 4, and Obayashi, who had succeeded Komura as ComCarDiv 1 in December, hauled down their flags. The anchored carriers became the administrative property of Kure Naval District: *Amagi*, *Katsuragi*, *Ryuho*, *Ise*, *Hyuga*. The Imperial Japanese Navy was dead as a fighting fleet.

3. *Closing the Bottleneck*

The defeat of the Japanese fleet did not alter Japan's plans to hold Leyte and the rest of the Philippines. Vice Admiral Onishi's kamikazes so impressed Vice Admiral Fukudome that the latter combined the air forces for defense of the islands, began large-scale recruiting for suicide-plane units, and made Onishi his chief of staff. The raw carrier pilots then training shifted to the Kamikaze Corps, while conventional squadrons began hastening from all over Southeast Asia and Japan to the threatened point at Leyte. The kamikaze planes—human guided missiles—would have far greater success than the poorly piloted planes, as was illustrated by the story of the Japanese pilot who bailed out over Manila before his attacker even fired a shot at him.[1] Priority targets for the kamikazes were carriers, secondary targets escorting destroyers; the emphasis would shift from one to the other each day.[2]

The frenzied operations of Task Force 38 for the two weeks ending on 26 October 1944 had taxed fleet reserves and aviators' nerves to the limit. By the end of that day, the fast carriers had about reached the end of their ammunition and food, which could not be replenished at sea like fuel. But they managed to stay on for a few more days covering Leyte and attacking Philippine targets. Pilot fatigue was serious; the flight surgeon of *Wasp*'s Air Group 14 reported only 30 of his 131 pilots fit for further combat.[3] And when Halsey sent McCain's TG 38.1 and Sherman's TG 38.3 to Ulithi on the twenty-eighth for fresh air groups, two of the returning air groups had served only five of the required six months in the combat zone. Such emergencies led ComAirPac to order emergency replacement air groups to Manus and Guam, but these could not arrive before December.[4] Halsey wanted to rotate air groups between these bases and the carriers, but Admiral Murray disapproved since air and ships' crews had trained together.[5] None of this rotation included the ships' crews, which stayed on for the duration.

The air plan called for the Navy to pass control of air operations to the Army on 27 October, and so on that day Captain Whitehead turned over air support responsibilities to General Kenney. In addition General MacArthur directed the fast carriers to make no more strikes against land targets unless requested by Army commanders. However, General Kenney could get only one group of P-38 Lightning fighters into the one operating air strip on rainsoaked Leyte. This situation continued for many weeks, meaning that the ground forces got no air support from the AAF at all, since the P-38s were used for combat air patrol over Leyte. In a way, this was just as well in terms of efficiency, since Navy techniques were much preferred by the Army than those of the AAF. According to one Air Force observer with the troops, the Seventh Division found its first experience with Navy close air support "far more satisfactory" than that rendered by the AAF in New Guinea, and attributed it to Navy techniques and preassault rehearsals.[6]

Intensive Japanese air raids quickly caused General MacArthur to revise his plans and to request that both the fast and escort carriers remain on station, not only to support the Sixth Army but also to attack Japanese convoys and airfields. Bogan's TG 38.2 and

Davison's TG 38.4 were therefore ordered to strike Visayan and Luzon targets, which they did 28 to 30 October, but not without severe enemy counterattacks. After successfully warding off a Japanese submarine attack, these carrier forces received a determined attack by kamikazes. *Franklin* and *Belleau Wood* were crashed by suiciders, causing much damage and loss of life; *Intrepid* suffered a hit of lesser effect. Davison was released for Ulithi, along with the exhausted escort carrier groups. These departures on 29–30 October took place one week before the Fifth Air Force was scheduled to fly in four squadrons of medium bombers. But heavy rains so slowed airfield construction that those planes were kept away until the end of December. Remaining to cover Leyte on the thirty-first were Bogan's three carriers and a handful of P-38s and P-61 Black Widow night fighters.

Back at Ulithi, the long-awaited change of command of the fast carriers took place on 30 October. Vice Admiral Mitscher, physically pooped—how seriously few people realized—turned over Task Force 38 to Vice Admiral McCain. Considering how little Mitscher had been used by Halsey in the naval battle, he might as well have been spared the additional strain of staying on as long as he had. Mitscher would return with Spruance when they relieved Halsey and McCain at the completion of the Philippines operation. On the thirty-first Rear Admiral Alfred Montgomery (ComCarDiv 3) took over Task Group 38.1. On standby for task group command was Rear Admiral Arthur Radford, while Jocko Clark cut short his own leave to make himself available.

The meager air defense at the Leyte beachhead invited Japanese counterattacks, which struck with great effect on 1 November. In addition, decoy reports of a Japanese fleet movement of the Kurita–Shima remnants toward Surigao Strait raised Allied fears. Ted Sherman and TG 38.3 raced back to join Bogan's TG 38.2 in protecting the shipping off Leyte; Montgomery's TG 38.1 was close behind. These three groups attacked Japanese airfields on Luzon on the fifth and sixth, taking the Japanese by surprise to the tune of over 400 planes, most of them on the ground. Halsey lost 25 planes, while *Lexington* took one kamikaze hit. Vice Admiral McCain, who shifted his flag from *Lexington* to *Wasp*, returned to Ulithi with the latter ship so it could change air groups. Only one week in command of Task Force 38, he turned it over to his senior cardiv commander, Sherman, until the thirteenth. On the eleventh a carrier strike of several hundred planes sank a convoy of five transports carrying 10,000 Japanese troops to Leyte and four escorting destroyers. The coordination of 300 attacking planes was so difficult, however, that many midair collisions were barely missed.[7]

These continuous operations in support of Sixth Army bothered the carriermen, especially the aggressive Bull Halsey, who wanted first to attack those surviving gun ships at Brunei Bay, Borneo, then to go all the way for a crack at Tokyo itself. But MacArthur, Kenney, and Forrest Sherman, meeting at Leyte on 10 November, decided "the support of fast carriers essential" to the Sixth Army, and so Task Force 38 continued to attack Luzon airfields and shipping throughout November. On the thirteenth and fourteenth carrier planes sank a light cruiser and five destroyers plus seven merchant ships, destroying over 75 planes. Five days later the carriers returned to shoot up an equal number of planes on the ground. Sherman's TG 38.3 then returned to Ulithi, joined by Davison's TG 38.4 after it unsuccessfully tested napalm in a 22 November attack on Yap Island in the western Carolines.[8]

One final Luzon strike on 25 November by Montgomery's TG 38.1 and Bogan's TG 38.2 completed fast carrier operations in support of Leyte. The bombing planes bagged their usual quota of enemy planes and ships, including a heavy cruiser, but the Japanese lashed back. Kamikazes plummeted into *Intrepid*, *Essex*, and *Cabot*, and a near-miss damaged *Hancock*. Such damage led to the cancellation of a strike against the Visayas for the twenty-sixth, and led Admiral Halsey to insist the fast carriers not be exposed in such routine operations until better anti-kamikaze methods could be devised. Task Force 38 returned to Ulithi, and General Kenney assumed full responsibility for Leyte's defense. At least he now had a second airfield operating for his P-38s and P-40 Warhawks, which were heavily engaged every day in repeling Japanese air raids. His P-61s being too slow for enemy night raiders, Kenney begrudgingly obtained Marine Corps night Hellcats from the new air base at Palau.[9]

Before the fast carriers could again confront the deadly kamikazes, techniques had to be devised that could insure 100-per-cent protection, and this meant more fighters. The more defensive fighters that were used on combat air patrol, the fewer fighters there were to escort the bombing planes. Carrier air groups would have to trade in more bombers for fighters, but where were these fighters and pilots to come from? Since Admiral Mitscher rejected breaking in a new plane, the F8F Bearcat, under these intensive combat operations, he could get only more F6Fs or F4U Corsairs from the Marines.[10] With pilot training already cut back since June 1944, and pilot fatigue suddenly straining the availability of reserve air groups, pilots would also be hard to come by. But planes and pilots were needed by the fast carriers—immediately!

One ready source was the Marine Corps, and in August 1944 three Marine generals had flown from Washington to Pearl Harbor to sound out Admiral Towers. Towers recalled their earlier attitude, that the Marines "didn't want carriers," but the Marines said times had changed and their pilots were sick of flying rear guard milk runs over bypassed Rabaul and other nearby islands. The Marines especially wanted their own escort carriers to support their infantry during landings. After Forrest Sherman studied the matter, it was adopted. In late October a special Marine Carrier Groups Command was established to begin training escort carrier pilots, final approval coming in December.[11]

The first suggestion to put Marine pilots aboard the fast carriers was made by Jocko Clark to Admiral Mitscher in San Diego early in November. Mitscher went on to Washington to fight for it, and when Admirals King and Nimitz met with various stateside air admirals in San Francisco at the end of the month the measure was adopted. On 2 December King ordered that ten Marine Corps fighter squadrons (18 planes each) be given "immediate carrier qualification" and temporarily assigned to the fast carriers. This was easier said than done, for although the "gyrenes" were eager for battle, landing a hot Corsair on a small, rolling carrier deck took great skill. Admirals Towers and Murray decided to have each Marine pilot make twelve landings aboard *Saratoga*, *Ranger*, or one escort carrier to qualify. The first units to qualify were Marine Fighting Squadrons 124 and 213, under Lieutenant Colonel William A. Millington, and these reported aboard *Essex* two days before the year ended. The sudden buildup required more air combat intelligence officers and mechanics to service a plane new to the carriers. The Marines brought their own "mechs," which, like the planes, would remain aboard once the pilots were eventually relieved by fresh Navy air groups.[12]

As soon as these planes became available, each carrier air group would change from 54 fighters, 24 bombers, and 18 torpedo planes to 73 VF, 15 VB, and 15 VT. Admiral King reversed pilot training cutbacks from 6000 to 8000 pilots per year, with the 1.67 air groups per carrier raised to two per carrier, which would meet emergencies caused by pilot fatigue from constant air operations and kamikaze alerts aboard ship. The faster F4Us would eventually have precedence as fighters, the F6Fs as fighter-bombers, with four of the Hellcats to be night fighters. As a temporary expedient to battle kamikazes, Ted Sherman recommended and got—for January 1945 only—air groups of 91 VF and 15 VT aboard *Essex* and *Wasp*. So many planes, 73, and pilots, 110, proved too difficult to administer as a single squadron so that on 2 January 18 fighter squadrons were divided into two administrative units, one of which was recommissioned a fighter-bomber squadron (VBF) of 36 planes.[13]

Devising defensive techniques for the many fighters became the primary task of Admiral McCain, his operations officer Jimmy Thach, and the rest of the fast carrier staff at Ulithi. Utilizing the advice of Jocko Clark—who had returned to the Pacific in mid-November—McCain enlarged his cruising formation horizontally by stationing radar picket ships, TOMCATs, 60 miles ahead of the carriers. Vertically, McCain instituted special dawn-to-dusk combat air patrols at all altitudes: JACKCAP—two to four fighters flying at low altitude in each of the four quadrants, with five to six such units outside the screen; DADCAP—dawn-to-dusk launched at dawn and relieved at sunset by BATCAP for dusk patrol; RAPCAP radar picket planes and SCOCAP scouting line planes stationed over the TOMCAT picket destroyers. When a returning strike reached these ships, it would circle them; snooping kamikazes that failed to circle would be picked off by the defensive fighters.

Defensive measures over the target required other innovations. Commander Thach devised the "Three Strike" system which facilitated McCain's "Big Blue Blanket." One fighter patrol stayed over an enemy airfield while a second prepared to take off and a third was en route to or from the target or was being rearmed. This "constant cap" would be continued at night by heckling fighters over enemy airfields to discourage Japanese planes from taking off. All these anti-kamikaze measures occupied Task Force 38 in simulated "MOOSETRAP" training strikes on the carriers during maneuvers off Ulithi in late November and early December 1944. It was hoped that the combination of more fighters and new tactics would protect the carriers from more kamikaze hits.[14]

One other necessary change to implement these tactics concerned the night carriers. *Enterprise* spent December at Pearl

Harbor converting to a night flattop with Bill Martin's Night Air Group 90, while *Independence* continued with Task Force 38. On the tenth Admirals Towers, McMorris, Murray, and Sherman recommended that Night Carrier Division 7 be formed from *Enterprise* and *Independence* with Rear Admiral Matt Gardner in command. On 19 December this was done, and five days later the "Big E" sailed for combat. The fliers trained en route. Some question arose of how best to use the night carriers, whether dispersed among the several task groups or concentrated as one night task group. The latter course was adopted so that crews on the day carriers could get some sleep.[15]

Continuous operations also taxed the strength of the admirals, Halsey and McCain foremost. At least one command change was therefore necessary, though rugged Fightin' Freddie Sherman never yielded his post of ComCarDiv 1. Dave Davison continued as ComCarDiv 2 and Gerry Bogan ComCarDiv 4, but Monty Montgomery after long duty deserved a rest. At the end of the Philippines operation, he was earmarked to return to Hawaii to command the training CarDiv 11. The incumbent Rear Admiral Tommy Sprague, himself resting after the nightmare off Samar–Leyte, would then replace Montgomery as ComCarDiv 3. At Ulithi, Jocko Clark, ComCarDiv 5, and Raddy Radford, ComCarDiv 6, were available for task group command. The other fast cardivs were Gardner's for night operations, CarDiv 7, and a second training unit at Pearl, CarDiv 12, Rear Admiral Ralph Jennings, recent skipper of *Yorktown*.

The first test of these new techniques would be the Mindoro operation, and on 1 December Task Force 38 sortied from Ulithi in three task groups. But Leyte had been getting such a pounding from Japanese planes and kamikazes that the AAF could not eliminate enemy air in the central Philippines, a necessary preliminary before the Mindoro assault could take place on 5 December. This being the case, General MacArthur was persuaded by the admirals on 30 November to postpone the operation for ten days. Task Force 38 got the word on the afternoon of 1 December and returned to Ultihi. The Luzon operation was changed from 20 December to 9 January.

Given another week's respite, the fast carrier forces continued MOOSETRAP maneuvers to prepare more extensively for the second half of the Philippines campaign. All admirals got a chance to practice handling task groups, but the heavy damage incurred during November restricted Halsey to three groups of four day carriers each:

FLEET ORGANIZATION

Commander Third Fleet—Admiral W. F. Halsey, Jr.
Chief of Staff—Rear Admiral R. B. Carney*
Commander Task Force 38—Vice Admiral J. S. McCain (Com2nd FasCarForPac)
Chief of Staff—Rear Admiral W. D. Baker*
CTG 38.1—Rear Admiral A. E. Montgomery (ComCarDiv 3)
Yorktown—Captain T. S. Combs; Air Group 3
Wasp—Captain O. A. Weller; Air Group 81
Cowpens—Captain G. H. DeBaun; Air Group 22
Monterey—Captain S. H. Ingersoll; Air Group 28
CTG 38.2—Rear Admiral G. F. Bogan (ComCarDiv 4)
Lexington—Captain E. W. Litch; Air Group 20
Hancock—Captain R. F. Hickey; Air Group 7
Hornet—Captain A. K. Doyle; Air Group 11
Cabot—Captain S. J. Michael; Air Group 29
Independence—Captain E. C. Ewen; Night Air Group 41
CTG 38.3—Rear Admiral F. C. Sherman (ComCarDiv 1)
Essex—Captain C. W. Wieber; Air Group 4
Ticonderoga—Captain Dixie Kiefer; Air Group 80
Langley—Captain J. F. Wegforth; Air Group 44
San Jacinto—Captain M. H. Kernodle; Air Group 45

* Nonaviator.

This two-week break at Ulithi gave the fast carrier officers their first real chance to study their new commander, Vice Admiral McCain, since he had relieved Mitscher one hectic month before. The general impression was not favorable. Personally likable, salty, profane, and messy even to the point of dribbling tobacco down his shirt while he rolled his own cigarettes, Slew-foot McCain issued not only vague communications but often contradictory ones. "Order, counter-order, disorder" one admiral summarized McCain's techniques; the new TF 38 commander even managed to get into a squabble with Admiral Halsey during this rest period at Ulithi. His new defensive tactics were not well received by his subordinates, who tended to feel that Ernie King had forced McCain on them. Particularly bitter and jealous was Ted Sherman, who would easily have commanded the fast carriers had not Ernie

King stepped in. Sherman complained on 7 December that McCain "asks the impossible and gets some fancy idea that is contrary to the principle of simplicity. As Ching Lee says, a lot of these new brooms come out here and think they know more than people that have been doing it out here for years. They just make it a lot harder for us." [16]

Because of the kamikaze menace, the fast carriers would remain mobile, striking at strategic targets and leaving close support at Mindoro to the escort carriers. In December the new Escort Carrier Force Pacific Fleet was created, under the command of Rear Admiral Cal Durgin, who had come all the way from the Mediterranean to administer the growing numbers of "jeep carriers." For Mindoro six escort carriers of this Force were provided, under tactical command of Felix Stump.

Task Force 38 sortied from Ulithi on 10–11 December and headed for Luzon targets; General Kenney's air forces would cover all targets south of Manila. Its task being to keep enemy fighters grounded during the landings at Mindoro, the fast carriers struck and "blanketed" Luzon continuously day and night 14–16 December. Although Ted Sherman could lament hitting "cow pastures" instead of shipping,[17] Task Force 38 kept Luzon planes generally grounded and shot up over 200 enemy planes, some in the air. Losses were 27 planes, average for operations of two or three days' duration over the Philippines; if shot down, the airmen carried "pointee-talkers" to assist them in Filipino, Formosan, or Chinese dialects and wore CBI (China–Burma–India theater) shoulder patches familiar to the natives.[18] Task Force 38 then withdrew to refuel, after which air strikes were to be resumed in support of the Seventh Fleet landing on Mindoro, which was carried out successfully on the fifteenth.

While searching for a fueling rendezvous in heavy weather on the night of 17–18 December, the leaders of Task Force 38 tried to avoid a tropical disturbance that was difficult to pinpoint. As the seas worsened, it became apparent to some that a very severe storm was making up; in fact, a typhoon.[19] Admirals Montgomery and Bogan had good information, while Captain M. H. Kernodle of *San Jacinto* in Sherman's group "received warnings for 24 hours before I got into the storm, from my aerographer, from the action of the ship, and condition of the sea." "Ugly Mike" Kernodle later told the Court of Inquiry, "I was fully aware of the storm, and that it was going to be severe. In addition to that, I also heard reports from other vessels who were in desperate trouble, and I was not. I had all the warnings any one could possibly have." [20]

Admiral Montgomery did not pass on his "pretty accurate" information, assuming that Halsey and McCain had "later and better" information, but they did not. Lacking solid data from Pacific Fleet Weather Central, Halsey could not decide on the exact course of the small, tight typhoon—and he did not consider the storm a typhoon until after noon of the eighteenth. He took no precautions except a voice transmission to his task groups during the night "to secure everything." Halsey earnestly wanted to clear the heavy weather, refuel his destroyers, now dangerously low on fuel after dawn, and get off his scheduled strikes to Luzon. After 4 A.M. Halsey told his aerologist, Commander George F. Kosko, to call McCain for an estimate of the weather. McCain only replied he could not fuel, so Kosko called Bogan, who placed the storm close to Kosko's own estimate, with which McCain agreed. But all were wrong, and the fast carriers drifted toward the center of the storm. Neither Halsey nor McCain again exchanged weather information with each other or with their three carrier admirals. Nor did Halsey consult McCain on his refueling rendezvous, the last one of which Ted Sherman did not like at all. But Halsey was calling the shots.[21]

Not until noon of 18 December did Halsey cancel his attempt to refuel as well as his Luzon strikes, and at 1:45 he finally informed Nimitz of the typhoon. By then, Task Force 38 was in the thick of it heading south into a storm blowing roughly east to west. Planes broke their lashings on the light carriers, and rolled around to start fires (on *Monterey* and *Cowpens*) or to fall overboard, while the fast carriers plunged wildly in the mountainous waves; luckily, their exposed girders supporting the flight deck overhang did not buckle. Tragedy engulfed three of the destroyers low on fuel. Without ballast to stabilize them, they turned turtle and sank with nearly all hands, nearly 800 men. The task force and oilers rode out the storm throughout the afternoon, clearing it by evening.

The Court of Inquiry, consisting of aviator Vice Admirals Hoover and Murray and batdiv commander Rear Admiral Glenn B. Davis, put the "preponderance of responsibility" squarely on Halsey, for "errors in judgment under stress of war operations and not as offenses." Admiral Nimitz concurred, emphasizing the lack of adequate information given to Halsey and requesting that older and more experienced aerological officers be assigned to the fleet.[22] Interestingly, however, Commander Kosko, who had only just reported three weeks before, stayed on, only to encounter another typhoon six months later. Halsey's desire to keep his commitment in supporting MacArthur's troops on Mindoro won the praise of Nimitz, but Cincpac also issued a letter to the Fleet in February 1945 advising naval commanders to pay more respect to the weather. This meant that courses for fueling should be secondary to safety of the ships, which included operating independently if necessary.

Poor weather information notwithstanding, Halsey's conduct during the night of 17–18 December was typically sloppy. He consulted McCain, who was no help at all, only once, and made no effort to keep his task group commanders advised of developments. He might also have learned something from Sherman, Montgomery, Bogan, or even Mike Kernodle. But Halsey did not operate that way. Like the bull he was when he charged north at Leyte, he had tried to defy the elements by maintaining his fueling and attack schedules. His errors in judgment were compounded by errors in administration. Slew McCain played no positive role during the typhoon, and gave little evidence that he would have helped the situation. His own aerologist never figured in the affair, and McCain did not try to communicate with the task group commanders. Like Mitscher, McCain probably felt more like an observer with Halsey in command, yet one wonders how Mitscher and his expert weatherman, Jim Vonk, might have handled the situation.

The damage caused by the storm kept the fast carriers out of action for many days, but the AAF had begun to operate in sufficient strength from Leyte to cover Mindoro. Task Force 38 returned to Ulithi on 24 December, and Admiral Nimitz arrived to spend Christmas Day with Halsey aboard *New Jersey*. Next day Monty Montgomery got caught between a motor launch and the hull of an escort carrier he was visiting; the accident cracked several of his ribs and put him out of action one month ahead of schedule. Arthur Radford, in standby status, assumed command of TG 38.1. Admiral Gardner and *Enterprise* arrived to form Night Task Group 38.5 with *Independence* on 5 January 1945. Also, the first Marines flew aboard, but during January they were to lose seven pilots killed and 13 F4U Corsairs wrecked from deck crashes. Said Colonel Millington: "We just can't learn navigation and carrier operations in a week as well as the Navy does it in six months." [23]

Fast carrier operations resumed 30 December 1944 for strikes in support of MacArthur's landing at Lingayen Gulf, Luzon, 9 January 1945. Beginning on the third, Task Force 38 lived up to Halsey's "conception of carrier warfare [which] rejects passive defense of an area in favor of stifling the opposition at its source." [24] For six days carrier planes pounded Japanese airfields on Luzon, Formosa, the Pescadores Islands, the Sakishima Gunto, and Okinawa. Heavy weather created holes in McCain's "Big Blue Blanket," so that several kamikazes got through to sink an escort carrier near Mindoro, damaging and sinking many more ships off Lingayen. But over 150 enemy planes were destroyed, and on the ninth others stayed grounded, thanks to carrier strikes on Formosa and the Ryukyus. On the same day, Sixth Army went ashore at Lingayen covered by Vice Admiral Oldendorf's six old battleships and Rear Admiral Durgin's 17 escort carriers (unit commanders Ralph Ofstie, Felix Stump, and George Henderson). Also, Seventh Fleet now had its own air support commander, Captain Ford N. Taylor, Jr.

This week of activity had its problems. Losses were unusually high—86 aircraft, 40 of them operationally, and many of these Marine pilots inexperienced in carrier landings. Furthermore, Slew McCain was issuing more vague, contradictory, and critical orders, trying the patience of Halsey and the task group commanders, especially in regard to fueling plans, which were often confusing. After these many messages, on 8 January McCain sent out a pep talk cheering on the troops; this was so corny that Captain Cat Brown, chief of staff to Ted Sherman, offered his boss a helmet "as a vomit bowl when he read it." [25] Also unhappy were the night carriermen, who, covered by Bogan's TG 38.2 during the day and operating independently as TG 38.5 at night, found no targets or opportunity to defend the fleet from night attack.

No enemy carriers and only one minor surface-ship sortie off Mindoro challenged Seventh Fleet operations. The destruction of Japan's carriers and other vessels in the battle for Leyte Gulf had paid off, but Halsey still wanted to eliminate those surviving battleships and cruisers near Singapore. So did MacArthur, who feared a surface shelling of the Lingayen beachhead by the Japanese or an enemy attempt to cut his supply route to Mindoro if Task Force 38 pulled out of its support role. But Halsey and Nimitz had the answer: fast carrier strikes on those fleet units. Merchant shipping would also be plentiful in the South China Sea; a fast carrier sortie there would be the first direct stroke in driving the cork into the Luzon bottleneck. On the morning of the ninth Nimitz released Task Force 38 from covering the beachhead to strike westward.

Halsey's big target was *Ise* and *Hyuga*, those elusive half-battleships that had escaped his guns off Cape Engaño in October. Navy intelligence placed them at Camranh Bay, French Indochina, and Commander Third Fleet hoped to preserve the element of surprise so that they would not run south to Singapore. On the night of 9–10 January, as Task Force 38 passed through the Luzon Strait into the South China Sea, a report came in of a huge Japanese convoy of over 100 ships moving up the coast of China toward the Formosa Straits, whence probably to Japan. But Halsey passed it by, considering the *Ise*s bigger game.[26] Following another of McCain's not-too-well-planned fueling operations on the eleventh, Halsey split Task Force 38 into two parts. Completely bypassing McCain, whose ineptness irritated Halsey, the fleet commander gave Ted Sherman command of TGs 38.1 and 38.3, while Gerry Bogan led the nighttime approach with TGs 38.2 and 38.5.[27] But Camranh Bay, after all of Halsey's preparations, had no battleships. *Ise* and *Hyuga* had kept moving: Saigon in mid-December, Camranh for two weeks till 1 January, then back to Lingga Roads and Singapore. They returned to Japan in mid-February.[28]

Targets in Southeast Asia were otherwise plentiful. On 12 January alone fast carrier planes sank 44 enemy ships totaling 132,700 tons and destroyed over 100 planes at the cost of 23 carrier planes, though most of the pilots were rescued by natives and smuggled to China. Heavy weather hampered refueling, but Halsey ran north for unimpressive strikes against Formosa and the nearby Chinese coast on the fifteenth. The next day Task Force 38 planes attacked Hong Kong, Hainan, Canton, Swatow, and Macao with meager results; Japanese antiaircraft fire claimed 22 planes, and the neutrality of Portuguese Macao led to a Court of Inquiry and formal apology to Portugal. Very heavy monsoon weather forced Task Force 38 southward, and Halsey wanted to exit the South China Sea by going all the way south to Surigao Strait. This ridiculous idea would have taken the fast carriers out of the war for a week, and placed them in very confined waters exposed to enemy air attack. Nimitz told Halsey to wait for the weather to clear, then pass over the top of Luzon. He did.[29]

Steaming northward after the weather lifted, the three task groups of Radford, Bogan, and Sherman (Gardner's night group had been dissolved on the twelfth) spent 21 January bombing Formosa, the Pescadores, and the Sakishimas. Hitting Japan's vitals, the carriers came under fierce kamikaze attacks. Two smacked into the new *Ticonderoga*, killing 143, wounding 202, including Captain Dixie Kiefer, and causing severe enough damage to force *Ticonderoga*'s retirement to Ulithi. Another suicider crashed a TOMCAT destroyer, a conventional attacker dropped a bomb on *Langley*, and a stray bomb from a landing Avenger caused bad fires and 52 deaths on *Hancock*. That night seven Avengers sank one tanker off Formosa, and the next day Task Force 38 planes attacked and photographed the Sakishimas and Ryukyu Islands targets, especially Okinawa. These activities ended fast carrier support for Philippine opertions, and Task Force 38 reached Ulithi on the twenty-fifth.[30]

Meanwhile, Sixth Army moved inland at Lingayen, seizing the airfields so that General Kenney could fly in his planes to support the drive overland to Manila. On 17 January General Kenney relieved Admiral Kinkaid and Captain Taylor of responsibility for covering the beachhead from the air, although the last escort carrier did not depart until the thirtieth. As elsewhere in the Pacific, the Army Air Forces excelled in interdiction bombing—"tactical isolation"—by attacking enemy lines of communication, but its close support of ground forces left much to be desired. General MacArthur therefore called in seven Marine Corps squadrons of old SBD Dauntlesses from the Solomons to support Sixth Army. Marine techniques of bombing to within 300 yards of friendly lines with these planes, said one Army general, kept the enemy underground, "and have enabled our troops to move up with fewer casualties and with greater speed. I cannot say enough in praise of these men of the dive bombers. . . ." [31] Soon the Fifth Air Force picked up some of the Marines' tricks for mopping-up operations on Luzon and for the capture of bypassed central and southern Philippine Islands. The Allies liberated Manila on 3 February, and the Japanese ceased major organized resistance on Luzon 14 April. Operations in the south continued into the summer.

By early February 1945, with the Army Air Forces operating from Luzon airfields and with the Navy using Manila and building a major base and anchorage, which the fast carriers would eventually use, at Leyte–Samar, the plugging of the bottleneck was nearly complete. From that time forward, Japanese ships made the long run from the East Indies to the homeland only at great peril to themselves. If they were not attacked by Philippine-based air, they ran the risk of being torpedoed by an American submarine. Surviving these hazards, enemy ships then faced a hazardous voyage through key waterways, including harbors, now being aerially mined by B-29 bombers from the Marianas and by medium bombers based at Leyte. With the fall of Manila, the long-range blockade of Japan began.

For the Fast Carrier Task Force, the Philippine campaign had been remarkable for the endurance of the carriers and the damage they inflicted on the enemy. From September 1944 through January 1945 its planes had destroyed literally thousands of enemy aircraft, had sunk or put out of action the major strength of the enemy fleet, and had supported Sixth Army single-handedly, alongside the valiant escort carriers, against Japanese human guided missiles for weeks on end. One task group, except for a three-day visit to Ulithi, kept the sea for a record 84 days. Strategically, Japan had spent her surface fleet and last effective naval air squadrons in trying to hold the Philippines, and had given away the secret of her suicide corps when it might have been harbored for a more opportune moment. In losing the Philippines, Japan lost the war, for the oil, rubber, and gasoline were cut off down in Indonesia.

For all their triumphs, the fast carriers had not been commanded as efficiently as in previous operations. Halsey and McCain, though they were dashing fighters, did not work as an effective team nor did they carry out their operations as meticulously and carefully as did Spruance and Mitscher. Singlemindedness in sinking the enemy carriers and in supporting an exposed beachhead are credits to Halsey's leadership, but not at the expense of leaving Leyte uncovered in the one case and leaving the fleet exposed to a typhoon in the other. Halsey's obsession with sinking Japanese warships led to rather fruitless searching in the South China Sea at the expense of juicier targets. Bull Halsey was a carrier task force commander and nothing else in these operations; after hauling down his flag on 26 January 1945 he concerned himself primarily with plans for covering amphibious operations with the carriers rather than their amphibious aspects, which was left to keener minds.[32] Slew McCain was nothing more than a deputy to Halsey.

He never enjoyed tactical command in any crucial situation, and relied heavily on his operations officer, Jimmy Thach, for tactical innovations.[33]

With Japan's petroleum supply sealed off at Luzon, Admiral King looked to the final encirclement of Japan by the U.S. Fifth Fleet. The conquest of the bypassed East Indies Ernie left to America's ally, Great Britain, and her steadily growing Eastern Fleet.

Nine:
British Fast Carrier Forces

The Second Anglo-German War, begun in 1939, did not allow for a major British naval commitment in the war against Japan until after 1943. By the end of that year, the requirement for British capital ships in the Atlantic and Mediterranean was greatly reduced. Italy—and her Navy—had surrendered in September, while Germany had ceased surface-ship operations and construction altogether, though a few hidden, isolated battleships had to be watched. American carrier *Ranger* joined the British fleet for operations against occupied Norway in October, and British and American hunter-killer groups of escort carriers had practically driven the U-boat from the seas by the end of the year. As the date for D-Day at Normandy approached, Royal Navy carriers could be released for operations against Japan.

That contribution would probably be made in the Southeast Asia theater, after October 1943 commanded by Admiral Lord Louis Mountbatten RN, equivalent in rank and authority to MacArthur and Nimitz. In September 1943, Admiral Sir James Somerville RN returned with the British East Indies Fleet from Madagascar to Colombo, Ceylon, from which place the Japanese had driven this fleet in early 1942. Any British counteroffensive in the East Indies would be directed toward Singapore, Malaya, which Britain had considered the key to her Far Eastern defenses since World War I. At the Cairo conference in November 1943 Prime Minister Winston Churchill supported the idea of a drive through Malaya and the Dutch East Indies, while some of his advisers advocated an Australia-based fleet operating on MacArthur's left flank during the push from New Guinea to the Philippines.[1] Such a drive would liberate Borneo and culminate at Hong Kong on the coast of China, where, in December 1943, at least Admiral Nimitz was headed.

The British at Cairo also introduced the idea of eventually placing a British fleet in the Pacific to fight alongside Nimitz's Pacific Fleet. Admiral Ernie King, like many of his predecessors and fellow officers who had served during days of not-so-cordial relations between the two countries, rejected the idea. King just "assumed" that with the defeat of Germany all U.S. naval units would redeploy to the Pacific and those of the Royal Navy to the Indian Ocean.[2] Churchill agreed to use his Navy to keep the Japanese at Singapore tied down while the American Navy crossed the Pacific, but the idea of a fleet in the Pacific was appealing. President Roosevelt, in an effort to stall a decision, pointed out that the problem need not be treated as urgent until Germany gave up, perhaps in the summer of 1945.[3]

Having planted the idea of a British Pacific fleet, the British began during the summer of 1944—with the German Navy practically destroyed—to press for their own task force in the Pacific. Ernie King fought it, on the basis, or so he told Nimitz in June 1944, that the British Eastern Fleet should recapture the oil-rich Indies, thus easing the fuel situation in the western Pacific. But in August, when Admiral Mountbatten was asked by Churchill if he could spare fleet carriers from Southeast Asia for the Central Pacific, Mountbatten replied that modern carriers and battleships *belonged* in the open Pacific. He anticipated that the Japanese fleet would move from Singapore anyway—as it did in October 1944—whereupon land-based planes could deal with any ships left at Singapore. But Mountbatten did not have to wait until the enemy fleet moved to release his carriers, for at the Allied conference at Quebec in September the Combined Chiefs of Staff agreed—over Ernie King's protests—to form the British Pacific Fleet.[4]

Admiral King, whatever his much-discussed feelings toward the British, believed the Royal Navy had no real appreciation of the requirements of waging naval warfare in the vast distances of the Pacific. At San Francisco in late July 1943 Savvy Cooke had briefed King and Nimitz on the British concept of war in the Pacific: the recapture of Singapore and a drive up the coast of Southeast Asia toward the China Sea, with no concrete thoughts about the problems of supply and air support.[5] By the fall of 1944 the British had not changed this strategy, and they still knew little of Pacific logistics. But they had learned about air support as early as the North African invasion and most recently from the escort carriers of Troubridge and Durgin at the invasion of southern France during the summer. Mountbatten would depend on the escort carriers of Rear Admiral G. N. Oliver's 21st Aircraft Carrier Squadron during the invasion of Malaya, eventually scheduled for 9 September 1945.

Unreconciled to a course he thought would certainly end up as a burden on American logistics, Admiral King continued to fight the deployment of the British Pacific Fleet until that fleet actually stood ready to sail from its forward base into battle.

1. Emergence of the Fleet Air Arm

Completion of the 1937 transfer of British naval aviation from the Royal Air Force to the Royal Navy in May 1939 could not overcome the losses sustained by 20 years of divided control. British Naval aircraft were by all standards inferior to those of the RAF, Japan, and the United States. By the date of America's entry into the war, Britain had but four new fleet carriers with only two more under construction. Furthermore, like U.S. personnel before 1927, few flag officers had ever flown. But many had become naval air observers, enabling them to command air units, though aviation experience was not required for carrier force command. Nevertheless, the British used well what little they had—disrupting the Italian fleet at Taranto, for instance, and contributing importantly to the sinking of *Bismarck*.

At least British fleet air entered the war with adequate representation at the Admiralty: the post of Fifth Sea Lord and Chief of Naval Air Services with the rank of vice admiral. Such a place of prominence was not achieved by American naval aviation until mid 1943 with the creation of DCNO (Air). As in the U.S. Navy, naval air underwent administrative reorganization as operations shifted from mobilization and the defensive to the offensive with sufficient material. In January 1943 the functions of naval aviation were split into two posts at the Admiralty. One of them, Fifth Sea Lord and Chief of Naval Air Equipment, Rear Admiral Denis W. Boyd RN, whose post compared in the USN with DCNO (Air), assumed all material activities of the Fleet Air Arm. The other new billet, Assistant Chief Naval Staff (Air), "was primarily responsible for coordinating the work of the Naval Staff dealing with air matters and for advising on questions of staff policy in connection with Naval Air work." An air admiral to influence policy was just what American naval aviators wanted, but could not get during the war thanks to Ernie King. But the First Sea Lord, Admiral Sir Andrew Cunningham RN, was no Ernie King and had no desire to check the rising influence of wartime aviation at Navy headquarters. Rear Admiral R. H. Portal RN was Assistant Chief Naval Staff (Air) until November 1944 when he took command of Pacific Fleet air bases in Australia; his relief was Rear Admiral L. D. Mackintosh RN.[1]

Under this excellent division of responsibilities, the Fleet Air Arm grew over the next two years. For initial operations against Japan, Britain had its four 23,000-ton fleet carriers of the *Illustrious* class: *Illustrious*, *Victorious*, *Formidable*, and *Indomitable*, which compared with *Enterprise* except in shorter cruising radius, speed (30.5 knots to 33), armored flight deck, and a smaller complement of aircraft. Two modified versions, of the *Implacable* class, slightly larger and faster (32.5 knots), would be completed in time for incorporation into the British Pacific Fleet: *Indefatigable*, commissioned in May 1944, and *Implacable*, August 1944.

Britain adopted the American idea of a crash program for light carriers to augment the heavy ships, with one important difference: these CVLs would make only 25 knots, fulfilling the definition of a fast carrier only at top speed. Virtually one class, though half of them differed slightly internally from the other half, sixteen 14,000-ton light carriers of the *Colossus* and *Majestic* classes were projected. Especially equipped for operating in the Far East, mainly with air conditioning, some of these ships would actually fight in the Pacific if the war lasted to the end of 1945; the rest would help fulfill postwar requirements. *Colossus* was commissioned in December 1944, followed quickly by *Vengeance* and *Venerable* in January 1945 and *Glory* in April.[2]

Like the U.S. Navy, the Admiralty planned for its postwar fleet in the wartime carrier-building program. Along with the many *Colossus–Majestic* light carriers, the Royal Navy designed three new classes of fast carriers. Early in 1944 work commenced on the new *Hermes* class, eight 30-knot carriers of 18,000 tons each; four keels were laid before the war ended. Four carriers of the new 32-knot, 35,000-ton *Ark Royal* class were projected, and two keels laid by war's end, and in 1945 the Navy drew up plans for three battle carriers of the *Gibraltar* class, over 40,000 tons and comparable to the U.S. *Midways*. Though these ships could not affect the course of the war, they reflected the impact of naval air on the Royal Navy and the Air Arm's determination to make good after prewar reverses.

Existing British carriers could compare with their American counterparts in most respects, but their planes were sadly inferior, almost unsuitable for fast carrier task force operations in the Pacific. In fighters, the Fleet Air Arm had to depend on adaptations of existing land-based planes. Notably, the superb Spitfire was converted into the Supermarine Seafire, folding wings and all in later models, but it had neither the range nor the undercarriage strength of specially designed carrier planes. The replacement for the Seafire, the two-seat Fairey Firefly, proved a versatile fighter-bomber, but it was slower and less maneuverable than the single-seaters. The Navy kept both planes, as they certainly surpassed previous models of carrier aircraft. In bombers, by 1943 the Fleet Air Arm had only one new plane to replace the ancient Swordfish, the Fairey Barracuda, slow, heavy, underpowered, short-ranged, unpredictable. Such planes could not match their counterparts in the U.S. Navy, though their performance against the Japanese was still an open question.[3]

The obvious solution to the dilemma was to equip British fast carriers with American-built carrier planes. Under Lend Lease, during the winter of 1942–1943 the United States began supplying Great Britain with F4F Wildcats (renamed Martlets), followed by F4U Corsairs, F6F Hellcats, and TBF/TBM Avengers. In fact, the British put Corsairs on carriers in August 1943, over one year before the U.S. Navy finally did it. Corsairs from *Victorious* covered an attack on the German battleship *Tirpitz* in April 1944. Many British carrier squadrons using American planes trained at Naval Air Station Quonset Point, Rhode Island. By obtaining such modern naval planes, the Fleet Air Arm was able to erase the many years during which it had fallen behind under RAF control; after the war Britain could again compete in the design and construction of new naval aircraft.

The British had a great deal to learn from the Americans in carrier tactics, also. Rear Admiral Alva Bernhard, who had commanded an American carrier force with the British Home Fleet, wrote in December 1943 that the British "know less of the proper use of carrier air power than we did when the *Langley* was our only carrier."[4] To learn more, the British attached several observers to key American staffs in the Pacific. In October 1943 Commander H. S. Hopkins RN relieved Captain M. B. Laing RN on Nimitz's staff, but as foreigners were regarded with suspicion Hopkins was not allowed to attend Cincpac meetings or see secret documents until January 1944. With the creation of the British Pacific Fleet, the Admiralty decided to place a vice admiral on the Cincpac staff, but Nimitz—already burdened with a large staff—would not have it. So Harry Hopkins was promoted to acting captain and assigned to stay on as British liaison officer; he was relieved in July 1945 by Captain Anthony Pleydell-Bouverie RN.[5]

Liaison officer to both Admirals Spruance and Halsey on Fifth–Third fleet staffs was Commander Michael LeFanu RN, who reported to Spruance aboard *Indianapolis* early in January 1945. In addition, Commander C. E. A. Owen RN reported to Admiral Mitscher's staff about a month later. Fittingly, LeFanu reported directly from gunnery duty aboard a battleship, while Owen was an aviator. Direct arrangements between Spruance and the British Pacific Fleet began early in February when that Fleet's cruiser commander, Rear Admiral E. J. P. Brind RN, visited Spruance at Ulithi. But much had to be learned before the two fleets would ever operate together.[6]

In aviation, two British naval officers, one an aviator and the other an aviation observer, visited Vice Admiral Towers in September 1943 as part of the Lethbridge mission "sent out to acquaint themselves with methods of warfare in the Pacific Ocean areas."[7] The same month Commander Richard M. Smeeton RN reported as British liaison officer to ComAirPac. Smeeton served on board various carriers and at Pearl Harbor until being ordered to the British Pacific Fleet as air plans officer late in 1944; his relief was Commander F. H. E. Hopkins RN. As well as looking and learning, these men were able to pass on some British aviation practices to the Americans. As early as February 1944 new staff officers began arriving to form the nucleus of the British Pacific Fleet, while observers joined American carriers, and British reserve pilots trained with carrier air groups in Hawaii.[8]

The one overriding weakness in any prospective British carrier operations in the Pacific Captain Hopkins perceived very soon. "Logistics is the most important aspect of the war at sea, in the Pacific," he reported home, hammering away on this subject when he visited the Admiralty during the late summer and early fall of 1944.[9] This being so, Rear Admiral C. S. Daniel RN made a study of American naval supply and administration in the Pacific during the year, obtaining information that would facilitate British preparations. Daniel reported in May as administrative officer of the British Pacific Fleet.

Aviation became even more prominent in the Royal Navy as British warships and base personnel gathered at Ceylon and Australia preparatory to sending a carrier force into battle. Then, in May 1945, after the British Pacific Fleet had gone into action, Fleet Air administration underwent a final wartime reorganization. All material functions held by the Fifth Sea Lord-Chief of Naval Air Equipment were assumed by the new Vice Controller (Air)-Chief of Naval Air Equipment, Rear Admiral M. S. Slattery RN. Over-all naval air policy matters, formerly the responsibility of the Assistant Chief Naval Staff (Air), passed up to the new Fifth Sea Lord (Air), "now broadly responsible for the general direction and coordination of all Naval air policy."[10] The first Fifth Sea Lord (Air) was Rear Admiral Troubridge, ably assisted by the downgraded ACNS (Air), Rear Admiral Mackintosh. This important step placed an aviation policy billet on the Board of Admiralty, or in American terms on the Cominch staff, something American naval aviators still did not have, for their DCNO(Air) was roughly equivalent to Vice Controller (Air).

Finally, in June 1945, as more British carriers joined the fleet and their squadrons worked up in the British Isles for eventual assignment in the Far East, the Admiralty established another new post, that of Admiral (Air). Vice Admiral Boyd, the first Admiral (Air), assumed authority over all fleet aviation and air training at home. The Fleet Air Arm now enjoyed a senior air admiral in the naval command hierarchy, another advancement over the American organization.

Before battle could be joined in the far-flung reaches of the Pacific, however, British carriers had to practice, learn new techniques, and build up their logistics. The early lessons were learned by the Eastern Fleet.

2. *British Pacific Fleet*

Aside from *Victorious*' brief tour in the South Pacific during the summer of 1943, the first fleet carrier assigned to fight Japan after the reverses of 1941–1942 was *Illustrious.* Dispatched from the Atlantic with two battleships and one battle cruiser, *Illustrious* joined Admiral Somerville's rather small Eastern Fleet at Trincomalee, Ceylon, in January 1944. Shortly thereafter, Task Force 58 drove the Japanese fleet from Truk to the Palaus and Singapore, leading Somerville to ask for more carriers. *Victorious* was not due until July, but the U.S. Navy offered to provide *Saratoga* and its veteran Air Group 12 fresh from Rabaul and the Marshalls. Everyone agreed, and as soon as Eniwetok was taken Admiral Nimitz detached "*Sara*" and three destroyers as Task Group 58.5 to Colombo, Ceylon, via Espiritu Santo and Perth, Australia.

The joint operation between the two carriers commenced with their rendezvous in the Indian Ocean 27 March 1944. The carrier admiral, Rear Admiral Clement Moody RN, a nonpilot, had already captained one carrier, headed the Naval Air Division after the outbreak of war, and served as Rear Admiral, Aircraft Carriers, Home Fleet, before his similar assignment with the Eastern Fleet. Captain R. L. B. Cunliffe RN was the veteran skipper of *Illustrious*, and Captain John H. Cassady that of *Saratoga*. But neither Clem Moody, Smiler Cunliffe, nor Hopalong Cassady would coordinate the air operations of this combined fast carrier task force. Air operations depended on Commander Jumpin' Joe Clifton, skipper of Air Group 12, and on Lieutenant Commander Dickie Cork RN, fighter wing leader on *Illustrious*, and on Lieutenant Commander Bob Dosé of *Sara*'s Fighting 12.

Joint operations required certain adjustments at first. The 80 American pilots' first social call to the "wet" British carrier ended in a drunken spree to the tune of 700 bottles of beer, and three dozen bottles each of whiskey and gin—except for Jumpin' Joe, a fanatic on ice cream.[1] Fighting 12, the first American squadron to fly Corsairs from a carrier deck but now equipped with Hellcats, enjoyed seeing Cork's squadron using them, but the gawky, lumbering Barracuda bombers brought from one irreverent American swab the crack, "The Limeys'll be building *airplanes* next!"[2] Joint air operations in early April revealed the British taking all hour and a half to launch and rendezvouz one deckload of planes, so Clifton took the British aviators in hand and soon had rendezvous time down to 25 minutes. By mid-month both groups were working as a team, an achievement marred, however, by the tragic loss of the popular Dickie Cork in an air collision while landing at a shore base.[3]

The joint Allied carrier operation in the Indian Ocean involved *Illustrious* and *Saratoga* in an attack on the Japanese base at Sabang, which guarded the Malacca Straits and the northern sea approach to Singapore. The raid was timed at General MacArthur's request to coincide with his landings at Hollandia, New Guinea, in the hope that Japanese planes in Malaya would then not attempt to reinforce New Guinea.[4] Admiral Somerville, an old hand at carrier strikes from his Force H days, commanded the operation, which was truly international. It included one British carrier and one American carrier; one French and two British battleships; one British battle cruiser; one Dutch, one New Zealand, and four British cruisers; eight British, one Dutch, three Australian, and three American destroyers.

Commander Clifton led the strike, launched at 5:30 A.M. 19 April 1944, from a point 100 miles southwest of Sabang. In the combined squadrons were 24 Hellcat and 13 Corsair fighters escorting 18 Dauntless, 17 Barracuda, and 11 Avenger bombers. Arriving over the target about 7 A.M., these planes caught the Japanese completely by surprise. No enemy planes were aloft, but Dosé's fighters, following their Rabaul precedent, accompanied the bombers in their dives. For ten minutes, 30 tons of bombs fell on Sabang, destroying three or four oil tanks; the fighters shot up 21 parked aircraft. One *Saratoga* Hellcat was shot down by antiaircraft fire, but the British—veterans at air-sea rescue—had a lifeguard sub ready to pick up the pilot though under fire from an enemy shore battery. During the day, "*Sara*'s" combat air patrol splashed three enemy snoopers. The carrier force then headed to Trincomalee, mission accomplished, though it is doubtful that the Japanese would have sent planes all the way from Malaya to New Guinea to try to stop MacArthur.

Although *Saratoga* was due to return to the United States for an overhaul, Admiral King suggested—and Admiral Mountbatten readily concurred—that *Saratoga* might attack the Japanese-occupied naval base at Soerabaya, Java, on her way home. Admiral Somerville therefore led the same naval forces out of Colombo on 6 May 1944, but—because of two British deficiencies—headed first for the British anchorage at Exmouth Gulf, Australia. Having always depended on bases for their short-range ships, the British had not developed a sophisticated refueling technique at sea. Therefore, six tankers refueled the anchored ships at Exmouth on 15 May. The other trouble was the Barracuda; because the attacking planes would fly 180 miles over land and water to hit Soerabaya from the south and then return, the short-range Barracuda could not participate. As a result, a squadron of American-built Avengers flew aboard *Illustrious*, and the Barracuda flew ashore.

The air strike on Soerabaya on 17 May 1944 repeated the success at Sabang, with Joe Clifton again coordinating the attack. The fighters easily shot down the two airborne Japanese planes, while the bombers paired off into two main groups. One hit the shipping and dock installations, the other bombed the Bratt Engineering Works and Java's only refinery of aviation gas. Fires were started at the latter places, two small ships were sunk, and Torpedo 12 lost its skipper, Lieutenant W. E. Rowbotham, along with his crew, to antiaircraft fire. A second deckload strike would have completed the destruction, but Admiral Somerville could not know this until the planes returned, too late for a second launch. Admiral Nimitz later censured Captain Cassady of *Saratoga* for his failure to recommend such a strike earlier. The next day, the British and Allied ships passed in review for "*Sara*" and her escorts, which afterward departed for home.

As American forces thrust westward through the Marianas to the Philippines, Admiral Nimitz stressed "the desirability of aggressive air action by the British Eastern Fleet." [5] Admiral Mountbatten, anxious to help, was hampered by the poor carrier procedures and inadequate training in Far Eastern operations. Nevertheless, Admirals Somerville and Moody carried out several air raids as new carriers reported. Adverse weather prevented severe damage to Japanese installations in the Andaman Islands when *Illustrious* planes struck in June 1944, but the next month the newly arrived *Victorious* (Captain M. M. Denny RN), *Illustrious* (now under Captain C. E. Lambe RN), and other ships carried out a very effective air-surface bombardment of Sabang. In late August and early September Clem Moody led *Victorious* and *Indomitable* (Captain J. A. S. Eccles RN), fresh from the Atlantic, in air strikes on Japanese coastal positions in Sumatra, but their inefficient Barracudas and inexperienced air crews inflicted little damage. In a vain effort to divert Japanese attention away from Leyte, Vice Admiral Sir Arthur Power RN led these same two carriers on 17–19 October in undramatic raids on the Nicobar Islands.[6]

Throughout the summer of 1944 the Admiralty prepared for major naval action against Japan by dispatching more ships to Ceylon and by making command changes to create the British

Pacific Fleet. Admiral Somerville, retired years before for medical reasons (but now returned officially to the active list) and weary from many years in combat, was relieved as Commander-in-Chief East Indies Fleet on 23 August by Admiral Sir Bruce Fraser RN, a nonpilot who had commanded a carrier before the war. When the new fleet was agreed upon at Quebec in October, Fraser returned to London for discussions. Simultaneously, Mountbatten agreed to release the carriers from his Southeast Asia Command. The decision was also made to establish the new fleet's base at Sydney, Australia, while British carriers would trade in their Barracudas for American-built Avengers. All six of Britain's fleet carriers would go to the Pacific. On 22 November 1944 Admiral Fraser hoisted his flag at Ceylon as Commander-in-Chief British Pacific Fleet. Admiral Power took over the Eastern Fleet as full admiral, and Clem Moody became Flag Officer (Air), East Indies Station, with the rank of vice admiral.

Since Admiral Fraser, like his counterpart Nimitz, would remain ashore, experienced commanders afloat were needed. Appointed Second-in-Command, BPF was Vice Admiral Sir H. Bernard Rawlings RN, a leading figure in the revival of the Fleet Air Arm before the war although not himself a pilot. The man who would actually command the British fast carriers was Admiral Commanding 1st Aircraft Carrier Squadron (the same as ComCarDiv 1), Rear Admiral Sir Philip L. Vian RN, hero of early surface operations in the Atlantic and convoy-air battles of the Malta campaign; he had also used escort carriers to cover the Salerno landings. Not a pilot, Vian would somewhat reluctantly depend on his staff for advice in air matters. As with most good British combat leaders, Vian had served at sea almost continuously since 1939. In addition to this long tiring duty, compounded by a bout with fever, he was normally a rigid, formal officer; even in the tropics he would shun khakis for the white tunic and long trousers. Fearless and calm in battle, Vian was usually cold, efficient, and demanding. One writer described Vian briefing the pilots aboard *Illustrious*: he "stood there, foursquare and uncompromising, stiff and unsmiling, with a brown, lined seaman's face, and gave them the benefit of his blunt wisdom." [7]

Admiral Fraser acted quickly to utilize and equip his new fleet. Rear Admiral Vian hoisted his flag in the new fleet carrier *Indefatigable* (Captain Q. D. Graham RN) in England and sailed for Ceylon in November. Vice Admiral Rawlings reported to Ceylon and after studying American carrier tactics and procedures could only conclude: "We have to go to school again." Vice Admiral Daniel found Sydney in need of hasty expansion for a fleet base; his greatest shortages were in fast fleet tankers and aircraft-replenishment ships. The latter problem was solved in January 1945 by the arrival of three British escort carriers and the activation of a Mobile Operating Naval Air Base (MONAB) at Sydney. But forming a fleet train (service squadron) was something else. First, since Sydney was the rear base like Pearl Harbor, Britain needed advanced bases. Secondly, its simple train of oilers, half of which were commercial tankers with civilian crews, had never operated in the open ocean so far from friendly bases. Nor had they replenished large warships by coming alongside under way as was the American practice; instead, they dragged hoses off the stern, refueling in tandem, an inefficient and time-consuming practice.

These shortcomings hardened Ernie King's resolve to keep the BPF away from American fast carrier operations. He told Admiral Nimitz at San Francisco in November that "the more desirable solution would be for the British Pacific Fleet to be assigned certain tasks in the Pacific to carry out independently, rather than for ships of the Royal Navy and the United States Navy to be maneuvered together." [8] Logistically, King insisted, the BPF had to be self-sustaining, but it could share advanced American bases at Manus, Ulithi, and Leyte. To standardize operations, the British would have to adopt U.S. tactical and communications procedures (as the American Battle Squadron of the British Grand Fleet had done in 1917–1918), but the USN would supply liaison, communications, and air combat intelligence officers to facilitate the changes.

Admiral Fraser journeyed from Ceylon to Pearl Harbor via Australia to open discussions with Admiral Nimitz on 17 December. Fraser discovered that Nimitz shared King's reluctance to include the BPF in the Central Pacific,[9] but the two men managed to agree upon the above changes. Nimitz assigned two veterans as liaison officers to the British: Captain C. Julian Wheeler, who had commanded a cruiser in fast carrier screens, to Vice Admiral Rawlings; and Captain Eddie Ewen, skipper of the night *Independence*, to Rear Admiral Vian. Wheeler did not share Ernie King's hard-line attitude, and on the last day of the year he told Jack Towers "that he felt a broader interpretation of the [self-sufficiency] directive would have been most desirable both for efficiency and for preservation of friendly relations." [10] Towers agreed and suggested to Nimitz that all British and American stores, especially oil and aviation gas, should be pooled.[11] Nimitz fell into line and informed Wheeler before he left for Sydney that he could tell Admiral Fraser that "we would make it work regardless of anything." [12] When operations began, the British, supplied on "a very frayed and tatty shoe string," were pleasantly surprised to receive "actual American support, strictly under the counter!" [13]

Before the British fast carriers could hope to tackle a major target, they needed a battle-training period, as the American flattops had had in raiding Marcus and Wake in 1943. Admiral Power, commanding the Eastern Fleet at Trincomalee, therefore assembled the four available carriers for several operations "primarily to weld the force together." [14]

Admiral Rawlings being severely ill, Power assigned the missions to Admiral Vian, who shifted his flag from *Indefatigable* to *Indomitable.* The first target was the Japanese oil refinery at Pangkalan Brandan in northwest Sumatra, to be attacked by *Indomitable* and *Illustrious*, which sortied with escorts from Trincomalee on 17 December. Three days later 27 bomb-laden Avengers escorted by 28 Hellcats and Corsairs found the target obscured by clouds and instead bombed the port facilities at Belawan Deli, while the fighters strafed the port of Kota Raja and the airfield at Sabang. They did little damage.[15]

Dissatisfied with these results, Vian sortied from Trincomalee with *Indomitable*, *Victorious*, and *Indefatigable* and escorts on 31 December for a second crack at the Pangkalan Brandan refinery. On 4 January 1945 Vian's planes attacked in clear skies. The Corsairs and Hellcats shot down seven airborne interceptors and were followed by 12 rocket-firing Fireflies and 32 bomb-carrying Avengers. The attack planes struck the refinery accurately, setting it ablaze; the fighters strafed several parked planes. No British planes were lost to enemy action, though two crashed in operational mishaps. One could say that these two forays were the Marcus–Wake phase of the BPF's battle training. Now these ships and planes needed a Rabaul to really test their mettle.

Palembang, southern Sumatra, housed the two largest oil refineries in southeast Asia; "between them they were capable of meeting three-quarters of Japan's needs for aviation fuel." [16] Furthermore, Palembang shared with Tarakan and Balikpapan, both in Borneo, the responsibility of supplying oil to what was left of the Japanese fleet. Admiral Nimitz therefore specifically asked the

British to knock out Palembang. On 16 January 1945—the same day Task Force 38 planes were ranging up and down the coast of China and Indochina—Admiral Vian departed Trincomalee with the greatest carrier striking force in the history of the British navy: *Indefatigable*, *Indomitable*, *Illustrious*, *Victorious*, 238 airplanes, one battleship, three cruisers, and ten destroyers.

Enemy fighters, barrage balloons, and heavy antiaircraft fire greeted the British carrier planes over Palembang at dawn, 24 January 1945. The fighter sweep shot down fourteen Japanese planes, then attacked the airfields around the well-defended city. Lieutenant Commander W. J. Mainprice RN led the Fireflies and Avengers to successfully bomb the Pladjoe refinery. Retiring, the carriers took two entire days to refuel, plus two in transit, which gave the Japanese ample time to stage in more planes to Palembang. On the twenty-ninth Vian returned. The Fireflies paved a path for the Avengers by shooting down the barrage balloons guarding the Soengei Gerong refinery, but many Japanese fighters gave battle. Commander Mainprice was shot down and lost, along with ten other British planes. The Japanese also sustained heavy losses in aircraft, including those which attacked the carriers but were shot down by antiaircraft fire. But the bombers got through to pound the refineries.[17]

The Palembang operation was the BPF's Rabaul; it qualified the British fast carriers for Central Pacific operations, for they had maneuvered in a close tactical four-carrier formation under major combat conditions. The damaged refineries of Palembang produced only one-third their total capacity in February and March, while the Soengei Gerong plant did not produce at all until May. By this time, the Indies were cut off from Japan by the air-sea-mining blockade of the Allies. During the strikes, Vian had lost 16 planes in combat, 25 operationally—these losses no doubt due in large part to the fragile undercarriages of the Seafires. Sad to relate, the pilot losses became all the more tragic when, after the war, it was learned that several pilots had parachuted, been captured, and then executed by the Japanese. The empty oil tankers returned to Trincomalee, leaving the carriers with only enough fuel to reach Sydney instead of completing the destruction of Palembang with a third strike.[18]

Vice Admiral Rawlings hoisted his flag aboard battleship *King George V*—the "Cagey 5" to American sailors—at Fremantle,

Australia, on 5 February, then proceeded with the carriers to Sydney, arriving on the tenth. The ships were replenished, losses replaced, and preparations made to advance to Manus before joining the United States Fifth Fleet. As agreed between Fraser and Nimitz, Fraser would supply and maintain these ships, and Rawlings would operate under tactical command of Spruance or Halsey—the first time in modern British history that a British fleet operated under command of a foreign officer. In fact, however, Rawlings would be little more than an observer, for Vian would take his orders as a four-carrier task group commander from Mitscher or McCain (though Fraser resumed tactical command at night). In actual strength, the BPF was 50 planes weaker than a four-carrier American fast carrier task group. The three *Illustrious*es each carried about 35 Corsairs or Hellcats and 15 Avengers (to *Essex*'s 73 VF, 15 VB, 15 VT), and the larger *Indefatigable* 40 Seafires, 20 Avengers, and nine Fireflies.[19]

Early in March most of the ships formed British Task Force 113 and moved up to Manus, though *Illustrious* remained briefly at Sydney for repairs. Only 27 of the required 69 service vessels of Task Force 112—the fleet train—had reached Manus, partly as a result of a longshoremen's strike at Sydney; one of the absent vessels was the water boat, forcing each ship to distill its own water, a laborious task for large ships. Swells at Manus made refueling difficult, and the heat was oppressive. Mountains of paperwork accompanied the transition to American procedures and signals and seriously burdened British communications and staff officers. Said Admiral Vian later, "None of us pretended to like it."[20]

To make matters even more irritating, Ernie King adamantly refused to allow the BPF to operate in the Central Pacific. Meeting with Admiral Nimitz early in March at San Francisco, King said he preferred it to be used in Southeast Asia or in the invasion of Borneo being planned for the summer. Nimitz replied that he was willing to employ the British carriers in the second phase of the Okinawa campaign, to which King finally agreed, but Cominch insisted that the BPF remain self-supporting, a doctrine to which Nimitz paid lip service.[21] Until King could make up his mind to comply with the Quebec decision, the British carriers were delayed at Manus. Finally, on 14 March, Admiral Fraser received orders to send his fleet into combat, but with the qualification that it could be withdrawn on seven days' notice.

Task Force 113 departed Manus 19 March for Ulithi: four carriers, two battleships, five cruisers, and 18 destroyers. Part of the Fleet Train remained at Manus, and a major portion of it moved up to Leyte–Samar. At Ulithi, the BPF was redesignated Task Force 57. The ships refueled, final conversations were held, and on 23 March the British fast carrier force sortied to join Task Force 58 in support of the Okinawa campaign. Two days later, British tankers passed their lines astern for a final refueling of the carriers before combat. One pleasant surprise was the absence of Japanese submarines to take advantage of the situation, an opportunity the Germans had rarely passed up.

Initially, the BPF operated tactically separated from Task Force 58 so that the British could break in without affecting the rest of the carrier forces. Consequently, Admiral Vian was assigned the neutralization of Japanese airfields in the Sakishima Gunto, which his planes first attacked on 26 March. "The actual technique of attacking airfields and the aircraft upon them was something fairly novel to the majority of the Fleet Air Arm," and better photography and bombs than the British were then using were required.[22] As the BPF began to deal with the kamikazes, it soon became apparent to Americans and British alike that the British fighter direction techniques were superior. Used to intercepting the excellent pilots and planes of the Luftwaffe, Commander E.D.G. "Drunkie" Lewin RN, Vian's experienced fighter director officer, found he needed only a portion of the many defensive fighters to which the Americans had become accustomed. Of course, if their fighter direction allowed a "bogie" or two to crash a carrier, the British enjoyed the advantage of armored flight decks, through which no kamikaze could penetrate.[23]

Okinawa was the BPF's final shakedown. This fleet would form an integral part of Third Fleet in the final operations against the Japanese mainland. Looking to that campaign, scheduled to begin during the summer, the Admiralty continued sending service vessels to Sydney; a sufficient number would be available by August. Because of the need of air service ships, the first two *Majestic*-class light carriers, *Pioneer* and *Perseus*, completed in August, were finished as "aircraft maintenance ships."[24] But by autumn Britain would have carriers to spare. On 1 March 1945 Rear Admiral C. H. J. Harcourt RN, a nonaviator, was appointed Admiral Commanding 11th Aircraft Carrier Squadron and was ordered to assemble four new *Colossus*-class light carriers at Sydney to participate in the invasion of Japan.

After 8 May 1945—the day Germany surrendered to the Allies—Great Britain could devote her full military energies to the war in the Pacific.

3. Canadian Pacific Fleet

To add to Admiral King's problems, the Canadian government announced at the Quebec Conference in September 1944 its desire to enter the war against Japan as soon as Germany surrendered.[1] As early as October 1943 a Canadian Navy-Air Force proposal "that carriers be acquired and operated by the Navy" had initiated Canada in the field of fast carrier operations. But the following January the Canadian Naval Staff learned that Britain could not spare a fast carrier until January 1945. In the meantime, however, Canada received two escort carriers on loan from the Royal Navy, and in March 1944 the Navy established an air section headed by a Director of Naval Air Division, Lieutenant Commander J. S. Stead RCN.[2]

During the summer of 1944, as the American fast carriers swept westward, the British Admiralty agreed to consider Canadian requests for two new light carriers of the *Colossus* class. The British needed Canadian manpower to supply their convoy escort needs in the Atlantic, but finally in November the Admiralty agreed to commission into the Royal Canadian Navy two light carriers then building, *Ocean* in July 1945 and *Warrior* in September 1945. Beset by continued manpower problems, due partly to Prime Minister W. L. Mackenzie King's insistence that only volunteers be sent to the Pacific, the Canadians regretfully announced they could not man a light carrier before September 1945. So *Ocean* was eliminated as a Canadian ship and replaced by light carrier *Magnificent*, due for commissioning in November 1945. Britain made the formal offer—which was accepted—on 14 January 1945.[3]

Plans for an RCN Carrier Task Force went forward in Canada, but Commonwealth problems in Britain delayed action until the spring of 1945. Britain finally agreed on 23 April to proceed with the transfer of the two ships to Canadian control. In May, Commander Stead was relieved as Director of Naval Air Division by Lieutenant Commander John H. Arbick RCN, a former RCAF squadron leader without "an atom of experience in carrier based aircraft." With the end of the war in Europe, however, Arbick could begin to crystallize Canada's plans for a Pacific fleet.[4]

Arbick's problems were many, but he visited Britain and the United States during the spring to obtain relevant information. Prime Minister Mackenzie King did not make matters easy; along with the volunteer rule, this erratic gentleman opposed the idea of offensive naval aviation in general and his government refused to allow Canadian warships to operate outside the North or Central Pacific. The British insisted upon retaining operational control over the Canadian ships, but now they could not use them in the recovery of Southeast Asia and the East Indies. Also, the United States offered Canada outright 200 TBM Avengers as a gift, but since Canada did not receive Lend Lease and since her capital had to be kept within the Commonwealth, the Canadians instead purchased second-best British-built carrier bombers—Barracudas. Finally, construction was slowing down with the end of the war in Europe, and even the first carrier, *Warrior*, would not be ready for action until early in 1946.[5]

Nevertheless, planning for the Canadian Pacific Fleet continued successfully during the summer of 1945. On 11 June Commander Arbick called for two front-line fighter squadrons of Seafires and two of Fireflies for bombing. All would be trained in Great Britain. Four days later the first Seafire squadron was recommissioned in Scotland for duty aboard Canadian carriers, followed on 1 July by the first torpedo-bombing-reconnaissance squadron. Instead of getting Fireflies, however, this unit flew the lumbering Barracudas. A second Barracuda squadron was reformed on 15 August. Sixty vessels of various types would comprise the Canadian Pacific Fleet which would be based, "tropicalized," overhauled, and trained at Vancouver and Esquimalt, British Columbia. The two-carrier fleet would be integrated into the British Pacific Fleet, "due mainly to the communications and mechanical parts supply."[6]

Canada's carriers could not hope to participate in the war against Japan until the last stages of the Kyushu operation or the invasion of Honshu in the late winter or early spring of 1946. *Warrior*, launched in May 1944, might join the BPF early in the new year, but *Magnificent*, launched in November 1944, was not expected to be commissioned until the spring of 1946 and therefore would probably miss seeing action.[7] With the absorption of the CPF into the BPF for the final operation against Japan, the RCAF would be integrated into the RAF in the Pacific and Canadian ground forces would comprise part of MacArthur's American armies invading Honshu.[8]

Great Britain was hitting back at Japan with all the naval might she could muster, joined by all the Commonwealth nations. Even so, these forces would form only one small part of the mightiest fleet in history, the United States Pacific Fleet—or, as it was coming to be called in 1945, "the fleet that came to stay."

Ten:
Changing Missions: Peripheral War

The unexpected speed of the advance across the Pacific and the many facets of fast carrier activities outdistanced official Navy thinking on the roles and missions of the Fast Carrier Task Force. At the beginning of 1945, Washington-based officers were just starting to absorb the lessons of the recent carrier battles of the Philippine Sea and Cape Engaño–Leyte. To these men, destruction of the enemy fleet was still the paramount objective. In March, Bureau of Aeronautics Chief Rear Admiral Duke Ramsey told a New York audience the war would not end until the Japanese fleet came out and thus allowed the fast carriers to attack "their legitimate targets." [1] The same month in Washington, visiting Admiral Halsey was amused to learn that "certain high officials" feared a possible Japanese carrier raid on San Francisco during the United Nations Conference there. On 27 March, therefore, Admiral Nimitz appointed Halsey Commander Mid-Pacific Striking Force, "charged with interception and destruction of enemy raiding forces," and composed of carriers *Bon Homme Richard* and *Ranger* and all available surface units at Hawaii and West Coast ports.[2]

But the Japanese surface fleet was dead, and by mid February 1945 Japan was cut off from her major fuel stores. Three actual missions therefore faced the fast carriers. First, the proverbial noose had to be tighted on enemy communications, by air strikes on Japanese merchant shipping in the East China Sea. Second and most time-consuming, the carriers had to support Army and Marine Corps landing forces as they seized the last island bases surrounding Japan. This task was made monumental by the relative proximity of enemy kamikaze bases. Third, the carriers would take the war directly to Japan with pinpoint air strikes on Japanese industry, airfields, and coastal traffic. This latter mission, undertaken on a large scale after the first two were completed, would complement the massive strategic bombing campaign of Marianas-based B-29s.

The Pacific Fleet's strategic orientation thus shifted from widespread islands and the open ocean to the periphery of the Asian continent. Instead of lightning strikes to knock out one big air base like Truk or to support a landing as at Kwajalein, the fast carriers now had to destroy or neutralize massive enemy land-based air power and continental bases. This new function of carrier air forces, as one Cincpac staff officer observed, added "a new dimension to the strategic use of a fleet." [3] Task Force 58 became to the Japanese Empire what the airdromes of the British Isles were to Nazi Germany. In the Pacific, land-based tactical air could not join in the attack until new bases were seized and constructed at Iwo Jima and Okinawa. Then they could operate at relatively close range to Japan.

No actual break in the hostilities heralded new tactical requirements, but the changes were unmistakable: many more fighters, combat air patrols, picket radar destroyers, night carriers, and a greatly expanded at-sea replenishment organization. The new requirements meant the carriers had to do the one thing their admirals hated more than anything else: remain tied to a beachhead, virtually immobile, and be subjected to relentless kamikaze and bombing attacks. Losses off the Philippines in November and at Lingayen in January had given a hint of things to come.

To direct this war being fought on the periphery of Asia, Cincpac moved his headquarters forward from Pearl Harbor to Guam. During the fighting for that island in the summer of 1944 Admirals Nimitz and Forrest Sherman had gone ashore to consider moving up, and Nimitz got Admiral King to agree late in September.[4] In December Nimitz announced that Vice Admiral Towers, Deputy Cincpac-Cincpoa, would remain at Pearl Harbor to "act at my stead on all matters requiring local action," mainly logistics and administration.[5] The move began in mid-January 1945; Advanced Headquarters Guam was established on the twenty-ninth.

As of 27 January 1945, when Admirals Spruance and Mitscher resumed command from Halsey and McCain, the Pacific Fleet counted on three more Central Pacific operations. Iwo Jima, necessary as an emergency field for crippled B-29s and as an air base for long-range fighters to escort the Superforts, would be assaulted 3 February. Okinawa, followed by the seizure of other nearby Ryukyu Islands, was to be assaulted 1 March. Because General

MacArthur needed fleet units at Luzon longer than expected, these two target dates were changed respectively to 19 February and 1 April. The third operation would be a landing along the coast of China, near Shanghai, during the late summer.

The question of post-Okinawa operations led to a heated debate between the Army and Navy, with the Army Air Forces siding with the Navy. The Army, its strategy for victory based upon invasion and occupation, believed the American public would not stand for a long-drawn-out air-sea blockade of Japan. Supported by the British but opposed by the U.S. Navy, the Joint Chiefs of Staff on 11 July 1944 had decided on invasion of the main Japanese islands.[6] The Navy, however, believed that a tight air-sea blockade of Japan would neutralize that country's war-making capability, just as the Navy had done to Rabaul, Truk, and other key bypassed islands. Japan would be forced to surrender by starvation and by the devastation wrought by the B-29 raids, which included aerial mining of Japanese waters. Admiral King concluded late in September 1944 that such a blockade required an advanced base along the coast of China.[7]

Advocates of the blockade and China landing included most of the Navy's best minds, Ernie King and Savvy Cooke in Washington; Nimitz, Spruance, and Forrest Sherman in the Pacific. Bull Halsey, intellectually outside this class of strategists but assigned to study post-Okinawa operations during his rest in the two-platoon command scheme, opposed the idea of "gradual encirclement and strangulation" of Japan as "a waste of time." Alone among high-ranking admirals, Halsey advocated the direct invasion of Kyushu, Japan.[8]

Studying post-Philippines operations during the autumn of 1944, Spruance told Nimitz a landing should take place "on the China coast someplace north of Formosa." He recommended the area of Ningpo peninsula–Chusan Archipelago–Nimrod Sound just south of Shanghai and the mouth of the Yangtze River. Airfields at Ningpo and a deepwater anchorage at Nimrod would allow air attacks on occupied China and on Japan from the west. Savvy Cooke immediately agreed, and by November had sold Ernie King on the idea. At San Francisco at the end of the month, Admiral Nimitz suggested the JCS order him to carry out the operation, code-named LONGTOM. King agreed, expecting it could be done in July 1945. But Forrest Sherman pointed out that flooded rice fields at that time made 1 October a better date. Since the JCS had decided to assault Kyushu about this time, King observed that the Joint Chiefs would have to decide upon either Chusan or Kyushu—meaning either blockade or invasion. The next major landing after Okinawa should take place about six months after the surrender of Germany so that redeployed ground forces from Europe could be used. On 17 January 1945 the JCS again decided for Kyushu and told Nimitz to leave LONGTOM for future reference.[9]

The Navy would not be dissuaded; its leaders knew what a blockade could do and that countless American lives would be lost invading Japan. Savvy Cooke went one further, suggesting in March that strangulation of Japan be augmented by landings on the Shangtung peninsula of China in the Yellow Sea and the opening of a sea route to Soviet Russia through La Pérouse Strait north of Hokkaido, northernmost of the Japanese home islands. All these operations would be under over-all Navy command, being in the Central or North Pacific. The Army did not agree with these as alternatives to the Kyushu landings, tentatively set for 1 November 1945, although Admiral King pointed out that forces earmarked for Chusan could be switched to Kyushu as late as 5 August.[10]

Nimitz's planners under Forrest Sherman presented a tentative operation plan for Chusan on 27 February 1945. With the landing to take place on 20 August 1945, fast carrier forces would attack Japan until "shortly before the assault," when surprise strikes would be carried out against the Shanghai–Ningpo area. As early diversions, the four-carrier British Pacific Fleet would attack Hong Kong and Canton on 7–8 July and again on 17–18 July. These ships would then return to Ulithi, where the fast carriers were to be divided into two forces. Commencing 14 August, the "Eastern Carrier Force" (one British, two U.S. day carrier task groups) would attack targets on Kyushu and Honshu from the south. On the same day the "Western Carrier Force" (one night, two day task groups, all U.S.) would enter the East China Sea for a week of strikes against Kyushu, southern Korea, and the Shanghai–Ningpo area. Land-based air from the Marianas, Luzon, Allied China, and newly taken Iwo and Okinawa would join in.[11]

Enthusiastic about the proposed operation, the Navy submitted a formal recommendation for its implementation. Using the Cincpac study, Admiral Cooke on 8 March recommended to King that the Chusan–Ningpo landing be scheduled for 20 August. King passed it on to the Joint Chiefs officially on 20 March. Early in

April Admiral Spruance again requested its implementation. The JCS studied the proposal, along with the Army's for landing on Kyushu, and on 25 May made its decision. Kyushu would be assaulted on 1 November 1945, Chusan indefinitely postponed. Nimitz, who officially deferred further action on the plan on 30 May, in July revived LONGTOM in the event that the Kyushu landings were postponed until 1946.[12] But the project was dead, though the admirals fought on against any invasion of Japan.

Key to Navy strategic thinking was the Fast Carrier Task Force. Along with land-based air power, it was ringing Japan with enemy air forces and effectively supporting every beachhead assaulted. Between them, Allied carrier and land-based air would pound Japan into submission. The Navy and AAF believed invasion unnecessary. But the senior service, the Army, along with the British, disagreed.

1. Fast Carrier Fleet in 1945

Four new heavy fast carriers joined the Pacific Fleet during the Iwo Jima–Okinawa operations, *Bennington, Randolph*, *Shangri-la*, and *Bon Homme Richard*, and many more new carriers neared completion for participation in final operations against Japan. New commissionings of *Essex*-class carriers during the first half of 1945 were *Antietam* (CV-36) in January, *Boxer* (CV-21) in April, and *Lake Champlain* (CV-39) in June. New launchings of *Essex*es included *Kearsarge* and *Tarawa* in May. The first two *Midway*-class battle carriers were also launched, *Midway* in March and *Franklin D. Roosevelt* in April, named for the President who died that month. With even more carriers building, in March the Navy canceled the projected construction of six additional *Essex*es and two other *Midway*s.

In aircraft, the shift to more fighters and the fighter-bombers had created difficulties. Admiral King's ceiling of about 38,000 aircraft proved unrealistic as production of fighters grew, and in January Admiral Fitch asked for 5000 more planes. Though the SBD had been retired and many SB2Cs were being taken off the carriers to make room for fighters, these planes could be used as trainers or kept in reserve. But King refused to lift the ceiling, despite repeated requests by Fitch in February and again in April. The pampered aviators would simply have to economize.[1]

The major question involving fighters was the proposed changeover from F6F-5 Hellcat to the F8F-1 Bearcat. ComAirPac Admiral Murray, following Mitscher's reasoning, did not want Hellcat production stopped until after August 1945, when air superiority over Japan would be assured. But in February the Navy ordered over 2000 Bearcats from Grumman and over 1800 (redesignated F3M-1) from General Motors' Eastern Aircraft Division. To work out a satisfactory production program, on 16 February Assistant Secretary Di Gates held a conference in his office, attended by Admirals Fitch, Ramsey, and Cassady and representatives of the Grumman company. They agreed to keep up the full production of the F6F through August, about 300 per month. Thereafter production would fall off to nothing by February 1946. F8F production would increase, bypassing that of the Hellcat in November 1945. Two to four dozen F7F Tigercats would come off the assembly lines each month of 1945. Though not destined for the carriers, the F7F did qualify aboard *Antietam* in April. Still, the trusty Hellcat would remain the top carrier fighter type to the end of the year.[2]

Other fighters, especially the Corsair, figured in Navy plans. The F4U-4 Corsair, at 446 miles per hour faster than the F8F-1's 421 mph or the F6F-5's 386 mph, had begun to reach the fleet in October 1944 and was gradually being assigned to the carriers. Some were equipped with 20mm cannon, though most kept the .50-caliber machine gun. The F4U-4 went into action in April 1945. With speed so important, the Navy also held high hopes for its two jet types. In January 1945 1000 FR-1 Fireball turbojets were ordered. The same month, McDonnell's XFD-1 purely jet Phantom flew for the first time, leading to a contract for 100 of them in March.[3]

In attack planes, the Navy had reached something of a crisis. Existing fighters could not carry heavy bombloads, though the 5-inch Holy Moses rocket was a definite boon. The powerful 11.75-inch Tiny Tim, pushed by Admiral Towers, "is not what we hoped it would be," Jimmy Flatley reported to Jimmy Thach. Its accuracy was less than that of a torpedo or low-level bomb, and it created stowage problems on the carriers. Nevertheless, reorganized Air Groups 5 on *Franklin* and 10 on *Intrepid* carried Tiny Tims into the Okinawa campaign in March.[4]

Existing bombers did not have the versatility of a fighter-bomber, leading Admiral Fitch to inform Secretary Gates in December 1944: "A faster, more powerfully armed dive-bomber type aircraft is urgently required by the Fleet." Gates agreed, reinforced by Admiral McCain's request for "a suitable single seater dive bomber" in February 1945. Fitch placed great hope in the XBTM Mauler, purchased by the Navy in January, but Douglas' XBT2D Dauntless II made such a dramatic demonstration in its first flights in March 1945 that the next month the Navy ordered 548 Dauntless IIs. In February, the Navy, disappointed in the twin-engine Grumman XTB2F which it had canceled the month before, contracted Grumman to develop another new attack plane, the single-engine, two-seat XTB3F Guardian, to be fitted with a turbojet booster and to carry two torpedoes; this plane would eventually join the postwar arsenal as the antisubmarine AF-2. Douglas' XTB2D, which first flew in February, was not accepted by the Navy.[5]

For 1945, then, the fast carriers would rely upon the latest models of old standbys, the F6F-5 Hellcat, TBM-3 Avenger, SB2C-5 Helldiver, and the newly arrived F4U-4 Corsair. Late in the year the F8F-1 Bearcat would appear, to replace the Hellcat completely in 1946. If the war lasted until spring of the latter year, the BT2D Dauntless II might replace the Avengers and Helldivers altogether. One or two squadrons of FR Fireballs and BTM Maulers would also be operational by that time.

A more pressing need was fresh pilots. Until the end of 1944 attrition figures had been based on casualties alone, ignoring the factor of fatigue created by kamikaze attacks and constant air operations. The inability of air groups to finish the normal six months' combat tour led to emergency replacements. Cutback pilot training programs had to be reaugmented, forcing the Navy to admit to "one of its most embarrassing mistakes of the war." Staff medical officers were assigned to Mitscher and McCain to watch pilot health, but no permanent changes could be made under existing personnel and rotation schedules. Two studies were initiated during the spring of 1945. Rear Admiral Slats Sallada headed a board that applied a "flow principle" of replacement pilots based on the flow of aircraft logistics recommended by the Radford boards. ComAirPac laid plans for cutting the combat tour of a carrier air group to four months. But neither of these proposals could be implemented before the end of the war.[6]

Nevertheless, the carrier pilots waiting to begin the Iwo Jima operation in February 1945 were the best. All air groups were commanded by veterans, and all pilots averaged 525 hours flying time in training before combat assignment. By pitiable comparison, the average Japanese pilot had trained 275 hours in the air in December 1944. The high attrition rate would whittle this figure down to 100 hours by July 1945. In total, Task Force 58 could launch over 1000 aircraft piloted by experts.[7]

Logistically, the Pacific Fleet had achieved new heights by February 1945. So successful had been fuel and aircraft replenishment of the fast carriers by Service Squadron 10 that the concept of at-sea supply was now expanded to include food, ammunition, clothing, general stores, personnel, and salvage services. The general logistics support group, Servron 6, was created on 5 December 1944 and earmarked for first use during the Iwo Jima operation. Servron 10 fuel storage and service ships remained at Ulithi, but ships' stores and repair base facilities were being transferred to the new naval base at Leyte–Samar, then under construction. As before, Servrons 6 and 10 remained under Commander Service Force Pacific, Vice Admiral Calhoun, with aviation personnel and material under ComAirPac, Vice Admiral Murray. With Calhoun's pending relief in March 1945, Secretary of the Navy Forrestal wanted Vice Admiral Towers to coordinate the great logistics machine, but the admirals wanted him to remain as Nimitz's deputy. Instead, Vice Admiral W. W. "Poco" Smith got the job.[8]

This expanded replenishment system would give the fast carrier task force even greater mobility. Servrons 6 and 10 gave up using the bases at Saipan, Guam, and Kossol Passage in February 1945 in favor of concentrating at Ulithi. When the base at Leyte–Samar was completed in April, the headquarters of the logistics support groups would be moved there. Until June, however, the fast carriers continued to use Eniwetok, Guam, and Ulithi.[9] The British Fleet would also use these bases, along with Manus. With new bases to support its very sophisticated fleet of supply vessels, Task Force 58 could remain at sea weeks, even months, before returning to base. However, the limiting, unknown factor would again be fatigue of the crews.

The Navy's command structure began significant personnel changes as the war entered what had to be its last full year if not less. Starting at the top, Congress in December 1944 authorized the new rank of Fleet Admiral for four of the Navy's top commanders. So promoted were Admiral Leahy, Chief of Staff to the President and chairman of the JCS; Admiral King, Cominch-CNO; and Admiral Nimitz, Cincpac-Cincpoa. A fourth name was not put forth by the Navy, though several politicians wondered why Admiral Halsey, Commander Third Fleet, did not rate promotion. There were at least three reasons: Halsey's fumble at Leyte Gulf, his December typhoon, and the fact that Admiral Spruance, Commander Fifth Fleet, rated the promotion equally if not more. The Navy could not promote both, so it promoted neither. New five-star Generals of the Army were George C. Marshall, Army Chief of Staff; Dwight D. Eisenhower, Supreme Commander Allied Expeditionary Force (Europe); MacArthur, Commander-in-Chief Southwest Pacific; and H. H. Arnold, Chief of the Army Air Forces.[10]

The aviators still blamed Ernie King for keeping a high-ranking pioneer flyer off the Cominch staff or from reaching four-star rank. To a lesser degree they blamed Secretary Forrestal and personnel chief Admiral Jacobs, and they felt Jake Fitch was too weak as DCNO (Air).[11] Their obvious choice was Jack Towers, who still did not see eye-to-eye with King. In November 1944 Secretary Forrestal and King had agreed that the advisory General Board should be flushed of its ancient, retired members and made up of younger combat-experienced admirals.[12] Aviators would certainly qualify. One such individual due for leave and rumored for the General Board was Rear Admiral Ted Sherman. But such a leader could hardly be spared from combat, and his leave was postponed until July.[13] In fact, an air admiral in high places and a youthful General Board would have to wait until the postwar period.

In the Pacific a major controversy was developing over the divided command. MacArthur would complete the Luzon–Philippines mop-up by the summer, while Nimitz would direct the Iwo, Okinawa, and possible Chusan operations. After that, Southwest and Central Pacific theaters would merge for the final campaign against Japan. Unity of command was essential, and both MacArthur and Nimitz wanted it, while the AAF preferred autonomy alongside Army and Navy. General Marshall in the winter of 1944–45 advocated that Nimitz command all naval forces and MacArthur all ground forces in the Pacific, a solution the JCS finally approved in April.

At the fleet level, Spruance's Fifth Fleet staff now became well-balanced. Rear Admiral Arthur C. Davis, a veteran naval pilot, became chief of staff. Captain Bobby Morse, fleet aviation officer, with nothing to do under the old regime, managed a transfer. His relief was a celebrated hunter-killer leader from the Atlantic, Captain A. B. Vosseller. These respresentatives of aviation on Spruance's staff led to a new closeness between Fifth Fleet and Task Force 58 staffs. Art Davis and Abe Vosseller enjoyed a great deal of contact with Mitscher, Arleigh Burke, and Jimmy Flatley. Flatley, Mitscher's operations officer, and Vosseller saw each other constantly, as both—along with Jimmy Thach—had gone through flight training together.[14]

All fast carrier division commanders by February 1945 were combat veterans. ComCarDiv 1, Ted Sherman, had his leave postponed to command TG 58.3. ComCarDiv 2, Dave Davison, took over TG 58.2. ComCarDiv 3, Tommy Sprague, had already reported in "makee-learn" status. ComCarDiv 4, Gerry Bogan, went home on one month's leave. ComCarDiv 5, Jocko Clark, returned to be Mitscher's right-hand man as CTG 58.1. ComCarDiv 6, Arthur Radford, continued to command at sea as CTG 58.4. ComCarDiv 7, Rear Admiral Matt Gardner, led the night carriers as CTG 58.5. On 1 January 1945 the Carrier Training Squadron Pacific was established to control carrier air group training operations out of Hawaii and San Diego. Training CarDivs 11 and 12 were commanded by Rear Admiral Ralph Jennings during the spring and by Rear Admiral Freddy McMahon during the summer.

Escort Carriers Pacific remained under the command of Rear Admiral Cal Durgin, and its task units were again commanded by former fast carrier captains: Ziggy Sprague, Felix Stump, Bill Sample, Ernie Litch, George Henderson, and Harold Martin.

Other air admirals held down rear areas, either because they deserved a rest from combat, because they had failed to measure up as combat leaders, or because they could not pull the right strings to get assigned to combat jobs. They all lent their administrative expertise as backup to the combat operations. For instance, Rear Admiral Black Jack Reeves took over the new Naval Air Transport Service, based in San Francisco. Six rear-area air admirals conferred on aviation matters at San Diego on 9–11 February: Monty Montgomery, reporting after his injury as Commander Fleet Air West Coast; Keen Harrill, being detached from that post to virtual exile as atoll commander at Kwajalein; Sam Ginder, Commander Carrier Transport Squadron, which ferried planes across the Pacific; Van Ragsdale, Fleet Air Commander at Alameda; John Ballentine, Fleet Air Commander at Seattle; and John Dale Price, whom Ernie King wanted in carriers but who never broke in despite his ability.[15] Finally, isolated throughout the United States in various training and fleet air commands were such long-forgotten air admirals as Pownall, Bernhard, Hardison, and McFall.

Tactically, the Fast Carrier Task Force underwent no major changes for Iwo and Okinawa. Current Tactical Orders and Doctrine, reissued on 1 May 1945 for the last time during the war, again stressed tactical concentration for mutual antiaircraft protection.[16] The night carrier task groups changed slightly. Light carrier *Independence* had proved too small for such rugged operations; said night air group commander Caldwell: "All I can say is that we got away with it!"[17] *Independence* was therefore ordered back to Pearl to reconvert to a day carrier. *Bataan*, working up as a night carrier, received similar orders. Instead, the two prewar heavy carriers *Enterprise* and *Saratoga* comprised Night CarDiv 7, although "*Sara*" reported to Ulithi with two dozen day fighters along with her night planes. Kamikazes required round-the-clock flight operations.

On 7 February 1945 Vice Admiral Mitscher issued a memorandum to his admirals concerning fast carrier tactics. It contained nothing new, but summarized the need for concentration, which Ted Sherman took somewhat as criticism, for he had the bad habit of constantly falling out of formation behind the other task groups. Mitscher concluded that the optimum size of each fast carrier task group should be four carriers: three CV and one CVL. With this Sherman disagreed, since he believed that more concentrated carriers required a comparatively smaller combat air patrol. Sherman's veteran operations officer, Commander R. H. Dale, replied to the memo by noting to Sherman: "To increase the striking force and efficiency I believe that up to 8 carriers can be operated efficiently in one task group." But as long as Mitscher commanded, four was the theoretical limit.[18]

Tactical mobility, maximum defense, and intelligent command would be absolutely essential for in the next operation Task Force 58 would attack not only Formosa, the Ryukyus, and Kyushu, but Tokyo itself.

The other tactical concern of the carriers would be supporting the amphibious forces. Close air support reached full maturity at Iwo Jima, with Commander Air Support Control Units now administratively subordinate to the amphibious commander, Vice Admiral Turner, rather than to ComAirPac. Captain Dick Whitehead remained in over-all control of air support from the amphibious command ship, while Captain E. C. Parker controlled "advanced" air support prior to the landing and Colonel Vernon E. Megee USMC led the Landing Force Air Support Control Unit which went ashore. After excellent performances in close support at Bougainville, Peleliu, Leyte, and Luzon, the Marine aviators would take command of all tactical air—Navy, Marine, and AAF—after the beachhead had been secured, at Iwo, Okinawa, and Chusan if it took place. Duplicating Whitehead's shipboard organization in a tent ashore, Colonel Megee would experience the same problems.[19]

The last two island targets would be attacked by the Fast Carrier Task Force at its peak in efficiency, tactics, training, and experience. These attributes would be more important than ever before, thanks to the fanatical Japanese defenders of Iwo and Okinawa and to the unrelenting attacks by the Kamikaze Corps.

2. *Kamikazes at Iwo and Okinawa*

The day before he plummeted into the sea in glory, kamikaze pilot Yoshi Miyagi wrote: "I am nothing but a particle of iron attracted by a magnet—the American aircraft carrier."[1] Vice Admiral Onishi, kamikaze leader, believed one to three kamikazes could sink an enemy carrier or battleship, whereas it took eight bombers escorted by 16 fighters to achieve the same result by conventional bombing.[2] Against this philosophy, the fast carrier support of Iwo Jima and Okinawa would require the most tedious and exhausting carrier air operations of the war.

Air defense was half the problem; softening the beach and supporting the troops demanded equal attention. The Marines wanted ten days of prelanding bombardment of Iwo Jima by gun ships and carriers, but Admiral Spruance gave only three. His reason was twofold. First, Iwo had received intensive shelling and bombing from ships and long-range medium bombers for ten weeks prior to the assault, so that the island seemed already heavily damaged. Secondly, Spruance wanted to strike Tokyo with the fast carriers, a project Halsey had not been able to carry out earlier because of heavy commitments in the Philippines. Along with the sheer satisfaction of attacking Japan's capital city with single-engine planes, the raid would tie up Japanese planes at home and prevent their interference with the landings.

The carrier pilots got the best prelanding briefings to date. At Ulithi from 3 to 9 February 1945 Whitehead's and Megee's air support experts worked out details with ground commanders and briefed carrier pilots on close air support techniques. Colonel Megee and Lieutenant Colonel Millington of *Essex,* both Marine flyers, formulated a low-level strafing attack to take place as the troops went ashore. Combined with Marine-air-sea rehearsals held since the previous November, the Air Support Control Units were ready to assist ground forces at Iwo. Said Admiral Turner, the amphibious commander, after the operation: "Briefings such as these have, by universal concurrence among those concerned, proved highly beneficial and have resulted in well conducted and coordinated attacks. . . ." [3]

Task Force 58 sortied from Ulithi on 10 February, and held a rehearsal with Marines at Tinian. Then it headed for Tokyo:

FLEET ORGANIZATION

Cincpac-Cincpoa—Fleet Admiral C. W. Nimitz*
Commander Fifth Fleet—Admiral R. A. Spruance*
  Chief of Staff—Rear Admiral A. C. Davis
 CTF 58—Vice Admiral M. A. Mitscher (Com1stFasCarForPac)
   Chief of Staff—Commodore A. A. Burke*
  CTG 58.1—Rear Admiral J. J. Clark (ComCarDiv 5)
   Hornet—Captain A. K. Doyle; Air Group 11
   Wasp—Captain O. A. Weller; Air Group 81
   Bennington—Captain J. B. Sykes; Air Group 82
   Belleau Wood—Captain W. G. Tomlinson; Air Group 30
  CTG 58.2—Rear Admiral R. E. Davison (ComCarDiv 2)
   Lexington—Captain T. H. Robbins, Jr.; Air Group 9
   Hancock—Captain R. F. Hickey; Air Group 7
   San Jacinto—Captain M. H. Kernodle; Air Group 45
  CTG 58.3—Rear Admiral F. C. Sherman (ComCarDiv 1)
   Essex—Captain C. W. Wieber; Air Group 4
   Bunker Hill—Captain G. A. Seitz; Air Group 84
   Cowpens—Captain G. H. DeBaun; Air Group 46
  CTG 58.4—Rear Admiral A. W. Radford (ComCarDiv 6)
   Yorktown—Captain T. S. Combs; Air Group 3
   Randolph—Captain F. L. Baker; Air Group 12
   Langley—Captain J. F. Wegforth; Air Group 23
   Cabot—Captain W. W. Smith; Air Group 29
  CTG 58.5 (night)—Rear Admiral M. B. Gardner (ComCarDiv 7)
   Enterprise—Captain G. B. H. Hall; Night Air Group 90
   Saratoga—Captain L. A. Moebus; Night Air Group 53

* Nonaviator.

To the chagrin of the Marines, after he had promised to leave two battleships with the bombardment force, Spruance took all eight of his battleships with him, plus his one new "battle cruiser," five heavy and 11 light cruisers. The Marines could appreciate that "antiaircraft gun platforms are essential ingredients of a fast carrier force," but they saw no need for arming all these battleships for a fleet action. Carrying armor-piercing shells, six of the eight battlewagons would be unable to provide shore bombardment when Task Force 58 returned to Iwo from Tokyo.[4] A surface battle was highly unlikely since Japan had no major fleet left to fight; Admiral Spruance and Admiral Lee, who was now reduced to the battleship squadron commander, should have taken appropriate measures to arm their battleships for shore bombardment. Fleet doctrine was changing rapidly, making it difficult for men like Spruance to realize and accept the fact that surface battles were probably a thing of the past.

Heavy weather, scouting submarines, and land-based patrol planes helped Task Force 58 keep its approach to Japan a secret from the enemy. Then, at dawn on 16 February, 60 miles off the coast and twice that distance from Tokyo, Mitscher launched his planes. As skipper of the old *Hornet*, Pete Mitscher had been the last carrier captain to send planes against Tokyo—Doolittle's raiders almost three years before. The sky over Honshu was overcast and cold; machine guns tended to freeze in these northern latitudes. Mitscher had warned his new pilots to concentrate on teamwork, but seemingly reluctant enemy Zeroes caused green Hellcat pilots to break formation to seek "dogfights." "The old lesson was learned the hard way again," lamented Commander F. J. Brush of *Wasp*'s Air Group 81; five of his best pilots were lost as a result of their eagerness for aerial combat. The fighter sweep battled Japanese planes from the coast to Tokyo. So preoccupied were the fighters that they had no time to strafe, but the bombers that followed delivered their attacks successfully. The Japanese lost over 300 planes in the air that day, including several that were deloused over the TOMCAT destroyer pickets. But Task Force 58 lost 60 aircraft, a high loss rate after comparable successes in the Philippines. One pilot loss was Air Group 9's skipper, Phil Torrey, who had led the group over Rabaul and Truk.[5]

The rest of the Tokyo operation was anticlimactic. Matt Gardner's night fighters kept enemy planes around Tokyo grounded, but his night radar-equipped Avengers failed to uncover any shipping. Foul weather permitted only one strike on the morning of the seventeenth. The visit to Tokyo accomplished comparatively little, thanks to the weather and active Japanese interceptors. But some carrier commanders blamed Mitscher's tactics as well. With so many fighters allowed for combat air patrols, the many new fighters could not be employed offensively. Admirals Radford and Clark and Captain Artie Doyle of *Hornet* brought up the old idea that the nine Avengers on each light carrier be transferred to the heavy carriers and that the light carriers carry all fighters, a full 36-Hellcat squadron. This change would eliminate special training for the oddly comprised light carrier air groups and raise the morale of their pilots as they became equal partners in attack roles rather than absorbing mostly routine patrol duties. The recommendation began its trip up through channels.[6]

Swinging south, the fast carriers shifted to close support at Iwo. Radford's planes bombed Chichi Jima on 18 February, and two battleships and three cruisers peeled off to join the bombardment force of five old battleships, 11 escort carriers, four cruisers, and ten destroyers. After dawn on the nineteenth, just as the Marines prepared to land, Millington's Marine Corsairs from *Essex* and planes from the rest of Sherman's and Davison's task groups swept in to strafe and bomb the beach and the menacing Mount Suribachi. Each Hellcat carried six 5-inch rockets and one 500-pound bomb, the Helldivers and Avengers all bombs and some napalm that did not always ignite. The Marines welcomed the fast carrier pilots, whom they felt to be better-trained and more knowledgeable about close support tactics than those on the escort carriers. From 8:05 to 8:15 A.M. the naval gunfire stopped, allowing the planes to deliver their excellent strafing attack. *Cowpens* fighters discovered that the eastern side of Suribachi "was so pockmarked from Naval shells and aerial bombs that it resembled a lunar landscape from the air." [7]

But Iwo was barely scratched; digging into caves, the Japanese came out when the Marines stepped into the murderous shifting volcanic sand at the edge of the beach. Inch by inch, suffering terrible casualties, the Marines pushed inland. Task Force 58 remained on station for three days, providing the most effective air support of the operation. Marine Corps artillery observers flew off escort carriers during the day and from *Saratoga* at night to spot targets, an old Mediterranean practice being put to good use in the Pacific for the first time at Iwo. Despite the fact that the support air request radio net from air liaison teams ashore to Captain Whitehead was always overcrowded, as long as Task Force 58 was on hand every request for air support was answered.[8]

Japanese air attacks were minor and easily broken up by defensive day fighters and by *Enterprise* fighters at night on the nineteenth and twentieth. On the morning of the twenty-first Admiral Mitscher detached *Saratoga* to provide night defensive cover for the landing forces; she was assigned to Admiral Durgin's escort carrier task group in the afternoon. The men of the jeep carriers regarded "*Sara*'s" presence with misgivings; her less-maneuverable 40,000 tons provided an inviting target for enemy bombers and kamikazes. These fears were well founded. Shortly after *Saratoga* joined Durgin, a 50-plane attack struck the Iwo shipping. Staged through the Bonins, at 5 P.M. the kamikazes dived on "*Sara.*" Within three minutes, three bombs and two suicide planes smacked into the old ship, but she got underway and survived another bomb hit two hours later. *Saratoga* lost 123 men killed, many others wounded, and 36 planes destroyed. The same attack claimed one escort carrier, sunk by a lone kamikaze.[9]

Although night carriers provided Task Force 58 with a defensive and strike capability at night, they had to be protected round the clock. *Saratoga*, not covered at Iwo, limped to Eniwetok, then to the United States for major repairs, and out of the war. Even if she were repaired in time for return to the Pacific, she could never again be exposed to another enemy air attack. *Saratoga*, like *Ranger*, would be useful only as a training carrier. "*Sara*'s" departure also ended the two-carrier night task group. *Enterprise*, reporting to Admiral Durgin, kept planes aloft for 174 consecutive hours over Iwo between 23 February and 2 March—a terrific strain on pilots and ship's crew. This also stripped Task Force 58—which departed Iwo late on the twenty-second—of any night carrier. The forthcoming trials of the "Big E" would further tax its personnel. The new *Bonhomme Richard*, still in the United States, was designated as a night carrier to replace *Saratoga*, but any two-carrier night task group could not be reformed until the fall of 1945.

Effective close support at Iwo slacked off in the absence of the fast carriers. Fortunately, the Japanese launched no other large air attack, but the escort carriers still could not meet all requests. On 1 March Colonel Megee set up his control unit ashore, which improved the situation somewhat, and on the sixth the first P-51

Mustangs of the Seventh Air Force landed at the captured air strip on Iwo. Ignorant of close air support techniques, these eager AAF jockeys took lessons from the gyrenes and were soon winning praises for their precision low-altitude work. On 11 March the escort carriers withdrew to prepare for Okinawa, and three days later the P-51s flew their last support missions. Major Japanese resistance on Iwo Jima ended on 26 March.[10]

Iwo Jima was a resounding success. Despite the heavy Marine losses due to the dug-in Japanese troops, the new air base became a godsend for the B-29s. On 4 March, while the fighting still raged, the first crippled Superfort landed at Iwo; scores more followed until the end of the war. On 7 April 100 long-range P-51s arrived to begin escorting the B-29s to Japan. Fast carrier air support had been near-perfect, and AAF performance excellent after proper instruction by Marine Corps target coordinators. So important had air support become that the Navy decided to upgrade that command billet to flag rank. At the end of the operation, Rear Admiral Mel Pride, former skipper of *Belleau Wood*, reported to Captain Whitehead in "makee-learn" status.

Fulfilling their strategic role, the fast carriers returned to strike Japan. But bad weather led to canceled strikes for Tokyo on 25 February and for Nagoya the next day. Heading south toward Okinawa, Task Force 58 paused to refuel from Servron 6. This inactivity was something of a waste and led Ted Sherman to lament: "Ho hum, this war is getting awfully tame, as far as we carriers are concerned." [11] Mitscher sent Radford's task group back to Ulithi, then on 1 March used the other carriers to bomb and to take good photographs of Okinawa beaches in clear weather. Then the other groups turned south. TF 58 anchored at Ulithi on the fourth, ending fast carrier support of the Iwo Jima operation.

At Ulithi Admiral Mitscher reshuffled his forces and prepared for the ominous forthcoming campaign. Conferring with his task group commanders aboard flagship *Bunker Hill* on 10 March, Mitscher remarked that he was at a complete loss about what the Japanese might do next. For all he knew, he said, they might employ poison gas. The enemy came up with such a surprise the following night when a long-distance kamikaze flew all the way to Ulithi and crashed into *Randolph*, lighted while taking on ammunition. The big carrier was put out of action for a month. In addition, along with *Saratoga*'s departure, *Lexington* and *Cowpens* went home for overhaul. Many air groups rotated out, and with the new ones arrived overhauled *Franklin*, *Intrepid*, and *Bataan*. Though Mitscher strongly believed in the three CV–one CVL task group for optimum antiaircraft defense, he agreed to let Ted Sherman—backed by Radford—operate a larger task group if the occasion arose. He also rejected the idea of a night carrier task group, using *Enterprise* only for dusk combat air patrol. But Okinawa might lead to other changes, depending on the Japanese reaction to this landing so close to their homeland.[12]

Though Mitscher kept the same task group commanders, Clark, Davison, Sherman, and Radford, he wanted two admirals on standby status to take over in any emergency. He therefore recalled Gerry Bogan, cutting short Bogan's leave at 16 days, which was obviously displeasing to the pugnacious Bogan, who hoisted his flag in *Franklin* in Davison's group. Tommy Sprague wore his flag in *Wasp*, in Clark's group; he was scheduled to relieve Clark in the middle of the operation. Matt Gardner remained aboard *Enterprise*, attached to Radford's group. The reshuffled Task Force 58 sortied from Ulithi on 14 March.

Again Mitscher headed for Japan, this time to strike airfields on

FLEET ORGANIZATION

CTF 58—Vice Admiral M. A. Mitscher
- CTG 58.1—Rear Admiral J. J. Clark
  - *Hornet*—Captain A. K. Doyle; Air Group 17
  - *Bennington*—Captain J. B. Sykes; Air Group 82
  - *Wasp*—Captain O. A. Weller; Air Group 86
  - *Belleau Wood*—Captain W. G. Tomlinson; Air Group 30
- CTG 58.2—Rear Admiral R. E. Davison
  - *Hancock*—Captain R. F. Hickey; Air Group 6
  - *Franklin*—Captain L. E. Gehres; Air Group 5
  - *San Jacinto*—Captain M. H. Kernodle; Air Group 45
  - *Bataan*—Captain J. B. Heath; Air Group 47
- CTG 58.3—Rear Admiral F. C. Sherman
  - *Essex*—Captain C. W. Wieber; Air Group 83
  - *Bunker Hill*—Captain G. A. Seitz; Air Group 84
  - *Cabot*—Captain W. W. Smith; Air Group 29
- CTG 58.4—Rear Admiral A. W. Radford
  - *Yorktown*—Captain T. S. Combs; Air Group 9
  - *Intrepid*—Captain G. E. Short; Air Group 10
  - *Langley*—Captain J. F. Wegforth; Air Group 23
  - *Enterprise*—Captain G. B. H. Hall; Night Air Group 90

Kyushu and the remnants of the Japanese fleet at Kure; but the Japanese were waiting. While carrier planes bombed and strafed Kyushu on 18 March, Japanese kamikazes and bombs scored near-misses and damage to *Enterprise*, *Yorktown*, and *Intrepid*. The next day Mitscher's strikes were met over Kure by a special squadron of new well-armored, fast Shiden-kai fighters piloted by veteran instructors under the leadership of distinguished carrier tactician Captain Minoru Genda. The sudden appearance of aggressive enemy fighters, superior to the Hellcats and flown by professionals, surprised the American planes, several of which were shot down.[13] These few planes, however, could not stop the hundreds of U.S. carrier aircraft, and Mitscher's bombers attacked their first enemy carriers since Leyte, five months before. They heavily damaged light carrier *Ryuho* and inflicted light damage to the new heavy carrier *Amagi* and battleship *Yamato*.

Simultaneously, on the morning of 19 March, Japanese bombers and kamikazes counterattacked with devastating effect. Covered by a low layer of haze, enemy planes within minutes of each other dropped two bombs on *Franklin* and one on *Wasp*. Turned into a blazing inferno of exploding ammunition, including the new big Tiny Tim rockets, *Franklin* seemed on the verge of sinking. But the heroic efforts of Captain Les Gehres and the crew, of whom over 700 perished, saved the valiant ship.[14] One of those lost was Captain Arnold J. Isbell, the famed Atlantic hunter-killer leader and prospective skipper of *Yorktown*. *Wasp* suffered much damage and over 200 dead. Task Force 58 withdrew slowly to cover its wounded vessels and remained under sporadic air attack. On the afternoon of the twentieth friendly antiaircraft guns started fires that caused damage to *Enterprise*, and the next day Jocko Clark's fighters shot down a flight of 18 enemy bombers carrying Oka, or baka, piloted rocket bombs 60 miles from the force.

Badly hurt by these attacks, TF 58 was reorganized on 22 March. Admiral Mitscher made TG 58.2 a "crippled" task group of *Franklin*, *Wasp*, and *Enterprise* bound for Ulithi. Clark kept four carriers, *Hornet*, *Belleau Wood*, *San Jacinto*, and *Bennington*, to which ship Tommy Sprague shifted his flag from *Wasp*. Radford also commanded four carriers, *Yorktown*, *Intrepid*, *Langley*, and newly arrived *Independence* (Captain N. M. Kindell; Air Group 46), now a day carrier. But Ted Sherman got the five-carrier task group, *Essex*, *Bunker Hill*, *Hancock*, *Bataan*, and *Cabot*. Sherman was jubilant, for he could test his tactical theory: the larger a task group the better. "I have long advocated carriers," he observed, "and now have a chance to work with 5 to see how it works out. I believe 6–8 CV's can be efficiently operated in one task group and maybe more [*sic*]." [15]

Thus reformed, Task Force 58 began the prelanding shelling of Okinawa. With three fast carriers taken out of the war inside of one month—*Saratoga*, *Franklin*, and *Wasp*—small wonder that Admirals Nimitz and Spruance welcomed the arrival of the four British carriers on 25 March.

FLEET ORGANIZATION

Task Force 57—Vice Admiral Sir H. B. Rawlings RN*
  CTG 57.2—Rear Admiral Sir Philip L. Vian RN*
    Chief of Staff—Captain J. P. Wright RN**
    Indomitable—Captain J. A. S. Eccles RN*
    Victorious—Captain M. M. Denny RN*
    Illustrious—Captain C. E. Lambe RN*
    Indefatigable—Captain Q. D. Graham RN*

* Nonaviator.
** Naval Aviation Observer.

With 500 enemy planes destroyed during these strikes on Japan, the fast carriers slowed down to give Okinawa a week of bombing prior to the 1 April assault. The task groups rotated between fueling and striking until the first, maintaining almost constant alerts as kamikazes and conventional bombers continually approached the force. Visual fighter direction took precedence over that of radar, as the Japanese had discovered U.S. radar could not see them coming in low singly or in small groups at very high altitude.[16] No enemy hits occurred, however, whereas Jocko Clark's planes sank an eight-ship convoy north of Okinawa on 24 March.[17] Four days later a false report of an enemy fleet sortie added to the excitement. While combat air patrols fended off airborne attackers, dive bombers and torpedo planes worked over Okinawa. *Intrepid* planes, the only air group left with the new Tiny Tim rockets after *Franklin*'s departure, fired eight Tims on the twenty-fourth and more on succeeding days. Results were inconclusive, and the big, inaccurate 11.75-inch rocket was thereafter withdrawn from the carriers. With the carrier attacks, Okinawa got seven days of shelling by the bombardment ships. Beginning 24 March, and for exactly three months, Durgin's escort carriers—always numbering between 12 and 17—stood off the island.

Task Force 57, the British carriers, undertook the neutralization of the Sakishima Gunto, a staging base of islands south of Okinawa for Japanese planes shuttling between Kyushu and Formosa. On the twenty-sixth and twenty-seventh Admiral Vian launched his short-range Seafires on combat air patrol and sent his Hellcats, Corsairs, Fireflies, and Avengers to bomb Miyako Island. While the British ships withdrew to fuel on the twenty-eighth, Durgin's escort carriers filled in the gap. Resuming its Sakishima strikes on the thirty-first, Task Force 57 came under its first kamikaze attack. Duncan Lewin's fighter direction was superb, though it quickly became apparent that the British 20mm and two-pounder antiaircraft guns could not stop a kamikaze after it began its dive. The British needed 40mm Bofors and more experienced gunners.[18] But their armored flight decks saved them. A kamikaze crashed *Indefatigable* at the base of the island superstructure, killing several men, but did not seriously impair flight operations. The British continued on station until 3 April, when relieved by TG 58.1 to retire for replenishment. The British Pacific Fleet had shown its mettle, and Admiral Nimitz congratulated it for its "illustrious" performance. To which Vice Admiral Rawlings replied that the enemy would be pursued "indomitably, indefatigably, and victoriously." [19]

Lieutenant General Buckner and Tenth Army, including two Marine divisions, went ashore on 1 April against comparatively light opposition under cover of more than 500 planes from the escort and fast carriers. Though the pilots had had no real chance to rehearse the operation, the experience at Iwo Jima was fresh in their minds, and Whitehead's people had been able to prebrief them at Ulithi 10–15 March and some escort carrier squadrons at Leyte on the nineteenth. So close support was carried out efficiently.[20] To intercept incoming enemy strikes, Whitehead had 19 specially trained fighter director teams stationed aboard radar picket destroyers around Okinawa for his "radar-defense-in-depth" when the enemy air forces counterattacked. These ships became prime targets.[21] The enemy, however, as at Peleliu and Iwo, was dug in to the rear waiting to hit the troops after they were established ashore. This relative breather ashore allowed Task Force 58 to concentrate on its own defense during a first hectic week of April.

The Japanese hesitated before reacting to the invasion, partly because they believed their own overblown accounts of damage to the U.S. fleet, but on 6 April they struck back at Task Force 58.[22] Over 350 kamikazes attacked in small groups, leading Mitscher to stow his bombers below and to scramble all fighters. Jocko Clark's and Ted Sherman's carriers were under constant attack, despite the many airborne fighters. Superb gunnery saved the force, although *Belleau Wood* suffered a near-miss. That ship's two dozen Hellcats of Fighting 30 shot down 47 of the 355 Japanese planes destroyed, leading Captain Red Tomlinson to signal Admiral Clark: "Does this exceed the bag limit?" "Negative," Jocko answered. "There is no limit. This is open season. Well done." [23]

At the height of this free-for-all, Mitscher learned that Japanese superbattleship *Yamato* had sortied from the Inland Sea for a one-way suicide run to Okinawa. With bombers inactive on the sixth, a surface battle would have been necessary. But the big ship and its retinue of one light cruiser and eight destroyers posed no threat until the seventh. That day Mitscher launched search-strikes, arming the Helldivers with 1000- and 250-pound bombs and the fighters with 500-pounders. After the demonstrated effectiveness of torpedoes against the Japanese fleet in June and October, Mitscher loaded the Avengers with "fish." This would probably be the last chance for torpedo planes to battle an enemy capital ship. Early in the afternoon Jocko Clark's Turkeys planted four torpedoes into *Yamato*, which developed a list. Overcast skies eliminated any chance for coordinated attacks, but an hour later Arthur Radford's TBMs dropped six more fish into *Yamato*. At 2:23 P.M. the great ship rolled over, exploded, and sank. For naval aviation, the sinking of *Yamato* was final proof of the obsolescence of the battleship. In addition, the carrier planes sank the light cruiser and four of the destroyers.

During the night of 7–8 April Rear Admiral Davison returned from Ulithi with two repaired carriers, leading Mitscher to reorganize Task Force 58 for the second time in the operation. Clark's TG 58.1 and Sherman's TG 58.3 remained the same, while Radford's TG 58.4 gave *Independence* to Davison's reformed TG 58.2: *Randolph*, *Enterprise*, and *Independence*.[24]

The kamikazes, mostly based at Kyushu, were relentless, however, and while Task Force 58 tried to support the now-heavily engaged troops on Okinawa, Japanese air forces inflicted more damage to the fast carriers. Kamikazes rammed into *Hancock* on 7 April, *Enterprise* on the eleventh, and *Intrepid* on the sixteenth, in addition to many picket destroyers. On 17 April Mitscher again altered his task composition, dissolving TG 58.2 and sending Davison back to Ulithi with the damaged *Hancock* and *Enterprise;* TF 58 had again lost its night carrier. *Cabot* was also detached for an overhaul, as was *Illustrious,* relieved on the fourteenth by *Formidable* (Captain Phillip Ruck-Keene RN).

From 17 April to 28 May 1945 the fast carriers underwent no further major task reorganization. On 28 April, however, Mitscher sent TG 58.1 back to Ulithi for a ten-day rest; Jocko Clark was scheduled to be relieved by Tommy Sprague after a long tour at sea. But Mitscher would not let his right-hand man go until the completion of the operation, and Clark stayed on.

FLEET ORGANIZATION

Task Force 58—Vice Admiral M. A. Mitscher
  TG 58.1—Rear Admiral J. J. Clark
    Hornet, Belleau Wood, San Jacinto, Bennington (Rear Admiral T. L. Sprague aboard)
  TG 58.3—Rear Admiral F. C. Sherman
    Essex, Bunker Hill, Bataan, Randolph (Rear Admiral G. F. Bogan aboard); *Monterey* joined on 12 May
  TG 58.4—Rear Admiral A. W. Radford
    Yorktown, Intrepid, Langley, Independence;
    Shangri-la (Captain J. D. Barner; Air Group 85) joined 24 April; *Langley* went home for overhaul 18 May
  TG 57.2—Rear Admiral Sir Philip Vian RN
    Indomitable, Victorious, Formidable, Indefatigable

On Okinawa, the Army and Marines battled fanatical Japanese troops, especially at the almost impregnable Shuri Castle. The carriers flew all air support missions until the second week after the assault when Colonel Megee's air support unit got ashore and over 100 Marine Corps F4Us occupied the two operational airstrips on Okinawa. This was the vanguard of the Tactical Air Force Tenth Army (TAF), commanded by a major general of Marines. But these planes were needed to combat the increasing kamikaze attacks, so that the carriers had to be tied down at the beach to do most of the close support work. On 18 April Rear Admiral Pride relieved Captain Whitehead—who was due for a carrier command—as Commander Air Support Control Units. The next day he coordinated a massive air strike planned by Whitehead on the Shuri defenses. The strike consisted of 650 planes—300 from Task Force

58—but these could not reach the caves which protected the enemy ground forces, and Shuri held.[25]

"In general, ground troops of both services preferred land-based planes to those from the carriers" at Okinawa,[26] but the fact was that the carriers *had* to remain on station as long as land-based Marine air could not fill close support requirements alone. Upon going ashore initially, Colonel Megee had taken his authority from General Buckner and had refused to work through Navy channels and Captain Whitehead. When Admiral Nimitz learned this, he informed Admiral Turner: "Tell Megee to report to Whitehead or return to Pearl Harbor." [27] Megee fell into line, and channeled all requests through command ship *Eldorado*, contrary to the Marines' preference to coordinate their own air. When Nimitz visited Okinawa, General Buckner told him the campaign was on *terra firma,* hence an Army affair. Replied Cincpac: "Yes, but ground though it may be, I'm losing a ship and a half a day. So if this line isn't moving within five days, we'll get someone here to move it so we can all get out from under these stupid air attacks." [28]

Admirals Spruance and Mitscher were similarly fed up with the Army engineers' failure to construct airfields ashore as rapidly as the Navy's Construction Battalions (Seabees) had done on other islands. Until more fighter strips were available, the fast carriers and picket destroyers had to carry the hazardous burden of defending and supporting the Okinawa landing forces. During a periodic check on the construction of the airfields, Captain Abe Vosseller of Spruance's staff learned one day that General Hap Arnold, AAF Chief, had been writing private letters to the engineer general in charge of airfield construction exhorting him to ease up on the fighter strips and to concentrate on completing the bomber fields, which would be used for bombing Japan. When Vosseller passed on this piece of news to his boss, Spruance refused to believe it. Going ashore, however, Spruance learned the facts for himself and "turned that situation around in about fifteen minutes." [29]

Quite apart from their differences in Washington, Navy relations with the AAF in the Pacific had not always been cordial, the worst conflict being between Vice Admiral John H. Hoover, Commander Forward Area and a naval aviator, and Major General Willis H. Hale, commanding the Seventh Air Force. Jack Towers had tried unsuccessfully to get Hoover transferred,[30] and the two men continued to direct land-based air operations in the Central Pacific. The situation vis-à-vis General Kenney in the Southwest

Pacific was similarly bumpy, again because of personalities as well as differing philosophies of air power. Admiral Spruance felt Kenney's Philippine-based planes were destroying sugar mills rather than enemy planes on Formosa.[31] In technique, the AAF in the Pacific had to learn close air support from the Marines, which it did well. Its generals also recognized the shock value of carriers in amphibious operations, "provided land-based air power was in a position to take over promptly the primary responsibility." [32] But without airfields, the AAF could do nothing at Okinawa, and TF 58 proved carriers could assume the role of land-based planes, though only at great risk and cost to themselves.

The Marines had one airfield throughout April; the other was rained out, then shelled by Japanese artillery, making it inoperable. The offshore islet of Ie Shima was captured, and on 13 May P-47 Thunderbolts arrived there. The rains halted airfield construction in May, but in June work resumed and Okinawa received 750 planes by 1 July, date of the first Okinawa-based bombing strike on Kyushu.

Meanwhile, the fast carriers continued to attack Japan, Okinawa, and the Sakishima Gunto while fending off the deadly human guided missiles. Even with these heavy commitments, however, Mitscher was still able to rotate his task groups for rest periods at Ulithi: when, on 12 May, after ten days of rest, TG 58.1 returned to battery, Mitscher detached TG 58.4. Upon the return of this group at the end of May, TG 58.3 could retire to the new base at Leyte for a rest.

The British carriers under Vice Admiral Vian (so promoted on 8 May) replenished at Leyte Gulf late in April, then returned to the fight. Without night fighters, they could not keep the Japanese from filling in the cratered airfields in the Sakishimas at night. On 4 May, while Vice Admiral Rawlings' battleships and cruisers were away shelling Miyako Island, kamikazes plunged onto *Formidable* and *Indomitable*. Captain Phillip Ruck-Keene of *Formidable* sent a signal from the smoke and confusion to Vian: "Little Yellow Bastard!" To which Vian replied: "Are you addressing me?" Though the armored flight decks prevented serious damage to the innards of these ships, several aircraft were destroyed and the radar equipment badly damaged; *Indomitable* had the only radar in the BPF equal in performance to that of the USN. On the ninth two more kamikazes hit, again on *Formidable* and *Victorious*. Their antiaircraft tactics obviously weak, the British quickly adopted the American tactic of picket destroyers, which they first deployed on 14 May.[33]

Armored flight decks were not enjoyed by Mitscher's ships, which reeled under the attacks. On 11 May *Bunker Hill*, Mitscher's flagship, took a kamikaze that killed over 350 men, including 13 of the admiral's staff and most of Fighting 84, asphyxiated in the ready room. After passing tactical command to Ted Sherman, Mitscher shifted his flag to night carrier *Enterprise*, which had rejoined TF 58 on the sixth, and *Bunker Hill* limped home and out of the war. Following some poor advice from advisers Burke and Flatley, Mitscher took his carriers north to attack Kyushu. Commander Bill Martin got off the first successful night heckle mission of the war with 16 night TBMs from *Enterprise* on 12–13 May, followed by day strikes. But on the fourteenth a kamikaze found the old veteran and crashed into her. Good damage control saved the "Big E," but she was out of the war for months. Amid the smoke, the bald Mitscher remarked to Jimmy Flatley: "Jimmy, tell my task group commanders that if the Japs keep this up they're going to grow hair on my head yet." The next day he shifted to *Randolph*, where Gerry Bogan loaned him several staff officers.[34]

On 18 May Mitscher formally requested Admiral Spruance to detach Task Force 58 from its 60-mile-square operating area less than 350 miles from Kyushu, where it had been for two months. Being held to the beach at Tarawa in November 1943 or at Saipan in June 1944 had been one thing, but Okinawa was murder! Unlike the two other operations, however, the troops could not rely on the escort carriers, which themselves had to launch occasional strikes against Kyushu. The fast carriers had become close support escort carriers, and the cost was great. Pilot efficiency was down to four months (from nine one year before), while ships' crews were exhausted. *Bunker Hill* had been at sea 59 days when hit on 11 May. And 17 days later Ted Sherman recorded, "Everybody is dead tired, we have been out of Ulithi 76 days now." But Spruance had no choice. Much as he hated to do it, he turned down Mitscher's request and kept TF 58 on station.[35]

However, the worst was over. No more serious kamikaze attacks threatened the carriers. After the withdrawal of *Enterprise*, no other carriers were hurt, except *Indomitable*, which sustained damage from a collision with a destroyer in the fog and had to retire for Sydney on 20 May. The same day Ted Sherman sent a strike of 12 TBMs loaded with 500-pound bombs to hit Shuri Castle on

Okinawa. In a dramatic demonstration of Navy precision close air support, the Turkeys placed their bombs on the enemy's position only 50 yards ahead of friendly troops, dislodging the enemy in that sector. With pressure from the advancing American ground forces, Shuri was finally evacuated on 29 May. The kamikazes now thrust themselves at American airfields on Okinawa and at offshore shipping; the carriers were no longer targets.

Task Force 57 flew its last strikes against the Sakishima airfields on 25 May, then withdrew to Sydney to replenish and prepare for the final campaign against Japan. Satisfied that the BPF had learned the art of fast carrier operations in the Pacific, Admiral Spruance now recommended it be integrated into the U.S. Fast Carrier Task Force. Admiral Nimitz agreed.

With nine-tenths of the job completed at Okinawa, Admiral Nimitz made his last two-platoon shift of the war. He had wanted Halsey to relieve Spruance about 1 May 1945 in order for his brilliant fleet commander to begin planning the Kyushu operation, but Spruance's tact and perseverance were needed at Okinawa until victory there was nearly complete.[36] Now, on 27 May while at sea, Halsey finally relieved Spruance, who returned immediately to Nimitz's advance headquarters at Guam. Fifth Fleet became Third Fleet; Task Force 58 became TF 38.

On 28 May Pete Mitscher handed over command of the fast carriers to Slew McCain, who raised his flag in the new *Shangri-la*, which had been in battle for one month. The changeover in mid-operation took the task group commanders by surprise; to a man they preferred working with the efficient Mitscher and still regarded the inefficient McCain as Ernie King's man, though Sherman did not mind serving under Halsey.[37] But Mitscher was through with sea duty. Seriously exhausted by long, tedious months in combat, sitting for long periods in silence, depending more and more on his excellent staff to run the task force, Mitscher had been ill—how ill no one would ever know, for his medical officer, Captain Ray Hege, had been killed on *Bunker Hill*. The strain of combat command had taken its toll, and Mitscher would soon relieve Jake Fitch as DCNO (Air) in Washington.

The task group commanders remained the same until the scheduled return to Leyte in June, with one slight exception. Jocko Clark had TG 38.1 (*Hornet*, *Bennington*, *Belleau Wood*, *San Jacinto*), Ted Sherman TG 38.3 (*Essex*, *Randolph*, *Bataan*, and *Monterey*), and Arthur Radford TG 38.4 (*Yorktown*, *Shangri-la*,

Ticonderoga, Independence). Ralph Davison had been relieved as ComCarDiv 2 by Rear Admiral Clifton A. F. Sprague; a jovial but not obnoxious drinker when relaxing, Davison had managed to miss an important airplane flight and was forthwith removed from command for his error. Ziggy Sprague hoisted his flag in makee-learn status in the repaired *Ticonderoga* (Captain William Sinton; Air Group 87), which, after a practice strike on bypassed Maloelap in the Marshalls on 17 May, had rejoined the task force. Also, Matt Gardner, without a night carrier, had been detached as ComCarDiv 7 in late April. Tommy Sprague remained aboard *Bennington* and Gerry Bogan on *Randolph*.

Another change came about when Vice Admiral Ching Lee, battleship squadron commander with the fast carriers, departed for home 18 June. Lee insisted he be returned to command after this trip, so the senior battleship admiral, Rear Admiral John F. Shafroth, became acting battleship commander. Two months before, Lee's chief of staff, fiery aviator Commodore Tom Jeter, had been relieved by Commodore Joseph C. Cronin, an escort carrier captain who now shifted to Shafroth's staff. By this point in the war, however, the fast battleships had lost their role as battle line vessels; they were floating antiaircraft platforms.

Admiral Halsey, resuming the role of fast carrier tactical commander, did not need to remain tied to the beach at Okinawa. He detached Sherman's task group to Leyte for a rest and ran north to strike Kyushu with Clark's and Radford's task groups. Ironically, since Halsey had had such bad luck with weather before, he immediately began to encounter heavy seas. After getting off strikes against Kyushu airfields on 2–3 June, he managed—of all things—to drag the task force into another typhoon.

The typhoon,[38] tight like the one encountered the preceding December, was discovered on the morning of 3 June. As in the December fiasco, however, intelligence was often vague and communications delayed, but Admiral Radford recommended to McCain that the task force steer clear of the heavy weather belt altogether. McCain replied only that Halsey had to decide.[39] During the early evening of 4 June, Halsey received better information from Cincpac, but he and aerologist Commander Kosko—who had been in the first storm—drew unsound conclusions regarding the track of the typhoon. The storm was heading north, the task force eastward away from it when Halsey asked the advice of Kosko.

Kosko recommended the force reverse course to the west to cross in front and ahead of the storm. Using the bad evidence of how only Radford's group, including Halsey's flagship, would be affected, he ignored the effect of such a change on Clark's group, then refueling from Rear Admiral Donald B. Beary's Servron 6 oilers.[40] With this misinformation, at 1:30 P.M. 5 June Halsey ordered both task groups back into the path of the typhoon.

As the two task groups reversed course westward after midnight, the barometer dropped and the weather worsened. Admirals Clark and Beary saw what was happening, and at 2:46 A.M. Beary signaled McCain: "Believe this course is running us back into the storm." McCain changed course due north. This was fine for Radford's group, 16 miles away from Clark's, and including both Halsey's and McCain's flagships, but Clark and Beary needed 20 precious minutes to get sea room to begin the maneuver. The typhoon was closing rapidly from the south behind Clark and Beary, causing heavy swells and rain and making some ships roll badly. At 4:01 Clark informed McCain his radar had the eye of the storm pinpointed 30 miles to the west, but McCain made no answer. At 4:20 Clark requested a course change to the southeast, to which McCain replied his radars showed nothing. When Clark reaffirmed that his had for one and a half hours, McCain took another precious 20 minutes debating with his own weatherman, Commander John Tatom, "to find out if I know anything that Admiral Clark did not know." Finally, at 4:40, McCain replied: "We [Radford's task group] intend holding present course. Use your own judgment." "If twenty minutes' delay made any difference," McCain rather feebly told the Court of Inquiry later, "I'm sorry."[41]

Clark, however, did not change course. Like Admiral Bogan in the December typhoon, Clark naturally assumed his superiors, Halsey and McCain, had more complete information than he did.[42] But they had less data than Clark, who tried to maintain course in vain until 5:07, when he began to maneuver to find a better course. He had been sucked into the inferno and at 5:35 ordered all ships to maneuver independently; at 7:00 TG 38.1 reached the eye of the storm. So completely did Radford's group miss the storm that at 4 A.M. Halsey had remarked to Mick Carney, his chief of staff, that the storm "possibly was not a typhoon after all."[43]

No ships were lost, but the flight deck overhangs on *Hornet* and *Bennington* collapsed, heavy cruiser *Pittsburgh* lost her bow,

76 planes were destroyed, and six men were lost overboard, while lesser damage was sustained by a number of other ships. Clark's task group cleared the storm during the afternoon of 5 June.

The Court of Inquiry which met at Guam on 15 June included two of the men who had sat at the December investigation, Vice Admirals Hoover and Murray, as well as Vice Admiral C. A. Lockwood. Halsey blamed the lack of information and slow communications for his troubles.[44] Though partially agreeing, the Court was fed up with Halsey's shenanigans. It blamed Halsey, McCain, and Kosko and recommended that they be transferred to other duty; it assigned lesser blame to Clark and Beary. Fleet Admiral King agreed with the verdict. "The record shows conclusively that there was ineptness in obtaining, disseminating, and acting upon meteorological data." He added that, with the experience of the previous storm, Halsey and McCain could have avoided the worst part of this one, "had they reacted to the situation as it developed with the weatherwise skill to be expected of professional seamen." [45]

Neither King nor Nimitz agreed with the sentence for morale purposes, although Secretary Forrestal was ready to retire Halsey. Reviewing both typhoons, King concluded "the primary responsibility for the storm damage and losses in both cases attaches to Commander Third Fleet, Admiral William F. Halsey, Jr., U.S. Navy." Since Cincpac was responsible for weather reporting, Nimitz "to a lesser degree" shared responsibility. King recommended no further action, except that corrective measures in weather reporting be initiated.[46] Halsey would never get his fifth star during the war.

Refueling and heading south, Clark's carriers—by backing down for air operations off the sterns of the damaged *Essex*-class carriers —and Radford's launched close support strikes to Okinawa on 6 June. The same day, TG 38.1 was reinforced by the new night carrier, *Bonhomme Richard* (Captain A. O. Rule, Jr.; Night Air Group 91). Next day the ships ran north to bomb the big Kanoya airfield on Kyushu, which they did on the eighth. Jocko Clark detached *Bennington* to return to Leyte for repairs, and on the ninth the remaining carriers launched planes to drop napalm on heavy enemy emplacements at Okino Daito Island. A short bombardment of Minami Daito Island by Jack Shafroth's three battleships on the tenth concluded these operations. Reaching Leyte Gulf on 13 June, 92 days after the start of the Okinawa campaign, the men of Task Force 38 were appalled to see the damaged flight deck of anchored *Randolph,* crashed by a stunt-flying AAF P-38 pilot.[47]

Plans for the seizure of additional islands near Okinawa, such as Okino Daito and Kikai Jima, were canceled as unnecessary early in June, as was the Chusan operation late in May. Okinawa had been expensive, but hundreds upon hundreds of Japanese planes had been destroyed, and Kyushu brought within easy range of land-based medium bombers and fighters. In August, B-29s would also begin operating from Okinawa. By mid-June organized enemy resistance ended on the island, and regular air strikes to Kyushu began early in July. The fast carriers were finally released from their close support role.

The kamikaze had proved a perplexing challenge, leading to several crash programs to design countermeasures. An unsuccessful attempt was made to convert rockets to antiaircraft surface-to-air missiles using rocket launchers and special proximity fuzes.[48] The Bureau of Aeronautics initiated two formal missile programs, for the rocket-powered Lark in March and for the jet-assisted Little Joe, designed to stop baka bombs, in May.[49] The latter was test-flown successfully on 20 July, but implementation in the fleet took time.

The real countermeasures would have to be in tactics, and Commodore Arleigh Burke was given command of the Special Defense Section under Cominch at Casco Bay, Maine, "to expedite readiness to defeat Jap suicide attacks." On 15 June Burke and two other officers began work, drafting men, ships, and planes into the effort to assist them under the direct authority of Fleet Admiral King. One individual Burke selected was Vice Admiral Ching Lee, ComBatron Two, who took command of the operational ships—Experimental TF 69—on 1 July, remaining at this post until his sudden death on 25 August. Devising various maneuvers and new positions for antiaircraft guns on ships, this section issued its first and only "Anti-Suicide Action Summary," on 31 July 1945. It was issued to all relevant Pacific commands immediately.[50]

Ferocious as the kamikazes had been at Okinawa, one could only assume that the Japanese defense of the homeland would be even more determined. But much damage could be done to Japan's air forces between July and the Kyushu landings scheduled for 1 November. This became the primary task of the fast carriers during the summer of 1945.

Eleven: Target Japan

Even as the Navy made preparations for the invasion of Japan, the admirals continued to oppose it in principle. Only the Army, "with its underestimation of sea power," insisted on invading Kyushu and Honshu. Fleet Admirals Leahy and King voted for it on the JCS only to achieve unanimity; both men believed Japan would surrender to the air and sea blockade before the landings could take place.[1] On 25 May 1945 the Joint Chiefs directed that Operation OLYMPIC—the landings on Kyushu—be implemented, target date 1 November 1945 [2] Operation CORONET, scheduled tentatively for 1 March 1946, involved landings on the Honshu coast near Tokyo for the drive across the Kanto Plain to the capital city. "For planning purposes," the Allied Combined Chiefs of Staff determined that organized resistance in Japan should cease by 15 November 1946.[3]

Despite the possibility that Japan might surrender before any of these dates, planning went forward as usual. For the Fast Carrier Task Force, OLYMPIC meant the culmination of all tactical and technical developments since the uncertain summer of 1943, the fulfillment of two decades of planning and dreaming by American naval aviators. By the summer of 1945, therefore, the U.S. Navy had become an air navy. And aviation not only controlled the destiny of the fleet but also the future of American defense policy. For this reason, the antagonist of the air admirals was no longer the Gun Club but the surging, independent-minded U.S. Army Air Forces.

1. Battle of Washington

The United States Congress and AAF crusaders brought the question of unification into the open during the first half of 1945.

A Congressional bill in January called for a unified department of defense, with autonomy for the Army, Navy, and a new Air Force. On 11 April the Richardson Board made its report, supporting this view, except for Admiral Richardson himself who submitted his own minority report. Richardson feared that the new Air Force would inevitably pull naval aviation out of the "fabric of the Navy into which it is ultimately woven." [1] Remembering the British experience between the wars, he felt that the American military would be weakened by such a decision. Other admirals reacted similarly, leading Admiral McCain to write to Secretary Forrestal that same month: "It is beginning to look to me that the war after the war will be more bitter than the actual war. Which, of course, is a shame." [2]

Navy postwar planning was not as positive as that of the AAF. Vice Admiral Edwards, assisted by planning officers Donald Duncan from October 1944 to July 1945 and Matt Gardner thereafter, issued his Navy Basic Post-war Plan No. 1 the day before Germany surrendered in May. The USN would keep ten fast carriers active to patrol the Pacific and the Caribbean; Britain could police European waters and the Atlantic after the war. This makeshift plan did not please the aviators, who continued to blame Ernie King and his chief deputies Edwards and Horne for checking the rise of aviation in the Navy. For example, though several studies by DCNO(Air) between May and July advocated raising the aircraft inventory to 39,000 or more planes, King insisted the ceiling stay at 37,735 planes. This made air planners frantic, as the Navy had jumped to more than 42,000 aircraft by April. In June, therefore, certain airmen in Washington, led by Rear Admiral Slats Sallada—reporting as new Chief of BuAer—began drawing up their own suggestions for the postwar Navy. Simultaneously, Secretary Forrestal appointed administrative expert Ferdinand Eberstadt to make an independent, unbiased examination of the proposals for unification and to suggest a positive position for the Navy to take.[3]

The Navy and its airmen shuddered at the thought of unification because it implied unified air forces, or—equally bad—the employment of Navy air under over-all command of Army or Air Force generals. General MacArthur's willingness in 1942 to expend the carriers to serve Army purposes still gnawed in Navy memories; Navy men found ominous confirmation of their fears in Army and AAF dependence on the carriers at Okinawa with seemingly little regard for their safety. This being so, when General Hap Arnold visited Pearl Harbor in June, Admiral Towers and his Navy advisers made it quite clear that the Pacific was the Navy's responsibility. On 16 July the U.S. Army Strategic Air Forces in the Pacific was created under General Carl Spaatz, giving the AAF virtual autonomy and equality with the Army and Navy in the Pacific. Also, it was well known that General Arnold wanted unified command in the Pacific, with General Spaatz to control all air operations including the carriers and Navy land-based air. The AAF had asked for this and been turned down in July by Admirals King and Nimitz. But in August General Spaatz and Kenney agreed they should try again as soon as Kyushu fell.[4]

With the destruction of the Japanese Navy, however, the Navy was faced with a crisis. Its traditional mission accomplished, its *raison d'être* seemingly eliminated, it now had to justify its existence. Also, Okinawa was the last amphibious operation, except for the invasion of Japan (which the Navy opposed), so that mission no longer counted. The AAF faced no such dilemma; its strategic bombers had pounded German industry into near-collapse and now its great B-29s were similarly smashing Japanese industry into submission. To capitalize on these successes, AAF propagandists began to advertise that their planes had paved the road to victory in the Pacific.

But what role did the Navy have by the summer of 1945? Normally the silent service, the Navy had now to supply an answer. The one the admirals chose gave tacit recognition to the victory of aviation within the fleet. The Navy, said its propagandists, was built around its air arm—which, having swept the Pacific of the enemy fleet, was now projecting naval power inland. In other words, the Navy was shifting from a maritime, peripheral strategy to a continental strategy. Unfortunately, though, the projected invasion of Japan was a European concept; Germany had been driven underground by *land*-based planes. This realization was difficult for the Navy to accept, but it had little choice if it was to resist subordination to an independent Air Force.[5]

The changing mission was also recognized by the admirals in the Pacific, though they had little concern about the unification struggle—yet. Admiral Radford told a reporter in June that the role of the carrier had "changed completely." "Our job now," said Radford, "is to keep our lines of communication open and to assure the strict blockade of Japan. . . . Working with the B-29s, we can do

Blockading the Homeland

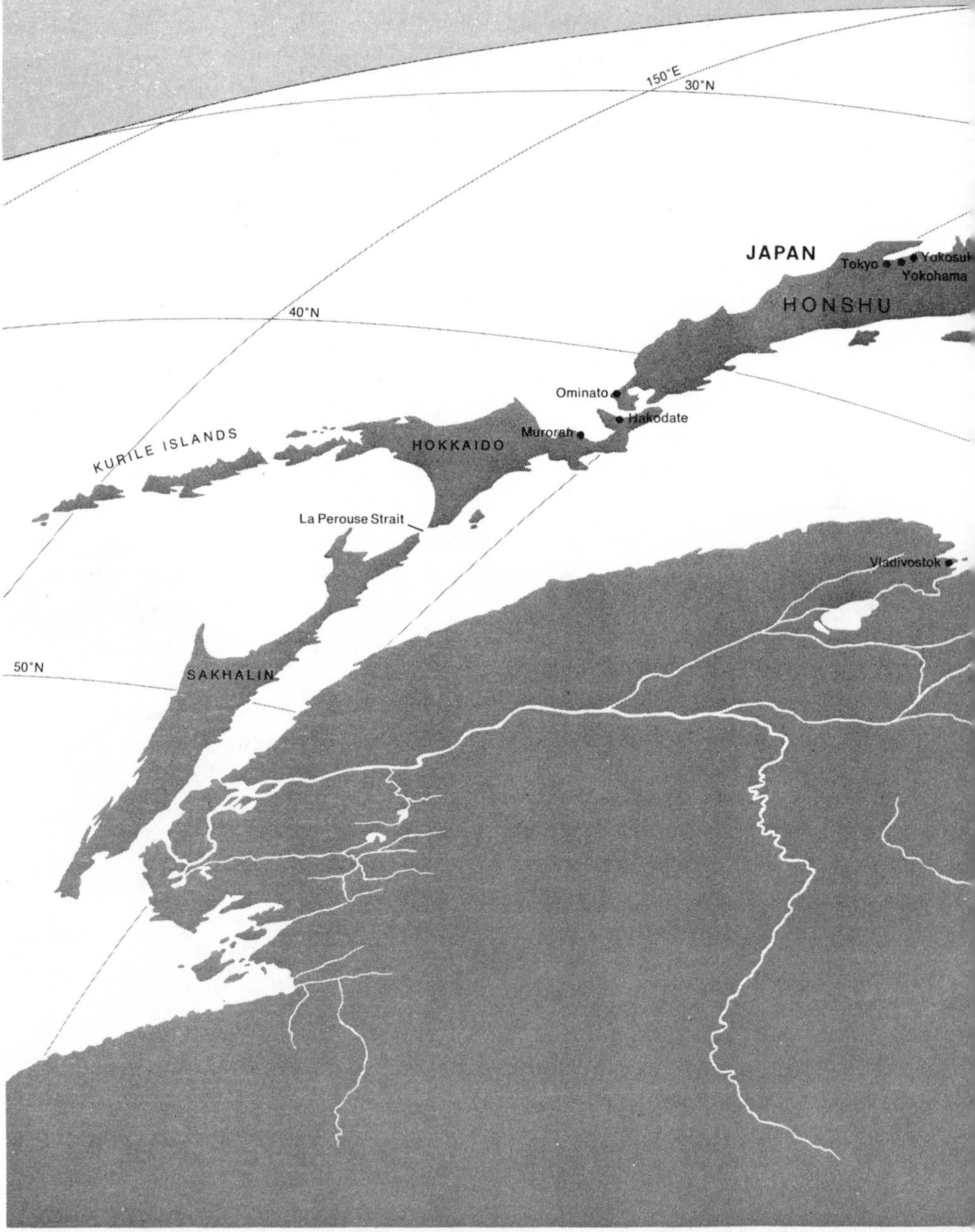

150°E
30°N
JAPAN
Tokyo
Yokohama
HONSHU
40°N
Ominato
Hakodate
Muroran
HOKKAIDO
KURILE ISLANDS
La Perouse Strait
Vladivostok
50°N
SAKHALIN

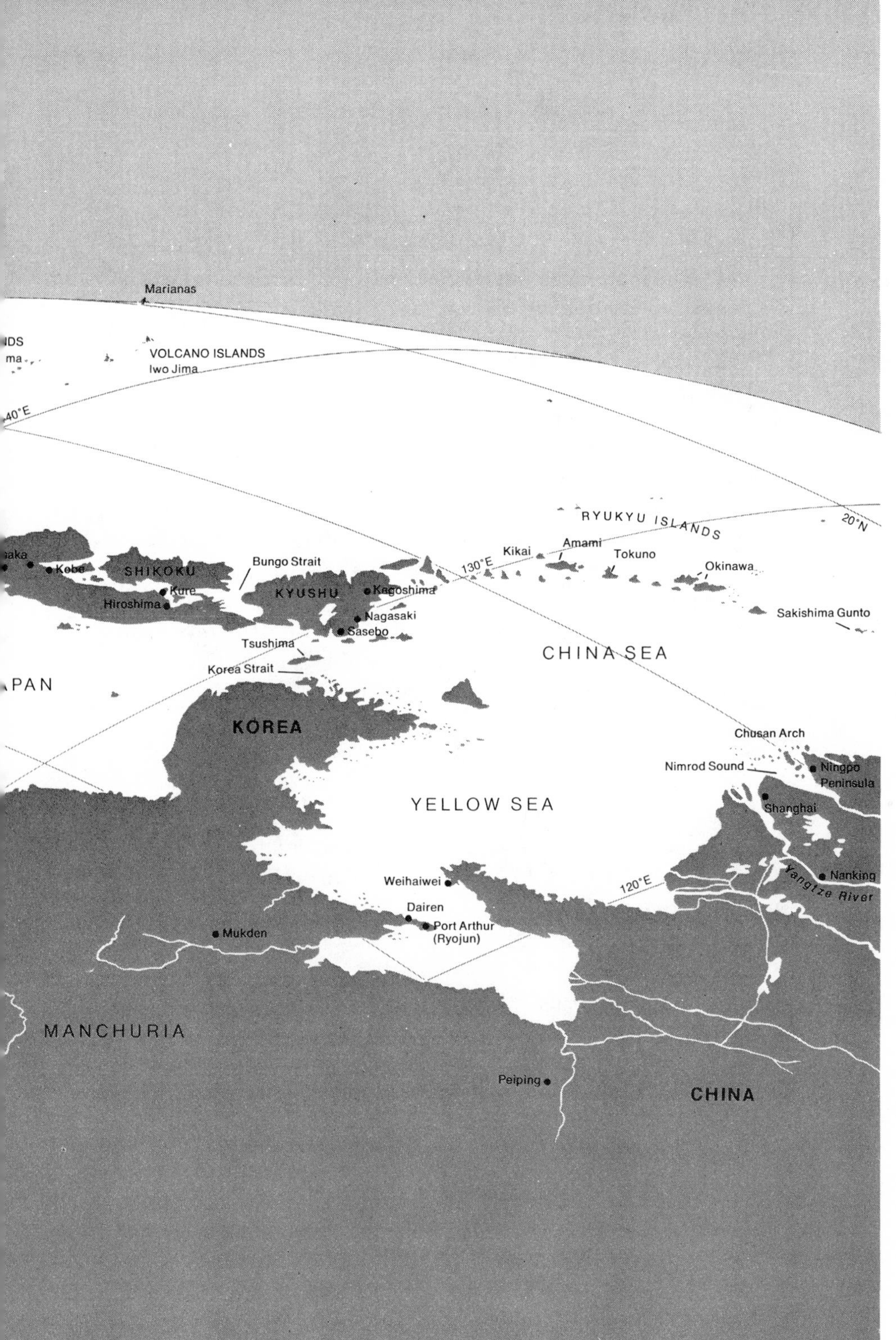

Marianas
VOLCANO ISLANDS
Iwo Jima
RYUKYU ISLANDS
20°N
Kikai
Amami
Tokuno
Okinawa
130°E
Bungo Strait
SHIKOKU
Kobe
Kure
Hiroshima
KYUSHU
Kagoshima
Nagasaki
Sasebo
Sakishima Gunto
Tsushima
Korea Strait
CHINA SEA
KOREA
Chusan Arch
Nimrod Sound
Ningpo Peninsula
Shanghai
YELLOW SEA
Weihaiwei
120°E
Nanking
Yangtze River
Dairen
Port Arthur (Ryojun)
Mukden
MANCHURIA
Peiping
CHINA

the pinpoint work on small targets, while the big bombers go after large industrial establishments."[6] These tasks in mid-1945 were definitely secondary and less glamorous than those of the AAF. Admiral Halsey was even less encouraging. Writing to Admiral Nimitz in June, he pointed out that the B-29s were offensive and the carriers defensive. The Kyushu invasion armada required "constant fighter cover for defense against violent and powerful kamikaze attack. . . . The fast carrier force will be required to contribute heavily to the defense and for many weeks will be tied to the direct support of a major invasion. . . ." Somewhat nostalgically, Halsey admitted the obvious: "The glorious days of the carrier spearheading the Pacific offensive ended when the spear entered the heart of the Empire. Targets are scarce."[7]

Nevertheless, the Fast Carrier Task Force would reach full flower in Operation OLYMPIC, blockading Japan; attacking enemy airfields, shipping, and industry; fending off kamikazes; and providing close air support for the landing forces. These tasks could be accomplished by no other fighting force and were vital to the succesful completion of World War II. Whatever differences over air power policy and command existed at this time had to be postponed until the postwar period.

2. *Preparations for Final Victory*

The great size of the Allied carrier fleet for the Kyushu operation testified to the ascendancy of naval aviation in the United States and Royal navies. In addition to the many carriers at Leyte–Samar and Sydney in mid-June 1945, several more were en route to join them before the November assault. Three new American *Essex*-class carriers were *Antietam*, *Boxer*, and *Lake Champlain*, along with their repaired or overhauled sisters *Intrepid*, *Hornet*, and *Wasp*. Also returning were *Enterprise* and *Cabot*, while *Saratoga* and *Langley* reported for training chores at Pearl Harbor. The British were sending new fleet carrier *Implacable* and new light carriers *Colossus*, *Vengeance*, *Venerable*, and *Glory*.

Projected commissionings for the second half of 1945 were British light carrier *Ocean* in August, American battle carriers *Midway* (CVB-41) in September and *Franklin D. Roosevelt* (CVB-42) in October, and five *Essex*-class carriers, the new *Princeton* (CV-37) due in October, *Kearsarge* (CV-33) and *Tarawa* (CV-40) in November, and *Leyte* (CV-32) and *Philippine Sea* (CV-47) in December. American shipbuilding was accelerated, *Leyte* being launched in August and *Philippine Sea* in September. Under extended repair were the battered sisters of these new ships, *Bunker Hill* and *Franklin.* First of a new class of two *Saipan*-class light carriers, *Saipan* (CVL-48), was launched in August and was due for the fleet in December.

Only the remotest possibility for combat existed for other new carriers then building. *Valley Forge* (CV-45) and *Saipan*-class light carrier *Wright* (CVL-49) were due in February 1946, followed by *Oriskany* (CV-34) and battle carrier *Coral Sea* (CVB-43) in May. Also in this category were three *Colossus*-class light carriers, the British *Theseus* and *Triumph* and the Canadian *Warrior*, all launched in mid-1944.

Other carrier construction was obviously for postwar purposes, so that on 12 August the U.S. Navy canceled construction on two of its *Essex*es, *Reprisal* (CV-35), to have been completed in July 1946, and *Iwo Jima* (CV-46), due in November 1946. Besides the two British *Majestic*-class light carriers commissioned as maintenance ships in August, six more had been launched in 1944 and 1945, with commissioning expected in the distant future. Larger British carriers were only in the earliest stages of construction.[1]

Blue water navies had embraced the fast carrier as the capital ship of their surface fleets. As long as Japan refused to capitulate, she would be ringed by increasing numbers of fast carriers, together with airfields and escort carriers. The British were beginning to approach the Americans in technique if not quantity, while the first British naval pilots were beginning to reach positions where they could command aircraft carriers. No British fast carrier captain had ever been a qualified pilot, although Captain (later Rear Admiral) L. D. Macintosh RN, who had commanded *Victorious* in 1943 and had brought *Implacable* into commission in August 1944, was a naval aviation observer. The first pilot to command a British fast carrier was Captain Caspar John RN, skipper of light carrier *Ocean,* commissioned on 8 August 1945.[1a]

In defensive armament, the British still enjoyed the armored flight deck, which had also been incorporated into the American *Midway*-class battle carriers. For its vulnerable *Essex*es, the U.S. Navy added more 40mm antiaircraft guns, which could knock a kamikaze out of the sky. The lighter 20mms were kept at a minimum. Also, two new guns were being developed. The radar-controlled 5-inch/54 caliber, which had greater range and altitude, joined the U.S. Fleet in April 1945. It was installed aboard *Midway* and *FDR*. The other weapon was the new 3-inch/50 caliber rapid-fire dual-purpose gun. Longer-range and twice as effective as the 40mm, this gun used proximity-fuzed shells. Production was hastened by the kamikaze threat, and the 3-inch/50 was first test-fired on 1 September 1945.[2]

In fighter aircraft, with the great emphasis on defense, Admiral Halsey advocated 80 per cent of a heavy carrier's planes be fighters. Admiral Mitscher wanted the F6F-5 Hellcat taken off the light carriers altogether, because it was not fast enough on combat air patrol to intercept high-altitude enemy snoopers; he recommended the F4U-4 Corsair as a temporary replacement until the F8F-1 was available. The first Bearcats in the Pacific operated for a day off *Langley* at Pearl Harbor, 24 August. On the heavy carriers Mitscher wanted Hellcats and Corsairs to remain aboard "until the Japanese air force is reduced to the point where it can no longer put more than three or four small raids (3 or 4 planes per raid) in the air at a time. This will be true when our carrier forces and land-based squadrons can cover the whole of Japan, Korea, Manchuria and Japanese-held China." In actual time, this would have to be sometime around the middle of 1946. Then the F8F Bearcat would replace the F6F and F4U as fighters altogether.[3]

New developments in fighters were few. Late-model F6Fs carried two light 20mm cannon in place of two of their six 50-caliber machine guns, evidence that the 50 would eventually be replaced by the 20mm. One squadron of FR Fireballs and one of F8F Bearcats reported to Hawaii, and in July an XFD-1 Phantom jet became the first pure jet to fly from a carrier deck.[4]

In bombing planes, Mitscher recommended the SB2C and TBM be kept until a new VBT type joined the fleet, probably the BT2D Dauntless II. When that happened—early 1946?—Mitscher thought the F4U could become solely a bomber and the new plane a bomber-torpedo type. These changes led the Navy to cancel its contract for the TBY Seawolf in July. About equal in performance to the TBM Avenger, the Seawolf cost more, would complicate fleet logistics, and was unproved in combat. With the torpedo plane vanishing, the Seawolf was unnecessary.[5] The Avenger did have a new function as a scout, however. The bulky "Turkey" could house new airborne early-warning radar gear which could spot enemy planes up to 75 miles away. Several TBMs were thus equipped and plans laid to place corresponding equipment in four carriers. If successful, these planes would eliminate the need for destroyers as radar pickets and thus remove that hazardous duty.[6]

One other separate plane type was the new helicopter, but more experimentation was needed before it could be employed tactically.[7]

When Admiral Mitscher returned from combat, the existing *Essex*-class carrier air group included 73 fighter types (VF, VBF: Corsairs and Hellcats), 15 dive bombers (SB2C Helldivers), and 15 torpedo bombers (TBM Avengers). The light carrier air group remained 24 Hellcats (two of them photographic planes) and nine Avengers. Fighters were key to the defense against the kamikazes, but the aviators also wanted additional bombers to destroy parked enemy planes and shore installations. Mitscher therefore recommended the light carriers turn in all their Avengers and Hellcats for 36 F4U Corsair fighters, these to be replaced "as soon as practicable" by 48 of the smaller, speedy F8F Bearcats. These all-fighter light carriers could provide the combat air patrols. The heavy carriers he recommended carry an air group of 48 VF (F6F or F4U), 24 VBF (F4U eventually replacing the SB2C), 18 VT (TBM to be replaced by the BTM or BT2D), two photographic fighters, and a night composite squadron of six night Hellcats and six night Avengers. The night carrier program he wanted discontinued.[8]

In July most of his ideas were accepted. Henceforth, as new carrier air groups formed or came home to be reformed, they would adopt new proportions of aircraft. Air groups aboard carriers at sea would make changes whenever possible. The heavy carrier air groups would be comprised of 32 VF (24 day VF, four photo VF, four night VF), 24 VBF, 24 VB, and 20 VT; with the air group commander in a fighter this was a 101-plane air group. The light carriers would go all fighters, 36 total, some immediately to F6F, the rest very soon to F4U. The night carriers remained 37 VFN, 18 VTN. The new battle carriers would carry huge air groups of 73 fighters (65 F4U, four photo F6F, four night F6F) and 64 bombers (SB2C). *Saipan*-class light carriers would have 48 Hellcats (24 VF, 24 VBF).[9]

Tactically, Mitscher still advocated the fast carrier task group of three heavies and one light carrier, although he noted to Admiral Nimitz that Ted Sherman's experience with five and six carriers led that officer to advocate the larger task group of up to eight carriers. Sherman believed the larger task group allowed larger and better-coordinated air strikes, a smaller percentage of fighters for combat air patrol, a smaller number of supporting ships, and improved communications. Mitscher disagreed on the grounds that more than four carriers reduced combat efficiency because of smaller air space available for each air group. Also, airborne communication circuits would be overloaded, carrier maneuverability would be restricted because of increased steaming time into the wind, and larger formations were less compact for antiaircraft defense. As at Okinawa, however, both four- and five-carrier task groups would be used, enabling more experimentation.[10]

The problem of night operations was temporarily solved during the summer of 1945. Mitscher, who had always loathed night activity, recommended that each heavy carrier carry its own night fighters and bombers—six of each—and thus eliminate the waste of entire carriers being used solely at night. The temporary losses of *Saratoga* and *Enterprise* between February and May seemed to forecast the end of the night carriers. Rear Admiral Gardner had hauled down his flag in April, and Rear Admiral Donald Duncan, prospective ComCarDiv 7, shifted to a day billet. The night admiral's staff returned to Pearl Harbor and did not go back to Task Force 38 until the end of June when Rear Admiral J. J. Ballentine reported aboard *Bon Homme Richard* as temporary ComCarDiv 7. Simultaneously, the decision was made to retain the two night carriers, "Bonnie Dick" and "Big E," but in separate day groups, not as one night carrier task group. Also, each day carrier would have its own four night fighters.[11]

The Royal Navy, frustrated without night carriers, took measures to achieve a night air capability. Pilots of No. 828 Squadron, TBM Avengers, arrived in the Pacific aboard *Implacable* in June; along with several Hellcat pilots, these planes could operate at night. For a longer-range program, light carrier *Ocean*, commissioned early in August, was designated "a night flying carrier," to work up in the United Kingdom before transit to the Pacific. There was even talk of forming a night carrier task group of one heavy and two light carriers in the fall, but much depended on the actual need during the final operation against Japan.[12]

The summer brought more personnel changes in the U.S. Navy and in the fast carriers. At the highest level, President Roosevelt had died in April; this strong advocate of sea power was succeeded by Harry S Truman, who not only knew next to nothing about navies but also actively endorsed unification. Civilians in the Navy

Department, however, were forceful advocates of naval aviation, including Secretary Forrestal, a warm admirer of Pete Mitscher and several air rear admirals. On 1 July Di Gates was promoted from Assistant Secretary (Air) to Under Secretary of the Navy, where he continued to fight for naval aviation. His replacement as Assistant for Air, John L. Sullivan, had served five years as Assistant Secretary of the Treasury and knew little about aviation; but Sullivan got into the spirit of his new job by being sworn in by Jake Fitch aboard fast carrier *Shangri-La* off the coast of Japan on 4 July.

Ernie King resisted any new aviation post in Washington, although Admiral Fitch felt a Deputy Cominch (Air) ought to be established, perhaps to be held by returning Pete Mitscher.[13] Nevertheless, many important aviators reported from combat to Washington where their records and ideas would enhance the position of naval aviation. Many of the appointments were announced publicly —breaking wartime precedent—on 14 July, to take effect one month later. Consequently, on 14 August Vice Admiral Mitscher relieved Fitch as DCNO (Air). Fitch then became Superintendent of the U.S. Naval Academy, the first naval aviator and vice admiral to hold that post. He relieved a rather inconspicuous battleship admiral who had been Superintendent during most of the war. Simultaneously, Captain S. H. Ingersoll, skipper of *Monterey* at the Turkey Shoot and Leyte Gulf, became Commandant of Midshipmen. Fitch immediately initiated a stronger program of aviation; the Navy's future admirals would be flyers.[14]

On 1 June Rear Admiral Slats Sallada relieved Duke Ramsey as Chief of BuAer; Ramsey went to the Pacific. Rear Admiral Allan R. McCann, a submariner who had also commanded a battleship in TG 38.2 at Leyte before directing the final campaign against Germany's U-boats, relieved Malcolm Schoeffel as Ernie King's operations officer on 20 August. Rear Admiral Matt Gardner relieved Wu Duncan as Cominch Plans Officer in July, bringing with him two top Pacific air planners, Captains George Anderson and P. D. Stroop. Captain Wallace Beakley was relieved in May as King's air officer by Captain Robert B. Pirie, for many months Gerry Bogan's chief of staff.

In the Pacific, Fleet Admiral Nimitz remained as Cincpac-Cincpoa, and he wanted Admiral Spruance to command the Kyushu landings.[15] As Spruance gathered his Fifth Fleet staff at Guam to begin the planning, new aviators reported to him. Rear Admiral

Duke Ramsey relieved Art Davis as chief of staff on 13 July, and Captain Jack Moss, former chief of staff to Monty Montgomery, relieved Abe Vosseller as fleet aviation officer. Davis took over a carrier division, and Vosseller became aide to Di Gates. Captain Savvy Forrestel, operations officer, took command of a battleship, relieved on the staff by another "black shoe," Captain E. M. Thompson.

The Pacific Fleet also underwent some important command changes. Vice Admiral Jack Towers, long due for a sea command, turned over his post of Deputy Cincpac-Cincpoa temporarily to Vice Admiral John H. Hoover, on 26 July, who was followed by Vice Admiral Newton one month later. On 14 July Rear Admiral Montgomery handed over the West Coast Fleet Air job to Rear Admiral Ragsdale and six days later relieved George Murray as ComAirPac (but not as a vice admiral). Murray stepped down to be Commander Marianas, and late in August Hoover replaced Ragsdale. New Deputy ComAirPac was Rear Admiral Cato Glover, reporting in August to relieve Rear Admiral Freddie McMahon, who took over the Carrier Training Squadron.

The first major change in the fast carriers was the appointment of a relief for Mitscher. The logical choice in terms of experience, seniority, and ability was Ted Sherman. Late in April Sherman began to despair that his outspokenness had offended Ernie King and therefore his chances for promotion. On 2 May he concluded, "I am tired of this job," and that he would try to relieve George Murray as ComAirPac and hope for a third star in the process. One week later he wrote to Nimitz on the subject, sending copies to Towers, Mitscher, Fitch, and Savvy Cooke. On 21 May Sherman wrote to Halsey and again to Fitch: "I am perfectly willing and eager to stay at sea and fight the Japs. But I want to do it in a position in keeping with my talents, my experience, and my seniority. At present, I do not believe that is the case." On the thirtieth he wrote to personnel chief Randall Jacobs on the matter.[16]

Having earlier come so close to being part of the two-platoon shift, Sherman's frustration was understandable. He learned, however, on 1 June, that Nimitz had recommended him to relieve Mitscher, and two days later Halsey did the same. On 14 June Sherman got the word; he was to get 30 days' leave, promotion to vice admiral, and appointment as Commander First Fast Carrier Force Pacific and Commander Task Force 58. Leaving Leyte on 19 June, he went to Guam where on the twentieth he visited Nimitz, who told him to be back after 15 August. Sherman then journeyed to Washington, where he was warmly received by Ernie King. On 13 July he was promoted to vice admiral.[17]

For his staff, Sherman was assigned a nonaviator cruiser commander, Captain M. E. "Germany" Curts, as chief of staff. For operations officer Sherman selected Captain Herbert D. Riley, skipper of an escort carrier and earlier replacement of George Anderson in the BuAer-DCNO(Air) plans post.

The other key carrier job, Commander Second Fast Carrier Force Pacific, held since August 1944 by Vice Admiral Slew McCain, was also in question. McCain had not given an especially outstanding account of himself in the June typhoon, not to mention the December typhoon and other difficulties during his first command tour with the fast carriers. Furthermore, McCain's health was not much better than Mitscher's, as a result of the strain of combat and continuous operations. No doubt Jack Towers had a low opinion of McCain's abilities as carrier commander, which was an indirect slap at Ernie King for pushing McCain to the Pacific in the first place. Nimitz therefore decided to remove McCain from command of Task Force 38 after the first stages of OLYMPIC. On 14 July the Navy announced that one month hence McCain would be relieved to return to Washington as deputy head of the Veterans Administration. It was the end of the line for McCain; he would have no place in the postwar air Navy.[18]

McCain's relief posed a real problem for Ernie King, because Admiral Nimitz wanted Jack Towers for the job. Nearly three years before King had sent Towers to the Pacific more or less under fire and Towers had locked horns with Nimitz over air policy during the late summer of 1943. However, Nimitz had soon discovered the correctness of Towers' thinking and had made Towers his own deputy. Since then, Towers had performed excellent work, including most Pacific Fleet administrative chores since February 1945. Ernie King did not like the idea of giving his old antagonist a sea command; he even told Ted Sherman, soon to relieve Mitscher, on 26 June that it was too bad Sherman "was not twins." However, Nimitz convinced King when they met at San Francisco on 30 June and 1 July. Nimitz gave Towers the news on the second, and Towers went on leave on 26 July.[19]

Vice Admiral Towers was scheduled to relieve McCain in command of Task Force 38 on 14 August, but he took his time to gather a good staff and therefore spent a week longer at it before reporting. As the acknowledged leader of American naval aviation, Towers had his pick, and what a staff it was! For chief of staff he selected nonaviator Captain John E. Gingrich, an old friend who had served four years as a superb naval aide to then Under Secretary Forrestal and then had brought his own ship, cruiser *Pittsburgh*, out of the June typhoon after it had lost its bow.[20] For operations, Towers broke precedent by appointing an aviator with the rank of captain, Eddie Ewen, veteran skipper of *Independence* in her "night" days and liaison officer with the British carrier force. Three other crack officers would assist Ewen: Commander Noel A. M. Gayler, who had led *Randolph's* Air Group 12 to Iwo Jima, and Commander James H. Hean, both from McCain's staff; and Lieutenant Commander William N. Leonard, a veteran combat pilot and air ordnance expert. Towers brought his flag secretary of many months, Lieutenant Commander W. W. Grant, but failed to get back Commander Willing Pepper, who had been captured by Nimitz to organize the Cincpac operational intelligence section at Guam.

Since summer operations would consist only of air strikes on Japan and no complex amphibious affair, several changes could be made in the cardiv commands. No officer immediately replaced Ted Sherman as ComCarDiv 1, while Ziggy Sprague remained in makee-learn status as ComCarDiv 2. Tommy Sprague as ComCarDiv 3 assumed command of TG 38.1. Donald Duncan headed west in July to relieve Gerry Bogan as ComCarDiv 4, and Art Davis relieved Jocko Clark as ComCarDiv 5. Longtime veterans Bogan and Clark were earmarked for shore billets, as was Arthur Radford, but his experience was needed and Radford was retained as ComCarDiv 6. John Ballentine reported as ComCarDiv 7. Vice Admiral Sir Philip Vian RN remained as Admiral Commanding 1st Aircraft Carrier Squadron, and Rear Admiral C. H. J. Harcourt RN reported to Sydney as Admiral Commanding 11th Aircraft Carrier Squadron.

As in the past, fast carrier captains continued to be drawn from escort carriers in the Atlantic and Pacific. From the Atlantic came several distinguished U-boat hunter-killers to take command of fast carriers during the summer: Harold F. Fick to *Bon Homme Richard* and Dan V. Gallery to *Hancock*, while James R. Tague brought out *Antietam* and Logan C. Ramsey, who had written on carrier tactics in 1943, brought out *Lake Champlain*. Two of Ted Sherman's former tacticians got carriers: Cat Brown, chief of staff in the Philippines and Okinawa, took command of *Hornet;* H. S. Duckworth, chief of staff during the formative days of mid-1943, got command of *Cowpens.* Air support expert Dick Whitehead reported to *Shangri-La.*

The Fast Carrier Task Force would execute the final campaign against Japan with the best men and machines available. After victory and liquidation of the Japanese Empire, the aviators might not have the opportunity to show their stuff again.

3. OLYMPIC: The Concept Fulfilled

The fight for Japan would be more or less settled at the Kyushu beachhead. Abandoning their defense-in-depth used at Peleliu, Iwo, and Okinawa, the Japanese planned to throw no less than 3000 kamikazes into the amphibious shipping off Kyushu *before* troops and cargo could be unloaded. Only 350 suicide planes would challenge the fast carriers directly; Japan's generals cared only for the troop and supply ships. The planes, ranging from simple trainers to new, jet-propelled "special attackers," would be flown by generally poorly trained aviators, some with as little as 20 hours of instruction. If the initial kamikaze attack failed, another 3500 conventional and suicide Army and Navy planes would be rushed to the threatened area, supported by over 5000 suicide boats, 19 destroyers, and 38 submarines—the last of the Navy's operating fleet. If these mass counterattacks failed to stop the American invasion armada at Kyushu, only 3000 planes would be left to defend Honshu and specifically Tokyo. Kyushu would be defended to the last—as usual.[1]

As in the great Allied invasion of Europe, the Army wanted its leading general in the Pacific to have over-all command of the invasion of Japan. General of the Army MacArthur was not about to commit 40 or 50 divisions to the care of an admiral, and rightly so. Since the Pacific had been primarily the Navy's show, however, Fleet Admiral Nimitz was not about to commit two dozen fast carriers and 16 escort carriers to the jurisdiction of an unappreciative general, and rightly so. In March 1945 the JCS decided to give Nimitz supreme command of the naval aspects of the operation, while MacArthur would command all operations ashore. For the first time during the war Admiral Richmond Kelly Turner would command a landing that included MacArthur's forces. Then, on 3 April, the Joint Chiefs declared Nimitz commander of all naval forces in the Pacific, including Seventh Fleet; at Kyushu he would be served by four four-star admirals: Spruance, Halsey, Turner, and Kinkaid. The same day General MacArthur assumed command of all Army forces in the Pacific, including those of the Pacific Ocean Areas which on 1 July became U.S. Army Forces, Middle Pacific.[2] The AAF, again, was split between Spaatz and Kenney; tactical air was still under Nimitz.

So the divided command remained, though it was somewhat improved. Nimitz would remain at Guam and MacArthur at Manila, except for short visits to the beachhead.

Fast carrier logistics were influenced by the over-all supply load. With the landing forces to gather at Guam, Leyte–Samar, and Okinawa, the fast carriers would reestablish their main base at Eniwetok in the Marshalls. On 1 July the service forces of the Pacific Fleet were reorganized. Servron 6 remained the at-sea logistic support group of the fast carriers, and Servron 10 incorporated all other fleet logistics. Advanced service headquarters shifted in July from Leyte to Eniwetok, though the servrons continued to use Saipan, Ulithi, and occasionally Okinawa. The British left their main fleet train at Manus and sent a detachment to Eniwetok. With the fast carriers and Servron 6 operating from Eniwetok, they would avoid the typhoon belt, be closer to commercial tanker routes from California and Panama, and not interfere with the large numbers of assault craft staging up from the south.[3]

In aircraft logistics, fast carrier air groups had begun to back up on the West Coast because of the unscheduled return of damaged carriers during the Okinawa campaign, but the flow continued with the end of that operation. In June, four new heavy and three light carrier air groups arrived at Leyte. Then all air groups that started OLYMPIC in July, save No. 85 aboard *Shangri-La*, would remain in combat until the landings, barring sinkings, heavy pilot losses, or the unpredictable factor of fatigue. In July, Radford's Integrated Aeronautic Program of replacing and maintaining combat aircraft in the forward areas reached its full inventory of 1500 airplanes, dispersed at the Marshalls, Manus, Leyte–Samar, and the Marianas. Three CASUs maintained 300 planes at Saipan, and aircraft replacement pools were being established at Guam.[4]

The operation was scheduled to start with only the three fast carrier task groups that had completed the Okinawa operation, but more would be added as new, repaired, and overhauled carriers joined the fleet. And, as was the custom for new air and ship crews, each would first engage in battle practice on a live target. The first to arrive was Britain's newest heavy carrier, *Implacable*, which sortied from Manus in a task group under Rear Admiral Brind on 10 June to bomb long-forgotten Truk. On the fourteenth and fifteenth *Implacable*'s Seafires, Fireflies, and Avengers attacked Truk, while night Avengers continued the fight both nights. The second night, the fifteenth, flares were dropped to light the target for six Avengers bombing visually. In addition, cruisers and destroyer shelled the islands. The operation, despite meager targets, was successful. Losses were one Seafire shot down by antiaircraft fire, and four Avengers lost operationally.

American fast carriers were similarly active, doing all their work on an old favorite, Wake Island. On 20 June Task Group 12.4 under Rear Admiral Ralph Jennings attacked Wake. Three carriers participated: *Lexington*, *Hancock*, and *Cowpens*. On 18 July *Wasp* bombed Wake, followed by *Cabot* on 1 August and by *Intrepid* five days later. On 12 August the new *Antietam* sortied from Pearl Harbor for strikes on Wake scheduled for the sixteenth. Next in line was the new *Boxer*, which departed San Diego for Hawaii on 1 August.

The first phase of OLYMPIC would consist of air strikes on the Japanese coast, to be conducted from early July to mid-August 1945. When these operations began, the Fleet and fast carriers would be organized thus:

FLEET ORGANIZATION

Cominch-CNO—Fleet Admiral E. J. King
  Deputy Cominch-CNO—Vice Admiral R. S. Edwards*
  Vice CNO—Vice Admiral F. J. Horne**
  Chief of Staff—Vice Admiral C. M. Cooke*
Cincpac-Cincpoa—Fleet Admiral C. W. Nimitz*
  Deputy Cincpac-Cincpoa—Vice Admiral J. H. Towers
  Chief of Joint Staff—Vice Admiral C. H. McMorris*
    Deputy Chief of Staff—Rear Admiral F. P. Sherman
  ComAirPac—Vice Admiral G. D. Murray
Commander Third Fleet—Admiral W. F. Halsey, Jr.
    Chief of Staff—Rear Admiral R. B. Carney*
  CTF 38—Vice Admiral J. S. McCain (Com2ndFasCarForPac)
    Chief of Staff—Rear Admiral W. D. Baker*
    CTG 38.1—Rear Admiral T. L. Sprague (ComCarDiv 3)
      Lexington—Captain T. H. Robbins, Jr.; Air Group 94
      Hancock—Captain R. F. Hickey; Air Group 6

Bennington—Captain B. L. Braun; Air Group 1
Belleau Wood—Captain W. G. Tomlinson; Air Group 31
San Jacinto—Captain M. H. Kernodle; Air Group 49
CTG 38.3—Rear Admiral G. F. Bogan (ComCarDiv 4)
Essex—Captain R. L. Bowman; Air Group 83
Ticonderoga—Captain William Sinton; Air Group 87 (joined 21 July after three weeks at Guam)
Randolph—Captain F. L. Baker; Air Group 16
Wasp—Captain W. G. Switzer; Air Group 86 (joined 26 July after Wake strike)
Monterey—Captain J. B. Lyon; Air Group 34
Bataan—Captain W. C. Gilbert; Air Group 47
CTG 38.4—Rear Admiral A. W. Radford (ComCarDiv 6)
Yorktown—Captain W. F. Boone; Air Group 88
Shangri-la—Captain J. D. Barner; Air Group 85
Bon Homme Richard—Captain A. O. Rule, Jr.; Night Air Group 91
Independence—Captain N. M. Kindell; Air Group 27
Cowpens—Captain G. H. DeBaun; Air Group 50
CTF 37—Vice Admiral Sir Bernard Rawlings RN* (Force joined 16 July)
CTG 37.2—Vice Admiral Sir Philip Vian RN*
Chief of Staff—Captain J. P. Wright RN**
Implacable—Captain C. C. Hughes-Hallett RN*
Indefatigable—Captain Q. D. Graham RN*
Victorious—Captain M. M. Denny RN*
Formidable—Captain Phillip Ruck-Keene RN*

* Nonaviator.
** Naval aviation observer.

Though not present during the first month of OLYMPIC, Ted Sherman could rejoice that Halsey and McCain had agreed to try his five- or six-carrier task group. Two other admirals were in "makee-learn"-standby status should the task force be expanded or their services be otherwise required. Ziggy Sprague (ComCarDiv 2) was one, J. J. Ballentine (ComCarDiv 7) the other; Ballentine would direct any necessary night operations with "Bonnie Dick" but not as a formal task group commander. Changes in ship command during or at the end of this period were Dick Whitehead to *Shangri-La*, 16 July; Captain J. R. Tate to *Randolph*, 26 July; Captain H. F. Fick to *Bon Homme Richard*, 23 August; Captain H. H. Goodwin to *San Jacinto*, 24 August; and Captain J. C. Annesley RN to *Victorious* in August.

Following these operations, Task Force 38 would retire in mid-August to Eniwetok to replenish, reorganize, and change commanders.[5] There Towers would relieve McCain as CTF 38, Ziggy Sprague would relieve Bogan at CTG 38.3, and a new TG 38.2 would be formed under Ballentine. The newly arrived *Intrepid*, *Antietam*, and *Cabot*, along with *Randolph*, would comprise this task group. *San Jacinto* would depart for home and overhaul, trading air groups with *Bataan*. *Essex* would also leave the combat area for the same reason. Throughout late August and September 1945 Task Force 38 would again attack Japan, with the British launching diversionary strikes against Hong Kong and Canton late in September. Makee-learn admirals would be Donald Duncan (ComCarDiv 4) and Art Davis (ComCarDiv 5).

FLEET ORGANIZATION

Commander Third Fleet—Admiral W. F. Halsey, Jr.
CTF 38—Vice Admiral J. H. Towers (Com2ndFasCarForPac)[6]
CTG 38.1—Rear Admiral T. L. Sprague (ComCarDiv 3)
Bennington, Lexington, Hancock, Belleau Wood
CTG 38.2—Rear Admiral J. J. Ballentine (ComCarDiv 7)
Randolph, Intrepid, Antietam, Cabot
CTG 38.3—Rear Admiral C. A. F. Sprague (ComCarDiv 2)
Ticonderoga, Wasp, Monterey, Bataan
CTG 38.4—Rear Admiral A. W. Radford (ComCarDiv 6)
Yorktown, Shangri-la, Bon Homme Richard, Independence, Cowpens

Halsey's and Towers' operations would be restricted to points east of the 135th meridian, that is to Honshu Island east of Tokyo, including Tokyo, Nagoya, Yokohama, and other great Japanese industrial cities, and to Hokkaido Island. Admiral Nimitz had wanted the fast carriers to have freedom to operate in the Philippine, East China, and Yellow seas and the Sea of Japan. But General MacArthur wanted the isolation of Kyushu left to General Kenney's Far Eastern Air Forces, which would be directed to targets to the west of the 135th meridian—Kyushu, Shikoku, and western Honshu, including the ports of Hiroshima and Kure. On 1 August, at a meeting in Manila with MacArthur, Nimitz finally agreed with this arrangement. B-29s from the Marianas and Okinawa would be coordinated into both areas against major strategic targets.[7]

Throughout September and October 1945 available carriers would be assigned to Task Force 38, until 24 October when—for the first time in the war—the Fast Carrier Task Force would be divided into two separate parts, Task Forces 38 and 58. Several of Towers' carriers would be drawn out of TF 38 to comprise TF 58. The former would be used solely for long-range operations against strategic targets up and down the Japanese coast, the latter only for air defense and support at the beach. This ideal division had been made possible by the overwhelming number of available carriers; it was to be the ultimate fulfillment of evolving fast carrier tactics.

Admiral Spruance, commanding the Fifth Fleet, would arrive off Kyushu with Turner's landing forces and the embarked Sixth Army on 24 October. The air forces would include Ted Sherman's Task Force 58 and Cal Durgin's 16 escort carriers, including four with Marine Corps air groups and one to three night escort carriers. The latter could cover the beach and landing craft at night, leaving night fast carriers *Enterprise* and *Bon Homme Richard* free to cover Task Force 58 and possibly to launch night bombing strikes. From the twenty-fourth the Navy would assume all responsibility for the target area, and General Kenney's fliers would do what they knew best, interdiction bombing of enemy lines of communication on northern Kyushu to the assault area in the south. So sold was MacArthur on Navy air coverage of the beaches at Leyte and Okinawa that he insisted the Navy have sole responsibility for defending and supporting the landing area. Furthermore, Kenney's Army planes could operate over the target area only when "managed by a naval commander." This would be Rear Admiral Mel Pride, Commander Air Support Control Units.[8]

Tactically, Ted Sherman naturally preferred the five-carrier task group for maximum antiaircraft defense with a minimum of planes. His task organization would therefore be:

FLEET ORGANIZATION

Commander Fifth Fleet—Admiral R. A. Spruance*
  Chief of Staff—Rear Admiral D. C. Ramsey
 CTF 58—Vice Admiral F. C. Sherman (Com1stFasCarForPac)
   Chief of Staff—Commodore M. E. Curts*
  CTG 58.4—Rear Admiral A. W. Radford (ComCarDiv 6)
   Bennington—Captain B. L. Braun; Air Group 1

Ticonderoga—Captain William Sinton; Air Group 87
Hancock—Captain D. V. Gallery; Air Group 6
Enterprise—Captain G. B. H. Hall; Night Air Group 52
Bataan—Captain W. C. Gilbert; Air Group 49
CTG 58.5—Rear Admiral D. B. Duncan (ComCarDiv 4)
Intrepid—Captain G. E. Short; Air Group 10
Lake Champlain—Captain L. C. Ramsey; Air Group 14[9]
Bon Homme Richard—Captain H. F. Fick; Night Air Group 91
Cowpens—Captain H. S. Duckworth; Air Group 50
Cabot—Captain W. W. Smith; Air Group 32
Commander Air Support Control Units—Rear Admiral A. M. Pride

---

* Nonaviator.

The admirals had no illusions about Japanese resistance in the air. While four early-warning carriers with similarly equipped Avengers might be ready for the operation, Admiral Pride would rely on a greatly expanded anti-kamikaze force of 13 shipboard (amphibious command ship) and five landing force fighter director teams. Air strikes would commence on 24 October, reaching their peak on the day of the landing, 1 November. Throughout the operation, strike groups from Task Force 58, the escort carriers, and some from the Far Eastern Air Forces would be kept over the beach continually from 7 A.M. to 5 P.M. At night 12 night Hellcats and six P-61 AAF Black Widows would remain on station. Whether such an elaborate air support-defensive system could withstand hundreds of kamikaze attacks was an open question, but Navy and Marine Corps air support techniques would be near-perfect after the many months of striving for improvement.[10]

Halsey's Third Fleet would continue to range north and eastward, keeping open Allied lines of communications to the beach and to Russia—which ought to be in the war against Japan by then—by attacking Japanese air, naval, and ground forces in Hokkaido and the southern Kuriles. Admiral Towers would use Mitscher's standard task group organization of one light and three heavy carriers for Task Force 38. Vice Admiral Rawlings' Task Force 37 would operate with Third Fleet, and would include the four new but slower 25-knot British light carriers. These ships carried the rather unusual air group of 21 speedy Corsairs and 12 sluggish Barracudas.

FLEET ORGANIZATION

- Commander Third Fleet—Admiral W. F. Halsey, Jr.
    - Chief of Staff—Rear Admiral R. B. Carney*
  - CTF 38—Vice Admiral J. H. Towers (Com2ndFasCarForPac)
      - Chief of Staff—Commodore J. E. Gingrich*
    - CTG 38.1—Rear Admiral A. C. Davis (ComCarDiv 5)
      - *Hornet*—Captain C. R. Brown; Air Group 19
      - *Wasp*—Captain W. G. Switzer; Air Group 86
      - *Boxer*—Captain D. F. Smith; Air Group 93
      - *Monterey*—Captain J. B. Lyon; Air Group 34
    - CTG 38.2—Rear Admiral T. L. Sprague (ComCarDiv 3)
      - *Yorktown*—Captain W. F. Boone; Air Group 88
      - *Lexington*—Captain T. H. Robbins, Jr.; Air Group 94
      - *Antietam*—Captain J. R. Tague; Air Group 89
      - *Belleau Wood*—Captain W. G. Tomlinson; Air Group 31
    - CTG 38.3—Rear Admiral C. A. F. Sprague (ComCarDiv 2)
      - *Randolph*—Captain J. R. Tate; Air Group 16
      - *Shangri-La*—Captain R. F. Whitehead; replacement air group
      - *Independence*—Captain N. M. Kindell; Air Group 27
      - *Langley*—Captain H. E. Regan; Air Group 51
  - CTG 37—Vice Admiral Sir H. B. Rawlings RN*
    - CTG 37.6—Vice Admiral Sir P. L. Vian RN (Com1st A.C. Sqdn)*
      - *Implacable*—Captain C. C. Hughes-Hallett RN*
      - *Indefatigable*—Captain Q. D. Graham RN*
      - *Indomitable*—Captain J. A. S. Eccles RN*
      - *Formidable*—Captain Phillip Ruck-Keene RN*[11]
    - CTG 37.7—Rear Admiral C. H. J. Harcourt RN (Com11th A.C. Sqdn)*
      - *Venerable*—Captain W. A. Dallmeyer RN*
      - *Vengeance*—Captain D. M. L. Neame RN*
      - *Glory*—Captain A. W. Buzzard RN*
      - *Colossus*—Captain G. H. Stokes RN*

* Nonaviator.

It was hoped that a sufficient foothold would be established by 4 November so that the first land-based AAF and Marine Corps planes could be brought in to Kyushu airfields to help cover the beachhead and to assist the escort carriers in supporting Sixth Army. As this happened, Task Force 58 would be released to join Third Fleet for strikes in the north. By December, the Allied Pacific Fleets—barring losses—could have 30 fast carriers ranging the coast of Japan. Earmarked as possible replacements or supplementary carriers by the end of the year were veterans *Essex, Franklin*, *Bunker Hill*, *San Jacinto*, *Victorious*, *Illustrious*, and the new British night light carrier *Ocean*.

If Japan continued the war after the fall of Kyushu—which few Allied leaders expected—MacArthur and Nimitz would implement Operation CORONET, landings on the Honshu coast 50 miles from Tokyo tentatively set for 1 March 1946. The amphibious ships carrying the First, Eighth, and Tenth armies would be confronted by suicide glider bombs catapulted from inside caves ten miles away, and all operations would have to be conducted during a continuous snowfall that did occur in early March 1946. How different this would be from the steaming tropical heat of the South Pacific![12]

Carrier staff planners for CORONET had not gone into any details by the summer of 1945, but MacArthur would undoubtedly rely again upon the fast carriers to support his assault.

4. *Final Operations*

Phase One of the Kyushu operation began with the sortie of Task Force 38 from Leyte on 1 July 1945. Fueling east of Iwo Jima on the eighth, the fast carriers picked up a weather front for the run in to strike Tokyo. Geared for severe counterattacks from kamikazes, Admiral Halsey launched his strikes on the tenth. But only two snoopers approached the force, and they were easily splashed by the combat air patrol. The attacking carrier planes were equally surprised to find no Japanese aircraft over Tokyo, rather that the Japanese had degassed and scattered their planes in widely dispersed revetments at least ten miles from any airfield. Still, the fighter-bombers were able to destroy over 100 grounded planes from the trouble-free skies over the capital of Japan.[1]

When the results of the 10 July strikes were in, Assistant Secretary (Air) Sullivan, riding aboard *Shangri-La*, concluded "that the Japanese had reached the irreducible minimum of planes to resist an invasion of the mainland." Requesting immediate passage home, he boarded a destroyer at 5:30 P.M. for Iwo Jima, where he caught a plane for the States and Washington. Arriving there, Sullivan proceeded to cancel several contracts for Navy aircraft, a process already begun by Di Gates. The major cutback was the F8F Bearcat; the Hellcat would do—especially as a fighter-bomber —if there were no enemy planes left to shoot down.[2]

The reason for lack of Japanese aerial opposition—though antiaircraft fire had been stiff—was simply that Japan had given up trying to destroy the fast carriers. The Army decreed that all remaining aircraft should be harbored until October, the month Japan guessed the United States would land, then be thrust against the American invasion shipping armada when it appeared off Kyushu.

Swinging north, Task Force 38 selected targets in northern Honshu and Hokkaido. Admiral Halsey seemed to attract foul weather, however, and strikes scheduled for 13 July could not be launched until two days later. Again, enemy planes rose nowhere and were difficult to locate on the ground, but the carrier planes sank over 50,000 tons of coastal shipping and light naval craft. The destruction was accompanied by very effective battleship-cruiser bombardments of the valuable Kamaishi and Muroran iron factories.

At the refueling rendezvous on 16 July, Third Fleet was joined by the British Pacific Fleet which had departed Sydney on 28 June. For the first time, Admiral Vian's task group became part of the American fast carrier tactical formation directly under Halsey's command. Aware of the shortcomings of British logistics and the lower fuel capacity of their ships, Halsey expected TF 37 to conduct strike operations on two days for every three undertaken by TF 38. By refueling from Servron 6 fast tankers, however, the British carriers "were able to match us strike for strike." [3] What did bother Rawlings and Vian, however, was night maneuvering, "constantly altering course to keep clear of the erratic and unpredictable movements of the *Bon Homme Richard.*"[4]

After inconclusive strikes and shelling on and near Tokyo 17–18 July, more refueling, and the intermittent heavy weather, the fast carriers launched their last strikes of the war against the immobile Mobile Fleet on 24 and 28 July 1945—an action which, incidentally, Admiral McCain considered a waste of time. Joined by AAF B-24s, the carrier planes severely damaged several capital ships at Kure, some of which sank until they settled on the shallow bottom. Halsey could rest now that *Ise* and *Hyuga*, which had escaped him at Leyte and the South China Sea sweep, were among those bottomed, as was battleship *Haruna*. Severely damaged were heavy carriers *Amagi* and *Katsuragi* and light carrier *Ryuho*. Also hit were uncompleted carriers *Kasagi*, *Aso*, and *Ibuki*. Night attacks assisted in the destruction. On Mick Carney's advice, Halsey routed the British planes to other targets; the U.S. Navy wanted full credit for sinking the Japanese surface fleet. However, the British did their work well, with night Hellcats from *Formidable* shooting down three enemy planes under a full moon the night of the twenty-fifth. Heavy antiaircraft fire cost Task Force 38 133 planes and 102 airmen—a frightful loss. Even so, fortunately, no enemy interceptors attacked the Fleet.[5]

July ended with heavy weather, a shore bombardment of southern Honshu on the twenty-ninth, and air strikes on Kobe and Nagoya the following day. The presence of typhoons prolonged refueling, and a special order from Admiral Nimitz prevented further combat sorties for over a week. Nimitz instructed Halsey to take the Third Fleet far away from southern Japan, for on 6 August a B-29 from the Marianas dropped an atomic bomb on Hiroshima on the western end of Honshu. The fleet had to stand clear to avoid the unknown effects the radiation fallout might have on the air and water in that area. The bomb, a highly guarded and well-kept secret, took the carrier admirals by complete surprise. None of them had known such a weapon existed. What its implications were for the aircraft carrier could only be guessed. A second such bomb was dropped by another B-29 on Nagasaki, Kyushu, on 9 August.

Meanwhile, General MacArthur requested carrier strikes on Misawa air base in northern Honshu, where intelligence reported the Japanese were massing a large air fleet and airborne troop unit for a large-scale suicide landing on Okinawa—a tactic already tried there unsuccessfully on a limited scale. The Japanese were in fact collecting about 200 medium bombers and 300 select troops, but for a suicide attack on B-29 bases in the Marianas.[6] After his heavy ships bombarded the Kamaishi factory on the eighth, Halsey sent his planes to Misawa on the ninth. They broke up the Marianas suicide force, destroying over 200 planes in revetments. More strikes were flown over and targets shelled in northeast Honshu on the tenth, during which the fledgling Canadian naval air arm was well represented. Lieutenant R. H. Gray RCN, senior pilot of 1841 Squadron on *Formidable*, pressed an attack with his Corsair against a Japanese destroyer at Onegawa Harbor despite heavy antiaircraft fire. Gray succeeded in scoring a direct hit on the vessel, but he himself was shot down. For his exploit, Gray was posthumously awarded the Victoria Cross—Britain's highest honor for bravery.[7]

These operations on 9–10 August broke the pattern of the July strikes. On the ninth the Soviet Union declared war on Japan, and its armies swept into Manchuria. Halsey reasoned that the airfields in northern Honshu and Hokkaido were the only ones close enough to Russia for long-range air strikes by Japan against her new enemy. So these raids were designed also to assist the Russians. In addition, for the first time since June, the Japanese counterattacked with about 20 planes on the ninth. Most were shot down, but one crashed a picket destroyer, causing heavy casualties.[8]

Until the evening of 10 August Third Fleet operations had conformed to the OLYMPIC timetable. That night Task Force 37 was to retire to Manus to replenish, while Task Force 38 was to withdraw to refuel, then retire to Eniwetok as planned. But that night Japan indicated she had accepted Allied surrender terms in principle, and was now discussing details. Admiral Rawlings decided to stay another day to await developments, and during refueling on the eleventh he conferred with Halsey. For lack of fast fleet tankers, Rawlings said that he had to withdraw immediately but wanted at least a token force in on the kill if Japan did surrender. Halsey agreed, and Rawlings selected *Indefatigable* and several escorts.

The end was coming quickly. Submarines operating in the Sea of Japan had closed shipping traffic from China and Korea, while the aerial mining of Japanese coastal waters and harbors by B-29s had virtually stopped all intercoastal shipping by the first of August. The devastating fire raids and atomic bombings by the strategic bombers brought Japan's economy to a virtual standstill. Okinawa-based and carrier air strikes, battleship-cruiser-destroyer bombardments, and a series of fierce typhoons ravaged the east coast from Hokkaido to Kyushu, further frustrating the futile attempt of Japan to continue her national life.

On 14 June 1945 the Joint Chiefs of Staff had ordered Generals MacArthur and Arnold and Admiral Nimitz to make plans "to take immediate advantage of favorable circumstances, such as a sudden collapse or surrender, to effect an entry into Japan proper for occupational purposes." [9] On Nimitz's staff, Forrest Sherman and his new assistant, Malcolm Schoeffel, initiated studies to occupy Japan and China, and had them ready on 9 and 13 August respectively. On the eleventh Rear Admiral Louis E. Denfeld, a fast battleship division commander, hauled down his flag for transit to Iwo Jima by destroyer, escorted by carrier *Independence.* As Ernie King's genius in personnel administration throughout most of the war, Denfeld would be needed to direct the emergency demobilization of the huge wartime Navy. Dodging a typhoon, *Independence* delivered her cargo for passage home by plane, then returned to TF 38 on the fourteenth. On 12 August Halsey placed Rear Admiral Ballentine, who had no real job as night carrier commander, in charge of naval landings from Third Fleet for the occupation. Simultaneously, Halsey resolved not to retire as planned but to press Japan until she surrendered, even though fuel shortages limited operations only to short ranges and ships' cooks "were reduced to serving dehydrated carrot salad." [10]

On 12 August a typhoon caused Halsey to stand clear of his proposed operating area off Tokyo; also, Task Force 37 under Vice Admiral Vian departed for Manus. Remaining were *Indefatigable* and her escorts, reorganized into Task Group 38.5 under Rawlings and joined by Admiral Fraser, Commander-in-Chief, BPF, on the sixteenth.

The last air operations of the Fast Carrier Task Force against Japan took place on 13 and 15 August 1945 with a refueling in between. On the thirteenth full-deckload strikes claimed over 250 planes on the ground, while the combat air patrol splashed 18 more. A smaller strike of 103 planes hit Tokyo after dawn on the fifteenth, shooting down 30 to 40 airborne enemy planes. Another 73 carrier planes were enroute to the target when Halsey got the word from Nimitz: "Suspend air attack operations." A few uninformed Japanese pilots continued the attack, shooting down four *Yorktown* Hellcats over the coast, but none got through the defensive fighters to reach the task force. Off Wake Island, *Antietam*'s strikes, scheduled for the next day, were also cancelled.

The war was over, yet Task Force 38 had to maintain a constant vigil against any Japanese treachery. Halsey ordered TF 38 to "Area McCain," 100 to 200 miles southeast of Tokyo, where the three task groups maintained their normal wartime air patrols through the twenty-third. For over an hour on the sixteenth and seventeenth the ships maneuvered in abnormally tight formations for aerial photographs to be taken of sprawling Fast Carrier Task Force. On the twenty-second and twenty-third the planes massed overhead for photos. On the nineteenth Admiral Ballentine hauled down his flag and reported to Guam as Nimitz's liaison officer to General MacArthur for the Japanese surrender, officially set for 2 September in Tokyo Bay. On the eighteenth Vice Admiral Ted Sherman hoisted his flag in *Lexington*, then shifted to *Wasp* two days later. On the twenty-second Vice Admiral Jack Towers raised his flag in *Shangri-La*. Slew McCain, bitter over his relief, was ready to leave, but Halsey convinced him to stay for the ceremony. Towers formally relieved McCain as Commander Task Force 38 on the morning of 1 September.

The early capitulation of Japan caused some confusion in the fleet, as Admiral Nimitz put his plans into effect immediately. Admiral Spruance at Guam ordered all Fifth Fleet units gathering for OLYMPIC to go to Okinawa, while he boarded a battleship for passage to Manila, 16–21 August, formulating occupation plans en route. He remained at Manila, conferring with MacArthur, for a week, then went to Okinawa on the thirtieth. His Fifth Fleet, the amphibious craft which would have landed troops at Kyushu, was to occupy the Inland Sea as soon after the surrender as practicable. Third Fleet would carry out the emergency occupation of Tokyo Bay.[11]

The China occupation was not as simple, due to the unrelenting advance of the Russians from the north and the quick takeover by the Chinese Communists. President Truman ordered Nimitz to occupy Dairen on the Liaotung peninsula ahead of the Russians, the important base they had lost to Japan in 1905.[12] This was not possible, however, since the Russians and the Nationalist Chinese government had signed a mutual defense pact on 14 August, and both countries jointly occupied the base. The United States did, however, help the Nationalists reoccupy their other ports from Shanghai to Korea. Air cover was provided by the three fast carriers which reached Eniwetok in mid-August, *Intrepid*, *Antietam*, and *Cabot*. On the twenty-first Halsey formed these ships into a task unit under Rear Admiral Art Davis, who had hoisted his flag in *Antietam* the day before. *Antietam* went first to Guam to repair an operational difficulty, while the other two ships joined Bogan's TG 38.3 on 25–27 August. On the twenty-ninth the three ships rendezvoused at Okinawa and next day were designated Task Force 72 under Davis—the first fast carriers to operate as part of Seventh Fleet. On 1 September TF 72 departed Okinawa for the Yellow Sea.

Late on 23 August Halsey assigned his carriers to new operating areas. While some planes flew aerial surveillance over Japanese airfields, others dropped food and supplies to prisoners of war. Halsey planned to take many of his surface ships into Sagami Wan, Tokyo's outer bay, on the twenty-sixth, but two typhoons appeared on the day before to discourage him. Unhappily, one of the storms made radical turns and bumped into Gerry Bogan's TG 38.3 off Shikoku. Half of the task group was fortunately 200 miles away under Ziggy Sprague, but the storm fell full force on *Randolph, Wasp,* and *Indefatigable. Randolph* lost steering control for four minutes, and the flight deck overhang of *Wasp* buckled, collapsing 20 feet of the forward deck—the same fate suffered by the heavy carriers in the June typhoon. Admiral Towers exonerated Bogan because of the storm's unpredictable movements, but *Wasp* had to be detached for home and repairs on the thirty-first. Ted Sherman, riding on *Wasp*, shifted his flag back to *Lexington.* The next day Donald Duncan boarded *Randolph*—as previously arranged—to stand by to relieve Bogan.[13]

Heavy weather was all the fast carriers had to fight. On the twenty-seventh many ships of Third Fleet entered Sagami Wan, but Task Force 38 was represented only by light carrier *Cowpens* because Halsey feared Japanese wrongdoing which the vulnerable carriers might not be able to avoid. Ted Sherman voiced a loud protest, feeling that the fast carriers had earned a place of honor at the surrender ceremony. Halsey, however, sent him a stinging rebuke to mind his own business.[14] The same day a bold Fighting 88 pilot landed at Atsugi airfield and ordered the Japanese to erect a banner: WELCOME TO THE U.S. ARMY FROM THE THIRD FLEET. The next day arriving Army paratroopers saw it.[15] On the twenty-eighth two of Towers' staff officers landed at Atsugi in a Torpedo 85 Avenger to begin preparatory talks. Night Fighting 91 from "Bonnie Dick" flew its last combat air patrol over Third Fleet the night of 27–28 August; next night the entire fleet lighted ship.[16]

As these preliminaries to surrender occurred, the last wartime "business-as-usual" routine took place. Admiral McCain completed his last action report on 31 August, concluding that since the new air group reorganization had not been tried in combat, "optimum striking power was never reached." [17] The changes came only days too late; ComAirPac Montgomery on 5 August had ordered all light carriers to have 36 Hellcat fighters and no more Avengers by the fifteenth. But since the fast carriers did not return to Eniwetok by that date, the change could not take place. The only light carrier at Eniwetok at the time was *Cabot*, whose Torpedo 32 was decommissioned on the eighteenth and more F6Fs flown aboard the next day. *Cabot* became the first and only wartime all-fighter light carrier.[18] As previously arranged, *San Jacinto* traded air groups with *Bataan* on the twenty-first and departed for home and an overhaul ten days later.

On 30 August the ships in Sagami Wan moved into Tokyo Bay, and Halsey shifted his flag from *Missouri* ashore to Yokosuka naval base. With Bull Halsey on Japanese soil, the war was surely over.

The Japanese surrender would be signed aboard battleship *Missouri* on 2 September, upon which the carriermen looked with disdain. To them the fast carrier symbolized victory far more than did the battleship; in fact one particular carrier, the "Big E," had survived the whole Pacific war and had participated in most of its battles. But *Enterprise* was still under repair in the United States and could not be present. There were nine other heavy carriers to choose from, but Secretary Forrestal played a bit of politics by suggesting *Missouri* in honor of President Truman's home state.[19] The President happily accepted, and it was at least a small feather in Navy's cap for the forthcoming battle over unification.

Britain used her carriers to facilitate the surrender and occupation of several places. Rear Admiral Harcourt, assembling his 11th Aircraft Carrier Squadron at Sydney, dispatched *Glory* to Rabaul; the bypassed garrisons in the South Pacific surrendered to Allied representatives aboard her flight deck in Simpson Harbor on 6 September. Harcourt hoisted his own flag aboard freshly repaired *Indomitable* and departed for Hong Kong via the Philippines in company with *Vengeance* and several escorts. Leaving his flagship outside the harbor for fear of mines, Harcourt transferred to a cruiser for the entry into Hong Kong on 30 August. Going ashore, Harcourt became Commander-in-Chief, Hong Kong and passed command of the task group to Rear Admiral C. S. Daniel RN.[20] The next day carrier planes sank a suicide boat trying to escape, but no further incidents occurred, and Hong Kong surrendered on 16 September. Other Japanese forces surrendered to whatever Allied ships or troops were present, but none were carriers.

The main event took place on schedule with no mishaps. General of the Army MacArthur represented the Allied powers as Supreme Commander, perhaps final recognition of Army superiority in Far Eastern affairs over the Navy. Fleet Admiral Nimitz signed the surrender agreement for the United States, flanked by two naval aviators, Admiral Halsey, who symbolized the fighter, and Rear Admiral Forrest Sherman, whose excellent mind had contributed so importantly to American strategy in the Pacific war. Standing in the front rank of witnesses alongside other Allied representatives and officers were Fast Carrier commanders Jack Towers, Ted Sherman, and Slew McCain. Only Pete Mitscher was missing.

Just as the ceremony ended, 450 carrier planes from Task Force 38 roared in from the sea over Tokyo Bay in a final demonstration of carrier air power. The war of the fast carriers had come to an end.

Twelve: Action Report

General Tojo told General MacArthur after the war that the three major factors in the defeat of Japan were the far-ranging operations of the Fast Carrier Task Force, the leapfrogging and neutralization of major bases (made possible by the fast carriers), and the destruction of Japan's merchant shipping by American submarines.[1] During the autumn of 1945, the United States Strategic Bombing Survey (USSBS) interrogated Japanese military and naval officers and found a similar appreciation for these aspects of American strategy. Two leading questioners, incidentally, were naval aviators, Rear Admiral Ralph Ofstie, the Senior Naval Member, and Commander Thomas H. Moorer, who had served in patrol planes and then for the last year of the Atlantic war as Admiral Bellinger's tactical officer.

The USSBS findings, released in 1947, criticized two military concepts which had originally dominated the war in the Pacific, but "which had become outmoded prior to our entry into the war through the rapid evolutionary advance of air weapons." One was the belief that naval surface engagements would decide the course of the war, the other that the invasion of Japan was necessary for victory.[2]

Strict Navy adherence to the battle line concept before and during the war USSBS criticized as "founded on tradition, precedent, custom, and classic example and influenced by service-pride and a study of military history which emphasized technique and results achieved, rather than cause and effect." Until 1943 money and industrial effort was wasted on building battleships, while aircraft carriers had to protect the battle line so that it could fight its Jutland. If the battle line concept had not dominated naval thinking at the Gilberts, Marianas, and Leyte, fleet warships and tactics could have focused entirely on air power. Evolution of naval tactics, said USSBS, "had passed from control of the sea to control of the air—control of the air as a prerequisite to control of the sea and all surface operations." [3]

USSBS concluded that the aircraft carrier, unlike land-based air forces, "was designed to an objective which was sound and which was achieved . . . to further the over-all mission of the fleet." This was to command the sea and its air, to cover and support landings, and to provide search and reconnaissance; its mobility was a major asset in fulfilling these missions. Vulnerable to air attack, expensive, and insufficient to launch mass attacks, carrier aviation "was not intended to operate against the enemy's sustaining industry. . . ." Carriers could do the latter, as in mid-1945, but only after complete domination of the air had been achieved with the constant help of land-based air. As a matter of fact, USSBS reminded the carrier's supporters, "Major carrier operations in World War II against land-based aircraft were conducted after the Japanese Air Forces had been reduced to a relatively impotent and ineffective force [excepting, of course, for the human guided missiles of the kamikaze corps]." [4]

The Army's own battle line concept, USSBS observed, had been employed in Europe successfully, "to move ground forces into the enemy homeland for the decisive struggle." Since modern history "contained no examples of a military victory without an invasion and . . . occupation of enemy's vital areas . . . ," the Army had concluded it should also use its traditional strategy in the Pacific. Important islands should be taken and developed as bases for attacks on other islands until the final jumps to Kyushu and Honshu. Air forces would be used to augment this strategy, interdicting enemy lines of communication, destroying enemy tactical air, and providing logistical airlift.[5]

This latter criticism by USSBS was severe. Had U.S. strategy "been oriented toward airpower and air weapons," the Survey noted, "and had our air, sea, and land forces been combined in one powerful thrust," all military forces in the Pacific could have been directed along the most direct route to Japan: from the Solomons to the Admiralties, Truk, the Marianas, and Iwo Jima. Militarily speaking, MacArthur's entire Philippines campaign was unnecessary, especially since Manila was wrecked and many Filipinos killed or maimed. Similarly, Nimitz's landings in the Gilberts, Marshalls, and at Okinawa were all unnecessary. Had the invasion of

Japan never been contemplated, these islands could have been bypassed and neutralized. From the Marianas, over 1000 B-29s could and would have pounded Japan into submission, while aerial mining would have closed her harbors.[6]

The USSBS report herein cited, one of 200 made after the war, is testimony of the impact of aviation on postwar analysts. Written by advocates of "airpower" (one word, no less), this summary not surprisingly overstated its case. Its criticism of American military leaders for failing to immediately recognize the full potential of strategic bombing, fast carrier strikes, and aerial mining was unfair Monday-morning quarterbacking. Such techniques had to be *tried* first. The very-long-range B-29 was not available until the summer of 1944, and its early missions from China to Japan were downright unimpressive. Only after the first incendiary raids of March 1945 did Japan begin to feel the severity of all-out strategic bombing. The first real trials of the Fast Carrier Task Force in November 1943 were both impressive (Rabaul) and unimpressive (Gilberts); only in the Marshalls under Mitscher did the fast carriers mature.

After the new air weapons had been proved, of course, USSBS was correct in its criticism. Battle line tactics were unnecessary at the Marianas, for which Spruance is to blame, and the concept of invasion of Japan was obsolete by the summer of 1945, meaning General Marshall and other Army leaders were at fault. After the Marianas—except for Halsey plodding north from Leyte and forming his battle line—the fast carriers broke away from the battle line to achieve tactical perfection by the end of the war. The AAF was not as fortunate, being unable to convince the Army that air-sea blockade would force Japan's surrender without invasion, until of course it did.

USSBS failed to appreciate the importance of sealing off the Luzon bottleneck. Submarines and aerial mines alone might have done great damage, but unless Japanese warships and planes were tied down elsewhere they could have been concentrated in the defense of shipping lanes, as they had been during the winter of 1941–1942. Hence the value of the South and Southwest Pacific campaigns in eating up Japanese air and thus enabling the Central Pacific offensive to proceed more expeditiously. Whether Nimitz was wrong in attacking the Gilberts and Marshalls is open to doubt, since his real objective was gaining airfields for the anticipated attack on Truk. Also, if MacArthur had not landed at Leyte and then Luzon, Nimitz would have gone to Amoy–Formosa; the bottle simply had to be corked for the strangulation of Japan to begin. Long-range air forces and submarines alone might have finished the job, but probably not for many more years.

A tight air-sea blockade was essential to any noninvasion strategy, which explains the Navy's desire to seize Okinawa and the Ningpo–Chusan area, with Savvy Cooke even advocating landings north of Japan. So Okinawa, an excellent staging base for the invasion of Kyushu, also doubled as a base for ships and planes in the blockade of Japan. As a matter of fact, had the war lasted until the end of 1945, OLYMPIC might well not have been carried out, for in September a devastating typhoon struck Okinawa, destroying many planes and valuable landing craft.[7] Had this calamity set back the Kyushu landings even one week, OLYMPIC might have been written off, for the tides at Kyushu were too strong for a landing after 1 November. Conceivably, the JCS might have then allowed Nimitz to implement LONGTOM for a landing in the Nimrod–Chusan–Ningpo area of China in October or November. Waiting for the spring of 1946 to stage OLYMPIC might have forced the Joint Chiefs to revise their strategy from invasion to air-sea blockade.

But all this speculation is academic, for Japanese officials when interrogated "indicated that Japan would have surrendered to the air attack [by 1 November, some said] even if no surface invasion had been planned, if Russia had not entered the war, and if the atomic bombs had not been dropped." [8]

After all the "what-might-have-been-ifs," the facts of the Fast Carrier Task Force success remain. Any final appraisal of the fast carriers must be based on the Force as it existed on the last day of the war. Admiral Montgomery noted this in the final wartime ComAirPac Analysis, quoting from *Belleau Wood*'s Action Report:

> With respect to recommendations[,] experience embraced in this report in no way changes the recommendations made within the past six months. But like the suggestions contained herein these are only applicable to *this war*, will soon be obsolete and if absorbed will focus the naval mind at a point [2 September 1945] which will soon be in the past and therefore misleading. . . .[9]

In fact, however, the immediate postwar fleet Tactical Instructions were virtually identical to PAC 10, written "with a wartime viewpoint as representing the best knowledge as to dispositions, number of ships, and tactical procedure that obtained in 1945." [10]

In the over-all picture, the aviators could—and did—congratulate themselves on the fact that in the Central Pacific offensive "the carrier task force with its extreme flexibility and mobility had been the dominant factor." Few analysts could disagree with the airmen's summary, signed by Forrest Sherman, that the mobility of the Fast Carrier Task Force "gave to the attacker the advantages of continuous initiative and surprise. No weapon is equally good at all times or in all places, but for the Pacific war the carrier task force was ideal." [11]

Tactically, only two major problems remained unsettled at war's end, task group composition and close air support techniques. With regard to the former, task groups larger than four carriers had been insufficiently tested, leading one supporter of Ted Sherman to conclude it was "not logical to assume that the fast carrier task force had reached the peak of its development when the enemy capitulated." [12] To Mitscher's supporters of the 3 CV, 1 CVL group, however, the five-carrier formation was "too unwieldy," especially during large-scale air operations or in bad weather.[13] As for air support, the Marines continued to criticize the Navy's control as "too inflexible." They wanted shipboard control transferred ashore, where requests for air strikes could be filled more quickly.[14] However, with large Army forces to support as well as coordinating the air defense of the beach and fleet, the Navy maintained its system.[15]

The future mission of the fast carriers as of mid-1945—with the enemy fleet destroyed and his major islands captured—was not encouraging. One observer concluded that "the chief mission of the Fast Carrier Task Force was completed . . . with the securing of Okinawa" as a base for land-based air; "the historic mission of the carrier was completed." The fast carrier strikes on Japan had been an "extra dividend"; "the principal job had been done." [16] Admiral Montgomery asked the unpopular but obvious question of whether close support was not now the primary function of the fast carriers.[17] The postwar Navy would have to take up this question.

As for the fast battleship as the backbone of the fleet, the end had come after Leyte when the last chance for a battle line action with the new battlewagons had been missed, and the type command of ComBatPac abolished. Within one month of Japan's surrender, Admiral Mitscher noted to Secretary Forrestal that it was "fallacious" to keep the battleships as support ships in the fast carrier formations. They could not use their main and antiaircraft batteries simultaneously, they required air protection when out of formation in their battle line, and they would not need their big guns anyway in the presence of carrier air—as proven at Saipan and during the run north from Leyte.[18] V-J Day marked the end of the old Gun Club; the final *coup de grâce* came in December 1950 when aviator Rear Admiral Malcolm Schoeffel became Chief of the Bureau of Ordnance, home of the Gun Club.

Before going on to a consideration of the postwar period in light of wartime developments, let us pause for a final appraisal of the men who had shaped these events and who in all probability would never fight again.

Fleet Admiral King will always remain a controversial figure whose single-minded determination to build up the wartime Navy and to win the war provided the Navy with strong command at the very top. His continued refusal to grant the aviators special status within the naval establishment did no great harm to the war effort, although his playing favorites (for example McCain over Towers or Ted Sherman) was inexcusable. Since King knew the Navy was changing to air, he must be credited with making the transition as evolutionary as possible in those two short years—bringing in junior flag aviators to key staff posts and pushing through in 1943 the new nuts-and-bolts post of DCNO (Air).

The war over, King moved to reorganize the Department. Using a study begun in August 1945 under Di Gates, in October King had the title of Cominch abolished, its functions absorbed into one over-all Chief of Naval Operations.[19] He also established five Deputy CNO posts: Personnel, Administration, Operations, Logistics, and Air. His major work completed, Ernie King stepped down as CNO on 15 December 1945. There would never be another quite like him.

Fleet Admiral Nimitz was literally the man of the hour in the Pacific war. His identification with submarines perhaps enabled him to weigh the dispute between his battleship and carrier admirals more objectively. In addition, his natural patience led him to admit mistakes and to make changes unhesitatingly. Without this side of Nimitz's personality, the fast carriers might not have been released from the Gilberts beaches or the post of Deputy Cincpac-Cincpoa redefined and given to Towers. As over-all Fleet commander in the Pacific, Nimitz sagaciously selected the right people to advise him. Two men stand out: Spruance and Forrest Sherman, while Nimitz left air matters to Towers. By the end of the war, Sherman was

Nimitz's right arm if not a major part of his brain. Peerless as wartime strategist and theater commander, Nimitz rated postwar appointment as CNO. However, Secretary Forrestal preferred a younger man and aviation officer and wanted to remove the old "black shoes" from the top postwar commands. Forrestal offered Nimitz chairmanship of the antiquated General Board or an advisory role, but Cincpac wanted to be CNO. With public and professional opinion supporting him, Nimitz won his case and relieved King in December.[20] He well deserved the post.

General of the Army MacArthur deserves evaluation in this history, because like Nimitz he learned first-hand the important role of the Fast Carrier Task Force, and by the end of the war had come to prefer naval air support at the beaches to that of the AAF. Apart from his irritating vanity and his obsession about returning to the Philippines, MacArthur came to accept the Pacific war for what it was, an air-sea-land war of vast distances that made final victory possible by blockade and bombing alone. "By the time we had seized the Philippines," he told Congress in 1951, "we were enabled to lay down a sea and Navy blockade so that the supplies for the maintenance of the Japanese armed forces ceased to reach Japan. . . . At least 3,000,000 of as fine ground troops as I have ever known . . . laid down their arms because they didn't have the materials to fight with. . . . When we disrupted their entire economic system . . . they surrendered." [21] MacArthur, truly a Pacific-oriented general, remained in command of the occupation and reconstruction of Japan.

Admiral Spruance, a brilliant strategist and coordinator of large naval forces afloat, commanded all the amphibious operations of the Central Pacific campaign, from the Gilberts to the planned Kyushu landings. His well-ordered, calculating mind was a major factor in the success of these operations, as was his close association with his tactical amphibious commander, Admiral Turner. Preferring to leave details to his subordinates, Spruance exercised tactical command over the fast carriers only twice—holding Pownall to the beaches in the Gilberts and doing the same to Mitscher at Saipan, and both actions resulted in the misuse of carriers. Tactically, Spruance, Turner, and Carl Moore, chief of staff, were the last inheritors of battle line formalism. By early 1945 Fifth Fleet staff included key aviators, and Spruance never again interfered with Mitscher.

Quiet and unassuming, Spruance deserved more than he got

after the war. As an honorarium, he was appointed Nimitz's successor in the post of Cincpac-Cincpoa, 24 November 1945 to 1 February 1946. He served out his last two and a half years on active duty as President of the Naval War College where, incidentally, he unrealistically continued the study of gunnery tactics and ignored aviation. Still virtually unknown by the public, he did not receive the rewards that Halsey did and that Spruance richly deserved: popular acclaim and the rank of fleet admiral. Perhaps only coincidentally, Spruance faded from the limelight as inconspicuously and rapidly as did other battleship-oriented officers, including the amphibious leaders, for who could envision battle line or amphibious operations in a world dominated by atomic-armed strategic bombers? Carl Moore retired from the Navy on the first day of 1947, followed shortly thereafter by Kelly Turner.

Admiral Halsey proved to be an embarrassment to the Pacific Fleet after his arrival in the Central Pacific in mid-1944. At sea aboard *Enterprise* when the first bomb had fallen on Pearl Harbor, Halsey had served in the forward areas continuously except during a short illness. He needed a rest, but being the bull he was he wanted a job after the victory in the Solomons. Backed by public opinion, he won command of one platoon in the Central Pacific command shift, but except for Peleliu Halsey was never entrusted with the command of an amphibious operation. Acting virtually as tactical commander of the Fast Carrier Task Force in strategic support of Army operations in the Philippines and at Okinawa, Halsey managed to leave the Leyte beachhead uncovered to a Japanese fleet bombardment and then took the carriers into two typhoons. Sloppy and careless in their command habits and communications, Halsey and his lieutenant Vice Admiral McCain became more inefficient as time passed. As Jocko Clark suggested to this writer on numerous occasions, the war simply became too complicated for Halsey. Also, the strain of his long service was a factor. Within a week of the surrender, Ted Sherman—Halsey's loyal follower and friend—and Duke Ramsey discussed Halsey's problems: "We both agreed that Halsey had not been thinking straight lately." [22] McCain, who had commanded the fast carriers only six months to Mitscher's 14, was similarly exhausted; he died four days after Japan signed the surrender.

Neither Halsey nor McCain had a place in the Navy's postwar plans. McCain was en route to the Veterans Administration when he died. Halsey handed over all his duties to Spruance on 19 September and went home for speaking tours. In a final tribute to Halsey's exploits earlier in the war, the Navy in December promoted him to fleet admiral. He retired from active duty in April 1947. In this generous spirit of victory, Congress also promoted McCain posthumously to admiral. Concerning the record of Halsey and McCain with the fast carriers, however, this writer can only conclude that both men were inferior third-act heroes in the Central Pacific offensive and might best have served elsewhere. Their Central Pacific commands belonged to more competent officers.

Vice Admiral Towers directed the formation of the Pacific Fleet air forces, including the Fast Carrier Task Force, in 1943, and deserves credit as the leader who battled the Gun Club and Nimitz to gain for carrier aviation its rightful place in the Pacific Fleet. Long considered a crusader, however, Towers had to buck the resentment of Ernie King and the reservations of Nimitz to gain his objective. But gain them he did, becoming Nimitz's deputy in February 1944 and then Commander Task Force 38 just before the war ended. Full recognition of his and aviation's victory came swiftly after the Japanese surrender. On 31 October 1945 Towers left the fast carriers to accept the honorarium appointment of Commander Fifth Fleet. He relieved Admiral Spruance on 8 November in the full rank of admiral. The crowning achievement came on 1 February 1946 when Towers relieved Spruance as Cincpac-Cincpoa, being sworn in aboard carrier *Bennington.* Virtually unknown to the public, Jack Towers was one of the unsung heroes of the carrier war. In pressing the cause of naval aviation, he completed the task begun by Admiral Moffett a quarter of a century before.

Vice Admiral Mitscher emerged from the war as the acknowledged leader of carrier aviation. Providing inspiring leadership to the previously misused fast carriers, he led the Fast Carrier Task Force in all its major operations. His first tour lasted an exhausting ten months, January through October 1944, followed later by four more strenuous months under the kamikaze deluge. Of Mitscher Nimitz could say, "He is the most experienced and most able officer in the handling of fast carrier task forces who has yet been developed. It is doubtful if any officer has made more important contributions than he toward [the] extinction of the enemy fleet."[23] The first high-ranking aviator to return home from the wars, the normally softspoken Mitscher immediately opened fire against the battleship and the AAF. Secretary Forrestal wanted him to be CNO, but Mitscher refused; he hated desk jobs. Promoted to admiral early in 1946, Mitscher briefly commanded the new Eighth Fleet and then the Atlantic Fleet, bringing the fast carriers into that ocean for the first time. The rigors of the war finally caught up with him, however, and he died in February 1947. For the Fast Carrier Task Force, Mitscher had been The Leader.

Vice Admiral Ted Sherman, the only air admiral to lead fast carrier forces from late 1942 to the end of the war almost continually, deserves special credit for advancing the multicarrier task formation and for his dynamic leadership at Rabaul, Leyte, and Okinawa. His appointment to command Task Force 58 as a vice admiral was a year overdue; McCain had gotten the job Sherman deserved. A Halsey-type slugger and influenced by an explosive personality, Sherman was by any measure the best of the latecomer air admirals to command carriers in battle. He relieved Towers as Commander Fifth Fleet at Tokyo 18 January 1946 and in April brought that famous fleet to its new home at Los Angeles. But as a fighter, little remained for Sherman to do after the war, and early in 1947 he retired.

Rear Admiral Forrest Sherman, though he never went to sea during the Central Pacific offensive, had perhaps more influence on the strategy of that theater and its over-all direction than any other air admiral. His keen mind had already sufficiently impressed Ernie King and Jack Towers when Nimitz made him his closest adviser. Sherman's cold intellect and ruthless ambition irritated and frightened his peers, but these traits in no way minimized his contribution to victory and to cementing the cleavage between Nimitz and Towers during the fall and winter of 1943–1944. He served briefly as the first battle carrier (*Midway*-class) division commander after the war, but his star was tied to Nimitz. As vice admiral, Sherman became DCNO (Operations) when Nimitz became CNO in December 1945.

Rear Admirals Montgomery and Clark, for their fine abilities as fighting admirals, were kept either in the Pacific or on call during most of the offensive. Montgomery tested many of the earlier tactical formations, then distinguished himself at Rabaul, the Marianas, and the Philippines. Commanding West Coast fleet air and AirPac in 1945 after his injury, Montgomery became vice admiral and in August 1946 relieved Ted Sherman as Commander Fifth Fleet.

Clark, like Halsey and Ted Sherman a well-known fighter, made the new *Yorktown* a model fast carrier and then became Mitscher's first lieutenant in battle. His unfortunate position in the second typhoon in no way diminished his exploits in the Marianas and off Okinawa. At sea or under orders for duty afloat since mid-1941, Clark took a training command in 1945 and the next year became embroiled in the troubles over demobilization and unification.

Rear Admirals Radford and Duncan did not serve at sea continuously simply because their superb administrative skills were needed in Washington. Radford organized aviation training in 1942–1943, then managed to get a fast carrier division before being drafted first by Towers and then by McCain for staff work. By careful string-pulling, he managed to return to the fast carriers in 1945. He distinguished himself off Okinawa and would have been the only veteran fast cardiv leader to have a task group in OLYMPIC. Going to Washington after the surrender, Vice Admiral Radford relieved Mitscher as DCNO (Air) in January 1946. Duncan was not as lucky in escaping desk jobs. His command and shakedown of *Essex* in 1943 laid the groundwork for bringing the other ships of this class into commission. Drafted by Ernie King later that year, Duncan lent his expertise to solving many problems in the Cominch office. Relieving Gerry Bogan of his task group in September 1945, Duncan stayed at sea for another year.

Rear Admiral Ramsey shared Duncan's fate in that he never served afloat after taking over the Bureau of Aeronautics in mid-1943. Adroitly manipulating the difficult procurement and technical development programs of naval aviation, Ramsey was not released to be Spruance's chief of staff until two full years had passed. Tremendously popular among aviators as well as a very talented officer, Ramsey was promoted first to vice admiral in November 1945, serving briefly as Deputy Cincpac-Cincpoa under Spruance, and then to admiral in December, beginning a two-year tour of duty as Vice CNO under Nimitz in January 1946. His contribution to the success of the fast carriers had been indirect but nevertheless significant.

Rear Admirals Reeves, Bogan, and Davison all turned in excellent scores as fast carrier task group commanders. Tough and informed leaders, each compiled a distinguished record. Due for duty ashore, Reeves and Bogan left the fast carriers in the summers of 1944 and 1945 respectively. Davison's untimely relief during Okinawa ended in a training command and shortened career for him.

By the autumn of 1944 the Pacific Fleet could depend on the availability of good, reliable, experienced carrier admirals. Some, as stated above, failed to get to sea in time to prove their mettle as combat fast carrier admirals, or circumstances kept them from exercising direct command. But their work as escort carrier admirals, fast carrier captains, or key staff officers was important. Others who fit into this category were Rear Admirals Gardner, Ballentine, Davis, Sallada, and the two Spragues.

The average American naval aviator below the rank of admiral had so much training and experience that after Rabaul the Japanese could not have hoped to match him. Many pilots achieved outstanding records, and a large number of them flying fighters became aces (five or more kills) as they encountered increasingly inferior enemy pilots and aircraft. The top World War II Navy ace was Commander Dave McCampbell of *Essex*'s Air Group 15, who shot down a total of 34 Japanese planes during the Turkey Shoot and Leyte battles. For his deeds he became the only pilot of the Fast Carrier Task Force to win the Medal of Honor (though Butch O'Hare had received one in 1942). His skill and bravery were typical of the fast carrier pilot.

The assignment of fast carrier admirals to the key postwar commands was no coincidence. Secretary Forrestal, welcoming the return of these carrier combat veterans from the wars, declared on 4 December 1945: "The actual fact is that the Navy is becoming an air Navy. It is becoming that by a natural evolution of its activities and a natural reflection of the increasing preponderance of Naval aviation in our activities. The leading commands of the Navy will in time be occupied by men who deal with air in one form or another." Forrestal gathered a clique of key airmen about him in beginning to make these changes. It included Mitscher, Radford, Forrest Sherman, Stuart Ingersoll, and Thomas H. Robbins (skipper of *Lexington* off Okinawa), also nonaviator Mick Carney.[24]

The changes came rapidly. By the summer of 1946, the Navy high command reflected the impact of the wartime fast carriers. Forrestal was still Secretary of the Navy and Sullivan Under Secretary. Under CNO Fleet Admiral Nimitz were Admiral Duke Ramsey, Vice CNO; Vice Admirals Louis Denfeld, DCNO (Personnel); Forrest Sherman, DCNO (Operations); Mick Carney, DCNO (Logistics); and Arthur Radford, DCNO (Air). Rear Admiral Slats Sallada was still Chief of BuAer, while Malcolm Schoeffel had become first aviator Deputy Chief of the Bureau of Ordnance.

Admiral Jack Towers commanded the Pacific Fleet, Admiral Pete Mitscher the Atlantic Fleet.

Even the old advisory General Board underwent overhaul, as Forrestal and King had been planning since late 1944. As the Board was comprised of old battleship admirals awaiting retirement (among them Fletcher, Ghormley, Hustvedt), Forrestal picked Jack Towers early in 1947 to revitalize it with younger combat veterans who would undertake good, forward-looking studies. By April 1947 Towers had such a Board: Vice Admirals Soc McMorris and Pat Bellinger, Captains Truman Hedding and Arleigh Burke, and Colonel Randolph Pate of the Marines. Towers chaired the Board until his retirement from the Navy in December 1947, followed by Soc McMorris, Jack Shafroth, and Harry Hill, all nonaviators. Many bright younger flag officers and senior captains were brought in, but with Navy policy so confused in the midst of unification and the Cold War the General Board could accomplish little; it passed out of existence in 1951.[25]

For the ten years after V-J Day the fast carrier admirals dominated key posts within the U.S. Navy, joined by nonaviators who had become identified in some capacity with the wartime carrier force. For instance, DCNOs (Air) were Vice Admirals Radford (1946), Duncan (1947), Price (1948), Durgin (1949), Cassady (1950), Gardner (1952), Ofstie (1953), and Combs (1955). Chiefs of BuAer until the Bureau was abolished in 1959 were Rear Admirals Pride (1947), Combs (1951), Apollo Soucek (1953), James S. Russell (1955), and Bob Dixon (1957). Soucek had brought *FDR* into commission, Russell had been chief of staff to Ralph Davison, and Dixon operations officer to Ted Sherman. ComAirPacs were Vice Admirals Price (1946), Sallada (1948), Tommy Sprague (1949), Martin (1952), and Pride (1956). ComAirLants were Vice Admirals Bogan (1946), Stump (1948), Ballentine (1951), and McMahon (1954).

The immediate postwar organization of fleets underwent several changes. Effective 1 January 1947, all numbered fleets were abolished, leaving only the "Pacific Task Fleet" under Vice Admiral Montgomery and the "Atlantic Task Fleet" under Vice Admiral Spike Blandy. The divided strategic command in the Pacific was perpetuated. General MacArthur controlled Japan, the Ryukyus, and U.S. forces in the Philippines, and the Navy's Cincpac controlled the rest. Admiral Towers held this supreme post only one month, until relieved in February by Louis Denfeld.[26] The post of

Deputy Cincpac, after the war held in succession by Vice Admirals Newton, Ramsey, Lynde D. McCormick, Duncan, and Sallada, was downgraded after 1948.

Then, in the summer of 1948, despite demobilization and the mothballing of all veteran wartime carriers, the numbered fleets reappeared as "task fleets," the word *task* being dropped early in 1950. The famous Third and Fifth fleets were retired, but Seventh survived in the Far East and a new Sixth was formed in the Mediterranean. As during the war, large fast carriers were not needed in the Atlantic, but they were in the Mediterranean area. Consequently, after Admiral Mitscher's death, several distinguished nonaviators (Blandy, Fechteler, McCormick, Jerauld Wright to 1960) but no airmen commanded the Atlantic Fleet until Admiral Thomas H. Moorer took it over in 1965. The Sixth Fleet became a carrier fleet: Vice Admirals Forrest Sherman (1948), Ballentine (1949), Gardner (1951), Cassady (1952), Combs (1954), and Ofstie (1955).

The Pacific remained the Navy's theater, where the mobility of the fast carriers provided quick military response to any challenge. Cincpacs after Towers were Admirals Denfeld (1947), Ramsey (1947), Radford (1949), and Stump (1953–1958). In 1958 the area was divided between the over-all Pacific Command and the Pacific Fleet, both four-star Navy billets. Commander Seventh Fleet, as during the Pacific war, was a nonaviator until early in the Korean War, when the Fast Carrier Task Force was rejuvenated to be its main striking arm. It then became an aviation billet: Vice Admirals Martin (1951), Clark (1952), Pride (1953), Ingersoll (1955), and Beakley (1957).[27]

The top post in the Navy, CNO, reflected the change to aviation most profoundly. Not always an aviator, the CNO required close contact with air, and if he himself did not fly his Vice Chief had to be a pilot. At the end of the Nimitz–Ramsey reign in 1947, a rivalry over the next CNO arose between the old Gun Club, supporting Spike Blandy, and the aviators (including Nimitz and Forrest Sherman), supporting Duke Ramsey. With the unification controversy raging, President Truman wanted a compromiser and picked a compromise candidate, Louis Denfeld, who selected Arthur Radford as Vice CNO.[28] Denfeld was followed by aviator Forrest Sherman in 1949, nonaviators Bill Fechteler in 1951 (Donald Duncan Vice CNO), Mick Carney in 1953, and Arleigh Burke in 1955, and aviators thereafter: George Anderson in 1961, David

L. McDonald (air officer and exec of *Essex*, 1944–1945) in 1963, and Tommy Moorer in 1967. Admiral Radford served as Chairman of the JCS, 1953-57, as did Moorer, 1970-74.

The British Navy also underwent rapid transformation into an air orientation. Despite Admiral Fraser's remark that "the British Fleet is seldom spectacular, never really modern, but always sound," [29] the Fleet Air Arm took a leading role in postwar carrier technical developments. The real deficiency was in quantity, for Britain's decline as a great power led to a reduced fleet. Several of the *Majestic*s and larger carriers then building were not completed, while some *Colossus*-class light carriers were sold or loaned to Canada, Australia, France, and Holland. Work on near-finished heavier carriers was suspended for several years, until 36,800-ton *Eagle* was commissioned in 1951, followed in the mid-1950s by sister ship *Ark Royal* and four 22,000-ton light carriers of the new *Hermes* class.

After its experiences in running down German battleships in the Atlantic and in prolonged carrier operations in the Mediterranean and Pacific, the Royal Navy had no illusions about its future. The BPF shifted its base from Sydney to Hong Kong early in 1946, and in June the Fleet Air Arm's leading spokesman, Vice Admiral Sir Denis Boyd RN, relieved Admiral Fraser in command of that fleet. Hoisting his flag aboard carrier *Venerable*, Boyd announced the BPF would have no battleships. Fraser imitated Nimitz, becoming First Sea Lord (1947–1951) as admiral of the fleet. Vice Admiral Vian, after a brief tour as Second-in-Command, BPF, served as Fifth Sea Lord (Air) in 1946–1947, being eventually promoted to admiral of the fleet.

Most of the wartime British fast carrier captains went on to high flag rank in the postwar Royal Navy. Charles E. Lambe of *Illustrious* stayed in air another decade and ended his career in 1960 as Admiral of the Fleet Sir Charles Lambe, First Sea Lord. ComAirPac observers Richard Smeeton and Frank Hopkins rose to be full admirals, as did former Third/Fifth Fleet liaison officer Michael LeFanu. British naval aviators finally caught up with their USN counterparts when the first British pilot to command a fast carrier (*Ocean*), Admiral of the Fleet Sir Caspar John RN, served as First Sea Lord and Chief of Naval Staff, 1960–1963.

The takeover by the American air admirals in 1945 did not diminish the fact that it was made possible by victory over Japan in a sea war which by any stretch of the imagination would never again be repeated. Continental nations like Germany might die in battle and be reborn within one generation to fight again; armies can be raised and trained easily and quickly. But navies are much more sophisticated and require years of continuous growth and warship construction. Japan's naval demise came 50 years after her first modern fleet victory over China in the Yalu River; her achievements in 1941–1942 were remarkable but could not be sustained against an industrial power such as the United States. Neither Japan nor any other nation which survived World War II entertained the faintest hope of ever challenging American supremacy at sea. This being so, the apparent need for the Fast Carrier Task Force immediately disappeared.

The atomic bomb made matters worse for the Navy. When A-bombs flattened Hiroshima and Nagasaki less than ten days before the Japanese quit fighting, the obvious conclusion was that the A-bomb—dropped from a strategic bomber—had been the direct cause of Japan's surrender. The public believed this, the military believed it—contrary to the findings of the USSBS study, which assigned equal weight for the immediate capitulation to the Russian declaration of war and the atomic bombs, but over-all defeat also to the tight air-sea blockade of Japan maintained by mines, subs, and conventional land- and carrier-based aircraft. The AAF had dropped the Bomb from B-29s; the Navy had no carriers large enough to carry planes of that size. The Bomb had ended the war —or so the reasoning went— and would do the same in all future wars, *ergo* the Air Force was to be the new first line of defense, and the Navy and carriers were obsolete. Furthermore, when carrier *Saratoga* was sunk and light carrier *Independence* gutted by an experimental nuclear blast near Bikini Atoll, Marshall Islands, in July 1946, carriers appeared suddenly vulnerable to the new weapon.

When continental Soviet Russia loomed up as the new potential enemy in 1946–1947, two questions plagued the Navy: of what possible use could Pacific-oriented fast carriers be against Moscow or the Ukraine, and how vulnerable were they to land-based atomic air attack?

The unification issue, already put off for postwar consideration, was made all the more bitter by the appearance of the Bomb. The AAF wanted independence to maintain its virtual monopoly over strategic bombing and nuclear weapons. The Navy, which had developed its wartime air arm in complete ignorance of the Bomb, felt it would now become subordinated to the new Air Force. And well it might—for the traditional American postwar letdown was in full swing. Unschooled in the responsibilities of world leadership, the American public and government had but one thought, to demobilize the armed forces and bring the boys home. Having one miracle weapon to depend upon in the future made this attitude all the more convenient. The U.S. would return to its shell, covered by strategic bombers—economical, efficient, simple.

The Navy had no really convincing argument to counter this viewpoint or to oppose unification with a separate Air Force. Ferdinand Eberstadt, appointed by Forrestal to formulate a Navy position on unification, completed his report in September 1945. He recommended three separate departments, War, Navy, and Air, but not unified under a single head. The next month Senate hearings pitted the Navy against the Army and AAF, both of which advocated a single Secretary over all three services; Arthur Radford and Forrest Sherman spoke for the Navy. The Richardson Report was presented, showing that such luminaries as Nimitz and Halsey had supported unification during the war; these two men quickly changed their minds. But the Army and AAF, experts in management and politics, were too effective. After they won President Truman over to their side in December, unification became only a matter of time.[30]

The Navy continued to fight unification in 1946. Admiral Nimitz opposed it outright, but convinced by Forrest Sherman that unification was inevitable, he joined Sherman and Ramsey in supporting it. The admirals insisted, however, that naval aviation and the Marine Corps be kept within the Navy. Admiral Radford did not agree with the Nimitz group, and he was joined by several other airmen, especially Jocko Clark. Nevertheless, unification and the U.S. Air Force became law in July 1947, and Forrestal was appointed the first Secretary of Defense. John Sullivan became Secretary of the Navy, now a downgraded post. Demobilization and cutbacks in the Navy's budget continued, however, leading Radford and the air admirals to "revolt" late in 1949. Criticizing the Air Force's new B-36 strategic bomber as vulnerable, CNO Denfeld and several younger veteran Navy pilots presented their case to Congress, including Vice Admiral Carney (non-air), Rear Admiral Ofstie, Brigadier General Megee, Captains Burke (non-air), Thach, and Fred Trapnell (Radford's wartime chief of staff), and

Commanders Bill Martin and Bill Leonard. The only tangible result of this squabble was the replacement of the ineffective Denfeld with the brilliant Forrest Sherman as CNO.

The overriding concern of the admirals was to share the strategic bombing role and nuclear capability of the Air Force. But with the completion of the last wartime-constructed *Essex*es and *Midway*s immediately after the war, no new carriers had been programmed. Yet, a new design offered encouragement: the 60,000-ton "supercarrier" *United States* (CVB-58). The keel for this great ship was laid in April 1949, followed within days by its sudden cancellation, which was a major cause behind the "revolt of the admirals." The coming of the Korean War in 1950 reversed the situation, and the next year Congress appropriated funds for the new, large 56,000-ton *Forrestal*-class carriers, which could launch nuclear air attacks. These and larger models began joining the fleet in the mid-1950s, culminating in the giant nuclear-powered 85,000-ton flattops of the new *Enterprise* variety of the 1960s and 1970s.

In addition to its new carriers, the Navy seized the strategic bombing priority enjoyed by the Air Force, which had depended upon manned long-range bombers and intercontinental ballistic missiles launched from hardened silos in the United States. In 1960, the Navy made operational the first of many submarines armed with new Polaris ICBMs to be fired from beneath the surface of the ocean. Virtually impossible to detect, the Polaris sub enjoyed flexibility and security whereas the striking forces of the Air Force did not. But what effect did this new weapon have on the attack carrier?

Ironically, with the preoccupation of the American armed forces with developing strategic weapons with which to confront the Soviet Union, the serious possibility of total nuclear war began to pass in the mid-1950s. Instead, Communist revolutionary wars inspired by Russia and China, which had been overrun by the insurgent Communists in 1949, broke out and required American participation. But atomic or hydrogen bombs could hardly be dropped on civilian villages infiltrated by guerrillas, nor could they be used to precipitate another war. Flaring up in the Far East–Southeast Asia area—the same region attacked by the Fast Carrier Task Force in 1944–1945—these wars were ideally suited to air operations by fast, mobile carrier forces. Unfortunately, the air admirals, like their counterparts in the Army and Air Force, took 20 years before they could accept the fact these wars demanded equal, if not more, attention than the effort to deter Soviet Russia from waging world war.

American military leaders, like the government and people, considered the Korean War an oddity or mistake—a "police action"—that should never be repeated. But it was *Essex*-class carriers which provided the most effective air support for ground forces in Korea between 1950 and 1953. During the immediate postwar search for a mission, the Navy in November 1946 had abolished its old dive bomber (VB) and torpedo (VT) squadrons for the common attack (VA) squadrons. Also, it abandoned the special night forces in favor of a total, all-weather capability. The main all-purpose attack plane became the Douglas BT2D Dauntless II, in February 1946 renamed Skyraider and two months later redesignated AD-1. Designed for use against Japan, this aircraft and the veteran F4U Corsair provided ideal close air support for the Army and Marines in Korea. The Air Force, completely oversold on strategic bombing, had abandoned propeller-driven attack planes in favor of jets. These swift craft, used with the old AAF tactics of deep support, proved entirely inadequate in Korea.[31] Conversely, Air Force jet fighters in Korea were excellent, while those of the Navy, developed during the postwar budget squeeze, were inferior to those of the enemy.

Since Korea had apparently been an emergency crisis—which had, however, provided the Navy with a lever for obtaining appropriations for more carriers—the air admirals were not strongly influenced by techniques used in Korea. Their concern, like that of the government, the two sister services, and the public at large, was Russia. The four-carrier Task Force 77 which provided close support and some strategic bombing in Korea was replaced by widely dispersed single *Forrestal*-class attack carriers armed for nuclear attack only. Many older *Essex*es were recommissioned as antisubmarine carriers (CVS) to track down far-ranging Soviet subs. The fast battleships, down to one in commission by 1950, had been bolstered to four to provide very effective shore bombardment in Korea. But again regarded as obsolete, these excellent amphibious support ships were all returned to mothballs by 1958. The trusty old Corsair was immediately phased out after Korea; 90 of the last F4U-7 model were sold to France for use against guerrillas in Vietnam. The prop-driven XA2D-1 Skyshark, designed to replace the AD, developed mechanical troubles which the Navy did not consider worth correcting; the plane was canceled in 1953. Production of the versatile AD Skyraider ceased in 1957. The Navy went to jets designed to carry heavy, even nuclear payloads from *Forrestal*-class carriers in order to bomb key continental targets—not to provide slow, low close support for amphibious or ground forces in the jungles of Asia.

The Navy's position during the 1950s typified traditional American attitudes toward war and the world at large, though it was also conditioned by the bitter struggles with the Air Force. American wars were always to be aimed at complete military victory, this time by strategic bombing. Also, Europe remained the prime concern, as it had been during World War II. Hence "massive retaliation" formed the basis of American defense policy during the 1950s, while major U.S. ground forces remained in Europe as part of the North Atlantic Treaty Organization. But the world and traditional political objectives in war were changing. The rise of communism in Asia on the heels of Japanese imperialism drastically altered the world balance of power and called for military techniques then being sacrificed in the nuclear arms race. Perhaps General MacArthur had not exaggerated when in 1944 he said that "the history of the world will be written in the Pacific for the next ten thousand years." [32]

By 1960, when the first Polaris submarine went to sea, American leaders feared involvement in any conflict in Southeast Asia because of the "lack of an American capacity to fight a limited war, especially an unconventional or guerrilla one." [33] Air bases in Japan, the Philippines, Okinawa, and Guam were too distant from Southeast Asia for efficient tactical support in such countries as Thailand, Vietnam, or Indonesia, while Seventh Fleet's three carriers were too spread out—one off Japan, one off Formosa–Okinawa, and only one in the South China Sea. Such was the situation when the United States became involved in the Vietnam crisis early in the 1960s. New requirements there demanded a general reassessment of American military objectives and capabilities.

The Vietnam War, which became an American conflict in February 1965 with carrier air strikes on North Vietnam, brought the U.S. Navy back to its tactical situation as of V-J Day. The three-to-four-carrier Task Force 77 off Vietnam duplicated Task Force 58 off Okinawa by cruising offshore, but without serious threat of enemy air attack, to launch air strikes against targets along the Vietnamese coast and to support ground forces ashore. The rapidly disappearing Skyraider (redesignated A-1H) remained the most reliable fixed-wing close-support airplane, just as when designed as the XBT2D 20 years before, though too often it was wasted in strategic bombing chores. The jets proved best as fighters but were really too fast for optimum efficiency in close support. The new armed helicopter, flown into battle by a revitalized Army air service, added a new dimension to air support, but also old C-47 cargo planes and even B-52 jet strategic bombers were pressed into the business of tactical air support while the Navy and Air Force re-examined the possibilities of building a successor to the Skyraider and its TBM, SB2C predecessors.

In ships, familiar vessels such as *Ticonderoga* and *Hancock* and some of the very same destroyers that had battled kamikazes off Okinawa accompanied new carriers and lighter ships into the fight. Simultaneously, new carrier construction was ordered. Additional evidence that the old problems had reappeared came when finally, in 1968, the Navy recalled one of its four battleships to active duty for offshore fire support.

Fleet requirements in the late 1960s closely resembled those of 1944 and 1951, and the same men were in command—only at higher echelons—to direct the carrier-centered fleets. Two such men each commanded the Seventh Fleet and then the Pacific Fleet in 1965–68, Admirals Roy L. Johnson, air officer of *Hornet* in 1944, and J. J. Hyland, Commander Air Group 10 on *Intrepid* in 1945. The same Bill Martin who had led Mitscher's night Avengers from the "Big E" in 1944 and a year later from the "Bonnie Dick" was vice admiral in command of the two-carrier Sixth Fleet during the Arab-Israeli war of 1967.

The aviators had successfully forged an air Navy by V-J Day 1945, using as their vehicle the Fast Carrier Task Force. After sinking the Japanese surface fleet, the mission of the air Navy became close support of amphibious forces and air-sea blockade of the enemy coast by sinking shipping and bombing key targets, especially airfields, ashore. With only slight variations, dictated by the absence of enemy aircraft, this mission remained intact during the Korean and Vietnam wars. By the summer of 1967, the Navy believed, as reported by the editors of *The New York Times*, "that other Vietnams are at least as likely to develop as a nuclear war against the Soviet Union and China, and having the mobility and striking power of the carriers would therefore seem at least as important as having intercontinental missiles." [34]

The U.S. Navy continued to be led by its aviators through the 1970s. The last World War II–weaned "brown shoes" attained the senior commands just as their fast carriers bombed North Vietnam in the closing days of that war (1972–73), as those in the Sixth fleet stood by during the Arab-Israeli War of 1973, and all continued to police the world's oceans under the *Pax Americana,* even as the Soviet Union began to float a modest carrier force of its own. Admiral Noel Gaylor, once of Towers's staff, held the Pacific Command, 1972–76. Indeed, the continuity of America's air-centered Navy has remained intact as the backbone of *Pax Americana* down to the end of the century, including the Persian Gulf War of 1990–91.

Between each of the Navy's three Pacific conflicts, however, the naval aviators had confused their mission by adopting a continental strategy with which to confront Russia. Once the Polaris submarine absorbed that requirement, the modern fast attack carrier could resume its special mission of waging warfare along the periphery of the continental landmasses. Since the character of the Polaris subs of necessity remains passive, the major active combat by the Navy is done by naval forces built around aircraft carriers. And with the rapid decline of British fleet aviation, the naval aspects of these limited wars became primarily the responsibility of the U.S. Navy.

Twenty years passed between the creation of Admiral Moffett's Bureau of Aeronautics in 1921 and the first large-scale fast carrier task force attack on Pearl Harbor. Another 20 years elapsed between the victory of the U.S. Fast Carrier Task Force over Japan's navy and the final realization of the mission of the modern fast carrier force: to wage naval warfare systematically in America's limited wars. The peak years of this near-half-century were 1943 to 1945, when the air admirals battled opponents inside and outside the Navy and enemies at sea to forge the air Navy. The victory of the fast carriers was their victory.

Appendices

Appendix A:
Allied Carrier Statistics, 1943–1945[1]

	Saratoga (1927)	*Enterprise* (1938)	*Essex* (1942)	*Ticonderoga*[2] (1944)
Standard displacement (in tons)	33,000	19,800	27,100	27,100
Over-all length	888′	809′6″	872′	888′
Extreme width of flight deck	130′	109′6″	147′6″	147′6″
Draft	24′2″	28′	28′7″	28′7″
Top speed (knots)	33.91	32.5	33	33
Complement (air and ship crews)	2,122	2,919	3,448	3,448
Number of aircraft (maximum)	90	85	100	100
Antiaircraft guns (total barrels)	100+	100+	80+	85+
Catapults	1	3	2	2
Horsepower	180,000	120,000	150,000	150,000
Number in commission, 1 August 1943– 1 November 1945	1	1	10	7

[1] *American Naval Fighting Ships*, II, 462, 464–67; Admiralty Records, provided by Lieutenant Commander P. K. Kemp RN.

[2] Modified *Essex*-class.

Midway (1945)	*Independence* (1943)	*Saipan* (1945)	*Illustrious* (1940)	*Implacable* (1944)	*Colossus*[3] (1944)
45,000	11,000	14,500	23,000	23,000	14,000
986′	622′6″	684′	753′	766′	695′
136′	109′2″	115′	96′	96′	80′
35′	26′	28′	29′3″	29′4″	23′
33+	31	33	30.5	32.5	25
4,104	1,569	1,721	1,600	1,650	950
137	45	50+	55	70	33
108	24	40	120	125	88
2	2	2	1	2	1
212,000	100,000	120,000	111,000	148,000	40,000
2	9	0	4	2	5

[3] The *Majestic*-class light carrier varied in none of the essentials from this class.

Appendix B:

Carrier Aircraft, 1943–1945[1]

These figures should be used as comparative data, since flat statistics

Airplane (Model)	*Max. range (mi.)*	*Speed (mph)*	*Service Ceiling*
FIGHTERS			
U.S. F6F-3 (July 1943)	1620	376	38,400 ft.
U.S. F6F-5 (Nov 1944)	1650	386	37,300
U.S. F4U-1D (Aug 1945)	1500	409	40,000
Br. Seafire (Mk. III)	771	341	31,500
Br. Firefly	1300	316	28,000
Jap. Zero-32 (Dec 1944)	1435	346	39,800
DIVE BOMBERS			
U.S. SBD-5 (June 1944)	1345	252	26,100
U.S. SB2C-4 (Nov 1944)	1420	295	29,100
Jap. "Betty" (May 1945)[2]	3075	283	30,400
TORPEDO PLANES			
U.S./Br. TBM-3 (Jan 1944)	1665	267	25,300
Jap. "Judy" (Mar 1945)	2580	339	33,100
Br. Barracuda (Mk. II)	1150	228	16,600

[1] WSEG Study, Appendix G, Enclosure A, pp. 228–29: "Statistical Information on World War II Carrier Experience," prepared by Aviation History Section, DCNO (Air), October 1950; performance characteristics of U.S. Naval aircraft from "U.S. Navy Service Airplane Characteristics and Performance Data Sheets" issued

do not take into account such variables as the requirements of combat.

Crew	*Guns*	*Bombs*	*or*	*Rockets and Torpedoes (T)*
1	6	none		none
1	6	2/1000 lb.		6/5″
1	6	2/1000		8/5″
1	6	2/250		none
2	4	2/1000		8/60 lb.
1	4	2/132		none
2	4	1/1600		8/5″
2	4	2/1000		8/5″; one T.
5–7	5	1/2200		one T.
3	4	2/1000		8/5″; one T.
2	3	1/1100		one T.
3	2	6/250		one T.

by BuAer; those of Japanese aircraft from reports of Technical Aircraft Intelligence Center; also, Owen Thetford, *British Naval Aircraft*, pp. 152, 160–61, 303–4.

[2] Generally used as a torpedo bomber from land bases.

Appendix C: *United States Navy, 1943–1945*

I. Naval Air Administration

A. NAVY DEPARTMENT

1. Commander-in-Chief United States Fleet–Chief of Naval Operations: Fleet Admiral Ernest J. King, 1942–end of war
2. Deputy Chief of Naval Operations (Air)
   a. Vice Admiral John S. McCain, August 1943–August 1944
   b. Vice Admiral Aubrey W. Fitch, August 1944–August 1945
   c. Vice Admiral Marc A. Mitscher, August 1945–end of war
3. Assistant Chief of Staff (Operations), Cominch
   a. Rear Admiral Arthur C. Davis, March 1943–August 1944
   b. Rear Admiral Malcolm F. Schoeffel, August 1944–August 1945
   c. Rear Admiral A. R. McCann (non-air), August 1945–end of war
4. Assistant DCNO (Air)
   a. Rear Admiral Frank D. Wagner, August 1943–April 1944
   b. Rear Admiral Arthur W. Radford, April 1944–October 1944
   c. Rear Admiral John H. Cassady, October 1944–end of war
5. Assistant Operations Officer (Air), Cominch
   a. Captain Thomas P. Jeter, November 1942–December 1943
   b. Captain Wallace M. Beakley, December 1943–May 1945
   c. Captain Robert B. Pirie, May 1945–end of war
6. Assistant Secretary of the Navy (Air)
   a. Artemus L. Gates, 1941–July 1945
   b. John L. Sullivan, July 1945–end of war
7. Chief of the Bureau of Aeronautics
   a. Rear Admiral John S. McCain, 1942–August 1943
   b. Rear Admiral DeWitt C. Ramsey, August 1943–June 1945
   c. Rear Admiral Harold B. Sallada, June 1945–end of war

B. PEARL HARBOR

1. Commander-in-Chief Pacific Fleet and Pacific Ocean Areas:
   Fleet Admiral Chester W. Nimitz, 1941–end of war
2. Deputy Cincpac-Cincpoa (including aviation matters)
   a. Vice Admiral John H. Towers, February 1944–July 1945
   b. Vice Admiral John H. Hoover, July 1945–August 1945
   c. Vice Admiral John H. Newton, August 1945–end of war
3. Assistant (later Deputy) Chief of Staff (Plans), Cincpac:
   Rear Admiral Forrest P. Sherman, November 1943–end of war
4. Commander Air Force Pacific Fleet (ComAirPac)
   a. Vice Admiral John H. Towers, 1942–February 1944
   b. Rear Admiral Charles A. Pownall, February 1944–August 1944
   c. Vice Admiral George D. Murray, August 1944–July 1945
   d. Rear Admiral Alfred E. Montgomery, July 1945–end of war
5. Chief of Staff, ComAirPac (Deputy after December 1944)
   a. Captain Forrest P. Sherman, 1942–November 1943
   b. Rear Admiral Arthur W. Radford, December 1943–February 1944
   c. Rear Admiral J. J. Ballentine, February 1944–September 1944
   d. Commodore Frederick W. McMahon, October 1944–end of war
   e. Rear Admiral Cato D. Glover, Jr., reporting August 1945

C. COMBAT ZONE

1. Commander Fast Carrier Forces Pacific
   a. Rear Admiral Charles A. Pownall, November 1943–January 1944
   b. Vice Admiral Marc A. Mitscher, January 1944–August 1944
2. Commander First Fast Carrier Force Pacific
   a. Vice Admiral Marc A. Mitscher, August 1944–July 1945
   b. Vice Admiral Frederick C. Sherman, July 1945–end of war
3. Commander Second Fast Carrier Force Pacific
   a. Vice Admiral John S. McCain, August 1944–September 1945
   b. Vice Admiral John H. Towers, September 1945–end of war
4. Commander Carrier Division One
   a. Rear Admiral DeWitt C. Ramsey, 1942–July 1943
   b. Rear Admiral Frederick C. Sherman, July 1943–March 1944
   c. Rear Admiral William K. Harrill, March 1944–August 1944
   d. Rear Admiral Frederick C. Sherman, August 1944–July 1945

5. Commander Carrier Division Two
   a. Rear Admiral Ralph E. Davison, July 1944–April 1945
   b. Rear Admiral C. A. F. Sprague, April 1945–end of war
6. Commander Carrier Division Three
   a. Rear Admiral Charles A. Pownall, August 1943–January 1944
   b. Rear Admiral Marc A. Mitscher, January 1944–March 1944
   c. Rear Admiral Alfred E. Montgomery, March 1944–December 1944
   d. Rear Admiral Thomas L. Sprague, March 1945–end of war
7. Commander Carrier Division Four
   a. Rear Admiral John H. Hoover, August 1943–October 1943
   b. Rear Admiral John W. Reeves, Jr., October 1943–July 1944
   c. Rear Admiral Gerald F. Bogan, July 1944–end of war
   d. Rear Admiral Donald B. Duncan, reporting August 1945
8. Commander Carrier Division Five
   a. Rear Admiral Frank D. Wagner, April 1944–June 1944
   b. Rear Admiral J. J. Clark, August 1944–July 1945
   c. Rear Admiral Arthur C. Davis, July 1945–end of war
9. Commander Carrier Division Six
   a. Rear Admiral Harold B. Sallada, August 1944–November 1944
   b. Rear Admiral Arthur W. Radford, November 1944–end of war
10. Commander Carrier Division Seven
   a. Rear Admiral Matthias B. Gardner, December 1944–April 1945
   b. Rear Admiral J. J. Ballentine, June 1945–August 1945
11. Commander Carrier Division Eleven
   a. Rear Admiral Arthur W. Radford, July 1943–December 1943
   b. Rear Admiral Samuel P. Ginder, December 1943–April 1944
12. Commander Carrier Division Twelve
   Rear Admiral Alfred E. Montgomery, August 1943–March 1944
13. Commander Carrier Division Thirteen
   Rear Admiral J. J. Clark, March 1944–August 1944

D. RELATED AGENCIES

1. Commander Fleet Air West Coast
   a. Rear Admiral Charles A. Pownall, 1942–August 1943
   b. Rear Admiral Marc A. Mitscher, August 1943–January 1944
   c. Rear Admiral William K. Harrill, January 1944–March 1944
   d. Rear Admiral Frederick C. Sherman, March 1944–August 1944
   e. Rear Admiral William K. Harrill, August 1944–February 1945

f. Rear Admiral Alfred E. Montgomery, February 1945–July 1945
g. Rear Admiral Van H. Ragsdale, July 1945–August 1945
h. Vice Admiral John H. Hoover, August 1945–end of war

2. Director of Marine Corps Aviation
Major General Field Harris, July 1944–end of war

3. Commander Air Force Atlantic Fleet
Vice Admiral Patrick N. L. Bellinger, March 1943–end of war

II. Fast Carriers in Commission August 1943–November 1945

	Date of Commissioning
1. Prewar	
a. *Saratoga* (CV-3)	16 November 1927
b. *Enterprise* (CV-6)	12 May 1938
2. *Essex* class	
a. *Essex* (CV-9)	31 December 1942
b. *Yorktown* (CV-10)	15 April 1943
c. *Intrepid* (CV-11)	16 August 1943
d. *Hornet* (CV-12)	29 November 1943
e. *Franklin* (CV-13)	31 January 1944
f. *Lexington* (CV-16)	17 February 1943
g. *Bunker Hill* (CV-17)	25 May 1943
h. *Wasp* (CV-18)	24 November 1943
i. *Bennington* (CV-20)	6 August 1944
j. *Bon Homme Richard* (CV-31)	26 November 1944
3. *Ticonderoga* (modified *Essex*) class	
a. *Ticonderoga* (CV-14)	8 May 1944
b. *Randolph* (CV-15)	9 October 1944
c. *Hancock* (CV-19)	15 April 1944
d. *Boxer* (CV-21)	16 April 1945
e. *Antietam* (CV-36)	28 January 1945
f. *Shangri-La* (CV-38)	15 September 1944
g. *Lake Champlain* (CV-39)	3 June 1945
4. *Midway* class	
a. *Midway* (CVB-41)	10 September 1945
b. *Franklin D. Roosevelt* (CVB-42)	27 October 1945
5. *Independence* class	
a. *Independence* (CVL-22)	14 January 1943
b. *Princeton* (CVL-23)	25 February 1943
c. *Belleau Wood* (CVL-24)	31 March 1943

d. *Cowpens* (CVL-25)	28 May 1943
e. *Monterey* (CVL-26)	17 June 1943
f. *Langley* (CVL-27)	31 August 1943
g. *Cabot* (CVL-28)	24 July 1943
h. *Bataan* (CVL-29)	17 November 1943
i. *San Jacinto* (CVL-30)	15 December 1943

Appendix D:
Royal Navy, 1943–1945

I. Fleet Air Administration

A. Fifth Sea Lord and Chief of Naval Air Equipment:
  Rear Admiral Denis W. Boyd, January 1943–May 1945

B. Fifth Sea Lord (Air):
  Rear Admiral T. H. Troubridge, May 1945–end of war

C. Vice Controller (Air) and Chief of Naval Air Equipment:
  Rear Admiral M. S. Slattery, May 1945–end of war

D. Assistant Chief of Naval Staff (Air)
  1. Rear Admiral R. H. Portal, June 1943–November 1944
  2. Rear Admiral L. D. Mackintosh, November 1944–end of war

E. Admiral Commanding, First Aircraft Carrier Squadron:
  Vice Admiral Sir Philip L. Vian, November 1944–end of war

F. Admiral Commanding, Eleventh Aircraft Carrier Squadron:
  Rear Admiral C. H. J. Harcourt, March 1945–end of war

II. Fast Carriers in Commission August 1943–November 1945

	Date of Commissioning
A. *Illustrious* class	
1. *Illustrious*	25 May 1940
2. *Formidable*	24 November 1940
3. *Victorious*	15 May 1941
4. *Indomitable*	10 October 1941
B. *Implacable* (modified *Illustrious*) class	
1. *Indefatigable*	3 May 1944
2. *Implacable*	28 August 1944

C. *Colossus* class

1. *Colossus*	16 December 1944
2. *Vengeance*	15 January 1945
3. *Venerable*	17 January 1945
4. *Glory*	2 April 1945
5. *Ocean*	8 August 1945

Appendix E:
Imperial Japanese Navy

I. Naval Air Administration

A. Chief of the Bureau of Aeronautics
   1. Vice Admiral Nishizo Tsukahara, 1942–September 1944
   2. Vice Admiral Michitaro Totsuka, September 1944–April 1945
   3. Vice Admiral Shigeyoshi Inoue, April 1945–May 1945
   4. Vice Admiral Misao Wada, May 1945–end of war

B. Commander-in-Chief Mobile Fleet:
   Vice Admiral Jisaburo Ozawa, 1942–February 1945

C. Commander Carrier Division One
   1. Vice Admiral Jisaburo Ozawa, 1942–October 1944
   2. Rear Admiral Keizo Komura, October 1944–December 1944
   3. Rear Admiral Sueo Obayashi, December 1944–February 1945

D. Commander Carrier Division Two:
   Rear Admiral Takaji Joshima, August 1943–July 1944

E. Commander Carrier Division Three:
   Rear Admiral Sueo Obayashi, February 1944–September 1944

F. Commander Carrier Division Four:
   Rear Admiral Chiaki Matsuda, May 1944–February 1945

II. Japanese Carriers, 1943–1945[1]

Ship	Displacement (tons)	Horse-power	Speed (knots)	Planes	Date Completed
Shokaku	29,800	160,000	34.2	75	8 August 1941
Zuikaku	29,800	160,000	34.2	75	25 September 1941
Junyo	27,500	56,250	25.5	54	3 May 1942
Hiyo	27,500	56,250	25.5	54	31 July 1942
Taiho	34,200	160,000	33.3	75	7 March 1944
Unryu	20,400	152,000	34	63	6 August 1944
Amagi	20,400	152,000	34	63	10 August 1944
Katsuragi	20,200	104,000	32	63	15 October 1944
Shinano	68,060	150,000	27	54	19 November 1944
Zuiho (CVL)	13,950	52,000	28	30	27 December 1940
Ryuho (CVL)	15,300	52,000	26.5	36	28 November 1942
Chiyoda (CVL)	13,600	56,800	29	30	31 October 1943
Chitose (CVL)	13,600	56,800	29	30	1 January 1944

[1] These figures and full-load tonnages are based on Japanese official records used by Okumiya and Horikoshi in *Zero!*, p. 176. However, in the text the writer used the standard tonnages given in *Japanese Aircraft Carriers and Destroyers* (Pocket Pictorial Vol. II), pp. 6–61, which should be consulted for other details on Japanese carriers.

Bibliographic Essay

The framework of this study is based upon official documents of the United States Navy, supplemented by those of the Royal Navy, Royal Canadian Navy, and the Imperial Japanese Navy. Official materials and histories and other secondary works greatly facilitated the task of structuring this period of naval history. Histories built entirely on official sources, however, often amount to little more than chronicles or simple narratives of combat actions—great fun to read but wholly inadequate for understanding the interrelationships of historical forces. The writer has therefore consulted several private collections of papers and has corresponded with or interviewed numerous individuals associated with the history and development of the Fast Carrier Task Force during World War II.

The Division of Naval History, later renamed the Naval Historical Center, is the main source of documents for this study. Of especial help in locating the pertinent material was Mrs. Mildred D. Mayeux, a tireless archivist. Documents included action reports of fleet, task force and group, and ship commanders, naval intelligence interviews, campaign summaries, war diaries and rosters of major commands, fleet fighting instructions, official correspondence and memoranda, type command monthly analyses, and unit histories. The important monographs and official summaries in this Archives are:

Weapons Systems Evaluation Group, WSEG Study No. 4: "Operational Experience of Fast Carrier Task Forces in World War II," 15 August 1951. Designed to measure "the general effectiveness" of fast carriers, this study provided excellent statistics and some insights; a good compendium.

"United States Naval Administration in World War II: Commander in Chief, United States Fleet" (1945). Prepared by Commander W. M. Whitehill, USNR, and criticized by Jeter A. Isely as incomplete and its sections not correlated, this history was nevertheless valuable in providing rosters of the Cominch office.

Commander-in-Chief, United States Pacific Fleet and Pacific Ocean Areas, "Command History, 7 December 1941–15 August 1945" (1945). A good administrative history, tracing key wartime changes.

"History: Commander Air Force Pacific Fleet" (002238, 3 December 1945). A minutely detailed, excellent administrative history.

"United States Naval Administration in World War II: DCNO(Air): Air Task Organization in the Pacific Ocean Areas, Ship-based Aircraft" (1945). Rosters of all carrier task forces; indispensable to the writer.

Office of the Commander, Air Support Control Units, Amphibious Forces, U.S. Pacific Fleet, "Air Support Command History, August 1942 to 14 August 1945" (1945). A copy of this valuable summary-outline history was loaned to the writer by Vice Admiral R. F. Whitehead, USN (Ret).

Documents from this Archives have led to several published sources, including:

Furer, Rear Admiral Julius Augustus, USN (Ret.). *Administration of the Navy Department in World War II.* Washington, 1959. A bulky, thorough volume.

Rowland, Lieutenant Commander Buford, USNR, and Lieutenant William B. Boyd, USNR. *U.S. Navy Bureau of Ordnance in World War II.* Washington, 1953. A particularly useful history, especially with regard to aviation ordnance.

U.S. Naval Aviation in the Pacific: A Critical Review. Washington, 1947. Nothing critical about it.

The Aviation History Unit, headed by Adrian O. Van Wyen, produced several monographs after the war, all of them part of the overall series *United States Naval Administration in World War II,* but subtitled, "DCNO (Air) Essays in the History of Naval Air Operations."

"Carrier Warfare."

Part I: "Remarks on the Development of the Fast Carrier Task Force," by Lieutenant Andrew R. Hilen, Jr., USNR (October 1945). A good discussion, but heavily biased in favor of the theories of Admiral Frederick C. Sherman, on whose staff author Hilen had served for over one year.

Part III: "History of Naval Fighter Direction," by Lieutenants William C. Bryant, USNR, and Heith I. Hermans, USNR (February 1946). Indispensable for understanding the problems of air defense of the carriers.

Dittmer, Lieutenant (jg) Richard W., USNR. "Aviation Planning in World War II" (n.d.). Traces the problems of procuring Navy planes and maintaining production levels.

Grimes, Lieutenant J., USNR. "Aviation in the Fleet Exercises, 1923-1939" (n.d.). Good in what it does include, but there are big gaps for the 1920s.

Land, Lieutenant W. G., USNR, and Lieutenant A. O. Van Wyen, USNR. "Naval Air Operations in the Marianas" (early 1945). Meant as a case study to assist in future operations, this study was outdated when completed but is a valuable tool for the historian.

Seim, Commander Harvey B., USN. "U.S.S. *Independence*—Pioneer Night Carrier" (January 1958). A sound summary of one aspect of the carrier war.

This same Aviation History Unit has produced four publications worthy of note:

Buchanan, Lieutenant A. R., USNR (ed.). *The Navy's Air War: A Mission Completed.* New York, 1946. A useful outline summary of American wartime naval aviation.

Duncan, Donald B., and H. M. Dater. "Administrative History of U.S. Naval Aviation." *Air Affairs,* I (Summer 1947), 526–39. A "ghosting" by historian Dater for Admiral Duncan in a magazine that shortly became defunct; useful, however, for the researcher.

MacDonald, Scot. *Evolution of Aircraft Carriers.* Washington, 1964. A collected series of articles from *Naval Aviation News,* examining carriers of all nations. Complete and useful.

United States Naval Aviation, 1910–1960 (NAVWEPS 00-80P-1). Washington, 1961. An invaluable reference work done primarily by A. O. Van Wyen and Lee M. Pearson for naval aviation's fiftieth anniversary.

Lee M. Pearson, historian for the Naval Air Systems Command, was very generous in providing technical data on U. S. aircraft and radar. Also, K. Jack Bauer, while assisting in the Morison histories (discussed below), provided data from primary sources. Finally, the Office of the Judge Advocate General of the Navy allowed the writer to examine the proceedings of the Courts of Inquiry investigating the two typhoons of 1944–1945.

Special credit is due two midshipmen from the United States Naval Academy Class of 1966 for outstanding original research papers that proved of value to this history: Charles E. Jones, III, "The SB2C Helldiver—An Historical Development and Analysis," and James T. Petillo, "Japanese Air Defense of the Philippine Islands."

Information on the British, Canadian, and Japanese navies taken from primary documents was provided by individuals with official access in those countries. Lieutenant Commander P. K. Kemp RN (Ret.), and Captains R. S. D. Armour RN (Ret.) and Donald Macintyre RN (Ret.) provided material from British Admiralty records, now administered by their Naval Historical Branch, Ministry of Defence. Along with vital statistics on ships and miscellaneous information, most valuable was the staff monograph "Notes on the Administrative Organization for Air Matters within the Admiralty, 1912 to 1945." The original Canadian documents were provided by Commander John H. Arbick, RCN (Ret.), after security clearance from Naval Intelligence. Material from Susumu Nishiura, Chief, War History Office, Defense Agency, Japan, mostly concerned rosters and biographies of Japanese officers. However, the writer was provided with an excellent monograph by General Minoru Genda, written by him, "Evolution of Aircraft Carrier Tactics of the Imperial Japanese Navy."

Private collections of papers, mostly diaries, were utilized, a task made somewhat difficult by wartime Navy regulations prohibiting diaries. However, some men ignored the order; as Admiral Frederick C. Sherman prefaced his own diary, after the first one went down with the old *Lexington* in the Coral Sea, "Seaman order prohibits all persons in the Navy from keeping a diary. I believe the order is illegal. . . . However, being entitled to keep secret papers, I am going to keep a War Record for future use but will keep it secure so that the enemy can never get possession of it."

Two collections and diaries were used extensively, those of Sherman and Admiral John H. Towers. Towers kept his "Memoranda for Files" by dictating each day's activities to a yeoman to serve as reminders for future meetings. The result is an unparalleled, straightforward record of the Cincpac meetings during 1943 and 1944. Sherman, a highly emotional individual, kept a superb diary relating the frustrations of carrier command. Despite Sherman's biases, there is no reason to suspect the validity of his observations. Both collections were kindly furnished the writer by the widows of these two officers. Where Sherman's papers are is not (as of 1991) known, while Mrs. Towers deposited her husband's papers at the Library of Congress.

Related collections are those of Admirals C. M. Cooke and H. E. Yarnell. Cooke's, in the possession of Major C. M. Cooke, Jr., USAF, gives details of the San Francisco meetings between King and Nimitz, while taped conversations between father and son in 1964 cover the broader aspects of the war. Yarnell's papers, administered by the Naval Historical Foundation, are concerned with prewar matters and the 1943 study he made of naval aviation.

The diary of the late Lieutenant Joseph E. Kane, VB-14 (*Wasp*), 10 May 1944 to 12 February 1945, gives excellent insight into the thoughts of the individual pilot; it was kindly furnished the writer by Midshipman Joseph E. Kane, II, USNA 1966. The papers of the late Vice Admiral James H. Flatley, Jr., loaned by Midshipman Brian A. "J" Flatley, USNA 1966, contain mostly official documents but also several private letters concerning the carrier war. Two poor collections are those of Admirals M. A. Mitscher and D. C. Ramsey. Mitscher's papers, at the Library of Congress, testify to the admiral's silence; sympathy letters over his death are the most prominent items. Ramsey's are at the Library of Congress.

Among the living (some of whom, however, have since passed away) who provided significant information from their own wartime experiences are the following. The writer either interviewed or corresponded with them, while in two instances tape recordings were mailed, and in two other cases telephone conversations sufficed; the period of research was February 1961 to June 1968. Ranks given are those of the correspondents at the time of contact with the writer, though most were at that time already retired from active duty. Also given are the pertinent wartime carrier or related posts held by each individual.

Anderson, George W., Jr., Admiral, USN. Navigator, *Yorktown* 1943; AirPac, Cincpac, Cominch staffs 1943–1945.

Arbick, John H., Commander, RCN. Director of Naval Air Divison, Canadian Naval Staff 1945.

Beakley, Wallace M., Vice Admiral, USN. AirPac, Cominch staffs, 1943–1945.

Beebe, Marshall U., Captain, USN. CO VF-17 1944–1945.

Blackburn, J. T., Captain, USN. CO VF-17 1943–1944; BuAer 1944; CO VF-74 1945.

Bogan, Gerald F., Vice Admiral, USN. ComCarDiv 4 1944–1945.

Boone, W. Fred., Admiral, USN. CO *Yorktown* 1945.

Burke, Arleigh A., Admiral, USN. C of S CTF 58/38 1944–1945.

Cheek, M. C., Rear Admiral, USN. Staff ComThird Fleet 1942–1945.

Clark, J. J., Admiral, USN. CO *Yorktown* 1943–1944; ComCarDivs 13 and 5, 1944–1945.

Clifton, Joseph C., Rear Admiral, USN. CO VF-12 1943; CO CVG-12 1944; XO *Wasp* 1945.

Cronin, Joseph C., Rear Admiral, USN. C of S ComBatRon 2 1945.

Dale, Roland H., Captain, USN. CO VF-24 1943; CO CVG-17 1944; Operations Off. ComCarDiv 1 1944–1945.

Day, Barton E., Captain, USN. Staff ComCarDiv 3 1945.

Dixon, Robert E., Rear Admiral, USN. Ops. Off. ComCarDiv 1 1943–1944; BuAer 1944–1945.

Dodson, O. H., Rear Admiral, USN. Staff ComCarDiv 12 1943–1944.

Dosé, Robert G., Captain, USN. CO VF-12 1944.

Farrington, Robert F., Captain, USN. CO VT-12 1943.

Fitch, Aubrey W., Admiral, USN. DCNO(Air) 1944–1945.

Gardner, Matthias B., Admiral, USN. CO *Enterprise* 1943–1944; ComCarDivs 11 and 7, 1944–1945; Cominch Staff 1945.

Genda, Minoru, Captain, IJN, and General, Japan Self-Defense Air Force. Naval General Staff 1942–1944; CO 343rd Navy Air Corps 1945.

Gould, Samuel B., Lieutenant Commander, USNR. Staff ComCar-Div 6 1945.

Goodwin, Hugh H., Vice Admiral, USN. C of S ComCarDiv 6 1944.

Hill, Harry W., Admiral, USN. Amphibious commands 1943–1945.

Jeter, Thomas P., Rear Admiral, USN. CO *Bunker Hill* 1944; C of S ComBatPac, ComBatRon 2 1944–1945.

Johnson, Roy L., Admiral, USN. CO CVG-2 1944; AO *Hornet* 1944–1945.

Kirn, L. J., Rear Admiral, USN. Ops Off. ComCarDiv 2 1944–1945.

Lawrence, R. E., Commander, USN. Staff ComCarDiv 6 1944–1945.

LeFanu, Michael, Admiral, RN. Staff ComFifth/Third Fleets, 1945.

Lewin, E. D. G., Captain, RN. Staff Com1st A.C. Sqdn. 1944–1945.

McCampbell, David, Captain, USN. CO CVG-15 1944.

McCrary, Douglas A., Lieutenant, USNR. VT-5 1943–1944; Staff ComCarDivs 13 and 5, 1944–1945.

McKay, J. C. Goodyear Aircraft Corporation.

McManus, J. W., Captain, USN. CO VB-75 1945.

Malstrom, A. I., Rear Admiral, USN. CO *Tarawa* 1945.

Molteni, P. G., Captain, USN. Staff CTF 38 1945.

Moore, C. J., Rear Admiral, USN. C of S ComFifth Fleet, 1943–1944.

Morse, R. W., Rear Admiral, USN. Staff ComFifth Fleet 1943–1944.

Pennoyer, F. W., Jr., Vice Admiral, USN. AirPac staff 1943–1945.

Pepper, G. Willing, Captain, USNR. Staff AirPac, Cincpac 1942–1945.

Phillips, R. A., Captain, USN. Staff ComCarDivs 12 and 3 1943–1945.

Potter, E. B., Professor of History, U.S. Naval Academy.

Pownall, Charles A., Vice Admiral, USN. ComCarDiv 3, CTF 50 1943; ComAirPac 1944.

Raby, John, Rear Admiral, USN. CO CVG-9 1943.

Radford, Arthur W., Admiral, USN. ComCarDiv 11 1943; C of S

ComAirPac 1943–1944; Asst DCNO(Air) 1944; ComCarDiv 6 1944–1945.

Rayner, H. S., Vice Admiral, RCN. Canadian Naval Staff 1944–1945.

Reeves, J. W., Jr., Admiral, USN. ComCarDiv 4 1943–1944.

Regan, H. E., Rear Admiral, USN. C of S ComCarDiv 1 1944; CO *Langley* 1945.

Reynolds, F. Robert, Lieutenant Commander, USNR. On *Yorktown*, 1943–1944; Staff ComCarDivs 13 and 5, 1944–1945.

Ridgway, C. D., Captain, USNR. On *Yorktown*, 1943–1944; Staff ComCarDivs 13 and 5, 1944–1945.

Riley, Herbert D., Vice Admiral, USN. Ops. Off. CTF 58 1945.

Russell, James S., Admiral, USN. C of S ComCarDiv 2 1944–1945.

Russell, William H., Professor of History, U.S. Naval Academy.

Sallada, H. B., Admiral, USN. ComCarDiv 6 1944; Chief BuAer 1945.

Schaeffer, V. H., Rear Admiral, USN. CO *Bataan* 1943–1944; C of S ComSeventh Fleet 1944–1945.

Smeeton, Sir Richard, Vice Admiral RN. Staff ComAirPac 1943–1944; Staff Com1st A.C. Sqdn. 1944–1945.

Smith, Dan F., Rear Admiral, USN. CO CVG-20 1944–1945; XO *Independence* 1945.

Sowerine, Owen E., Captain, USNR. Staff ComCarDivs 13 and 5, 1944–1945.

Spruance, Raymond A., Admiral, USN. ComFifth Fleet 1943–1945.

Stassen, Harold E., Captain, USNR. Staff ComThird Fleet 1942–1945.

Stump, Felix B., Admiral, USN. CO *Lexington* 1943–1944.

Stebbins, E. E., Captain, USN. CO VB-5, 1943–1944; CO CVG-5 1944.

Sullivan, John L. Assistant SecNav (Air) 1945.

Thach, J. S., Admiral, USN. Ops Off. CTF 38 1944–1945.

Torrey, Mrs. P. H., Sr. Mother of CO CVG-9 1943–1945.

Towers, Mrs. J. H. Widow of Admiral J. H. Towers.

Trapnell, F. M., Vice Admiral, USN. C of S ComCarDiv 6 1944–1945.

Vonk, J. J., Lieutenant, USN. On *Yorktown*, 1943–1944; Staff CTF 58/38 1944–1945.

Vorse, A. O., Captain, USN. CO CVG-80 1944–1945; AO, Navigator *Cabot* 1945.

Vosseller, A. B., Vice Admiral, USN. Staff ComFifthFleet 1945.

Waller, R. R., Rear Admiral, USN. XO *Yorktown* 1943; Staff AirPac 1943–1944; C of S ComCarDiv 5 1945.

Wheeler, C. J., Rear Admiral, USN. CO *Mobile* 1943–1944; Staff BPF, 1944–1945.

Whitehead, Richard F., Vice Admiral, USN. ComAir Support Control Units 1944–1945; CO *Shangri-La* 1945.

Williamson, T. B., Vice Admiral, USN. Staff ComCarDiv 2 1945.

Wilson, E. E. President, United Aircraft Corporation 1931–1945. (Also used Columbia Univ. Oral History transcript at USNA).

Wilson, Ralph E., Vice Admiral, USN. Staff ComThirdFleet 1943–1945.

Wright, J. P., Captain, RN. C of S Com1st A.C. Sqdn 1944–1945.

Individuals who provided general background information which proved useful were:

Ansel, W. C., Rear Admiral, USN.
Arnold, M. E., Rear Admiral, USN.
Baldwin, G. C., Captain, RN.
Bauer, L. H., Captain, USN.
Blythe, George, Chief Pharmacist's Mate, USNR.
Bolger, J. F., Vice Admiral, USN.
Briggs, Cameron, Rear Admiral, USN.
Bright, Cooper B., Captain, USN.
Childers, K. C., Captain, USN.
Combs, T. S., Vice Admiral, USN.
Cornwell, D. S., Vice Admiral, USN.
Cunningham, C. J., Commander, RN.
Fechteler, W. M., Admiral, USN.
Felt, Harry D., Admiral, USN.
Glover, Cato D., Jr., Admiral, USN.
Griffin, C. D., Vice Admiral, USN.
Hoskins, J. M., Vice Admiral, USN.
Knight, Page, Captain, USN.
Lee, Fitzhugh, Vice Admiral, USN.
MacComsey, H. F., Captain, USN.
Martin, H. M., Admiral, USN.
Miller, Max, Lieutenant Commander, USNR.
Parker, R. W., Captain, USN.
Trexler, B. R., Commander, USN.
Triebel, C. O., Rear Admiral, USN.

Published works on the U.S. Navy vary in quality, most being plagued by what historian Theodore Ropp so aptly describes as the "oh, gee whiz" or blood-and-guts approach. The outstanding naval history of the war is Samuel Eliot Morison's semi-official 15-volume *History of United States Naval Operations in World War II*. Morison's greatest shortcoming, however, was his superficial treatment of naval aviation; as evidence, he mentioned Admiral Towers but three times in eight volumes on the Pacific war. Friend of many battleship admirals, Morison never served on carriers during the war, preferring battleships, cruisers, destroyers, and even a Coast Guard cutter. Receiving his formal education even before the battle of Jutland, Morison's orientation is understandable, but it does not excuse this gap in his monumental history. Volumes consulted were (all published in Boston):

Coral Sea, Midway and Submarine Actions (IV). 1949.
The Struggle for Guadalcanal (V). 1949.
Breaking the Bismarcks Barrier (VI). 1950.
Aleutians, Gilberts and Marshalls (VII). 1957.
New Guinea and the Marianas (VIII). 1957.
The Invasion of France and Germany (XI). 1957.
Leyte (XII). 1958.
The Liberation of the Philippines (XIII). 1959.
Victory in the Pacific (XIV). 1960.
Supplement and Index (XV). 1962.

General volumes on the U.S. Navy and the Pacific war considered significant were:

Adamson, Colonel Hans Christian, USAF (Ret.), and Captain George Francis Kosko, USN (Ret.). *Halsey's Typhoons.* New York, 1967. An unimaginative rehashing of the subject.

Albion, Robert Greenhalgh, and Robert Howe Connery. *Forrestal and the Navy.* New York, 1962. Excellent administrative study.

Arpee, Edward. *From Frigates to Flat-tops: The Story and Life of Rear Admiral William Adger Moffet, USN.* Chicago, 1953. The only biography of Moffet, but a good one.

Baldwin, Hanson. "The Battle for Leyte Gulf." *Sea Fights and Shipwrecks* (with notes by Fleet Admiral W. F. Halsey, Jr., and Admiral T. C. Kinkaid). New York, 1955. A good general account of the Leyte affair, enhanced by the comments of Admiral Kinkaid.

Brodie, Bernard. *A Guide to Naval Strategy* (3rd ed.). Princeton, 1944. A solid examination of naval warfare during World War II. Subsequent editions have changed little, are therefore inadequate as history and for modern use.

———. *Sea Power in the Machine Age.* Princeton, 1941. Good for the prewar period, but some bad guesses about the future importance of aviation in war.

Bryan, Lieutenant J., III, USNR, and Philip G. Reed. *Mission Beyond Darkness.* New York, 1945. Exciting events of 20 June 1944 retold in detail.

Buchanan, A. Russell. *The United States and World War II,* 2 vols. New York, 1964. The best summary of all facets of the war, especially useful for its technological slant in places. The author is intimately informed about naval aviation, having edited the Air History Unit's book in 1946.

Carter, Rear Admiral Worrall Reed, USN (Ret.). *Beans, Bullets and Black Oil.* Washington, 1953. A sound narrative of fleet logistics in the Pacific by one of the commanders.

Clark, Admiral J. J., USN (Ret.), with Clark G. Reynolds. *Carrier Admiral.* New York, 1967. If I may say so—as collaborator—this is a very good first-person account of task group command of the fast carriers; I only wish there were others like it.

Davis, Vincent. *Postwar Defense Policy and the U.S. Navy, 1943–1946.* Chapel Hill, 1966. Or the original version, "Admirals, Policies and Postwar Defense Policy: The Origins of the Postwar U.S. Navy, 1943–1946 and After." Unpublished Ph.D. dissertation, Princeton University, 1962. An indispensable source for the present work, covering many administrative and policy subjects of the Navy; written by a political scientist, the narrative sometimes is confused as history in the interest of maintaining the theme, but on the whole is a key work.

Denlinger, [Henry] Sutherland, and Lieutenant Commander Charles B. Gray, USNR. *War in the Pacific: A Study in Navies, Peoples and Battle Problems.* New York, 1936. An interesting prewar treatment of problems in the Pacific.

Dictionary of American Naval Fighting Ships, Vol. 2. Washington, 1963. Appendix I is an excellent list of U.S. carriers and their characteristics from 1922 to 1962. Appendix I of Vol. 1 (Washington, 1959) contains a similar list for battleships.

Falk, Stanley L. *Decision at Leyte.* New York, 1966. The latest work on that operation, but mistitled, since it is not focused on Halsey's momentous decision but is instead a summary of the campaign.

Forrestel, Vice Admiral E. P., USN (Ret.). *Admiral Raymond A. Spruance, USN: A Study in Command.* Washington, 1966. Not a very penetrating study, which is a disappointment because of Forrestel's unique position as Spruance's operations officer from August 1943 to July 1945.

Green, William. *War Planes of the Second World War: Fighters*, Vol. 4. Garden City, 1961. This book is superb on the history and characteristics of all U.S. fighter aircraft during World War II.

Halsey, Fleet Admiral William F., Jr., USN, and Lieutenant Commander J. Bryan III, USNR. *Admiral Halsey's Story.* New York, 1947. Halsey's defense of his several wartime activities, with interspersed anecdotes by former staff officers. All in all, a flimsy, journalistic piece of work.

Jensen, Lieutenant Oliver, USNR. *Carrier War.* New York, 1945. A good picture history of the fast carriers between Marcus and Leyte, with heavy emphasis on the carrier *Yorktown* (CV-10).

Karig, Captain Walter, USNR, *et al. Battle Report*, 6 vols: *The End of an Empire*, IV. New York, 1948. A pop history with a few good anecdotes and first-hand accounts. Also consulted, *Victory in the Pacific*, V (1949). Undocumented.

King, Fleet Admiral Ernest J., USN. *U.S. Navy at War, 1941–1945*. Washington, 1945. The bound collection of Cominch's yearly wartime reports to the Secretary of the Navy.

———, and Commander W. M. Whitehill, USNR. *Fleet Admiral King*. New York, 1952. A very good autobiography written in the third person and emphasizing the major decisions and broad aspects of the Navy's war. See also Whitehill's "A Postscript to *Fleet Admiral King: A Naval Record*," *Proceedings* of the Massachusetts Historical Society, LXX, 203–26.

Leahy, Fleet Admiral William D., USN. *I Was There*. New York, 1950. Good on high-level decision-making.

Lockwood, Vice Admiral Charles A., USN (Ret.), and Colonel Hans Christian Adamson, USAF (Ret.). *Zoomies, Subs and Zeros*. New York, 1956. Tales of air-submarine cooperation in the Pacific war, from the submariners' point of view; some good tales.

———. *Battles of the Philippine Sea*. New York, 1967. These prolific gentlemen have added nothing really new to the subject, except perhaps for a defense of Spruance's use of his battleships off Saipan.

Meakin, Bob. *50th Anniversary of Naval Aviation*. El Segundo, Calif., 1962. Douglas Aircraft reminiscences.

Miller, Lieutenant Max, USNR. *Daybreak for Our Carrier*. New York, 1944. A day-to-day pop account of life aboard a typical fast carrier in 1943 by one of those journalists.

Millis, Walter, and E. S. Duffield (eds.). *The Forrestal Diaries*. New York, 1951. Solid source material on administrative changes in the Navy from 1943 to 1949, but of limited use for present work.

Mizrahi, J. V. *U.S. Navy Dive and Torpedo Bombers*. N.p., 1967. Good pictorial rundown on prewar and wartime attack planes.

Morison, Elting E. *Admiral Sims and the Modern American Navy*. Boston, 1942. An excellent biography of one of the Navy's great leaders and early supporters of fleet aviation.

Morison, Samuel Eliot. *The Two Ocean War*. Boston, 1963. A summary of Morison's epic 15-volume semi-official history discussed above. Useful because of Morison's more subjective thoughts and opinions in this book.

O'Callahan, Father Joseph, S.J. *I Was Chaplain on the Franklin*. New York, 1956. A heroic story, pure and simple; death and bravery in the raw by a Medal of Honor holder.

Potter, E. B., and Fleet Admiral C. W. Nimitz, USN. *Sea Power*. Englewood Cliffs, N.J., 1960. The standard Naval Academy textbook history of navies, used for its good treatment of the formalist-meleeist tactical controversy during the Age of Sail.

Pratt, Fletcher. *Fleet Against Japan*. New York, 1946. A collection of writer Pratt's wartime articles for *Harper's*, consequently inaccurate but very good on personalities.

Pyle, Ernie. *Last Chapter*. New York, 1946. An excellent first-person version of life aboard a fast carrier off Okinawa, written just before this wonderful little guy was killed ashore on Ie Shima.

Ropp, Theodore. *War in the Modern World*. New York, 1962. Asks the right questions about warfare in general.

Roscoe, Theodore. *United States Submarine Operations in World War II*. Annapolis, 1949. The last word on the subject, regarding narrative accounts of the actions themselves.

———. *United States Destroyer Operations in World War II*. Annapolis, 1953. Ditto.

Roskill, Captain Stephen W., RN (Ret.). *The Strategy of Sea Power*. London, 1962. An excellent series of lectures covering the broad spectrum of naval history, used for the present work for its updating of the formalist-meleeist tactical controversy between 1816 and 1918.

Sherman, Admiral Frederick C., USN (Ret.). *Combat Command: The American Aircraft Carriers in the Pacific War*. New York, 1950. A sorry disappointment, in light of Sherman's revealing wartime diary.

Stafford, Commander Edward P., USN. *The Big E*. New York, 1962. The wartime career of the celebrated *Enterprise* (CV-6), with lots of excitement and action; unique in its subject and coverage.

Taylor, Theodore. *The Magnificent Mitscher*. New York, 1954. Not a magnificent book, but probably as good as anyone will ever be able to do on the quiet man; undocumented.

Tuleja, Thaddeus V. *Statesmen and Admirals: Quest for a Far Eastern Naval Policy*. New York, 1963. Good on the prewar period.

Turnbull, Captain Archibald D., USNR, and Lieutenant Commander Clifford L. Lord, USNR. *History of United States Naval Aviation*. New Haven, 1949. An excellent coverage of the history of naval air up to 1940; the omission of the wartime period makes the title misleading.

Wagner, Ray. *American Combat Planes*. Garden City, 1960. A good outline of U.S. warplanes, giving their characteristics, from the beginnings to the late 1950s.

Waters, Sydney D. *The Royal New Zealand Navy*. Wellington, 1956. The best of the Commonwealth histories on naval operations in the wartime Pacific.

Wheeler, Gerald E. *Prelude to Pearl Harbor: The United States Navy and the Far East, 1921–1931.* Columbia, Mo., 1963. Good on the 1920s, should be read first in tandem with Tuleja's *Statesmen and Admirals.*

Wilson, Eugene E. *Slipstream: The Autobiography of an Air Craftsman.* New York, 1950. Good on naval aviation in the 1920s, when aviator Wilson served on the staffs of Admirals Moffett and Reeves.

Woodward, C. Vann. *The Battle for Leyte Gulf.* New York, 1947. An early, thorough though undocumented account of the big battle.

Articles from the *United States Naval Institute Proceedings* particularly useful were, as they appeared:

Sherman, Lieutenant Forrest, USN. "Air Warfare," 52 (January 1926), 62–71.

Woodhouse, Henry. "U.S. Naval Aeronautic Policies, 1904–42," 68 (February 1942), 161–75.

Percival, Lieutenant Franklin G., USN (Ret.). "Wanted: A New Naval Development Policy," 69 (May 1943), 655–66.

Ramsey, Captain Logan C., USN. "The Aero-Amphibious Phase of the Present War," 69 (May 1943), 695–701.

Stanford, Peter Marsh. "The Battle Fleet and World Air Power," 69 (December 1943), 1533–39.

Hessler, Lieutenant William H., USNR. "The Carrier Task Force in World War II," 71 (November 1945), 1271–81.

Eckelmeyer, Captain Edward H., Jr., USN. "The Story of the Self-Sealing Tank," 72 (February 1946), 205–19.

Halsey, Lieutenant Commander Ashley, Jr., USNR. "The CVL's Success Story," 72 (April 1946), 523–31.

Steinhardt, Jacinto. "The Role of Operations Research in the Navy," 72 (May 1946), 649–55.

Gray, Commander James S., USN. "Development of Naval Night Fighters in World War II," 74 (July 1948), 847–51.

Halsey, Fleet Admiral William F., Jr., USN. "The Battle for Leyte Gulf," 78 (May 1952), 487–95.

Hamilton, Captain Andrew, USNR. "Where is Task Force Thirty-Four?" 86 (October 1960), 76–80.

Reynolds, Clark G. " 'Sara' in the East," 87 (December 1961), 74–83.

Potter, E. B. "Chester William Nimitz, 1885–1966," 92 (July 1966), 31–55.

Dyer, Vice Admiral George C., USN (Ret.). "Naval Amphibious Landmarks," 92 (August 1966), 51–60.

Other articles are:

"Air Group Nine Comes Home." *Life* (1 May 1944).

Bauer, K. Jack, and Alvin C. Coox. "OLYMPIC vs. KETTSU-GO." *Marine Corps Gazette,* 49 (August 1965), 32–44.

Brodie, Bernard. "Our Ships Strike Back." *The Virginia Quarterly Review,* XXI (Spring 1945), 186–206.

———. "The Battle for Leyte Gulf." *The Virginia Quarterly Review,* XXIII (Summer 1947), 455–60.

Bywater, Hector C. "The Coming Struggle for Sea Power." *Current History,* 41 (October 1934), 9–16.

Crichton, Kyle. "Navy's Air Boss." *Collier's* (23 October 1943).

Demme, Robert E. "Evolution of the Hellcat," *The Second Navy Reader* (ed. by Lieutenant William Harrison Fetridge, USNR). New York, 1944.

Hayes, John D. "Joseph Mason Reeves '94 (1872–1948)." *Shipmate,* 25 (May 1962), 10–11.

Jones, George E. "Brain Center of Pacific War." *The New York Times Magazine* (8 April 1945).

McCain, John Sidney. "So We Hit Them in the Belly." *Saturday Evening Post* (14 July and 21 July 1945).

Morris, Frank D. "Our Unsung Admiral." *Collier's* (1 January 1944).

Waite, Elmont. "He Opened the Airway to Tokyo." *Saturday Evening Post* (2 December 1944).

Certain materials are difficult to classify. Cruise books of ships, air groups, and squadrons fall into this category. Usually these works are nothing more than yearbooks meant for reminiscing only. However, the writer consulted some of them for the value of their flavor. For a carrier, *Into the Wind* [*Yorktown*], edited by Lieutenant Robert L. Brandt, USNR, is good, also the published diary of Lieutenant Commander J. Bryan, III, USNR, of the same ship, *Aircraft Carrier* (New York, 1954). For air groups, the writer consulted *Carrier Air Group 9* (March 1942–March 1944) edited by Lieutenant Robert Giroux, USNR (1945); *Carrier Air Group Ten* (September 1944–November 1945), edited by Lieutenant R. L. Browne, USNR (n.d.); and *Carrier Air Group Eighty-Six,* edited by Lieutenant Robert Camp, Jr., USNR (1946). For squadrons, see especially Robert Olds, *Helldiver Squadron* [VB-17] (New York, 1944), also *Odyssey of Fighting Two* by Lieutenant Thomas L. Morrissey, USNR (1945), and *History of Fighting Squadron Forty-Six* by Lieutenant Commander Hibben Ziesing, USNR (1946).

Unique in its category is the tape recording by Commodore A. A. Burke, USN, in August, 1945, transcribed onto microfilm as "The

First Battle of the Philippine Sea: Decision Not to Force an Action on the Night of 18–19 June [1944]." The statement gives an unusual and revealing insight into the attitudes of Task Force 58 staff that fateful night of Spruance's momentous decision.

Also, the U.S. Naval War College rosters from 1935 to 1944 are available in the College library.

The Marine Corps produced several official histories excellent in their thoroughness and generally complete in their treatment of carrier air support of Marine Corps forces:

Bartley, Lieutenant Colonel Whitman S., USMC. *Iwo Jima: Amphibious Epic.* Washington, 1951.

Boggs, Major Charles W., Jr., USMC. *Marine Aviation in the Philippines.* Washington, 1951.

Hoffman, Major Carl W., USMC. *Saipan: The Beginning of the End.* Washington, 1950.

———. *The Seizure of Tinian.* Washington, 1951.

Hough, Major Frank O., USMCR. *The Assault on Peleliu.* Washington, 1950.

Lodge, Major O. R., USMC. *The Recapture of Guam.* Washington, 1954.

Nichols, Major Charles S., Jr., USMC, and Henry I. Shaw. *Okinawa: Victory in the Pacific.* Washington, 1955.

Stockman, Captain James R., USMC. *The Battle for Tarawa.* Washington, 1947.

The outstanding work on the U.S. Marine Corps and one that is often very critical of Navy close air support control procedures is Jeter A. Isely and Philip A. Crowl, *The U.S. Marines and Amphibious War* (Princeton, 1951). Also substantial is Robert Sherrod, *History of Marine Corps Aviation in World War II* (Washington, 1952), especially in its treatment of carrier-based Marine squadrons. For an effective criticism of AAF tactical air, see Major Frank O. Hough, USMCR, *The Island War* (New York, 1947). General Holland M. Smith, USMC (Ret.), and Percy Finch, *Coral and Brass* (New York, 1949), is best for illustrating the fight of the Marines to gain recognition within the Pacific command structure.

The official historical program of the U.S. Army by far exceeds those of the other services put together. For this study, the outstanding volume of this series, *United States Army in World War II*, is Maurice Matloff, *Strategic Planning for Coalition Warfare, 1943–1944* (Washington, 1959), which gives a complete coverage of all high-level strategic planning for the Pacific. Several other volumes from this series were also useful, though they generally avoided criticism of Navy or AAF air support measures.

Cannon, M. Hamlin. *Leyte: The Return to the Philippines.* Washington, 1954.

Cline, Ray S. *Washington Command Post: The Operations Division.* Washington, 1951.

Crowl, Philip A., and Edmund G. Love. *Seizure of the Gilberts and Marshalls.* Washington, 1955.

Crowl, Philip A. *Campaign in the Marianas.* Washington, 1960.

Morton, Louis. *Strategy and Command: The First Two Years.* Washington, 1962.

Smith, Robert Ross. *Triumph in the Philippines.* Washington, 1963.

———. "Luzon versus Formosa," in Kent Roberts Greenfield (ed.), *Command Decisions.* Washington, 1960.

See also Louis Morton, *Pacific Command: A Study in Interservice Relations* (U.S. Air Force Academy, 1961), and Gwenfred Allen, *Hawaii's War Years, 1941–1945* (Honolulu, 1950).

The U.S. Air Force produced only one official history, Wesley Frank Craven and James Lea Cate (eds.), *The Army Air Forces in World War II,* 6 vols. The forewords to Vol. 4, *The Pacific: Guadalcanal to Saipan, August 1942 to July 1944* (Chicago, 1950), and Vol. 5, *The Pacific: Matterhorn to Nagasaki, June 1944 to August 1945* (Chicago, 1953), reveal AAF policies toward tactical air warfare in the Pacific, with occasional snipes at the Navy. These volumes are less thorough than those of the other services, though several essays were very useful:

Futrell, Frank. "Prelude to Invasion," V.

———. "Leyte," V.

———. "Mindoro," V.

———. "Luzon," V.

———, and James Taylor, "Reorganization for Victory," V.

Olsen, James C. "The Gilberts and Marshalls," IV.

———, and Captain Bernhardt L. Mortensen, USAF. "The Marianas," IV.

———, and James Lea Cate. "Iwo Jima," V.

R. Earl McClendon produced two good monographs: *The Question of Autonomy for the United States Air Arm, 1907–1946* (Air University Documentary Research Study, 1948), and *Army*

Aviation, 1947–1953 (Air University Documentary Research Study, 1954). The best book on General Mitchell is Major Alfred F. Hurley, USAF, *Billy Mitchell: Crusader for Air Power* (New York, 1964). Good for Pacific strategic discussions is George C. Kenney, *General Kenney Reports* (New York, 1949). General of the Air Force H. H. Arnold, *Global Mission* (New York, 1949), is worth a look.

The British naval histories are generally good, especially the official set: Captain Stephen W. Roskill RN, *The War at Sea, 1939–1945*, 3 vols., in particular Vol. 3, *The Offensive* (London: Part One, 1961; Part Two, 1962). Sound general histories are Lieutenant Commander P. K. Kemp RN, *Fleet Air Arm* (London, 1954), and Ian Cameron [pseud. of Donald Gordon Payne], *Wings of the Morning* (London, 1962), though the latter should be used with caution. For aircraft, the only complete work is Owen Thetford, *British Naval Aircraft, 1912–1958* (London, 1958). The prewar period is best covered by Captain Roskill again, *Naval Policy Between the Wars*, 2 vols. (London, 1968, 1976); the draft manuscript of Vol. One was generously loaned by Captain Roskill to the writer. Also see the general yearly reference works, *Jane's Fighting Ships* and *Brassey's Naval Annual.*

For the British Pacific Fleet, the best treatment is by the wartime fast carrier commander, Admiral of the Fleet Sir Philip L. Vian RN, *Action This Day: A War Memoir* (London, 1960). Three sources shed light on the problems of Anglo-American liaison in the Pacific: Captain Harold [S.] Hopkins RN, *Nice to Have You Aboard* (London, 1964); Captain E. M. Evans-Lombe RN, "The Royal Navy in the Pacific," *Royal United Service Institution Journal*, 92 (August 1947), 333–47; and Captain C. Julian Wheeler USN, "We Had the British Where We Needed Them," *U.S. Naval Institute Proceedings*, 72 (December 1946), 1583–85. Two helpful pieces from the *RUSI Journal* on strategy are Admiral the Viscount Mountbatten of Burma RN, "The Strategy of the Southeast Asia Campaign," 91 (November 1946), 479–83, and Martin Halliwell, "The Projected Assault on Japan," 92 (August 1947), 348–51. An excellent ship history-cruise book is Kenneth Poolman, *Illustrious* (London, 1955).

Canadian wartime naval matters are thoroughly examined by Gilbert Norman Tucker, *The Naval Service of Canada: Its Official History*, 2 vols (Ottawa, 1952). For naval aviation, J. D. F. Kealy and E. C. Russell, *A History of Canadian Naval Aviation* (Ottawa, 1967), is superb. Less useful but containing pertinent information is Colonel Stanley W. Dziuban, USA, *Military Relations Between the United States and Canada, 1939–1945* (Washington, 1959), part of the official U.S. Army series.

The Japanese Navy suffers from a lack of complete histories, simply because, for obvious reasons, the war after 1942 does not interest Japanese writers. However, a reasonably good history is Masanori Ito, with Roger Pineau, *The End of the Imperial Japanese Navy* (New York, 1956). Two reliable source materials are United States Strategic Bombing Survey (Pacific), *Interrogations of Japanese Officials*, 2 vols (OpNav-P-03-100; Washington, 1946), and Joel C. Ford, Jr., "The Development of Japanese Naval Administration in World War II with Particular Reference to the Documents of the International Military Tribunal for the Far East" (Unpublished Master of Arts thesis, Duke University; Durham, N.C., 1956). The material of the former provided the basis for U.S. Strategic Bombing Survey, *The Campaigns of the Pacific War* (Washington, 1946), and James A. Field, Jr., *The Japanese at Leyte Gulf* (Princeton, 1947). See also USSBS, *Japan's Struggle to End the War* (Washington, 1946).

The best Japanese battle study is Captain Mitsuo Fuchida and Commander Masatake Okumiya, *Midway: The Battle that Doomed Japan* (Annapolis, 1955). Several good books by Japanese writers have emphasized ships and airplanes or aerial tactics: *Japanese Aircraft Carriers and Destroyers* (Pocket Pictorial Vol. 2; London, 1964); "Aireview" Staff, *General View of Japanese Military Aircraft in the Pacific War* (Tokyo, 1956); Katsu Kohri, Ikuo Komori, and Ichiro Naito, Aireview's *The Fifty Years of Japanese Aviation, 1910–1960* (Tokyo, 1961); Captain Rikihei Inoguchi, IJN (Ret.), Commander Tadashi Nakajima, IJN (Ret.), and Roger Pineau, *The Divine Wind* (Annapolis, 1958); Masatake Okumiya and Jiro Horikoshi, with Martin Caidin, *Zero!* (New York, 1956); and Saburo Sakai, with Martin Caidin and Fred Saito, *Samurai* (New York, 1957). Japanese monographs prepared at General MacArthur's headquarters after the war by former Japanese officers vary in quality; the author had access to them, but finally used only one for its detail: No. 23, *Air Defense of the Homeland*.

Key Japanese articles include:

Fukaya, Hajima (ed. by Martin E. Holbrook and Gerald E. Wheeler). "Japan's Wartime Carrier Construction." *U.S. Naval Institute Proceedings*, 81 (September 1955), 1031–43.

Kiralfy, Alexander. "Japanese Naval Strategy." From Edward Mead Earle (ed.), *Makers of Modern Strategy* (Princeton, 1943). See also Kiralfy's *Victory in the Pacific* (New York, 1942).

Moore, Lynn Lucius. "*Shinano:* The Jinx Carrier." *U.S. Naval Institute Proceedings*, 79 (February 1953), 142–49.

"Professional Notes" (published comments by Admiral Tossio Matsunaga, IJN). *U.S. Naval Institute Proceedings*, 68 (June 1942), 885–86.

Sekine, Captain Gumpei, IJN. "Japan's Case for Sea Power." *Current History*, 41 (November 1934).

Yokoi, Rear Admiral Toshiyuki, IJN (Ret.). "Thoughts on Japan's Naval Defeat." *U.S. Naval Institute Proceedings*, 86 (October 1960), 68–75.

Prewar Japanese policy in the Far East is in Herbert Feis, *The Road to Pearl Harbor* (New York, 1962). Other items of interest were found in Toshikazu Kase, *Journey to the Missouri* (New Haven, 1950), on infighting within the Japanese high command; in Jean Lartéguy (ed.), *The Sun Goes Down* (London, 1956), which contains letters from kamikaze pilots; and in a news item on Japanese aviation training in the *North-China Herald*, CLXIII (28 May 1927).

The only document to examine the air war from Japanese and American records is U.S. Strategic Bombing Survey, *Air Campaigns of the Pacific War* (Washington, July 1947).

Much secondary information was gleaned from the always reliable *New York Times*, especially from articles and columns by military editor Hanson W. Baldwin, plus occasional items from *Time*, *Naval Aviation News*, *U.S. Naval Institute Proceedings*, and the *Royal United Service Institution Journal*.

Three commercial motion pictures provided excellent flavor and are recommended for late-show television viewing as good representations of the fast carrier war. *The Fighting Lady* (1944) is a color documentary of films taken aboard *Yorktown* April 1943 to February 1944 and in *Ticonderoga* during the summer of 1944, also gun camera shots and scenes of the Battle of the Philippine Sea. *Wing and a Prayer* (1945), starring Dana Andrews (VT commander), Don Ameche (air officer), and Charles Bickford (carrier captain), traces *Enterprise* going into the battle of Midway, but using vintage 1944 aircraft and ships. *Task Force* (1949), starring Gary Cooper (carrier captain), Walter Brennan (carrier admiral), and Wayne Morris (pilot), traces the development of U.S. naval aviation from *Langley* days to the enemy hits on and the retirement of *Franklin* in 1945. Actor Morris actually served as a Hellcat pilot in Dave McCampbell's Fighting 15 aboard *Essex* during the war.

A dearth of fictional literature exists regarding the fast carriers, but a good beginning was made by Richard Newhafer, *The Last Tallyho* (New York, 1964). Ensign Newhafer flew Hellcats in Fighting 5 aboard *Yorktown*.

Even in the realm of music, one may enjoy "The Theme of the Fast Carriers," part of Richard Rodgers' score for the excellent television serial of the 1950s, *Victory at Sea.*

The maps of the present work are based on the projections in Richard Edes Harrison's superb wartime atlas, *Look at the World* (New York, 1944).

The fascination of the reading public and of the major navies of the world for aircraft carriers has continued from World War II to the present, and with it has appeared a plethora of works on the subject. Listed here are those books and articles published between 1969 and 1991 (and a few earlier ones that the writer missed), which, in the opinion of the writer, most importantly amplify certain aspects of *The Fast Carriers.*

Baker, Richard. *Dry Ginger: The Biography of Admiral of the Fleet Sir Michael LeFanu.* London, 1977.

Belote, James H. and William M. *Titans of the Sea.* New York, 1975. Carrier operations, 1941–44.

Brown, David. *Carrier Fighters, 1939–1945.* London, 1975.

———. *The Seafire: The Spitfire that Went to Sea.* Annapolis, 1989. An encyclopedic treatment of the best wartime British-built carrier fighter.

Brown, Eric. *Wings of the Navy,* 2nd ed. Annapolis, 1987. Sixteen carrier planes of World War II evaluated.

Buell, Thomas B. *Master of Sea Power: A Biography of Fleet Admiral Ernest J. King.* Boston, 1980.

———. *The Quiet Warrior: A Biography of Admiral Raymond A. Spruance.* Boston, 1974. About as good a biography as will probably ever be written about Spruance and which naturally defends its subject's decisions. As for Towers, "one of the few men he [Spruance] ever hated" (pp. 216–18), Buell almost ignores him, suspecting the Towers diary to be "self-serving nonsense" (p. 465). The discussion of Spruance and the transports at Saipan (pp. 178–80) is excellent, as is the treatment of the decision by King before the Marianas operation to relieve Moore when it was over. Aside from one mention in a footnote, *The Fast Carriers* is not included in Buell's bibliography.

Cagle, M. W. "Arleigh Burke—Naval Aviator," Naval Aviation Museum *Foundation,* vol. 2, no. 2 (September 1981), 2–11.

———. "Mr. Wu, Part 2," NAM *Foundation,* vol. 10, no. 2 (Fall 1989), 43–51. Donald B. Duncan of the *Essex.*

Caldwell, Turner F. "We Put the Flattops on the Night Shift," *The Saturday Evening Post* (11 August 1945), 26–27, 41–42. Night carrier operations.

Dansereau, Raymond J. *Tomorrow's Mission: World War II Diary of a Combat Aircrewman.* Privately published, 1990. An aviation radioman with VT-5 and VT-3 on the new *Yorktown* (CV-10).

Dyer, George C. *The Amphibians Came to Conquer: The Story of Admiral Richmond Kelly Turner*, 2 vols. Washington, 1972.

Evans, David, and Mark R. Peattie. *The Rising Sun at Sea: Japanese Naval Doctrine, Technology, and Leadership, 1887–1945.* Annapolis, forthcoming. The definitive work on this subject, utilizing major Japanese sources.

Francillon, René J. *Japanese Aircraft of the Pacific War.* Annapolis, 1987.

————. *U. S. Navy Carrier Air Groups, 1941–45.* London, 1978.

Frank, Benis M. *Halsey.* New York, 1974.

Friedman, Norman. *Carrier Air Power.* Annapolis, 1981. A superb doctrinal treatment of the first six decades of carrier operations in all navies that had them.

————. *U. S. Aircraft Carriers: An Illustrated Design History.* Annapolis, 1983.

Heinemann, Edward H., and Rosario Rausa. *Ed Heinemann: Combat Aircraft Designer.* Annapolis, 1980. Autobiography of the designer of Navy Douglas dive bombers and other planes.

Hezlet, Sir Arthur. *Aircraft and Sea Power.* New York, 1970.

————. *The Electron and Sea Power.* London, 1975.

Hoehling, A. A. *The Franklin Comes Home.* New York, 1974. CV-13.

Hoyt, Edwin P. *McCampbell's Heroes.* New York, 1983. VF-15.

————. *How They Won the War in the Pacific: Nimitz and his Admirals.* New York, 1970. Very useful for details of Nimitz's meetings with the senior admirals, also one version (pp. 316–18) of Jocko Clark's attempt to get Pownall relieved; at Clark's request, I never printed any version during Clark's or Pownall's lifetimes. This book shows Towers's respect for Spruance (p. 395 and elsewhere).

Hyams, Joe. *Flight of the Avenger: George Bush at War.* New York, 1991. The future President as TBM pilot with VT-51 on the *San Jacinto.*

Jentschura, Hansgeorg, Dieter Jung, and Peter Mickel. *Warships of the Imperial Japanese Navy, 1869–1945.* London, 1977.

Jurika, Stephen, Jr., ed. *From Pearl Harbor to Vietnam: The Memoirs of Admiral Arthur W. Radford.* Stanford, 1980.

Lamb, Charles. *War in a Stringbag.* London, 1977, 1987. Superb memoir by a British torpedo plane pilot, mostly on early Swordfish operations but culminating on the *Implacable* off Truk in 1945.

MacIsaac, David. *Strategic Bombing in World War Two: The Story of the United States Strategic Bombing Survey.* New York, 1976. MacIsaac, after a thorough and excellent analysis, properly cautions against accepting the final conclusions of parts of the USSBS (p. 135).

Marder, Arthur, Mark Jacobsen, and John Horsfield. *Old Friends, New Enemies: The Royal Navy and the Imperial Japanese Navy, 1942–1945.* Oxford, England, 1990. Excellent for the British Eastern and Pacific Fleets.

Melhorn, Charles M. *Two-Block Fox: The Rise of the Aircraft Carrier, 1911–1929.* Annapolis, 1974.

Merrill, James M. *A Sailor's Admiral: A Biography of William F. Halsey.* New York, 1976.

Mersky, Peter. *The Grim Reapers: Fighting Squadron Ten in WW II.* Mesa, Ariz., 1986.

Miller, Edward S. *War Plan Orange: The U.S. Strategy to Defeat Japan, 1897–1945.* Annapolis, 1991.

Miller, H. L. "The Last Dogfights of World War II—A Correction," NAM *Foundation,* vol. 6, no. 2 (Fall 1985), 67. *Hancock* kills on 15 August 1945.

Millot, Bernard. *Divine Thunder: The Life and Death of the Kamikazes.* New York, 1970.

Monsarrat, John. *Angel on the Yardarm: The Beginning of Radar Defense and the Kamikaze Threat.* Newport, 1986.

Phillips, Christopher. *Steichen at War.* New York, 1981. Photography on the fast carriers.

Polmar, Norman. *Aircraft Carriers.* New York, 1969.

Potter, E. B. *Admiral Arleigh A. Burke: A Biography.* New York, 1990. Adds a few details about Mitscher and Burke.

———. *Bull Halsey.* Annapolis, 1985.

———. *Nimitz.* Annapolis, 1976. Excellent, balanced work. "Nimitz never warmed to Towers' personality, but he recognized the man's ability and the general correctness of his professional thinking." (p. 361). Fascinating account of Nimitz's message to Halsey at Leyte (p. 339).

Raven, Alan. *Essex-Class Carriers.* Annapolis, 1988.

Reynolds, Clark G. *Admiral John H. Towers: The Struggle for Naval Air Supremacy.* Annapolis, 1991. The biography of Admiral John H. Towers, including much new and important information on his role in forging the fast carriers.

———. *The Carrier War.* Alexandria, Va., 1982. A handsomely illustrated overview in the Time-Life "Epic of Flight" series.

———. *Command of the Sea: The History and Strategy of Maritime Empires.* New York, 1974; revised ed., Robert Krieger, 2 vols., 1983.

———. *Famous American Admirals.* New York, 1978. A reference work that includes complete biographical essays on several fast carrier admirals and pilots who became admirals.

———. *The Fighting Lady: The New* Yorktown *in the Pacific War.* Missoula, 1986. A socio-operational history of CV-10 during 1943–45 and based on several dozen diaries as well as official documents and oral interviews.

———. "Forrest P. Sherman," in R. W. Love, ed., *The Chiefs of Naval Operations.* Annapolis, 1980.

———. "Halsey," in Jack Sweetman, ed., *The Great Admirals: Centuries of Command at Sea.* Annapolis, forthcoming.

———. *History and the Sea: Essays on Maritime Strategies.* Columbia, S.C., 1989. By the writer, these essays include analyses of Ernest J. King and Douglas MacArthur as maritime strategists in the Pacific war but especially the 1983 essay on the continental strategy of Imperial Japan.

———. "Mitscher," Stephen Howarth, ed., *Men of War: Great Naval Leaders of World War Two.* London, 1992.

———. *The Saga of Smokey Stover.* Charleston, S.C., 1980. The edited diary of Lieutenant E. T. Stover, USNR, of CV-10 and featured in the film *The Fighting Lady.*

————. "Taps for the Torpecker," *U. S. Naval Institute Proceedings,* 112, no. 12 (December 1986), 55–61. Last attack on the *Yamato* by VT-9.

————. *War in the Pacific.* New York, 1990. Primarily an illustrated history, it balances the role of the Soviet Union and the Chinese Communists with the United States and Britain in the struggle against Japan.

————. "William A. Moffett: Steward of the Air Revolution," in James C. Bradford, ed., *Admirals of the New Steel Navy: Makers of the American Naval Tradition, 1880–1930.* Annapolis, 1990.

Roberts, John. *Anatomy of the Ship: The Aircraft Carrier Intrepid.* Annapolis, 1982. CV-11.

Sakaida, Henry. "The Last Dogfights of World War II," NAM *Foundation,* vol. 6, no. 1 (Spring 1985), 27–34. 15 August 1945.

Smith, Perry McCoy. *The Air Force Plans for Peace, 1943–1945.* Baltimore, 1970.

Smith, Peter C. *Dive Bomber! An Illustrated History.* Annapolis, 1982.

Spurr, Russell. *A Glorious Way to Die.* New York, 1981. Sinking of the *Yamato,* but must be balanced with Richard K. Montgomery, "We Watched a Battleship Die," in *Liberty* (1 September 1945). Some errors too.

Steichen, Edward. *The Blue Ghost.* New York, 1947. CV-16.

Swanborough, Gordon and Peter M. Bowers. *United States Naval Aircraft Since 1911.* New York, 1968; Annapolis, 1976.

Thetford, Owen. *British Naval Aircraft Since 1912,* 2nd ed. London, 1962.

Thruelsen, Richard. *The Grumman Story.* New York, 1976.

Tillman, Barrett. *Avenger at War.* New York, 1980.

————. "Coaching the Fighters," *U. S. Naval Institute Proceedings,* 106, no. 1 (January 1980), 39–45. Fighter director officers.

————. *Corsair: The F4U in World War II and Korea.* Annapolis, 1979.

————. *The Dauntless Dive Bomber in World War II.* Annapolis, 1976.

————. *Hellcat: The F6F in World War II.* Annapolis, 1979.

Warner, Oliver. *Admiral of the Fleet: The Life of Sir Charles Lambe.* London, 1969. Captain of HMS *Illustrious* during 1944–45.

Wheeler, Gerald E. *Admiral William Veazie Pratt, U. S. Navy: A Sailor's Life.* Washington, 1974. Interwar carrier doctrine.

————. "Thomas C. Kincaid: MacArthur's Master of Naval Warfare," in William M. Leary, ed., *We Shall Return! MacArthur's Commanders and the Defeat of Japan, 1942–1945.* Lexington, Ky., 1988. A full biography of Kincaid is forthcoming.

"Wings over Water: A History of Naval Aviation and its Relationship to American Foreign Policy," 1986. An educational television special to which the writer contributed (and appears) and which includes excellent footage on the Japanese. Available on videotape.

Winston, Robert A. *Fighting Squadron.* New York, 1946. Reprint. Annapolis: Naval Institute Press, 1991. VF-31 on the *Cabot* by the squadron commander.

Winters, T. Hugh. *Skipper: Confessions of a Fighter Squadron Commander, 1943–1944.* Mesa, Ariz., 1985. Excellent autobiography of the skipper of VF-19 on the *Lexington* (CV-16).

Winton, John. *Find, Fix and Strike! The Fleet Air Arm at War 1939–45.* London, 1980.

———. *The Forgotton Fleet: The British Navy in the Pacific, 1944–45.* New York, 1970.

Y' Blood, William T. *Red Sun Setting: The Battle of the Philippine Sea.* Annapolis, 1981. A sound treatment and review of the battle, which "could have been decisive . . . had Spruance been more aggressive" (p. 211).

Notes

Chapter One: Fast Carriers, 1922–1942

1. Quoted in Scot MacDonald, *Evolution of Aircraft Carriers* (Washington, 1964), p. 22.
2. Quoted in Elting E. Morison, *Admiral Sims and the Modern American Navy* (Boston, 1942), p. 506.
3. Henry Woodhouse, "U.S. Naval Aeronautic Policies, 1904–42," *United States Naval Institute Proceedings*, 68 (February 1942), 164.
4. Katsu Kohri, Ikuo Komori, and Ichiro Naito, Aireview's *The Fifty Years of Japanese Aviation, 1910–1960* (Tokyo, 1961; Book Two of Eng. tr. by Kazuo Ohyauchi), p. 8.

1. GREAT BRITAIN

1. Naval Historical Branch, Ministry of Defence, "Notes on the Administrative Organisation for Air Matters within the Admiralty, 1912 to 1945," Appendix XIII to a staff history (London, 1965), p. 2. Cited hereafter as "Admiralty Air Administration."
2. *Ibid.*, pp. 3–4.
3. Ian Cameron [Donald Gordon Payne], *Wings of the Morning* (London, 1962), p. 237; *Jane's Fighting Ships, 1944–45* (London, 1946), pp. 31–33.

2. JAPAN

1. See Captain S. W. Roskill, *Naval Policy Between the Wars: The Period of Anglo-American Antagonism, 1918–1928* (London, 1968), pp. 310ff.
2. *Japanese Aircraft Carriers and Destroyers* (London, 1964), pp. 6–17.
3. Joel C. Ford, Jr., "The Development of Japanese Naval Administration in World War II with Particular Reference to the Documents of the International Military Tribunal for the Far East" (Unpublished Master of Arts thesis, Duke University, Durham, N.C., 1956), pp. 61–62. Cited hereafter as "Japanese Naval Administration."

4. Reuters news bulletin, 23 May 1927, from *North-China Herald*, CLXIII (28 May 1927), 368. Courtesy of A. B. Pearson.
5. Admiral Tossio Matsunaga, inspector of the Naval Air Service, in *The Aeroplane* (London, 20 March 1942), reprinted in "Professional Notes," *U.S. Naval Institute Proceedings*, 68 (June 1942), 886.
6. *Ibid.*, p. 885; also Saburo Sakai, *Samurai* (New York, 1957), p. 26. Sakai was a celebrated Japanese ace (five kills) many times over during World War II.
7. Minoru Genda, "Evolution of Aircraft Carrier Tactics of the Imperial Japanese Navy," pp. 1–2. This essay is a private manuscript provided the writer by General Genda in 1965.
8. Captain Gumpei Sekine, IJN, "Japan's Case for Sea Power," *Current History*, 41 (November 1934), 130.
9. Hector C. Bywater, "The Coming Struggle for Sea Power," *Current History*, 41 (October 1934), 15.
10. Biographical data furnished by Susumu Nishiura, Chief, War History Office, Defense Agency Japan, and by *Japan Biographical Encyclopedia and Who's Who*.
11. Captain Mitsuo Fuchida and Commander Masatake Okumiya, *Midway: The Battle that Doomed Japan* (New York, 1958), p. 74.
12. Rear Admiral Toshiyuki Yokoi, "Thoughts on Japan's Naval Defeat," *U.S. Naval Institute Proceedings*, 86 (October 1960), 72–74.
13. Fuchida and Okumiya, *Midway*, p. 26; Minoru Genda, "Japanese Carrier Tactics," pp. 3–7, 10; Alexander Kiralfy, "Japanese Naval Strategy," in Edward Mead Earle (ed.), *Makers of Modern Strategy* (Princeton, 1943), pp. 457–84, *passim;* see also J. C. Ford, Jr., "Japanese Naval Administration," pp. 90–91, on Japanese island defenses.
14. Minoru Genda, "Japanese Carrier Tactics," pp. 7–9.
15. See Herbert Feis, *The Road to Pearl Harbor* (New York, 1962), pp. 191, 217.
16. Fuchida and Okumiya, *Midway*, pp. 107–08.
17. Minoru Genda, "Japanese Carrier Tactics," pp. 9–10.
18. Fuchida and Okumiya, *Midway*, pp. 32–34; on Onishi, see Captain Rikihei Inoguchi, Commander Tadashi Nakajima, and Roger Pineau, *The Divine Wind* (New York, 1960), pp. 159–63.
19. *Ibid.*, p. 34; Herbert Feis, *Road to Pearl Harbor*, p. 217.
20. Minoru Genda, "Japanese Carrier Tactics," p. 11; General Genda to the writer, November 1965; Fuchida and Okumiya, *Midway*, pp. 34–36; J. C. Ford, Jr., "Japanese Naval Administration," pp. 120–21.
21. Minoru Genda, "Japanese Carrier Tactics," p. 9.
22. Nagumo Report, quoted in Fuchida and Okumiya, *Midway*, p. 43.

23. Minoru Genda, "Japanese Carrier Tactics," p. 10.
24. See Herbert Feis, *Road to Pearl Harbor, passim.*
25. Alexander Kiralfy, *Victory in the Pacific* (New York, 1942), p. 75.
26. Fuchida and Okumiya, *Midway*, pp. 93, 108–9, 200–2.
27. *Ibid.*, pp. 150, 204; see also Samuel Eliot Morison, *Coral Sea, Midway and Submarine Actions* (Boston, 1950), Commander Thaddeus V. Tuleja, USN, *Climax at Midway* (New York, 1960), and Walter Lord, *Incredible Victory* (New York, 1967).
28. Masatake Okumiya and Jiro Horikoshi, with Martin Caidin, *Zero!* (New York, 1956), pp. 165–66.
29. United States Strategic Bombing Survey (USSBS), *Interrogation of Japanese Officers* (Washington, 1946), II, 176. Testimony of Captain Toshikazu Ohmae, a top fleet staff officer.

3. UNITED STATES

1. Donald B. Duncan and H. M. Dater, "Administrative History of U.S. Naval Aviation," *Air Affairs*, I (Summer 1947), 528–30.
2. S. W. Roskill, *Anglo-American Antagonism*, p. 116, also 234–268 and 356–399.
3. Gerald E. Wheeler, *Prelude to Pearl Harbor: The United States in the Far East, 1921–1931* (Columbia, Mo., 1963), p. 96.
4. Sims to Senator Henry Cabot Lodge, 10 February 1921, from the Lodge papers, quoted in S. W. Roskill, *Anglo-American Antagonism*, p. 248. Sims wrote to a friend in March 1922, "The battleship is dead." E. E. Morison, *Admiral Sims and the Modern American Navy*, p. 506. He retired from the Navy in October 1922.
5. Duncan and Dater, "Administrative History," p. 530.
6. See Major Alfred F. Hurley, USAF, *Billy Mitchell: Crusader for Air Power* (New York, 1964), pp. 56–72.
7. Captain Archibald D. Turnbull, USNR, and Lieutenant Commander Clifford L. Lord, USNR, *History of United States Naval Aviation* (New Haven, 1949), pp. 255–56.
8. *Ibid.*, pp. 260–61.
9. Lieutenant J. Grimes, USNR, *Aviation in the Fleet Exercises, 1923–1939* (Manuscript history, Navy Department, n.d.), pp. 5–7, 10–12.
10. Turnbull and Lord, *Naval Aviation*, pp. 217–18.
11. J. Grimes, *Aviation in the Fleet Exercises*, pp. 16–18.
12. "V" is the U.S. Navy symbol for heavier-than-air craft, "C" in this case carrier, hence CV-1 was carrier *Langley*, VF-1 Fighter Plane Squadron 1, etc. The Navy began numbering its vessels in 1920.

13. J. Grimes, *Aviation in the Fleet Exercises,* p. 48.
14. *Ibid.,* pp. 62–63 and *passim.*
15. Yarnell to J. V. Forrestal, 17 November 1944. Yarnell papers, Naval Historical Foundation.
16. J. Grimes, *Aviation in the Fleet Exercises,* p. 106.
17. *Ibid.,* pp. 157–65.
18. *War Instructions, United States Navy, 1934* (F.T.P. 143). This and all other official documents, unless otherwise noted, are from the Classified Operational Archives, Division of Naval History, Navy Department, Washington, D.C.
19. Admiral J. J. Clark, USN (Ret.) with Clark G. Reynolds, *Carrier Admiral* (New York, 1967), pp. 49–50. See also Fleet Admiral E. J. King, USN, and Commander Walter Muir Whitehill, USNR, *Fleet Admiral King: A Naval Record* (New York, 1952), p. 232.
20. *Fleet Admiral King,* p. 260.
21. Lieutenant A. R. Buchanan, USNR (ed.), and the Aviation History Unit, *The Navy's Air War: A Mission Completed* (New York, 1946), p. 16.
22. Fleet Admiral E. J. King, *U.S. Navy at War, 1941–1945* (official wartime reports) (Washington, 1945), p. 23.
23. "Current Tactical Orders and Doctrine, U.S. Fleet Aircraft, Vol. One, Carrier Aircraft, USF-74 (Revised), March 1941," prepared by Commander Aircraft Battle Force, 20 April 1941.
24. *United States Naval Aviation, 1910–1960* (NAVWEPS 00-80P-1) (Washington, 1961), p. 76. An American battleship did not refuel at sea until July 1940.
25. J. Grimes, *Aviation in the Fleet Exercises,* pp. 216–17.
26. Duncan and Dater, "Administrative History," p. 534.
27. Lieutenant (jg) Richard W. Dittmer, USNR, *Aviation Planning in World War II* (Manuscript history, n.d.), pp. 12–13.
28. Bernard Brodie, *Sea Power in the Machine Age* (Princeton, 1941), p. 433.

Chapter Two: Weapon of Expediency, 1942–43

1. ON THE DEFENSIVE

1. Along with *Fleet Admiral King,* see Walter Muir Whitehill, "A Postscript to *Fleet Admiral King: A Naval Record,*" *Proceedings* of the Massachusetts History Society, LXX, 203–26.
2. Fletcher Pratt, *Fleet Against Japan* (New York, 1946), pp. 49–50. Vice

Admiral William S. Pye lent his excellent mind to high-level staff work most of the war; Rear Admiral Robert A. Theobald suffered from a fiery personality that eventually cost him his North Pacific command.

3. King to Captain D. C. Ramsey, Head of Plans Division, BuAer, 6 December 1941 (an informal handwritten note). Ramsey papers, researched at the Air History Unit, Navy Department. Ramsey had such an active career during the war that this was the last item he saved in his personal papers.
4. Samuel Eliot Morison, *The Rising Sun in the Pacific* (Boston, 1957), pp. 235–37; see also *Carrier Admiral*, pp. 83–85.
5. Admiral Frederick C. Sherman, *Combat Command: The American Aircraft Carriers in the Pacific War* (New York, 1950), p. 87.
6. Files, Air History Unit; Turnbull and Lord, *History of United States Naval Aviation*, pp. 320–21.
7. Samuel Eliot Morison, *Coral Sea, Midway and Submarine Operations* (Boston, 1953), pp. 29–30.
8. Weapon Systems Evaluation Group (Office of the Secretary of Defense), *Operational Experience of Fast Carrier Task Forces in World War II*, WSEG Study No. 4, 15 August 1951, p. 21. Classified Operational Archives. Cited hereafter as WSEG Study.
9. S. E. Morison, *Coral Sea, Midway . . . .*, pp. 113–23.
10. The Award, as quoted by the official Navy Department mimeographed biography of Rear Admiral Browning.
11. *U.S. Naval Aviation in the Pacific: A Critical Review* (Washington, 1947), p. 2; *United States Naval Aviation, 1910–1960*, p. 199; files, Air History Unit.
12. Cominch Secret Informations #1, #2, and #3, taken from Lieutenant A. R. Hilen, Jr., USNR, "Remarks on the Development of the Fast Carrier Task Force," *Carrier Warfare* (Manuscript history, October 1945), p. 10.
13. Most biographical information on officers above the rank of commander is taken from mimeographed biographies printed by the Biographies Branch, Office of Information, Navy Department.
14. Jeter A. Isely and Philip A. Crowl, *The U.S. Marines and Amphibious War* (Princeton, 1951), pp. 89–90.
15. *Ibid.*, p. 96.
16. *Ibid.*, pp. 92–93, especially Nimitz to King on the future employment of carriers in the Pacific, 2 September 1942.
17. Samuel Eliot Morison, *The Struggle for Guadalcanal* (Boston, 1949), pp. 27–28, 58–63.
18. *Ibid.*, p. 107.
19. *Ibid.*, p. 137n.

20. F. C. Sherman to Ramsey, 27 October 1942. Admiral Frederick C. Sherman personal diary, courtesy of Mrs. Frederick C. Sherman. Sherman papers at California Western University, San Diego, California. See also S. E. Morison, *Guadalcanal,* p. 223.
21. Rear Admiral Robert C. Giffen, a nonaviator commanding two escort carriers and a convoy relieving Guadalcanal, ignored normal antiaircraft precautions and lost the heavy cruiser *Chicago* to air attack at the battle of Rennell Island in January 1943. S. E. Morison, *Guadalcanal,* pp. 351–63.
22. F. C. Sherman diary, entries of 10 and 20 January and 15 March 1943.
23. H. M. Dater, "Memorandum for Files," recording a conversation between Dater, head of the Aviation History Unit, and Rear Admiral H. S. Duckworth, Sherman's 1943 chief of staff, 18 January 1951. Cited hereafter as the Dater-Duckworth memorandum.
24. ComCarDiv 1 War Diary 1943; ComCarDiv 2 War Diary 1943. Classified Operational Archives.
25. See Samuel Eliot Morison, *Breaking the Bismarcks Barrier* (Boston, 1957), pp. 118–27.
26. F. C. Sherman diary, 15 April 1943.

2. BATTLE OF WASHINGTON

1. Duncan and Dater, "Administrative History," p. 535.
2. A. R. Buchanan, *The Navy's Air War,* p. 17.
3. R. W. Dittmer, *Aviation Planning in World War II,* pp. 16–17.
4. *Ibid.,* pp. 28–29.
5. *Ibid.,* pp. 21, 57–69.
6. Data on carriers taken from *Dictionary of American Naval Fighting Ships,* II (Washington, 1963), Appendix I, "Aircraft Carriers, 1908–1962," 461–86; Lieutenant Commander Ashley Halsey, Jr., USNR, "The CVL's Success Story," *U.S. Naval Institute Proceedings,* 72 (April 1946), 523–31.
7. Rear Admiral W. R. Sexton, Chairman, General Board, to Secretary of the Navy Frank Knox, Serial 174, 14 March 1942, and First Endorsement, 18 March 1942. Hereafter the word *serial* is omitted from Classified Operational Archives documents.
8. *Dictionary of American Naval Fighting Ships,* I (Washington, 1959), Appendix I, "Battleships, 1886–1948," 198–99.
9. Robert Greenhalgh Albion and Robert Howe Connery, *Forrestal and the Navy* (New York, 1962), p. 11.
10. *Ibid.,* p. 10.
11. *Ibid.,* p. 97.

12. *Ibid.*, pp. 98–101.
13. See Appendix C for the naval aviators on King's staff from 1943 to 1945.
14. Kyle Crichton, "Navy Air Boss," *Collier's*, 112 (23 October 1943), 21; see also *Time*, 42 (26 July 1943), 68.
15. Duncan and Dater, "Administrative History," p. 536.
16. Rear Admiral Julius Augustus Furer, USN (Ret.), *Administration of the Navy Department in World War II* (Washington, 1959), pp. 165, 392.
17. Albion and Connery, *Forrestal and the Navy*, p. 101.
18. King's directive, quoted in J. A. Furer, *Administration of the Navy Department*, p. 164.
19. Furer, *op. cit.*, pp. 16, 392.
20. Conversation with Vice Admiral W. M. Beakley, USN (Ret.), 20 February 1965.
21. Albion and Connery, *Forrestal and the Navy*, pp. 124–25; *Fleet Admiral King*, p. 629.
22. Yarnell to King, 13 October 1943. Yarnell papers, Naval Historical Foundation. This letter, addressed to "Dolly"—King's early nickname—could well have been instigated by Knox, Forrestal, or others.
23. Yarnell to Nimitz, 7 September 1943. Classified Operational Archives. Unless otherwise noted, all letters, summaries and manuscript histories are from this Archives.
24. Captain Logan C. Ramsey, USN, "The Aero-Amphibious Phase of the Present War," *U.S. Naval Institute Proceedings*, 69 (May 1943), 700.
25. Yarnell to Towers, 4 August 1943.
26. Sallada to Yarnell, 7 September 1943.
27. Thach to Yarnell, 15 September 1943.
28. Durgin to Yarnell, 30 August 1943.
29. Brown to Yarnell, 9 August 1943.
30. Gardner to Yarnell, 25 August 1943.
31. Nimitz to Yarnell, 1 September 1943.
32. Cincpac Confidential letter, 01945, 19 August 1943.
33. F. C. Sherman to Nimitz, 0111, 5 September 1943. The copy the writer used was from the papers of Vice Admiral James H. Flatley, Jr., courtesy of Midshipman Brian A. "J" Flatley. It had been mailed to Commander Flatley at Jacksonville, Florida, which demonstrates that Sherman was circulating his thoughts. Sherman elaborated on his ideas for a "Flying Navy" in a letter to Yarnell, 19 September 1943.
34. Towers to Yarnell, 7 September 1943. Admiral John H. Towers papers, courtesy of Mrs. Towers.

35. And they had not. See, for instance, Lieutenant Forrest Sherman, "Air Warfare," *U.S. Naval Institute Proceedings,* 52 (January 1926), 62–71.
36. F. P. Sherman to Yarnell, 8 September 1943.
37. Yarnell to Nimitz, 7 September 1943.
38. Towers to Nimitz, 4 October 1943, forwarded by Nimitz to Yarnell, 7 October 1943.
39. Admiral H. E. Yarnell, "Report on Naval Aviation," 6 November 1943, pp. 1, 3, 11–12.
40. Brown to Yarnell, 9 August 1943.
41. R. Earl McClendon, *The Question of Autonomy for the United States Air Arm, 1907–1946* (Maxwell Air Force Base, Alabama, December 1948), pp. 225–27.
42. Vincent Davis, "Admirals, Policies and Postwar Defense Policy: The Origins of the Postwar U.S. Navy, 1943–1946 and After" (Unpublished Ph.D. dissertation, Princeton University, 1962), pp. 15–18). Cited hereafter as "Postwar Defense Policy." In book form, see Davis' *Postwar Defense Policy and the U.S. Navy, 1943–1946* (Chapel Hill, 1966), p. 10.
43. *Ibid.*, pp. 23–33.

Chapter Three: Mobilizing the Carrier Offensive

1. Maurice Matloff, *Strategic Planning for Coalition Warfare, 1943–44* (official U.S. Army history; Washington, 1959), p. 191. This Committee, which advised the Joint Chiefs of Staff "on broad questions of national policy and world strategy" (*ibid.*, p. 108) was composed of the Army's Lieutenant General S. D. Embick, the Army Air Forces' Major General Muir S. Fairchild, and the Navy's Vice Admiral Russell Willson, a former Deputy Cominch.
2. *Ibid.*, pp. 186–91.
3. *Ibid.*, p. 207.
4. *Ibid.*, pp. 207–8.

1. THE NEW WEAPONS

1. *Into the Wind* (*Yorktown* cruise book, 1945), p. 74. For life aboard a typical fast carrier, see Commander James Shaw, USN, "Fast Carrier Operations, 1943–1945," in Samuel Eliot Morison, *Aleutians, Gilberts and Marshalls* (Boston, 1957), pp. xxvii–xxxix, and Lieutenant Max Miller, USNR, *Daybreak for Our Carrier* (New York, 1944).
2. A. H. Hilen, Jr., "Remarks on Carrier Development," p. 15.
3. Lieutenant William C. Bryant, USNR, and Lieutenant Heith I. Hermans, USNR, "History of Naval Fighter Direction," *Carrier Warfare* (Vol. I of Essays in the History of Naval Air Operations), manuscript

history, Air History Unit, February 1946, pp. 191, 194. Cited hereafter as "Fighter Direction." Also, Lieutenant Commander Buford Rowland, USNR, and Lieutenant William B. Boyd, USNR, *U.S. Navy Bureau of Ordnance in World War II* (Washington, 1953), pp. 426–27.

4. *Ibid.*, p. 192; A. R. Buchanan, *The United States in World War II* (New York, 1964), pp. 376–78.
5. Rowland and Boyd, *Bureau of Ordnance*, pp. 218–39, 268; see also Bernard Brodie, "Our Ships Strike Back," *The Virginia Quarterly Review*, XXI (Spring 1945), 186–206.
6. *Ibid.*, pp. 258, 272–87.
7. Robert E. Demme, "Evolution of the Hellcat," reprinted from *Skyways* magazine in *The Second Navy Reader* (New York, 1944), p. 193.
8. Okumiya and Horikoshi, *Zero!*, pp. 161–62. This information is given by Okumiya, during the Alentians campaign air staff officer to Rear Admiral Kakuta, ComCarDiv 4.
9. See Appendix B.
10. Okumiya and Horikoshi, *Zero!*, p. 163; R. H. Demme, "Evolution of the Hellcat," pp. 194, 198, 200–1; see Captain Edward H. Eckelmeyer, Jr., USN, "The Story of the Self-Sealing Tank," *U.S. Naval Institute Proceedings*, 72 (February 1946), 205–19.
11. Rowland and Boyd, *Bureau of Ordnance*, pp. 303–4, 332–33.
12. Midshipman 1/c Charles E. Jones, III, USN, "The SB2C Helldiver—An Historical Development and Analysis," (Unpublished research paper, United States Naval Academy, 1966), p. 15 and *passim;* J. J. Clark, *Carrier Admiral*, pp. 113–14.
13. Samuel Eliot Morison, *Supplement and General Index* (Boston, 1962), pp. 112–13.
14. *Ibid.*, p. 113.
15. Quoted in *The New York Times*, 13 September 1943.
16. Admiral M. B. Gardner, USN (Ret.) to the writer, 21 May 1966. Then Captain Gardner was chief of staff to McCain.
17. Transcript of interview of Lieutenant Colonel Edward A. Montgomery, USMC, "Night Fighter Operations in Great Britain," at BuAer, June 1943.
18. William Green, *War Planes of the Second World War: Fighters, IV* (Garden City, 1961), p. 106.
19. Towers to Nimitz, 00329, 29 August 1943.

2. THE JAPANESE

1. Toshikazu Kase, *Journey to the Missouri* (New Haven, 1950), pp. 67–70.
2. ComAirPac "Analysis of Air Operations: Solomons, New Guinea, and

Netherlands East Indies Campaigns, March 1943," 00171, 21 April 1943. This monthly secret periodical covered the Central Pacific after August 1943 and is hereafter referred to as ComAirPac Analysis.

3. "Japanese General Outline of the Future War Direction Policy, Adopted at the Imperial Conference, 30 September 1943," in Louis Morton, *Strategy and Command: The First Two Years* (official U.S. Army history; Washington, 1962), pp. 655–56.
4. Data on Japanese ships from Okumiya and Horikoshi, *Zero!*, pp. 176–77; Pocket Pictorial 2, *Japanese Aircraft Carriers and Destroyers, passim;* Lynn Lucius Moore, "*Shinano*: The Jinx Carrier," *U.S. Naval Institute Proceedings,* 79 (February 1953), 142–49.
5. WSEG Study, p. 21.
6. Masanori Ito, with Roger Pineau, *The End of the Imperial Japanese Navy* (New York, 1956), p. 84.

3. COMMAND AND DOCTRINE

1. Matloff, *Strategic Planning for Coalition Warfare,* pp. 313–14.
2. Gwenfred Allen, *Hawaii's War Years, 1941–1945* (Honolulu, 1950), pp. 185–86.
3. Matloff, *op. cit.,* p. 314: Cincpac Command History, pp. *55,* 60–61; General Holland M. Smith, USMC (Ret.), and Percy Finch, *Coral and Brass* (New York, 1949), p. 115.
4. Vice Admiral George C. Dyer, USN (Ret.), "Naval Amphibious Landmarks," *U.S. Naval Institute Proceedings,* 92 (August 1966), 60.
5. Major Frank Hough, USMCR, *The Island War* (New York, 1947), p. 9.
6. *Ibid.,* quoting AAF Field Service Regulations FM 100–20, "Command and Employment of Air Power," July 1943.
7. W. F. Craven and J. L. Cate in the foreword to their semi-official *The Army Air Forces in World War II* (Chicago, 1950), IV, viii, xiii–xiv.
8. Lieutenant Franklin G. Percival, USN (Ret.), "Wanted: A New Naval Development Policy," *U.S. Naval Institute Proceedings,* 69 (May 1943), 655–57.
9. Pacific Fleet Confidential Letter 31CL-42 and 33L-42, 02490, 13 August 1942.
10. F. C. Sherman diary, 30 March 1943.
11. Vice Admiral E. P. Forrestel, USN (Ret.), *Admiral Raymond A. Spruance, USN: A Study in Command* (Washington, 1966), p. 69.
12. Fletcher Pratt, *Fleet Against Japan,* p. 56.
13. Data based on conversation between Rear Admiral F. C. Sherman and Captain Forrest Sherman at Espiritu Santo, 25 May 1943, recorded in F. C. Sherman diary, 25 May 1943.

14. Entries in the F. C. Sherman diary throughout June and July 1943.
15. Current Tactical Orders and Doctrine, U.S. Pacific Fleet, PAC-10, 01338, 10 June 1943, Pt. IV, pp. 5–7.
16. *Ibid.*, Pt. IV, p. 4.
17. F. C. Sherman diary, 25 July 1943.
18. *Ibid.*, 16, 25 July 1943. After Sherman attended the Cincpac morning meeting of 17 July, Nimitz bade him farewell, "stating he had not recommended me to go down." Diary entry of 25 July.
19. *Admiral Raymond A. Spruance*, p. 69.
20. F. C. Sherman diary, 25 July 1943.
21. *Ibid.*, 31 July; 5, 26, 30–31 August; 1–2, 30 September; 10 October 1943.
22. Nimitz to Towers, 001011, 11 August 1943.
23. "History: Commander Air Force Pacific Fleet," 002238, 3 December 1945, p. 14.
24. Towers to Nimitz, "Organization and Employment of Aircraft Carriers Pacific Fleet," 00318, 21 August 1943.
25. Towers to Yarnell, 7 September 1943. Towers papers.
26. Towers diary, 23 August 1943.
27. Towers to Yarnell, 7 September 1943. See p. 489 below.
28. Towers diary, 26 August 1943.
29. *Ibid.*, 28 August 1943.
30. Which made Sherman furious, as Duckworth was never returned to him. F. C. Sherman diary, 22 August 1943.
31. Dater-Duckworth memorandum; Pownall Action Report, no serial, 4 September 1943.
32. One year later the Navy officially announced: "The introduction of the fast carrier task force to combat occurred August 31, 1943, with the raid on Marcus Island. . . ." *The New York Times*, 30 August 1944.
33. *U.S. Naval Aviation, 1910–1960*, p. 7.
34. Quoted in *The New York Times*, 30 August 1943.
35. Oliver Jensen, *Carrier War* (New York, 1945), p. 47.

Chapter Four: Fast Carrier Task Force on Trial

1. Isely and Crowl, *Amphibious War*, p. 200.
2. *Coral and Brass*, p. 136.
3. Isely and Crowl, *op. cit.*, p. 200.

1. BATTLE TRAINING AND DOCTRINE

1. Vice Admiral Charles A. Lockwood, USN (Ret.), and Colonel Hans Christian Adamson, USAF (Ret.), *Zoomies, Subs and Zeros* (New York, 1956), pp. 12–14.
2. Pownall Action Report, no serial, 4 September 1943.
3. Conversation with Vice Admiral Beakley, USN (Ret.), 20 February 1965.
4. *Ibid.*
5. Pownall Action Report, 4 September 1943.
6. Oliver Jensen, *Carrier War*, p. 51; Rear Admiral Charles O. Triebel, USN, *Snook*'s captain, to the writer, 17 April 1961.
7. *Carrier Admiral*, pp. 123, 125.
8. *Ibid.*, pp. 125–26; conversation with Vice Admiral Beakley, 20 February 1965.
9. WSEG Study, p. 17.
10. Pownall Action Report, 4 September 1943.
11. Samuel Eliot Morison, *Aleutians, Gilberts and Marshalls* (Boston, 1957), pp. 95–96.
12. Pownall Action Report, 005, 22 September 1943.
13. Towers diary, 9 September 1943.
14. Cincpac-Cincpoa "Command History, 7 December 1941–15 August 1945" (1945), p. 70.
15. Towers diary, 8–9 September 1943.
16. See *Carrier Admiral*, pp. 126–27.
17. ComAirPac Analysis, September 1943, 00413; also Pownall Action Report, 0017, 3 October 1943 and conversation with Vice Admiral Beakley, 20 February 1965.
18. Philip A. Crowl and Edmund G. Love, *Seizure of the Gilberts and Marshalls* (official U.S. Army history; Washington, 1955), pp. 68–69.
19. Isely and Crowl, *Amphibious War*, p. 201
20. *Lexington* Action Report, 009, 22 September 1943; Pownall Action Report, 3 October 1943.
21. Towers diary, 5 October 1943.
22. *Ibid.*, 28 September 1943.
23. *Ibid.*, 19 September 1943.
24. *Ibid.*, 20 September 1943.
25. Dater-Duckworth memorandum.

26. *Fleet Admiral King*, pp. 490–91.
27. Towers diary, 25 September 1943.
28. Dater-Duckworth memorandum.
29. "United States Naval Administration in World War II: DCNO(Air): Air Task Organization in Pacific Ocean Areas, Ship-based Aircraft" (1945), pp. 20–22.
30. ComAirPac Analysis, October 1943.
31. *Skate* was strafed by a Japanese plane, which mortally wounded one of her officers, leading Admiral Towers in December to assign fighters to cover lifeguard submarines. ComAirPac History, p. 108.
32. Dater-Duckworth memorandum.
33. Crowl and Love, *Gilberts and Marshalls*, p. 69.
34. ComAirPac Analysis, October 1943.

2. DEBATE OVER DOCTRINE

1. J. Grimes, *Aviation in the Fleet Exercises*, p. 18.
2. Towers to Nimitz, 4 October 1943, forwarded by Nimitz to Yarnell, 7 October 1943.
3. Towers diary, 5 October 1943.
4. History of Fleet Air Command, West Coast, 0255, 22 January 1945.
5. Towers diary (kept by Forrest Sherman), 6, 9 October 1943.
6. *Carrier Admiral*, p. 129.
7. F. C. Sherman diary, 10 October 1943.
8. Rear Admiral Robert W. Morse, USN (Ret.) to the writer, 29 June 1966.
9. Towers diary, 12, 20 October 1943.
10. For changes to *Enterprise* see Commander Edward P. Stafford, USN, *The Big E* (New York, 1962), pp. 255–57.
11. Lee M. Pearson, *Naval Confidential Bulletin* (based on BuAer files, n.d.), p. 75.
12. ComAirPac History, p. 1.
13. Crowl and Love, *Gilberts and Marshalls*, pp. 36–37.
14. See, for instance, Lieutenant Thomas L. Morrissey, USNR, *Odyssey of Fighting Two* (published by the author, 1945), p. 31.
15. Crowl and Love, *op. cit.*, p. 162.
16. *Admiral Raymond A. Spruance*, p. 74.
17. "General Instructions to Flag Officers, Central Pacific Force, for Galvanic," 29 October 1943, quoted in *Admiral Raymond A. Spruance*, p. 74.

18. *Ibid.*

19. Originally, Tarawa and Nauru were to have been assaulted. Nauru's airfield worried nonaviator Captain James M. Steele, Nimitz's planning officer, and Admiral Turner. But Admiral Spruance and Major General H. M. Smith felt it was too heavily defended to be worth the cost, while the aviators felt it could be easily neutralized. The latter reasoning influenced Nimitz and King, who substituted Makin for Nauru on 27 September 1943. Conversation with Admiral George W. Anderson, Jr., in May 1964; *Coral and Brass,* p. 114; S. E. Morison, *Aleutians, Gilberts and Marshalls,* pp. 84–85; *Admiral Raymond A. Spruance,* pp. 70–71.

20. Towers diary, 14 October 1943.

21. *Ibid.*, 17 October 1943.

22. *Ibid.*, 21 November 1943.

3. BATTLE

1. Fleet Admiral William F. Halsey, Jr., USN, and Lieutenant Commander J. Bryan, III, USNR, *Admiral Halsey's Story* (New York, 1947), pp. 177–78.

2. Samuel Eliot Morison, *Breaking the Bismarcks Barrier* (Boston, 1957), pp. 286–87.

3. *Admiral Halsey's Story,* p. 181.

4. Quoted by Lieutenant Commander R. F. Farrington, commanding VB-12, in an Air Intelligence Group Interview, 18 February 1944, Director of Naval Intelligence (OpNav-16-V-#E38), 23 March 1944.

5. Admiral Carney, recalling the occasion in *Admiral Halsey's Story,* p. 181.

6. Dive bombing varied from 60° to 90°, glide bombing 30° to 55°, skip or masthead bombing was at 20°, horizontal bombing below that. From Aviation Training Division, *Introduction to Naval Aviation* (NavAer-80R-19, January 1946).

7. Oliver Jensen, *Carrier War,* p. 59; S. E. Morison, *Breaking the Bismarcks Barrier,* pp. 326–27; conversations with Rear Admiral J. C. Clifton, USN, and Captain R. G. Dosé, USN (VF-12) in 1961.

8. F. C. Sherman diary, 6 November 1943.

9. Crowl and Love, *Gilberts and Marshalls,* p. 70.

10. F. C. Sherman diary, 12 November 1943.

11. *Admiral Halsey's Story,* p. 183.

12. Robert Olds, *Helldiver Squadron: The Story of Carrier Bombing Squadron 17 with Task Force 58* (New York, 1944), p. 51.

13. See Commander James C. Shaw's account in S. E. Morison, *Breaking the Bismarcks Barrier,* pp. 332–36.

14. Lieutenant Commander Arthur Decker in Air Intelligence Group Interview, 18 March 1944, Director of Naval Intelligence (OpNav-16-V-#E42), 10 April 1944.

15. Oliver Jensen, *Carrier War*, p. 65.

16. "As a matter of history, those ships formed the first actual Fast Carrier Task Force. . . ." Turnbull and Lord, *History of United States Naval Aviation*, p. 320.

17. E. P. Stafford, *The Big E*, pp. 261–62; conversation with Admiral Arthur W. Radford, USN (Ret.), in December 1964; Admiral Gardner to the writer, 21 May 1966.

18. Isely and Crowl, *Amphibious War*, pp. 224–25, 230–31, 248–49; Crowl and Love, *Gilberts and Marshalls*, pp. 159–62; S. E. Morison, *Aleutians, Gilberts and Marshalls*, pp. 156–58.

19. Bryant and Hermans, "Fighter Direction," p. 197.

20. Towers diary, 21 November 1943.

21. *Ibid.*

22. The same night of 13–14 November a severe fire caused by a deck crash on *Yorktown*'s flight deck almost claimed that ship. See *Carrier Admiral*, pp. 133–135.

23. The best account of this action is E. P. Stafford, *The Big E*, pp. 280–85. Ted Sherman regarded night air battles as "a hell of a way to operate and none of us like it." F. C. Sherman diary, 30 November 1943.

24. Crowl and Love, *Gilberts and Marshalls*, p. 211.

25. ComAirPac Analysis, November 1943.

26. WSEG Study aircraft statistics; see Appendix B of this book.

27. *Carrier Admiral*, pp. 138–40.

28. In Air Intelligence Group Interview, 4 January 1944, Director of Naval Intelligence (OpNav-16-V-#E28), 3 February 1944. In addition, Stump said, "Admiral Pownall did everything that I, as an ex-torpedo-plane pilot, think he could have done in maneuvering. . . ."

29. See S. E. Morison, *Aleutians, Gilberts and Marshalls*, pp. 193–97, and *Carrier Admiral*, pp. 140–41, for vivid descriptions of that hectic night.

30. "Lee is a good man but command of combined air and surface forces should be under Air." F. C. Sherman diary, 7 December 1943.

31. Which Sherman criticized: "All those CV's at Pearl not doing a thing since Galvanic." *Ibid.*, 28 December 1943.

32. See Admiral F. C. Sherman, *Combat Command*, pp. 209–12.

33. Captain James R. Stockman, USMC, *The Battle for Tarawa* (official Marine Corps history; Washington, 1947), p. 68.

4. BATTLE OF WASHINGTON

1. Peter Marsh Stanford, "The Battle Fleet and World Air Power," *U.S. Naval Institute Proceedings,* 69 (December 1943), 1538.
2. Vincent Davis, "Postwar Defense Policy," p. 52.

Chapter Five: Task Force 58

1. These conclusions are from "Overall Plan for the defeat of Japan: Report by the Combined Staff Planners, Approved in Principle, 2 December 1943," in Louis Morton, *First Two Years,* pp. 668–71.
2. Okumiya and Horikoshi, *Zero!,* p. 308.
3. Originally the Marshalls were to have been assaulted on 1 January 1944, but on 25 October 1943 Nimitz had asked Admiral King for permission to move the date back, giving him time to build up his airfields in the Gilberts, train his troops, assemble more equipment, and to repair damage received in capturing the Gilberts. The JCS agreed, and the target date was eventually set at 31 January. Crowl and Love, *Gilberts and Marshalls,* pp. 167–68.
4. Maurice Matloff, *Strategic Planning for Coalition Warfare,* p. 377.
5. Admiral Harry W. Hill, USN (Ret.), in an address to midshipmen of the United States Naval Academy, 13 January 1965. Hill, who attended this meeting as one of the bombardment commanders, regarded Nimitz's dramatic pronouncement as Hill's "greatest thrill of the war."
6. Marshalls strategy from Crowl and Love, *Gilberts and Marshalls,* pp. 168–70; Isely and Crowl, *Amphibious War,* pp. 255–56; S. E. Morison, *Aleutians, Gilberts and Marshalls,* pp. 201–6; *Coral and Brass,* pp. 112–14, 141.
7. S. E. Morison, *Breaking the Bismarcks Barrier,* pp. 226–27; F. G. Percival, "Wanted: A New Naval Development Policy," *Proceedings* (May 1943), *passim*; *Admiral Halsey's Story,* pp. 170–71; conversation with Vice Admiral Beakley, 20 February 1965. Commander Beakley and Admiral Towers stopped at Samoa on the return to Hawaii from a Christmas trip to Guadalcanal, and from his bedroom Beakley overheard Towers and Price discussing leapfrogging most of the night.
8. Minutes of Pacific Conference, San Francisco, 3–4 January 1944. Cooke papers.
9. *Admiral Halsey's Story,* pp. 187–88.
10. Towers diary, 7 November 1943.
11. ROADMAKER [capture of Truk] Joint Staff Study, 00023, 26 February 1944; Towers to Nimitz, 00088, 5 January 1944.
12. Towers to Nimitz, 5 January 1944. Italics Towers'.

13. *Ibid.*, memos of McMorris and Sherman attached, also Nimitz to King, 0005, 16 January 1944.
14. Matloff, *Strategic Planning for Coalition Warfare,* p. 455.
15. *Ibid.*, pp. 455–56; George C. Kenney, *General Kenney Reports* (New York, 1949), pp. 346–48.
16. *General Kenney Reports,* p. 348.
17. MacArthur to Marshall, 2 February 1944, in Matloff, *Strategic Planning for Coalition Warfare,* p. 456.

1. COMMMAND SHAKEUP

1. Albion and Connery, *Forrestal and the Navy,* pp. 125–26.
2. *Coral and Brass,* pp. 138–39.
3. King to Knox, 516, 29 January 1944, First Endorsement of Yarnell report of 6 November 1943; Horne to King, 0402, 6 January 1944.
4. *The New York Times,* 24 January 1944.
5. Pacific Command History, pp. 70–71.
6. George E. Jones, "Brain Center of Pacific War," *The New York Times Magazine* (8 April 1945), p. 10.
7. *Carrier Admiral,* p. 142.
8. Towers diary, 27 December 1943; numerous conversations with Admiral Clark and several former *Yorktown* officers involved.
9. Towers diary, 23, 25 December 1943; Theodore Taylor, *The Magnificent Mitscher* (New York, 1954), pp. 169–70.
10. *Admiral Raymond A. Spruance,* p. 102.
11. Towers diary, 27 December 1943.
12. *Ibid.*, 30 December 1943–2 January 1944.
13. *Ibid.*, 3–4 January 1944. Later, during the actual bombardment, Spruance insisted on two days of shelling, which illustrates his shift to the Towers–Radford viewpoint. See *Admiral Raymond A. Spruance,* p. 103.
14. *Ibid.*, 5–7 January 1944.
15. Admiral Gardner to the writer, 21 May 1966.
16. F. C. Sherman diary, 16 January 1944.
17. See Vincent Davis, *Postwar Navy,* pp. 199–201.
18. *The Magnificent Mitscher,* pp. 171, 178; conversation with Admiral A. A. Burke, USN (Ret.), 3 June 1966; Vice Admiral G. D. Murray to Henry Suydan, February 1947, and Suydan's obituary of Mitscher in the *Newark Evening News,* 4 February 1947, both in the Marc A. Mitscher collection, Library of Congress.

19. Captain R. H. Dale, USN (Ret.), to the writer, 14 April 1966. Commander Dale was air group commander on *Bunker Hill,* Sherman's flagship.
20. *Admiral Raymond A. Spruance,* pp. 83, 102.
21. Quoted in *The Magnificent Mitscher,* p. 202.
22. *Coral and Brass,* pp. 115–16.

2. OPEN SECRET WEAPON

1. S. E. Morison, *Aleutians, Gilberts and Marshalls,* p. 107.
2. From the orders outlining Service Squadron 10, in Rear Admiral Worrall Reed Carter, USN (Ret.), *Beans, Bullets, and Black Oil* (Washington, 1951), p. 96.
3. S. E. Morison, *op. cit.,* pp. 107–8.
4. Towers diary, 26 August 1943; ComAirPac History, p. 1.
5. WSEG Study, pp. 35–40.
6. Yarnell to Knox, "Report on Naval Aviation," 6 November 1943.
7. Conversation with Admiral Radford, December 1964; Towers diary, 9 February 1944. Towers wanted to send J. J. Ballentine, but McCain insisted on Radford.

3. KWAJALEIN TO TRUK

1. Current Tactical Orders and Doctrine, U.S. Fleet—USF 10A—Cominch 1944, pp. 4–22. PAC 10 had incorporated the general tactical instructions issued by Cominch earlier in the war as USF 10, now also superseded by USF 10A.
2. Towers to Naval Air Force Pacific Fleet, 02330, 16 December 1943 (signed by Radford).
3. Towers to Nimitz, 0030, 8 January 1944.
4. Commander James S. Gray, Jr., "Development of Naval Night Fighters in World War II," *U.S. Naval Institute Proceedings,* 74 (July 1948), 848–49.
5. ComAirPac History, p. 22; ComAirPac memorandum for carrier divisions, 0050, 13 January 1944.
6. Towers diary, 31 December 1943. Fighter distribution was a major topic of discussion at the San Francisco meeting. See Vice Admiral McCain's remarks quoted in *The New York Times,* 9 January 1944.
7. Interview of Lieutenant Commander J. E. Vose, USN, Commanding Bombing 17, 16 February 1944, Air Intelligence Group (Op-Nav-16-V-#40), 23 March 1944.
8. Turner Action Report, 00165, 4 December 1943.

9. *Ibid.;* also Turner Action Report, 00371, 23 December 1943.
10. Craven and Cate, Foreword to Vol. V, *AAF in World War II,* p. xvii.
11. "Air Support Command History, August 1942 to 14 August 1945," (1945), p. 5.
12. *Ibid.,* pp. 4–5.
13. Isely and Crowl, *Amphibious War,* p. 249.
14. See S. E. Morison, *Aleutians, Gilberts and Marshalls,* pp. 218–21.
15. Air Support History, p. 5. Some of these air support sorties were antisubmarine patrols.
16. WSEG Study, pp. 9–10.
17. Isely and Crowl, *Amphibious War,* p. 292.
18. Cincpac Command History, pp. 137–38.
19. *Coral and Brass,* p. 149.
20. Isely and Crowl, *Amphibious War,* pp. 291–92. After GALVANIC and FLINTLOCK code names were used but seldom referred to in the Pacific; the writer follows this practice.
21. F. C. Sherman diary, 27 February 1944. See also the entries of 11, 23, and 24 February 1944.
22. *Ibid.,* 11 February 1944.
23. Elmont Waite, "He Opened the Airway to Tokyo," *Saturday Evening Post* (2 December 1944), p. 20.
24. Oliver Jensen, *Carrier War,* p. 97. Remarked one Bombing 17 pilot jokingly to his comrades, "Just give me your last letters and I'll deliver them to your next-of-kin." Robert Olds, *Helldiver Squadron,* pp. 182–83.
25. F. C. Sherman diary, 23 February 1944; *The Magnificent Mitscher,* p. 182.
26. W. R. Carter, *Beans, Bullets, and Black Oil,* p. 121.
27. S. E. Morison, *Aleutians, Gilberts and Marshalls,* p. 320. A strike, opposed to a sweep, was a prebriefed mission against prearranged targets.
28. "Air Group Nine Comes Home," *Life* (1 May 1944), pp. 92–97; Oliver Jensen, *Carrier War,* p. 101.
29. Oliver Jensen, *Carrier War,* p. 105; see S. E. Morison, *Aleutians, Gilberts and Marshalls,* pp. 326–29.
30. Bryant and Hermans, "Fighter Direction," p. 205.
31. Isely and Crowl, *Amphibious War,* p. 301.
32. *The Magnificent Mitscher,* p. 186.
33. Cincpac, "Operations in the Pacific Ocean Areas," February 1944.
34. *The Magnificent Mitscher,* p. 187.

35. See Samuel Eliot Morison, *New Guinea and the Marianas* (Boston, 1953), pp. 154–55.

36. *Carrier Air Group 9* (Chicago, 1945), p. 23.

37. ComAirPac Analysis, February 1944, 00280, 24 March 1944; ComAirPac Supplementary Report on Carrier Operations, 30 January–24 February 1944. See *Fleet Admiral King*, p. 536n.

38. Oliver Jensen, *Carrier War*, p. 41.

4. STRIKING WESTWARD

1. Moore to Spruance, ComCenPac File A16-3, 19 February 1944; Rear Admiral C. J. Moore, USN (Ret.), to the writer, 5 August 1961; conversation with Vice Admiral C. A. Pownall, USN (Ret.), in June 1961.

2. Nimitz to King, 00025, 1 March 1944, cited in Cincpac Command History, p. 140.

3. Fleet Admiral William D. Leahy, USN, *I Was There* (NewYork, 1950), p. 228; see *Admiral Halsey's Story*, pp. 189–90.

4. *Ibid.*, p. 230.

5. See Cincpac Command History, pp. 140–41; Robert Ross Smith, "Luzon versus Formosa," in Kent Roberts Greenfield (ed.), *Command Decisions* (Washington, 1960), p. 465; *Fleet Admiral King*, p. 537.

6. General Kenney was "dumbfounded." *General Kenney Reports*, p. 371.

7. Hanson Baldwin, "Navy Shift in Pacific," *The New York Times*, 11 February 1944.

8. Towers diary, 22 February 1944.

9. *Ibid.*, 22, 28 February 1944.

10. F. C. Sherman diary, 4, 6 March 1944.

11. *The Magnificent Mitscher*, pp. 190–91 and *passim;* conversation with Admiral Burke, 3 June 1966.

12. *Ibid.*, pp. 196–97, 247–48.

13. Sherman to Rear Admiral Lynde D. McCormick, 31 March 1944, cited in Cincpac Command History, p. 137; *General Kenney Reports*, pp. 376–77; *Admiral Halsey's Story*, pp. 189–90. See Chapter Nine for British carrier operations in the Far East.

14. *Carrier Admiral,* pp. 149–50, 154, 157–58. Also pp. 489–90 below.

15. J. S. Gray, "Night Fighters," *Proceedings*, p. 850; ComAirPac History, p. 23; see my "Day of the Night Carriers," *The Royal United Service Institution Journal*, CX (May 1965), 148–54.

16. ComAirPac Analysis, April 1944, 00613, 1 June 1944; *The Magnificent Mitscher*, pp. 193–94; S. E. Morison, *New Guinea and the Marianas*, p. 33n; Oliver Jensen, *Carrier War*, pp. 122–27.

17. The Ginder problem, Clark's appointment, and Mitscher's attitudes about command are from the Towers diary, 10, 19 April 1944; conversations with Admirals George W. Anderson, Jr., in 1964 and A. A. Burke in 1966 and former Lieutenant J. J. Vonk, TF 58 meteorologist, in December 1965; and *Carrier Admiral, passim.*
18. Air Support History, pp. 5–6.
19. *The Magnificent Mitscher*, p. 205.
20. ComAirPac Analysis, March 1944, 00468, 30 April 1944.
21. Oliver Jensen, *Carrier War*, p. 131.
22. Clark Action Report, cited in Bryant and Hermans, "Fighter Direction," p. 213.
23. Towers to AirPac Distribution List, 0057, 16 January 1944; Pownall to King, 00361, 14 April 1944.
24. ComAirPac Analysis, May 1944, 00740, 29 June 1944.

Chapter Six: Battle of the Fast Carriers

1. THE JAPANESE FLEET

1. Biographical data from the Director of the Japanese Defense Agency for Military History, and *USSBS*, II, 548–73.
2. Masanori Ito, *End of the Imperial Japanese Navy*, p. 95.
3. Okumiya and Horikoshi, *Zero!*, p. 323.
4. *USSBS*, I, 10 (Ozawa).
5. Ito, *op. cit.*, p. 108.
6. These figures are from Captain Toshikazu Ohmae, senior staff officer to Vice Admiral Ozawa, in Apprendix II, S. E. Morison, *New Guinea and the Marianas*, p. 146. Allied code names of these planes were, respectively, Zeke, Judy, Jill, Val.
7. Okumiya and Horikoshi, *Zero!*, p. 324.
8. Ito, *op. cit.*, p. 96.
9. WSEG Study, p. 21.
10. *USSBS*, I, 7 (Ozawa).
11. See Okumiya and Horikoshi, *Zero!*, pp. 322–23.
12. Mitscher (CTF 58) Operations Plan No. 7-44, Intelligence Annex, 24 May 1944; Clark (CTG 58.1) Operations Plan No. 7-44.

2. AMERICAN BATTLE TACTICS

1. Quoted in *The New York Times*, 21 June 1944.
2. That battle, fought 15 August 1545, curiously falls exactly 400 years to

the day (barring calendar changes and time differences) before, as we shall see, the guns of the last great battleship line fell silent, 15 August 1945.

3. Admiral Sir John Byng, executed for failing to do "his utmost" at the battle of Minorca, May 1756.

4. For a balanced textbook discussion of formalism and meleeism, see E. B. Potter and C. W. Nimitz (eds.), *Sea Power* (Englewood Cliffs, N.J., 1960), pp. 21–167, for the period to 1815, and Captain S. W. Roskill, *The Strategy of Sea Power* (London, 1962), pp. 80–81, 101–22, for the period 1816 to 1918.

5. *Admiral Raymond A. Spruance*, pp. 12–13, and the Naval War College rosters for 1936 to 1938. Very junior aviators began to serve at the War College in 1936. In the Junior Tactics class were Lieutenant Commanders Miles Browning, T. P. Jeter, and T. H. Robbins, Jr. Robbins served as Spruance's assistant in 1937–38. The War College class of 1940 included two future distinguished aviators, Captain Frederick C. Sherman and Commander C. A. F. Sprague.

6. *Coral and Brass*, p. 165.

7. E. J. King, *U.S. Navy at War*, p. 34.

8. Towers diary, 14 June 1944.

9. *Ibid.*, 14–15 June 1944; conversation with Admiral George W. Anderson, Jr., USN (Ret.), in May 1964.

3. ATTACK ON THE MARIANAS

1. Theodore Roscoe, *United States Submarine Operations in World War II* (Annapolis, 1949), p. 365.

2. Rowland and Boyd, *Bureau of Ordnance*, p. 427.

3. Bryant and Hermans, "Fighter Direction," p. 203.

4. This was the ASB radar. *Hancock*'s Helldivers carried the new ASH scope which could detect a ship 35 miles away. Captain Frank Akers to Vice Admiral J. S. McCain, "Information on Carrier Based Planes, Radar and other Electronics Equipment," 12 July 1944.

5. The fighter radar was the AIA. Akers to McCain, 12 July 1944; "Pilots Operating Manual for Airborne Radar AN/APS-6 Series for Night Fighters" (CO NAVAER 08-5S-120, 17 February 1944), p. 5.

6. Clark Action Report, 0029, 10 May 1944.

7. Ofstie, "Operations against Marcus and Wake Islands, 19–23 May 1944" from "Performance and Operational Data, U.S. Navy Planes in the Pacific, January–May 1944" (OpNav-16-V-E#122), August 1944; Litch in "Performance and Operational Data . . ., July–October 1944" (OpNav-16-V-E#345), December 1944.

8. Lieutenant John F. Gray to Commander James H. Flatley, 13 June 1944. Flatley papers.
9. Mitscher Action Report, 00388, 11 September 1944.
10. Lieutenants W. G. Land, USNR, and A. O. Van Wyen, USNR, "Naval Air Operations in the Marianas," mimeographed by the Air History Unit, Washington, 1945 (irregular pagination); Mitscher Action Report, 29 June 1944.
11. VF-24 Action Report and Commander J. D. Blitch, VB-14 Action Report, cited in Land and Van Wyen, "The Marianas." Several documents of this chapter are from the Land-Van Wyen study.
12. VT-16 Action Report complained that "the rocket is a weapon of dubious merits penalizing an airplane already vulnerable to the attacks demanded of it." See also Mitscher Operations Plan 7-44, 00255, 24 May 1944.
13. S. E. Morison, *New Guinea and the Marianas*, pp. 179–80.
14. Isely and Crowl, *Amphibious War*, p. 331, says Spruance feared for the loss of these antiaircraft batteries so he stationed them far from the beach. For a defense of Lee's battleship gunnery see Vice Admiral C. A. Lockwood, USN (Ret.) and Colonel H. C. Adamson, USAF (Ret.), *Battles of the Philippine Sea* (New York, 1967), pp. 69–71.
15. Philip A. Crowl, *Campaign in the Marianas* (official U.S. Army history: Washington, 1960), p. 46; *Coral and Brass*, p. 162.
16. See Isely and Crowl, *Amphibious War*, pp. 331–34; Air Support History, pp. 6–7.
17. Cincpac-Cincpoa Item #10,238, quoted in Major Carl W. Hoffman, USMC, *Saipan: The Beginning of the End* (official Marine Corps history: Washington, 1950), p. 36.
18. Conversation with Admiral Burke, June 1966.
19. Captain R. H. Dale to the writer, 14 April 1966. Commander Dale was then operations officer to Rear Admiral Harrill.
20. *Carrier Admiral*, pp. 162–63.
21. Numerous conversations with Admiral Clark; Captain Dale to the writer, 14 April 1966.

4. SPRUANCE'S DECISION

1. The best hour-to-hour account of these events is Samuel Eliot Morison, *New Guinea and the Marianas*, pp. 170ff. Beyond the times and chronological statements, however, this source suffers from certain inaccuracies and superficial assessments regarding fleet doctrine and Spruance's tactics, influenced no doubt by necessary limitations of time, space, and contemplation in preparing such a multivolume history and by the

fact that most participants were still living when Morison published the Marianas volume. See also my critique later in the present chapter.

2. *Admiral Raymond A. Spruance*, p. 138.
3. Fifth Fleet battle plan, 17 June, quoted in *ibid.*, p. 243.
4. Towers diary, 14–15 June 1944.
5. *Carrier Admiral*, p. 165.
6. Spruance to Mitscher, 17 June 1944, in S. E. Morison, *New Guinea and the Marianas*, p. 243.
7. All this from *Carrier Admiral*, pp. 166–68.
8. Oliver Jensen, *Carrier War*, p. 150.
9. The writer is indebted to Professor William H. Russell of the United States Naval Academy for some of the ideas herein expressed.
10. *Carrier Admiral*, p. 166.
11. *Ibid.*, p. 167; *Magnificent Mitscher*, pp. 212–13.
12. Mitscher Action Report, 11 September 1944.
13. *Admiral Raymond A. Spruance*, p. 137.
14. Admiral R. A. Spruance, USN (Ret.), to the writer, 17 February 1961.
15. Commodore A. A. Burke, USN, *The First Battle of the Philippine Sea: Decision Not to Force an Action on the Night of 18–19 June* (Transcribed interview, 1945), p. 8. Cited hereafter as the Burke transcript.
16. Captain Harold (S.) Hopkins, RN, *Nice to Have You Aboard* (London, 1964), p. 140. Commander Hopkins at the time was British liaison officer on the Cincpac staff.
17. Mitscher Action Report, 11 September 1944.
18. Spruance to Mitscher and Lee, 18 June 1944, in *Admiral Raymond A. Spruance*, p. 137.
19. Burke transcript, p. 9.
20. *Magnificent Mitscher*, pp. 215–16; see Fletcher Pratt, *Fleet Against Japan*, p. 159.
21. Diary of Lieutenant Joseph E. Kane, VB-14, 10 May 1944 to 12 February 1945. Entry of 18 June 1944. Courtesy of Midshipman Joseph E. Kane, II, USNA Class of 1966.
22. Burke transcript, p. 7, says that Mitscher felt this as early as the afternoon of the seventeenth.
23. *Ibid.*, p. 8.
24. *Ibid.*, p. 4; S. E. Morison, *New Guinea and the Marianas*, p. 253.
25. *Ibid.*, pp. 4–5.
26. *Ibid.*
27. *Carrier Admiral*, pp. 168, 175–76.

28. *Magnificent Mitscher*, pp. 220–21.
29. Mitscher Action Report, 11 September 1944.
30. *Admiral Raymond A. Spruance*, p. 137.
31. Rear Admiral Morse to the writer, 29 June 1966.
32. Mitscher Action Report, 11 September 1944.
33. Burke transcript, p. 10.
34. Spruance Action Report, 00026, 13 July 1944.
35. S. E. Morison, *New Guinea and the Marianas*, pp. 254–55.

5. BATTLE OF THE PHILIPPINE SEA

1. Or so he told Professor Morison's historical staff in 1952. *New Guinea and the Marianas*, p. 232n.
2. Masanori Ito, *End of the Imperial Japanese Navy*, pp. 108–9.
3. Montgomery Action Report, 000223, 6 July 1944.
4. Again, S. E. Morison, *New Guinea and the Marianas*, pp. 257–304, is the best source, but see also Ito, op. cit., pp. 103–7.
5. Montgomery Action Report, 6 July 1944.
6. Overheard and quoted by Lieutenant Commander Paul D. Buie, skipper of *Lexington*'s VF-16. *Magnificent Mitscher*, p. 227.
7. Conversation with former Lieutenant Douglas A. McCrary, USNR, June 1966, TBF pilot in *Yorktown*'s VT-5 from August 1943 to April 1944 and thereafter air operations officer to Rear Admiral Clark.
8. *Magnificent Mitscher*, p. 227.
9. Spruance Action Report 00398, 14 July 1944.
10. Nimitz to Spruance, 19 June 1944 (see item 5 in Documentary Addendum).
11. *Carrier Admiral*, p. 171.
12. S. E. Morison, *New Guinea and the Marianas*, p. 268; A. R. Buchanan, *The United States and World War II*, p. 521, says that the "one flaw in [the] American performance was [this] failure to send out search planes."
13. In 1955 Admiral Spruance claimed incorrectly that the carrier planes had no search radar at all. P. A. Crowl, *Campaign in the Marianas*, p. 122.
14. *Admiral Raymond A. Spruance*, p. 52.
15. The first quote is from the Burke transcript, p. 17. The second quote is from Lieutenant J. Bryan III, USNR, and Philip G. Reed, *Mission Beyond Darkness* (New York, 1945), p. 15.
16. *Ibid.*, p. 23.

17. *Hornet* Action Report, 0020, 1 July 1944, report of Commander Air Group 2.
18. "Action Narrative Carrier Air Group Fourteen Strike vs. Japanese Fleet, 20 June 1944."
19. Kane diary, 23 June 1944.
20. See S. E. Morison, *New Guinea and the Marianas*, p. 299.
21. *USSBS*, I, 10 (Ozawa).
22. Lieutenant (jg) John Denley Walker in Walter Karig *et al*, *Battle Report*, IV (New York, 1948), p. 248.
23. "History of VF-1" (mimeographed), p. 4.
24. Bryan and Reed, *Mission Beyond Darkness*, pp. 63–64.
25. Kane diary, 25 June 1944.
26. Bryan and Reed, *op. cit.*, p. 69.
27. ComAirPac, Current Tactical Orders Aircraft Carriers U.S. Fleet, USF-77(A), February 1943 (Prefaced by Admiral E. J. King, 10 May 1943), p. 20.
28. Kane diary, 24 June 1944.
29. Bryan and Reed, *Mission Beyond Darkness*, pp. 72–73; *Magnificent Mitscher*, pp. 234–35; *Carrier Admiral*, p. 173; S. E. Morison, *New Guinea and the Marianas*, pp. 302–4; conversation in 1965 with Captain O. E. Sowerwine, USN (Ret.), communications officer to Rear Admiral Clark.
30. Montgomery Action Report, 6 July 1944; Bryan and Reed, *Mission Beyond Darkness*, pp. 71, 78, 98–99.
31. Kane diary, 25 June 1944.
32. Bryan and Reed, *op. cit.*, pp. 103, 105.
33. Summarized in S. E. Morison, *New Guinea and the Marianas*, p. 304.

6. ANOTHER JUTLAND?

1. *The New York Times*, 23 June 1944.
2. Hopkins, *Nice to Have You Aboard*, p. 146.
3. Conversation with Admiral George Anderson in 1964. Commander Anderson in June 1944 was special assistant to Vice Admiral Towers, Deputy Cincpac, and therefore close to all Pacific policymaking.
4. Mitscher Action Report, 11 September 1944; conversation with Admiral Burke in 1966.
5. Admiral Spruance to the writer, 17 February 1961.
6. *Admiral Raymond A. Spruance*, p. 137.

7. Montgomery Action Report, 6 July 1944.
8. F. C. Sherman, *Combat Command* (1950), p. 243. In his diary for 5 July 1944 Sherman said only of the Battle of the Philippine Sea: "It must have been a mess."
9. *Carrier Admiral* (1967), pp. 175–76.
10. *Fleet Admiral King*, p. 563.
11. Harrill (CTG 58.4) Operations Plan No. 1-44, Annex I.
12. Reeves (CTG 58.3) Operations Order No. R-3-44, Part III, Annex F.
13. Burke transcript, pp. 11–12.
14. Davis' official title until relieved was Cominch Assistant Chief of Staff (Operations).
15. S. E. Morison, *New Guinea and the Marianas* (1953), pp. 310–19.
16. *Ibid.*
17. See *ibid.*, p. 314, n. 16, then Alfred Thayer Mahan, *The Influence of Sea Power Upon History, 1660–1783* (1890; American Century Series, 1957), p. 481: ". . . prolonged control of the strategic centers of commerce [in our case, the waterways and Japanese seaports girdling the Chinese mainland] . . . can be wrung from a powerful navy only by fighting and overcoming it."
18. A. T. Mahan, *Influence of Sea Power*, pp. 444–49. If the reader will pardon this bit of historical fun, Mahan quotes an anonymous critic of Rodney (1809) who asserted that Rodney (Spruance?) would have preferred "to rest his reputation" upon actions against "the best" of the French admirals, de Guichen (Yamamoto?) in the action off Dominica (Midway?) exactly two years before, April 1780 (June 1942?). No doubt Spruance's reputation, whether he likes it or not, will rest upon Midway.
19. Captain S. W. Roskill, *The Strategy of Sea Power*, p. 79.
20. J. Grimes, *Aviation in the Fleet Exercises*, p. 157.

Chapter Seven: Emergence of the Air Admirals

1. Bernard Brodie, *A Guide to Naval Strategy* (3rd ed., Princeton, 1944), pp. 57–58.
2. ComAirPac Analysis, June 1944, 00888, 27 July 1944.
3. ComAirPac Analysis of Marianas Operations, 11–30 June 1944, 001224, 20 September 1944.
4. See Samuel Eliot Morison, *The Invasion of France and Germany* (Boston, 1957), p. 280. Escort carriers had been present at Salerno, but only in a reconnaissance and covering capacity.

1. BATTLE OF WASHINGTON

1. Albion and Connery, *Forrestal and the Navy,* pp. 125–26, 232–35.
2. J. A. Furer, *Naval Administration,* p. 165.
3. *Fleet Admiral King,* pp. 573–74.
4. Vincent Davis, "Postwar Defense Policy," p. 322.
5. *Ibid.,* pp. 67–71, 73–74, 151–52, 210.
6. Towers diary, 14 July 1944.
7. King to Nimitz, 002159, 31 July 1944, "Requirements for Naval Aviation in the Pacific Ocean Areas."
8. Fitch to Horne, 0178031, 17 August 1944.
9. Vincent Davis, "Postwar Defense Policy," pp. 226, 240–43.
10. *Ibid.,* pp. 109, 114, 119, 317.
11. R. E. McClendon, *Separate Air Arm,* pp. 228–33; Towers diary, 28 November–10 December 1944.
12. Vincent Davis, "Postwar Defense Policy," pp. 164–66.
13. *The New York Times,* 30 August 1944.

2. JAPAN

1. J. C. Ford, Jr., *Japanese Naval Administration,* p. 126.
2. USSBS, *Japan's Struggle to End the War* (Washington, 1946), p. 10.
3. USSBS, II, 356. Interrogation of Fleet Admiral Osami Nagano, IJN.
4. Toshikazu Kase, *Journey to the Missouri,* p. 78.
5. Most of these data are from Hajime Fukaya (ed. by Martin E. Holbrook and Gerald E. Wheeler), "Japan's Wartime Carrier Construction," *U.S. Naval Institute Proceedings,* 81 (September 1955), 1031–43.
6. Katsu Kohri, *et al., Fifty Years of Japanese Aviation,* pp. 122, 130.
7. Quoted in Captain Rikihei Inoguchi, Commander Tadashi Nakajima, and Roger Pineau, *The Divine Wind* (Annapolis, 1958), p. 27. See also Masanori Ito, *End of the Imperial Japanese Navy,* pp. 180–81.
8. ComAirPac Analysis, June 1944.

3. INNOVATIONS AND ADMIRALS

1. Rowland and Boyd, *Bureau of Ordnance,* p. 245.
2. Mitscher Action Report, 11 September 1944.
3. Air Officer's Report in *Hornet* Action Report, 0020, 1 July 1944.
4. USSBS, I, 12 (Ozawa).

5. "Rough Draft (Re4f) Fire Control Radar Equipment History—Installations," and other Bureau of Ordnance documents, courtesy of Lee M. Pearson, historian, Naval Air Systems Command.
6. William Green, *Fighters,* IV, 103–5.
7. *The New York Times,* 19 September 1944.
8. Commander R. E. Dixon to Commander J. H. Flatley, 30 November 1944. Flatley papers.
9. Minutes of San Francisco Conference, 13–22 July 1944, Cooke papers; unsigned memorandum for Rear Admiral Radford (Op-03): "Proposed re-equipping of 23 CVAGs with 72 VF and 18 VTB," 0129331, 19 June 1944; King to Nimitz, 31 July 1944. For one example of agitation from the fleet to increase fighters, see Clark Action Report, 0070, 16 August 1944.
10. ComAirPac Analysis, September 1944, 001809, n.d.; Kane diary, 28 August 1944, when VB-14 pilots checked out in F6Fs; Towers diary, 12 October 1944, when Halsey's request was granted.
11. William Green, *Fighters,* IV, 192–94; conversation with Vice Admiral Beakley, 20 February 1965.
12. *Ibid.*, IV, 106–8.
13. Memo for Radford, 19 June 1944; *The New York Times,* 11 June 1944.
14. Towers diary, 28 August 1944; Major General Field Harris, USMC, Director of Marine Corps Aviation, to Fitch, 271500, 26 December 1944.
15. William Green, *Fighters,* IV, 109.
16. Dixon to Flatley, 30 November 1944.
17. Towers diary, 28 August 1944.
18. William Green, *Fighters,* IV, 88–89, 132–33, 186.
19. Jacinto Steinhardt, "The Role of Operations Research in the Navy," *U.S. Naval Institute Proceedings,* 72 (May 1946), 654.
20. Rowland and Boyd, *Bureau of Ordnance,* pp. 333–34, 339–40.
21. *Ibid.*, pp. 306–9.
22. Ray Wagner, *American Combat Planes* (Garden City, 1960), pp. 348, 351–52; for the XTB2D see J. V. Mizrahi, *U.S. Navy Dive and Torpedo Bombers* (Sentry Books, 1967), pp. 56–57.
23. Captain H. F. Fick, Plans Division of DCNO (Air), to Fitch, "Substitution of SB2C Aircraft for TBM Aircraft," 0212331, 28 September 1944; Towers diary, 28 August 1944.
24. Ray Wagner, *American Combat Planes,* pp. 351–52; Memorandum, Fitch to Gates, 0288331, 30 December 1944; Bob Meakin, *50th Anniversary of Naval Aviation* (El Segundo: Douglas Aircraft Corporation, 1962), p. 15; *U.S. Naval Aviation, 1910–1960,* p. 106.
25. ComAirPac History, p. 146.
26. Towers diary, 5 July 1944.

27. Mitscher Action Report, 11 September 1944.

28. Memorandum, Captain C. W. Wieber to McCain, 0150231, 15 July 1944; King to Nimitz, 31 July 1944; Towers diary, 13 July 1944.

29. ComCarDiv 7, "History of the Navy's First Night Fighter Division," 0189, 27 August 1945.

30. Akers to McCain, 12 July 1944; Wieber to McCain, 15 July 1944. Adapting of ships' radar to night operations was left to Cincpac, who relied upon Admiral Gardner.

31. R. W. Dittmer, *Aviation Planning in World War II,* pp. 179–204, 219–20; J. A. Furer, *Naval Administration,* pp. 394–95; conversation with Admiral Radford, 21 December 1964.

32. ComAirPac History, p. 145; WSEG Study, p. 33.

33. *Ibid.*, pp. 125–37; Captain G. Willing Pepper, USNR (Ret.) to the writer, 16 August 1966.

34. *Ibid.*, pp. 2–4.

35. Gwenfred Allen, *Hawaii's War Years,* pp. 185, 187; James C. Olsen and Captain Bernhardt L. Mortensen, "The Marianas," in Craven and Cate, *AAF in World War II,* IV, 693; *Coral and Brass,* p. 201.

36. Tape-recorded interview by Admiral C. M. Cooke, USN (Ret.), in July 1964. Cooke papers.

37. *Fleet Admiral King,* p. 540.

38. *Admiral Halsey's Story,* pp. 193–94.

39. F. C. Sherman diary, 20 November 1944; the entry of 24 June 1944 relates Sherman's visit with McCain in Washington early in May to discuss Mitscher's relief.

40. *The New York Times,* 25 May 1944; Towers diary, 30 May, 1 June 1944; conversation with Admiral Radford in 1964; Admiral Aubrey W. Fitch, USN (Ret.), to the writer, 29 December 1966.

41. A variation of W. S. Gilbert's famous Act I statement from *H.M.S. Pinafore,* quoted by Rear Admiral Joseph C. Cronin, USN (Ret.), former chief of staff to Shafroth, in a letter to the writer, 8 September 1965.

42. Minutes of the San Francisco Conference, 24–26 November 1944. Cooke papers.

43. Towers diary, 13, 14, 22 July 1944.

44. Towers' diary notes Pownall defended the position of Sam Ginder, while the Cooke tape notes Pownall objected to the two-platoon system of command in the Pacific as it meant constant operations and therefore "working 'em too hard" ("them" being commanders and staffs).

45. *Ibid.*, numerous entries in March and April 1944, also 22 and 31 July 1944, the information of the latter entry being told to Towers by For-

rest Sherman, who with McMorris had witnessed Pownall's protest to Nimitz.

46. F. C. Sherman diary, 21 December 1944.
47. Minutes of San Francisco Conference, 29 September–1 October 1944. Cooke papers.
48. ComCarDiv 1 War Diary 1944; Towers diary, 22 July 1944.
49. Minutes of San Francisco Conference, 13–22 July 1944. Cooke papers. Nevertheless, island group commanders included Bernhard, Ginder, Harrill, Reeves, Sallada, and Murray, among others, during 1944–45. See pp. 489–90 below.
50. Murray to Nimitz, 001252, 24 September, 1944.
51. Savvy Cooke wanted to adopt the amphibious practice and name them Commanders Fifth and Third Fast Carrier Forces respectively. Cooke to King, 31 July 1944.
52. *Magnificent Mitscher,* p. 248; Towers diary, 8–9 August 1944.
53. Towers diary, 15–16 August 1944.
54. *Carrier Admiral,* pp. 194–95; Commander Second Carrier Task Force Roster, 1 September 1944.
55. *Ibid.,* pp. 196–97; Towers diary, 21–22 August, 2, 3, 5, 7 October 1944; ComCarDiv 3 War Diary 1944; conversation with Admiral Burke, 8 March 1966.

4. STRATEGY AND CARRIER SWEEPS

1. *Carrier Admiral,* pp. 181–83.
2. S. E. Morison, *New Guinea and the Marianas,* pp. 312–13.
3. *Ibid.,* pp. 379–80.
4. Isely and Crowl, *Amphibious War,* pp. 384–85. See also Major O. R. Lodge, USMC, *The Recapture of Guam* (official Marine Corps history; Washington, 1954), pp. 33–36, 109.
5. *Ibid.,* pp. 359–64. See also Major Carl W. Hoffmann, USMC, *The Seizure of Tinian* (official Marine Corps history; Washington, 1951), pp. 127, 129.
6. *Carrier Admiral,* pp. 186–87, which is partially based on Clark's Action Report.
7. *Ibid.,* pp. 189–90.
8. Saburo Sakai, *Samurai,* p. 198.
9. *Magnificent Mitscher,* p. 245.
10. *Admiral Halsey's Story,* pp. 194–95.
11. R. R. Smith, "Luzon vs. Formosa," p. 465.
12. Matloff, *Strategic Planning for Coalition Warfare,* pp. 480–81.

13. ComAirPac Analysis, September 1944, 001756, 11 December 1944.
14. Frank Futrell, "Prelude to Invasion," in Craven and Cate, *AAF in World War II*, V, 281.
15. Matloff, *Strategic Planning for Coalition Warfare*, pp. 481–82; Samuel Eliot Morison, *Leyte* (Boston, 1958), p. 7; R. R. Smith, "Luzon vs. Formosa," pp. 468–69.
16. Frank Futrell, "Prelude to Invasion," p. 286; R. R. Smith, "Luzon vs. Formosa," pp. 467–69.
17. *Ibid.* Admiral King preferred a straight shot at Kyushu rather than Luzon. Minutes of 29 September–1 October 1944 Conference.
18. *Ibid.*, pp. 286–87; S. E. Morison, *Leyte*, p. 11; Matloff, *Strategic Planning for Coalition Warfare*, pp. 486–87.
19. *Admiral Halsey's Story*, pp. 199–200; *Carrier Admiral*, pp. 194–95.
20. R. R. Smith, "Luzon vs. Formosa," pp. 470–76; S. E. Morison, *Leyte*, p. 17.
21. *Ibid.*, pp. 476–77; Matloff, *Strategic Planning for Coalition Warfare*, pp. 530–31.
22. Matloff, *op. cit.*, p. 487.
23. A. R. Buchanan, *The Navy's Air War*, pp. 218–20; Major Frank O. Hough, USMCR, *The Assault on Peleliu* (official Marine Corps history; Washington, 1950), p. 198.
24. O. R. Lodge, *The Recapture of Guam*, p. 169; F. O. Hough, *The Assault on Peleliu*, pp. 25, 192–93; Isely and Crowl, *Amphibious War*, pp. 416–22.
25. Air Support History, pp. 8–9.
26. ComAirPac Analysis, September 1944; *Admiral Halsey's Story*, p. 204; *U.S. Naval Aviation, 1910–1960*, p. 107.
27. W. R. Carter, *Beans, Bullets, and Black Oil*, p. 212.
28. All of the above from S. E. Morison, *Leyte*, pp. 74–80.

Chapter Eight: The Philippine Campaign

1. USSBS, I, 219 (Ozawa).
2. *Ibid.*, I, 317 (Toyoda).
3. James A. Field, *The Japanese at Leyte Gulf* (Princeton, 1947), p. 18.

1. BATTLE FOR LEYTE GULF

1. Conversation with Admiral George Anderson in May 1964.
2. Air Support History, p. 9; Vice Admiral Whitehead to the writer, 14 October 1966. Whitehead was attached to Seventh Fleet 4 October to 6 November 1944.

3. Minutes of San Francisco Conference, 29 September–1 October 1944. Cooke papers.
4. See S. E. Morison, *Leyte*, p. 58.
5. Minutes of San Francisco Conference, 29 September–1 October 1944.
6. *Admiral Halsey's Story*, p. 198.
7. "Special Notes" by Halsey to the article by Hanson Baldwin, "The Battle of Leyte Gulf," in Don Congdon (ed.), *Combat: Pacific Theater* (New York, 1958), p. 357, reprinted from Baldwin's *Sea Fights and Shipwrecks* (New York, 1955).
8. Captain Harold E. Stassen, USNR, to the writer via the Reverend Glen H. Stassen, 16 June 1964.
9. Kane diary, 21 October 1944.
10. Masanori Ito, *End of the Imperial Japanese Navy*, p. 209; S. E. Morison, *Leyte*, p. 91; J. A. Field, *Japanese at Leyte Gulf*, p. 27.
11. Kane diary, 18 October 1944.
12. USSBS, I, 219 (Ozawa).
13. J. A. Field, *Japanese at Leyte Gulf*, p. 36n.
14. S. E. Morison, *Leyte*, pp. 165–69; USSBS, I, 60 (Captain Rikihei Inoguchi).
15. Report of Captain Raymond D. Tarbuck, USN, of General MacArthur's staff, 3 November 1944, cited in M. Hamlin Cannon, *Leyte: The Return to the Philippines* (official U.S. Army history; Washington, 1954), p. 45.
16. Kinkaid's notes to Baldwin, "Battle of Leyte Gulf," p. 348; *Admiral Halsey's Story*, p. 215.
17. USSBS, II, 500 (Fukudome).
18. *Magnificent Mitscher*, p. 260.
19. *Admiral Halsey's Story*, p. 214; Hanson Baldwin, "Battle of Leyte Gulf," p. 344.
20. Sherman Action Report, 0090, 2 December 1944.
21. *Ibid.*
22. Vice Admiral Ralph E. Wilson, USN (Ret.), Halsey's operations officer, to the writer, 15 August 1967.
23. Harold E. Stassen, Halsey's flag secretary, to the writer, 25 June 1964.
24. ComAirPac Analysis, August 1944, 001354, 14 October 1944.
25. *Admiral Halsey's Story*, p. 216.
26. Halsey Action Report, 0088, 13 November 1944.
27. *Ibid.;* Rear Admiral M. C. Cheek, USN (Ret.), Halsey's intelligence officer, to the writer, 16 June 1966; Halsey's notes to Baldwin's "Battle of Leyte Gulf," p. 363; Stassen to the writer, 12 August 1964.

28. Stassen to the writer, 25 June 1964. In his own autobiography Halsey tones down his statement, saying he addressed Rear Admiral Carney, "Here's where we're going. Mick, start them north." *Admiral Halsey's Story*, p. 217.
29. *Admiral Halsey's Story*, p. 217.
30. Hanson Baldwin, "Battle of Leyte Gulf," p. 327.
31. Kinkaid notes in *ibid.*, p. 349.
32. *Ibid.*, pp. 348–49.
33. S. E. Morison, *Leyte*, pp. 194n, 195; *Magnificent Mitscher*, p. 262.
34. *Admiral Halsey's Story*, p. 217.
35. *Ibid.*; *Magnificent Mitscher*, pp. 262–63; conversation with Admiral Burke in March 1966; Vice Admiral G. F. Bogan, USN (Ret.), to the writer, 11 May 1964.
36. Conversation with Rear Admiral T. P. Jeter, USN (Ret.), in 1966.
37. C. Vann Woodward, *The Battle for Leyte Gulf* (New York, 1947), p. 113; USSBS, I, 157 (Ohmae); *Magnificent Mitscher*, p. 263; J. A. Field, *Japanese at Leyte Gulf*, pp. 47, 63–64, 72–73; Vice Admiral Bogan to the writer, 11 May 1964.
38. Whitehead Action Report, 2 November 1944; Vice Admiral Whitehead to the writer, 14 October 1966; S. E. Morison, *Leyte*, p. 245.
39. Kinkaid's notes to Baldwin's "Battle of Leyte Gulf," p. 354.
40. Related to the writer by William H. Russell, a professor of history at the United States Naval Academy since 1946.
41. Naval War College rosters kindly furnished by the College librarian.
42. Observations of C. V. Woodward in *Battle for Leyte Gulf*, p. 133.
43. Captain David McCampbell, USN, to the writer, 5 March 1961; J. A. Field, *Japanese at Leyte Gulf*, p. 94.
44. See S. E. Morison, *Leyte*, pp. 322–28, for details of the battle; also C. V. Woodward, *Battle for Leyte Gulf*, p. 125.
45. *Admiral Halsey's Story*, p. 219.
46. Kinkaid to Jacobs, Chief of Personnel, 9 May 1945.
47. "It is felt that the Allied Air Forces did not fully realize the problem encountered in defense of [the objective] area." Whitehead Action Report, 2 November 1944.
48. *Carrier Admiral*, p. 201. Admiral Spruance, watching events from Pearl Harbor, had concluded he would have kept the fleet off San Bernardino Strait had he been in command. *Admiral Raymond A. Spruance*, p. 167.
49. See Captain Andrew Hamilton, USNR, "Where is Task Force Thirty-Four?" *U.S. Naval Institute Proceedings*, 86 (October 1960), 76–80. At Ulithi, Arthur Radford got a chuckle from reading the dispatch. Conversation with Admiral Radford in 1964.

50. Kinkaid's notes to Baldwin's "Battle of Leyte Gulf," p. 350.
51. *Admiral Halsey's Story*, p. 220.
52. Ted Sherman shared his superior's frustration: "We ruled the sea in our vicinity, there were no enemy aircraft in the air to bother us, the enemy was in full retreat, and the only remaining objective was to prevent his cripples from getting away." Sherman Action Report, 2 December 1944.
53. Halsey to Nimitz, 250215, from Messages, Halsey Action Report, 13 November 1944.
54. S. E. Morison, *Leyte*, pp. 330–31.
55. Kurita interviewed by Masanori Ito, and quoted in *End of the Imperial Japanese Navy*, p. 166.
56. *Ibid.*, pp. 166–67; J. A. Field, *Japanese at Leyte Gulf*, pp. 125–28.
57. Commander Harvey B. Seim, USN, "U.S.S. *Independence*—Pioneer Night Carrier." Unpublished manuscript (January 1958) at the Air History Unit, Office of the Chief of Naval Operations, pp. 47–48, 66–71.
58. C. V. Woodward, *Battle for Leyte Gulf*, p. 185.

2. CRITIQUE AND CONSEQUENCES

1. Quoted in S. E. Morison, *Leyte*, p. 193.
2. Conversation with Admiral Radford, December 1964.
3. Halsey Action Report, 13 November 1944.
4. Harold Stassen to the writer, 16 June 1964.
5. "The Battle for Leyte Gulf," *U.S. Naval Institute Proceedings*, 78 (May 1952), 487–95.
6. *Magnificent Mitscher*, p. 265.
7. "Kinkaid Charges Blunder at Leyte," *The New York Times*, 26 April 1949.
8. Rear Admiral V. H. Schaeffer, USN (Ret.), to the writer, 27 October 1966.
9. M. H. Cannon, *Leyte*, p. 92.
10. Frank Futrell, "Leyte," in Craven and Cate, *AAF in World War II*, V, 364n.
11. Commander Harold S. Hopkins, RN, to Naval Attaché, Washington, 28 October 1944, cited in Hopkins, *Nice to Have You Aboard*, p. 193.
12. E. B. Potter, "Chester William Nimitz, 1885–1966," *U.S. Naval Institute Proceedings*, 92 (July 1966), 49. See p. 490 below.
13. Conversation with Admiral George W. Anderson, Jr., in May 1964.
14. ComAirPac Analysis, October 1944, 001883, 30 December 1944.
15. Minutes of San Francisco Conference, 24–26 November 1944. Cooke papers.

16. Taped interview of Admiral Cooke by his son, Major C. M. Cooke, Jr., July 1964. Cooke papers.
17. *Admiral Halsey's Story*, p. 226.
18. *Fleet Admiral King*, p. 580.
19. Ernie Pyle, *Last Chapter* (New York, 1945), p. 57.
20. Assistant Secretary of the Navy (Air) John L. Sullivan, *A Report on Naval Aviation in the Pacific War* (mimeographed press release, 22 September 1945), p. 26.
21. C. V. Woodward, *Battle for Leyte Gulf*, p. 109.
22. F. C. Sherman, *Combat Command*, pp. 313–14.
23. Bernard Brodie, "The Battle for Leyte Gulf," *The Virginia Quarterly Review*, XXIII (Summer 1947), 459–60.
24. Samuel Eliot Morison, *The Two Ocean War* (Boston, 1963), pp. 454, 475, 582.
25. Stanley L. Falk, *Decision at Leyte* (New York, 1966), pp. 209–11, 317.
26. *The New York Times*, 16 December 1944.
27. L. L. Moore, "Shinano," p. 148; Katsu Kohri, *et al*, *Fifty Years of Japanese Aviation*, p. 133.
28. Hajima Fukaya, "Japan's Carrier Construction," pp. 1032–35.
29. "Aireview," *Japanese Military Aircraft*, pp. 39, 43, 84–85.

3. CLOSING THE BOTTLENECK

1. Story by Rear Admiral George Murray, quoted in *The New York Times*, 12 November 1944.
2. USSBS, I, 62 (Inoguchi).
3. *Admiral Halsey's Story*, p. 228.
4. ComAirPac History, pp. 148–49.
5. Murray to Nimitz, 001835, 21 December 1944.
6. AAF Evaluation Board, Pacific Ocean Areas, Report 3, based on the observations of Brigadier General Martin F. Scanlon, USAAF, cited in M. H. Cannon, *Leyte*, p. 93. According to AAF Field Manual 100–20, 21 July 1943, "Command and Employment of Air Power," p. 16, close support of infantry was ranked third in priority by Fifth Air Force after attacks on enemy shipping and troop concentrations, and after interdiction of enemy lines of communication.
7. S. E. Morison, *Leyte*, pp. 343–53; ComAirPac Analysis, November 1944, 00286, 13 February 1945.
8. *Ibid.*, pp. 354–57; Frank Futrell, "Leyte," p. 373.
9. Major Charles W. Boggs, Jr., USMC, *Marine Aviation in the Philippines* (official Marine Corps history; Washington, 1951), p. 29.

10. Captain J. T. Blackburn, USN, to the writer, February 1961; Admiral Burke to the writer, 12 October 1961. Commander Tommy Blackburn was sent to the Pacific in October to hear Mitscher's opinion about the possible replacement of the F6F with the F8F as the basic carrier fighter.
11. Robert Sherrod, *History of Marine Corps Aviation in World War II* (Washington, 1952), pp. 326–29, 331.
12. *Ibid.*, p. 332; Murray to King, "Revision of Naval Aviation Program," 001685, 3 December 1944, endorsed with comments by Nimitz, 004227, 11 December 1944; Murray to Jacobs, 001706, 6 December 1944; Towers diary, 28 November 1944; *Magnificent Mitscher,* p. 269.
13. Murray to King, 3 December 1944; ComAirPac History, p. 18; Sherman Action Report, 0091, 8 December 1944; Halsey Action Report, 0081, 23 January 1945; Captain M. U. Beebe, USN, to the writer, 19 April 1961. Lieutenant Commander Beebe was then skipper of VF-17.
14. Data from ComAirPac Analysis, December 1944, 00495, 10 March 1945; A. R. Hilen, Jr., "Remarks on Carrier Developments," p. 19; WSEG Study, pp. 21–22; *Carrier Admiral,* p. 206; Vice Admiral John Sidney McCain, USN, "So We Hit Them in the Belly," *Saturday Evening Post* (14 July 1945), p. 44; *Admiral Halsey's Story,* p. 233; Vice Admiral J. S. Thach, USN, to the writer, 22 January 1962.
15. Towers diary, 10 December 1944; "History of the Navy's First Night Carrier Division"; Burke transcript, pp. 33–36.
16. F. C. Sherman diary, 20, 29 November; 5, 7, 9, 12, 17, 18 December 1944.
17. *Ibid.*, 14 December 1944.
18. ComAirPac History, p. 109.
19. The best account of this typhoon is Samuel Eliot Morison, *The Liberation of the Philippines* (Boston, 1959), pp. 59–87.
20. "Record of Proceedings of a Court of Inquiry, etc. . . ., 26 December 1944," pp. 54–57, 65–67, 69–71. Office of the Judge Advocate General of the Navy. Testimonies of Rear Admiral Bogan and Captains Kernodle and J. B. Moss, chief of staff to Rear Admiral Montgomery.
21. *Ibid.*, pp. 11–18, 67–73, 80. Testimonies of Vice Admiral McCain, Rear Admirals Sherman, Bogan, and Baker (CTF 38 chief of staff), Captain Moss, and Commander Kosko.
22. Nimitz to Judge Advocate General, 22 January 1945. Jacobs to Forrestal, 26 May 1945, pointed out that older, experienced aerological officers were hard to come by, but that they were being assigned. Kosko later wrote his own book, which adds nothing new and avoids the question of responsibility. Colonel Hans Christian Adamson, USAF (Ret.), and Captain George Francis Kosko, USN (Ret.), *Halsey's Typhoons* (New York, 1967).
23. Robert Sherrod, *Marine Corps Aviation,* p. 333.
24. *Admiral Halsey's Story,* p. 243.

25. F. C. Sherman diary, 5–8, 11 January 1945.
26. *Carrier Admiral*, p. 207.
27. F. C. Sherman diary, 10–12 January 1945. McCain tried to butt in, recorded Sherman on the eleventh, "but in general, it looks as if Halsey is side-tracking McCain as much as possible."
28. USSBS, I, 282 (Matsuda).
29. S. E. Morison, *Liberation of the Philippines*, pp. 168–73.
30. *Ibid.*, pp. 179–82.
31. Major General Verne D. Mudge, USA, commanding First Cavalry Division, quoted in A. R. Buchanan (ed.), *Navy's Air War*, pp. 268–69. See also Major C. W. Boggs, Jr., USMC, *Marine Aviation in the Philippines* (Washington, 1951) especially pp. 71–76, 81–85, 106; Frank Futrell, "Luzon," in Craven and Cate, *AAF in World War II*, V, 420–21, 426, 429; Robert Ross Smith, *Triumph in the Philippines* (official U.S. Army history; Washington, 1963), p. 655: Group commanders "were virtually unanimous in preferring" Marine Corps close support to that of the AAF.
32. *Admiral Halsey's Story*, p. 250.
33. The Halsey–McCain relationship compares administratively with that of Civil War Generals U. S. Grant and G. G. Meade in 1864–1865 during the final Virginia campaign.

Chapter Nine: British Fast Carrier Forces

1. Matloff, *Strategic Planning for Coalition Warfare*, p. 452.
2. King to Horne, 002739, 13 December 1943; see Vincent Davis, "Postwar Naval Policy," p. 59.
3. Matloff, *Strategic Planning for Coalition Warfare*, pp. 452–53.
4. *Ibid.*, p. 496; *Fleet Admiral King*, p. 562; Admiral the Viscount Mountbatten of Burma, "The Strategy of the South-east Asia Campaign," *Royal United Service Institution Journal*, 91 (November 1946), 479.
5. Minutes of Pacific Conference, San Francisco, 30 July–1 August 1943. Cooke papers.

1. EMERGENCE OF THE FLEET AIR ARM

1. "Admiralty Air Organization," pp. 5–6, 8.
2. Vital information on British carriers was generously furnished the writer by Lieutenant Commander P.K. Kemp RN, official historian of the Ministry of Defence. See his *Fleet Air Arm* (London, 1954).
3. Owen Thetford, *British Naval Aircraft, 1912–1958* (London, 1958), *passim.*

4. Bernhard to Admiral H. E. Yarnell USN (Ret.), 26 December 1943.
5. Harold Hopkins, *Nice to Have You Aboard,* pp. 38, 72, 199, 213.
6. Admiral Sir Michael LeFanu RN, to the writer, 28 July 1967; *Admiral Raymond A. Spruance,* p. 170.
7. Towers diary, 12 September 1943.
8. Harold Hopkins, *Nice to Have You Aboard,* p. 96; ComAirPac History, pp. 40–41.
9. *Ibid.,* pp. 94–95.
10. "Admiralty Air Organization," pp. 8–9.

2. BRITISH PACIFIC FLEET

1. Kenneth Poolman, *Illustrious* (London, 1955), p. 166, and numerous conversations over vanilla ice cream between Rear Admiral Clifton and the writer.
2. Ian Cameron, *Wings of the Morning,* p. 256.
3. Kenneth Poolman, *Illustrious,* pp. 169–70; conversations with Rear Admiral Clifton USN and Captain R. G. Dosé USN in 1961. See my " 'Sara' in the East," *U.S. Naval Institute Proceedings,* 87 (December 1961), 74–83. Cork was replaced by Lieutenant Commander Michael Tritton RN.
4. Captain S. W. Roskill RN, *The War at Sea,* III, *The Offensive* (Part I) (official history; London, 1960), 354.
5. Towers diary, 7 July 1944.
6. Captain S. W. Roskill RN, *The War at Sea,* III, *The Offensive* (Part II) (official history; London, 1961), 200–01; Owen Thetford, *British Naval Aircraft,* p. 151.
7. Kenneth Poolman, *Illustrious,* p. 204.
8. *Fleet Admiral King,* p. 581.
9. Admiral of the Fleet Sir Philip Vian RN, *Action This Day* (London, 1960), p. 159.
10. Towers diary, 31 December 1944.
11. *Ibid.,* 8 January 1945.
12. Captain C. Julian Wheeler USN, "We Had the British Where We Needed Them," *U.S. Naval Institute Proceedings,* 72 (December 1946), 1584.
13. Admiral LeFanu to the writer, 28 July 1967.
14. Captain E. M. Evans-Lombe RN, "The Royal Navy in the Pacific," *Royal United Service Institution Journal,* 92 (August 1947), 335. Captain Evans-Lombe was chief of staff to Admiral Fraser.
15. S. W. Roskill, *The War at Sea,* III (Pt. 2), 202.

16. *Ibid.*, III (Pt. 2), 309.
17. *Ibid.*, III (Pt. 2), 310; Philip Vian, *Action This Day*, pp. 163–67.
18. *Ibid.*, III (Pt. 2), 333–34; *Action This Day*, pp. 167–68.
19. *Ibid.*, III (Pt. 2), 344n. Add an occasional Walrus amphibian for air-sea rescue.
20. *Action This Day*, pp. 168–70, especially *Illustrious* Action Report.
21. Minutes of Pacific Conference, San Francisco, March 1945. Cooke papers.
22. E. M. Evans-Lombe, "The Royal Navy in the Pacific," p. 338.
23. *Action This Day*, pp. 190–91; E. D. G. Lewin to the writer, 22 April 1966.
24. *Jane's Fighting Ships, 1946–47*, p. 34.

3. CANADIAN PACIFIC FLEET

1. Colonel Stanley W. Dziuban, *Military Relations Between the United States and Canada, 1939–1945* (Washington, 1959), p. 268.
2. J. D. F. Kealy and E. C. Russell, *A History of Canadian Naval Aviation, 1918–1962* (Ottawa, 1967), p. 35.
3. *Ibid.*, pp. 35–36.
4. *Ibid.*, p. 36; Commander John H. Arbick, RCN (Ret.) to the writer, 3 January 1964.
5. Gilbert Norman Tucker, *The Naval Service of Canada: Its Official History* (Ottawa, 1952), II, 101–2, 104; conversation with Commander Arbick in 1964.
6. Minutes to Naval Staff Meeting, 11 June 1945, in regard to Arbick memorandum of 29 May 1945; RCN Press Release of 18 July 1945; Commander Arbick to the writer, 3 January 1964; Kealy and Russell, *Canadian Naval Aviation*, pp. 37–38. Canadian Naval documents courtesy of Commander Arbick by permission of Director of Naval Intelligence.
7. Vice Admiral H. S. Rayner RCN to the writer, 16 January 1964. Then Commander Rayner was Director of Plans on the Canadian Naval Staff, September 1944 to December 1945.
8. S. W. Dziuban, *Military Relations Between the United States and Canada*, pp. 269–71.

Chapter Ten: Changing Missions: Peripheral War

1. Ramsey to the Wings Club, 19 March 1945. *The New York Times*, 20 March 1945.

2. Halsey Action Report, "Operations of the Third Fleet, 26 January–1 July 1945," 00228, 14 July 1945; *Admiral Halsey's Story,* p. 249.
3. Lieutenant William H. Hessler, USNR, "The Carrier Task Force in World War II," *U.S. Naval Institute Proceedings,* 71 (November 1945), 1279.
4. *Fleet Admiral King,* p. 575.
5. Cincpac Staff Memorandum 47–44, 6 December 1944.
6. Matloff, *Strategic Planning for Coalition Warfare,* pp. 487–89.
7. Minutes of San Francisco Conference, 29 September–1 October 1944. Cooke papers.
8. *Admiral Halsey's Story,* p. 250.
9. *Admiral Raymond A. Spruance,* p. 209; Cooke to Sherman, 20 October 1944; Cooke to King, 16 October 1944 (Cooke papers); Frank Futrell and James Taylor, "Reorganization for Victory," in *AAF in World War II,* V, 677–78; Minutes of San Francisco Conference, 24–26 November 1944. Cooke papers.
10. Cooke to King, 13 March 1945; Minutes of San Francisco Conference, March 1945.
11. Cincpac Joint Staff Study LONGTOM 0005023, 27 February 1945, recommended the landing between 20 August and 15 September 1945, the interval between floodings of the rice fields. King and Cooke settled on 20 August, though Spruance advocated 15 August.
12. Vice Admiral T. S. Wilkinson to Vice Admiral H. W. Hill, 18 July 1945. Wilkinson and Hill were prospective amphibious commanders for LONGTOM.

1. FAST CARRIER FLEET IN 1945

1. R. W. Dittmer, *Aviation Planning in World War II,* pp. 226–30, 241.
2. Fitch to Gates, 052031, 27 February 1945.
3. William Green, *Fighters,* IV, 110–11, 133, 186, 194.
4. Flatley to Thach, 10 December 1944. Flatley papers. Also Towers diary, 19 November 1944.
5. Fitch to Gates, 30 December 1944; McCain Action Report, 00168, 7 February 1945; Ray Wagner, *American Combat Planes,* pp. 351–52.
6. Duncan and Dater, "Administrative History," pp. 537–38; ComAirPac History, p. 111.
7. WSEG Study, p. 21.
8. W. R. Carter, *Beans, Bullets, and Black Oil,* pp. 355–56; Minutes of San Francisco Conference, 24–26 November 1944.
9. WSEG Study, p. 33.

10. See *The New York Times,* 16 December 1944.

11. See Arthur Krock in *The New York Times,* 23 March 1945; also F. C. Sherman diary, 8 March 1945, describing conversation between Sherman and Radford.

12. Minutes of San Francisco Conference, 24–26 November 1944.

13. F. C. Sherman diary, 26 January 1945. The rumor was passed to Sherman by Fitch and Mitscher.

14. Rear Admiral Morse to the writer, 29 June 1966; tape recording for the writer by Vice Admiral A. B. Vosseller, USN (Ret.), February 1965.

15. King said so to Nimitz in the conference of 24–26 November 1944. From the minutes. Meeting listed in History of Fleet Air Command, West Coast, 0077, 13 March 1945.

16. Current Tactical Orders and Doctrine, U.S. Fleet (USF 10B), Cominch, 1 May 1945, pp. "4–29" and "4–45."

17. Air Intelligence Group Interview of Commander Turner F. Caldwell, Jr., USN, 23 March 1945 (OpNav-16-V-#E0706, 24 May 1945).

18. Commander First Carrier Task Force, "TACTICS—As applied to Fast Carrier Task Force *Now*," 7 February 1945, including penciled comments in the margin by Sherman. Dale to Sherman, 12 February 1945. F. C. Sherman papers.

19. Air Support History, pp. 10–11; telephone conversation with Vice Admiral Whitehead, 19 September 1966.

2. KAMIKAZES AT IWO AND OKINAWA

1. In a letter dated 18 May 1945, from Jean Lartéguy, ed., *The Sun Goes Down* (London, 1956), pp. 141–42.

2. Toshikazu Kase, *Journey to the Missouri,* pp. 247–48.

3. Turner to Spruance, 000146, 3 March 1945; Lieutenant Colonel Whitman S. Bartley, USMC, *Iwo Jima: Amphibious Epic* (official Marine Corps history; Washington, 1954), pp. 36–37, 39–40, 52n.

4. Isely and Crowl, *Amphibious War,* pp. 445–47.

5. ComAirPac Analysis of Air Operations, Tokyo Strikes, February 1945, 00931, 28 April 1945.

6. *Ibid.;* Clark Action Report, 0027, 15 March 1945.

7. [Lieutenant Commander Hibben Ziesing, USNR], *History of Fighting Squadron Forty-Six* (New York, 1946), p. 12; Isely and Crowl, *Amphibious War,* pp. 506–7, 509.

8. W. S. Bartley, *Iwo Jima,* pp. 42n, 52, 204–6; Isely and Crowl, *Amphibious War,* p. 506.

9. Samuel Eliot Morison, *Victory in the Pacific* (Boston, 1960), pp. 53–56.

10. W. S. Bartley, *Iwo Jima,* pp. 116, 118, 147, 187; Isely and Crowl, *Amphibious War,* p. 509.
11. F. C. Sherman diary, 28 February 1945.
12. *Ibid.,* 7, 10 March 1945; Mitscher Action Report, 0045, 13 March 1945.
13. See Okumiya and Horikoshi, *Zero!,* pp. 382–83; Saburo Sakai, *Samurai,* pp. 256–57.
14. See Father Joseph T. O'Callahan, S.J., *I Was Chaplain on the Franklin* (New York, 1956) for a superb account of the battle by one of the ship's Medal of Honor recipients.
15. F. C. Sherman diary, 22 March 1945.
16. Bryant and Hermans, "Fighter Direction," p. 216.
17. *Carrier Admiral,* p. 221.
18. *Action This Day,* p. 186.
19. Sydney D. Waters, *The Royal New Zealand Navy* (Wellington, 1956), p. 376.
20. Major Charles S. Nichols, Jr., USMC, and Henry I. Shaw, *Okinawa: Victory in the Pacific* (official Marine Corps history; Washington, 1955), pp. 27, 34, 63.
21. Air Support History, p. 12.
22. S. E. Morison, *Victory in the Pacific,* p. 101.
23. *Carrier Admiral,* p. 225.
24. Task Force 58 organization from Mitscher Action Report, 00222, 18 June 1945.
25. Nichols and Shaw, *Okinawa,* pp. 126–27.
26. Isely and Crowl, *Amphibious War,* p. 565.
27. Telephone conversation with Vice Admiral Whitehead, 19 September 1966.
28. E. B. Potter, "Chester William Nimitz," p. 52.
29. Tape recording by Vice Admiral Vosseller in February 1965; see *The Magnificent Mitscher,* p. 287.
30. Minutes of San Francisco Conference, 24–26 November 1944. Nimitz had refused to relieve Hoover.
31. Or so he told Halsey. *Admiral Halsey's Story,* p. 253.
32. Craven and Cate (eds.), *AAF in World War II,* V, ix–x.
33. *Action This Day,* p. 185.
34. *Magnificent Mitscher,* pp. 292–99; E. P. Stafford, *The Big E,* pp. 492–96.
35. *Ibid.,* pp. 290, 299; Mitscher Action Report, 18 June 1945; F. C. Sherman diary, 28 May 1945.
36. Cooke to King, 8 April 1945. Cooke papers.

37. F. C. Sherman diary, 28 May 1945; conversations with Admirals Radford and Clark in 1965.

38. For details, see S. E. Morison, *Victory in the Pacific*, pp. 298–309, and *Carrier Admiral*, pp. 232–38.

39. Conversation with Admiral Radford, December 1965.

40. Testimony of Commander Kosko, "Record of Proceedings of a Court of Inquiry, etc. . . ." convened 15 June 1945, pp. 64, 71–72. Office of the Judge Advocate General.

41. Testimonies of Vice Admiral McCain and Commander Tatum, pp. 54–55, 76; also *Carrier Admiral*, p. 233, based on Clark's Action Report.

42. Testimony of Rear Admiral Clark, p. 45.

43. Court of Inquiry summary narrative of typhoon, n.p.

44. Halsey Action Report, 00194, 18 June 1945.

45. King to Forrestal, 001897, 31 July 1945.

46. Letter to Forrestal, 14th Endorsement to Cominch-CNO Secret Letter, 00476 of 21 February 1945, 23 November 1945. Kosko argues rather feebly that Halsey did not want to separate his two task groups for fear of kamikaze attacks. Adamson and Kosko, *Halsey's Typhoons*, 6. 183.

47. *Admiral Halsey's Story*, p. 254.

48. Rowland and Boyd, *Bureau of Ordnance*, p. 322.

49. *U.S. Naval Aviation, 1910–1960*, p. 112.

50. Cominch History, pp. 140–41; conversation with Admiral Burke in 1966.

Chapter Eleven: Target Japan

1. *Fleet Admiral King*, pp. 598, 621.

2. See Admiral Leahy, *I Was There*, pp. 383–85, for other details regarding the decision. Early in August someone accidentally released the code name OLYMPIC for publication, so the JCS immediately changed it to MAJESTIC.

3. *Fleet Admiral King*, p. 611.

1. BATTLE OF WASHINGTON

1. R. Earl McClendon, *Separate Air Arm*, p. 236n.

2. Quoted in Albion and Connery, *Forrestal and the Navy*, p. 260.

3. *Ibid.*, pp. 262–63; Vincent Davis, "Postwar Defense Policy," pp. 263–64, 290, 294, 299, 308–9, 314–15; R. W. Dittmer, *Aviation Planning in World War II*, pp. 242–48.

4. General of the Air Force H. H. Arnold, USAF, *Global Mission* (New York, 1949), p. 561 and *passim;* Louis Morton, *Pacific Command: A*

Study in Interservice Relations (U.S. Air Force Academy, 1961), pp. 27–28; *General Kenney Reports*, pp. 566–67; Minutes of San Francisco Conference, 30 June–1 July 1945. Cooke papers.

5. Vincent Davis, "Postwar Defense Policy," pp. 372–74, 383–87.
6. Quoted in *The New York Times*, 22 June 1945.
7. Halsey to Nimitz, 9 June 1945, quoted in Halsey Action Report, 00228, 14 July 1945.

2. PREPARATIONS FOR FINAL VICTORY

1. Projected commissioning dates from Fitch to Distribution List, "Schedule of Naval Aeronautic Organization . . ." as of 31 July 1945, 047903, 11 August 1945. Keel-layings of *Reprisal* and *Iwo Jima* had been July 1944 and January 1945 respectively.

1a. The first pilot to command a *slow* British carrier was Captain T.O. Bulteel, skipper of the *Argus* and *Furious* before his death early in 1943. Information courtesy of Captain Donald Macintyre RN.

2. Rowland and Boyd, *Bureau of Ordnance*, pp. 246, 260–61, 267–68.
3. Mitscher to Nimitz, 00220, 31 May 1945.
4. Rowland and Boyd, *Bureau of Ordnance*, p. 334; William Green, *Fighters*, IV, 105, 133.
5. Cassady to Gates, 021003, 25 June 1945.
6. Bryant and Hermans, "Fighter Direction," p. 224.
7. Fitch to Gates, 06403, 28 May 1945.
8. Mitscher to Nimitz, 31 May 1945.
9. Fitch to Distribution List, 11 August 1945; ComAirPac Analysis, Okinawa Carrier Operations, 002144, 28 September 1945. Commander Tommy Blackburn, commanding *Midway*'s Air Group 74, wanted 36 F8F, 72 F4U, and 36 F7F, but maintenance difficulties kept the F8 off till 1946 and the F7 was going to the Marines for land-based operations. Captain J. T. Blackburn, USN, to the writer, 22 February 1961.
10. Mitscher to Nimitz, 31 May 1945; Sherman Action Report, 0069, 18 June 1945, and Mitscher's Endorsement, 2 August 1945.
11. ComCarDiv 7 War Diary, 1945.
12. Information generously supplied the writer by Captains A. S. D. Armour and Donald Macintyre RN, Naval Historical Branch, Ministry of Defence.
13. *Time* (18 June 1945), p. 14.
14. *The New York Times*, 15 July 1945.
15. Cooke to King, 8 April 1945. Cooke papers.
16. F. C. Sherman diary, 24, 25 April, 2, 8, 9, 30 May 1945. Sherman to Fitch, 21 May 1945. F. C. Sherman papers.
17. *Ibid.*, 7, 11, 13, 14, 15, 19, 20, 26 June 1945.

18. In his final message to TF 38 he said, "I am glad and proud to have fought through my last year of active service with the renowned fast carriers." Recorded in *Admiral Halsey's Story*, p. 283.
19. F. C. Sherman diary, 26 June 1945; Towers diary, 2 July 1945.
20. See Albion and Connery, *Forrestal and the Navy*, pp. 33–34.

3. OLYMPIC: THE CONCEPT FULFILLED

1. All available source material has been incorporated by K. Jack Bauer and Alan C. Coox into their excellent article, "OLYMPIC vs. KETTSU-GO," *Marine Corps Gazette*, 49 (August 1965), 33–44.
2. Futrell and Taylor, "Reorganization for Victory," *AAF in World War II*, V, 678; *Fleet Admiral King*, p. 598.
3. W. R. Carter, *Beans, Bullets, and Black Oil*, p. 379; WSEG Study, p. 33.
4. Fitch to Distribution List, 11 August 1945; WSEG Study, pp. 41–45; ComAirPac Weekly Availability Report, 3 July 1945.
5. Data on Operation OLYMPIC is drawn from Cincpac-Cincpoa Joint Staff Study OLYMPIC, 25 June 1945; OLYMPIC Operations Plan 10–45, no serial, 8 August 1945; Operations Plan 11–45, 0005812, 9 August 1945, "Forces under Fleet Admiral C. W. Nimitz, USN, to Conduct Operations in Support of the Invasion of Kyushu, Japan." The latter and Fitch to Distribution List, 11 August 1945, were used to determine task organizations for October and November 1945. See also Bauer and Coox, "OLYMPIC vs. KETTSU-GO," and *Admiral Halsey's Story*.
6. Cominch Weekly Memorandum, Composition of Task Forces, "Effective at Future Date," 16 August 1945.
7. Futrell and Taylor, "Reorganization for Victory," *AAF in World War II*, V, 690.
8. *Ibid.* Nimitz and MacArthur decided this at Manila, 3–7 August 1945.
9. The writer has taken the liberty of substituting this ship for *Bunker Hill*. Both carriers belonged to CarDiv 4, but repairs to the latter probably would not have been completed by late October.
10. Air Support History, p. 12; Turner Operation Plan No. A11–45 (Advance Draft).
11. The writer is assuming by October 1945 *Victorious* would be in need of upkeep. *Implacable* and *Indefatigable*, newer, larger, and carrying more planes, and probably *Formidable*—also late in arriving in the Far East—would have remained for the Kyushu landings. *Illustrious* had returned to England during the summer for refit.
12. See Martin Halliwell, "The Projected Assault on Japan," *Royal United Service Institution Journal*, XCII (August 1947), 348–51.

4. THE FINAL OPERATION

1. S. E. Morison, *Victory in the Pacific,* p. 311; *Admiral Halsey's Story,* p. 259.
2. Mr. John L. Sullivan to the writer, 28 January 1964; Vice Admiral Vosseller to the writer, 11 March 1965.
3. *Admiral Halsey's Story,* p. 262.
4. *Action This Day,* p. 197.
5. *Admiral Halsey's Story,* pp. 264–65.
6. Japanese Monograph No. 23, *Air Defense of the Homeland,* pp. 31, 73, 91.
7. S. W. Roskill, *The War at Sea: The Offensive,* III (Pt. 2), 377n.
8. *Admiral Halsey's Story,* p. 267; Commander Third Fleet War Diary 1945.
9. Ray S. Cline, *Washington Command Post* (official U.S. Army history; Washington, 1951), p. 344.
10. *Admiral Halsey's Story,* p. 269; ComThird Fleet and ComCarDiv 7 war diaries; Pacific Command History, p. 111.
11. ComFifth Fleet War Diary 1945.
12. Nimitz related this to Vice Admiral Sherman at Guam on 16 August 1945, recorded in F. C. Sherman diary, 24 August 1945.
13. ComCarDiv 4 War Diary 1945; Bogan Action Report on Typhoon off Honshu and Shikoku, 25 August 1945, 0542, 30 August 1945, and Towers endorsement, 01778, 10 September 1945.
14. Conversation with Vice Admiral Riley, November 1966. See also Halsey's preface to F. C. Sherman, *Combat Command,* p. 9.
15. *Admiral Halsey's Story,* p. 277.
16. ComThird Fleet War Diary 1945; CTF 38 War Diary 1945.
17. McCain Action Report, 00242, 31 August 1945.
18. Unit history of *Langley,* 0587, 16 October 1945; mimeographed ship's history of *Cabot* (1950), p. 28.
19. Albion and Connery, *Forrestal and the Navy,* p. 180.
20. *Action This Day,* pp. 215–16.

Chapter Twelve: Action Report

1. S. E. Morison, *Leyte,* p. 412.
2. United States Strategic Bombing Survey, *Air Campaigns of the Pacific War* (Washington, July 1947), p. 3.

3. *Ibid.*, pp. 3, 59–60.
4. *Ibid.*, pp. 66–67.
5. *Ibid.*, pp. 3, 59.
6. *Ibid.*, pp. 57–58.
7. Martin Halliwell, "Projected Assault on Japan," p. 349.
8. USSBS, *Air Campaigns of the Pacific War*, p. 53.
9. ComAirPac Analysis, Fast Carrier Empire Strike, July–August 1945, 002195, 23 October 1945. Italics in original.
10. Carrier Task Force Tactical Instructions, United States Fleet USF-4 (promulgated 19 August 1946), p. xv; almost identical words were used in General Tactical Instructions, USF-2 (28 April 1947), p. xiii.
11. Office of the CNO, *U.S. Naval Aviation in the Pacific* (Washington, 1947), p. 42.
12. A. H. Hilen, Jr., "Remarks on Carrier Development," p. 20.
13. Conversation with Admiral Radford, December 1965.
14. Isely and Crowl, *Amphibious War*, pp. 585–86.
15. Telephone conversation with Vice Admiral Whitehead, September 1966.
16. W. H. Hessler, "The Carrier Task Force in World War II," p. 1281.
17. ComAirPac Analysis, Okinawa Carrier Operations, March–June 1945, 002144, 28 September 1945.
18. Mitscher to Forrestal, 24 September 1945, in *Magnificent Mitscher*.
19. Albion and Connery, *Forrestal and the Navy*, pp. 237–39.
20. E. B. Potter, "Chester William Nimitz," p. 52.
21. Quoted in Theodore Ropp, *War in the Modern World* (New York, 1962), pp. 381–82.
22. F. C. Sherman diary, 8 September 1945.
23. Nimitz Fitness Report on Mitscher, quoted in *Magnificent Mitscher*, p. 304.
24. Vincent Davis, "Postwar Defense Policy," pp. 474–78; *Magnificent Mitscher*, pp. 320–21.
25. Minutes of San Francisco Conference, 24–26 November 1944; conversation with Admiral Burke, June 1966; General Board rosters, 1945–51.
26. Walter Millis and E. S. Duffield (eds.), *The Forrestal Diaries* (New York, 1951), p. 195. Entry of 21 August 1946. Also *The New York Times*, 13 November 1946, 1 January 1947.
27. Vice Admiral Robert P. Briscoe, a nonaviator, commanded Seventh Fleet briefly on a temporary, emergency basis for two months in 1952.
28. *The Forrestal Diaries*, p. 343. Entry of 12 November 1947. See also *Carrier Admiral*, pp. 252–53.

29. Quoted by Admiral Vian in *Action This Day*, p. 196.

30. See Albion and Connery, *Forrestal and the Navy*, pp. 263–67; R. E. McClendon, *Separate Air Arm*, pp. 236–42.

31. See R. Earl McClendon, *Army Aviation, 1947–1953* (Air University Documentary Research Study, 1954), pp. 12, 15.

32. *The Forrestal Diaries*, p. 18. Entry of 22 November 1944, quoting an article on MacArthur by Bert Andrews of the New York *Herald Tribune.*

33. John Spanier, *American Foreign Policy Since World War II* (2nd rev. ed.) (New York, 1965), pp. 215 and *passim.*

34. *The New York Times*, "News of the Week in Review," 6 August 1967, p. 2E.

Documentary Addendum

The personal correspondence file of Admirals King and Nimitz was not available originally but since has been opened by the Navy's Operational Archives, revealing five items of major relevance to the history of the Fast Carrier Task Force. They follow in chronological order.

1. King's refusal to allow Towers to command the fast carriers (pp. 68-71, 75-77, 124-25). King erupted in a letter to Nimitz dated 12 August 1943 against Towers going to sea. Without mentioning Towers by name, King told Nimitz that the latter's air "type commander"—ComAirPac—should not be at sea, absent from Fleet headquarters. "If the Chief of Staff can conduct affairs, what is the need of having a Principal? Where is the task force staff to come from? The absence would involve not only physical absence for the period of the 'excursion' [a combat operation], but 'mental absence' during the period of organization, preparation, and training!" Towers, if he wanted to see "active service," could always trade jobs with Fitch, air type commander in the South Pacific, which theater of course was not the main event for the carrier armada. As for Towers' relative seniority, King said this was "of no moment."
2. The relief of Miles Browning, skipper of the *Hornet* (p. 147). Mitscher, after holding mast on Browning for the loss of a sailor's life during a shipboard incident while at anchor, wrote Nimitz on 24 May 1944 that Browning's ship was not ready for action like the other carriers. He related how he had had Jocko Clark advising Browning during the Hollandia-Truk operations "as I considered Clark one of the best carrier captains that it has ever been my pleasure to serve with." Nevertheless, Browning had been a poor ship handler, had suffered high operational casualties, and was guilty of negligence in the above incident. "All things add up to the fact that the *Hornet* is a jittery ship." Mitscher recommended Browning's relief, and Admiral Lee, senior officer present, concurred.

3. New flag officers to command carrier division (pp. 235-39). In a memo to King dated 28 July 1944, Admiral Horne recommended Rear Admiral Ralph F. Wood for a carrier division command. When King passed this along to Nimitz, Forrest Sherman and Soc McMorris in separate undated memos, plus several other flag officers, made up a virtual chorus opposing Wood's assignment. Finally, Towers on 1 August 1944 wrote Nimitz saying that Wood was "overbearing towards his juniors," comparing him with Browning and Captain Shoemaker of the *Franklin.* Once earmarked to command the air forces of the Seventh Fleet, Wood had been kicked out by Admiral Carpender, Fleet commander. Concluded Towers, Wood was "disliked and distrusted pretty well throughout naval aviation."
4. Nimitz on Halsey's blunder at Leyte Gulf (pp. 275, 278-80). Nimitz wrote to King on 28 October 1944, two days after the battle, that he regretted that Lee's Task Force 24 had not been left off "the vicinity of Samar." Said Nimitz, "It never occurred to me that Halsey, knowing the composition of the ships in the Sibuyan Sea, would leave the San Bernardino Strait unguarded, even though the Jap detachments in the Sibuyan Sea had been reported seriously damaged." That all the escort carriers and screening vessels had not been completely destroyed "is nothing short of special dispensation from the Lord Almighty. . . ." Potter quotes this letter more fully in his *Nimitz,* p. 344.
5. Nimitz to Spruance, 19 June 1944, is from Spruance manuscript collection 12, Box 2, Folder 23, Naval War College archives (courtesy of Gerald E. Wheeler). It is reproduced here in full:

Index

About the Author

Clark G. Reynolds is author of several books on naval history, including *Command of the Sea: The History and Strategy of Maritime Empires, Famous American Admirals, History and the Sea: Essays in Maritime Strategies, War in the Pacific,* and *Admiral John H. Towers: The Struggle for Naval Air Supremacy*. He received a Ph.D. from Duke University and is currently professor of history at the University of Charleston in South Carolina.

The **Naval Institute Press** is the book-publishing arm of the U.S. Naval Institute, a private, nonprofit society for sea service professionals and others who share an interest in naval and maritime affairs. Established in 1873 at the U.S. Naval Academy in Annapolis, Maryland, where its offices remain, today the Naval Institute has more than 100,000 members worldwide.

Members of the Naval Institute receive the influential monthly magazine *Proceedings* and discounts on fine nautical prints and on ship and aircraft photos. They also have access to the transcripts of the Institute's Oral History Program and get discounted admission to any of the Institute-sponsored seminars offered around the country.

The Naval Institute also publishes *Naval History* magazine. This colorful quarterly is filled with entertaining and thought-provoking articles, first-person reminiscences, and dramatic art and photography. Members receive a discount on *Naval History* subscriptions.

The Naval Institute's book-publishing program, begun in 1898 with basic guides to naval practices, has broadened its scope in recent years to include books of more general interest. Now the Naval Institute Press publishes more than sixty titles each year, ranging from how-to books on boating and navigation to battle histories, biographies, ship and aircraft guides, and novels. Institute members receive discounts on the Press's nearly 400 books in print.

For a free catalog describing Naval Institute Press books currently available, and for further information about subscribing to *Naval History* magazine or about joining the U.S. Naval Institute, please write to: